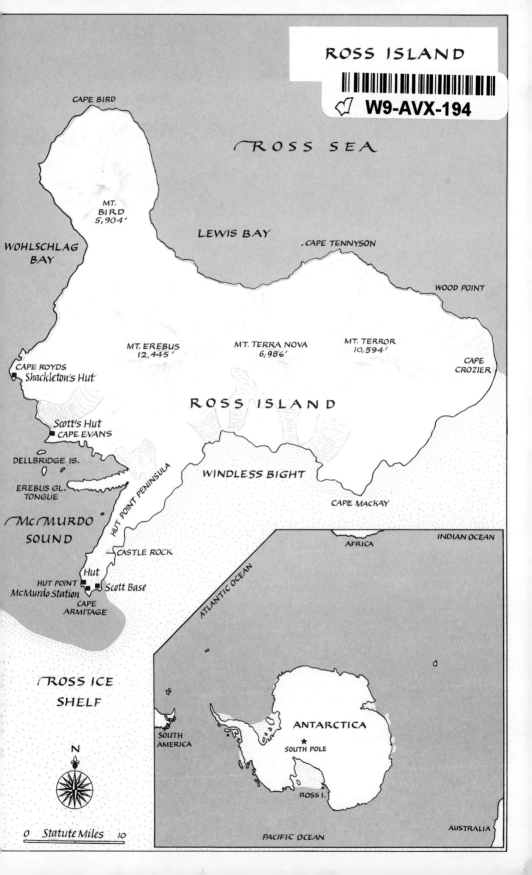

EDGE OF THE WORLD
Ross Island, Antarctica

OTHER BOOKS BY CHARLES NEIDER

FICTION

Naked Eye
The Authentic Death of Hendry Jones
The White Citadel

BIOGRAPHY

Susy: A Childhood

CRITICISM

Mark Twain
The Frozen Sea: A Study of Franz Kafka

BOOKS EDITED BY CHARLES NEIDER

Antarctica
The Autobiography of Mark Twain
The Complete Short Stories of Mark Twain
Short Novels of the Masters
Man Against Nature
Etc.

EDGE OF THE WORLD
Ross Island, Antarctica

~~~~~~

A Personal and Historical Narrative

*Illustrated with maps, black-and-white photographs,
and with thirty-three color photographs by the author*

by CHARLES NEIDER

DOUBLEDAY & COMPANY, INC.
Garden City, New York
1974

Chapter 2, in somewhat different form, was published in November 1971 by the National Science Foundation as a booklet titled *A Historical Guide to Ross Island, Antarctica*. A condensed version of Chapter 23, "A Walk in Taylor Valley," accompanied by photographs by the author, appeared in the November-December 1972 issue of the *Antarctic Journal of the United States*, published by the National Science Foundation. Appendix 4, "Taking Photographs in Antarctica," appeared, together with photographs by the author, in somewhat different form and under the title "Photography at the Edge of the World" in the July 1973 issue of *Industrial Photography*.

Black-and-white photographic credits: 1. Goddard Space Flight Center, National Aeronautics and Space Adminstration. 2, 3, 4, 10 and 11. Photography flown by the United States Navy for the United States Geological Survey. 5 and 8. Herbert G. Ponting. 6. Beresford, London. 7. Source unidentified. 9. H. R. Bowers. 12. Official United States Coast Guard photograph.
Color photographs: the author.

Map design: the author.
Cartography: Rafael D. Palacios.

The quotation in Chapter 1 from Maurice Herzog's article in the New York *Times* magazine of October 4, 1953 is © 1953 by The New York Times Company. Reprinted by permission. The quotations in Chapter 2 from Richard E. Byrd's article, "Our Navy Explores Antarctica," in the October 1947 issue of the *National Geographic* magazine are used by permission of the magazine. The quotations in the same chapter from George Dufek's *Operation Deepfreeze*, published in 1957, are used by permission of Harcourt Brace Jovanovich. The quotations in Chapter 11 from Margery and James Fisher's *Shackleton and the Antarctic*, published in 1958, are used by permission of Houghton Mifflin Co. The quotations in Chapters 2 and 16 from Apsley Cherry-Garrard's *The Worst Journey in the World* are used by permission of Constable & Co., London. The editorial from the New York *Times*, "The Example of Antarctica," reprinted in Chapter 13, is © 1969 by The New York Times Company. Reprinted by permission. The quotations in Chapter 16 from Edward A. Wilson's journal and in Chapter 23 from Griffith Taylor's report in the second volume of *Scott's Last Expedition*, published in 1913 by Dodd, Mead & Co., New York, are used by permission of the publisher. The quotation in Chapter 16 from Roald Amundsen's *My Life as an Explorer*, published in 1927 by Doubleday, Page & Co., New York, is used by permission of Doubleday & Co. The quotations from and references to the accident board's Findings of Fact in Chapter 28; the publication in the same chapter of Lcdr. Neil Nicholson's deposition; and the publication in Appendix 1 of the Search and Rescue Log have been authorized by the United States Coast Guard.

I wish to express my gratitude to the above organizations for their kindness in granting these permissions.
ISBN: 0-385-07090-X
Library of Congress Catalog Card Number 72–84936
Copyright © 1974 by Charles Neider
All Rights Reserved
Printed in the United States of America
First Edition

To
JIM BRANDAU,
remarkable pilot and friend,
with gratitude and affection

CONTENTS

Contents

ACKNOWLEDGMENTS

BY ITS NATURE the existence of a book such as the present one depends on the immeasurable good will and aid of many persons and institutions. No printed acknowledgment can hope to convey the gratitude I feel for all that was done on my behalf to make the research and the writing of this book possible. The names of certain persons are omitted here because acknowledgment to them is made either directly or implicitly in the text of the work.

My debt to the National Science Foundation for granting me a working residence in Antarctica (Project S-32 in the 1970–71 austral summer season) is most considerable. I am especially grateful to Thomas O. Jones and to Philip M. Smith. Mr. Jones responded to a special plea I made, as will be seen in the prologue. Mr. Smith encouraged me in my work, spoke to his colleagues about his enthusiasm regarding my project, took me on a private walking tour of McMurdo Station to give me the benefit of his valuable memories of the station's appearance in earlier years, and after my return from Antarctica entertained me in Washington and outlined for me at length the future plans of the United States Antarctic Research Program. I am also very grateful to Guy Guthridge, Kendall Moulton, Roland Paine, Richard Penney, Jack Renirie, K. G. Sandved, Walt Seelig and Chris Shepherd of the National Science Foundation for many important favors and services performed for me in Washington, in Christchurch, New Zealand and in Antarctica.

The United States Navy made it possible for me to visit the Antarctic in November 1969. Rear Admiral David F. Welch, Commander, and Lieutenant Dan Davidson, Public Affairs Officer, United States Naval Support Force, Antarctica (Operation Deep Freeze, also known as Task Force 43), extended innumerable courtesies to me in the United States, in New Zealand and in the Antarctic. Dan Davidson kindly drove me to Lyttelton, the port for Christchurch, to show me the place that had harbored the ships of Scott, Shackleton and Byrd. During my second visit to Antarctica the Navy played an indispensable role in providing my project with logistic support. It also unwittingly put in my way some rare and wonderful pilot friends, who not only helped me to see and enjoy Antarctica but lent invaluable moral support during many a wardroom evening at McMurdo Station. Among them were Commander John Dana, Lieutenant Commander Billy Blackwelder and Lieutenant Dan Biggerstaff. Several of Task Force 43's pilots repeatedly and beyond the course of duty risked their lives in a long search for me and my three companions when we were lost on a flight from McMurdo Station to Cape Bird on Ross Island. On this, my second visit to the white continent, Admiral Welch once again proved to be a good friend. Lieutenant Commander Kenneth Allison was of help to me in Washington.

I am grateful to the United States Coast Guard for countless favors, among them a stay on its icebreaker, the *Staten Island,* during which I was the recipient of many kindnesses. Coast Guard pilots, as part of Task Force 43, also risked their lives in the search for me and my three companions, and it was two Coast Guard helicopters that rescued us from the top of Mount Erebus, where we were stranded. The Coast Guard has kindly placed at my disposal parts of the Findings of Fact related to the crash episode, including the deposition made by Lieutenant Commander Neil Nicholson, and has made available to me for publication the relevant Search and Rescue Condition Log as well as a photograph of the crash terrain taken from a C-130. I offer profound thanks to Captain T. McDonald, Captain A. C. Pearce, Captain Stanley G. Putzke, Commander H. Haugen, Commander B. L. Meaux, Commander James N. Schenck, Lieutenant Commander Neil Nicholson and Lieutenant Commander Lawrence Schilling.

My stay at New Zealand's Scott Base on Ross Island was a memorably warm one despite the rather low temperature of my quarters. All hands casually made me feel welcome and many helped me in my research. I was the sole non-Kiwi at the base at the time. I wish in particular to thank Brian Porter, Jim Barker and Brian Jackson for many gentle courtesies extended to me. I wish also to thank the New Zealand Antarctic Research Program of the Department of Scientific and Industrial Research in Christchurch; the library of the University of Canterbury in Christchurch; the Christchurch Public Library; John C. Wilson of the Canterbury Museum in Christchurch; the Alexander Turnbull Library in Wellington; Anthony R. W. Mousley and B. M. Smyth of Kodak New Zealand Ltd. of Wellington; and the dedicated Antarctic scholar Les B. Quartermain of Wellington.

I wish to thank the Chapelbrook Foundation of Boston for awarding me a substantial grant of money in connection with my project, and those persons who so generously recommended me to the Foundation: the novelist Saul Bellow, the physicist George Cody of the RCA Laboratories in Princeton, New Jersey, the novelist Janet Frame, the novelist and critic Albert Guerard, Jr. of Stanford University, the critic and autobiographer Alfred Kazin, my editor Harold Kuebler of Doubleday & Company, and the novelist Wirt Williams of Los Angeles State College. I am additionally indebted to Harold Kuebler for valuable suggestions concerning the manuscript of the present work.

I am grateful to the MacDowell Colony of Peterborough, New Hampshire, for granting me five consecutive residence fellowships (1969 through 1973), during parts or all of which I devoted myself to intellectual and physical preparations for the trips to Antarctica and to the writing of the present work. The former director of the Colony, George Kendall, the present director, Conrad Spohnholz, and the secretary, Mrs. Jane Scheibe, were all very supportive of my project, as were my fellow colonists Carol Engelson, Mrs. Louise Varèse and Mrs. Virginia Sorensen Waugh. To Carol Engelson of New York I owe a very special debt for her sustained interest in the subject of this work.

Through the kindness of Alfred Bush of the Firestone Library, Princeton University, I was provided for many months with a library office looking out on the chapel. The Firestone Library also sent first editions of its Antarctic collection to Ross Island for my use. I utilized them at McMurdo Station, at Scott Base, on the *Staten Island* and while camping out on Capes Royds and Evans, Ross Island. They were with me when I slept in the historic Shackleton and Scott huts on the capes.

Princeton University also made available to me for a long time one of the more remarkable offices a writer has been blessed with: a basement laboratory illuminated by sixteen long fluorescent bulbs and containing a blackboard, two long stone counters, two arrays of sub-counter cabinets, various chemicals, glass jars, glass tubes and metal instruments, two large stone sinks, six small stainless steel sinks, ten water spigots, seven air spigots, seven vacuum spigots, three gas spigots, thirty-four electrical outlets, four large strapped-down tanks of gas (nitrogen, oxygen, helium and hydrogen), an exhaust system for radioactive chemicals, two large stainless steel filters for the system, a power control center console, a damper unit console, a precision magnet power supply console and an electro-magnet weighing almost six thousand pounds and capable of producing a field strength of fourteen thousand gauss at six and a half kilowatts. The place had contained radioactive materials just prior to my occupancy, so during the early part of my stay I used a Geiger counter to check that it was harmless. I worked happily in this office, one access to which was by a steeply pitched stairway composed of one cement and thirteen iron stairs.

It gives me great pleasure to thank Walter Bernstein, Mrs. Leigh Bienen, Mrs. Suzuko Brandau, Robert J. Buettner of Holmes & Narver, William Cobb, Jim Elder, Carl Faith of Rutgers University, Henry Franklin, Charles William Gregory, Louis Halle of The Graduate Institute of International Relations in Geneva, Laurence M. Gould of the University of Arizona, James Kitching of The University of the Witwatersrand in Johannesburg, Don Kobes of E. Leitz Inc., Walter Heun of E. Leitz Inc., who lent me photographic equipment to supplement my own equipment, John Lindstrom and John Sissala of the Goddard Space Flight Center, W. R. MacDonald of the Geological Survey, Gary Means, Jim Menick, Catharine Meyer of *Harper's* magazine, Howard Moss, Willis Nelson, Stuart Rawlinson, Jane Ross, David Rubinfine, Archibald Sheeran, Mrs. Beverly Vance, Reginald Vanderpool, Walter Teller, Robert Wood of The Johns Hopkins University, Sir Charles S. Wright and Miss Pat F. Wright.

I owe very special thanks to Robert Axtmann of Princeton University for his generous and unwavering support of my interest in Antarctica and of my effort to write this book.

I am extremely grateful to my wife, Joan Merrick, and our daughter, Susy, for graciously and supportively accepting my absence from home for relatively long periods of time. My debt, both human and professional, to Joan is beyond my ability to convey.

LIST OF ILLUSTRATIONS

BLACK-AND-WHITE PHOTOGRAPHS:
1. Ross Island from a Nimbus 4 satellite
2. Ross Island from the west
3. Ross Island from the east
4. Cape Evans and vicinity
5. Robert Falcon Scott
6. Ernest Shackleton
7. Shackleton's southern party
8. Wilson, Bowers and Cherry-Garrard
9. At the Pole: the Scott party
10. Ross Island from the south
11. Mount Erebus
12. The helicopter crash site

COLOR PHOTOGRAPHS:
1. Mount Erebus at midnight
2. The *Staten Island*
3. McMurdo Sound
4. Mount Bird
5. Pack ice
6. Beaufort Island
7. Ross Island from the north
8. Beaufort Island and Mount Bird
9. McMurdo Station from Observation Hill
10. The Discovery Hut
11. Interior of the Discovery Hut
12. Crevasses on a slope of Mount Erebus
13. Vostok Station
14. Shackleton's hut on Cape Royds
15. The Adélie rookery, Cape Royds
16. Shackleton's hut
17. The author in the hut
18. Cape Royds in November

EDGE OF THE WORLD
Ross Island, Antarctica

1

~~~~~~~~~~~~~~~~~~~~~~~~~~

PROLOGUE

THE CONTINENT of Antarctica and its surrounding seas have been the stage of extraordinary experiences during the last two centuries, eliciting remarkable behavior from men in conditions of extreme stress.

Renewed interest in Antarctica is timely now for several reasons: 1969 marked the tenth anniversary of the Antarctic Treaty and the fortieth of Richard E. Byrd's flight over the South Pole; 1971 the sixtieth anniversary of the attainment of the Pole by Roald Amundsen; 1972 the sixtieth anniversary of the death of the ill-fated Robert Falcon Scott and his four companions on their homeward trek from the Pole, and the fiftieth anniversary of the death of Ernest Shackleton in South Georgia during his fourth Antarctic expedition. The recent discovery of freshwater vertebrate fossils on the continent greatly strengthens the theory of continental drift. American women have recently been introduced into Antarctic life and work. Also, at a time of ecological crisis, the white continent serves as a benchmark of a still relatively undefiled frontier, and readers are perhaps now ready to encounter, if only vicariously, a world of simplicity and purity in which the struggle between man and man must be set aside so that mankind can better understand and endure nature.

My interest in Antarctica goes back to my boyhood in Richmond, Virginia. In 1931, when I was sixteen, I heard Byrd lecture on Antarctica. He became a boyhood hero of mine. I wanted very much to go to the Antarctic, so I wrote letters to the National Geographic

Society and the American Geographical Society, asking to be included in an expedition. Naturally I was turned down.

My dream of visiting the continent continued into my adult years but I never thought it would be realized. I have long been interested in man's behavior in conditions of great stress, especially when he is pitted against nature. In 1954 I edited a book titled *Man Against Nature*, published by Harpers, which included authentic accounts of exploration. In several of these Antarctica was the environment against which man struggled. It later struck me that the time had come for a literary person to go to the Antarctic.

We have had reports from the explorers, and innumerable highly technical papers from the scientists, both emanating from Antarctica, but no one, so far as I know, has brought out a detailed, aesthetic account of the novelistic texture of life as it has been and is lived and worked there. The reason for this lack is that literary persons, like other representatives of the humanities, have rarely been granted a working residence in Antarctica. Such a shortcoming of the United States Antarctic program is unfortunate for the taxpayer, who supports the program and who is culturally impoverished by the current limitations. Hopefully the present book will encourage a congressional broadening of the program to include the humanities. What I am saying about the United States Antarctic program is equally true of the Antarctic programs of other nations, as far as I am aware. There is much in that strange continent (beyond the scope of scientific research) that can enrich the general public.

There are tours that take you by ship from South America to the Antarctic Peninsula but these do not go to the high latitudes. (South of the equator "high latitudes" describes the more southerly ones.) Recently there have been a few, expensive tours by ship from New Zealand to Ross Island. The tourists spend only a brief time on the island but it is far better than no time at all. The usual way for an American to go to the high latitudes is to have the United States Navy fly him from its base in Christchurch, New Zealand, down to Ross Island in the Ross Sea. The main United States base in the Antarctic, McMurdo Station, is on Ross Island, whose latitude is close to 78°.

In November of 1969 I went to the Antarctic as a guest of the Navy, having been invited with three newsmen to observe Operation Deep Freeze, the Navy's logistic support activity on behalf of American scientific research on the continent. The research, which is entirely basic research as contrasted with applied research, is conducted by USARP, the United States Antarctic Research Program, under the supervision and with funds of the National Science Foundation. With us were four science writers who were guests of NSF.

But this is putting it coolly. What actually happened was that from the moment I learned I was a candidate for a trip to Antarctica, however brief, my boyhood hopes and memories welled up and I lived for a period in almost painful suspense. When a letter arrived from an admiral, informing me on behalf of the Navy Department, the Department of Defense and the State Department (I was puzzled by the State Department's being part of the sponsoring group) that I had been selected to go, I reached for the nearest bottle in the liquor cabinet, downed several shots and found my eyes tearful with incredulity and joy. Alone in the house, I waited for my wife Joan to return from an errand so she could be the first to hear the news. I was at the top of the stairs when she entered the door. I said casually, "I'm going to Antarctica." She rushed to the foot of the stairs to see if I was joking, saw my glass in hand and my beatific, bourbonized smile, and, beaming, congratulated me with a kiss.

The lure of Antarctica, that fabulous, awesome and in some ways exquisitely beautiful last frontier, is so great that the long first leg to New Zealand seemed even longer despite the speed of the huge Air Force jet (a C-141) that took us to Christchurch via California, Hawaii and Samoa. You travel with the suspense of a pilgrim eager to reach places sanctified by human and superhuman events. But the chief goal of the Antarctic pilgrim is to reach pure nature itself —from ancient, pre-human time, frozen in an incredible ice cap. Such a pilgrim goes to pay his respects to natural conditions; to take a breath of unpolluted air; and to sense how it all felt in the beginning, before the introduction of man. But he also goes to see how man survives in the world's most hostile place and does so by means of the very gadgetry which increasingly possesses and assails him. He travels, in short, from technological defilement for a glimpse of innocence, hoping to learn along the way a few things about himself.

Innocent he has no doubt the white continent is; because it has so far not been more than superficially degraded by man (although it is not entirely free of nuclear fallout and of traces of air pollution, it's as close to natural purity as one can attain in this world); because nations work there in tranquillity and cooperation under the re-markable Antarctic Treaty; because it is largely devoid of life, a fact which in some strange, not easily comprehended way is pleasant to contemplate, as if life itself and not only man is so problematical that it is astringently pleasant to take a vacation from it (perhaps by life the pilgrim tends to mean not those rare mosses and lichens and certain soil organisms which manage to hang on in the Antarctic's inimical climate but pestilential forms which he would gladly do without: cold, flu and pneumonia bugs, which are usually dormant in the extremes of cold and dryness); and because with the excep-tion of a few predatory examples such as the Killer whale and the leopard seal higher forms of life like penguins and seals regard man as a friend, not having had sufficient experience of him to develop inbred suspicion and fear, and because historically they have had no enemies on land—if you exclude the skua's preying on the Adélie penguin.

Read even the early explorers of Antarctica, such as Charles Wilkes and James Clark Ross, and you will understand that Ant-arctica can become an addiction. Wilkes commanded a United States exploring expedition in the years 1839–42, went very far south and made observations from which he correctly concluded that Antarctica was a continent. He marveled, as did Ross, at the continent's haunting beauty. His name is honored by a vast stretch of Antarctica south of Australia: Wilkes Land. If you read the Antarctic explorers of the early part of our own century you will see that Ant-arctica not only can but sometimes does become an addiction. Ant-arctica is a great proving ground. It tests ships, sledges, dogs, ponies, equipment and above all men. Even while you're there the place sometimes seems like a fantastic dream. After you've left it you want to return to make sure it really happened to you, in all its grandeur, rarity, purity and beauty.

I have sometimes been asked whether one is oppressed by a sense of danger while living and working in Antarctica, or even while making the long flights to the continent that is the windiest, coldest, driest, highest and most remote on earth. The answer, as far as I know it from personal experience and from the experience of some of my Antarctic friends, is that you leave much of your sense of physical danger behind in the temperate zone. You have a long and sometimes rather hazardous flight journey from the United States to Ross Island. In those thousands of miles you seem to take on a new set of values and feelings concerning your physical safety. It's as though you have two Chinese masks, one for the temperate zone, the other for Antarctica. In Antarctica, assuming you like the place (there are those who feel ill at ease in it or even dislike it), you usually wear the mask of euphoria and immortality. You know that accidents, some fatal, do occur, but you do not believe they will happen to *you*. Any other attitude would make working well there difficult.

The euphoria seems to be caused by a complex of reasons: the extreme dryness of the air; the fact that many places on the continent are high pressure areas; the great beauty of the place; the challenge of danger that so heightens one's sense of being alive. Personally, I also have to reckon with an unusual amount of aggression, which finds a clear and natural outlet against a form of nature that is extremely hostile to life. After my return to Princeton, New Jersey, it occurred to me that with one exception I had not used any medication whatsoever, not even an aspirin tablet, during my second and extended stay in Antarctica. Both mentally and physically I had rarely felt so harmonious and well. The exception was a muscle-relaxant pill prescribed for me because of severe cramps due to dehydration in my left thigh, the result of camping out.

Maurice Herzog, the French mountain climber and author, once wrote:

"The true value of life is never apparent until one has risked losing it. A man who has triumphed over mortal danger is born again. It is a birth without indebtedness to anything on earth. It endows one with a serenity and independence which are truly unutterable.

"Mountain climbers, polar explorers, pioneers in unknown, hostile regions, in the caves of the earth and the sea's depths, are all linked by the same vision. All of them stake their native, human gifts against the unknown. Their reward is to enrich mankind's heritage, and the sense of this is their common bond.

"When all the mountains in the world have been scaled, when the poles hold no more secrets, when the last acre of the last continent has been traversed, when, in short, everything on our planet is known and catalogued, the way will still be open for discovery. The world will never be conquered so long as the zest for conquest, for adventure, is in men's hearts."

During my 1969 visit to Antarctica I was the beneficiary of the usual grand tour: McMurdo Station, Pole Station, Byrd Station,

Scott Base, and Capes Evans and Royds, the latter two on Ross Island. I was tremendously moved by what I saw. Awaking in a Jamesway hut early one morning, I felt a desire to write a book about Ross Island and determined that I would do all I could to return to Antarctica to research the book.

Back home in Princeton, I made inquiries by mail regarding the possibility of obtaining a working residence in the Antarctic in connection with the book. I learned from my senators, my congressman and from the legal office of the State Department that such a residence was not available to a person like me. Nevertheless I wrote letters to the Navy and to the National Science Foundation, outlining my project and requesting that I be permitted to return to the ice for a relatively extended stay. Realizing that my chances for success were exceedingly slim, I developed as much leverage as I could by obtaining a grant from the Chapelbrook Foundation of Boston (a philanthropic institution) and contracts with prominent publishers for two books about Antarctica. I was going far out on a limb as more and more of my literary energy was being consumed in difficult and delicate correspondence. If I failed to return to Antarctica I would have nothing to show for the time I had spent.

Both the Navy and the National Science Foundation informed me they were having budgetary problems and that until these were resolved no decision could be made in my case. It seemed to me that the National Science Foundation if not the Navy had something to gain by letting me do my book, for although it had sponsored much important scientific research in the Antarctic most of its work was unknown to the general public. The Navy, in the form of Operation Deep Freeze, on the other hand, had looked consistently to the broader aspects of its public relations.

There came a time when I sensed that both organizations preferred that I drop the matter. I wrote to the White House, suggesting the desirability of broadening the United States Antarctic program and requesting help for my project. Possibly I would have lacked the temerity to do so had I not had behind me a curious experience of 1959, when I had successfully requested Premier Khrushchev of the Soviet Union to intervene on my behalf in a controversy I was having with *The Literary Gazette* of Moscow. Khrushchev had opened the pages of this magazine to me for a defense against an attack on me in connection with *The Autobiography of Mark Twain*, which I had arranged and edited. As a result of my letter to the President I received a reply, written on behalf of the White House, from an executive of the National Science Foundation informing me that my project would be seriously considered.

Some time later, after much silence from the National Science Foundation, I sensed that it was becoming dangerously late in the season for making a decision about my project. Feeling that a desperate move was necessary, I picked up the phone in my home study and called Thomas O. Jones of the National Science Foundation because he was the person who had replied for the White House. I had to deal with two secretaries before I got through to him. He barely remembered my name. I said that it seemed to me extremely important that the humanities had some representation in Antarctica; that the book I had in mind was a unique and good one; and I began to outline the kind of support I had for it. He interrupted by saying stiffly that he knew nothing about this, that he had staffs to handle this sort of thing.

I said, "There is absolutely no hope for my project unless you intervene on my behalf. I can't reasonably expect the Navy to do it. The Navy is not essentially an intellectual organization, as the National Science Foundation is. Only you can help me."

His tone grew more plastic. He said he would speak to his people about my proposal and that someone would be in touch with me about it.

Having taken this last-ditch step, I resolved to put the matter out of mind as much as possible.

Several days later I returned home from an afternoon walk to find a message that a Phil Smith had phoned me from Washington and had said he would either call again before five or in the morning. I had no idea who he was. I phoned NSF, learned that he was Philip M. Smith, Deputy Head of the Office of Polar Programs, and that he had already gone home. His secretary gave me his home telephone number, at which I reached him. He said he was an admirer of my books and that he was very enthusiastic about my Ross Island project. Could I come to Washington for a luncheon meeting?

The meeting, at which Roland Paine and Jack Renirie of the NSF press department were also present, was entirely successful. I knew Renirie from my 1969 trip to Antarctica and had already met Paine. On the Metroliner back to Trenton I studied a booklet called *Survival in Antarctica*, which Smith had given me. It helped me grasp

the fact that I had indeed become a member of the USARP team
for the upcoming austral season.

During September and October of that year, 1970, I had a residence fellowship at the MacDowell Colony in Peterborough, New
Hampshire. MacDowell is an old and honored artists' colony, where
I had lived several times previously. I was working on a book but I
used part of my time in preparations for my coming trip. During
previous stays I had driven daily to Keene, New Hampshire, some
twenty-two miles west of Peterborough, to swim a half mile of the
crawl nonstop at the Y there. This year I increased the distance to
three quarters of a mile. On weekends, when the pool was closed, I
cycled long distances in the New Hampshire hills. I had usually been
in hard physical condition. Now I meant to toughen myself further,
for my work in the Antarctic would be based on a rigorous life, with
periods of little sleep and with much physical exertion. My program
would be a very varied one. My stay would not be limited to Ross
Island. I regarded the island as the hub of United States activities,
both scientific and logistic, in Antarctica, and I meant to treat it
accordingly. In this view I had the complete support of Phil Smith.
Although I had come uncomfortably close to failing in my efforts to
return to Antarctica, now that I was a Usarp (pronounced you-
sarp) I was to have all the cooperation I could wish for, both from
the National Science Foundation and the Navy. I was fifty-five. I
hoped my age would not interfere with what I had to do.

There were several things I urgently wished to accomplish on this
second visit. I hoped to have the rare experience of camping at
Capes Royds and Evans on Ross Island and sleeping in the historic
Shackleton and Scott huts there; to live with the New Zealanders at
their Scott Base on the island; to observe the operation of the remarkable ice airfield, Williams Field, near the island; to live on an
icebreaker as it approached the island and cut a channel to
McMurdo; to hike in one of the fascinating Dry Valleys in Victoria
Land across McMurdo Sound from the island; to visit Vostok, the
Russian station deep in the continent's interior, on the annual diplomatic flight from McMurdo as a witness of the functioning of the
Antarctic Treaty; to study McMurdo and its environs at close range;
and in general to get to know as much of Ross Island as I could.

Also, I wanted to report as vividly as I was able on what the continent is like, this report being based on both of my visits. The Arctic

and the Antarctic are poles apart in more ways than one readily realizes. The North Pole is a frozen, floating point on a sea some ten thousand feet deep. The South Pole is at an elevation of ninety-two hundred feet and is located roughly in the middle of a continent whose average elevation is about seventy-five hundred feet. The Arctic is a sea surrounded by great land masses. The Antarctic is a land mass approximately as large as the United States and Mexico combined, containing great plateaus, vast mountain ranges and an ice cap that in places is almost three miles deep. Its average temperature is some 35° F. lower than that of the Arctic. It is surrounded by the unbroken confluence of the Pacific, Atlantic and Indian Oceans which, with the prevailing westerlies, comprise the world's most savage sea. The lowest temperature ever recorded on earth was noted at Vostok: −126.9° F. Whereas the North Pole is relatively close to places inhabited by man and is not very distant from highly developed forms of life, the South Pole is utterly remote on a continent that holds life at bay, allowing survival only minimally in its interior.

Above all I hoped to bring out a report in language of the awesome beauty of Antarctica; of the mystical spell one becomes addicted to there; and of the unusual persons and morale one is likely to encounter and to get to know in a very special way. The frame of my narrative would be, quite simply, what happened to me: what I did and saw, whom I met, what stories I heard. Within that frame I hoped to include some of the incredible highlights of the island's history. I would not have much time to accomplish all this. Only a bit more than a month had been allotted me on the ice. But still, as a non-scientist I was lucky to be going back at all.

In September I received a notice to appear at the naval base in Kittery, Maine, for a physical examination. I had an early morning appointment. The New Hampshire villages I drove through were still mostly asleep. I encountered fog as I approached the seacoast. The examination was lengthy and thorough. While lying on a table and having a cardiogram taken I fell asleep, to the surprise of the young male attendant. Weird, extremely high and barely audible sounds came through large earphones during the hearing tests. When a male nurse stabbed at my arm to draw blood from a vein it felt like a blow from a hammer. A medical officer was impressed by my low pulse rate: 62. I returned to the Colony with the sense that I was in excellent physical condition.

Shortly afterwards I attended an Antarctic orientation conference, lasting six days, in Skyland, Virginia. The purpose of the conference, sponsored by the National Science Foundation, was to acquaint new Antarctic hands with certain facts and problems and to permit USARP personnel to meet Navy people. Phil Smith had asked me to give a talk at Skyland. I had agreed to speak on some of the psychological aspects of a life of action. I was greatly surprised to learn from a printed brochure that mine was the main talk the first evening of the conference.

As an example of what I mean by the psychological side of action let me mention a repeated revelation I once had at the periscope of a submarine during diving practice. I could see the Atlantic's whitecaps gleaming in a bright sun, and the forward end of the submarine already submerged, and the rest of the craft disappearing rapidly. A part of me still seemed above water while the rest was beneath. I was reminded of Stevenson's imagined split personality as portrayed in *Dr. Jekyll and Mr. Hyde,* and of the equally split protagonist of Dostoyevsky's fictional *Notes from Underground,* and of stories I had read of surgeons performing major operations on themselves.

Some years later I was in the lava zone on Mount Etna in Sicily. The lava patches were hundreds of yards wide and often they were of considerable height, standing like hills. These cold ribbons stretched for miles, flinty, barren. I imagined the molten stuff streaming out of fissures, burying chunks of forest, setting fields afire, then slowly cooling, the gases erupting, the most porous stuff on top, and down beneath, the solidifying lava rock. I had been standing awe-struck when suddenly the place became intolerable, for I was in an entirely inorganic world, without life or souvenir of life: a pitted moon-world. I had a new sense of the awesome loneliness of man in the inorganic universe and felt a close affinity with all forms of life I momentarily remembered, however lowly.

What impelled Byrd to brave the Antarctic winter alone was not only the desire to make accurate and historic meteorological observations but also the opportunity to discover utter, sustained and dangerous solitude and in that solitude to take stock of himself, his future and his relations with the community of men. One of the most fascinating aspects of Jim Corbett's hunting of man-eating Indian tigers was that the man became the beast, with a cunning approximating the tiger's, while the tiger, in its ability to outguess

Corbett at times, even to the point of almost hunting him down, assumed the intellectual and instinctual contours of the human being. There is the beast in all of us and there is no sure borderline between the animal and his human brother.

Aside from the feat itself, the most remarkable thing about William Beebe's descent into the deep ocean was its experience of unimaginable darkness, broken by the flashes of phosphorescent fish that suggested the sparks of thought and image in our night dreams. It was beautiful and stunning. That the effect of great darkness is very profound can be attested to by those who have descended into the depths of vast caverns.

What I have been suggesting is that adventure, large or small, excites not only our physical selves but our imaginative ones as well, and that a true adventure is also a psychological and perhaps even a spiritual matter.

Many of the greatest adventures of the present century have occurred in Antarctica, a continent that perhaps more than any other in this period has been the scene of man's prolonged and at times incredibly persistent will to endure in the teeth of nature's hostility. The adventures have not solely involved geographical exploration. There has been interior exploration as well, as evidenced by Scott's and Shackleton's almost compulsive need to test the interior limits of man's endurance. Their belief in the nobility of manhauling sledges was not an expression of masochism (however, it did involve deep national and personal prejudices against the use of dogs in sledging) but at least partly of patriotic concern regarding Englishmen's manliness at a time when there was spreading wonder about the possible decadence of Britain's youth in the face of a rising threat from Germany. While they pushed forward the boundaries of geographical exploration they simultaneously explored the frontiers of their ability to endure severe physical and mental punishment.

At the conclusion of my talk, during the question and answer period, Rear Admiral David F. Welch, commander of Operation Deep Freeze (another name for this operation is Task Force 43), sitting in the front row and eying me steadily, asked, "In your opinion, was Scott's tragedy largely due to the fact he had a narrow Navy mind?"

I thought a moment, smiled, and said softly, "Admiral, I intend to return to McMurdo."

There was laughter, in which the admiral joined.

Then I said it was my view that Scott's greatness and his ability to keep writing up to the end were in some measure due to esprit de corps, to his career in the Royal Navy, his devotion to its tradition, his concern for matters larger than personal ones, his training in the importance of keeping logs. I added that it was no accident that he should have been gifted as a literary stylist. He was steeped in the works of his Royal Navy predecessors such as James Cook, the remarkable navigator, marine surveyor and expedition commander who was also a skilled observer, with an alert prose style. And I said that the partnership between science and naval logistic support, or between naval geographical discovery with the accompaniment and support of science, was a tradition going as far back as Cook of the eighteenth century and continuing through Bellingshausen, Ross and Wilkes of the nineteenth and Scott and Byrd of the twentieth.

I met many interesting people at Skyland. Among them were the British Antarctic explorer Sir Vivian Fuchs; Dale Vance of Boulder, Colorado, who would be spending a year as an American exchange scientist with the Russians at Vostok Station; Roy Cameron, a microbiologist of the Jet Propulsion Laboratory in Pasadena; Bill Cobb of Longmont, Colorado, a meteorologist who would spend about a week at Pole Station; Bob Wood of Johns Hopkins, who had worked several seasons with penguins at Cape Crozier, Ross Island, and who would be returning there; and Chris Shepherd, whom I had met at McMurdo Station in 1969 and who was now the station's USARP representative. I had met Admiral Welch the previous year. I renewed my acquaintance with him in his quarters after my talk. I also spoke at length with Phil Smith.

It was hot and humid at Skyland and the valley below us was obscured by mists except at night, when, looking out over it, you saw the lights of distant farms, cars, a town. We had three large meals daily. The only regular exercise we had was in climbing the trail through woods up to the dining hall. But on occasion a few of us, including Fuchs, who looked handsome and trim, played frisbee.

I heard some interesting anecdotes. Cameron had been the leader of a party camping in Taylor Valley, and one morning a young man, new to Antarctica, was found running and shouting around and around a tent because, as he explained, he could not stand the silence. Cameron had him shipped back to McMurdo. Another young man had been approved for wintering over at Byrd Station, which was underground, or rather undersnow. After a week there he mentioned to some buddies that he felt menaced because there was something above him. They repeated this to the station scientific leader and he was flown out because it was feared he might crack up. I asked several young men who were scheduled to winter over at Byrd Station and Pole Station (the latter was also undersnow) if during their physical examinations they had been asked by a psychiatrist if they had ever had claustrophobia. Their answer was no. They said that both the psychologists and the psychiatrists had behaved in a deliberately aggressive, provocative manner, posing such questions as, "What the hell do you want to winter over at the Pole for?" Their replies had been carefully moderate.

On my return to the MacDowell Colony I found a letter requesting that I appear at Kittery, Maine, for more chest X rays. It was a long drive for the few minutes it took to take two or three photographs. This time I was treated very specially by the attendants, one of whom was a young woman. There was too much solicitude in their handling of me.

I requested a meeting with the radiologist. He remained seated at his desk. He was about forty and wore Navy khakis. He was studying my films on a lighted screen in front of him.

He said casually, "I'm afraid your right lung is in pretty bad shape. I'm going to have to scratch you from the Antarctic program."

"What do you have in mind—cancer?"

"Frankly, yes."

What struck me most at this moment was not fear that I might have the disease and might require surgery and possibly removal of the lung or might have to face the possibility that the disease had spread fatally but a horror that after all my efforts I might not make it back to the Antarctic.

He wanted to settle the matter at once; he was already late in sending in the report on me. I explained what my return to Antarctica meant to me and begged him to give me a little time in which to have earlier chest X rays sent to him by Princeton Hospital for comparison.

Then I asked, "If there is something seriously wrong with my lung wouldn't I feel some pain during the long-distance nonstop swims in which I almost always push myself?"

He thought a moment, said, "Yes, that seems reasonable to assume," and agreed to wait for the Princeton films before reaching a decision.

This was on a Monday morning. He said he should have the Princeton plates by Wednesday if they were sent promptly. He suggested I phone him Wednesday at three.

During Monday and Tuesday nights I kept waking up and imagining that my right lung had collapsed. I went swimming in Keene on Wednesday but couldn't finish even half a mile. I felt my right lung wasn't working at all. When I returned to my MacDowell studio it was ten to two. I downed some scotch and told myself I'd just nap for a quarter of an hour. When I awoke it was almost four. I walked groggily to Colony Hall and got through to the radiologist.

He said coolly, "Oh yes, the plates have come. We're letting you go. Have a good trip."

"You can't imagine what this means to me."

"I think I can," he said. "Stay out of trouble down there."

2

~~~~~~

A HISTORICAL GUIDE TO ROSS ISLAND

Ross Island is one of the most fascinating places in Antarctica. Of volcanic origin, situated at a latitude of almost 78°, roughly triangular in shape and some forty-five miles wide and an equal distance long, it is the site of the continent's largest and most active volcano, Mount Erebus, 12,450 feet high. On its western side, at Cape Royds, it harbors a group of Adélies in the world's southernmost penguin rookery; at Cape Evans, several miles south of Cape Royds, the world's southernmost skua rookery; and on its eastern side, on the ice shelf just off Cape Crozier, the world's southernmost Emperor penguin rookery.

On the southern end of the island, the world's southernmost land accessible by ship, is the continent's largest and most populous station. McMurdo Station is the United States's prime logistic base for the nation's inland stations and is the center of the nation's scientific research in Antarctica. The station contains the continent's sole nuclear plant and its largest building. Some two miles east of McMurdo Station, on the opposite side of Cape Armitage, is its relatively small but scientifically very active and productive neighbor, New Zealand's Scott Base. Six or seven miles from McMurdo Station is one of the world's most remarkable airfields, Williams Field, built on the floating ice of the Ross Ice Shelf.

Above all, Ross Island is fascinating for the numerous and important historical events which have occurred on or near it and for the remarkable stature of certain of the actors in them. In this respect it surpasses any other place on the continent. The visitor to

Ross Island is fortunate to be intimately exposed to a profound sense of the Antarctic past and to the influence of heroic times and men. Both Robert Falcon Scott (1868–1912) and Ernest Shackleton (1874–1922) used the island as the base for their polar explorations. Scott's two huts at Hut Point and Cape Evans and Shackleton's hut at Cape Royds are still intact. All three are protected as historic sites under the Antarctic Treaty.

The island was discovered by James Clark Ross (1800–62), a British explorer who also discovered the Ross Sea and the Ross Ice Shelf and who named many of the most conspicuous features of the island and its vicinity: Mount Erebus, Mount Terror, Cape Crozier, Cape Bird, McMurdo Bay (renamed McMurdo Sound by Scott's first expedition), Victoria Land, Beaufort Island and Franklin Island. On his first expedition (the National Antarctic Expedition) Scott named the island in honor of Ross. The rare Ross seal is also named after him.

Ross entered the Royal Navy at the age of twelve. He was a member of several important Arctic expeditions. At the age of thirty-one he discovered the north magnetic pole. He commanded the *Erebus* and the *Terror* during the Antarctic expedition of 1839–43. On this voyage he conducted experiments in terrestrial magnetism and gathered much important data on the behavior of magnetic compasses in the high southern latitudes. Also, he attempted to reach the south magnetic pole. His hope of being the discoverer of both magnetic poles was frustrated by the fact that the south magnetic pole was not attainable by sea, being located in Victoria Land, and by the dangerous lateness of the season, which made it imperative that he return north without an attempt to winter over on the continent. It was while intrepidly drawing ever closer to the pole that he broke through a wide belt of pack ice into the unsuspected, large and clear sea that was to bear his name.

He discovered Ross Island in January 1841. Writing in his book, *A Voyage of Discovery and Research in the Southern and Antarctic Regions*, Ross described the first sighting of the island.

"With a favourable breeze, and very clear weather, we stood to the southward, close to some land which had been in sight since the preceding noon [January 26], and which we then called the 'High Island'; it proved to be a mountain twelve thousand four hundred feet of elevation above the level of the sea, emitting flame and smoke in great profusion; at first the smoke appeared like snow drift, but as we drew nearer, its true character became manifest."

This is still the largest eruption of Mount Erebus to be witnessed and recorded.

Although Ross made landfalls at Possession and Franklin Islands in the Ross Sea, he made none at Ross Island, which remained untouched by man for sixty-one more years. On January 21, 1902, Scott, in the ship *Discovery* (of about 700 tons and specially built for Antarctic work), with a crew of some fifty men, became the first explorer since Ross to make his way into McMurdo Sound. The Sound, which lies between Ross Island and Victoria Land, is forty miles wide at its entrance and is approximately fifty miles long. Its southern terminus is the Ross Ice Shelf and the ice sheet of the Koettlitz Glacier.

Scott's National Antarctic Expedition (1901–4), often referred to as the Discovery Expedition, was sponsored chiefly by the Royal Geographical Society. Like Ross's expedition and numerous Antarctic expeditions both before and after Ross's, it had two main goals: geographical and scientific exploration. During this visit to the Sound, Scott wondered about the possible advantages of setting up winter quarters to the eastward. He was seeking a sheltered place, yet one that would provide him with more than local meteorological data and that would afford him ready access to the south. He planned to explore the Ross Ice Shelf (known as the Ice Barrier or the Barrier at that time), as well as to sledge in the direction of the geographic pole.

Turning north, he sailed around Cape Bird to Cape Crozier, examining the coastline from the ship, then proceeded eastward for several days alongside the imposing cliffs of the ice shelf. Finding no satisfactory harbor, he returned to McMurdo Sound, where on February 8 he decided to winter at Hut Point, the southwestern extremity of Ross Island. The Discovery Hut was constructed during February and the early part of March.

Scott devoted almost his entire life to the service of the Royal Navy. He had become a naval cadet at thirteen, a midshipman at fifteen and a full lieutenant at twenty-three. He was reticent, sensitive and moody. His intelligence and admirable personal style marked him as a leader. He was a naval commander when he was selected to head the Discovery Expedition.

During the expedition he introduced a number of Fridtjof Nansen's Arctic techniques into Antarctic work and opened the era of full-scale land exploration of the continent, using sledging traverses. He made many geographical discoveries, among them Edward VII Land, which much later was found to be a peninsula and was renamed accordingly. He also discovered and named Mount Discovery, the Royal Society Range and many important landmarks among the "Western Mountains." The Western Mountains was the name often used by him for the chain of mountains (part of the Transantarctic Mountains), beautifully visible from McMurdo Station, on the western side of McMurdo Sound. He, Ernest Shackleton and Edward A. Wilson sledged to a new farthest south of 82°17′ on December 30, 1902.

It was the Discovery Expedition that named many of the features of Ross Island. Scott wrote in *The Voyage of the "Discovery"*:

"Names have been given to various landmarks in our vicinity. The end of our peninsula is to be called 'Cape Armitage,' after our excellent navigator. The sharp hill above it is to be 'Observation Hill'; it is 750 feet high, and should make an excellent look-out station for observing the going and coming of sledge-parties. Next comes the 'Gap,' through which we can cross the peninsula at a comparatively low level. North of the 'Gap' are 'Crater Heights,' and the higher volcanic peak beyond is to be 'Crater Hill'; it is 1,050 feet in height. Our protecting promontory is to be 'Hut Point,' with 'Arrival Bay' on the north and 'Winter Quarters Bay' on the south; above 'Arrival Bay' are the 'Arrival Heights,' which continue with breaks for about three miles to a long snow-slope, beyond which rises the most conspicuous landmark on our peninsula, a high precipitous-sided rock with a flat top, which has been dubbed 'Castle Rock'; it is 1,350 feet in height."

On the return trek from the new southing Shackleton came down with scurvy complicated by the coughing of blood, and Wilson, a doctor, had fears for his life. Scott seemed to feel that Shackleton had let the party down, even though he realized that Shackleton's illness was as disappointing and disagreeable to Shackleton as to himself. Shackleton was invalided home in March 1903 with a taint of disgrace, as if he had failed to meet the rigors of a polar traverse. After his recovery he mounted his own expedition although he had difficulty in getting it financed. When he asked Scott if he could use the latter's Discovery Hut as his base, Scott declined, explaining that he himself hoped to use it in the not distant future.

Shackleton's British Antarctic Expedition left England on the *Nimrod* in 1907. Shackleton hoped to base himself on the Ross Ice Shelf off the Bay of Whales but on examining the ice there decided it was too dangerous. He thereupon sailed to Ross Island, where he found he could penetrate the sea ice only as far south as Cape Royds, some twenty-two miles north of Hut Point. He settled on this cape, where he built his now famous hut. On January 9, 1909, he and three companions made a southing to within ninety-seven geographical miles (almost 112 statute miles) of the Pole, in the process pioneering the Beardmore Glacier route over the Transantarctic Mountains. The party barely made it back to Ross Island. In his work of laying depots and at the beginning and end of the great traverse Shackleton made use of the Discovery Hut. He first revisited the hut August 14, 1908.

"It was very interesting to me to revisit the old scenes," he wrote in *The Heart of the Antarctic.* "There was the place where, years before, when the *Discovery* was lying fast in the ice close to the shore, we used to dig for the ice that was required for the supply of fresh water. The marks of the picks and shovels were still to be seen. I noticed an old case bedded in the ice, and remembered the day when it had been thrown away. Round the hut was collected a very large amount of *débris,* including seal-skins and the skeletons of seals and penguins. Some of the seal-skins had still blubber attached, though the skuas had evidently been at work on them. . . . The old hut had never been a cheerful place, even when we were camped alongside it in the *Discovery,* and it looked doubly inhospitable now, after having stood empty and neglected for six years. One side was filled with cases of biscuit and tinned meat and the snow that had found its way in was lying in great piles around the walls. There was no stove, for this had been taken away with the *Discovery,* and coal was scattered about the floor with other *débris* and rubbish."

Shackleton's expedition accomplished important work in addition to the new southing. For example, it made the first ascent of Mount Erebus and it reached the south magnetic pole. At that time the latter was some 375 statute air miles northwest of Cape Royds.

Scott's second and last expedition (the British Antarctic Expedition, 1910–13), left England in June 1910 on the *Terra Nova* and reached McMurdo Sound in the first week of January 1911. Unable because of ice conditions that year to base himself again at Hut

Point, Scott chose a cape known as "The Skuary," some fifteen miles
to the north, for his base. He renamed the cape Cape Evans in
honor of his second in command, Lieutenant E. R. G. R. Evans. Like
the great eighteenth-century English explorer and navigator James
Cook, Scott was much interested in the scientific work of his expeditions, to such an extent that he often tempered the fevers of
geographical exploration in order to gather and retain the materials
for scientific investigation. But always his and the British nation's
prime hope for this expedition was the discovery of the South Pole.

The Discovery Hut was again destined to be used as a staging
post for depot-laying parties and as a jumping-off base in an attempt
to reach the Pole. Scott revisited it January 15, 1911. He was appalled by its condition. He wrote in his journal:

"Shackleton reported that the door had been forced by the wind,
but that he had made an entrance by the window and found
shelter inside—other members of his party used it for shelter. But
they actually went away and left the window (which they had
forced) open; as a result, nearly the whole of the interior of the hut
is filled with hard icy snow, and it is now impossible to find shelter
inside. . . . There was something too depressing in finding the old
hut in such a desolate condition. . . . To camp outside and feel that
all the old comfort and cheer had departed, was dreadfully heart-
rending. I went to bed thoroughly depressed. It seems a fundamental expression of civilised human sentiment that men who come
to such places as this should leave what comfort they can to welcome
those who follow, and finding that such a simple duty had been
neglected by our immediate predecessors oppressed me horribly."

By March 7, after some hard work, the hut had been put into
good condition again. On November 3, 1911, Scott and four companions—Edward A. Wilson, Henry R. Bowers, Lawrence E. G.
Oates and Edgar Evans—left the hut for the last time. They
reached the Pole January 18, 1912, only to find they had been bested
by Roald Amundsen, the Norwegian explorer. Their return journey
was beset by illness, hunger and blizzards. Evans died February 17
at the foot of the Beardmore Glacier. On March 16 Oates walked
out of the tent into a blizzard in the hope of saving those more
physically fit. Scott, Wilson and Bowers pitched their final camp
only some eleven miles from One Ton Depot on the Ross Ice Shelf
(about a hundred and fifty miles from Hut Point) but were hopelessly blizzarded in. In a great naval tradition of keeping logs under

the most adverse conditions, Scott kept writing his journal until close to the end. Also, he wrote several letters to friends and colleagues explaining what had gone wrong and crediting his sledging companions with noble behavior under heartbreaking conditions. He referred to himself and his companions as dead men but there was no self-pity and little self-concern in either the journals or the letters. His outlook remained broad to the end.

On November 12, 1912, a search party discovered the tent, containing his body and those of Wilson and Bowers, as well as his records, letters and journals. On the sledge were thirty-five pounds of geological specimens, gathered on the Beardmore Glacier, that the party had declined to abandon despite the fact that for a long time they had been exhausting themselves in manhauling.

The Discovery Hut was to play still other important roles during the heroic era of exploration of the continent. After hearing that Amundsen had reached the Pole, Shackleton concluded that "there remained but one great main object of Antarctic journeyings—the crossing of the South Polar continent from sea to sea." The route he chose was from the Weddell Sea to McMurdo Sound. In 1914 he commanded the British Imperial Trans-Antarctic Expedition in the hope of achieving this goal. He failed to achieve it but as with Scott the failure was in some respects a glorious one: a triumph of the human spirit over great adversities. His ship *Endurance* was trapped by ice in the Weddell Sea, drifted ten months and was eventually crushed. The crew thereupon lived on an ice floe for almost five months, drifting northward. Finally escaping by whaleboats which they had saved from the *Endurance*, they reached deserted Elephant Island. Shackleton and five companions then set out in an open boat to seek help, crossing eight hundred miles of Antarctic waters to South Georgia, where they became the first men to traverse the island's high, dangerous mountains in their journey to the Norwegian whaling station on the opposite side of the island. The men stranded on Elephant Island were rescued, but only on the fourth attempt. One of the extraordinary facts of the Weddell Sea part of the expedition is that not one life was lost.

The McMurdo Sound section, however, lost three men, including its leader, Aeneas L. A. Mackintosh, captain of the *Aurora*. Mackintosh had been charged by Shackleton with the task of laying depots from Ross Island to the foot of the Beardmore Glacier, down which Shackleton planned to make his traverse after reaching the

Pole. The depots were duly laid but under terrible conditions and with inexperienced dogs, many of whom died. The Discovery Hut was often used as a base of operations. Ironically, the Mackintosh party, ignorant of Shackleton's plight, did not know that the depots were now useless to him.

The major effort in depot-laying began in September 1915. It was carried out by six men, one of whom, the Reverend A. P. Spencer-Smith, died on the return trek from a combination of scurvy and exhaustion. The others, all suffering from scurvy, holed up in the Discovery Hut on March 18 with inadequate food, fuel and clothes. Their main base was Scott's hut at Cape Evans but they did not dare to venture toward it over the still soft sea ice. (The land route was considered to be even more treacherous than the sea one.) Mackintosh and V. G. Hayward, having grown impatient, set out on May 8 for Cape Evans despite the warnings of other members of the party. Expecting to reach Cape Evans in a matter of hours, they did not carry a tent or sleeping bags with them. Shortly after their departure a blizzard blew up. They were not heard from again. It was presumed that they either fell through the ice or were blown out to sea on a floe.

On July 15 the remaining three men at Hut Point made a safe traverse over the sea ice to Cape Evans, where, together with four other companions already on the cape, they spent the rest of their second winter in the Scott hut. They were all rescued in mid-January 1917 by the *Aurora*.

Shackleton died of angina pectoris in South Georgia at the beginning of his fourth Antarctic expedition. His death, on January 5, 1922, at the early age of forty-eight, may be said to mark the close of the heroic era.

As far as is known, man did not visit either Ross Island or McMurdo Sound for a full thirty years after the *Aurora* sailed in 1917 for New Zealand. Then, late in February 1947, members of the U. S. Navy's Operation High Jump, a task force that had recently established Little America IV at the Bay of Whales, landed at Hut Point to survey the possibility of setting up an auxiliary base there. Although Admiral Richard E. Byrd, accompanying the task force, did not himself land on Ross Island, he described the landing in the October 1947 issue of the *National Geographic* magazine.

"Scott's camp might have been abandoned only a few weeks ago.

The prefabricated cabin . . . still stood in perfect condition. The timbers looked as if freshly sawn. Printed directions for putting them together, which were found pasted on one wall, might just have come from the press.

"A hitching rope which Scott had used for his ponies was so completely undeteriorated after 43 years that it was used without hesitation to secure the helicopter in which Admiral Cruzen had flown from ship to shore. A few sealskins scattered about looked new. Cartons of biscuits still were edible, although rather tasteless.

"And there was the 'latest news.' A Russian army was invading the Pamirs, according to the headlines of a British news magazine found in the ice. Paper and print looked as if the publication had come from the press only a few days before. But this journal had been printed in 1892."

Members of the task force also landed at Cape Evans, and Admiral Byrd described the hut there.

"It appeared somewhat disorderly after the buffeting of 35 winters. Snow had drifted through cracks in the planks of the sealed cabin. Straw and debris were strewn over the nearly ice-free volcanic ash.

"The frozen carcass of a dog stood on four legs as if it were alive. Seal carcasses from which fresh steaks might have been cut lay about. Scattered around the cabin were cartons of provisions, still good to eat. A box of matches ignited easily."

A year later members of Operation Windmill toured the huts briefly, after which Ross Island was not visited by man until late in December 1955, when Operation Deep Freeze I established a base in preparation for the extensive and continent-wide scientific activities of the International Geophysical Year of 1957–58. Hut Point was selected as the site in January, and the base was called Naval Air Facility McMurdo, McMurdo being Archibald McMurdo, a lieutenant on the *Terror*, in honor of whom Ross named McMurdo Bay. Ten-man and thirty-two-man tents formed a tent camp until prefabricated buildings could be unloaded and erected. The camp rose in the immediate vicinity of the Discovery Hut. Then Clements huts went up, the chapel was built, a supply dump and a tank farm were constructed, and "downtown" McMurdo, today the westernmost part of the station, overlooking the historic hut across the anchorage of Winter Quarters Bay, was born. After the Richard T. Williams tragedy (referred to later), Admiral George J. Dufek, at the chaplain's suggestion, officially named the base Williams Air Operating Facility, McMurdo Sound, Antarctica.

That early form of the station comprised some thirty buildings, including the kennels, a parachute loft, an inflation shelter, VIP quarters and a hut designated as "Aerology." One of the easternmost buildings was the Quonset chapel. The first wintering-over party at the station (1956) consisted of ninety-three men.

The United States scientific program during the IGY was administered by the United States Committee for the International Geophysical Year of the National Academy of Sciences. The Antarctic part of the program was conducted with the logistic support of the United States Navy. At the conclusion of the IGY, the National Science Foundation, an independent federal agency established in 1950, assumed the responsibility for United States Antarctic research.

The great scientific successes of the IGY spurred new and continuous scientific work on the continent, and gradually what was at first envisioned as a temporary central base took on a look of semipermanence. The station began to climb the adjacent volcanic hills and experienced the introduction of metal-frame buildings, a nuclear plant, graded roads, power lines and even waves of "urban renewal." It was renamed McMurdo Station in 1961.

If one were to take a walking tour of the station and its environs, including Scott Base, one might do best to begin at Scott's Discovery Hut (see map) and work back toward the center of the station. In the austral summer there's a bustle as cargo ships unload near the hut but at other times the hut sits silent and remote. It is spacious (some thirty-six feet square) and has a pyramidal roof and overhanging eaves. It was brought from Australia and was the kind of bungalow used by Australian frontier settlers of the time. Inasmuch as the ship *Discovery* was iced in and available as living quarters, the hut was not lived in during Scott's first expedition. It was used for such purposes as drying furs, skinning birds, refitting awnings and for the rehearsal and performance of various theatrical entertainments, complete with scenes and footlights. It was also utilized for gravity observations made by the swinging of pendulums.

Both Hut Point and Hut Point Peninsula derive their names from the famous hut which stands here, overlooking Winter Quarters Bay, McMurdo Station, Observation Hill, Cape Armitage, McMurdo

Sound and the Western Mountains. During Scott's first expedition the hut had no formal name but when Scott returned for his second expedition he always referred to the hut as the Discovery Hut. The hut is probably the most important single historic site on the entire continent, and visitors to McMurdo are specially privileged to be able to enter and inspect it. Over the years it became filled with ice and compacted snow. It was restored in 1963 and 1964 by members of the New Zealand Antarctic Society, with the help of the United States Navy.

Scott wrote in *The Voyage of the "Discovery"*:

"It was obvious that some sort of shelter must be made on shore before exploring parties could be sent away with safety, as we felt that at any time a heavy gale might drive the ship off her station for several days, if not altogether. With the hut erected and provisioned, there need be no anxiety for a detached party in such circumstances. . . . We found, however, that its construction was no light task, as all the main and verandah supports were designed to be sunk three or four feet in the ground. We soon found a convenient site close to the ship on a small bare plateau of volcanic rubble, but an inch or two below the surface the soil was frozen hard, and many an hour was spent with pick, shovel, and crowbar before the solid supports were erected and our able carpenter could get to work on the frame.

"In addition to the main hut, and of greater importance, were the two small huts which we had brought for our magnetic instruments. These consisted of a light skeleton framework of wood covered with sheets of asbestos."

The smaller huts are no longer extant.

Approximately ninety yards southwest of the Discovery Hut is Vince's Cross (2), made of wood and erected in 1902 to commemorate Seaman George T. Vince, the first man to lose his life in McMurdo Sound. One of a party of nine that got caught in a blizzard and decided to make their way back to the ship instead of lying low, Vince, unfortunately wearing fur-soled boots, with little traction, slid down what was later to be called Danger Slope and plunged off its cliff into the Sound. His body was never recovered.

Scott wrote: "Tuesday, March 11, was to be one of our blackest days in the Antarctic. . . . From the moment when he joined us at the Cape of Good Hope, Vince had been popular with all; always obliging and always cheerful, I learnt that he had never shown these qualities more markedly than during the short sledge journey which brought him to his untimely end. His pleasant face and ready wit served to dispel the thought of hardship and difficulty to the end. Life was a bright thing to him, and it is something to think that death must have come quickly in the grip of that icy sea."

Almost miraculously, no other member of the group was permanently injured, although a seaman of eighteen named Hare fell asleep and lay under the snow for about thirty-six hours, yet was free of frostbite. He went forty hours without food and sixty without warm food.

Some 330 yards northeast of the Discovery Hut is Our Lady of the Snows Shrine (3), built by United States Navy personnel in 1956. The small rock cairn with the statue of the Virgin Mary honors the memory of Richard T. Williams, a Seabee tractor driver who drowned off Cape Royds when his Caterpillar D-8 tractor broke through the sea ice on January 6 of that year. Williams went down about two miles west of Royds while he was en route to Cape Evans. His tractor crossed a bridge over a crack in the bay ice and was twenty feet beyond when a section of ice broke and the vehicle fell through. The tractor weighed more than thirty tons. Its escape hatch and side door were locked open, but the machine went down so rapidly Williams was unable to escape. It was after this tragedy that the Navy decided to use a sea-ice runway at Hut Point for its aircraft rather than one that was planned for Cape Evans. When the McMurdo base became known as McMurdo Station, the station's unusual airfield was named Williams Field.

From the Discovery Hut one can make one's way to old McMurdo (4) over Hut Point Road, which flanks the western and northern shores of Winter Quarters Bay. The oldest parts of the station, excluding the chapel, are the western and southern sections. Here stood the original mess hall, the library, the administration building, the medical quarters and the kennels. Standing in front of the Press Hut, one can look out over the anchorage and the historic hut and see the Western Mountains, whose distant peaks and glaciers endlessly fascinate one because, as a result of variations in snowfall, cloud cover, humidity and the position of the sun, they seem to change almost hourly. The Press Hut is an example of one of the old Jamesways, a green, tentlike, round-topped structure of prefabricated wood and insulated canvas, almost windowless, heated by two oil-fired units and containing several tiny semi-private cubicles.

Of The Chapel of the Snows (5), Admiral George J. Dufek wrote in *Operation Deepfreeze*, "It had been planned to hold religious services in the mess hall [in 1956] because there were no plans or materials for a church. But as the construction of the buildings at McMurdo progressed, a mysterious pile of lumber, planks, nails, Quonset hut sections, and assorted materials began to accumulate on a knoll overlooking the camp." The chaplain and some volunteers had begun gathering odds and ends for a church that the chaplain believed to be the first ever to be erected in Antarctica. In that year Father John C. Condit's parish was by far the world's southernmost. The chapel was constructed by volunteer labor. Dufek wrote, "The men, after a hard day's work, would drift over to the church site. Before the main camp was finished a tidy neat church with a steeple was to stand on a ridge overlooking the dump. Later it even had a bell, procured from a small gasoline tanker."

The Richard E. Byrd Memorial (6), standing just south of the chapel, is a bronze bust of Admiral Byrd on a polished black Norwegian marble pedestal. It was donated by the National Geographic Society and erected in October 1965.

As almost everyone knows, Byrd (1888–1957) was one of Antarctica's greatest explorers. More than any other person, he was responsible for the introduction into and wide use of aircraft on the continent. He led five successive Antarctic expeditions, beginning with the expedition of 1928–30. During this expedition he constructed the station Little America on the Ross Ice Shelf near the site of Amundsen's old base off the Bay of Whales, and made numerous geographical discoveries, including the Rockefeller Mountains, Marie Byrd Land (named in honor of his wife), and the Edsel Ford Mountains (now called the Ford Ranges). It was on November 29, 1929, that he first flew over the South Pole and became the first person to fly over both geographic poles.

Returning to Antarctica in 1934, he made other significant geographical discoveries. It was during this second expedition that he wintered over alone at Bolling Advance Weather Station on the ice shelf some 125 miles south of Little America. It appears from his narrative that he not only wanted to take weather readings of the continent's interior but to experience the extreme solitude of a solitary winter over. This was the kind of human exploration reminiscent of Scott's insistent desire to see how far the human body could be pushed short of disaster during manhauled traverses.

An aloof, reserved member of an old Virginia family, Byrd was reluctant to publish the personal details of the near-tragedy that overtook him at Bolling station but was persuaded by friends and colleagues to do so. His narrative is one of the finest to come out of the continent. He belongs to that select group of well-educated, intelligent, gifted and imaginative naval officers (beginning with Cook and including Scott and Shackleton) who produced first-rate narratives out of their Antarctic experiences.

He came close to dying from carbon monoxide poisoning at Bolling station but tried to keep his condition a secret from Little America because he feared that men would risk their lives in a midwinter rescue attempt if his true state became known. His increasingly erratic and irrational radio messages during the scheduled radio contacts gave him away and a successful rescue attempt was made.

The more athletically inclined visitor to McMurdo will find a climb of Observation Hill (7), about 750 feet high, rewarding for the beautiful panoramic views it affords. Approximately halfway up the hill, reached by a modern road, are the buildings of the nuclear plant (PM-3A), whose construction was authorized by Congress in 1960. The plant arrived at its destination December 12, 1961, and went critical March 3, 1962. It has an electric output of 1,800 kilowatts gross. All nuclear wastes are returned to the continental United States for disposal in conformity with the requirements of the Antarctic Treaty.

On top of the hill stands a great cross, made of Australian jarrah wood, in memory of Scott and his four companions. It was erected by members of Scott's last expedition, who took two days to carry it to the hill's crest. Apsley Cherry-Garrard, a young member of the expedition and the author of the classic account, *The Worst Journey in the World*, wrote of the Polar Party Cross:

"There was some discussion as to the inscription, it being urged that there should be some quotation from the Bible because 'the women think a lot of these things.' But I was glad to see the concluding line of Tennyson's 'Ulysses' adopted: 'To strive, to seek, to find, and not to yield.' . . . We went up Observation Hill and have found a good spot right on the top, and have already dug a hole which will, with the rock alongside, give us three feet. . . . Observation Hill was clearly the place for it, it knew them all so well. Three of them were Discovery men who lived three years under its shadow: they had seen it time after time as they came back from hard journeys on the Barrier: Observation Hill and Castle Rock were the two which always welcomed them in. It commanded McMurdo Sound on one side, where they had lived: and the Barrier on the other, where they had died. No more fitting pedestal, a pedestal which in itself is nearly 1000 feet high, could have been found.

"*Tuesday, January 22.* Rousing out at 6 A.M. we got the large piece of the cross up Observation Hill by 11 A.M. It was a heavy job, and the ice was looking very bad all round, and I for one was glad when we had got it up by 5 o'clock or so. It is really magnificent, and will be a permanent memorial which could be seen from the ship nine miles off with a naked eye. It stands nine feet out of the rocks, and many feet into the ground, and I do not believe it will ever move. When it was up, facing out over the Barrier, we gave three cheers and one more."

From the cross one can see in all directions. Mount Erebus, not visible from McMurdo Station, is the great landmark in the north. One can see Crater Hill, Crater Heights, the Gap, Williams Field, and the green huts of Scott Base at Pram Point.

Even finer views of the environs are provided by the crest of Crater Hill (8), approximately one thousand feet high. On the way to Crater Hill the visitor may wish to pause at Fortress Rocks (8), located in the outlying area behind McMurdo, between the Gap and Middle Crater (Middle Crater is between Ski Slope and Crater Hill). The descriptive name for these rocks was supplied by members of Scott's last expedition. The rocks are now the station's quarry.

Scott climbed Crater Hill numerous times during his first expedition. In *The Voyage of the "Discovery"* he left a detailed description of the views from the hill the fourth week in August.

"With full daylight each detail of our landscape once more stands clear, and the view from Crater Hill is magnificent.

"From Arrival Bay a line of rocky ridges runs towards Castle Rock, facing the north-west and gradually rising in height, with four distinct eminences, of which two are well-formed craters; the fourth is almost on a level with Crater Hill, and therefore nearly touches the sky-line; behind it Castle Rock, rising to 1,350 feet, shows in sharp precipitous outline, a black shadow against the

snowy background of Erebus. It is a high, hilly country, this foreground, with many a black mass of rock and many a slope of smooth
white snow; in itself it might be called a fine rugged scene, but how
dwarfed it all is by that mighty mountain behind, which, in spite
of its twenty geographical miles of distance, seems to frown down
upon us. Even Castle Rock, with its near bold eminence, is but a
pigmy to this giant mass, which from its broad spreading foot-slopes
rises, with fold on fold of snowy whiteness, to its crater summit,
where, 13,000 feet above the sea [Mount Erebus is actually 12,450
feet high], it is crowned with a golden cloud of rolling vapour.

"The eastern slope of Erebus dips to a high saddle-backed
divide, beyond which the snowy outline rises to the summit of Terror, whence a long slope runs gradually down to sea-level far to the
east. From point to point these two huge mountains fill up nearly
90° of our horizon, and from this southern side offer almost a complete prospect of snow-covered land. Beyond Castle Rock commences the low isthmus which connects our small peninsula to the
main island, and as it bends slightly to the east it can be seen from
Crater Hill. In running towards the right slope of Erebus and gradually broadening to its foot-slopes, it sweeps out on either side a
huge bay. . . .

"Looking to the eastward from Crater Hill, one has Pram Point
almost beneath one's feet, and one gets a good view of the regular
parallel ridges that fringe the coast; beyond these ridges stretches
the immeasurable barrier surface, limited to the eye by one long
clear sweep of perfectly regular horizon stretching from the eastern
slopes of Terror through more than 70° of arc to the eastern slope of
White Island. . . .

"Meanwhile the eye has passed on to scan that great frowning
range of mountains to the west which has looked down on us in
such ghostly, weird fashion throughout the winter months. Seen
now in the daylight, what a wild confusion of peaks and prec-
ipices, foothills, snowfields, and glaciers it presents! How vast it all
is! and how magnificent must be those mountains when one is close
beneath them! . . .

"Finally, from the vantage point of Crater Hill one can now obtain an excellent bird's-eye view of our own snug winter quarters.
Even from this distance the accumulation of snow which has
caused us so much trouble can be seen; the ship looks to be half
buried, and a white mantle has spread over the signs of our autumn

labours and over the masses of refuse ahead of the ship. Hodgson's biological shelters show as faint shadowed spots, and numerous sharp black dots show that our people are abroad and that work is being pushed ahead.

"Over all the magnificent view, the sunlight spreads with gorgeous effect after its long absence; a soft pink envelops the western ranges, a brilliant red gold covers the northern sky; to the north also each crystal of snow sparkles with reflected light. The sky shows every gradation of light and shade; little flakes of golden sunlit cloud float against the pale blue heaven, and seem to hover in the middle heights, whilst far above them a feathery white cirrus shades to grey on its unlit sides."

Williams Field (9) is roughly half a dozen miles from McMurdo by bus. It comprises a large airfield complex that includes a skiway, the adjacent camp (both skiway and camp are on the ice shelf), ice runways for wheeled aircraft on the sea ice and, at a greater distance, also on the ice shelf. It is the focal point of aerial support provided to inland stations. Through it Antarctic Development Squadron Six (VXE-6) maintains air links between the interior of the continent and the outside world.

The site of Scott Base (10), which is about two miles by road from McMurdo Station, was selected by Edmund Hillary, one of the two men (the other was Tenzing Norkay) to make the first ascent of Mount Everest (May 1953). He selected it for two reasons: as a scientific station for the IGY, and as the Ross Island base of the British Commonwealth Transantarctic Expedition, whose goal was Shackleton's old one of traversing the continent from the Weddell Sea to the Ross Sea via the Pole. Hillary led his nation's section of the expedition. His main task was to set up depots from Ross Island to the Pole to support Vivian Fuchs's party, which would make the full traverse. Hillary reached the Pole in a tractor January 4, 1958, becoming, after Scott, the first man to reach the Pole overland.

The station was constructed in 1957. Hillary was a member of its first wintering-over team. During the IGY, Scott Base conducted almost all the scientific research in the McMurdo area. It was not until after the conclusion of the IGY that McMurdo Station began its scientific work.

If Ross Island is indeed one of the most fascinating places in Antarctica, as I hope this chapter has shown, it follows, given the

nature of the continent, that the island is also one of the most fascinating places in the world. I was almost painfully impatient to return to it and to experience it as richly and as fully as I was able so
I could bring back an authentic account not only of human life and
work there but of that awesome extra dimension that goes far beyond man: a sense of the primeval mystery, of unutterable beauty,
of unbelievable silence and solitude, of looking out into the universe's spaces while experiencing a humbling regeneration of one's
soul.

3

MCMURDO STATION: ONE

WHAT A CONTRAST there was between my two flights from the vicinity of Washington, D.C., to Christchurch! The first, as I have mentioned, was in an Air Force C-141, called the Starlifter. This giant craft squatted low, its wing almost touching the ground, suggesting the wing of a gull that has just landed. It had a very high tail.

Pipes, tubing, girders overhead; a raw metal floor; two tiers of rudimentary seats, three abreast, facing backwards for safety; very few windows; bright little spotlights everywhere; transparent plastic tubing hanging from the walls, attached to plastic masks in gray plastic cases (these were the auxiliary oxygen supply, to be used in case the craft's pressurization system failed); irregular heating; and a terrific ceaseless noise, a compound of grinding, hissing and bass roaring, rarely varying in pitch or intensity. (Take-offs sounded like a subway train rushing through a tunnel.)

At times the noise created a welcome solitude. You became a bit unapproachable when people had to risk hoarseness to converse with you, and they tended to select their words more carefully than usual. Still, some things had to be said even if shouted, such as the claim that Admiral Byrd had once asked, "How do you get a four-inch pecker out of six inches of Antarctic clothing?"

We faced our altar, a mountain of luggage and cargo chained, webbed and plastic-sheeted as though like a maniac it might go berserk and commit unspeakable crimes. At 35,000 feet, mostly on autopilot, we chewed up space in a hurry. Flight time between Dulles Airport and Travis Air Force Base in California: about five hours. A two-hour refuel stop at Travis. Flight time from Travis to Hickam Air Force Base in Hawaii: some six hours. We spent part of the night at Hickam. Flight time between Hickam and Pago Pago: about five and a half hours. Another two-hour refuel stop. Flight time from Pago Pago to Christchurch: approximately four and a half hours.

We mocked the globe's vastness. In doing so we mocked our human nature. Pago Pago had the quality of a dream. We took photographs which we hoped would tell us what we should have experienced.

Our quarters in Christchurch were at the luxurious White Heron Motel near Harewood Airport.

My second flight was in a beat-up C-121, Operation Deep Freeze's last surviving Super Constellation, called *Phoenix 6*. The Connie, which felt small and fragile, looked like a used-up sheep dog. Its triple tail, painted red and outlined in black, like the rest of the craft seemed to be begging for retirement.

A grooved, fluted aluminum floor; bucket seats with dirty orange cloth bags hanging on the backs; an arched, dusty-blue ceiling with a row of shielded lights down the middle; an emergency ladder hanging from the ceiling on one side. When eating (the craft was crowded) you felt on the verge of disaster: one wrong gesture and you could have a lapful of gravy to contend with. Your motions were as cautious as those of a brain surgeon.

We took almost eleven and a half hours to get from Andrews Air Force Base to Alameda Naval Air Station in California. Normal flight time for the Connie was ten hours but the plane bucked headwinds. I spent the night at Alameda, sharing a room with Bill Cobb, whom I knew from Skyland. At breakfast we met Dale Vance, who had flown in from Boulder. Vance was a tall, handsome man with a charming laugh that sometimes broke into a giggle. He said he was eager to begin his long stretch at Vostok Station.

We lifted off at 9:15 A.M. It took us ten hours and fifteen minutes to fly to Barber's Point Naval Air Station in Hawaii. We spent twenty-five hours at Barber's Point. Then came the long leg—twenty-two or twenty-three hours—to Christchurch, including a three-hour stopover in bucketing rain at Pago Pago. The Connie, cruising at 8,000 feet, droned on, on.

I noted in my journal:

"One feels impatient, one wants finally to *arrive*, to meet whatever it is that's going to happen. Talk between Sy Richardson and Bill Austin about Tom Berg's death in the helo crash last year. Sy accompanied the remains back to the States. Nobody still seems to know why Berg and Jeremy Sykes died in that crash. . . .

"Saw a circular rainbow seeming to lie upon the ocean. And beautiful coral isles from 8000′. The ocean as usual looks gray, dull, with flecks of bright white that are whitecaps. But the isles show pure pale greens, intensely white circular surf, patches of brown.

"Vance told me a story about a Usarp at Byrd Station. A valuable worker, he got sore over an argument in a poker game, left the station angrily and took a walk. His tracks were followed three miles. The stride was still long, so he was probably still angry. Then they disappeared. He was never found. Vance, who wintered over at Byrd, said there are no crevasses in the area. So the man must have been caught by sudden bad weather."

Landing in Christchurch, we drove downtown to Warner's Hotel on Cathedral Square. This is the old hotel that was known to Scott and Shackleton, the one that now had a huge bar on the ground floor. My room looked out on the back end of Canterbury Cathedral.

Early next morning Vance, Cobb and I went to the USARP warehouse at the airport for the clothing issue, tryout and weigh-in. The warehouse was unheated, the doors were wide open. Together with other Usarps we stripped to our underwear. Much of the clothing was new; tags and straight pins had to be removed and adjustments made—for example in the mukluks: you separated the mukluks, removed in each the double felt inner sole, inserted a plastic sole, inserted the double felt sole, inserted a large felt liner, stuck your foot in, squeezed, banged your heel against the floor to settle everything, laced the boot, walked around. It was very important that clothes fitted properly; they must be neither too loose nor too snug.

We spent three days and four nights in Christchurch. On our last day I walked rapidly to the narrow, winding, willow-shaded Avon and crossed to the Hagley Park side of the river. My gravel trail took me under large trees whose shade was welcome. Thick tan masses of recently cut high grass, dry yet still redolent, called forth childhood memories of Bessarabia, an antediluvian harmony of stable smells, poppy fields and expanses of warm, moist farmland. On my left the park's great fields, empty and virginal-looking, reminded me of days in the Bronx shortly after I arrived in the United

States in the early twenties, and a sense of uncrowded park lawns and of a milder time, when our population was a hundred and twenty million. By the time I returned to Warner's I had worked up a good sweat. I took a bath before going downstairs to the bar to drink warmish sweet Kiwi beer in the company of some Kiwi workmen.

Cobb and I dined together and afterwards took a leisurely stroll on sleepy residential streets and in a deserted, very dry park. I did some final packing before turning in.

I awoke at 4:30 A.M. and lay abed until 4:55, thinking how lucky I was to have reached this moment, to have not been frustrated, for example, by some unexpected illness such as the flu currently making the rounds of Christchurch. I was in the lobby by 5:20. Vance, Cobb and I took a cab to the USARP warehouse, where we donned our Antarctic clothes and stored our own clothes. My orange hold bag (a seabag; hold bag because it would go into the plane's "hold"), containing two pairs of mukluks, gloves, heavy socks, extra waffle-weaves and various other items—nothing essential to my survival in case we had an "incident"—was already aboard the Navy C-130. My survival gear was in my hand bag (this too was an orange seabag), which would stay close to me on the craft.

We lifted off at 8 A.M. I was wearing longjohns; a heavy, plaid wool shirt; my own Dacron-cotton trousers under black windpants minus liners; white woolen socks; and my own hiking boots. In my hand bag were the heavy windpants liners, bear paws, black thermal boots, my red USARP parka, gloves, my black pile-lined cap and my own green nylon knapsack with its jammed contents. We sat on canvas seats alongside the raw walls of the plane. There was a long, high stack of green Navy seabags, orange USARP seabags and pale green Scott Base seabags strapped down in front of me. Dirty bunny boots hung here and there. The plane, which had a silvery pylon tank under each wing, was, as usual, terrifically noisy. Pink ear wax was handed out by a crewman. We were flying at 22,000 feet over a great white, cottony world that pained your eyes when you tried to observe it through one of the few portholes. Some people read or slept. Vance and three men played bridge. After a while the bolts on the plane walls iced up, but I got so hot I removed my wool shirt. The pilot didn't chill the craft much on this flight.

Of my previous flight I had written:

"In Christchurch in the austral spring or summer you pick up a United States Navy plane, which in eight hours will take you the twenty-four hundred miles to 'the ice,' as Antarctic hands call the continent. As you board the aircraft the city is warm and it seems mildly funny to be wearing waffle-weave longjohns, Seabee green shirt and trousers, pile-lined cap, cushion-sole socks and huge white rubber thermal boots called bunny boots. (You have acquired Navy-issue dunnage.) You and your fellow passengers sit in two rows on red canvas seats, facing each other across a fence of strapped-down seabags, and wonder what Antarctica will be like and what you will be like in it. The antipodean waters below are so cold that if a person is immersed he can survive only eight to ten minutes. But a plane has never gone down on this flight and everyone is cheerful even as we pass the point of safe return, beyond which the C-130 Hercules, a great ski-equipped four-engine turbo-prop, cannot turn back. There's excitement as the first pack ice is sighted.

"The plane is cool now and you put on two pairs of gloves and a parka with a fur-trimmed flying hood. In your seabag are huge gauntleted furback mittens known as bear paws and lined over-pants called many-pockets trousers but these are for places where it's really cold. You will not wear them on your arrival. Meanwhile one can't help but think there's a certain humor in the fact he's approaching the world's quietest place (when the winds aren't blowing) in a craft so noisy one carries on a conversation, if at all, in shouts. The roar is varied by the sound of hissing somewhere and by the screams of wing and tail controls.

"One disembarks, and there is Williams Field. We boarded a bulky, fat-tired orange bus and bounced on a road carved on the annual ice of McMurdo Sound, viewing distant mountains half-veiled by luminous clouds. We reached McMurdo Station, the center of American logistic and scientific activity in Antarctica, whose winter population of two hundred and summer population of almost a thousand makes it the largest station on the continent. Perched on volcanic hills on the southern tip of Ross Island, it has a severe climate, with an all-time recorded low of $-59°$ F. and with winds clocked as high as a hundred and fifty-five miles an hour. Its black hills and roads give it the look of a mining camp."

Yesterday the *Phoenix 6*, heading for Williams Field, had had to turn back because of too strong headwinds. Now there were rumors that we too might have to abort our flight. Bill Heaphy, the soft-voiced, gentle Kiwi who managed the USARP warehouse, had told me that after the other Connie (the *Pegasus*) had crashed at Williams Field in October they had found a man on the plane manifest who wasn't even in New Zealand, much less on the ice. Hearing about this, Admiral Welch had ordered that dog tags be worn in Antarctica from then on, by civilians as well as by the military. So now I was wearing two of them.

When we were over the Ross Sea some handsome, tall Kiwis sitting near me took very seriously the business of preparing to step out onto the ice. They donned huge windpants (orange or pale green); great canvas-covered orange boots made in Japan, with long yellow laces that they tied briskly; parkas; and adjusted snow goggles on their foreheads. They did all this despite the information, given over the intercom, that the current temperature at Williams Field was 25° F. It was funny to watch them.

Suddenly we landed, with a few heavy bumps on the skis. The aft platform was lowered, bluish polar light streamed in, unloading began. We disembarked by the front door and there one was, on the ice of Williams Field, with plow trucks and huts all around, the sun cheery, and Mount Erebus looming like an unbelievable hill, its crest obscured by clouds. Cobb, Vance and I deposited our baggage in one red truck and proceeded to McMurdo Station by another, receiving views of the eastern side of Cape Armitage, of the Gap, Observation Hill, Mount Discovery, the Royal Society Range, and then of Hut Point and the Discovery Hut as we rounded Cape Armitage and saw Winter Quarters Bay and the station.

The station, dark, its background hills dark also despite their patchy mantle of snow, was much uglier than I remembered it to be, for now it lacked a benign covering of snow and ice. Porous volcanic rock was everywhere, crushed to gritty dust in the main roads. There were no streets, only lanes, unpaved, without sidewalks, gray, uneven. Littered as it was with much equipment, some of it on pallets—crates, cases, gas cylinders, sledges, huge fuel tires, generators, bulldozers, reels of heavy wire—the station suggested a wartime supply dump. One saw telephone poles, power lines and large silvery tubing on wooden trestles. The place was not without some color. In addition to the green Jamesway huts there were rust structures, wine-colored ones and crimson boxlike plywood shacks. Towering over the station was the brown-gray heap of Observation

Hill, a trail snaking from the nuclear plant to the crest with its Polar Party Cross. At times you wanted to spread something over the hill's embarrassing, ugly nakedness.

I was stunned by the quarters I now moved into. They were Room 104 in the new USARP personnel building, which I dubbed the Lodge. It was a large, blue, two-story prefabricated metal building with buff stripes and was set on heavy wooden timbers so that drift snow wouldn't pile against it but would blow under and past it, and because it was cheaper and quicker to build in this manner than to drill into volcanic permafrost. There were eighteen separate rooms on the first floor and single rooms and a couple of dormitory rooms on the second. A simple wooden stairway of six steps, with a wooden balustrade, stood at the main entrance. The Lodge was luxurious by comparison with most of the continent's structures.

My room was immediately on the right as you entered the heavy, foyered double doors. It was spacious, had two closets, two single beds, a Formica desk, an overhead light, a floor lamp, bed lamps, two red armchairs, red curtains to match, a coffee table, a linoleum floor, steam heat and—and this was very important to me, for privacy was often hard to come by on the ice—I would not have to share it even though it was designed for double occupancy. One view out of my windows was of a row of red Nodwells (a large, heavy, tracked vehicle) parked on the southern side of the USARP garage across the road. Another view, looking slightly to the north, was of a couple of the hills behind McMurdo, and of a Jamesway on a rise.

A year earlier I had lived in the Press Hut on the station's western edge. The toilet facilities in the hut consisted of a small metal cone located in the tiny, dark, unheated vestibule between the rear double doors. Waffle-weave longjohns were useful if you had to get up at night, and waffle-weaves were what everyone slept in. Other facilities in the hut were equally simple. There was no water except in a yellowish plastic jug which issued a yellowish liquid to be drunk out of a solitary green ceramic cup.

In the morning you dressed fully before venturing out and you carried your single, small towel, a small bar of yellow soap and your toilet articles up the street to the Officers' Head, where you wrestled with the huge steel door latch both on opening and on shutting the outer door. The head had two rooms, the first of which contained a number of semi-private cubicles. There were no flush toilets. In the inner or basin room you hung your parka, cap and shirt on a high wooden hook, selected a basin and set to work. Some men preferred to wash and shave with their shirt on, for despite the oil-fired stove working noisily nearby, the room was by no means overheated. One night a ceiling leak put out the stove and flowed onto the floor. By morning the floor was ice-covered. Having finished your ablutions, you put on your shirt, parka, cap and gloves and wrestled with the outer latch as you left. Back at the Press Hut you removed the cap, parka and gloves. At times Antarctic life struck you as being largely a matter of donning and shedding clothes and opening and shutting double doors, some of the latter heavy enough to remind you of refrigerator doors.

By contrast, across the corridor from my room in the Lodge was a drinking fountain and the floor's spacious head. In the head were four basins in a row, each with a stainless steel shelf and a single light above a mirror. To the left of these were two urinals. The two toilets, nice modern affairs, with doors, each had a sign reading ONE FLUSH PER SITTING. Some joker had enlarged the last word with a pencil. An adjoining room contained a sauna and two shower stalls. Looking out of one of the head's windows, you saw the station's helicopter pads, usually with one or more H-34s sitting on them. In the distance were the peaks of the Royal Society Range.

The Lodge was situated on the station's eastern extremity. A little way south of it was the new USARP administration building, known as the Chalet. The Chalet was a rare building in Antarctica because it had a bit of style, even though the style was imitation-Swiss. It sat on a hill above the helo pads and hangar. As you approached it from the Lodge you saw beyond it the sea ice of McMurdo Sound and the beautiful white cone of Mount Discovery. The structure, whose A-shaped roof was a lighter shade of brown than its sides, contained a foyer, three office rooms overlooking the Royal Society Range, a small auditorium, a lounge, a small kitchen, a bathroom and a mezzanine. To the right of the entrance door, in silver letters, was the legend: NATIONAL SCIENCE FOUNDATION.

Immediately after depositing our luggage in our rooms—Vance had a similar room on the second floor; Cobb, because he would be at the station only overnight, had been assigned to a dormitory—Vance, Cobb and I went to the wardroom for a couple of drinks, then to the chow hall for dinner. The chow hall was in the Navy personnel building, the largest on the continent. Work on the building had begun in October 1966 and had been completed in February 1970. It was a steel, insulated, panel structure, half single-story, half two-story, and contained a laundry, a library, a barber shop, the ship's store and had a berthing capacity of two hundred and fifty and a feeding capacity of a thousand. All ranks ate the same food but dined separately. There were two cafeterias, one for the enlisted men and one for the chiefs and officers. Civilians ate in the officers' section. I ate a great deal more than was usual for me: sardines, green beans, roast beef, hominy and foods I no longer remember. I kept feeling thirsty and drank much cold water.

After dinner I opened the two letters that had greeted me at the station. One was from Phil Smith of NSF. The other was from a stranger who asked me to sign, cachet and mail two self-addressed envelopes. On his lurid stationery the Californian identified himself as a writer on the subjects of science, nucleonics, engineering, postal history, polar exploration and naval history.

I turned in early. During the night I had my shade and curtains drawn to darken the room but enough light seeped through for one to see easily by. Going to the head once, I frowned at the brilliant outdoor light. Lights burned in the head at all times and the humidifier across the corridor from my room never stopped. Apparently there was no shortage of electric power, thanks to the nuclear plant. There was such a degree of comfort in the Lodge and increasingly in the station that at times it was difficult to realize that nothing lived or grew here that we readily recognized. There were no mosquitoes or flies; no spiders spinning webs; no scratching sounds of mice.

On the way to the chow hall next morning I ran into a friend, Bob Mullins, who was delayed on an early-morning flight to Byrd Station (as was Cobb on a flight to the Pole) by ice fog over Williams Field. The fog was only some five hundred feet thick; a C-130 could easily take off through it; but if for some reason the craft got into trouble it might be in for a dangerous landing; so Mullins, Cobb and others were standing by. I led Mullins to the station's western edge to point out the Discovery Hut across the horseshoe-shaped anchorage. Hut Point was barren, dark; the hut was sharp in the morning light. Heading back toward the chow hall, we saw fog mists slipping over the crest of Observation Hill and lying like smog to the right over the sea ice, the tip of Mount

Discovery showing gleaming white above it. The Royal Society
Range was majestic with snow. I experienced a thrill each time I
stared at its mountains—peaceful, remote, grand, unspoiled, with
clean whites and pale blues. The range was a striking visual relief
from gritty, dark-gray McMurdo. Meltwater rivulets, running down
the hills, crossed the station. Crusts of ice lay on some of the road-
side pools.

After breakfast I dusted and swept away the volcanic grit that
was everywhere in my room and that, as I soon learned, was the
price of leaving a window open. The grit, a summer phenomenon,
was caused by the vehicular traffic on the dry roads and by the
frequent and variable winds. I lunched with Dale Vance and his
friend Frank Merrem. The latter was just in from the Pole, where
he had wintered over. He had gone to the Pole Station in November
1969, when I was first on the ice. He was rather slightly built, had
graying hair, wore glasses and had a very pale forehead. He was
leaving on the first plane out for Christchurch and planned to tour
New Zealand a bit before returning home to Boulder, Colorado. At
the Pole he had worked in atmospheric physics. His little laboratory
had been situated about a quarter of a mile from the main station.
He had walked every day for at least twenty minutes, even when the
temperature was a hundred below. He had been frostbitten a few
times and once his plastic spectacle frames had suddenly snapped
but it hadn't been painful or even difficult to breathe at that temperature. He had felt he was "burning up" when he arrived at
Williams Field at 28° F. No one at the Pole Station had had a cold
during the wintering over, but two weeks before he departed he had
started packing boxes he had brought and he had developed a
whopper. There had been no significant medical problems except
those of a petty officer who seemed to have some sort of lung
trouble.

In the afternoon I met with Chris Shepherd (the station USARP
representative) in the Chalet, where, overheated and spending much
time working a 3M ⚡209 photocopier, I felt fretful and a fool to be
operating a machine when outdoors was glorious Antarctica. But
insurance against the loss of my journal was necessary to the security of my work in progress; I had determined to mail out pages
periodically. Vance picked me up and we went to the wardroom for
beer. The bar was out of ice; all three ice machines had broken
down. Some Navy officers joked that with all the ice in the world

down here, they couldn't get any for their drinks. Vance got caught up in rolling dice with the enlisted-man bartender and a Navy officer. They played Korean Threes. I went to my room, wrote some cards and met Vance for dinner, which consisted of tough steak, tiny shrimp in a bitter sauce, creamy pepper soup, prunes and mixed-fruit pie.

Afterwards I went to the chapel, where Chaplain John Q. Lesher (Protestant), a lieutenant commander, was practicing hymns on a little organ. He was the McMurdo custodian of the Discovery Hut key. I borrowed the key from him and walked down the long, cindery, curving road that flanked the anchorage on its way to Hut Point. A solitary skua circled above me and swooped at me several times before flying away. The hut's exterior wood was pale, bleached, but it had not rotted. I unlocked the door and let myself in, smelling an acrid odor like that of a stable. It was dark inside; the few windows were small. Black slabs of gleaming seal meat lay in a pile against a wall. There were splotches of milky ice on the floor. Not much if anything remained of the original contents. Some day the place would probably be cleaned up and made into a museum that would falsify with brightness and clarity.

A Navy captain had remarked to me in the morning, "Give it two or three more years and we'll have dependents down here."

Vance, when I had repeated this to him, had said, "Man, that's when I won't come back. I will have had it."

A howling wind came up and rattled the lock and door. Standing there alone, I found myself tending to underrate the place because Scott and his companions hadn't actually lived in it. I didn't visualize him in it readily, as I had in the Cape Evans hut last year. I reminded myself that this Discovery Hut was of the greatest importance in the human history of Antarctica.

The east wind blew harder. I stepped out to glance at the sky, then climbed the black hill to Vince's Cross. The wind was so strong I feared it might blow me off the soft ridge leading to the cross. On the station side the hill sloped gently; on the western side it fell like a cliff to the sea. The footing was loose. I saw the Sound, the tidal cracks, and skuas skimming over the sea ice. The wind began to bite. I decided not to linger at this time.

Returning to the chapel and seeing some flag markers moving in the wind, I had the illusion of the presence of ducks or chickens before remembering that there were no domestic animals here. No sound of a cat, a dog. No children's voices or women's voices either. I slipped the key under the door of the chaplain's office and visited the Biology Laboratory, where Beethoven's Ninth was being played on an expensive tape machine and where I ran into Robert Feeney, a bearded professor in biochemical research at the University of California, Davis, who was currently senior scientist at the Biolab.

This was Feeney's sixth working residence and the seventh year of his program in the Antarctic. At fifty-seven he was remarkably youthful in demeanor, interests, curiosity, friendliness and laughter, and he looked in fine physical condition. I had met him at McMurdo the previous year and at Skyland, Virginia, this year. When he asked me now if I cared to go fishing through the ice next morning out at the fish shack, which was located on the Sound about two and a quarter miles from Hut Point, I accepted with alacrity, for I had never fished through ice and had not visited the shack. We agreed to have breakfast together.

4

<hr />

FISHING THROUGH THE ICE

IT WAS a very pleasant meal, for Feeney was a jolly companion, and I was full of keen anticipation regarding the imminent new experience. At first we planned to walk to the shack, and Feeney and I wore windpants and mukluks for the purpose, but the wind proved too strong, so we went by Nodwell instead, riding with his postdoctoral colleague, Gary Means, and his three assistants, who were Feeney's graduate students. Feeney told me that the Navy people did not enjoy his habit of walking out to the shack alone but tolerated it because he had been here so often. Nor were they happy about the Nodwell's being driven to the shack so late in the season. The sea ice had softened and thinned, the tidal cracks had split wide, and just the other day a truck's front wheels had gone through the ice, and the truck had had to be pulled out by another truck. The Nodwell, which had metal tracks on eight tired wheels, was a heavy vehicle and the Navy people feared it would sink through a soft patch. Feeney told me that at the shack the ice was still fairly thick—6.9 feet—and that midway between the shack and the station it was 6.6 feet. Motor toboggans would have been the thing but they were all out in the field.

Means, who had gotten his Ph.D. degree in biochemistry at Davis under Feeney, was endlessly cheerful, had remarkably kind eyes and wore a beautiful, grandfatherly, reddish-gold beard. Before we went to the shack he and I drove up a hill behind McMurdo to a gas-storage depot, where he filled the Nodwell's tank. A large sign urged him to be sure to ground the fuel line before using it. This was designed to avoid accidents due to the considerable Antarctic static electricity.

As we descended from McMurdo to the ice, Feeney walked ahead and guided Means, who was driving. He pointed the way across the tidal cracks (bridged by heavy boards) and onto the firmer ice. The rear door of the vehicle was left open as an escape hatch. The assistants were Ahmed I. Ahmed, Jack R. Vandenheede and Charles Y. Ho. All five men were bearded. The Nodwell was full of gear—survival packs, a sled, metal equipment—and was smoky due to an oil leak (the engine was housed inside the cabin). It was a cloudy day, with an east wind that blew in gusts and brought the frigid air of the ice shelf. The Western Mountains looked somber; the glaciers there gleamed dully under long cloud banks. The sea ice, with patches of discoloration like eczema, was rough enough to throw us about. The Nodwell growled, whined and clanked. A couple of ice-scraping machines stood on the ice north of us. Feeney remarked that they looked like tanks abandoned on a desert of white snow.

The fish shack was a squat red plywood structure. A couple of small red flags stuck up out of the ice to the right of the door. North of the shack were the black features of Observation Hill, the Gap, Crater Hill and some of the slopes of McMurdo Station. The day was too overcast for one to see the Royal Society Range, but I could make out the lower part of Mount Discovery and a portion of Brown Peninsula. Some skuas, having seen us coming, flew to the shack and stood around waiting for odds and ends of fish to be thrown to them.

As you entered the shack you saw on the left a couple of bunks and an oil stove. On the right were a work table and some shelves. The shack was equipped with rations, sleeping bags, chemicals, retorts, test tubes, microscopes and dissection equipment. Its most prominent feature—this was near the door—was an uncovered hole, about four feet square, cut in the wooden floor and through the ice below. Looking down, you saw the irregular sides of the ice hole and the large, beautiful, many-faceted and seemingly phosphorescent crystals jutting out toward the center. The ice was luminescent with light refracted under the shack. Normally the stove was fired day and night to keep the hole from freezing over. It had gone out, so now there was a heavy ice skim on the water, which had to be broken up, scooped up with a long-handled net and dumped outside. After this was done, smaller nets were used to scoop up the finer stuff, which tinkled and which shone with rainbow colors. Then plastic buckets were lowered and water hauled up and poured into a large plastic tub that would hold the day's catch. When the skim was removed the water looked darkly clear, a brownish gray. I was told that the Sound here was about 1,500 feet deep. Meanwhile the stove was lit, and soon it was grunting heavily, and I wondered if it was working itself up to an explosion.

Feeney, Means and I sat on metal folding chairs and fished without bait, using light lines with multiple hooks. A school of silvery fish appeared: *Trematomus borchgrevinki*, named after C. E. Borchgrevink, an Antarctic explorer who built a hut, still extant, at Cape Adare, Victoria Land, at the end of the last century. The fish were divided into "keepers" (large enough to keep) and "leavers" (too small for efficient biological use). To avoid splashes that might frighten the school, "leavers" were placed on a little pale green ice shelf, from which they wriggled into the water. You could see the school hovering, or swimming as though in slow motion, their silver flashes outlined against the depths like the tracings of nuclear particles in a cloud chamber. They had very little experience with hooks; few persons had ever fished so far south. (It was hard to believe it but this was the world's southernmost fishing.) They didn't fight. The "keepers" were rather small this day, some eight to ten inches long. We handled them without gloves. They were slippery, felt scaleless and were very cold.

One marveled at the scene's strangeness: three men luring small exotic fish through pale green and pale blue ice almost seven feet thick, in water three degrees below the freezing point of fresh water, a couple of thousand miles from civilization and some 850 miles from the Pole; and three other men sitting at a long table and busily dissecting the freshly caught specimens and collecting blood, eyes, brains, muscles, livers and hearts. Part of the fish material would be studied at the Biolab and part would be frozen and shipped to the States for more leisurely study with more sophisticated equipment.

The Feeney team's chief interest was in the effect of temperature on biochemical reactions. They were looking for adaptive changes that occurred in cold-water fish but didn't take place in warm-water ones. They had already studied four of the enzymes involved in muscle energy and had made a detailed study of one of the critical respiratory enzymes in the heart muscle. They were currently studying blood clotting; brain enzymes; a red-cell enzyme that converted carbon dioxide to bicarbonate and vice versa; they were obtaining the mitochondria of hearts by differential separation; were working with respirometers; were collecting liver to use the liver enzymes on some of the blood proteins; and were gathering brains to study a brain enzyme involved in neural transfer.

They also had a major blood program going: they were studying the anti-freeze in the serum. This remarkable fish anti-freeze, which kept the blood from freezing in waters at a temperature of 29° F., worked about as glycerol did but was some hundred to three hundred times more efficient, and about a thousand times more efficient than the theory of colligative action called for. The freezing and boiling points of water were affected by materials through a process called colligative action.

The team was also interested in comparative biochemistry as a tool for studying molecular engineering, and in understanding how large polymers, particularly proteins, worked. They were looking for changes in protein structure caused by evolution, in the hope of better understanding function. One of the good places for obtaining proteins in significantly large quantities was egg white. Feeney had started the penguin egg-white program at McMurdo during his first visit to Antarctica seven years ago. He had begun with the Adélie, whose egg was about twice the size of a chicken egg and weighed an average of 120 grams. As for the huge Emperor penguin eggs, the drawback there was that you couldn't obtain fresh ones inasmuch as they were laid in midwinter, when conditions were too severe for human existence at Cape Crozier, at any rate for such a relatively minor purpose as collecting fresh eggs. So Feeney and his various colleagues and aides had collected frozen Emperor eggs in the austral summers and had made approximate corrections for changes they knew would be induced in the properties of the egg-white proteins by freezing. They had chopped the frozen eggs out of the ice with ice axes. These were eggs that the penguins had lost, presumably because of severe storms. The Biolab teams had also done much work in penguin taxonomy.

The Emperors, whose rookery was on the sea ice off Crozier, lived a very hazardous life. They had had a catastrophe earlier this year when a combination land and ice slide had fallen on the rookery and killed many birds. About four years ago the ice had gone out early from Crozier and had taken the rookery with it. The young birds hadn't molted yet and couldn't swim. When the ice melted as it traveled north they drowned.

No Weddell seals had come up through the ice hole in the shack this season. In some past seasons they had suddenly appeared, occasionally bringing with them from the great depths a large fish weighing from seventy-five to a hundred pounds. This was the *Dissostichus mawsoni,* known at McMurdo only because the Weddell would bring it to light. Waiting around the hole would be a rapper and a gaffer. The former would rap the seal on the head with a poker; the latter would gaff the fish when the seal opened its mouth to turn on its attacker. Some three dozen specimens had been obtained in this manner.

There are several kinds of seals in Antarctica, among them the rare Ross, the vicious leopard, the homely crabeater and the remarkable Weddell. The Weddell can dive two thousand feet in search of food and can stay submerged up to forty minutes. How does it withstand the pressure? How does it detect its prey in the blackness of the depths? How does it find its way back to a hole in the ice that it itself had cut with its teeth? Why doesn't it get the bends on coming up? These are some of the questions scientists studying Weddells are trying to answer. Studies of Weddells may, among other things, reveal how our bodies use oxygen.

I was reminded of the time last year when I had gone from McMurdo by Nodwell over the ice northward to Hutton Cliffs, whose ice colors at midnight were startling: aquamarine, turquoise, sapphire, cobalt. I had visited the hut there that was used as a seal station. It contained three beds in a tier, a desk and scientific equipment. A TV camera had been lowered through a hole in the ice and could be aimed by remote control. Standing in front of a small screen, I had observed Weddells in the water and heard their sounds with hydrophones: clucking, whistles, grunts, glottal clicks and pops. Outside, some mothers and pups basked on the ice. A large seal lay alone on her back, making coughing noises. Sometimes she blew air hard through her nostrils before closing them tightly with what sounded like a sigh. Or she took a deep, seemingly painful breath and made laughing motions with her throat. But the sounds that issued were comically inappropriate to her mass: they were parakeet whistles. When I drew close she mooed and showed her teeth. In the south the sun broke through in a molten white splash, saffron streamers flowing from it. The ice dimples and sastrugi were sharply revealed. A small, gentle white cape lay on the horizon's left side, showing bits of black like ermine tails.

As we fished in the red shack, suddenly, as if something in the water had struck a note or a scent, the school of *borchgrevinki* disappeared; and although we sat patiently, hoping to catch more, and tried fishing deeper to arouse new interest, the hole remained empty. One felt the movement of cold, heavy air from the hole like the exhalation of a giant refrigerator. Ahmed brought me an excellent cup of hot chocolate. There was a long, pleasant silence during which one stared into the beautiful hole and wondered how it would feel to fall in. It would probably be impossible to climb out without help. Yet Feeney had fallen in once while alone and had managed to save himself.

That was at a time when the Biolab had a shack smaller and a good deal more cramped than the present one. While waiting hopefully for a seal to surface with a large fish in its mouth, he attempted to go across the side of the hole, slipped and fell in. He had a fish trap on the bottom of the sea, and this was attached to a wire hanging from a nearby winch, and he was able to throw one knee onto an ice ledge, catch hold of the wire and pull himself out. He turned the stove up, took off his clothes and got into a sleeping bag. He often stayed at the shack alone at night. He loved going outside and observing the remarkable and often changing scenes all around him.

The worst scare he ever had on the ice was at Crozier while studying penguins. He was still new to Antarctica then.

"When you're green you're cautious about things you don't need to be cautious about, and not cautious about things you should be. One of the things you don't do is walk the penguin trails at the edge of the ice. The ice sometimes overhangs, and you weigh a lot more than a penguin, and if the ice breaks off you may have had it, for often there will be a drop and you won't be able to get out, and the leopard seals patrol there. I was out there in between our work periods, and I was trying to get some movies of a leopard seal eating an Adélie. The seal throws the penguin up in the air, catches it and slaps it on the water. He removes its skin in this way and blood shoots all over. Well, I saw a leopard seal come up right next to the ice, and I saw him start off, and I took after him on the trail. I was running. Then I got to this one spot and paused. I don't remember why. Maybe I had to climb over something. At that moment, when I was about two feet from the sea, a leopard seal threw his head and upper part of his body onto the ice and snapped at me. He missed me by a matter of inches. I was able to throw myself backwards after he slid back in, but not right at the moment. I got back about three feet from the edge and just lay there, sweating heavily, before I had the strength to get myself back another ten feet. All I could see were that great face and those jaws. It just scared the dickens out of me."

I sat there hoping for the fish to bite again, for I had many things to do while in Antarctica and would probably not have the time to return to the shack. I hoped in vain. We headed back for the station, Feeney as jolly as ever.

5

~~~~~~

MCMURDO STATION: TWO

ON RETURNING from the fish shack I lunched with Dale Vance, after
which I went to the chapel, borrowed the key to the Discovery Hut
and headed for the road that swung around the bend of Winter
Quarters Bay. There was a bitter wind on this gray afternoon. The
dry "streets" of the station looked particularly ugly and the black
hills felt ominous. Seabees were erecting a large metal building.
Occasionally a huge truck or bulldozer raised a cloud of dust that
gritted between one's teeth. As you descended the bend you saw
equipment stacked on the shore below: large vehicles, fuel lines, a
Jamesway, a roaring generator making electricity for a welding arc.
Seabees were bulldozing and grading, preparing the offloading
area for the ships that would soon be coming. The gray-green tidal
crack here was now some six feet wide. The rotten sea ice along the
shore had been shoved up by pressure.

The Royal Society Range was under cloud cover, but I could
see a number of the slate-blue planes of the craggy foothills, as well
as the cradles of small glaciers glinting in a source of light not visible
to me. I could make out Hobbs Peak (the northernmost part of the
Range), Hobbs Glacier and the outlet of the Blue Glacier. The combination of overcast in the west, together with the spotlighted,
white-cradled glaciers among blue hills that seemed to be in motion,
was quite dramatic. In the foreground was the subdued sea ice
with its lovely, unevenly glowing texture.

Reaching the hut, I removed my gloves and struggled to unlock
the small, seemingly frozen padlock that secured the lockless, latch-

less door. The wind, sweeping off the ice shelf and through the
Gap and over the station, made my hands cry out in pain. It was this
wind with which members of Scott's first expedition were so familiar.
When I was inside it gave the impression of being demonically intent on destroying the door: it kept exploding the latter open so violently I feared it would rip it off its hinges. I could pull the door
shut by a rawhide thong but I could not fasten it. I found a bit of
ancient rope near the blubber stove, tied one end to the thong and
knotted the other to a rusty nail above the door frame. This managed
to hold the door shut. Sounds of howling; of rattling of the padlock
against dry wood; of creaking, banging.

A Weather Bureau thermometer that I had brought with me registered 18° F. on the floor and 19° about twenty inches above it. I
poked a flashlight beam into rafter corners in the absent-minded
expectation of finding spider webs. On shelves were boxes of oat-
meal; cans of marmalade, sardines, damson jam, biscuit; an empty
old bottle of Courvoisier cognac. Here and there were sledge-haul-
ing harness; long wooden arcs that had probably been used in gravity experiments; the slabs of seal meat I had seen yesterday; and
sticky blubber in the blubber pot near the stove, the skin black, the
blubber orange.

On returning the key to the chaplain I saw two enlisted men on
their knees in the chapel corridor, scraping old wax off the linoleum
with razor blades in preparation for Christmas. One of them was
going to the Pole tomorrow for the rest of the austral summer. The
chaplain dropped to his knees and scraped away too. Walking
towards the Lodge and passing piles of equipment that looked
abandoned, I felt a sense of release in living in a place so casual
about neatness.

At the Lodge I sought out David Elliot, a geologist who had
made a spectacular fossil find the previous austral summer season,
and made an appointment with him to be interviewed in my quarters two days later in connection with my book. I had read about the
discovery in the New York *Times*. The find had a very important
bearing on the validity of the theory of continental drift, the increasing proof for which I had been following with keen interest for
years. Long ago, for my amusement, I had made plaster of Paris
templates of the continents from a globe, had arranged them like
the pieces of a jigsaw puzzle until they seemed to form a supercontinent, and had photographed the result. At McMurdo I had

heard many fine things concerning Elliot's competence as a scientist, his high intelligence, his articulateness, and his attractive English personality, so I was understandably eager to chat with him in private in the hope of learning from the most authoritative source the details of the discovery and what it had been like to make it.

At first, as I sensed, he was cool to my proposal, possibly because he was very busy. He asked probing questions about my project. I was relieved when, after I explained the purpose of my book, he consented to be interviewed. Still, I feared he would not be sufficiently communicative for a good interview. To my surprise and pleasure, he was to stay in my quarters for a long time and we were to chat on and on about matters unrelated to the discovery. He had an excellent grasp of the works of Scott and Shackleton and it was delightful to discuss the relative merits of the two men with him, although we disagreed strongly at times.

I was alone in my room when a friend knocked at the door and came in in a sour mood to complain of the Navy's reluctance to let him hike out on the sea ice.

"They have a wild hair up their ass," he said.

And he said he didn't like women to be at Cape Crozier. There was a German-born woman there now, with her husband.

"It's no good, goddammit. She even has her own crapper. The Navy built and flew it in. We had to rock it down against the wind. Crozier's windier than hell. After we finished—there were four of us —we dedicated it by pissing against it, one on each corner. We didn't piss low, either. We stood back and aimed high. That's how we dedicated her shit house. No disrespect meant to the lady. I like her."

I could not help being surprised by this open hostility to the woman's presence at Crozier, which I took to mean to her presence on the continent. The man was usually so uncomplaining and so temperate in his judgments. He was a highly respected senior scientist; a family man; and one of good humor and good will. I wondered if he was reacting to the fact that he was due to leave the ice in a day or two. And then I imagined the four men urinating on the portable outhouse and wondered what it was like to be a woman in Antarctica. My friend left to keep an appointment at the Chalet.

Vance was in his room, looking damp and tired from hard work. He showed me a package he had received from an uncle today: a six-pack of bloody-mary mix he would take to Vostok. We drank beer together in the wardroom, where we learned that the Connie had lost an engine yesterday on returning to Christchurch. The popcorn and mixed nuts were free; the drinks were very inexpensive. There was a huge photograph of a beautiful pinup girl on the wall facing the customers. She was lying on her back, breasts standing, one leg raised, her lips smiling sensually, her eyes staring at one. In one hand she held a back scratcher.

I got up late next morning (7:15), skipped breakfast and went to the radio-communications building on a hill behind the station, where a Lieutenant Parker asked me if I'd be willing to be the first to try out some new radio gear when I camped at Capes Royds and Evans. This was a compact radio with a whip antenna and was designed to operate on batteries. The question was if it would perform faithfully at a range of fifteen to twenty-five miles of McMurdo. I said I'd be glad to, although it struck me as funny that a novice at Antarctic camping should be asked to try out a new rig on his very first time out. I was given a course in radio communications and was presented with a unit called a Patrolfine H.F. Single Sideband Transceiver, known more simply as a Southcom 120, which was manufactured in Escondido, California. The unit had two extra sets of nickel-cadmium batteries. If all three sets failed to work I was to switch to a generator, which was good for 1,800 watts. If I couldn't get through to McMurdo directly I was to try an aircraft channel and ask that my messages be relayed. My call number would be McMurdo Three Two (S-32 being my USARP project number). Calling time would be 0800–1000 daily.

Judging by the degree of indoctrination I received on the use of the generator, I gathered that the lieutenant did not have his hopes up about the ability of the batteries to withstand Antarctic temperatures. I must be sure to open the fuel line first, then set the lever to CHOKE, and then crank with the rope. After three or four cranks I must set the lever to RUN. When I wanted to shut the generator off I must close the fuel line to empty the carburetor; this would prevent freezing in the latter. I must let the generator run about fifteen minutes so it could warm up thoroughly before I drew power from it. It was best to run it with the tank almost full; the more fuel, the more gravity would help to move the fuel through the line. Fuel, a mixture of gasoline and oil, would be provided by USARP.

As I left, the lieutenant remarked that we were currently in a communications blackout as a result of solar activity. We could rouse Pole and Byrd Stations but nothing else, so there would be no flights to or from Cheechee for a while, which meant, among other things, that mail would move neither in nor out until the blackout lifted.

Later in the day I attended a scientific briefing, which reminded me of briefings I had been given during my first visit to the ice, after which I had written:

"The equipment is frostily sedate even when it contains tiny colored lights, but at the cosmic ray station in a long red hut between McMurdo Station and Scott Base it goes into an antic dance. It does this every two minutes when the digital readout (an automatic counter) whirls lighted numerals faster than the eye can catch them and punches its findings on a roll of narrow tape to be sent to the States for analysis. The new Antarctica is accustomed to complex control and instrument panels. One sees them in the cockpits of aircraft, in the small nuclear plant at McMurdo where seawater is desalinated and electricity produced, in some of the scientific stations and at Williams Field. We heard discussions of the next logical step: unmanned automated stations that will radio their findings to polar satellites. Meanwhile, manned American research on the continent continues in numerous fields: glaciology, oceanography, biology, cartography, meteorology, geomagnetism, seismology, aurora, upper atmosphere physics (including cosmic ray and ionosphere opacity studies), paleontology and others.

"Why has Antarctica been chosen as the site upon which to conduct basic research? There are a number of reasons, among them the following: the continent comprises one-tenth of the earth's land mass; it contains significant clues to the earth's past; it greatly influences the weather patterns of the Southern Hemisphere; it is relatively free of radio static; and it is ideally suited to upper atmosphere studies.

"The scientists we encountered were young, eager, personable and very competent. We often saw them as a different breed from the Antarctic hands who wintered over in the old days. The tall, fit-looking young man at the cosmic ray station was about to return to the States after a stay on the ice of thirteen months, much of it in the hut. One remembered how winter-over personnel in the past felt the prolonged absence of sunlight, some growing morose, irritable, and a few breaking down. The young man had wintered over alone, had walked now and then to McMurdo on an errand and had received supplies and an occasional visitor. Had he ever been lonely or depressed? On the contrary, he asserted, he had enjoyed the winter. There had been fewer distractions, and being without mail had its advantages: there was no mail to upset him and no cause to be disappointed because someone hadn't written. Did he smoke, drink, play cards? No. 'I'm a straight arrow,' he said with an ironic smile. Then how had he spent his free time? Well, he had faced and stained the walls of his bedroom with veneered plywood, had kept a diary, had taken photographs. Occasionally he had spoken with his folks by ham radio. He was not only a different breed from his predecessors; he also lived under very different conditions. In the Antarctic, solitude has perhaps a less deleterious effect than the old condition of extreme crowding in tiny, primitive huts. He had electric light, a telephone, and the medical facilities at McMurdo."

The rest of the day was consumed by conversations and chores. At around nine o'clock, after drinking with Vance in the wardroom, I walked alone to a point quite close to Scott Base. The evening was extraordinarily warm. I removed my cap and left my parka unzipped. The road through the Gap, gravelly, gray, in spots soft, was well-traveled now that the sea-ice route was too rotten to be trusted. It was the main way to Williams Field: over the Gap; a brief distance northward of Scott Base; east past pressure ice and onto the ice shelf; and several miles east on the shelf to the field. A truck, coming downhill toward McMurdo, stirred a cloud of dust resembling steam. On my left the southern slope of Crater Heights still held much snow. Pools of meltwater marked the road shoulders. Those in the shadow of Observation Hill had ice skim forming on them. In the sun my ungloved hands were warm; in the shadow of the hill they turned painfully cold. A rivulet was scurrying across the road on its way to the Sound. The road was pockmarked as if by small explosives. Each hole contained milky water.

I reached the Gap's crest. Pressure ice on the left of silhouetted Cape Armitage rose in jagged masses, its crevices showing cobalt blue. On my right the lower portion of Observation Hill swooped down in a black plane. Beyond the hill lay the mottled, pale blue annual or sea ice, which, in the evening sun, had a faint, lilac, pearly cast. Directly ahead of me, some miles away on the ice shelf, the gray of White Island's cliffs and hilltops peeped through embayments of creamy snow. The little island looked almost idyllic, it rose so gently out of the shelf. I made out a faint, ribbon-like white line on the icescape, running approximately north and south. This was where the shelf and the sea ice met. At this point the shelf was barely ten feet higher than the Sound. The low-hanging sun illumined hills, ice and snow in a subtly dramatic, at times beautifully nostalgic way with a gentle ivory light. The sky was smoky except at the zenith, where it was azure.

I heard hillside snow and ice melting and occasionally a tinkle as of metal when a piece of ice broke loose and skittered down. The sun was lower at night than by day, so there was more glare during the night hours. At night it was painful to observe the Royal Society Range without sunglasses. My hands were atingle with warmth, yet earlier in the day they had felt like frozen claws, and the fingertips and nails had been very white.

I spotted Scott Base below me, with its handful of pale green huts on Pram Point. It seemed very strange to find a human settlement there. The sudden green of the base struck me as extraordinary, suggesting as it did young grass or spring leaves. For I was surrounded by a black wasteland that seemed to have been blasted into infertility. All around me were porous volcanic rocks, most of them black but some with a reddish hue. Yet the visual beauty was what one was chiefly aware of: the terrific contrasts between sweeping black shapes with the faintly blue ice; or between the rose-tinted powder-puff clouds with the sky's azure.

In the south Mount Discovery was tall, large, majestic, its cone suggesting a bald white head. In the north, beyond the great white stretch of Windless Bay, Mount Terror, a contemplative-looking mountain sweeping eastwardly into a cape, or so it seemed from where I stood, its bayside cliffs resembling chalk cliffs because of the way the snow was catching the light directly opposite them, its luminous gentle shadows the palest blue-grays, was thrillingly opalescent. It was a fairy world over there of pale blues, dappled grays and gleaming, glowing nacres. In the bay itself—this was the bay well known to Wilson, Bowers and Cherry-Garrard from their midwinter traverse between Capes Evans and Crozier—the shelf ice looked subdued, a twilight blue; but nothing was flat or dead there; everything was textured, even if only faintly, and was therefore alive.

When one turned one's head one experienced a tremendous sweep of space, and within the framework of this relatively monochromatic world there was the excitement of color: the sweet blue of the zenith, the lime above the horizon, the lavender, lilac and prune in the ice shelf, the slate blues of islands and mountains. The sea ice was a fiery mirror. The water rushing down the hillside gleamed like a stream of mercury. The unspoiled silence, the uncluttered views, the aloofness of the Royal Society Range, and the scene's incredible expanse worked profoundly on me. I felt in love with something or someone. Also, I felt loved, blessed, graced. "Lord, Lord," I kept saying to myself, "how lucky I am to be here," and my eyes filled with tears.

Later I hailed an orange bus, mounted it by the middle door and found myself among green-clad enlisted men with green survival bags. This was the Williams Field-McMurdo bus. Above the driver's head a sign urged TALK TO THE DRIVER. I was in a marvelously serene frame of mind when I reached the Lodge. But when I tried to work in my room I discovered that the walk had left me strangely pooped.

My alarm clock awoke me at 3 A.M. I dressed and went outside to see what the station looked and felt like in the middle of the night. It was still unusually warm, although in the shadows were ice-crusted pools. The shadows were very long. The sun was drawing close to Observation Hill. Soon it hid behind it. The Penguin Power and Light Company was thrumming with the never-pausing sound of generators. There was no one to be seen in the station.

6

NEW, MAJOR FOSSIL FINDS

IT HAD long been suspected by certain geologists that Antarctica had once had a temperate climate and had belonged to a southern supercontinent, named Gondwanaland after a region in India, whose other members were South America, South Africa, Australia and Peninsula India. It had seemed logical to include Antarctica in the concept of Gondwanaland despite the lack of Antarctic evidence, and Alfred Wegener did so in his classic presentation of the theory of continental drift. The significance of Antarctica in Gondwanaland lay precisely in its present isolation as a continent: it was separated from other continents by hundreds of miles of open sea. If land-living tetrapods should be discovered in Antarctica, the important question would be posed: how did they get there? Their presence could not be adequately explained by present-day geography. For much of geologic history the earth's climate was more temperate than the present one (we were still in an ice age), and the temperate climatic zones could well have reached the latitudes of the Antarctic Peninsula.

But it was unlikely that they extended to the Transantarctic Mountains within a few hundred miles of the Pole, and it was in those mountains that in February 1912 Edward Wilson of Scott's second expedition discovered *Glossopteris*, the Permian plant characteristic of the southern continents. *Glossopteris* was the first in-

I am greatly indebted to David H. Elliot for the materials in this chapter, which were gathered during an interview with him at McMurdo Station and in subsequent correspondence.

ternal evidence that Antarctica might indeed have been a part of Gondwanaland during the Permian Period, about 250 million years ago. However, plant seeds might possibly have been carried by winds across oceanic barriers; consequently *Glossopteris* was not considered to be hard evidence. Harder evidence would be the discovery of land-living tetrapods, for these could not have been carried by winds.

In December 1967 Peter J. Barrett, a New Zealand geologist participating in the United States Antarctic Research Program, while studying sedimentary rocks laid down by streams during the Triassic Period some 220 million years ago in the Transantarctic Mountains about 325 miles from the Pole, discovered the first Antarctic land vertebrate fossil. It was subsequently identified by Edwin H. Colbert, a vertebrate paleontologist of the American Museum of Natural History, as a jawbone belonging to a labyrinthodont amphibian, a large, salamander-like creature that had also lived on neighboring continents. A labyrinthodont amphibian belongs to a very broad grouping of amphibians and cannot be given any unusual significance. However, its discovery was important in indicating that Antarctica was not devoid of tetrapods during the Permian and Triassic Periods, the time for which there is most evidence for the existence of Gondwanaland. Before the discovery of the labyrinthodont amphibian, there had been no evidence of the existence of vertebrates that lived on land or in fresh water and were common both to Antarctica and to other Gondwana continents. Vertebrates had been found some fifty years earlier but they were fish and Devonian in age and therefore not really relevant to the argument about the existence of Gondwanaland.

As a consequence of Barrett's discovery, in November 1969 a team of four vertebrate paleontologists and nine geologists set up camp in the Central Transantarctic Mountains to see if other land vertebrate fossils could be found and to pursue geological studies. The paleontologists were led by Colbert. The geologists were led by David H. Elliot of Ohio State University. The geologists planned to map the geology of the area, to measure rock strata and to collect rock and fossil samples for later laboratory analysis. The camp, in the Queen Alexandra Range just west of the Beardmore Glacier, a mountainous, heavily glaciated region about midway between McMurdo Station and the Pole, was known as Coalsack Bluff Camp because it was near Coalsack Bluff, so named because the bluff contained coal seams. It consisted of four Jamesway huts that had been flown in and constructed by the Navy and it was supported by Navy personnel. The scientists could shuttle by Navy turbine helicopters from the camp to field work areas.

The scientists arrived at the camp November 22. The next morning, the very first day of field work, Elliot discovered a fossil site: bones in a sandstone bed laid down about 220 million years ago during the Triassic Period. Further search in the bed revealed the remains of labyrinthodonts and also those of thecodonts, the extinct reptiles ancestral to the dinosaurs. The scientists in Antarctica stated in a report to the National Science Foundation, "The presence of fresh-water amphibians and land-living reptiles in Antarctica, some 200 million years ago, is very strong evidence of the probability of continental drift because these amphibians and reptiles, closely related to the back-boned animals of the same age on other continents, could not have migrated between continental areas across oceanic barriers."

On December 4 one of the vertebrate paleontologists made a dramatic find: part of a skull identified by Colbert as *Lystrosaurus*, a reptilian counterpart of the hippopotamus in that it was probably an aquatic herbivore. *Lystrosaurus* had also lived in Africa. Its skull was distinctive: the eyes and nostrils were high on the head, possibly so the animal could see and breathe while wallowing. Scientists could not believe that *Lystrosaurus* was able to migrate across a great stretch of open ocean such as surrounds Antarctica. According to Laurence M. Gould, a famous geologist who was visiting the camp, and who had been chief scientist on Byrd's first Antarctic expedition in 1928, the *Lystrosaurus* was "the key index fossil of Lower Triassic in the major southern land masses." Gould said that the newest find "establishes beyond further question the former existence of the great southern continent of Gondwanaland," adding that the find was "not only the most important fossil ever found in Antarctica but one of the truly great fossil finds of all time." The New York *Times* ran a front-page story about the find on December 6.

A year later, in December 1970, while I was working at McMurdo, I met David Elliot, as I indicated in the previous chapter. And now, two days later, I had a fascinating talk with him in my room. He was attractive, young, lean, handsome, dark-haired and in excellent physical condition. He was on his way back to the United States after his fifth trip to Antarctica. His first had been to the Antarctic Peninsula with the British Antarctic Survey. His last four had been made in connection with the United States program. He was employed by the Institute of Polar Studies of Ohio State University and by the university's department of geology. Although he had made an important fossil find he was a geologist, not a paleontologist. I was intrigued by what seemed to me to be a discrepancy of fate. Dit it strike him in this way too?

Yes. Of course, if he hadn't found the fossils somebody else would have, sooner or later. The only edge he had had over anyone else was that he knew what the rocks looked like and what he might expect to find in them. The background for the find was something like the following. He had been involved in a mapping program which had been initiated by Peter Barrett, who had led the first two Antarctic expeditions that Elliot had been a member of under USARP. The base sheets for the geologic maps were the same as those used by the United States Geological Survey in the preparation of the topographic maps of the area. Some of the geology had been plotted from the geologic interpretation of air photographs inasmuch as it had not always been possible to go to the actual outcrops. Barrett and Elliot had worked together on these photographs, and last year Elliot had gone to Antarctica partly to check out some of the places where they had doubts, as well as to compile information for places where they had none. Barrett was also in Antarctica during the 1970–71 field season, but with the New Zealand program, not with the Ohio State University party in the Beardmore Glacier area.

The scientists, as we have noted, arrived at the camp November 22. The helos were not coming that day and they couldn't come the following day because of weather conditions, and in fact they didn't come for another five. Meanwhile what was a geologist to do? Obviously only one thing: head for the nearest outcrop. So Elliot hiked to some rocks a couple of miles away to see whether they were in fact Triassic, as Barrett and he had inferred from the air photographs. He looked for certain indicators but failed to find the principal one. Instead he came upon little fragments that he suspected were bone although they were unlike any bones he had previously seen. They were slightly knuckle-shaped and full of holes and they certainly weren't pebbles. He took a few back to camp and handed them to Colbert and asked, "What *about* these? Are they bones?" Colbert replied, "Yes, they are."

The find naturally created a stir in the camp. In the afternoon many members of the party went to the site, where it soon became obvious that there were a lot of bones there. Eventually about four hundred specimens were collected. But the collection suffered in one respect: complete skull material, the ideal material for precise identification of fossil reptiles, was absent; the bones from the sandstone bed had clearly come from some other source. The animals had probably died on a flood plain and been covered by fine-grained sediment deposited by floods. The river channel had subsequently migrated, cut across the flood plain, and the bones had been swept into the river and had been broken and water-worn. They had then been deposited in the slack water on the inside of a river bend and been covered by more sand. The finds made this year, 1970, at McGregor Glacier were superior to those of last year at Coalsack Bluff in that potentially better material was being recovered, including some complete skeletons. However, in this case it was proving much more difficult to separate the bones from the matrix than had been the case with the Coalsack Bluff material.

Was there another significant find in Antarctica one might hope for?

Yes: the discovery of mammal fossils, in particular marsupials, in the hope of demonstrating that marsupials migrated from South America across Antarctica and into Australia, and not from North America through Asia and down into Australia. (Fossil marsupials had been found in Australia and in both North and South America.) Although there were no clues at present, one had some idea of where to start looking, and again this depended to a certain extent on knowledge of the geology. If marsupials should be discovered, or even some mammals, this would rank as a third major Antarctic contribution to paleontology, and would have implications beyond the field of vertebrate paleontology. The other two major contributions were the discovery of fossil plant life and the finds of last year. It should be added that the important contributions of Antarctica to geology had to be seen in a historical context. The plants at Hope Bay in the northern part of the Antarctic Peninsula had been found in 1902. The impact of their discovery would not have been so great half a century later because advances in geological knowledge had amply indicated by then that there was no need to believe

Antarctica had always been an ice-covered continent. The tetrapod bones were significant because of their impact on the paleontological evidence for the existence of Gondwanaland and therefore for the reality of continental drift.

What were the present chances of finding mammals?

Not very good. Mammals had been found in Upper Triassic rocks in Europe, China, North America and Africa; a single mammal had been found in Triassic rocks of the Gondwana sequence of South Africa; and there was one Jurassic mammal from the southern hemisphere, from Tanzania. The rocks one was dealing with in the Transantarctic Mountains were part of the Gondwana sequence of Permian and Triassic ages, and the Jurassic rocks were mainly basalts, with only a few interbeds of tuff (a volcanic rock) or sediment. The mammalian fossil record from the other Gondwana continents was not very encouraging for finds in Antarctica. Elsewhere in Antarctica, on the Antarctic Peninsula, Jurassic rocks were, similarly, mainly volcanic, but there was perhaps some hope for discoveries in younger rocks.

Did the finds this year change the outlook concerning the theory of continental drift?

They strengthened the paleontological evidence supporting the theory. It had been argued by anti-drifters that a single specimen, of only one genus, was not sufficient proof, paleontologically speaking, of continental drift. It had been suggested by them (he thought this was a bit farfetched) that a few animals might have reached Antarctica by some chance mechanism such as floating on logs. However, if proponents of the theory could provide as evidence not only a single genus (*Lystrosaurus*) but components of a fauna with similar genera in the same proportions as in South Africa (for instance, large numbers of herbivores on which a small number of carnivores lived), they would immeasurably strengthen arguments for the theory. The recent fossil finds at McGregor Glacier suggested that the Antarctic fauna was very similar to that of South Africa in beds of equivalent age, although there *were* aspects of the fauna that James Kitching, the South African vertebrate paleontologist, who knew the South African fauna like the back of his hand, found unfamiliar to him. There were elements of the Antarctic fauna that were alien to South Africa but that might be closely related to elements of the fauna of South America or India or Australia; or the

alien elements of the Antarctic fauna might be endemic to Antarctica.

The fossil finds of this year did not have the popular impact of
those of last, but from the point of view of vertebrate paleontology
they were in many ways much more interesting. For example, one
of the fossil animals found this year was an advanced mammal-like
reptile, *Thrinaxodon*. It was quite close to being a mammal although
it still had to be classified as a reptile. Until this year only twenty-
five specimens had been known in the world, all found in South
Africa. Now we seemed to have twelve more, discovered in one locality of Antarctica. It was extraordinary that an animal of such
rarity should appear in such abundance in one locality, but this
paralleled the situation in South Africa, where the animals were
concentrated in a very few localities. We were fortunate to have hit
on the right place in Antarctica. We were also fortunate in another
way: we had the service this year of somebody who was probably
more skilled at the business of bone-finding than anyone else in the
world—a man with an international reputation, who had been at it
since the age of twelve and who was now approaching fifty. This
was, of course, James Kitching. Kitching could spot bone where nobody else saw it; he walked and tripped over bone all the time; he
had a remarkable eye for it.

What would Antarctica need to produce in order to win over
someone who was still severely critical of the theory of continental
drift?

There were two lines of evidence in support of the theory. One
was geophysical and came from the oceans. The other was paleontological and stemmed from the continents. It seemed to Elliot
that any other theory, given such a mass of evidence, would have
insurmountable difficulties. The anti-drifters used to say, "There is
no mechanism by which you can move continents. Therefore the
process is impossible." The oceans had by now given abundant
evidence that such a movement of the continents was possible, but if
this was still denied, then how did the animals get to Antarctica?
You could not postulate sunken land bridges; such things didn't exist. Even across the Scotia Arc there were wide areas in which you
could not simply resurrect land to make bridges: the gaps were too
large. So what would the anti-drifter argue now? Would he fall
back on separate and parallel lines of evolution? But as far as one
could tell from the fossil record there was no reason to believe you

could have separate lines of evolution leading to exactly the same animal. This had never occurred anywhere else in the world and there was no reason to believe it had occurred in Antarctica.

Was Antarctica an exciting place, geologically speaking?

Oh yes. It had several appeals. One was that it offered you the opportunity for genuine exploration. Another was that you were intimately involved with intercontinental correlations. The flat-lying rocks you saw everywhere in the valleys beyond McMurdo Sound and along the western side of the Ross Sea and the Ross Ice Shelf were part of the Gondwana sequence. The geology of the Antarctic Peninsula was very similar to that of southern South America. In addition, the Scotia Arc—South Georgia, the South Orkneys and so on—was a peculiar island arc system, in some ways simple, in others anomalous. The study and interpretation of the Scotia Arc might offer insight into the development of island arcs elsewhere, particularly the Caribbean.

I remarked that it was somehow "right" that he should have been at the core of this remarkable story of the finds. It would have been less of a good tale if he had been the fair-haired young paleontologist instead of a geologist. Life was full of fascinating dissonances. That was what made it difficult to be an inventor in adequate competition with life. It was what made a man like Tolstoy so wonderful in the field of literature. He gave you the sense of being able to invent all the curiosities, eccentricities and anomalies of life itself.

7

MIRACULOUS ESCAPE OF THE *PEGASUS*

On October 8, 1970, about two months before I arrived in Antarctica, the *Pegasus*, one of two C-121 Super Constellations owned by VXE-6, departed from Christchurch with favorable weather predicted for the McMurdo area. By the time it reached McMurdo almost twelve hours later on the first day of air operations for the season, the weather had deteriorated so badly that visibility was zero-zero in heavily blowing snow. The temperature was 6° F. After five attempts to land with the assistance of the GCA (Ground Control Approach) unit the pilot was forced to touch down. Veering off the ice runway, the Connie lost its right landing gear, its right wing and its nose-landing gear. Parts of it were scattered over several hundred yards. But the rest of the plane remained intact and all eighty persons aboard escaped serious injury. Passengers and crew broke out tents and other survival gear and waited for a rescue. The storm was so bad it took an hour for the first vehicle, a trackmaster parked four hundred yards away, to reach the aircraft. It took three hours for several vehicles to carry the occupants of the Connie to the McMurdo Dispensary.

When I flew from Washington to Christchurch in the *Phoenix*, the sister craft of the *Pegasus*, I sensed in some of my fellow passengers apprehension because of what had happened to the *Pegasus* and because it was thought we too might fly to the ice in an old Connie, and several times I heard the opinion that the *Phoenix* ought to be retired promptly from Antarctic service before a major tragedy occurred. Unlike the C-130s, which had both skis and wheels for landing gear and therefore possessed the capability of landing on many places on the ice shelf, the Connies had only wheels and could not land elsewhere than on the annual ice runway.

After interviewing Elliot I had a talk with Bobby Gene Russell, chief photographic officer of VXE-6, who had been aboard the *Pegasus* on October 8, and I heard his account of what had happened. I won't try to reproduce his North Carolina drawl.

The flights down here from Christchurch always cause a little concern on everybody's part, you know, particularly once you get up front and look out of the aircraft and all you see is just miles and miles of broken ice and water. You know that if you ever went down there you'd have a mighty poor chance of surviving. But you try to put that out of your mind and keep on going. The pilots face that every trip but they have faith in the aircraft and in the crewmen, and over the long haul VXE-6 has a mighty good safety record. So we put a little faith in that too. And some of us might put a little faith in our Maker, you know.

On the way down, this time that we had the crash, there were seven aircraft scheduled to come into McMurdo that day, and we were the last of the seven. The weather looked good and so we kept on going. Once you've passed the point of safe return there's no turning back on the Connie. When we got into the McMurdo Sound area the weather turned bad very rapidly, and as we came in for a landing we had something like thirty-five-knot cross winds that were 90° to the runway, and that's out of limits for the Connie. I think thirty knots is about max. So we not only had those heavy cross winds but the turbulence was something else too. The aircraft was heaving and tossing and turning, and during the initial approach you didn't know whether you just touched the deck or maybe hit an air pocket and dropped a hundred feet or what. On our way in, the pilot stated that things were a little out of tolerance there and everyone started to suiting up appropriately, getting all the foul weather gear on and putting loose gear in a safe position so it wouldn't go flying around the cabin.

Then we made our initial pass. We knew it was going to be a rough landing. We heard the engines backfiring a bit and everybody was anticipating a touch down. But it never came. Instead, he added power and pulled off to come around to make another pass.

Well, this went on six times, and I imagine it lasted something like maybe half an hour or forty-five minutes. Time tended to have little meaning then because we were all anticipating something pretty rough. It was so turbulent that a lot of people became airsick, and I was one of them, so I had a little brown paper bag I was throwing up in. I was sitting all the way aft, right adjacent to the regular entrance door.

The flight orderly, who was sitting right alongside where I was sitting, got airsick and had to unstrap himself and go to the door to use the plastic bag hanging from it. The only thing to keep him in one place during all the turbulence and the erratic attitude of the aircraft was the T bar at the end of the door, that he was hanging onto.

On the last two or three passes there was absolute silence on the part of everybody. That's the reason that I feel like there were more people praying to God than just myself. And I was sincerely praying to God. Finally, on the last pass we did touch down, and no sooner than we touched down than evidently the right wheel hit a snowbank and was sheared off, and then the right wing hit and broke off, and from the way it felt to me the tail of the aircraft slid around to the front, so to speak, and we were sliding down and off to the side of the runway tail first.

I thought that the aircraft had come to a stop and I was ready to get up out of my seat, but one of the helicopter pilots who was also a pax [passenger] back there thought that it hadn't, so he told everyone to keep their seats. Everybody seemed to be quite calm. Nobody was screaming or hollering or anything. I myself had said a very sincere prayer to the Lord to protect us and grant us a safe landing. About three or four seconds passed, then they said, "Okay, everybody out." The loudspeaker wasn't working but at that time it was so quiet you wouldn't need it. Once those engines were shut down it was very quiet except for the wind. I think they shut down everything to keep any electrical sparks from causing an explosion. Even though the fuel level itself was very low, we still had enough fumes to cause a big explosion.

The flight orderly twisted the T-bar handle on the door. Evidently the fuselage was in a warped state, and the door wouldn't slide open easily. So I unsnapped my belt and we pushed on the door and it slid open. And we all started getting out. The crew were making sure that all the pax were leaving. The emergency exits all opened up the way that they should. Everyone got out, both on the side where the wing had broken off and on the other side. I was able to see some of the crewmen for the first time. The copilot, Bill Avery, he did have a lot of blood down his face. It was hard for me to say how bad he was hurt but it looked pretty bad. But he had all his faculties and he was making sure everybody got off the aircraft in an orderly manner, and he was carrying out his routine as though there was nothing wrong at all.

From what I gather it took both Cliff Graue, the pilot, and Bill Avery, the copilot, to put the plane down. The pilot was trying to handle the aircraft on the passes, and he advised the copilot that if he could see the runway, to take it. Although I haven't heard it quoted between the two gents.

Once we all got off and got ourselves organized we regrouped in one central location. We almost all of us had our heavy gear on. It gets to be a nuisance, generally speaking, to put your heavy clothes on, on board, as you get near to McMurdo, but this time it paid off. As a matter of fact all of the survival gear that we could get our hands on, including tents, was taken out of the aircraft. You know, we didn't know just exactly where we were. We didn't know whether we were a hundred yards from the runway or maybe a couple of miles. There was nothing that we could see but just blowing snow, and at that time it *was* dark. It was a bit after ten o'clock at night and in October it gets dark down here. You have maybe four hours of what you would call darkness. It was the soft snow. It had everyone out there literally white. It was the kind that blew into your clothing and just stayed there. It was like paint out of a spray gun. It was real cold then.

Actually, as it turned out, we were lucky to be where we were. If it had been a Herc they could have had any set of alternatives that they could have gone to. And the Herc could head into the wind, he didn't have to touch down onto the runway. It just so happened that the wind was 90° to that runway. And it didn't matter which heading we had. It would have been equally rough both ways. He probably had the choice of landing on the snow somewhere with the wheels up, but he probably thought he would do a lot better on the runway because he knew that if he did have a fire, there were some people that were ready with fire-fighting equipment there. Whereas if he had gone off to some other location and maybe headed into the wind it would have been more difficult for anyone to find us.

The pilot decided that since there was no fire aboard the aircraft it appeared to him to be pretty safe, and maybe we should get back on for shelter. So at his decision we all climbed back aboard. There was no damage inside the cabin at all. Of course, the craft was sitting at an angle and it was a little awkward getting back in. At this time we discovered that one of the crewmen *had* been injured a little bit, and I guess the adrenalin had kept him going during that initial period after the crash. This was Billy Wilson, the flight engineer, and during the crash the nose wheel came up through the floor of the fuselage of the cockpit and pushed his seat up against the desk he was sitting adjacent to. So now he was in sort of a mild shock. He was chilling and what have you, and we broke out some sleeping bags and put him in one and tried to make him as comfortable as possible.

The people at Willy Field were having a rough time too. They *knew* that we were out there, they *heard* us making the passes, but they couldn't see us, and they didn't know where we had gone off the runway. All that they'd heard was the roar of the engines as one of them went wild—the control cables to the engine had sheared off. Then everything was dead quiet. So they were desperately trying to find the aircraft. The officer in charge of Willy Field then, Lieutenant Nelson, who was with the winter-over personnel, thought that he got a dark glimpse of something over off the runway, so he ventured off in the snow and sure enough he had caught a glimpse of the aircraft. And so he directed the rest of the vehicles on out to us.

Pat Creehan, the flight surgeon, was in the aircraft in very short order, taking a look at any of the people that were injured. Fortunately there were very few. Pat took a look at the flight engineer and we put the engineer in a litter and got him out into an ambulance, and we started the long trek up to McMurdo. We loaded aboard a Six-By, one of these canvas-covered trucks. They took us over to the ice runway parking lot and from there we transferred to the regular big orange buses that we have. Visibility was still very poor, and the drivers of the vehicles had to put someone out front to walk to the flags that we have marking the road, and go from one flag to the next and motion to the vehicle, because from inside the vehicle you couldn't see from one flag to another.

It seemed like it took at least two hours before we could get from the annual ice runway parking lot to McMurdo Station. There was no excitement to speak of. Everyone was very quiet. They seemed to be very well trained and well organized. There was no panic at any time that I can recall. The pilot couldn't have done a better job under the circumstances. However, I have to give a lot of credit to the prayers that were said on that flight. I truly think that it was an act of God that prevented any people from burning up. It was a big enough setback, the loss of the aircraft. If we had lost lives on top of that it would have hurt the Antarctic program. I honestly have to say that I don't think the whole Antarctic program is worth one injury to any man down here.

Everyone was taken to the chow hall. But before we went into the chow hall we passed through the Dispensary, and the admiral was there, and he inquired of every man whether he was hurt or not, and took a look at him. And then we went on over to the chow hall and had a good meal. We were hungry, because we had last eaten that morning at ten o'clock. Then, after we had sat down and talked to one another a little about what had happened, it seemed that a lot of people became a little shaky. I appeared to be a little trembly myself, and I noticed then that some of the other people were too.

The flight engineer was not seriously injured. He was put in sick bay just for observation. He was sore just from the bruises. And Bill Avery incurred a minor head injury. He bumped one of the instruments in the cockpit. Most facial or head injuries do bleed profusely. The very next Connie that came down, Cliff Graue flew it. And most of his crew with him. He's made a couple of trips down here since then. They towed the Connie out to Outer Willy, which is the ice runway located on the permanent ice shelf, quite far from here, and left it there.

You know, a lot of people say, "There was a lot of luck there." But I say there was no luck at all. It was a combination of skill on the pilot's part and God answering the prayers. We owe it to God to say that, don't we? I really believe that.

8

～～～～～～～～～

MCMURDO STATION: THREE

THE MORNING of December 17 I climbed Observation Hill, going from the Lodge by road up to the nuclear plant, then following the steep trail over volcanic gravel, soil and rock. It was not an easy climb for someone about to turn fifty-six but for one reason or another I was driven to go rapidly. My heart pounded; I sweated heavily. I had been indiscreet in coming alone and in not telling anyone where I was going. If I broke an ankle or had a heart attack I'd be in serious trouble, for I had climbed beyond shouting range of the station; and I would be invisible to the station in a sitting or prone position. Several times I felt like quitting. To look directly up or down raised questions better not asked and only drove me to climb more rapidly. Then quite suddenly I felt the steady, shockingly cold wind blowing off the ice shelf and realized I could be badly frostbitten or even frozen if I became immobilized. I put my cap back on and zipped up my parka. The sweat was rapidly chilling my body.

Near the summit of the hill was a visitors' register consisting of a lectern with a drawer containing two chained ballpoint pens that didn't work, a pencil and a ledger. Some of the comments written in the ledger intrigued me.

"Mountain climbing ain't my bag."

"November 25, 1970. I have come to the summit of Ob Hill this day with the help of God and rum cokes and a cold. This historic occasion marks the first accession of this hill by a graduate of Sacred Heart University, Bridgeport, Conn., 1968. Hurrah etc. for the Alma Mater and for all those who follow. Private [name illegible], Westport, Conn."

"Look around what you see."

"November 26, 1970. My name is Ahmed I. Ahmed and I am from U.A.R., Egypt. Actually it is the first time for me to climb such high mountain. I am so tired, especially after this heavy Turkey Thanksgiving dinner. Thank you. Ahmed I. Ahmed."

"Thanks God who has done a lot of wonderful things to me. Thanksgiving Day, 1970."

"November 26, 1970. Today may be Thanksgiving but there is nothing to be thankful for on this shitty mountain or at this shitty base. I dedicate this climb to all the poor souls who will be here for Thanksgiving of '71. Carl Ruffer." Someone had written above this, "Your a dumb shit. Your writing speaks for you."

"If you make this hill, ok, if not, tough shit."

"Nov. 26, 1970. To whom it may concern. I left that bottle up there. Good headaches to you. I climbed this hill for my wife Debby, whom I love very much."

"I still also hate the Navy but I'm too short to sweat it, in other words I'm no lifer, and furthermore just get back in Antarctica."

"Nov. 26, 1970. I'm a civilian at heart. I climbed this hill for my wife Millie, whom I love very much, and for Ralph, who will be born soon, whom I also love very much. Neither of them like the Navy and I don't blame them."

"Most of these ideas go for me but I'm in love with Pat, Jacqueline and Chippy."

From the crest of the hill, beside the Polar Party Cross, I had a view in all directions and saw at a glance almost the entire station and could gauge how much of McMurdo's stores were stacked outside and could hear the sounds of heavy truck and bulldozer engines. The nuclear plant halfway up the hill seemed far below me. Directly below me were gray, brownish and umber volcanic chunks, sharp, flinty, lying on a series of dead hillsides that were part of the hill. I could see four silver fuel tanks beside the Gap road, and Crater Heights, whose westernmost section was a concave ice sheet gleaming at the edges. The sun was directly above Erebus, which was beautifully visible and sported a plume of steam rising diaphanous and uncharacteristically straight. Clad as if in ermine, its pockets of blue-gray shadow resembling ermine tails, the volcano looked like a female breast, the kind that is still shapely even when a woman is on her back.

When I returned to the Lodge and went to the head I found to my astonishment that someone had left a faucet freely running. In Antarctica you use water as sparingly as possible. Despite the fact that the continent contains some 95 per cent of the world's permanent ice—if the ice were to melt, the oceans would rise an estimated two hundred or two hundred and fifty feet—there is little natural water during most of the year at McMurdo and none at all at the inland stations. As a consequence fire is probably the greatest single danger on the continent. Potable water is even scarcer than seawater and is expensive to make by the usual method: melting snow or ice. As for showers, everyone is honor-bound not to take more than one a week and a "Navy" shower at that: a quick dousing, a soaping with the water turned off, and a quick rinse. Because of the cold and the extreme dryness one isn't aware of inadequate hygiene.

Three Hawaiian repairmen entered the head, wearing only long-johns. They quartered in the Jamesway on the rise across the road from the Lodge. The Antarctic is an informal place. The waffle-weave longjohns are widely used as pajamas not only because the huts can be cold at night but because switching from one to the other is time-consuming and awkward in the extremely narrow, crowded and sometimes dim confines of a cubicle. The use of names is also informal. You hear Willy Field or Willy for Williams Field, helo for helicopter, Herc for Hercules, Connie for Constellation, O Head for Officers' Head, Ob Hill for Observation Hill, Cheechee for Christchurch, Kiwi for New Zealander, Hono for Honolulu. At first these may seem strange and, in the case of Willy Field, possibly insensitive. But in a day or two you become less aware of the strangeness and find yourself slipping into the same usage.

The Navy tends to downgrade formality in such a place, although it continues the tradition of the wardroom and of separate dining quarters for enlisted men, chiefs and officers. In the officers' section of the chow hall one receives a very pleasant impression of diversity within uniformity. People dress alike and eat the same food at the same informal tables but they may be sitting in Navy groups or scientist groups or visitor groups and discussing strikingly dissimilar matters in dissimilar language. But there is a certain formality too, as well as a university air because of the presence of numerous university-affiliated scientists.

Despite its primitive setting and still fairly primitive facilities, McMurdo is a sophisticated, intellectual and cosmopolitan outpost, where you see and hear foreigners, for example, as a matter of course in the spring and summer. What everybody seems to have in common are excellent morale and a sense of the ready and rather unreserved acceptance of each other. The latter is probably a result of a lively awareness of how hostile the environment can be and of how important therefore free cooperation is. There are many reasons why men become addicted to Antarctica—the adventure, the unspoiled freshness of it, the beauty, the excitement of scientific research—but ranked high among them, certainly, are the informal way of life, the acceptance of each other and the high morale.

Rear Admiral David F. Welch's quarters at McMurdo looked modest on a little knoll. The outside of the hut was rough but the inside was graced by touches, on the day I had visited in November 1969, uncommon in the Antarctic: a linen table cloth, place cards with names carefully hand-printed on them, and an unobtrusive servant. On the center of the table was a vase with plastic flowers. I had asked the admiral what problems kept him awake at night. He said there were two: the uncertain legal jurisdiction on the continent, and tourism. The admiral had complete criminal jurisdiction over the men in his command, but none over the civilians.

"If you shot one of my men I doubt that you could be tried for it," he said. "The U.S. has no sovereignty here. Nor would the laws of the high seas apply. Technically we're guests of the New Zealanders, who claim the Ross Dependency, which was turned over to them by Great Britain in the twenties. But all territorial claims were frozen for thirty years by the Antarctic Treaty. Also, the U.S. has never recognized any nation's claims in the Antarctic and has never made any. Of course, I'd fly you out of here even if I had to manhandle you, but that's all I'd do."

As for tourism, he had no doubt it would come to the Antarctic. The only question was how soon.

"I just hope it won't happen during *my* watch. I'm responsible for the safety of all Americans in the Antarctic, yet I can't tell tourists what they can or can't do. What if they started wandering around on the ice? There's a tourist agency which wants to bring a ship down here and use it as quarters for tourists whom they'd fly down in a chartered plane. This is completely open territory—anybody can come down here if he has the means of getting here and staying here. But if they start flying a plane down I'd have to be prepared for a rescue mission in case it got into trouble. What if somebody decides to fly across the continent alone, in a private plane? I couldn't stop him, yet I'd have to be ready to help if he needed help or to find him if he went down."

There was a discussion of the Antarctic Treaty. Signed originally by the United States, the Soviet Union and ten other nations, it provides for the free exchange of scientific information and for international inspection, and bans military bases and maneuvers, weapons testing, nuclear explosions and the disposal of radioactive wastes. The military role is restricted to logistic support efforts. This treaty is a relatively new but very important factor in Antarctic morale.

After climbing Observation Hill I phoned Jim Brandau, the helo pilot of Gentle 5 (an H-34) when it crashed in November 1969, and arranged to meet him in the wardroom at eight. Then Dale Vance, three other scientists, Jim Elder and I bounced and careened in a red USARP pickup truck over rutted, clogged, iced lava roads into the hills northwest of the station to a radio shack, called Pogo, near Arrival Heights. Elder, in charge of the Field Party Processing Center, drove crazily. I shared the cab with him. The others rode outside. Pogo was alone among black hills. From its doorway you saw Observation Hill: a brown pyramid beyond a black, pitted islandscape; and the Royal Society Range in the west; and glaciers gleaming over there on the seaward edge of Victoria Land. A great white plume seemed to stand like an ice shaft in Erebus's crater to the north of us.

In the shack, which was electrically heated, was Vance's ham radio rig that he planned to take to Vostok Station and to use to call his family during his year at the Russian base. He meant to test it now and to try for some phone patches for the rest of us as well as for himself. After warming up the rig he roused a friend at Byrd Station, then his good friend Steve Barnes in Boulder, Colorado. He spoke with his wife and two children in Boulder, then got me through via Barnes to my wife Joan in Princeton. It was 4:20 P.M. at McMurdo and 11:20 P.M. of the previous day in New Jersey. Barnes explained to Joan that it was a one-way call: when you temporarily finished speaking you said "Over" to notify your inter-

1. *Mount Erebus at midnight*

3. *McMurdo Sound*

2. *The Staten Island*

4. *Mount Bird*

5. *Pack ice*

6. *Beaufort Island*

7. *Ross Island from the north*

8. *Beaufort Island and Mount Bird*

9. *McMurdo Station from Observation Hill*

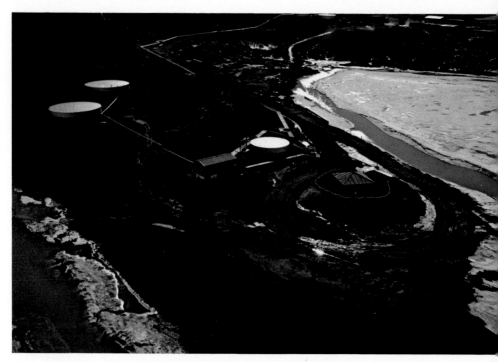

10. *The Discovery Hut*

11. *Interior view of the hut*

locutor it was his turn to talk. Joan sounded greatly surprised and excited.

Feeling like a nervous virgin, I sensed I wasn't being affectionate enough. I sounded too businesslike and too much a part of an exclusively male world. I kept saying how much I loved Antarctica and how my expectations of the ice, aroused by my first visit, had all proved true, and how much I admired the men I had met and how much I looked forward to camping in the field and how terrifically good I felt physically. Joan responded as I hoped she would: she stretched her imagination for me and understood my boyish enthusiasm and my great remoteness physically. Vance remained in Pogo with me, monitoring the equipment. The others had gone to a smaller, unheated shack to give me privacy.

I suggested to Joan that she wake Susy, which she did. Susy, almost thirteen, came on cool, affectionate and an instant master of "Over," to Vance's delight. I was tremendously elated all evening and into the next day as a result of the phone patch.

Everyone got a patch, which made Vance very proud. Jim Elder, grinning, said after his patch, "There's nothing like that to give you an ego boost."

After dinner Vance and I had a few drinks in the small, dim wardroom, which was in an old Jamesway near the Officers' Head and near another Jamesway (for DVs) named the Ross Hilton. Outside the wardroom was a dim, long corridor where you could hang your parka and cap. The wardroom was always warm, smoky and cozy, the drinks generous and cheap. A large bronze bell hung over the bar. If you pulled the clapper cord and sounded the bell, either deliberately or accidentally, you were obliged to buy drinks for all present. There were ruses to cause a novice to ring the bell. For example, a man at the bar's end might ask the novice to please pass the clapper cord over to him, giving the impression that the man meant to sound the bell and treat. The novice might oblige, causing the bell to ring to the general merriment and his cost. Also, it was a rule that anyone who entered the wardroom with his hat on had to buy drinks for the house. The wardroom was where you could mix freely with anyone, including the admiral. At one end of the room, near a dart game, was a door leading to a small movie theater, where movies were frequently shown. Admission was free.

Brandau did not show up at eight. At about eight-thirty Dave Murphy, a young friend of mine who was in the wardroom, phoned

Air Ops (Air Operations) and learned that Brandau was out on a mission. At about nine-thirty Vance and I went to Vance's room and drank from a bottle of bourbon, then I went downstairs with the intention of turning in at once, for I was very tired. There was a knock at my door. When I opened the door I saw an odd but interesting figure in a dirty, rumpled, khaki flight suit and heavy khaki boots. Bowing slightly as though nervously, he shyly said in an uncertain but deep voice that he was Jim Brandau. Dave Murphy had described him to me as resembling Burl Ives, the folk singer and actor, but Brandau was shorter and by no means as stout. As a matter of fact, he looked unusually powerful and fit. I was attracted to him at once and flattered he had come.

As I invited him into my room he said quietly, "I'd like you to have these," and handed me a large piece of Antarctic petrified wood and a piece of Antarctic coal, both of which he had picked up about a hundred and fifty miles from McMurdo. This generous and touching gesture was typical of the man, as I soon discovered. Remembering that Susy had asked me to bring back some interesting rocks, I gratefully accepted. He apologized for not having met me in the wardroom, explaining where he had been, and asked if I cared to go on a helo flight to Cape Evans in the morning to drop off two Kiwis from Scott Base and then stop off at Erebus Glacier Tongue to see an ice cave. I said I'd be delighted.

Then he said that Chris Shepherd wanted to see me now in the Chalet. It being after eleven, I wondered about the request but was glad to go. A party was in progress in the Chalet's mezzanine, with both USARP and Navy people present. Shepherd seemed quite relaxed and very different from the up-tight man he had been the last several days, when he had had to play host to a number of DVs. The clue to the party's meaning was scrawled on the blackboard near the lectern downstairs: two chalk drawings of a raised middle finger, one in full view, the other in profile. Above the drawings was the caption "DVs." Below them a sign read FUCK YOU.

Someone shouted, "Shall we sing a hymn for the DVs?"

There were cries of approval and everyone sang out, "Him! Him! Fuck him!"

Then somebody cried, "How about a folk song?"

And everybody sang loudly, "Folk! Folk! Folk him!"

Shepherd asked Brandau to fetch Vance, who soon joined us. Bottles of booze stood on the long conference table. The VXE-6 people had brought a red wine, served out of a Jim Beam bottle, that Brandau told me had been brewed at Willy Field. I got a shock when I took a large swallow. It tasted exactly like vinegar.

A memory game, a round, was played, led by Vance. It began, "A big red hen, a couple of ducks, three brown bears, four running hares, five fat females, six simple simons sitting on a stump, seven Sicilian sailors sailing the seven seas." Each time a new item was added you had to repeat the entire thing correctly when it came to your turn, or else drink some booze or wine.

Some 8mm stag films were projected. The first reel was too dark in places. There were boos. The sex act was shown very explicitly. There were groans and comments. When this reel was concluded, at about 1:15, Vance, Brandau and I left. Vance too had been invited to see the ice cave and the three of us were in for a short night.

We breakfasted together next morning, helicoptered to Scott Base to pick up the two Kiwis Brandau had mentioned, dropped them off at Cape Evans, then flew close to the entrance of an ice cave inside Erebus Glacier Tongue, causing some basking Weddells to writhe and hump away in alarm as we descended, hovered and landed. The Tongue cliffs, massive although from the air they seemed insignificant, resembled chalk. The Tongue, afloat but attached to Ross Island, thrust into the Sound with the appearance of a serrated knife from above. From our landing spot we could see white Hut Point Peninsula, Castle Rock jutting black out of it, black islands on the white snow-ice expanse of the Sound, the crisp Royal Society Range, and lovely, thin cloud formations in an azure sky. The day was utterly brilliant: cold if you were in shadow, warm if you weren't. We walked on patches of thick snow in which we descended to our shanks, and on gleaming, hard, uneven, treacherous, beautiful bluish and greenish ice.

The cave entrance was like a pelvic slit, gorgeously and startlingly blue. We climbed and clambered into the cave. The glowing light inside was an eerie, electric lavender. Strange ice formations clung like frozen whipped cream to the ceiling, and glistening ice crystals were encrusted high on the walls. I was the only member of the party not wearing gloves. Occasionally, in a narrow passageway on the rolling, slippery floor, I had to lean a hand against an ice hummock to avoid falling. My hand screamed immediately as though burned. The ice inside the cave was probably at close to mean temperature, many degrees below zero. The view toward the cave entrance showed patches of light, burning through long, thick icicles, that made both walls and ceiling dance.

When we were outside again Vance alluded to the amount of body heat I usually had and dared me to strip to the waist. We were in the lee of the Tongue cliffs, the sun was high and fierce and bouncing off everything, and I felt my face being razor-burned as in a desert. The weather, being now so fine, seemed as stable as that of New Zealand, but instability was precisely the Antarctic weather's hallmark. I stripped, and stayed stripped quite a while. I felt moderately warm in front (I was facing the sun) and cold in back, but I wasn't uncomfortable although my hands grew numb. But when I donned my waffle-weave top, which I had draped over the standing ice ax, it felt surprisingly cold; the cold then came as a small shock. The Weddells occasionally made a cowlike mooing call. It was fine to enter the helicopter and fly again and to see the horizon crazily tilting and the ice and snow passing swiftly below us: textured, lined, raked by natural forces.

On returning to McMurdo I went to the Chalet, where I decided with Chris Shepherd that I would go camping at Cape Royds in the morning, taking as my field assistant Dave Murphy of Holmes & Narver, the private contractors. I would stay two nights and be picked up at 1600 on December 21. Later in the day I met with Brian Porter (the Scott Base leader), Shepherd and a Navy commander with a thin face and flaming jug ears. Porter, very cordial, granted me permission to sleep in the historic Ross Island huts and asked me to act as their honorary custodian during my stay. After dinner with the chaplain I spent much time with Dave Murphy, preparing for our outing.

That night I awoke at 3 A.M., dressed, and walked down to the Discovery Hut, the key to which I had borrowed from the chaplain during the evening. I carried with me the first volume of Scott's *The Voyage of the "Discovery,"* which, along with a number of other valuable first editions, the Firestone Library of Princeton University had kindly let me ship to the ice. The hut is about thirty-six feet square and has a pyramidal roof and overhanging eaves. Scott described the eaves as resting "on supports some four feet beyond the sides, surrounding the hut with a covered verandah."

"The interior space," he wrote, "was curtailed by the complete double lining, and numerous partitions were provided to suit the requirements of the occupants. But of these partitions only one was erected, to cut off a small portion of one side, and the larger part which remained formed a really spacious apartment.

"It had been originally intended that the 'Discovery' should not attempt to winter in the Antarctic, but should land a small party and turn northward before the season closed; the hut had been provided for this party and carried south under the impression that circumstances might yet force the adoption of such a plan. Having discovered a spot in which we felt confident the 'Discovery' could winter with safety, the living-hut was no longer of vital importance; but, even retaining the ship as a home, there were still many useful purposes to which a large hut might be adapted."

Later in the volume he wrote again about the hut, this time drawing directly upon his diaries.

"'The main hut is of most imposing dimensions and would accommodate a very large party, but on account of its size and the necessity of economising coal it is very difficult to keep a working temperature inside; consequently it has not been available for some of the purposes for which we had hoped to use it. One of the most important of these was the drying of clothes; for a long time the interior was hung with undergarments which had been washed on board, but all these water-sodden articles became sheets of ice, which only dried as the ice slowly evaporated. When it was found that this process took a fortnight or three weeks the idea was abandoned, and the drying of clothes is now done in the living-spaces on board. . . . But although the hut has not fulfilled expectation in this respect, it is in constant use for other purposes. After the sledging it came in handy for drying the furs, tents, etc.; then it was devoted to the skinning of birds for a month or more, a canvas screen being placed close around the stove, whereby a reasonable temperature was maintained in a small space; then various sailorising jobs, such as the refitting of the awnings and the making of sword matting, were carried on in it; and finally it has been used both for the rehearsal and performance of such entertainments as have served to lighten the monotony of our routine, and in this capacity, when fitted with a stage and decked with scenery, footlights, etc., it probably forms the most pretentious theatre that has ever been seen in polar regions. Of late a solid pedestal of firebricks has been built in the small compartment and on this Bernacchi will shortly be swinging his pendulums for gravity observations; while

in the spring I hope that we may be able to use the larger apartment as a centre for collecting, weighing, and distributing the food
and equipment of the various sledge parties.

"'On the whole, therefore, our large hut has been and will be of
use to us, but its uses are never likely to be of such importance as
to render it indispensable, nor cause it to be said that circumstances
have justified the outlay made on it or the expenditure of space and
trouble in bringing it to its final home. It is here now, however, and
here it will stand for many a long year with such supplies as will
afford the necessaries of life to any less fortunate party who may
follow in our footsteps and be forced to search for food and shelter.'"

Still later in his volume Scott described in some detail two of the
theatrical performances produced in the hut, activities that greatly
brightened the winter.

"The idea of requisitioning our large hut as a place of entertainment had occurred to us early in the winter, and in this connection
it was first used for a concert given during the first week in May
[1902]. Royds, who took much pains in getting up this function,
arranged a long programme in order to bring forth all the available
talent; but although we were not inclined to be critical of our
amusements, one was fain to confess that our company had not
been chosen for their musical attainments. However, there were exceptions to the mediocrity, and some exhibition of dramatic talent,
which prompted the conception of a modified entertainment for a
future occasion; so Barne was entrusted with the task of producing
a play, and after much casting about succeeded in getting his company together. All became very diligent with rehearsals, and as
these were conducted in the hut with all due secrecy, the audience
remained in ignorance of even the name of the play until the night
of its production. It was decided that this should be immediately
after our mid-winter celebrations, and my diary for June 25 gives
some account of this great night:

"'At seven to-night we all journey across to the hut, forcing our
way through a rather keen wind and light snowdrift. The theatre
within looks bright and cheerful, but as there are no heating arrangements other than the lamps, one conquers the natural instinct
to take off one's overcoat and head covering, and decides that it
will be wise to retain these garments throughout the performance.
On one side of the large compartment a fair-sized stage has been

erected, raised some two feet above the floor; the edge is decorated with a goodly row of footlights, immediately behind which hangs a drop-curtain depicting the ship and Mount Erebus in glowing colours, and boldly informing one that this is the "Royal Terror Theatre." The remainder of the compartment forms an auditorium of ample size to accommodate all who are not performing, with a stray dog or two brought in to enliven the proceedings.

"'In front stands a row of chairs for the officers, and behind several rows of benches for the men; the apartment is lighted by a large oil lamp, and when all are seated one must own to having seen theatricals under far less realistic conditions. When all are seated also, and when pipes are lit, there is a perceptible improvement in the temperature, a condition that one feels will be very welcome to the lightly clad actors.

"'In due course programmes are passed round, informing us that Part I will consist of several songs rendered by popular singers, and that for Part II we shall have the "Ticket of Leave," "a screaming comedy in one act." These programmes, I may remark, are correct at least in one respect, in that there is some difficulty in picking out the information from amongst the mass of advertisements. Presently the curtain rolls up and discloses Royds at the piano and the first singers in true concert attitude. We have a duet, followed by several solos, and occasionally a rousing chorus, when one rather fears that the roof of the Royal Terror Theatre will rise. On the whole the first part passes decorously, and we come to the interval, when the wags advertise oranges and nuts.

"'Then we have Part II, which is what we are here for; the "screaming comedy" commences and proves to be fully up to its title. There is no need for the actors to speak—their appearance is quite enough to secure the applause of the audience; and when the representatives of the lady parts step on to the stage it is useless for them to attempt speech for several minutes, the audience is so hugely delighted. Thanks to Mr. Clarkson and his make-up box, the disguises are excellent, and it soon becomes evident that the actors have regarded them as by far the most important part of the proceedings, and hold the view that it is rather a waste of time to learn a part when one has a good loud-voiced prompter. As the play progresses one supposes there is a plot, but it is a little difficult to unravel. Presently, however, we are obviously working up to a situation; the hero, or perhaps I should say one of the heroes (for each actor at least attacks his part with heroism) unexpectedly sees through the window the lady on whom he has fixed his affections, and whom, I gather, he has not seen for a long and weary time. He is evidently a little uncertain as to her identity, and at this stirring moment he sits very carefully on a chair—he almost dusts the seat before he does so. Seated and barely glancing at the window, he says with great deliberation and in the most matter-of-fact tones, "It is—no, it isn't—yes, it is—it is my long-lost Mary Jane." The sentiment—or the rendering of it—is greeted with shouts of applause. Later on we work up to a climax, when it is evident that the services of the police force will be required. This part is much more to the taste of the players; somebody has to be chucked out; both he and the "chuckers-out" determine to make their parts quite realistic, and for several minutes there is practically a free fight with imminent risk to the furniture. And so at last the curtain falls amidst vociferous cheering, and I for one have to acknowledge that I have rarely been so gorgeously entertained. With renewed cheers we break up and wander back to the ship, after having witnessed what the "S.P.T." ["South Polar Times," the ship's paper, edited by Shackleton] may veraciously describe as "one of the most successful entertainments ever given within the Polar Circle"—and indeed they might with some truth add "or anywhere else." ' "

As I stood alone in the hut, feeling remote from the rest of the station, possibly because it was the middle of the night and the station had looked completely deserted, I opened Scott's volume and read the above pages. Then I read a paragraph that has always moved me:

" 'Beyond the large hut stand the smaller magnetic huts, and from the eminence on that point the little cluster of buildings looks quite imposing. In the midst of these vast ice-solitudes and under the frowning desolation of the hills, the ship, the huts, the busy figures passing to and fro, and the various other evidences of human activity are extraordinarily impressive. How strange it all seems! For countless ages the great sombre mountains about us have loomed through the gloomy polar night with never an eye to mark their grandeur, and for countless ages the wind-swept snow has drifted over these great deserts with never a footprint to break its white surface; for one brief moment the eternal solitude is broken by a hive of human insects; for one brief moment they settle, eat, sleep, trample, and gaze, then they must be gone, and all must be surrendered again to the desolation of the ages.' "

9

ADVENTURES OF SCOTT'S DISCOVERY

EXPEDITION

1. FARTHEST SOUTH

I HAVE GATHERED the materials for this chapter chiefly from the second volume of Scott's *The Voyage of the "Discovery."* Almost without exception the quotations are from his diary as published in that volume. In "Farthest South" I have added to these materials a few details from Edward Wilson's *Diary of the "Discovery" Expedition,* which was first published long after Scott's work.

It may be worth noting the difference, not only in tone but in content, between the two diaries. Wilson's diary is cooler, less prone to self-dramatization and to dramatization of the experience of sledging in the unknown, to such a degree that, when one compares the two documents as they describe this first extended southern sledge journey, at times one feels one is reading about two different events. For example, Wilson makes a good deal less of Shackleton's serious illness than Scott does, possibly because, unlike Scott the leader, he has much less at stake as an explorer, or because he feels less competitive with Shackleton, but also perhaps because he tends less to personalize the journey. Scott, for all his hard-headed ideas about sledging and his meticulous sledging plans and nature observations, was a romantic, and although he was genuinely inter-

The episodes (in Chapters 9, 11 and 16) from the three early expeditions of the so-called heroic age of Antarctic exploration have been selected because they are concerned with persons involved either with attempts on or with the attainment of the Pole.

ested in science and took most seriously the expedition's responsibilities in the field of scientific research, he lacked the scientist's temperament of Wilson, the medical doctor and vertebrate zoologist. On the other hand one can argue for the romantic strain in Wilson's illustrations, particularly in the matter of color. Both were complex men. It is obviously unwise to generalize about them. Still, it should be said that because by his outlook and literary gifts Scott was a romantic, to a significant extent he created the Antarctic world around him: of awesome beauty, great physical danger, unceasing fascination, endless challenge and human hardship. By his powerful and noble example he influenced not only his own two expeditions but many subsequent ones. He was one of the most gifted of all polar explorers, and the most gifted of Antarctic ones.

He wrote in *The Voyage of the "Discovery,"* "It might be said that it was James Cook who defined the Antarctic Region, and James Ross who discovered it." With typical modesty he refrained from adding that it was he himself who first systematically and extensively explored the continent, applying many of the techniques of northern sledging to southern conditions. The southern sledging journey in the austral summer of 1902–3 was a great milestone of Antarctic exploration. It was easily the farthest push south for its time. It pioneered the use of sledges and dogs in Antarctica. It provided a first inkling of what it was like to sledge on the Great Ice Barrier. It afforded a first indication of what the Barrier or ice shelf was like, and of how it was flanked on the west by the mountain ranges of Victoria Land, and of how enormously extensive it was. After a certain point each step was a step into the icy, monotonous and very dangerous unknown. The party was constantly seeing sights that no men had observed before and, with the exception of a few stray birds, no animals either.

The effect of this primal journey on subsequent sledging treks in Antarctica was very considerable. For one thing, the journey showed how great a difference there was between sledging in the north polar region and sledging in the south polar one. Sledging in the south was much more difficult and hazardous. On this journey both Scott and Shackleton came to conclusions that had important consequences for their later efforts to penetrate the southern unknown.

It is a curious and ironic fact that at least two members of the southern party were at earlier times in delicate health. Wilson had been troubled by tuberculosis and had spent some time in Davos, Switzerland, taking the cure. Shackleton as a youth had had some catarrhal trouble. And Scott too in his early years had not been in robust health. At the time of the journey Scott was thirty-four, Wilson was thirty and Shackleton was twenty-nine.

The English explorers of the first half of the nineteenth century had had much experience in northern sledging. But if Fridtjof Nansen's knowledge may be trusted, Scott was wrong to think that Englishmen were the pioneers of such sledging. In *Farthest North*, a classic work, Nansen wrote, "It was in Siberia that this excellent method of locomotion [sledges] was first applied to the service of polar exploration [in the seventeenth and eighteenth centuries]." Then Nansen continued in a vein which is of much interest to the present narrative: "While the Russians had generally travelled with a large number of dogs, and only a few men, the English employed many more men on their expeditions, and their sledges were entirely, or for the most part, drawn by the explorers themselves. . . . It would appear, indeed, as if dogs were not held in great estimation by the English."

Hugh Robert Mill, in his biography of Shackleton, wrote, "Now Shackleton was set the task, in no way alarming to a British sailor, of discovering by his own efforts in a week or two the art [of handling sledge dogs] that takes a northern Canadian years of apprenticeship to master. The result was better than one could have expected; but it served to strengthen the fine old British tradition which Sir Clements Markham [the "father" of the Discovery Expedition] set such store by, that the best polar draught animals are the human members of the expeditions. And in their hearts the *Discovery* people did not believe in dogs."

In *The Voyage of the "Discovery"* Scott discusses the pros and cons of using dogs as a means to an end: that is, not bringing them back "safe and sound." He admits that men can sledge farther if they sacrifice dogs but comes to the conclusion that it is for the men too painful a method.

"Probably our experience was an exceptionally sad one in this respect [they lost all their dogs on the southern sledging journey], but it left in each one of our small party an unconquerable aversion to the employment of dogs in this ruthless fashion. We knew well that they had served their end, that they had carried us much farther than we could have got by our own exertions; but we all felt that we would never willingly face a repetition of such incidents, and when in the following year I stepped forth in my own harness, one of a party which was dependent on human labour alone, it would not be easy adequately to convey the sense of relief which I felt in the knowledge that there could be no recurrence of the horrors of the previous season.

"I have endeavoured to give a just view of the use of dogs in polar enterprises. To say that they do not greatly increase the radius of action is absurd; to pretend that they can be worked to this end without pain, suffering, and death is equally futile. The question is whether the latter can be justified by the gain, and I think that logically it may be; but the introduction of such sordid necessity must and does rob sledge-travelling of much of its glory. In my mind no journey ever made with dogs can approach the height of that fine conception which is realised when a party of men go forth to face hardships, dangers, and difficulties with their own unaided efforts, and by days and weeks of hard physical labour succeed in solving some problem of the great unknown. Surely in this case the conquest is more nobly and splendidly won."

This is fine feeling but unfortunately it played a large part in the tragedy that overtook Scott and his four companions in March 1912. The national predisposition against the use of dogs was buttressed by Scott's experience during his first long sledge journey with dogs. When one compares these national and personal attitudes with those inherent in Amundsen, the contrast between the two nations and the two leaders, and between the two events which occurred during the South Pole treks, is greatly illuminated.

Scott's experience with dogs was a rather loaded one from the beginning: in the purchase of the dogs. A Russian named Trontheim had been commissioned to obtain between three and four hundred dogs for an American expedition intending to go to Franz-Josef Land in the north. The Discovery Expedition asked Trontheim to collect twenty dogs for it, on condition that the expedition be allowed to have first choice of the pack. Where Trontheim obtained the dogs Scott never came to know, but the latter assumed Trontheim got them in northern Russia. Twenty male dogs and three bitches were selected for the Discovery Expedition and housed in the London Zoo before being shipped to New Zealand. Scott did not examine the dogs thoroughly before the *Discovery* was settled in winter quarters at Hut Point. It was found that several of the dogs were very young and had probably never been in harness before. Also, there were three distinct types of dog: one large, the second short-legged and thick-set, and the third an animal with apparently much wolf in him, and very difficult to handle. It was a mixed lot, and they had not previously worked together. By the time the spring campaign of 1902 started, two dogs had been murdered by their comrades and three others had been lost in accidents. I mention these facts to suggest the pioneering and green nature of the Discovery Expedition in the use of dogs and to suggest also that Scott's conclusions on the value of dogs in polar sledging were not well based either on good materials or sufficient experience. The expedition had neither first-rate nor experienced dogs, as Amundsen had when he camped on the ice shelf and moved towards the Pole. The Discovery Expedition unfortunately lacked the services of Scandinavians well versed in the use of sledges, skis, polar clothing, sleeping bags, tents and above all in the use of sledge dogs. All might subsequently have been very different if this oversight had been avoided.

It would be incorrect and unjust to assume that the great Scandinavian explorers were insensitive to the lot of their dogs. In the second volume of *Farthest North* Nansen wrote: "It was undeniable cruelty to the animals from first to last, and one must often look back on it with horror. It makes me shudder even now when I think of how we beat them mercilessly with thick ash sticks when, hardly able to move, they stopped from sheer exhaustion. It made one's heart bleed to see them, but we turned our eyes away and hardened ourselves. It was necessary; forward we must go, and to this end everything else must give place. It is the sad part of expeditions of this kind that one systematically kills all better feelings, until only hard-hearted egoism remains. When I think of all those splendid animals, toiling for us without a murmur, as long as they could strain a muscle, never getting any thanks or even so much as a kind word, daily writhing under the lash until the time came when they could do no more and death freed them from their pangs—when I think of how they were left behind, one by one, up there on those desolate ice-fields, which had been witness to their faithfulness and devotion, I have moments of bitter self-reproach."

When one reads this passage one sympathizes with the position of the English and of Scott. Scott knew his Nansen well and had met the author and conferred with him before embarking on the Discovery Expedition. One can argue that if even a Norwegian felt like this, why not an Englishman who was inexperienced with sledge dogs and polar sledging, and with the terrific necessities of the latter? Perhaps Amundsen, who also expressed sorrow over the lot of sledge dogs, had the best answer: a very large number of good dogs, so large that for each animal there was much less of a load to pull, and consequently there was no need to beat the animals. Amundsen fed his dogs well on the South Pole march: by killing a certain number at specified points on the trek and feeding them to the live ones. This was probably a more humane situation regarding both dogs and men. And he and his companions did not shrink from eating dog cutlets in order to protect their own strength.

For all the horrors involved in the use of dogs, Scott the romantic found sledging a fascinating and charming life.

"Sledging draws men into a closer companionship than can any other mode of life. In its light the fraud must be quickly exposed, but in its light also the true man stands out in all his natural strength.

"Sledging therefore is a sure test of a man's character, and daily calls for the highest quality of which he is possessed. Throughout my sledging experience it has been my lot to observe innumerable instances of self-sacrifice, of devotion to duty, and of cheerfulness under adversity; such qualities appeared naturally in my comrades because they were demanded by the life."

The southern party began its great sledge journey November 2, 1902, with nineteen dogs, five sledges, one tent and a load of eighteen hundred and fifty pounds. Next day it caught up with the supporting party, which consisted of twelve men, including Michael Barne, its leader, and no dogs. The supporting party had started out from Hut Point October 30. The purpose of using this party was to increase the food allowance of the southern party from nine to thirteen weeks.

The following is the southern party's route in summary. They headed outward from Hut Point, passed close to the eastern side of White Island, swung around Minna Bluff, went south on the Great Ice Barrier to the 80th parallel, headed southeast towards Victoria Land, approaching it at about Cape Selborne, then marched approximately southward alongside the coast as far as

Cape Wilson, which is just north of Shackleton Inlet. On their return trek they stayed much closer to the land for reasons that will become apparent.

In the beginning the southern party enjoyed full meals. For breakfast each member had a cupful of bacon fried with pounded biscuit, two large cups of tea and a dry biscuit or two; for lunch two cups of hot Bovril chocolate and a dry biscuit; for supper a thick soup of pemmican, red ration (pea meal and bacon powder), pounded biscuit, a soup square, some powdered cheese boiled in water with salt and pepper, a cup of hot cocoa with plasmon, and some dry biscuit. They were not without intellectual fare: often, when they were comfortable in their sleeping bags after supper (each had a bag of reindeer skin), one of them would read aloud a chapter of the *Origin of Species.*

November 10–14. By the tenth the dogs had begun to feel the monotony of the march. On this day the party was visited by snow petrels, a beautiful, white, dovelike bird. On the twelfth the two parties camped for the night in slightly misty weather that caused Scott to feel as if lost on the great snow plain. "The feeling at first is somewhat weird; there is absolutely nothing to break the grey monotone about us, and yet we know that the mist is not thick, but that our isolation comes from the immense expanse of the plain." Wilson thought the dogs were pulling very well indeed. The following day, sights showed the parties to be very close to the 79th parallel and therefore farther south than anyone else had been. The parties pushed southward in thick snowy weather "in a terrible sameness of grey" that was responsible for many falls.

November 15–18. The fifteenth began with a beautiful, calm morning. The land to the north had grown dim. In the west one saw distant snow-covered mountain ranges. In all other directions there was only the seemingly infinite Ice Barrier. The southern party was very busy this morning making arrangements for the last parting. At about noon the farewells were said. Scott was very confident about his party's men, its equipment and its dogs. But trouble soon came. The southern party's load had been increased to twenty-one hundred pounds. The dogs began pulling so badly it was necessary to divide the load into two parts and haul half at a time, which meant that each gained mile had to be traversed three times. Before long the dogs seemed as reluctant to pull half the load as they had been to haul the whole one.

Scott, speculating as to the cause, did not attribute it to the heavy load. Was it the temperature, which rose at one time to 20° F. and made the heavy pulling very warm work? Was it the snow surface, which had grown softer? Was it the falling snow crystals, which increased the friction on the sledge-runners? Was it the absence of the supporting party, which had marched ahead of the dogs and had acted as an incentive for them to go forward? The dogs grew increasingly listless. Two men now always hauled on the traces. The third drove, which involved the hated use of the whip.

November 19–27. Gradually the men became convinced that the dog food—split and dried Norwegian codfish such as was normally used for human consumption—had gone bad during the passage through the tropics and was poisoning the animals; or, as Scott and Wilson thought, was giving them a form of scurvy. "Originally I had intended to take ordinary dog-biscuit for our animals, but in an evil moment I was persuaded by one who had had great experience in dog-driving to take fish. Fish has been used continually in the North for feeding dogs. . . . There is no doubt about the excellent food-value of this fish, and in every way it seemed well adapted to our purpose; and yet it was this very fish that poisoned our poor animals." The dogs sickened; some died. The lesson for future Antarctic explorers, Scott thought, was that they must safeguard the health of their dogs as carefully as that of their men. The barrier surface was growing smoother and had less sastrugi but the snow cover was thicker. One sank into the latter, and there was much friction on the sledge-runners. But at times the surface improved. Meanwhile the men grew sunburned. Their noses and lips blistered and cracked. Their appetite was increasing alarmingly.

On the twenty-fifth Scott took a meridian altitude reading and found the latitude to be 80°1'. "All our charts of the Antarctic Regions show a plain white circle beyond the eightieth parallel; the most imaginative cartographer has not dared to cross this limit, and even the meridianal lines end at the circle. It has always been our ambition to get inside that white space, and now we are there the space can no longer be a blank; this compensates for a lot of trouble."

A blizzard brought a day's enforced rest but the dogs seemed to derive little benefit from it. Scott decided it was necessary to reach the land soon—it was about fifty miles away—in order to set up a depot, so the party headed westward of southwest. The dog driving distressed the men. "It is sickening work, but it is the only way; we cannot stop, we cannot go back, we must go on, and there is no alternative but to harden our hearts and drive. Luckily, the turn for doing the actual driving only comes once in three days, but even thus it is almost as bad to witness the driving as to have to do it." By the twenty-sixth, Mounts Erebus and Terror were no longer in sight, and Mount Discovery resembled a molehill.

The surprisingly warm weather—at times the air temperature was in the plus twenties—caused the party to decide in favor of marching at night, when, because the sun hung lower in the sky, the temperature dropped. They would have breakfast between 4 and 5 P.M., begin marching at six and camp at three or four in the morning. There were certain disadvantages in this routine: they often had to march with the sun in their faces at midnight; at times the tent grew uncomfortably warm during sleep time; and they experienced a disturbing psychological effect, a disorientation, a sense of something being amiss.

December 2–5. At times the snow crust on the ice shelf cracked like pistol shots under the party, and the area would slowly sink with a long-drawn sigh. The dogs were terrified. Digging down, Shackleton found a rather hard crust two or three inches under the snow surface. Beneath this was an air space about an inch deep; then came about a foot of loose snow and a second crust. The men were now close enough to the land to discern some of its details. On their right was a magnificent mountain range, which Scott took to run in an east-west direction. The eastern end descended to a high snow-covered plateau. A feature of the coast were the rounded snow-capes, which could be seen both to the north and the south. The southern side of the range was bordered by "splendid high cliffs, very dark in colour." Scott noted carefully many other details of the unexplored Antarctic scape. Meanwhile the going grew so difficult it was hard to make even four miles a day. It was found that oil was being used too rapidly, so the hot luncheon meal would have to be exchanged for a cold one, and the two other meals would have to be economized.

December 6–14. On the morning of the sixth it was discovered that one of the dogs, Spud, had gnawed through his traces during the night and had made his way to the open seal-meat bag on one of the sledges, where he had gorged himself, consuming about a week's supply of the meat. The dogs were weakening. Some pulled hardly at all, five or six worked steadily, the rest hauled spasmodically. Snatcher died on the ninth. On opening him, Wilson found he had died of acute peritonitis. Snatcher was fed to his comrades. The coast must be ten or twelve miles away. Would the party reach it? And if so, in what condition would they be to continue the southward trek? On the tenth they were visited by a solitary skua. "We are nearly 180 miles from any possible feeding-ground it may have, and it is impossible to say how it found us, but it is curious that it should have come so soon after poor 'Snatcher' has been cut up." Hunger had begun to bite at the men, and conversation now had a way of turning to fine foods one would eat if only they were available. By the fourteenth the air temperature had risen to 27°, the snow surface temperature to 22°. The snow grew softer as the party drew near to the land. The sledge-runners sank three or four inches, and the men's legs went down over the ankles at each step. On the fourteenth the party completed the worst march they had yet had. Scott decided to depot the men's food tomorrow closer to the land so there would be no chance of missing it on the way home.

December 16. At the depot, named Depot B, were left three weeks' provisions and some dog food. The men counted on these to tide them over the homeward trek. All would be well if they could return here within four weeks and with a clear day to help them find the spot. They carried with them provisions for four weeks, some dog food, their camping gear and the clothes they were wearing. Scott noted the "blessed relief" of being free of relay work as they continued southward. "For one-and-thirty awful days have we been at it, and whilst I doubt if our human endurance could have stood it much more, I am quite sure the dogs could not. It seems now like a nightmare, which grew more and more terrible towards its end." During this time, as he calculated it, they had advanced not much more than half a degree of latitude, although they had covered some 380 statute miles. Vic was killed this night "for the common good."

December 18–20. "We are gradually passing from the hungry to the ravenous; we cannot drag our thoughts from food, and we talk of little else." The really bad times were the final hours of the day's march, and the nights. During the day the men felt a growing weakness. At night they would awake with a feeling of emptiness to contemplate with distress the four or five hours remaining until breakfast. Tightening one's belt before turning in helped reduce the pain. Scott, the only smoker of the three, had a theory his pipe mitigated the worst of the pangs. But two pipes a day did not go far on such a trek.

Wilson struck Scott as being indefatigable. At the end of a day's march, if the weather was fine Wilson would sit in the door of the tent and sketch for two or three hours the details of the western ranges. Scott tested Wilson's proportions by angular measurement and found them "astonishingly accurate." But Wilson sometimes paid with very painful attacks of snow blindness for these long hours spent in the glaring light.

Wolf died on the nineteenth. Fifteen dogs were left. The men resolved to save the nine best but they were using up so much energy in helping the dogs pull the sledges that Scott wondered if they wouldn't have been better off without dogs. Grannie died on the twentieth. She would provide the other animals with fresh meat for three days. "It is little wonder that we grow more and more sick of our dog-driving."

December 21. The party decided to see what they could accomplish without the use of dogs. Using skis, they could just barely move their own sledges. On foot they managed to do something under a mile an hour but only by pushing themselves hard. They calculated they were pulling about a hundred and seventy pounds per man. Scott decided that either the snow surface was extremely bad or that they were growing quite weak. "It is no use blinding ourselves to facts: we cannot put any further reliance on the dogs. Any day they might all give out and leave us entirely dependent on ourselves. In such a case, if things were to remain just as they are, we should have about as much as we could do to get home; on the other hand, will things remain just as they are?"

Each Sunday morning since the beginning of the sledge journey Wilson had examined the men's gums and legs for signs of scurvy but had found none. Tonight, however, he informed Scott in confidence that Shackleton had angry-looking gums that for some time had been getting worse. He and Scott decided to keep this news from Shackleton for the present; they needed to think matters out. "Certainly this is a black night, but things must look blacker yet before we decide to turn."

December 22. In the morning there was a bright sky. The high, snow-covered foothills no longer obstructed one's view to the west. The coastline there was now a deep bay beyond which the land rose to mountain ranges that Scott suspected formed "the backbone of the whole continent." Abreast of the camp was a pyramidal mountain some 9,000 feet high, whose uniformity and elevation made it an excellent landmark. Farther south was a conical mountain that would be the party's chief landmark for the coming week. "It is noticeable that along all this stretch of coast we can see no deep valley that could contain a glacier from the interior ice-cap (if there is one)."

Scott felt the scene's beauty, which was enhanced when the sun hung low in the south and formed "the most delicate blue shadows and purest tones of pink and violet on the hill-slopes. There is rarely an intensity of shade—the charm lies in the subtlety and delicacy of the colouring and in the clear softness of the distant outline."

Scott and Wilson, suspecting that bacon had brought on the symptoms of scurvy, decided to stop using it and to increase the allowance of seal meat. Shackleton was told this was a preventive measure but he seemed to have grown suspicious. The switch from bacon to seal was not quite equal in weight, so the party lost nourishment by it. They could not afford to lose more, for they were already on starvation rations. When they had left the ship their daily allotment had been about 1.9 pounds per man. This had been reduced by various circumstances, among them the incident of Spud and the seal-meat bag. The men were now experiencing acute hunger on 1.5 pounds per man-day. Great efforts were being made to conserve both food and fuel.

Breakfast:

You put the tea in long before the water boiled, and lifted it out and poured with the first bubbling. You immediately dropped the pemmican and biscuit into the pot and made a "fry," which took less time to prepare than a hoosh. Exactly twenty minutes after the primus lamp was lit it was put out, and two or three minutes later breakfast was over.

Lunch:

It consisted of half a biscuit, a small piece of seal meat and eight to ten lumps of sugar and was carried by each man in a small bag in a breast pocket, where it thawed during the first march. All three men found it very difficult not to filch from the bag. One believed, contrary to the evidence, that today's piece of seal meat was half an inch longer than yesterday's, therefore if one nibbled half an inch off, one would still have the equivalent of yesterday's lunch.

Supper:

This was by far the best meal of the day. Each man had from three-quarters to a whole pan of not very thick hoosh, heated in the central cooker. The hoosh boiled about thirty minutes after the primus was ignited. The cocoa was made simultaneously in the outer, colder cooker. As soon as the hoosh was ready the primus was turned off. The cocoa was not really warm or properly dissolved but it was the best drink the men could afford. No one criticized the quality of the food now. All one wanted was quantity. Half an hour after supper one seemed to feel as hungry as ever.

Wilson and Shackleton regularly had food nightmares, which were the subject of breakfast conversation. They were sitting at a table loaded with food, but their arms were tied. They picked up a dish, which slipped and broke. They lifted a bit of food to their mouths and fell off a precipice. They spent all their time shouting at waiters who ignored them. By the time a sirloin of beef reached them the meat was only ashes. So far Scott had been spared such dreams but he expected they would come.

Soon after leaving the ship the party had realized that the food had to be divided in a rigid system of shares. The divider had done his best to form three equal portions but had felt obliged to consume what he regarded to be the smallest. There had been numerous objections and arguments over the size of the portions until Shackleton had invented a game called "shut-eye." In this the rations were divided by anybody. Then one of the other men turned his head away while the divider pointed at a portion and asked, "Whose is this?" The man with the averted gaze would name the owner. The game, which left the matter of shares entirely to chance, was by now played at every meal as a matter of course. "One cannot help thinking how queer it would appear for a casual onlooker to see three civilised beings employed at it."

December 23. They were having trouble with their nostrils and lips, which were skinless in places. Their fingers were chapped and deeply cracked by the cold and by the very low humidity. Snow blindness attacked them frequently. There were times when all three men marched with one eye covered, the other peering through a goggle. But these discomforts were as nothing when compared with their hunger, which increased daily.

December 24. Wilson examined his companions again this morning. "The result?" asked Scott quietly. "A little more." They agreed it was not yet time to turn back. In the evening they were comforted by a new stretch of surface, which, although it was covered by an inch or two of feathery snow, was relatively firm. They camped on a hard spot. The sastrugi were now all from the south-southeast and parallel to the land.

Christmas Eve. They thought and talked about the folks at home and about how they, the sledgers, would celebrate tomorrow. For a week they had been planning the "gorgeous feed" they meant to have on Christmas Day. Every item of each meal had been gone over and over in great detail. Breakfast would be a "glorious spread." The primus would be kept lit ten or even fifteen minutes longer than usual. Lunch, for a change, would be warm, comforting.

Christmas Day. When they awoke this morning and wished each other a Merry Christmas they found the sun shining brightly on the green canvas roof of the tent. The sky was cloudless. There was no wind. The gleaming coastline stretched along the western horizon. For breakfast each man had a whole panful of biscuit and seal liver, the latter fried in bacon and in pemmican fat. This was followed by a large spoonful of blackberry jam from a can that had been brought along specially for this day. The meal comforted hunger pangs as they had not been soothed in weeks.

The trek was resumed at 11:30 A.M. The snow surface, which had improved last night, continued good. There was no need now for men to haul sledges or to whip dogs. At four o'clock came lunch, which consisted of hot cocoa, plasmon, a biscuit and a spoonful of jam. Another march from 5:30 to 8:30, when they camped, having covered almost eleven miles. It was the longest day's march they had made in quite some time.

They indulged themselves in the luxury of washing and brushing themselves for supper. Redolent of soap, they waited to begin the meal. Into the cooking pot went a double helping of everything. The result was a hoosh so rich one could stand one's spoon in it. The primus hissed on as the cocoa was brought to a boil. Shackleton, digging into his bundle, brought out a spare sock, the toe of which contained two surprises: a plum pudding about the size and shape of a cricket ball, and a crumpled piece of artificial holly. The pudding was heated in the cocoa. "For once we divided food without 'shut-eye.'"

After supper there was gay chatter. What was England like now?

Damp? Gloomy? And how did their friends picture them? As being on the sledge journey on the great snow plain? Which if any of them were capable of imagining the truth, that for the sledgers this had been "the reddest of all red-letter days"? The sun circled in the sky; the air was warm; all was very pleasant. There was a deep sense of comfort in the tent as Scott wrote in his journal over his second pipe. He expected that the party would sleep well tonight, without dreams and without tightening of the belt.

In his book Scott says that by this time he and his companions suspected they had made a serious error in not bringing more food along; that "the additional weight which we should have carried in taking a proper allowance of food would have amply repaid us on this occasion by the maintenance of our full vigour." But he does not explain how the party would have managed to pull a greater load, when they had already had grave difficulties in hauling their present one, even before weakness due to malnutrition set in. Nor does he mention the fact that the party had the option of eating dog cutlets to keep up their strength, as Amundsen and his companions were to do some ten years later on their triumphant journey to the Pole. National and personal prejudices regarding dogs were reinforced rather than examined during Scott's first great southern sledge journey, and this had serious consequences for him on his return from the Pole.

The hunger that assailed the men had strong social and psychological side effects. The party's thoughts and conversations seemed inexorably interwoven with the subject of food except for a half hour or so after supper, when "a desultory conversation would be maintained concerning far-removed subjects; but it was ludicrous to observe the manner in which remarks gradually crept back to the old channel, and it was odds that before we slept each one of us gave, all over again, a detailed description of what he would consider an ideal feast." The worst time was during the march; then the subject of food was reduced to the most minute and trivial questions and details. How many paces did you make per minute? How many before lunch? You began to count, and to lose count. What remained in the pemmican bag? Exactly how much could be used for tonight's hoosh? How much pemmican was there on the ship? What gorgeous streaks of yellow fat the ship's pemmican contained! How marvelous the seal meat on the ship had been, and the thick

soup and the thicker porridge! But what was such food when compared with London restaurant fare? You remembered having declined a particularly succulent dish in England. What an extraordinary thing to have done! You must have been a very different person
in those days.

But the men were not enduring hunger for nothing: there were
great rewards as they plodded southward into latitudes no human
beings had ever explored, while the superb western panorama slowly
changed. Skirting the coastline at a distance of eight to ten miles,
they had lost sight of the pyramidal and tabular landmarks that
had been abreast of them a week ago, and of the conical peak
toward which they had headed for days. "Perhaps the most interesting part of our view just at this time [Christmas Day] was the
coastline itself. . . . The undulating ice-cap fell gradually to a
height of one or two thousand feet and then abruptly to the barrier
level. In a few places this fall was taken by steep but comparatively
smooth snowslopes, in others the snow seemed to pour over in
beautiful cascades of immense ice-blocks, and in others, again, the
coast was fringed by huge perpendicular cliffs of bare rock."

December 26–31. On the twenty-sixth Wilson had such a severe
attack of snow blindness the party had to camp early. He writhed
in agony all afternoon. He put cocaine in his eyes, then zinc solution,
but neither remedy helped much. After supper, having tried but
failed to sleep, he gave himself morphine and slept soundly the entire night. Shackleton killed Brownie that night. Next day Wilson
pulled beside the sledges with his eyes completely covered. On the
twenty-eighth, sights showed the party to be at 82°11'. In Scott's
judgment they had about shot their bolt. The weather was fine, affording clear views of the beautiful southern scene. Scott was certain the change of diet had lessened the symptoms of scurvy. Next
day a blizzard kept the men in their tent. On the thirtieth, marching south-southwest in a thick fog, the party encountered many
cracks in the barrier surface and were obliged to make their last
camp, at between 82°16' and 82°17'. They had less than ten days'
provisions for the trek back to Depot B. When they turned homeward the following day, it seemed to make no difference to the dogs,
so lamentable was their condition.

January 1, 1903. Spud fell in his tracks, was carried awhile on
a sledge and died in the late afternoon. Using their tent floorcloth

and two bamboo ski poles, the men improvised a sail to take advantage of a southerly breeze.

January 3–8. Nell, too exhausted to walk further, was killed. Gus and Kid died. Dog food was fed freely to the remaining seven animals, there being little point in conserving and carrying it. On the sixth the temperature was 33° F. In Scott's opinion the skis the party had brought had failed to compensate in value for the extra weight they had added to the load. On the seventh the dogs, set free of their traces, walked beside the sledges while the party manhauled. "All day we have been steadily plodding on with the one purpose of covering the miles by our own unaided efforts, and one feels that one would sooner have ten such days than one with the harrowing necessity of driving a worn-out dog team." Next day the barrier surface made manhauling very tiring work. The party were about fifty miles from Depot B now, with less than a week's provisions left. Joe was killed and fed to the other animals. Four dogs remained. Wilson, as being probably the most expert at the job, did most of the killing. Scott was ashamed of his own "moral cowardice" in avoiding this "dirty work."

January 10–13. On the tenth a strong wind and the use of the sail helped the men to cover many miles. The course was erratic. At times the men had to run to keep up with the sledges. Birdie died. Shackleton was definitely unwell. The following day the barrier surface again was very difficult to sledge on. Lewis dropped behind and failed to catch up. It was snowing so heavily the party frequently did not know exactly where they were, and feared they would miss the depot. It continued to snow on the twelfth.

"The depot is a very small spot on a very big ocean of snow; with luck one might see it at a mile and a half or two miles, and fortune may direct our course within this radius of it; but, on the other hand, it is impossible not to contemplate the ease with which such a small spot can be missed. In a blizzard we shall certainly miss it; of course we must stop to search when we know we have passed its latitude, but the low tide in the provision-tank shows that the search cannot be prolonged for any time, though we still have the two dogs to fall back on if the worst comes to the worst. The annoying thing is that one good clear sight of the land would solve all our difficulties."

This is the first time Scott mentions the possibility of eating dogs; they are to be consumed as a last and desperate measure only.

At around midnight of the thirteenth, while trying to get a meridian altitude reading with the theodolite telescope, he saw a speck on the horizon: it was the depot. Hurrying to it, the men had a "fat hoosh." After experimenting with the sledges, they discovered that the latter moved more easily with wooden runners, so they stripped the runners of their covering of German silver. Depot A was about 130 miles away; the party had three weeks' provisions with which to reach it; so things looked much brighter. But there was no question that Scott's and Wilson's health had declined and that Shackleton's scurvy had seriously worsened. The men were sunburned black. They rarely washed now. They hadn't shaved or trimmed their hair in some time. Their clothes were tattered.

January 14–15. "Shackleton has very angry-looking gums—swollen and dark; he is also suffering greatly from shortness of breath; his throat seems to be congested, and he gets fits of coughing, when he is obliged to spit, and once or twice to-day he has spat blood." Scott himself had very red gums and a slight swelling of the ankles, and Wilson's gums were affected in one spot. After setting up camp Scott went to feed the dogs. Following him, Wilson confided he was alarmed about Shackleton's condition. Wilson and Scott decided it was absolutely necessary to keep Shackleton on his legs, for they doubted they were strong enough now to carry him by relay work. Scott emphasized to Shackleton that he must not pretend to be stronger than he felt and that, restless though he was by temperament, he must do as little work as possible. Next day the last two dogs were killed. "This was the saddest scene of all; I think we could all have wept. And so this is the last of our dog team, the finale to a tale of tragedy. I scarcely like to write of it. . . . Shackleton's state last night was highly alarming; he scarcely slept at all and had violent paroxysms of coughing, between which he was forced to gasp for breath."

January 16–28. Twice Shackleton slipped and fell heavily, and afterwards coughed, and spat blood. At the end of each march he was exhausted and dizzy. Visibility continued to be so bad that at times one felt one was marching blind. Wilson's eyes being on the point of giving out, Scott's were the only ones the party could depend on. On the afternoon of the eighteenth Shackleton had a severe attack of breathlessness, and the party were forced to camp. That night his condition was very serious. "He is very plucky about it, for he does not complain, though there is no doubt he is suffering badly." By the nineteenth the party had had overcast weather for some ten days. On the twentieth land was seen hazily in the west. Good progress was made next day by the use of the sail in a brisk southerly wind. Sometimes Shackleton rode on the sledges; mostly he walked. "Shackleton is improving, but takes his breakdown much to heart." The southerly breeze continued for several days and good marches were accomplished because of it; consequently the food allowance was increased slightly. On the twenty-fifth there was sunshine at last, and the smoke of Erebus was sighted about a hundred miles away. Familiar landmarks made their appearance, including Mount Erebus, Mount Terror and the Royal Society Range. Depot A was reached the afternoon of the twenty-eighth. Scott and Wilson wolfed too much food and as a consequence suffered from acute indigestion.

January 29. Shackleton had a relapse. "There is no doubt [he] is extremely ill; his breathing has become more stertorous and laboured, his face looks pinched and worn, his strength is very much reduced, and for the first time he has lost his spirit and grown despondent. It is terrible to have to remain idle knowing that we can do nothing to help. I have talked to Wilson tonight, who thinks matters are very critical, and advises pushing on to the ship at all hazards."

January 30. "Shackleton scarcely slept at all last night; his paroxysms of coughing grew less only from his increasing weakness. This morning he was livid and speechless, and his spirits were very low. He revived a little after breakfast, and we felt that our only chance was to get him going again. It took him nearly twenty minutes to get out of the tent on to his ski; everything was done in the most laboured fashion, painful to watch. Luckily the weather had cleared, and, though there was a stiff south-westerly breeze and some drift, the sun was shining brightly. At last he was got away, and we watched him almost tottering along with frequent painful halts."

February 1. "For two days the weather has been glorious, and has had a wonderful effect on our invalid, who certainly has great recuperative powers."

February 2. The party was now ten or twelve miles from Hut Point. The signs of scurvy had again increased in all three men.

February 3. The party reached the ship after having been in the field for ninety-three days and after having covered 960 statute miles.

"If we had not achieved such great results as at one time we had hoped for," Scott wrote, "we knew at least that we had striven and endured with all our might."

When the southern party reached the *Discovery* they found that the ship was still solidly frozen in. They also learned that a relatively small relief ship, the *Morning*, a wooden whaler purchased in Norway and refitted and overhauled in England, had recently arrived at Ross Island. The *Morning* had found the messages left hopefully for it in tin cans on a stout post at Cape Crozier. (Before departing from England, Scott had left word that he would deposit messages at certain designated places on his way to winter quarters.) The messages had been kept up to date by dangerous treks on the sea ice around Cape Armitage and along the western edge of the ice shelf up to the cape. Their purpose was to inform the relief ship of the whereabouts and condition of the *Discovery* and its crew. The *Morning* was now lying off the Dellbridge Islands some ten miles north of Hut Point, at the limit of the fast ice. It had brought news and letters from the outside world.

The journey had greatly strained the health of the southern party. Shackleton was immediately put to bed. Whenever he tried to move about he experienced a recurrence of his breathlessness and his fits of violent coughing. Regarding his illness, it may be noted that on November 6, only four days after the beginning of the journey, Wilson noted in his diary that Shackleton had "a most persistent and annoying cough." On the following day he wrote that Shackleton was coughing a great deal, and on the ninth he noted that Shackleton's cough "seems very troublesome." (It was not until December 21 that Scott learned from Wilson with dismay that Shackleton had symptoms of scurvy.) Add to these facts Shackleton's sickly, or at the very least gloomy, appearance in the photograph of the southern party (presumably taken before the start of the journey, for both Scott and Wilson look very fresh and fit) in the second volume of *The Voyage of the "Discovery,"* and one may wonder if Shackleton wasn't ill at the journey's beginning, not with scurvy then but possibly with a lung infection. Wilson did not speculate in his diary regarding the cause or nature of Shackleton's cough, nor did he mention taking Shackleton's temperature, or suspecting Shackleton of having a fever.

By the journey's end Wilson himself had prominent symptoms of scurvy. He rested in bed a full fortnight. And Scott, who at the end of the ordeal was the fittest of the three, had both legs swollen and his gums sore from scurvy. After they reached the ship the three men were overcome by an extraordinary lassitude that was mental as well as physical and that lasted for two or three weeks.

The *Discovery* was not destined to be freed from the ice until the following austral summer but it had ample supplies for the year, and Scott was never in doubt as to whether to abandon her. (Next summer, when it seemed he would be forced to do so, he suffered great anxiety and feelings almost of disgrace.) For him—and his crew by a large majority supported him—imprisonment, instead of being a major disappointment, was a great opportunity for continued, even more intensive and certainly more experienced scientific and geographical exploration of the Ross Island region. Having decided that the *Discovery* should remain at Hut Point with a reduced crew, he asked for a list of those men who wished to return to England on the *Morning*. Ironically, he received precisely the eight names he himself would have chosen. All the officers wanted to stay. "It has been a great blow to poor Shackleton, but I have had to tell him that I think he must go; he ought not to risk further hardships in his present state of health."

Shackleton was replaced by a twenty-one-year-old sub-lieutenant from the *Morning*, George F. A. Mulock, who was to do excellent surveying work for the Discovery Expedition. There were many young men on the expedition and Scott was delighted to have them for their energy and cheerfulness. The *Morning* left for New Zealand and England on March 3, 1903. Neither Scott nor Shackleton could have imagined then that the latter's Antarctic career was far from ended.

2. SCOTT'S WESTERN JOURNEY

During Scott's southern journey various reconnaissance journeys were made by other members of the expedition. One of these, led by Albert B. Armitage, was the first to reach the tremendous ice plateau west of the western ranges. Armitage found a way inland via the New Harbour Glacier, subsequently called the Ferrar Glacier after the expedition's geologist, but his pioneer journey, despite its considerable accomplishments, was unable to proceed far enough onto the ice cap to bring back sufficient and definite information about it. The ice cap, being in Scott's words "still wrapped in mystery," therefore posed a major challenge of exploration in the Ross Island area. Armitage's journey excited geological interest in the region of the Western Mountains, and this was an added reason for mounting another western journey the next sledging season. Scott wrote, "The interest centred in this region; there were fascinating problems elsewhere, but none now which could compare with those of the western land. It was such considerations that made me resolve to go in this direction myself, and I determined that no effort should be spared to ensure success."

In September 1903, during the austral spring, Scott led a depot-laying journey to the west, discovering a much easier route to the main portion of the Ferrar Glacier than Armitage had. The glacier served as a frozen highway up and through the mountains to the plateau. From it one had striking views of cross-sections of foothills and mountains. The area was thus an invaluable place for pioneer geological studies. On this relatively brief trek Scott's party encountered temperatures of −50° F. at night and almost equally low temperatures by day.

The western sledge party, including its supporting teams, left the *Discovery* October 12, 1903. Numbering twelve men, it was a combination of three separate teams: Scott's advance party, consisting of his chief engineer, Reginald W. Skelton, his boatswain, Thomas A. Feather, and Edgar Evans, William Lashly and Jesse Handsley; Hartley T. Ferrar and two men; and the carpenter (Fred E. Dailey) and two men. Scott's original plan was for all twelve men to sledge together, without dogs, onto the Antarctic plateau and as far west as possible within a given time. The advance party would then continue westward while the remainder turned back. Scott calculated that his party would be absent from the ship for nine weeks.

The following is Scott's western route in summary. Leaving Hut Point, he crossed McMurdo Sound in a slightly northwesterly direction, traversed the entire length of the Ferrar Glacier, emerging onto the ice plateau at about 160° E, headed almost due west as far as 152° E, then marched approximately southwest to 146°33′ E at a latitude of 78°. From this it will be seen that he made a tremendous foray onto the plateau. The distance covered in the western journey was almost as great as that of the southern one.

October 13–16. The men began the trek with four eleven-foot sledges. The loads averaged a little over two hundred pounds per man. In Scott's opinion all twelve men were in hard physical condition and up to the rigors of a fast start. By early on the fourteenth the teams reached New Harbour on the western side of McMurdo Sound. The spot was called Butter Point because a can of butter was cached here for each party in the expectation that on the return trip it was here that fresh seal meat could first be obtained. Despite Scott's confidence in the men's condition the parties had to camp prematurely on the fourteenth because two of the members were "a bit seedy." At supper a third man chopped off the top of his thumb while cutting frozen pemmican. He cheerfully showed the frozen bit of thumb to everyone as a sort of joke.

On the fifteenth the parties reached the snout of the Ferrar Glacier on its northern side and moved westward without much difficulty. "It was extraordinary, after we had discovered and travelled over this easy route, to remember what a bogey it had been to us for more than twelve months." On the following day they reached the depot that had been left under Cathedral Rocks, and camped in the vicinity. Scott was greatly impressed by the wild grandeur of the scenes around him and by the fact that it was easy to imagine oneself to be elsewhere than in a polar region. In many directions the hills and mountains were dark, bare rock. He saw grayish black rocks; reddish brown rocks; peaks; gullies; hanging glaciers; the blue ice of the Ferrar Glacier; and the glacier's ice cascades (white waves with deep blue shadows) to the west.

October 17. The parties slowly made their way up the glacier. At camp that night Scott was ecstatic about the scenic wonders of the day's trek. "Not one half-hour of our march has passed without some new feature bursting upon our astonished gaze. . . . Away beyond is the gorge by which we have come; but now above and beyond its splendid cliffs we can see rising fold on fold the white snow-clad slopes of Mount Lister. Only at the very top of its broad, blunt summit is there a sign of bare rock, and that is 11,000 feet above our present elevated position; so clear is the air that one seems to see every wrinkle and crease in the rolling masses of névé beneath. . . . For the main part we are surrounded with steep, bare hillsides of fantastic and beautiful forms and of great variety of colour. The groundwork of the colour-scheme is a russet brown, but to the west especially it has infinite gradations of shade, passing from bright red to dull grey, whilst here and there, and generally in banded form, occurs an almost vivid yellow. The whole forms a glorious combination of autumn tints, and few forests in their autumnal raiment could outvie it."

It was on this same night that Scott received the first reports of the trouble that was soon to force the parties to return to the ship. The German silver that covered the runners of two of the sledges had split. The unprotected wooden runners, although they could work a long time on snow, were incapable of surviving more than a few hours of running on the sharp glacial ice. As a result of the work of the previous sledging season, the German silver strips had worn thin, but without warning signs. The trouble was very unexpected.

October 18–26. On the eighteenth, after another sledge had split its runners, Scott ordered all the sledges unpacked and the runners examined, the result being his decision to turn back. But he was determined to make use of this adversity. Instead of sledging homeward at a normal pace he decided to test his own party "to the utmost," leaving it to the supporting parties to go at their own speed. He reached the ship at 8:30 P.M. of the twenty-first, having covered thirty-six miles that day, which he believed to be a record of Antarctic sledging. To his surprise, the supporting parties, led by Ferrar, reached the ship the same night, having marched thirty-seven miles that day.

On the twenty-sixth, after the sledge-runners had been repaired, Scott started out once again for the great ice plateau. This time he traveled with two parties, comprising nine men, himself included. He was not destined to be free of worries concerning the runners.

October 30–31. At breakfast on the thirtieth a sudden heavy wind scattered the camp's sleeping bags, finneskoes and various other important garments that had been left lying about rather carelessly on the ice outside the tents. The men ran to retrieve them. "The incident would have been extremely funny had it not involved the possibility of such serious consequences. The sleeping bags were well on towards the steep fall of the north arm [of the glacier] before they were recovered, and by good luck the whole affair closed with the loss of only a few of the lighter articles." By the time the parties had resumed the march they were faced by a full gale. Un-

able to push forward directly into the gale, they went westward
to find shelter, reaching a slope that ended in the glacier's perpendicular side. They descended the slope as far as safety permitted
and pitched camp in the moraine there. The wind kept them in the
moraine for two days. Scott saw much evidence of vast deglaciation.

November 1. Having reached the spring depot, Scott discovered
that a "violent gale" had forced open an instrument box at the depot and scattered some of its contents. "When we came to count
up the missing articles, we found that Skelton had lost his goggles
and that one or two other trifles had disappeared; but before we
could congratulate ourselves on escaping so lightly, I found to my
horror that the 'Hints to Travellers' had vanished.

"The gravity of this loss can scarcely be exaggerated; but whilst
I realised the blow I felt that nothing would induce me to return
to the ship a second time; I thought it fair, however, to put the case
to the others, and I am, as I expected, fortified by their willing con-
sent to take the risks of pushing on."

Hints to Travellers, published by the Royal Geographical Society, provided explorers with the data necessary to determine their
whereabouts when out of sight of landmarks, as Scott would be on
the plateau. In order to locate his exact position he would need, in
addition to taking sights of the sun or stars, to know the declination
of a heavenly body in order to find his latitude; and he would require certain logarithmic tables to fix his longitude. Without the
booklet he would trek into the unknown without knowing precisely
where he was or which was the exact way back.

That night the sledge-runners were found to be in very bad
condition. Skelton and Lashly, metalworkers, worked for hours on
them.

November 2–3. The morning of the second was calm and bright.
The temperature was 2° F. The parties carefully made a wide detour around Finger Mountain "and its dangerous ice-falls," passing
gradually from glacial ice to snow. They encountered heavy winds.
Next day the winds were still violent. Scott noted a golden rule for
traveling in this region: "Always take a long sweep around corners,"
adding, "We were often tempted to break this rule when a shorter
road looked easy, but we never did so without suffering. It was an
error of this sort that I made on the afternoon of the 3rd, and which
after an hour's work landed us in such a dangerously crevassed

region that we were very glad to struggle back by the way we had come. . . . The whole of this glacier can be made easy by taking the right course—a course such as a steamer takes in rounding the bends of a river." By the third the parties had reached an altitude of 7,000 feet.

November 4–10. Now began an extraordinary and punishing week. The morning of the fourth was sunny but cold, with an increasing west wind. After some marching the parties were faced by "an immense and rugged ice-fall, one of those by which the glacier signifies its entrance into the valley." Scott resolved to push on up the slope of the glacier to the icefall's foot despite the weather's having turned very bad. "The full force of the gale burst upon us, and the air became thick with driving snow." On reaching the slope's summit a search was made for a camp site but without immediate success. Everyone's face was being frostbitten. It was evident to Scott that shelter must be found soon if serious consequences were to be avoided. "I shall not forget the next hour in a hurry; we went from side to side searching vainly for a patch of snow, but everywhere finding nothing but the bare blue ice. The runners of our sledges had split again, so badly that we could barely pull them over the rough surface; we dared not leave them in the thick drift, and every minute our frost-bites were increasing. At last we saw a white patch, and made a rush for it; it proved to be snow indeed, but so ancient and wind-swept that it was almost as hard as the solid ice itself. Nevertheless, we knew it was this or nothing, and in a minute our tents and shovels were hauled off the sledges, and we were digging for dear life.

"I seized the shovel myself, for my own tent-party, but found that I could not make the least impression on the hard surface. Luckily, at this moment the boatswain came to my relief, and, managing the implement with much greater skill, succeeded in chipping out a few small blocks. Then we tried to get up the tent, but again and again it and the poles were blown flat; at last the men came to our assistance, and with our united efforts the three tents were eventually erected. All this had taken at least an hour, and when at length we found shelter it was not a moment too soon, for we were thoroughly exhausted, and fingers and feet, as well as faces, were now freezing. As soon as possible we made a brew of tea, which revived us greatly; afterwards we got our sleeping-bag in, and since that we have been coiled up within it.

"The temperature to-night is −24°, and it is blowing nearly a full gale; it is not too pleasant lying under the shelter of our thin, flapping tent under such conditions, but one cannot help remembering that we have come mighty well out of a very tight place. Nothing but experience saved us from disaster to-day, for I feel pretty confident that we could not have stood another hour in the open."

This site was later known as Desolation Camp, for the blizzard continued with undiminished violence for a full week, and the men were trapped in their tents. "If I were asked to name the most miserable week I have ever spent, I should certainly fix on this one." Twenty-two out of each twenty-four hours were spent in the sleeping bags. The other two were devoted to making and consuming the hot morning and evening meals. It was difficult to sleep much. A great deal of time was spent in lying with one's eyes open and "simply enduring." Scott's tent possessed a copy of Darwin's *Cruise of the "Beagle,"* from which the men would take turns reading aloud until their fingers froze.

By the fifth day the sleeping bags had become so icy it was hard to keep one's feet warm in them, and the continued inactivity was markedly affecting the men's health. On the evening of November 9 Scott resolved that, come what may, the parties would resume the trek in the morning, but when the attempt was made the blizzard drove a number of the men back into their tents in an alarming condition. "Skelton had three toes and the heel of one foot badly frost-bitten, and the boatswain had lost all feeling in both feet. One could only shout an occasional inquiry to the other tents, but I gather their inmates are in pretty much the same condition. I think the wind and drift have never been quite so bad as to-day, and the temperature is −20°."

November 11. The wind died down and the men were finally able to break away from the camp site. Ferrar's party turned back toward Depot Nunatak for some necessary geological work. The remaining six men headed for the icefall. "On starting we could not see half-a-dozen yards ahead of us; within a hundred yards of the camp we as nearly as possible walked into an enormous chasm; and when we started to ascend the slope we crossed any number of crevasses without waiting to see if the bridges would bear. I really believe that we were in a state when we none of us really cared much what happened; our sole thought was to get away from that miserable spot [the site]."

November 12–22. By the evening of the thirteenth the two parties had at last reached the snow plain of the great plateau and were camped at an elevation of 8,900 feet. On the fourteenth Scott, using the latitude of known landmarks still visible, as well as other information available to him, improvised on paper a curve of the sun's declination, which, when he returned to the ship, he found was "nowhere more than 4' in error." This chart was to be of much use to him in fixing the latitude of his various positions on the sledge journey over the plain. The temperature was falling. On the sixteenth it was −44°. And the surface became hard and slippery, necessitating the use of crampons. Also, there was a continuous wind. "It blew right in our teeth, and from the first it was evidently not the effect of temporary atmospheric disturbance, but was a permanent condition on this great plateau."

The men plodded on westward, Feather, Evans and Scott pulling one sledge, Skelton, Handsley and Lashly the other. The sledge party containing Handsley began to slacken badly, holding up Scott's party. Handsley was ill with some kind of chest condition but begged to be allowed to go on. "I tried to explain that I had no intention of reflecting on his conduct, but apparently nothing will persuade him but that his breakdown is in the nature of disgrace. What children these men are! and yet what splendid children! They won't give in till they break down, and then they consider their collapse disgraceful. The boatswain has been suffering agonies from his back; he has been pulling just behind me, and in some sympathy that comes through the traces I have got to know all about him, yet he has never uttered a word of complaint, and when he knows my eye is on him he straightens up and pretends he is just as fit as ever. What is one to do with such people?"

By the twenty-second Scott was forced to make a decision: Feather was transferred to Skelton's sledge and Lashly to Scott's; and the new Skelton party was ordered to return to the ship, while the advance party continued marching westward. The advance party was now due south of the south magnetic pole. The north end of their compass needle pointed toward the South Pole instead of toward the North Pole as it was designed to do. In directing Skelton toward the ship, Scott had told him to steer due west by the compass card even though Skelton would be marching eastward: the compass had reversed itself.

From now on the western party moved forward rapidly. Scott was greatly pleased with and impressed by his two sledging companions, one of them, Evans, a petty officer, the other, Lashly, a leading stoker, both members of the Royal Navy. The composition of this party was markedly different from that of the southern one. The latter was composed entirely of officers: Scott was a Royal Navy man, Shackleton belonged to the Royal Naval Reserve, and Wilson, a professional, was listed and regarded as an officer during the expedition. On the western journey Scott shared camp life with two members of the so-called lower deck, and he wrote that he learned much about lower-deck life from them. His ability to work and live successfully on such prolonged, difficult and close terms with lower-deck men, despite the starchiness with which he tended to regard his connection with the Royal Navy—we are speaking of a time when much greater formal differences existed between the ranks than now—is evidence of the plastic side of his sensitive character. However, the fact that they were lower-deck Navy men, accustomed to naval discipline and the differences between officers and seamen (often differences of birth, education and life style), rather than merchant seamen or simply civilians made it easier for him to get along with them.

He had early determined to obtain a naval crew for the expedition, being certain that the sense of discipline of such a crew "would be an immense acquisition," and he had succeeded in doing so despite considerable opposition from the expedition's originators and backers. Also, he had had what he had called grave doubts about his ability "to deal with any other class of men." Strictly speaking, the *Discovery* was not in the employment of the government. It sailed under the Merchant Shipping Act, whose regulations for enforcing discipline were designed to serve the needs of commerce, not war. In Scott's opinion such regulations failed "to provide that guarantee for strict obedience and good behavior which I believe to be a necessity for such exceptional conditions as exist in Polar service." Probably his belief was largely due to his extensive reading in the literature of English exploration in the northern polar regions during the first half of the nineteenth century, at which time it was customary, for example, for naval seamen to haul the sledges, often at the price of extreme exhaustion.

Scott explained in his book, "Throughout our three-years' voyage in the 'Discovery' the routine of work, the relations between officers and men, and the general ordering of matters were, as far as circumstances would permit, precisely such as are customary in His Majesty's ships. We lived exactly as though the ship and all on board had been under the Naval Discipline Act; and as everyone must have been aware that this pleasing state of affairs was a fiction, the men deserve as much credit as the officers, if not more, for the fact that it continued to be observed." It was at his strong insistence that the Discovery Expedition was run on this basis. It was a very different attitude or need from the one Shackleton would evidence when he mounted the Nimrod Expedition several years later.

Edgar Evans, who was to die with Scott on the return trek from the Pole, "was a man of Herculean strength, very long in the arm and with splendidly developed muscles." He weighed 178 pounds. "Lashly, in appearance, was the most deceptive man I have ever seen. He was not above the ordinary height, nor did he look more than ordinarily broad, and yet he weighed 13 st. 8 lbs. [190 pounds], and had one of the largest chest measurements in the ship. He had been a teetotaller and non-smoker all his life, and was never in anything but the hardest condition." Scott's own weight was 160 pounds. "It fell so far short of the others that I felt I really did not deserve such a large food allowance, though I continued to take my full share."

This "democratic" notion of food allowances, which favored the smaller and lighter men in any hard-pressed sledging party, was a fixed idea of Scott's that was to have, in my opinion, disastrous consequences for Evans during the South Pole trek.

The party was by now well out of sight of landmarks. There was nothing to be seen but the immense plain, with its undulations, sastrugi and smooth, glazed snow. "We were like a small boat at sea: at one moment appearing to stand still to climb some wave, and at the next diving down into a hollow. It was distressing work, but we stuck to it, though not without frequent capsizes, which are likely to have a serious effect on our stock of oil, for I fear a little is lost with each upset."

November 26–30. During the marching hours the temperature rarely rose much above −25°. At night it fell to −40° or below. There was a constant wind. On the twenty-sixth Scott wrote, "The wind is the plague of our lives. It has cut us to pieces. We all have deep cracks in our nostrils and cheeks, and our lips are broken and raw; our fingers are also getting in a shocking state; one of Evans's thumbs has a deep cut on either side of the nail which might have been made by a heavy slash with a knife. We can do nothing for this as long as we have to face this horrid wind. . . . The worst task of all is the taking of observations. I plant the theodolite as close as possible to the tent to gain what shelter I can, but it is impossible to get away from the wind, which punishes one badly at such times." On the twenty-eighth the sky was overcast, making visibility very uncertain.

On the thirtieth the party completed its last outward march, crossing heavy sastrugi. "At last we got through, and found on looking back that we must have descended into a hollow, as the horizon was above us on all sides. Ahead the slope was quite smooth, and, in spite of all the dreary monotony of the plain we have crossed, I felt distinctly excited to know what we should see when we got to the top. I knew it was the end of our effort, and my imagination suggested all sorts of rewards for our long labours. Perhaps there would be a gradual slope downward, perhaps more mountains to indicate a western coast for Victoria Land. . . . I journeyed up this slope with lively hopes, and had a distinct sense of disappointment when, on reaching the summit, we saw nothing beyond but a further expanse of our terrible plateau.

"Here, then, to-night we have reached the end of our tether, and all we have done is to show the immensity of this vast plain. The scene about us is the same as we have seen for many a day, and shall see for many a day to come—a scene so wildly and awfully desolate that it cannot fail to impress one with gloomy thoughts. I am not an imaginative person, but of late all sorts of stupid fancies have come into my mind. The *sastrugi* now got on my nerves; they are shaped like the barbs of a hook, with their sharp points turned to the east, from which direction many look high and threatening, and each one now seems to suggest that, however easy we may have found it to come here, we shall have a very difficult task returning.

"But, after all, it is not what we see that inspires awe, but the knowledge of what lies beyond our view. We see only a few miles of ruffled snow bounded by a vague, wavy horizon, but we know that beyond that horizon are hundreds and even thousands of miles which can offer no change to the weary eye, while on the vast expanse that one's mind conceives one knows there is neither tree, nor shrub, nor any living thing, nor even inanimate rock—nothing but this terrible limitless expanse of snow. It has been so for countless years, and it will be so for countless more. And we, little human insects, have started to crawl over this awful desert, and are now bent on crawling back again. Could anything be more terrible than this silent, wind-swept immensity when one thinks such thoughts?"

Scott wrote in his book (but now he was not quoting from his diary), "The interior of Victoria Land must be considered the most desolate region in the world. There is none other that is at once so barren, so deserted, so piercingly cold, so wind-swept or so fearsomely monotonous. . . . For me the long month which we spent on the Victoria Land summit remains as some vivid but evil dream. I have a memory of continuous strain on mind and body lightened only by the unfailing courage and cheerfulness of my companions."

The party turned homeward December 2. On that day they had so much trouble with a combination of poor visibility and sastrugi (which caused many falls) that they had to camp early. They were about seventeen marches from the Ferrar Glacier and had a bit more than fourteen days' full rations left and about twelve days' supply of oil. Scott had not counted on overcast skies at such an altitude. He was worried that if they continued, the consequences would be very serious for the party. But the sun reappeared and the trek was quickly resumed. "My companions are undefeatable. However tiresome our day's march or however gloomy the outlook, they always find something to jest about."

December 6–9. On the sixth Scott, alarmed about the dwindling oil supply, decided to march half an hour extra each day. He and his companions were now troubled by insomnia. Hunger had increased to such an extent that recourse was being had to Shackleton's game of "shut-eye." Still, good progress was being made on the marches, although on the ninth everything seemed to go wrong. "Our sledge weight was reduced almost to a minimum, and we ourselves were inured to hard marching if ever three persons were, yet by our utmost exertion we could barely exceed a pace of a mile an hour. I have done some hard pulling, but never anything to equal this. The sledge was like a log; two of us could scarcely move it, and therefore throughout the long hours we could none of us relax our efforts for a single moment—we were forced to keep a continuous strain on our harness with a tension that kept our ropes rigid and made conversation quite impossible. So heavy was the work that I may remark we once tried pulling on ski and found we simply couldn't move the sledge."

The party now had about a week's provisions and were well into their last can of oil. Scott proposed that they increase their marching time by an hour and cut their daily use of oil by half. If they didn't sight landmarks in a couple of days they would have to reduce their rations. "I have been struggling with my sights and deviations table, but although I believe we cannot be far off the glacier the sense of uncertainty is oppressive. We are really travelling by rule of thumb, and one cannot help all sorts of doubts creeping in when the consequences are so serious."

December 10–14. But next day Evans sighted the land and this cheered the party, although Scott still wondered where they were. They caught glimpses of land on the eleventh and twelfth but because of the bad weather Scott was unable to recognize a landmark and was therefore very uncertain about their exact position. His companions looked gaunt and wild but everyone was fit and there was no sign of the dreaded scurvy. Bad weather or not, the men could not afford to stand still; they continued to march eastward. On the fourteenth their puzzlement as to their whereabouts came to an abrupt end. They reached some ice disturbances, and although the wind was high and the air thick with snowdrift the decision was to go on. "To stop might mean another spell in a blizzard camp, when starvation would soon stare us in the face." Although all three men were wearing crampons, Lashly suddenly slipped and slid downward on his back. Evans followed. Scott braced himself to stop them but was jerked off his legs. At first the party slid smoothly, then they bounced violently. "At length we gave a huge leap into the air, and yet we travelled with such velocity that I had not time to think before we came down with tremendous force on a gradual incline of rough, hard, wind-swept snow. Its irregularities brought us to rest in a moment or two, and I staggered to my tent in a dazed fashion, wondering what had happened.

"Then to my joy I saw the others also struggling to their legs, and in another moment I could thank heaven that no limbs were broken. But we had by no means escaped scatheless; our legs now show one black bruise from knee to thigh, and Lashly was unfortunate enough to land once on his back, which is bruised and very painful. . . .

"As soon as I could pull myself together I looked round, and now to my astonishment I saw that we were well on towards the entrance of our own glacier; ahead and on either side of us appeared well-remembered landmarks, whilst behind, in the rough broken ice-wall over which we had fallen, I now recognised at once the most elevated ice cascade of our valley. In the rude fashion which I have described we must have descended some 300 feet; above us the snow-drift was still being driven along, but the wind had not yet reached our present level, so that all around us the sky was bright and clear and our eyes could roam from one familiar object to another until far away to the eastward they rested on the smoke-capped summit of Erebus.

"I cannot but think that this sudden revelation of our position was very wonderful. Half an hour before we had been lost; I could not have told whether we were making for our own glacier or for any other, or whether we were ten or fifty miles from our depot; it was more than a month since we had seen any known landmark. Now in this extraordinary manner the curtain had been raised; we found that our rule-of-thumb methods had accomplished the most accurate 'land fall,' and down the valley we could see the high cliffs of the Depot Nunatak where peace and plenty awaited us."

On the way to the depot Scott and Evans fell into a crevasse. "By a miracle he [Lashly] saved himself from following, and sprang back with his whole weight on the trace; the sledge flashed by him and jumped the crevass [sic] down which we had gone, one side of its frame cracked through in the jerk which followed, but the other side mercifully held. Personally I remember absolutely nothing until I found myself dangling at the end of my trace with blue walls on either side and a very horrid-looking gulf below; large ice-crystals dislodged by our movements continued to shower down on our heads."

Evans was hanging just above Scott. When Scott asked him if he was all right Evans characteristically replied casually that he was. Meanwhile Lashly held onto the sledge with one hand while with the other he disengaged two skis, which he slid beneath the sledge to make the latter more secure as a support. There was nothing more Lashly could do to help, for as soon as he relaxed his grip the sledge began to slip. After several attempts Scott climbed out of the crevasse by swarming up the rope with naked hands. "For a full five minutes I could do nothing; my hands were white to the wrists, and I plunged them into my breast, but gradually their circulation and my strength came back, and I was able to get to work. With two of us on top and one below, things had assumed a very different aspect, and I was able to unhitch my own harness and lower it once more for Evans; then with our united efforts he also was landed on the surface, where he arrived in the same frost-bitten condition as I had. For a minute or two we could only look at one another, then Evans said, 'Well, I'm blowed'; it was the first sign of astonishment he had shown."

At six o'clock the party reached the depot. "As long as I live I can never forget [that] night. Our camp was in bright sunshine, for the first time for six weeks the temperature was above zero, but what we appreciated still more was the fact that it was perfectly calm; the canvas of our tent hung limp and motionless, and the steam of our cooking rose in a thin, vertical shaft. All Nature seemed to say that our long fight was over, and that at length we had reached a haven of rest."

And so the party made their way downward and eastward, and felt strengthened and secure enough by the seventeenth to make a detour to explore what was later to be called Taylor Valley. It was delightful to experience the warmth and dryness of this valley and the clear, fresh meltwater that ran off some of the hanging glaciers. "I was so fascinated by all these strange new sights that I strode forward without thought of hunger until Evans asked if it was any use carrying our lunch further; we all decided that it wasn't, and so sat down on a small hillock of sand with a merry little stream gurgling over the pebbles at our feet. It was a very cheery meal, and certainly the most extraordinary we have had. We commanded an extensive view both up and down the valley, and yet, except about the rugged mountain summits, there was not a vestige of ice or snow to be seen; and as we ran the comparatively warm sand through our fingers and quenched our thirst at the stream, it seemed almost impossible that we could be within a hundred miles of the terrible conditions we had experienced on the summit."

By climbing, Scott tried but failed to catch a glimpse of McMurdo Sound. "But from our elevated position we could now get an excellent view of this extraordinary valley, and a wilder or in some respects more beautiful scene it would have been difficult to imagine. Below lay the sandy stretches and confused boulder heaps of the valley floor, with here and there the gleaming white surface of a broken lake and elsewhere the silver threads of the running water; far above us towered the weather-worn, snow-splashed mountain peaks, between which in places fell in graceful curves the folds of some hanging glacier. . . .

"I cannot but think that this valley is a very wonderful place. We have seen to-day all the indications of colossal ice action and considerable water action, and yet neither of these agents is now at work. It is worthy of record, too, that we have seen no living thing, not even a moss or a lichen; all that we did find, far inland amongst the moraine heaps, was the skeleton of a Weddell seal, and how that came is beyond guessing. It is certainly a valley of the dead; even the great glacier which once pushed through it has withered away."

On the afternoon of December 23 the party started to cross McMurdo Sound. Late on Christmas Eve they reached the ship, to be greeted by four persons who were the only ones on board. The party had been absent from the ship for eighty-one days and had marched 1,098 miles. "We may claim, therefore, to have accomplished a creditable journey under the hardest conditions on record, but for my part I devoutly hope that wherever my future wanderings may trend, they will never again lead me to the summit of Victoria Land."

Eight years later Scott was again to be struggling for his life on the immense inland plateau, although not in the region of Victoria Land. It was characteristic of him that he tried to reach the limit of human performance under very hard conditions, and it is partly for this reason, whether he realized it or not, that he preferred man-hauling to the use of dogs. Inasmuch as he persisted in marching the hairline between life and death which makes its sinuous way throughout the Antarctic, it was only a question of time before his luck would give out, and with it the luck of his companions, for whom he was the indomitable leader.

10

~~~

CAMPING AT CAPE ROYDS

CAPE ROYDS, a dark volcanic mass, the westernmost part of Ross Island, located approximately midway between the island's northern and southern extremities, is noteworthy for at least two reasons. It was the base of Shackleton's British Antarctic Expedition, the Terra Nova Expedition of 1907–9; and it is the site of the world's southernmost penguin (Adélie) rookery. In addition, it is fascinating because of its eerie, moonlike beauty.

A friend of mine recently asked me, "What's special about the fact that Royds is the home of the *southernmost* penguin rookery?"

The answer is that the farther south you go in these latitudes, in general the more extreme are the weather conditions you encounter. The Adélies feed in the sea; there is nothing on land to sustain them. They return to their old nests. Each October the Royds Adélies leave the pack ice and the open sea and walk and toboggan southward over the frozen Sound to their rookery. There is a certain raw courage, even though based on ancient habit, in their being the southernmost of their kind, and not only of *their* kind but of all penguins as well.

The prospect of returning to Royds excited me. (I had spent part of a day there the previous year.) I wanted to check my memory with respect to the cape's beauty as well as to learn if the place was as lovely late in December, when much of the snow would have melted, as it was in November, when it sported a thick mantle of snow. And I looked forward to observing the Adélies again, this time at leisure. But above all I was eager to live in the field.

Few people have the opportunity to camp out in Antarctica who do not have either scientific or logistic work to do there. Yet it is only in the field, away from the comforts of stations, that you can hope to get an authentic feel for the continent. Also, I wanted to go over the terrain until I no longer felt a stranger to it. The reason I planned to sleep in the historic hut was that I hoped thereby to lessen the awe I had for it, and the sense of distance I felt between me and its early residents, who had dared and endured so much. It seemed to me that awe and a sense of distance would not be conducive to sober and hopefully illuminating writing about such a place.

I knew of three kinds of previous residents at Royds: the original ones—indigenous so far as one can be indigenous in a place so hostile to land life; scientists in modern times; and the huts restoration parties (New Zealanders), who lived and worked there about a decade ago with the logistic support of the United States Navy. All had one element in common: functional work. Dave Murphy and I were to be something new to the place: extended visitors. If before we went to Royds we had notions of ourselves, as some of our friends had, as being idle vacationers we soon became disabused of them. We learned that camping at Royds was bone-tiring. When, having lost weight and been badly sunburned, we returned to McMurdo, the heated buildings came as a bodily shock. Our friends were puzzled.

The gap between visitors and residents at Cape Royds as well as at Cape Evans is considerable. Visitors stop by for an hour or two to tour the rookery and the hut. Few people have resided for a substantial time at Cape Royds since Shackleton's day. All in modern times have been scientists, studying the penguins, skuas and the cape's geology. In Shackleton's time the cape meant home. To modern residents home is McMurdo Station or Scott Base, with which, normally, they are in daily touch by radio. The early residents wintered over. No one in modern times winters over at any of the capes of Ross Island.

Neither Murphy nor I had camped out in Antarctica before. We asked many questions about what camping at Royds would be like but rarely received firm replies. For a while we could not elicit so simple a fact as whether the cape contained a wanigan (refuge hut). At last the deputy leader of Scott Base, Jim Barker, assured me there was one there, although he hadn't seen it. What did it contain? What was the temperature inside it and inside the Shackleton hut likely to be this time of year? What steps ought I to take to keep my cameras, tape recorder and batteries from freezing? We encountered a surprising ignorance regarding these and similar questions. Part of the reason was the lack of continuity of personnel. People came and went, and many failed to leave records.

One day at dinner three microbiologists from California asked me if it was true that I planned to sleep in the historic huts. When I said it was, they professed to be concerned about me. The huts, they asserted, were loaded with viable fungi, bacteria and viruses in conditions capable of supporting good cultures. Blubber decayed into energy and water; the water could keep certain microorganisms alive. In addition to blubber the huts contained old unwrapped biscuits, pony fodder, dead penguins, seal meat. The microbiologists named a fungal lung disease, aspergillosis, that you could contract by breathing in spores. The chances of my becoming infected were probably slight but I should not discount them, I was told.

I heard some lively anecdotes about the viability of microorganisms. For example, there was a house in California that sixty years ago had been occupied by a tubercular family. Recently some bedroom baseboards had been ripped out and had been found to be harboring live bacilli. Viable bacteria had been discovered in feces deposited during the Scott and Shackleton expeditions. A group of graduate students had rummaged around in old Indian sites in the San Joaquin Valley in California. Twenty had come down with Valley Fever and one had almost died of it. One of the microbiologists expressed the strong suspicion that the population decline of the Royds rookery since Shackleton's time was largely due to the presence of the hut, which in his opinion was probably a source of infection. He counseled me not to sleep in the huts; if I insisted on doing so I should spend a minimum of time in them and avoid stirring up dust and touching things.

I had never thought of the huts as a form of man's pollution of Antarctica. I had conceived of them only as historic shrines. The microbiologists were experts at obtaining and analyzing air samples. When I asked them to analyze samples of air from the Discovery Hut they said they were too busy, which probably was true but which alerted me to the possibility they were pulling my leg out of its socket.

One other bit of intellectual-emotional baggage accompanied us to Royds. This was the matter of the untried radio. Would the rig operate successfully on batteries? Or would the latter be too weak for the distance, or fail because of the cold? Would the radio work on the generator if necessary? The rule for field parties was that they check in daily with McMurdo by radio. If a party was not heard from for seventy-two hours McMurdo would send a plane to seek the reason. If your radio went bad you were advised to exercise special caution in anything unusual you did, for a minor accident could be serious if it occurred relatively far from shelter and was followed by bad weather. We knew this but paid little attention to it. Also, we were told unofficially that as long as the weather was bad enough to cause risk to pilots' lives we would not be rescued in case we were in trouble. We didn't bother to ask ourselves if this was hyperbole, for we really didn't care if it was or not. There is something about Antarctica that gives you a feeling akin to the self-confidence of the punchy boxer about to enter the ring for the victory he knows he so richly deserves.

On Saturday, December 19, after an early breakfast, Murphy and I walked up to the Field Center, loaded our gear onto a pickup truck and drove down to the helo pads, where some enlisted men were warming helo engines with huge pre-heater hoses. A strong wind was blowing. Murphy inquired if the helos would fly in it this morning. The men thought not, but when one of them asked Murphy who his pilot was and Murphy replied, "Brandau," the man said, "Oh, *he'll* fly in anything."

A little later Brandau, wearing a rumpled flight suit and a tan woolen hat like a skull cap, and with an old sheath knife strapped to his left leg, walked up from the helo hangar and said, "Mr. Neider, you'll sit in the cockpit."

He told the crewman to show me how to climb up to the cockpit on the port side. The crewman warned me not to touch a small yellow handle, which was designed to eject part of the canopy in an emergency, and to avoid another handle, which would do something else I wouldn't enjoy at the moment. It felt like more of a climb than I had expected. I slipped my right leg into the cockpit, got my torso to follow it, then drew my left leg in and sat down. My toes rested on a small platform but my heels were in the space of the cabin below me. The crewman, having climbed up behind me, cautioned me not to interfere with the motion of the control stick between my knees and not to touch the pedals or any of the levers. He showed me how to harness and belt myself in and how to don the communications helmet and plug it into the intercom system.

Brandau climbed aboard and spoke briefly over the intercom, checking to see if we could hear each other clearly. His face could change quickly from an impish smile to a look of seriousness. He started the engine, waited for it to warm up, checked the panel and the controls, flipped a couple of toggle switches. When the rotors began spinning, the cockpit was filled with a heavily flickering light. The instrument panel shook. At a signal from Brandau the crewman, who had been standing in front of the craft and signaling with his arms, came aboard. We lifted off. The sky was serene. The sun was an explosion of light.

Brandau flew inland to show me black Castle Rock, that historic landmark, at close range. Passing to the right or east of it, we got shoved about by strong gusts. His sun vizor was always pulled down. Inasmuch as mine interfered with the use of my cameras, I utilized it only rarely. Whenever the heading of the craft brought the sun to my eyes I was instantly blinded and had to slip the vizor out of the helmet's forward compartment. Mostly I was shooting through my open hatch in the direction away from the sun. Brandau had told me I was free to slide the hatch open or shut as I pleased. Usually, in the Navy H-34, I had marvelously unobscured views when the hatch was open, even when I looked down. But when we were too close to the ice, the rotor blast caused the air directly below us to vibrate and shimmy, and scenes there were distorted as if by heat waves. The open hatch let in a raw, cold airstream, which pained my naked hands and immediately chilled the cockpit, but Brandau never complained. On rare occasions I leaned far out and into the stream; it was difficult to catch one's breath then, and tears ran copiously.

At one point Brandau said something which I failed to make out, for there was much static on the intercom. Pointing toward the wall on my left, he motioned for me to pull one of the levers. I indicated a large, long lever to the left of my seat, similar to the one he was holding with his left hand (he handled the control stick with his right). Did he mean that one? He nodded. I pulled the lever up. We banked with a lurch to starboard. Shaking his head and smiling, he pointed again. Then I grasped that he wished me to pull a small lever which would release my shoulder harness and let me lean forward for better views through the windshield.

"Sorry about that," I said.

He nodded, smiling.

We flew over Erebus Glacier Tongue, over Cape Evans, then out over the Sound off Cape Royds, where he hoped to show me some whales in the pack ice. This was as far south as the pack went at this time. No whales were visible. We saw slices of green or oil-brown water. We flew over Backdoor Bay (so named because it's behind Shackleton's hut) and landed on a hilltop pad marked by a circle of red-painted volcanic rocks. This prescribed route for helicopters avoided the rookery. Adélies are terrified by helos that fly low over them. They scatter in a panic, leaving eggs and chicks as easy prey for the always waiting skuas.

Brandau shut down the engine and descended to the rookery while Murphy and I off-loaded our gear with the crewman's help. We carted the lighter things to a lower area behind a ridge, thus sheltering them from the rotors, which on take-off would make a wind of some thirty or thirty-five knots. The heavier ones we placed on the plateau near the pad. Brandau returned and then, as we waved good-by, the helo abruptly lifted off.

Some of our gear, such as the 1,800-watt generator, the five-gallon plastic jugs of water, the five-gallon fuel drum, the cartons of food, was quite heavy. With the exception of the generator, which we left near the pad, we carried the gear over uneven terrain down a long, curving black slope to the door of the Nimrod (Shackleton) Hut. From the hut the way sloped gently downward to the thawed eastern shore of Pony Lake, then northward and upward some two hundred feet to the wanigan. Intent on securing ourselves against the possibility of the weather's souring, we moved water, food and survival gear into the wanigan and staked down a heavy handline between the two structures, hammering short black metal stakes into the black volcanic soil. I had promised Brian Porter, the Scott Base leader, that only I would sleep in the hut and that I would bring nothing into it that might endanger it. The historic huts, being located in the Ross Dependency, were technically under the jurisdiction of New Zealand. I had visions of a New Zealand headline: Yank's Carelessness Destroys Shackleton's Antarctic Hut.

If, while I was asleep in the hut, a long-lasting blizzard blew up, I might be trapped without food, heat and water. In that case it would be uncomfortable to crawl alongside the yellow line to the wanigan, but without the line I might conceivably not survive. At the moment, the sky being cloudless, I felt a bit foolish to be hammering at the stakes. I hoped Murphy did not think I was unduly cautious. But I knew from reading that men had come close to dying within feet of a door or a handline during Antarctic blizzards. An Antarctic blizzard had the capacity not merely of animalizing you; it could make a vegetable of you; it could disorient you to the point where you behaved in a manner that seemed suicidal. The winds could bowl you over and over, and the particles they blew about might have more of the consistency of sand than snow.

We spent much of that first day in tiring chores. By leaving some of our sweat at Royds we came to feel we had earned the right to call the place home. The work, sapping us physically, thereby set a sober or at least a non-superficial tone to our stay. We both were ready for a greater physical price than we had been paying at McMurdo and for the deeper experience we hoped would accompany it. Also, we got to know each other during those long hours. I felt very lucky in my choice of Dave Murphy as a field assistant and companion. I had gotten to know him almost accidentally. On the day of my arrival at McMurdo he and Vance had helped me lug my cartons of gear, shipped ahead of me from Davisville, Rhode Island, down the cindery hill to my room in the Lodge. I had encountered him casually here and there and had invariably been impressed by his good humor, modesty, brightness and by the aura of quiet competence which emanated from him. Twenty-four, he was strong, had a fine if somewhat raucous laugh, and was keenly aware of and sympathetic to the work I had to do.

Turning to the radio, we tested it from inside the wanigan, for an icy wind was now blowing. We heard scientific data and various comments being exchanged. All had in common the fact that the purveyors and receivers were oblivious of our battery existence. We could receive but not transmit. Had the batteries so soon been drained by the cold? Or was the trouble perhaps in the whip antenna, that long, rapier-like appendage that threatened one's eyes, especially in the confined space of the shack?

We tried to transmit from outside the wanigan but still without success. We were without communication with the world but this seemed fine to us, for it left us free after the encroachments on one's privacy and freedom inherent in the life of an Antarctic station. On the other hand, as long as we were without radio contact we could not leave Royds ahead of schedule should we find it urgent to do so. An escape on foot was not possible, even in the best of weather. We might swing around the farther shore of Backdoor Bay and make our way southward down to Cape Barne. But there we would come up against the slippery and crevassed expanse of the Barne Glacier. Presuming we crossed the glacier safely and reached Cape Evans, we could not hope to proceed farther south, for arrayed against us would be snow slopes, icefalls, glaciers, crevasses and ice headlands, all issuing from Erebus. Our sole road south was the sea ice, which by now was too rotten to be trusted. Northward to Cape Bird, where some Kiwis were camping, it would be equally impossible to go.

As for the weather, if we got socked in we could hold out in the wanigan a long time. In addition to our own food we had the emergency supplies on the shelves, in the form mainly of dehydrated foodstuffs packaged in New Zealand and Australia. There were also such items as canned goods, sugar, flour, biscuits and lots of hard candy. The weather was still good although a wind from the direction of Erebus was bringing heavy clouds.

We carried the radio to the helo pad and tried it up there, hoping the hilltop position would get us through. No dice. We hooked up and started the generator, letting it warm up for the required fifteen minutes before drawing power from it. Over and over I said, "McMurdo Station. McMurdo Station. This is McMurdo Three Two requesting a radio check. This is McMurdo Three Two at Cape Royds, trying out some experimental gear. Do you read me? Over."

At last we heard McMurdo—he came in booming and clear, startling us—telling us we were extremely weak. For a moment we failed to grasp he was addressing *us*.

But dependence on the generator wouldn't do. Our task was to try to get the radio to work on batteries alone. We carried the radio to the crest of a black hill just south of the hut, in the lee of which the hut had been built so it would be sheltered from the biting southeasterlies. We saw the sweep of Backdoor Bay; the vividly marked helo pad (the red was the only warm color visible); and the southern view, which included black Cape Barne, the Barne Glacier and black Cape Evans on the left, and the four black Dellbridge Islands on the right. We also saw the Glacier Tongue, Castle Rock, the backbone of Hut Point Peninsula, but not Hut Point, which was behind Inaccessible Island. McMurdo could receive us, but again he said we were very weak.

It was time now for lunch. Carrying the rig, we returned to the wanigan. Standing, completely dressed except for gloves, we wolfed salt crackers and unlabeled canned butter; tea with Pream; and unlabeled canned strawberry jam with the consistency and appearance of pink axle grease. Meanwhile Murphy fried some frozen steaks on a bed of salt and heated some vegetable soup, but only after much fussing with the Coleman stove, which refused at first to throw a blue flame, giving us instead a long yellow one that threatened to blacken the inside of the shack. For dessert we sucked frozen peaches. There was nothing to heat the shack with except the cooking stove, and we had to keep the door ajar as a precaution against monoxide fumes. We could have sat on the double bunks or on the crates visible beneath them. It was simpler and warmer to stand and shift about.

The wanigan was a plywood box which I judged to be $8' \times 12' \times 8'$. It was secured against winds by a staked-down wire hawser looped over it. The side farthest from the door had the two bunks. Murphy now chose the upper one for sleeping in, generously leaving me the lower for a work space. The southern wall (on the door's right as you entered) contained the shelves of foodstuffs; the northern had a work table for preparing food. The quarters were cramped but cozy and snowtight. There were no pinups. Instead, there were little pinned pieces of paper telling you who had lived here and when.

From the door you had a view of the black cape's seaside end; the guano-tan rookery on some last hills to the left; the lilac-white Sound beyond; the Western Mountains; and some piedmont glaciers at the eastern edge of Victoria Land, stretching and gleaming along the horizon and looking unbelievably close in the crystal air.

We washed dishes and utensils in warm water, then set up a dipole antenna behind the wanigan, failed to get through with it, found a break in a connection, mended it with adhesive tape and failed again. We brought the antenna with its poles and long wire to the vicinity of the Nimrod Hut, lugged the generator downhill to the south of the hut and tried the radio with both dipole and generator, working oudoors so the generator's power line was at a safe distance from the historic structure. At last we roused McMurdo but so weakly he said he would see if he couldn't improve things for us. He asked us to call him next at 6 P.M.

Free now to visit the rookery, we headed for it along the feather-strewn north shore of Pony Lake, passing dead Adélie chicks whose stomachs had been pierced by skua beaks; a few dead adult penguins; some dead skuas; and some skeletons of both. The shore's rocks and soil were thinly crusted over in places by a whitish substance that we took to be salt from evaporated spume and scud blown inland from the Sound when the latter was ice-free. The lake, about the size of a pond, contained bird debris as well as algae in the shallower, thawed parts we were able to observe.

At one point, to the right or north of the rookery, the cape plunged from a height into the Sound. The dark terrain was not forbidding, for it was brightened by the pure sky and the Sound's whiteness. The Sound looked marbled at close range because of contrasts between the sea ice and the latter's thin mantle of snow. The ragged snow splotches were whiter than the ice, which was tinged with a faint wash of bluing. The tidal crack, reflecting the sky's blue, was some ten to fifteen feet wide. Half a dozen Weddells lay just beyond it, and a group of some twenty Adélies were waddling far out, heading north.

The penguins in the rookery paid little or no attention to us. Their eyes looked unreal, jewels stuck in black velvet. Their beaks were mottled brown, like tortoise shell, and were flesh-colored inside. From places in the rookery you could see the birds backgrounded by Erebus, a white plume flying from the volcano's crest. In the rookery were hard, guano-crusted trails between boulders. Some of the birds were nesting high up on boulder conglomerate that looked like giant loaves of black bread mashed upon each other. A lone skua stood placidly within the rookery, now and again making a little quacking sound. The penguins dozed on their nests. When they occasionally shifted they revealed one or two pale blue eggs, or a pair of very young gray chicks with spindly necks, whose heads wobbled uncertainly as the beaks opened wide for a meal of regurgitated food. The parents kept looking down to make certain the eggs and chicks were securely in place. When a skua flew low over the rookery or landed in it, angry grunting was elicited from the nearest Adélies.

I had written earlier about this rookery:

"The Adélie is about eighteen inches high and weighs some fourteen pounds. (The Emperor is much larger, being about three feet high and weighing about sixty pounds.) Penguins are marvelous navigators. They navigate by the sun, but exactly how is not yet understood. They have been known to attack men (comically) and dogs (tragically), with the manner of a person strong on moral indignation. Everyone has read about their comical behavior, their curiosity about man's doings, their innocence in the presence of huskies, their being preyed upon by leopard seals and skuas.

"There were hundreds of them already egg-sitting but there was a great bustle as individuals sought little gray pumice-textured stones for their nest, picking them up earnestly and waddling proudly away, their flippers working like primitive arms. If a nest is temporarily vacant a neighbor doesn't hesitate to steal stones from it. The occupant on returning seems blissfully unaware of the loss. When a bird wanders too close to an occupied nest the nester squawks furiously and makes threatening gestures, causing the trespasser to retreat in haste. There is a great quacking and squawking but with no suggestion of chaos, rather of the patient, endless bustle of a flea market. Their food is in the unfrozen sea miles to the north and they wait unfed until their mate returns from the sea to spell them. I had expected to visit immaculate citizens in formal dress but this was not an immaculate time. The white breasts were stained brown, tan and green and the areas around the nests were colored by guano. I had read in the accounts of the early explorers how strong the guano smell is but it seemed mild today, hardly more pungent than that of cormorants at their hangouts on Point Lobos in California.

"Occasionally a bird points its beak at the zenith, stretches its neck to the utmost, flaps its flippers and makes a clucking, chattering sound which begins slowly and softly and rises to considerable speed and volume before dying out. Sometimes as it fades it ends with sounds of choking or gargling, reminding one of a death rattle. This exercise, moving from individual to individual, is almost continuous in the group. When several birds display simultaneously the effect is cacophonous."

A year earlier I had headed from the hut towards the rookery. The way then was over thick snow and across Pony Lake with its treacherously hidden green ice. After that first visit to Royds I had written, "Both Scott and Cherry-Garrard have commented on the great beauty of Cape Evans, with its western views of glaciers and snow-capped mountains and with its proximity to the striking snout of the Barne Glacier."

But Royds too looks out on the Western Mountains. And when Scott wrote in his journal so enthusiastically about Evans he had not had a chance to live at Royds. It's true that the Royds hut is not elementally close to the shore, as the Evans one is, and lacks the proximity to something so dazzlingly raw as the Barne Glacier, and is humanized by the humanoid Adélies, but these facts only place it in a tamer setting than that of Evans, not a less beautiful one.

"On my brief visit," I continued, "I was more impressed by the beauty of Royds. Royds is admittedly less spectacular but its subtle beauty is very rewarding. If the sky had had its usual brilliance the scenes might have been less remarkable. Full of heavy snow clouds yet containing luminous patches, it softened the light majestically. Royds seemed to be outmastering the most gifted old Chinese water-colorist. There was a great variety of design and composition, and scenes were wondrous in their simplicity. It was a graphic artist's paradise. Black pebbly lines flowed like sinuous brush strokes over the virginal white. Black hills blown partially clear of snow stood against a white foreground. One stared at the frozen Sound between two meeting slopes and, far away, at a brilliant white ribbon on the dead-level flatness of the sea ice. A group of penguins like round-shouldered tuxedoed men seemed to be conferring at the cape's edge, a mass of blue and green pressure ice behind them."

The sky now, on my visit with Murphy, was brilliantly blue, yet Royds was as lovely as ever. It was strikingly black or oxford gray, and its hills and projections, contrasting with the Sound, the Western Mountains, the sky, the Dellbridge Islands, Mount Erebus with its icefalls, and the tan of the rookery, afforded an infinite variety of visual pleasure. The wealth of its plasticity and invention, almost entirely within a monochromatic frame, reminded me of the sculptured forms of the Carlsbad Caverns of New Mexico. It was badlands country. The lava levels seemed to be piled on top of each other as though they were black mud bricks. Looking inland, you saw only this weird land abutting against Erebus's ice slopes.

Heading north along shore rocks to have a closer view of some pressure ice, we broke through crusted ice into fish-stinking muddy water almost to our ankles, Murphy in his mukluks, I in my hiking boots. Then I slid and almost fell into thawed guano on a small hillside. We gave up trying to go further along the shore in that direction, for we might break through into the sea itself. We returned to the rookery.

While Murphy, fascinated, lingered there, I went to the Nimrod
Hut to prepare my sleeping accommodations, which consisted of a
green canvas cot with an aluminum frame, a striped cot mattress
and a green Bauer sleeping bag. The temperature in the hut was
29° F. on the floor and 30° on the large table near the stove on the
hut's eastern side. I set up the cot between the table and a pewlike
bench south of it. The bench was covered with dusty burlap and
held four and a half pairs of battered old shoes. Above it were photographs of Edward VII and Queen Alexandra, the sovereigns who
had given Shackleton's expedition their public blessing by visiting
the *Nimrod* just before it left England in 1907. I thought of
Shackleton's bitter disappointment in being invalided home; of the
great difficulties he had experienced in obtaining financial support
for an expedition of his own; and of his persistence, persistence and
unsinkable optimism. The table rested on unopened, heavy venesta
crates. On it were old copies of the *Illustrated London News*, a
visitors' register, two chipped enameled mugs and a couple of
candles.

The hut was more substantial than I remembered it to be from
my visit of a year ago. It was about nine of my paces wide and,
excluding the porch, about fifteen of them long. The floor, of neatly
joined boards, showed much wear, discoloration and the marks of
hobnailed boots, yet it was still so solid it didn't creak. Many of the
original bunks, as indicated in the hut plan in Shackleton's *The
Heart of the Antarctic*, were no longer extant, so the interior was
more spacious than it had been. In Shackleton's time some of the
bunks had been set at right angles to the walls. Now there were
two cots and a cratelike bunk parallel to the northern wall, and a
similar bunk parallel to the southern one.

When new, the structure had had two southern and two northern
windows. The southwestern window had been boarded up long ago.
From the remaining southern window you saw, as Shackleton and
his companions had seen and as Scott had later seen, a small, more
or less free land area, past which, some fifty feet away, was a falling
crest of lava rock. From the northern windows you looked out over
the remains of the pony stable: bales of fodder, piles of corn kernels,
rusted tin cans, sacks of wheat and flour. Past the stable was a wasteland of black hills suggesting a moonscape. The hut was well illuminated. It looked neat. And although it had the inevitable odors of

such a place—of dankness, of a stable, of fishy rot—they were not strong enough to be overly offensive.

On the north side were a pair of finneskoes; white canvas sacks; socks worn through at the heels. On a cot were two large dark reindeer-skin sleeping bags. Here and there were a book on a shelf, its covers gone; a hobnailed boot hanging from a nail; bits of netting; canvas shoes; jackets and trousers; a great pair of navy blue trousers. Hanging from a shelf was something resembling a white prayer shawl, dirty, red-striped, with tassels. Harness hung everywhere. A ski leaned against a wall. Patches of dirty white canvas lay on crates or on the floor. Suspended from a beam above the table was an old Nansen sledge as well as heavy iron bars from which gear could be hung. The stove and its pots were deeply rusted but bits of the original black paint still clung to the oven doors. Beyond the stove (that is, east of it), was a tiny cubicle, originally a darkroom, separated from the rest of the place by a sheet of striped burlap. In it were dusty jars and test tubes. On a shelf to the right of the cubicle were enameled metal plates and trays as well as some crockery. There was no photograph of Shackleton visible but his presence seemed to me to linger strongly in the hut.

I was fascinated by the foods still intact in their unopened cans and jars; foods that brought one's thoughts to an earlier, simpler time, that of his first expedition, before the First World War. Bird's Concentrated Egg Powder, "a complete substitute for though not made from eggs." Colman's Mustard. Heinz Preserved Sweet Midget Gherkins. Arrowroot. Ox tongues. Ham loaf. Kippered mackerel. Chicken and veal pâté. Consolidated pea soup. Pure preserved beet roots. Pure preserved scarlet runners (no soaking required). Preserved carrots. Pure preserved celery. Cabbage. Scotch kale. Chicken and ham pâté. Gravy soup. Ox tails. Kidney soup. Cloves. Calavances. Valencia raisins. Split peas. Marrow-fat peas. Flaked tapioca. Hops. Mixed pickles. Gooseberries. Parsnips. Cocoa. Apple jelly. Red plum marmalade. Tripe. Boiled mutton. Minced steak. Bacon rations. Stewed kidneys. Irish Brawn. Boiled mutton. Roasted veal. Mutton cutlets. Cod roes. Many foods, such as Huntley & Palmer's Digestive Plain Biscuits, were still in their sealed crates. Three unopened hams hung from hooks.

All these foods reminded me forcefully of Shackleton's personality, his trials, and above all his great achievement, the incredible farthest southing made with this hut as its base. It was wonderful to be alone in the hut—I had lacked the privilege the previous year—and to feel, slowly, the place changing for me from a shrine to a structure that was, temporarily and in a tiny sense, my home, which would shelter me for the night. I had a protective feeling about it. I had the key to its doorlock in my pocket. It still seemed strange to me that by the decision of Brian Porter, for this season the chief New Zealand representative in Antarctica, I was the hut's custodian.

Murphy joined me in the hut and looked around. The outside of the hut had weathered to a lovely off-white that contrasted well with the dark hills. We stood admiring it. Then, almost before we knew it, it was time to call McMurdo. We couldn't get through on the dipole but managed to rouse him with the whip antenna. We decided that the break in the dipole needed solder, not adhesive tape, and that the dipole would be useless to us until it was repaired at McMurdo.

From my journal:

"When the penguins aren't quack-squawking and the wind is down the silence is miraculous. The air is superb and very dry. You are alternately very cold or comfortable, depending on the wind and on where you are. The floors of both huts are very cold. Dave put on mukluks for this reason. I brought along black thermal boots but prefer to use my own hiking boots. We eat standing. I could carry in the brand-new collapsible plastic crapper with its aluminum legs, or drag out a small crate from under the bunks, but one is fed up with chores, one is lazy, very tired, one's back literally aches from bending, squatting, stooping, *carrying*—and one doesn't give a damn whether one sits or stands, the main thing is that one is *here*, in all this incredibly photogenic landscape."

For dinner we had dehydrated shrimp that tasted like softly compacted sawdust. After downing some of it we threw the rest out in front of the wanigan. Two skuas came and gorged themselves. Always hungry, we filled up on beef stew, canned bread, more frozen peaches and on some of the wanigan's hard candy, then sat silent in the shelter of the front of the refuge hut (the wind was still blowing behind us, from the east), resting in the warmth of the evening sun. It was wonderful to sit there like that, suddenly with nothing to do, really warm at last, gazing at the black cape's-end hills on the right, which, razorbacked against the sky, harbored skuas; at the beachlike dip between these and the rookery hills;

staring with wonder at the chain of mountains beyond the frozen Sound; and thinking of Shackleton and of the fact that this was really his cape now and forever would be; no matter that it was named for Charles Royds; and that the hut to the south was his hut; and remembering how well he had kept his journals during the trek that had discovered the Beardmore Glacier, and how vividly the journals could still bring all that experience back.

We turned in early. Undressing in the Nimrod Hut, I was momentarily shy about the windows being uncovered, then realized how sensational it would be if a stranger peeked in. The uncertain radio communications added to the sense of our autonomy. I hoped no visitors would descend upon us tomorrow to spoil our splendid isolation and our proprietary sense of the place. On an impulse I shone my flashlight beam into some of the dark upper corners, expecting to see cobwebs. Then I remembered. "No webs down here. No spiders. No insects. This is Antarctica."

I crawled into my sleeping bag, bunched my wool shirt into a pillow and zipped myself in. I fell quickly asleep. I awoke twice during the night and lay awake a bit and thought of all the chores I had to do and about the microbiologists' warnings and about whether I was breathing in the spores which might give me aspergillosis and whether Murphy and I would ever find the contact lens he had lost in front of the hut and I realized that the bright light, shifting with the unsetting sun's circular motion, had been bothering me, and I looked around for ghosts but there were none.

11

~~~~~~~~~~~~~~~~~~~~~~~~~~~~~~~

ADVENTURES OF SHACKLETON'S NIMROD

EXPEDITION

1. SHACKLETON'S FARTHEST SOUTH

By the time Shackleton was invalided home by Scott he was thoroughly under the spell of an Antarctic addiction; also, he was hopeful of winning great fame on the continent as the leader of his own expedition, financial backing for which was to prove very difficult and trying for him to obtain. In England he became involved in the fitting out of the relief ships *Morning* and *Terra Nova,* which went to the rescue of the men of the presumably permanently frozen in *Discovery;* by this means he kept his hand in Antarctic work. Once his own expedition was a reality he resolved that, unlike the Discovery Expedition, it would have no committee to control it; he would personally supervise all the arrangements himself. And it would have a distinctly non-naval tone. From the very beginning his idea was to leave a party in winter quarters without having a ship frozen in. His ship would return the following summer to pick up the men. Such a plan dispensed with the necessity of a relief ship, as had not been the case on the Discovery Expedition.

In *Shackleton and the Antarctic* his biographers, Margery and James Fisher, speak of a privately printed four-sheet pamphlet in

The materials for this chapter have been gathered to a large extent from the first volume of Shackleton's *The Heart of the Antarctic.* It may be noted that both this work and his *South* were written in collaboration with Edward Saunders, a New Zealand journalist, although only Shackleton's name appears as the author of the works.

which he outlined early plans for his expedition. They say it is un-
dated but infer from internal evidence that it was written during the
first months of 1906. They presume he had the document printed in
the hope of attracting financial support. In it he announced he
would use dogs, ponies "and a specially designed motor car" for the
hauling of sledges. "But though I propose taking a motor," he asserted, "I would not rely entirely upon this, as, with sixty dogs and
a couple of ponies, I am quite certain the South Pole could be
reached." The Fishers report he also stated it had been "an insufficient number of dogs, and consequently a great over-strain and
lack of food, that made us turn back on our Southern Journey," and
that "dogs were only taken as a sort of stand-by on the remote
chance of their being useful. If we had had sixty dogs I believe we
should have reached the South Pole."

Not long afterwards he became very critical of the value of dogs
in Antarctic exploration, for reasons the Fishers were unable to
discover, and counted on Manchurian ponies to get him to the Pole.
My guess is that his plan for a large number of dogs was an intuition only and that he mistrusted it as not being based on personal experience and fell back on the sad experience of Scott's
southern journey. Sixty dogs in themselves would not have given
him the Pole. Attaining the Pole would have depended, among
other factors, on how good they were and how well trained and
managed. It is clear from the record that Scott's Discovery Expedition was not equipped to handle so large a number of dogs, and it is
equally obvious that Shackleton's Nimrod Expedition was also un-
prepared in the matter. However, judging by Amundsen's subsequent and brilliant success, Shackleton was on the right track. His
change of mind, which probably had much to do with the national
predisposition against the use of dogs in polar work, may have cost
him the Pole. It also may have cost the lives of Scott and the latter's
four companions, who would not have gone to the Pole (and with
ponies) if Shackleton had reached it before them.

Shackleton made no effort to conceal his bias against the use of
dogs. In *The Heart of the Antarctic* he wrote, "Our experience on
the *Discovery* expedition, especially during the long southern journey
when we had so much trouble with our mixed crowd of dogs, rather
prejudiced me against these animals as a means of traction, and we
only took them as a stand-by in the event of the ponies breaking
down."

As for the value of Manchurian ponies, he wrote, "I had seen these ponies in Shanghai, and I had heard of the good work they did on the Jackson-Harmsworth expedition [in the Arctic]. They are accustomed to hauling heavy loads in a very low temperature, and they are hardy, sure-footed and plucky. I noticed that they had been used with success for very rough work during the Russo-Japanese War. . . ."

He did not state where he had heard of the good work the ponies had done on the Jackson-Harmsworth expedition but the likelihood is that he had gotten the word from his friend Albert B. Armitage, Scott's second in command on the Discovery Expedition and the navigator of the *Discovery*. In *Two Years in the Antarctic*, an account of his experiences during the latter expedition (published in 1905), Armitage wrote: "Over such a surface as that of the barrier I believe that Siberian ponies would do better than dogs, from what I have experienced with both animals in the North. [Armitage had served with the Jackson-Harmsworth expedition.] The Siberian pony can stand the severe cold, and can drag a heavier load in proportion to the amount of food he requires than the dogs. Moreover, the pony is far more palatable, in case of need, than the dog."

There are at least two shortcomings in such an opinion: Armitage had not experienced a barrier surface in the north inasmuch as no barrier surface existed there, and he had not had much firsthand experience of the Great Ice Barrier of the south.

It may be worth noting that in his autobiography, *Cadet to Commodore*, published in 1925 after Shackleton's death, Armitage spoke of his warm regard for "Shackles" and claimed that both he (Armitage) and the ship's senior surgeon (unnamed by Armitage but presumably this was Reginald Koettlitz) protested to Scott Shackleton's being invalided home after the farthest southing of 1902. Armitage further stated that both Scott and Shackleton were ill with scurvy and that the senior surgeon told Scott that Shackleton was not so ill as Scott himself. However, Armitage made neither of these claims in his earlier book. In his autobiography he suggested that Scott, in conjunction with Sir Clements Markham, was interested in making the expedition a Royal Navy show by hopefully excluding the two officers of the merchant marine, Armitage and Shackleton. Scott, Armitage wrote, asked him to return to England on the *Morning* because he, Armitage, had a wife and child; but Armitage, having been appointed to his position independently of

Scott, was able to refuse. However, such a charge made little sense in view of the fact that Scott had chosen Shackleton to share in the glory of the farthest south trek.

Shackleton had a qualified man go to Tientsin on his behalf to select fifteen ponies for him. The animals were shipped to Australia and then to New Zealand and were landed on Quail Island near Lyttelton, where they were broken. They were over twelve and under seventeen years old, were about fourteen hands high and of various colors. Shackleton ordered fifteen ponies to allow a margin for losses on the voyage to New Zealand. He took along only ten, together with nine dogs, when the *Nimrod* left New Zealand for the ice. The dogs, purchased in New Zealand, were descendants of Siberian dogs used on the Southern Cross Expedition at the turn of the century.

The Fishers believed the use of ponies was a mistake.

"Certainly," they wrote, "they could not stand the Antarctic temperatures as well as could the dogs, and consequently they delayed the start of the summer journeys. Their weight caused them to sink in any soft surface, so that their speed was far less than that of dogs would have been. They needed greater care all round and their food was heavy to transport."

Nevertheless it was the ponies that got Shackleton so very close to the Pole.

There is a fascinating link of bias and prejudice connecting Scott and Shackleton in their Antarctic work. Shackleton shared Scott's prejudice against dogs, reinforced by the experience of Scott's first southern journey, and Scott picked up Shackleton's preference for ponies, strengthened by their use on the Nimrod Expedition. All the while Amundsen, standing in the wings, benefited from both men's mistakes.

There was also a link of dissonance between the two great explorers. Shackleton quite naturally wanted to base his expedition at a southernmost point as well as at a place he was familiar with, and he desired to make use of McMurdo Sound, specifically Ross Island, for his winter quarters. But Scott, who was planning to return to the Antarctic and who entertained his own private hopes of attaining the Pole, argued that McMurdo Sound was his proper domain and that Shackleton should try elsewhere in his efforts. Shackleton made the unfortunate mistake of agreeing to Scott's request. He promised to use either the Barrier Inlet or King Edward VII Land as his winter quarters. Finding that the Barrier had calved away at the inlet, he concluded it would be foolhardy to camp there or anywhere else on the Barrier. (Amundsen camped on the Barrier off the Bay of Whales and made his way triumphantly to the Pole.) Shackleton then tried to base himself on King Edward VII Land, located at the Barrier's northeastern extremity, but was unable to reach the land because of severe ice conditions, and he had in desperation to retreat westward to Ross Island, where he selected Cape Royds as his winter quarters. The broken promise cost him the treasured friendship of Edward Wilson.

Of the hut on Cape Royds he wrote, "I thought then that [it] would have to accommodate twelve men, though the number was later increased to fifteen, and I decided that the outside measurements should be thirty-three feet by nineteen feet by eight feet to the eaves. This was not large, especially in view of the fact that we would have to store many articles of equipment and some of the food in the hut, but a small building meant economy in fuel. The hut was specially constructed to my orders by Messrs. Humphreys, of Knightsbridge, and after being erected and inspected in London was shipped in sections in the *Nimrod*.

"It was made of stout fir timbering of best quality in walls, roofs, and floors, and the parts were all morticed and tenoned to facilitate erection in the Antarctic. The walls were strengthened with iron cleats bolted to main posts and horizontal timbering, and the roof principals were provided with strong iron tie rods. The hut was lined with match-boarding, and the walls and roof were covered externally first with strong roofing felt, then with one-inch tongued and grooved boards, and finally with another covering of felt. In addition to these precautions against the extreme cold the four-inch space in framing between the match-boarding and the first covering of felt was packed with granulated cork, which assisted materially to render the walls non-conducting. The hut was to be erected on wooden piles let into the ground or ice, and rings were fixed to the apex of the roof so that guy ropes might be used to give additional resistance to the gales. The hut had two doors, connected by a small porch, so that ingress and egress would not mean the admission of a draught of cold air, and the windows were double, in order that the warmth of the hut might be retained. There were two louvres in the roof, controlled from the inside. The hut had no fittings, and we took little furniture, only some chairs. I proposed to use cases for the construction of benches, beds and other necessary articles of internal equipment. The hut was to be lit with acetylene gas, and we took a generator, the necessary piping, and a supply of carbide."

The cases he mentioned were the venesta cases, an early form of plywood. "These cases are manufactured from composite boards prepared by uniting three layers of birch or other hard wood with waterproof cement. They are light, weather-proof and strong, and proved to be eminently suited to our purposes. The cases I ordered measured about two feet six inches by fifteen inches, and we used about 2500 of them. The saving of weight, as compared with an ordinary packing-case, was about four pounds per case, and we had no trouble at all with breakages, in spite of rough handling given our stores in the process of landing at Cape Royds after the expedition had reached the Antarctic regions."

The expedition took along a complete printing press, from which issued *Aurora Australis*, the first book printed and bound in Antarctica.

In the austral spring of 1908 Shackleton began his final preparations for his attempt on the Pole. A maize depot for the ponies was established approximately one hundred and twenty geographical miles south of winter quarters. On an August sledge journey on the Barrier he concluded that the car wouldn't work efficiently on the Barrier's soft snow surface and that therefore he could not rely on it for the southern journey. By mid-September he had stored in the Discovery Hut all the supplies needed for the journey, his intention being to start from the southernmost base available.

By the time the attempt on the Pole was about to begin he had only four ponies left. Of the ten taken from New Zealand, two had died on the voyage and four had perished within a month of their arrival at Cape Royds, three of the latter dying as the result of eating large quantities of sandy soil with salt in it and the fourth probably succumbing to some sort of chemical poison in wood shavings it had consumed. The four surviving ponies were exercised regularly on the sea ice. "I felt that the little animals were going to justify the confidence I had reposed in them when I had brought them all the way from Manchuria to the bleak Antarctic." Shackleton decided that the maximum load each pony could pull was six hundred and fifty pounds.

As for the dogs: "The dogs, whose numbers had been increased by births until we had a fairly large team, were trained, but I did not see much scope for them on the southern journey. I knew from past experience that dogs would not travel when low drift was blowing in their faces, and such drift was to be expected fairly often on the Barrier surface even in the summer." Just how well trained the dogs were, say, by Amundsen's standards, is a moot point.

Shackleton selected Adams, Marshall and Wild to accompany him on the great journey. Lieutenant Jameson Boyd Adams, of the Royal Naval Reserve, was a meteorologist and the expedition's second in command. Eric Stewart Marshall was a surgeon and cartographer. Frank Wild, in charge of provisions, had been granted leave by the Royal Navy so he could join the expedition. He was destined to become one of the most experienced of Antarctic explorers. The four men would have two tents and each would have his own sleeping bag. Four eleven-foot sledges were to be taken, one for each pony. A depot party was scheduled to store sufficient food off Minna Bluff on January 15, 1909, "to provide for the return of the Southern Party from that point."

Shackleton decided on a daily ration of thirty-four ounces per man for the journey. He followed Scott in this "democratic" allotment of food, which ignored differences in human weight and therefore in the need for calories. He would take human food designed to last for ninety-one days. Its weight would be 773½ pounds. The staple items were to be pemmican and biscuits. The pemmican, made in Copenhagen, consisted of dried and powdered beef, and 60 per cent beef fat. The biscuits were made of wheat meal, with 25 per cent plasmon added. Each man's daily allowance on full rations would consist, in addition to the pemmican and biscuits, of cheese or chocolate, cocoa, plasmon, sugar, Quaker Oats, tea, salt and pepper.

The supporting party was to consist of Ernest Joyce, George Edward Marston, Raymond E. Priestley, Bertram Armytage and Sir Philip Brocklehurst, and was to accompany the southern party for ten days. Joyce had left the Royal Navy to join the expedition. Like Shackleton and Wild, he had participated in the work of the Discovery Expedition. These three were the only members of the Nimrod Expedition with previous polar experience. On the Nimrod Expedition Joyce was "in charge of general stores, dogs, sledges and zoölogical collections." Marston was the expedition's artist. Priestley was the geologist of the expedition. Armytage (not to be confused with the Armitage of the Discovery Expedition), was born in Australia and was at thirty-nine one of the oldest members of the expedition. Shackleton did not define his duties when he listed him in *The Heart of the Antarctic*. Brocklehurst, a young man of twenty or twenty-one, was an assistant geologist.

Scott had managed to march far south on the Barrier. Going much farther with the use of ponies and a more direct route, Shackleton discovered a great range of mountains and a route over the mountains onto the Antarctic plateau. Then he marched southward on the plateau to within a hundred geographical miles of the Pole. The following is his party's route in summary. They left Cape Royds for Hut Point; made their last preparations in the Discovery Hut; swung around the northeast side of White Island; headed almost due south past Minna Bluff and out onto the Barrier, not hugging the land as Scott had done; encountered what are now known as the Transantarctic Mountains; headed up the Beardmore Glacier and reached the plateau; and marched due south as far as latitude 88°23′ longitude 162° East before turning back. Their homeward march was almost exactly the reverse of their outward one.

In Shackleton's words, his party "ascertained that a great chain of mountains extends from the 82nd parallel, south of McMurdo Sound, to the 86th parallel, trending in a south-easterly direction; that other great mountain ranges continue to the south and south-west, and that between them flows one of the largest glaciers in the world [the Beardmore], leading to an inland plateau, the height of which, at latitude 88° South, is over 11,000 ft. above sea-level."

At the conclusion of the first volume of *The Heart of the Antarctic* Shackleton noted, "Subsequent calculations have shown that the distances given in my diary of the Southern Journey were not always quite accurate. The calculations were made under circumstances of special difficulty, and were not checked until after my return to civilisation. The reader will notice that some of the distances are given in statute miles and others in geographical miles. After the last meridian altitude was taken at the plateau depot and until the return to the same depot the distances were noted in geographical miles. I have thought it best to let the diary figures stand. . . ." I too have let them stand.

Shackleton began his southern journey the morning of October 29, 1908. This was a moment he had longed for since being invalided home by Scott. The supporting party left Cape Royds the same morning. At 1 P.M., during a halt to feed the ponies, Grisi, one of the animals, lashed out and struck Adams just below the knee, fortunately not inflicting a serious injury. Adams's leg was stiff and sore that night, which was spent in the vicinity of Erebus Glacier Tongue. Next day both parties reached Hut Point. Shackleton's party slept in the hut. The supporting party spent the night "at the very spot where the *Discovery* wintered six years ago." On the thirty-first the southern party returned to the Tongue to pick up the remainder of the pony fodder that had been depoted there. Finding neither a message from the Nimrod Hut nor the gear he had asked to be sent to him at the Tongue, Shackleton correctly suspected that a light storm was blowing at Cape Royds. After dinner he hiked to the cape, arriving at about 11:30 P.M. In the morning he rode in the car south as far as Tent Island, from which, with the other members of his party, he proceeded again to Hut Point. "We arranged the packing of the sledges in the afternoon, but we are held up because of Socks [a pony]. His foot is seriously out of order. It is almost a disaster, for we want every pound of hauling power."

November 2. "When we awoke we found that Quan had bitten through his tether and played havoc with the maize and other fodder. Directly he saw me coming down the ice foot, he started off, dashing from one sledge to another, tearing the bags to pieces and trampling the food out. It was ten minutes before we caught him. Luckily, one sledge of fodder was untouched. He pranced around, kicked up his heels, and showed that it was a deliberate piece of destructiveness on his part, for he had eaten his fill. His distended appearance was obviously the result of many pounds of maize." Socks seemed better, and Adams's leg had improved a good deal.

November 3–5. Heading south from Hut Point at 9:30 A.M., the southern party had not gone far on the sea ice before they encountered a surface that was "terribly soft," in which the ponies sometimes sank up to their bellies "and always over their hocks." The Barrier surface was even softer. The ponies' little hoofs often broke through the thin ice crust beneath the snow. Inasmuch as the supporting party were not marching as fast as his own, Shackleton decided to keep them with him for only two more days. The parties moved southeastward all day, avoiding the crevasses to the north of White Island. The weather on the fourth was fine. The fifth was overcast, with bad visibility. First sastrugi and then crevasses troubled the parties. Camp was pitched at 3 P.M., an hour before a strong wind blew up, bringing drifting snow.

November 6–7. The sixth was spent in the sleeping bags. "It is very trying to be held up like this, for each day means the consumption of 40 lb. of pony feed alone. We only had a couple of biscuits each for lunch, for I can see that we must retrench at every set-back if we are going to have enough food to carry us through. We started with ninety-one days' food, but with careful management we can make it spin out to 110 days. If we have not done the job in that time it is God's will." The temperature was 18° F. Shackleton read *Much Ado About Nothing.* "This is our fourth day out from Hut Point, and we are only twenty miles south. We must do better than this if we are to make much use of the ponies. I would not mind the blizzard so much if we had only to consider ourselves, for we can save on the food, whereas the ponies must be fed full."

The seventh was another bad day. The supporting party turned back in the morning. White Island and Observation Hill could be seen in the north. To the south there "lay a dead white wall." The southern party wore goggles with green and red glasses, a combination that lent a yellow tint to the scenes, but the glasses often fogged up from perspiration due to exertion, and it was necessary to remove and wipe them frequently. Consequently the men were beginning to suffer from snow blindness. Getting caught in a maze of crevasses, they had to stop. Camp was made between two crevasses. "Thus ended our day's march of under a mile, for about 1 P.M. it commenced to snow, and the wind sprang up from the south-west with drift." Shackleton and Adams were sharing one tent, Marshall and Wild the other. The plan was to take turns as tent mates. As reading material Shackleton had Shakespeare's comedies, Marshall had Borrow's *The Bible in Spain,* Adams had Arthur Young's *Travels in France,* and Wild had *Sketches by Boz.*

November 8–9. The eighth was yet another bad day, spent in the sleeping bags. The noon temperature was 8° F. "It is a sore trial to one's hopes and patience to lie and watch the drift on the tent-side, and to know that our valuable pony food is going, and this without benefiting the animals themselves. Indeed, Socks and Grisi have not been eating well, and the hard maize does not agree with them. . . . This standing for four days in drift with 24° of frost is not good for them, and we are anxiously looking for finer weather." The ninth was a clear, calm day. The light showed many crevasses.

"A lump of snow thrown down one would make no noise, so the bottom must have been very far below. . . . At 8.30 A.M. we got under way, the ponies not pulling very well, for they have lost condition in the blizzard and were stiff. We got over the first few crevasses without difficulty, then all of a sudden Chinaman went down a crack which ran parallel to our course. Adams tried to pull him out and he struggled gamely, and when Wild and I, who were next, left our sledges and hauled along Chinaman's sledge, it gave him more scope, and he managed to get on to the firm ice, only just in time, for three feet more and it would have been all up with the southern journey. The three-foot crack opened out into a great fathomless chasm, and down that would have gone the horse, all our cooking gear and biscuits and half the oil, and probably Adams as well. But when things seem the worst they turn to the best, for that was the last crevasse we encountered, and with a gradually improving surface, though very soft at times, we made fair headway."

Camp was made at 6 P.M. "Quan is now engaged in the pleasing occupation of gnawing his tether rope. I tethered him by the hind leg to prevent him attacking this particular thong, but he has found out that by lifting his hind leg he can reach the rope, so I must get out and put a nose-bag on him."

November 10–14. On the tenth Quan ate the straps on his rug. Grisi and Socks fought over the rug. Quan chewed Chinaman's tether. Chinaman gnawed away at the ropes of one of the sledges. In the afternoon the surface grew "appallingly soft" and the ponies sank up to their hocks. On the eleventh the familiar land behind the party was still visible. On the twelfth and thirteenth Shackleton was badly troubled by snow blindness.

"Snow-blindness is a particularly unpleasant thing. One begins by seeing double, then the eyes feel full of grit; this makes them water and eventually one cannot see at all. All yesterday afternoon, though I was wearing goggles, the water kept running out of my eyes, and, owing to the low temperature, it froze on my beard. However, the weather is beautiful, and we are as happy as can be, with good appetites, too good in fact for the amount of food we are allowing ourselves. We are on short rations, but we will have horse meat in addition when the ponies go under."

The fourteenth was another clear day. The men were suffering from burst lips. Shackleton noted that the Barrier, with its sastrugi and soft snow, was "as wayward and as changeful as the sea."

November 15. The party reached Depot A, which Wild, using binoculars, had spotted the day before. There was much work to do at the depot. After a noon lunch they headed due south. Unlike Scott, Shackleton was not hugging the western land but going directly over the ice shelf toward the Pole. As a precaution against losing his way on the homeward stretch he constructed at intervals snow mounds six or seven feet high. He was uncertain as to whether the mounds would survive the effects of sun and wind but believed the effort worthwhile. Two shovels had been brought for the purpose. As it turned out, the sledge tracks disappeared; the mounds remained and were a great comfort to the party.

November 16–18. The weather on the sixteenth was excellent and the ponies were pulling well. "All the western mountains stood up, miraged in the forms of castles. Even the Bluff [Minna Bluff] could be seen in the far distance, changed into the semblance of a giant keep." The party covered seventeen miles this day, a record for them so far. "It has been a wonderful and successful week, so different to this time six years ago, when I was toiling five miles a day over the same ground." The men were economizing on sugar. "The great thing is to advance our food-supply as far south as possible before the ponies give out." Everyone was in good condition. There were only minor troubles, such as split lips, which restrained laughter. Quan was still troublesome. Within the past week he had consumed part of a horsecloth, about a fathom of rope, several pieces of leather, and other odds and ends. On the seventeenth the weather was a dead white wall again.

The next day the surface was "simply awful." "We seem to have arrived at a latitude where there is no wind and the snow remains where it falls, for we were sinking in well over our ankles, and the poor ponies are having a most trying time. They break through the crust on the surface and flounder up to their hocks, and at each step they have to pull their feet out through the brittle crust. It is telling more on Chinaman than on the others, and he is going slowly. The chafing of the snow crust on his fetlocks has galled them, so we will have to shoot him at the next depôt in about three days' time. . . . It is possible that we have reached the windless area around the Pole, for the Barrier is a dead, smooth, white plain,

12. *Crevasses on a slope of Mount Erebus*

13. *Vostok Station*

14. *Shackleton's hut on Cape Royds, with the wanigan in the background*

15. *The warm color is due to the guano of the Adélie penguin rookery, Cape Royds.*

16.   Shackleton's hut

17.   The author in the hut

18.   *Cape Royds in November*

19.   *Adélie penguins, Cape Royds*

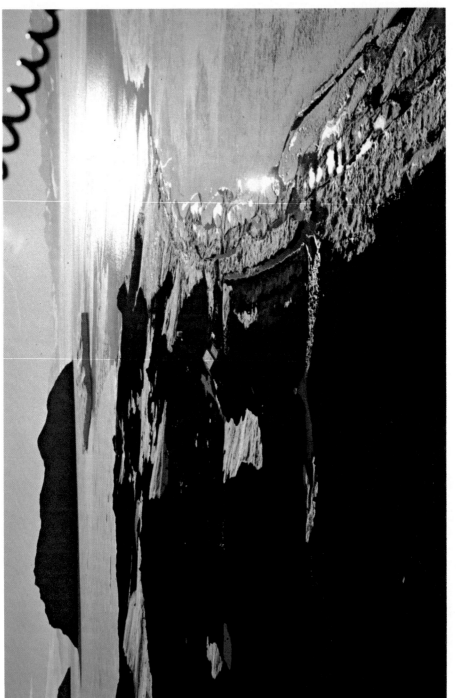

20. *Cape Evans and Inaccessible Island*

21. *Pack ice and the snout of the Barne Glacier*

22. *Scott's hut and Mount Erebus*

weird beyond description, and having no land in sight, we feel such tiny specks in the immensity around us."

November 19–21. Shackleton was making much better time than Scott had made on the latter's southern journey. This was due to his use of ponies and to the fact that he was heading directly south. On the nineteenth he was at 80°32', a latitude Scott had not reached until December 16, although Scott had left Hut Point on November 2, a day earlier than Shackleton had.

On the twentieth Shackleton wrote, "It is as though we were truly at the world's end, and were bursting in on the birthplace of the clouds and the nesting home of the four winds, and one has a feeling that we mortals are being watched with a jealous eye by the forces of nature. To add to these weird impressions that seem to grow on one in the apparently limitless waste, the sun to-night was surrounded by mock suns and in the zenith was a bow, turning away from the great vertical circle around the sun. These circles and bows were the colour of the rainbow. . . . The ponies are all fit except poor old Chinaman, and he must go to-morrow. He cannot keep up with the others, and the bad surface has played him out."

Chinaman was shot the next evening. A depot was made of about eighty pounds of pony meat, a can of biscuits weighing twenty-seven pounds, some sugar and a can of oil. When a pony was shot its throat was immediately cut so that its blood would run out. Then Marshall and Wild would skin the animal and remove meat from legs, shoulders and back. The men would cut the meat into small pieces as rapidly as possible, before it quickly froze solid. In time they discovered that the meat was fairly tender if it was only warmed; if it was boiled it became very tough. Only stewing, which required quantities of oil that couldn't be spared, would thoroughly soften it.

November 22–26. Depot B was marked with a sledge stuck upright in the snow, to which was lashed a bamboo pole flying a black flag. The three ponies were now hauling five hundred pounds each. Shackleton thought they were doing "splendidly." He began to see land he hadn't seen on Scott's southern journey because the latter journey had proceeded close to the western foothills. Adams had a bad tooth that was keeping him from sleeping. When his companion tried to pull it out it broke. Next day Marshall succeeded in extracting it. On the twenty-fourth a blizzard came up but blew itself out during the night. On the twenty-sixth Shackleton wrote,

"A day to remember, for we have passed the 'furthest South' previously reached by man. To-night we are in latitude 82°18½' South, longitude 168° East, and this latitude we have been able to reach in much less time than on the last long march with Captain Scott, when we made latitude 82°16½' our 'furthest South.' . . . To the south-south-east ever appear new mountains. I trust that no land will block our path. . . . One wonders what the next month will bring forth. We ought by that time to be near our goal, all being well."

November 27–30. The following day Shackleton grew anxious because he saw more new mountains arise, which trended increasingly to the east, meaning that he would have to alter his course from due south. But he was hopeful of finding some strait which would allow him to pass through them. The party were regularly eating pony meat. Shackleton was confident the meat would ward off scurvy. (No attacks of scurvy marred this farthest southing.) Grisi appeared unfit and snow-blind. He was shot on the night of the twenty-eighth. Depot C was made, containing one week's provisions and oil, together with pony meat; enough, it was hoped, to last the men to Depot B on their return march. On the twenty-ninth Shackleton wrote, "During the day still more great mountains appeared to the south-east, and to the west we opened up several huge peaks, 10,000 to 15,000 ft. in height. The whole country seems to be made up of range after range of mountains, one behind the other. The worst feature of to-day's march was the terribly soft snow in the hollows of the great undulations we were passing. During the afternoon one place was so bad that the ponies sank in right up to their bellies, and we had to pull with might and main to get the sledges along at all." Both Quan and Socks were snow-blind on the thirtieth, and Quan seemed to be very shaky. The men improvised shades for the ponies' eyes and took turns helping Quan haul his sledge.

December 1. Quan was shot next day. The party were in latitude 83°16'. "Ahead of us we can see the land stretching away to the east, with a long white line in front of it that looks like a giant Barrier, and nearer a very crusted-up appearance, as though there were great pressure ridges in front of us. It seems as though the Barrier end had come, and that there is now going to be a change in some gigantic way in keeping with the vastness of the whole place. We fervently trust that we will not be delayed in our march south. We are living mainly on horse-meat now, and on the march, to cool our throats when pulling in the hot sun, we chew some raw frozen meat. . . . The surface of the Barrier still sparkles with the million frozen crystals which stand apart from the ordinary surface snow. One or two new peaks came in sight to-day, so we are ever adding to the chain of wonderful mountains that we have found. At one moment our thoughts are on the grandeur of the scene, the next on what we would have to eat if only we were let loose in a good restaurant. We are very hungry these days, and we know that we are likely to be for another three months."

December 2–3. The four men now hauled one sledge. Socks followed them with the other. On the second Shackleton noted that Socks was lonely. "He whinnied all night for his lost companion." The party were approaching great pressure ridges that were heavily crevassed. They hoped to ascend tomorrow a red hill about 3,000 feet high in order to view the surrounding country and find a way up a glacier through the mountains. On the third, leaving camp immediately after breakfast, the men roped up and went in single file, each carrying an ice ax. Reaching the little mountain, they ascended it to a high ridge.

"From the top of this ridge there burst upon our view an open road to the South, for there stretched before us a great glacier running almost south and north between two huge mountain ranges. As far as we could see, except towards the mouth, the glacier appeared to be smooth, yet this was not a certainty, for the distance was so great. Eagerly we clambered up the remaining ridges and over a snow-slope, and found ourselves at the top of the mountain, the height being 3350 ft. according to aneroid and hypsometer. From the summit we could see the glacier stretching away south inland till at last it seemed to merge in high inland ice. Where the glacier fell into the Barrier about north-east bearing, the pressure waves were enormous, and for miles the surface of the Barrier was broken up. This was what we had seen ahead of us the last few days, and we now understood the reason of the commotion on the Barrier surface. To the south-east we could see the lofty range of mountains we had been following still stretching away in the same direction, and we can safely say that the Barrier is bounded by a chain of mountains extending in a south-easterly direction as far as the 86th parallel South."

Shackleton subsequently named the glacier the Beardmore after

William Beardmore, a former employer of his and a major sponsor of the expedition. The men returned to camp at 7 p.m.

December 4–5. Next morning the party proceeded toward the glacier. Socks was not feeling well. In the evening he was offered thaw water but refused it in favor of snow. On the fifth, camp was broken as usual at 8 a.m. The men came upon "massed-up, fantastically shaped and split masses of pressure" and then upon crevassed blue ice. They lunched near thaw water under granite columns more than 2,000 feet high. Here Shackleton, still troubled by snow blindness, was left behind with Wild while Adams and Marshall went ahead to spy out the afternoon route. On their return they reported a remarkable sight: "a bird, brown in colour, with a white line under each wing, flew just over their heads and disappeared to the south." They were certain it wasn't a skua. The afternoon march was over treacherous blue ice. In some places the crevasses were snowbridged, in others they were naked, razor-edged. Camp was made at 6 p.m. on a little patch of snow among crevasses, "and even that bridges some crevasses." The tent was under a huge granite pillar.

"Providence will look after us to-night, for we can do nothing more. One feels that at any moment some great piece of rock may come hurtling down, for all round us are pieces of granite, ranging from the size of a hazel-nut to great boulders twenty to forty tons in weight, and on one snow slope is the fresh track of a fallen rock. Still we can do no better, for it is impossible to spread a tent on the blue ice, and we cannot get any further to-night. I guess we will sleep soundly enough. My eyes are my only trouble, for their condition makes it impossible for me to pick out the route or do much more than pull."

December 6–7. It was heavy going next day as the men slowly ascended the huge glacier. "There is a wonderful view of the mountains, with new peaks and ranges to the south-east, south and southwest." The weather was fine. The temperature in the evening was 17° F. During the seventh Socks kept sinking up to his belly in deep snow. Wild, leading the pony, was following Shackleton and Adams over a snowbridged crevasse they had just crossed. Suddenly the pony, breaking through, disappeared. "Wild had a miraculous escape. . . . [He] says he just felt a sort of rushing wind, the leading rope was snatched from his hand, and he put out his arms and just caught the further edge of the chasm. Fortunately for Wild and us,

Socks' weight snapped the swingle-tree of the sledge, so it [the sledge] was saved, though the upper bearer is broken. We lay down on our stomachs and looked over into the gulf, but no sound or sign came to us; a black bottomless pit it seemed to be." Although its forward end was down the crevasse the sledge was safe.

"When I think over the events of the day I realise what the loss of the sledge would have meant to us. We would have had left only two sleeping-bags for the four of us, and I doubt whether we could have got back to winter-quarters with the short equipment. Our chance of reaching the Pole would have been gone. We take on the maize to eat [it] ourselves. There is one ray of light in this bad day, and that is that anyhow we could not have taken Socks on much further. We would have had to shoot him to-night, so that although his loss is a serious matter to us, for we had counted on the meat, still we know that for traction purposes he would have been of little further use. When we tried to camp to-night we stuck our ice-axes into the snow to see whether there were any more hidden crevasses, and everywhere the axes went through. It would have been folly to have pitched our camp in that place, as we might easily have dropped through during the night. We had to retreat a quarter of a mile to pitch the tent. It was very unpleasant to turn back, even for this short distance, but on this job one must expect reverses."

December 8–15. Shackleton's eyes recovered by the next day. The men struggled up the glacier, dodging crevasses and pits. The fine weather continued on the ninth. Occasionally the party had to relay their gear. Marshall fell into a crevasse but was saved by his harness. Then Adams fell through and then Shackleton. The sledges were showing the effects of work on "the sheer, knife-like edges of some of the crevasses." The men thought and talked mainly of food now. They camped at 3,000 feet. The tenth was a day of "falls, bruises, cut shins, crevasses, razor-edged ice." By the eleventh the party were 340 geographical miles from the Pole. Next day was one of relay work, for the men could handle only one sledge at a time. While two men pulled a sledge the two others steadied it. They made only three miles this day. On the thirteenth Shackleton bruised his knee in a fall. By evening the knee was better. A serious injury to one of them would probably have meant death for all. Camp was at 4,370 feet. The evening temperature was 19° F. The day's march was five miles, not including four miles of relay work.

The following day was very hard, with a high temperature that made everything wet.

On the fifteenth Shackleton wrote, "We have been going steadily uphill all the afternoon, but on a vastly improved surface, consisting of hard névé instead of blue ice and no cracks only covered-in crevasses, which are easily seen. Ahead of us really lies the plateau. We can also see ahead of us detached mountains, piercing through the inland ice, which is the road to the south for us. Huge mountains stretch out to the east and west. After last week's toil and anxiety the change is delightful. The distance covered to-day was 13 miles 200 yards."

December 16. The party camped for a noon lunch at 84°50'. (Whenever Shackleton noted his latitude in his diary he always added the word "South," as if to reinforce for himself the notion that he was really moving south, or as if he loved the look and sound of the word.) At the evening camp they were at an elevation of 6,000 feet.

"One more crevassed slope, and we will be on the plateau, please God. We are all fit and well. . . . There are splendid ranges of mountains to the west-south-west, and we have an extended view of glacier and mountains. Ahead of us lie three sharp peaks, connected up and forming an island in what is apparently inland ice or the head of the glacier. The peaks lie due south of us. To the eastward and westward of this island the ice bears down upon the inland ice-sheet, and joins the head of the glacier proper. To the westward the mountains along the side of the glacier are all of the bluff type, and the lines of stratification can be seen plainly. Still further to the westward, behind the frontal ranges, lie sharper peaks, some of them almost perfect cones. . . . We are travelling up the west side of the glacier. . . . These mountains are not beautiful in the ordinary acceptance of the term, but they are magnificent in their stern and rugged grandeur. No foot has ever trod on their mighty sides, and until we reached this frozen land no human eyes had seen their forms."

December 17–19. On the seventeenth there was more hard marching on the glacier. Sometimes it was necessary to cut steps on the icy slopes and to drag sledges up by alpine rope. In the afternoon the men depoted "everything except the barest necessities," even warm clothing. After dinner Wild climbed some land and returned with the report that the plateau at last was in sight. He had found rocks that turned out to be poor-grade coal. The altitude at the evening camp was, according to the hypsometer, 6,100 feet. On the eighteenth Shackleton wrote, "We have been saving food to make it spin out, and that increases our hunger; each night we all dream of foods. We save two biscuits per man per day, also pemmican and sugar, eking out our food with pony maize, which we soak in water to make it less hard. All this means that we have now five weeks' food, while we are about 300 geographical miles from the Pole, with the same distance back to the last depôt we left yesterday, so we must march on short food to reach our goal. The temperature is plus 16° Fahr. to-night, but a cold wind all the morning cut our faces and broken lips."

Each man was hauling about two hundred pounds. At noon of the nineteenth their latitude was 85°5'. "We seem unable to get rid of the crevasses, and we have been falling into them and steering through them all day in the face of a cold southerly wind, with a temperature varying from plus 15° to plus 9° Fahr. The work was very heavy, for we were going uphill all day, and our sledge runners, which have been suffering from the sharp ice and rough travelling, are in a bad way. . . . This glacier must be one of the largest if not the largest in the world. The sastrugi seem to point mainly to the South, so we may expect head winds all the way to the Pole." The weather continued to be excellent. The evening camp was at 7,888 feet.

December 20. "Not yet up, but nearly so. We got away from camp at 7 A.M., with a strong head wind from the south, and this wind continued all day, with a temperature ranging from plus 7° to plus 5°. Our beards coated with ice. It was an uphill pull all day around pressure ice, and we reached an altitude of over 8000 ft. above sea-level. The weather was clear, but there were various clouds, which were noted by Adams. Marshall took bearings and angles at noon, and we got the sun's meridian altitude, showing that we were in latitude 85°17' South. We hope all the time that each ridge we come to will be the last, but each time another rises ahead, split up by pressure, and we begin the same toil again. It is trying work and as we have now reduced our food at breakfast to one pannikin of hoosh and one biscuit, by the time the lunch hour has arrived, after five hours' hauling in the cold wind up the slope, we are very hungry. At lunch we have a little chocolate, tea with plasmon, a pannikin of cocoa and three biscuits. To-day we did 11 miles 950 yards (statute) having to relay the sledges over the last bit, for the ridge we were on was so steep that we could not get the two sledges up together."

December 21–24. The twenty-first: more climbing. "It is a wonderful sight to look down over the glacier from the great altitude we are at, and to see the mountains stretching away east and west, some of them over 15,000 ft. in height. We are very hungry now, and it seems as cold almost as the spring sledging. Our beards are masses of ice all day long. Thank God we are fit and well and have had no accident, which is a mercy, seeing that we have covered over 130 miles of crevassed ice." They made only six miles this day, reaching an altitude of over 8,000 feet. The twenty-second was a day of relaying the sledges over crevasses and pressure hummocks. Only the fact that the men were roped together kept them from disappearing forever into crevasses. "Wild describes the sensation of walking over this surface, half ice and half snow, as like walking over the glass roof of a station. The usual query when one of us falls into a crevasse is: 'Have you found it?' One gets somewhat callous as regards the immediate danger, though we are always glad to meet crevasses with their coats off, that is, not hidden by the snow covering. . . . Please God, ahead of us there is a clear road to the Pole."

On the twenty-third Shackleton wrote, "To-day's crevasses have been far more dangerous than any others we have crossed, as the soft snow hides all trace of them until we fall through. Constantly to-day one or another of the party has had to be hauled out from a chasm by means of his harness, which had alone saved him from death in the icy vaults below." On the twenty-fourth the surface began to improve to such a degree that the party abandoned one of their two sledges after lunch. At night they were at 9,095 feet.

Christmas Day, 1908. More climbing, now over soft snow. "We had a splendid dinner. First came hoosh, consisting of pony ration boiled up with pemmican and some of our emergency Oxo and biscuit. Then in the cocoa I boiled our little plum pudding, which a friend of Wild's had given him. This, with a drop of medical brandy, was a luxury which Lucullus himself might have envied; then came cocoa, and lastly cigars and a spoonful of *crème de menthe* sent us by a friend in Scotland. We are full to-night, and this is the last time we will be for many a long day. After dinner we discussed the situation, and we have decided to still further reduce our food. We have now nearly 500 miles, geographical, to do if we are to get to the Pole and back to the spot where we are at the present moment. We have one month's food, but only three weeks' biscuit, so we are going to make each week's food last ten days. We will have one biscuit in the morning, three at mid-day, and two at night. It is the only thing to do. To-morrow we will throw away everything except the most absolute necessities. Already we are, as regards clothes, down to the limit, but we must trust to the old sledge-runners and dump the spare ones. One must risk this. We are very far away from all the world, and home thoughts have been much with us to-day, thoughts interrupted by the pitching forward into a hidden crevasse more than once. Ah, well, we shall see all our own people when the work here is done. Marshall took our temperatures tonight. We are all two degrees subnormal, but as fit as can be. It is a fine open-air life and we are getting south."

December 26. "We lost sight of land to-day, having left it all behind us, and now we have the waste of snow all around. Two more days and our maize will be finished. Then our hooshes will be more woefully thin than ever. This shortness of food is unpleasant, but if we allow ourselves what, under ordinary circumstances, would be a reasonable amount, we would have to abandon all idea of getting far south."

December 27–31. On the twenty-seventh they reached 86°19′. On the twenty-eighth they were at an elevation of 10,199 feet. "The last sixty miles we hope to rush, leaving everything possible, taking one tent only and using the poles of the other as marks every ten miles, for we will leave all our food sixty miles off the Pole except enough to carry us there and back." On the evening of the twenty-ninth their elevation was 10,310 feet. Shackleton had a bad headache, his companions had nosebleed. Everyone's temperature was 94°. "We are only 198 miles off our goal now. If the rise would stop the cold would not matter, but it is hard to know what is man's limit. We have only 150 lb. per man to pull, but it is more severe work than the 250 lb. per man up the glacier was. The Pole is hard to get."

On the thirtieth the party made only four miles before being held up by a blizzard. "Our precious food is going, and the time also, and it is so important to us to get on. We lie here and think of how to make things better, but we cannot reduce food now, and the only thing will be to rush all possible at the end. We will do, and are doing all humanly possible. It is with Providence to help us."

At the year's end their latitude was 86°54′. The altitude was 10,477 feet. The temperature was −7° F. "We can only do our best. . . . Please God the weather will be fine the next fourteen days. Then all will be well. The distance to-day was 11 miles."

January 1–2, 1909. On the second day of the new year, at an altitude of 11,034 feet, Shackleton wrote, "A cold wind, with a temperature of minus 14° Fahr., goes right through us now, as we are weakening from want of food, and the high altitude makes every movement an effort, especially if we stumble on the march. My head is giving me trouble all the time. Wild seems the most fit of us. God knows we are doing all we can, but the outlook is serious if this surface continues and the plateau gets higher, for we are not travelling fast enough to make our food spin out and get back to our depôt in time. I cannot think of failure yet. I must look at the matter sensibly and consider the lives of those who are with me. I feel that if we go on too far it will be impossible to get back over this surface, and then all the results will be lost to the world. We can now definitely locate the South Pole on the highest plateau in the world, and our geological work and meteorology will be of the greatest use to science; but all this is not the Pole. Man can only do his best, and we have arrayed against us the strongest forces of nature. This cutting south wind with drift plays the mischief with us, and after ten hours of struggling against it one pannikin of food with two biscuits and a cup of cocoa does not warm one up much. I must think over the situation carefully to-morrow, for time is going on and food is going also."

January 3–4. On the fourth he wrote, "The end is in sight. We can only go for three more days at the most, for we are weakening rapidly. Short food and a blizzard wind from the south, with driving drift, at a temperature of 47° of frost [−15° F.], have plainly told us to-day that we are reaching our limit, for we were so done up at noon with cold that the clinical thermometer failed to register the temperature of three of us at 94 degrees. We started at 7.40 A.M. leaving a depôt on this great wide plateau, a risk that only this case justified, and one that my comrades agreed to, as they have to every one so far, with the same cheerfulness and regardlessness of self that have been the means of our getting as far as we have done so far. Pathetically small looked the bamboo, one of the tent poles, with a bit of bag sewn on as a flag, to mark our provisions, which has to take us back to our depôt, 150 miles north. We lost sight of it in half an hour, and are now trusting to our footprints in the snow to guide us back to each bamboo until we pick up the depôt again. I trust that the weather will keep clear. To-day we have done 12½ geographical miles, and with only 70 lb. per man to pull it is as hard, even harder, work than the 100 odd lb. was yesterday, and far harder than the 250 lb. were three weeks ago, when we were climbing the glacier. This, I consider, is a clear indication of our failing strength. The main thing against us is the altitude of 11,200 ft. and the biting wind. Our faces are cut, and our feet and hands are always on the verge of frost-bite. Our fingers, indeed, often go, but we get them round more or less. I have great trouble with two fingers on my left hand. They had been badly jammed when we were getting the motor up over the ice face at winter quarters, and the circulation is not good. Our boots now are pretty well worn out, and we have to halt at times to pick the snow out of the soles. Our stock of sennegrass is nearly exhausted, so we have to use the same frozen stuff day after day. Another trouble is that the lamp-wick with which we tie the finnesko is chafed through, and we have to tie knots in it. These knots catch the snow under our feet, making a lump that has to be cleared every now and then. I am of the opinion that to sledge even in the height of summer on this plateau we should have at least forty ounces of food a day per man, and we are on short rations of the ordinary allowance of thirty-two ounces. We depôted our extra underclothing to save weight about three weeks ago, and are now in the same clothes night and day. One suit of underclothing, shirt and guernsey, and our thin Burberries, now all patched. When we get up in the morning, out of the wet bag, our Burberries become like a coat of mail at once, and our heads and beards get iced-up with the moisture when breathing on the march. There is half a gale blowing dead in our teeth all the time. We hope to reach within 100 geographical miles of the Pole; under the circumstances we can expect to do very little more. I am confident that the Pole lies on the great plateau we have discovered, miles and miles from any outstanding land. The temperature to-night is minus 24° Fahr."

January 5. "Hunger grips us hard, and the food-supply is very small. My head still gives me great trouble. I began by wishing that my worst enemy had it instead of myself, but now I don't wish even my worst enemy to have such a headache; still, it is no use talking about it. Self is a subject that most of us are fluent on. We find the utmost difficulty in carrying through the day, and we can only go for two or three more days. Never once has the temperature been above zero since we got on to the plateau, though this is the height of summer. We have done our best, and we thank God for having allowed us to get so far." Shackleton increased the daily food allowance, realizing that unless he did so the party would be unable to accomplish much more.

January 6. "This must be our last outward march with the sledge and camp equipment. To-morrow we must leave camp with some food, and push as far south as possible, and then plant the flag. To-day's story is 57° of frost [−25° F.], with a strong blizzard and high drift; yet we marched 13¼ geographical miles through soft snow, being helped by extra food. This does not mean full rations, but a bigger ration than we have been having lately. The pony maize is all finished. The most trying day we have yet spent, our fingers and faces being frost-bitten continually. To-morrow we will rush south with the flag. We are at 88°7′ South to-night. It is our last outward march. Blowing hard to-night. I would fail to explain my feelings if I tried to write them down, now that the end has come. There is only one thing that lightens the disappointment, and that is the feeling that we have done all we could. It is the forces of nature that have prevented us from going right through. I cannot write more."

January 7. "A blinding, shrieking blizzard all day, with the temperature ranging from 60° to 70° of frost. It has been impossible to leave the tent, which is snowed up on the lee side. We have been lying in our bags all day, only warm at food time, with fine snow making through the walls of the worn tent and covering our bags. We are greatly cramped. Adams is suffering from cramp every now and then. We are eating our valuable food without marching. The wind has been blowing eighty to ninety miles an hour. We can hardly sleep. To-morrow I trust this will be over. Directly the wind drops we march as far south as possible, then plant the flag, and turn homeward. Our chief anxiety is lest our tracks may drift up, for to them we must trust mainly to find our depôt; we have no land bearings in this great plain of snow. It is a serious risk that we have taken, but we had to play the game to the utmost, and Providence will look after us."

January 8. Another day spent in the sleeping bags, with attacks of frostbite. Temperature: −40° F. "The wind has been blowing hard all day; some of the gusts must be over seventy or eighty miles an hour. This evening it seems as though it were going to ease down, and directly it does we shall be up and away south for a rush. I feel that this march must be our limit. We are so short of food, and at this high altitude, 11,600 ft., it is hard to keep any warmth in our bodies between the scanty meals. We have nothing to read now, having depôted our little books to save weight, and it is dreary work lying in the tent with nothing to read, and too cold to write much in the diary."

January 9. "Our last day outwards. We have shot our bolt, and the tale is latitude 88°23′ South, longitude 162° East. . . . It was strange for us to go along without the nightmare of a sledge dragging behind us. . . . Homeward bound at last. Whatever regrets may be, we have done our best."

January 10–20. During the next three days the party made good marches although they encountered "enormous sastrugi." The night of the twelfth Shackleton could not sleep, for both his frostbitten heels had cracked open and there were cracks under some of his toes. Still, the men were moving very rapidly. "We must continue to do so, for we have only about 20 lb. of biscuit to last us over 140 miles, and I expect there will be little in the locker by the time we strike our glacier head depôt. The surface has been very severe to-day." On the fourteenth a strong tail wind (they were using a sail) gave them the best day's march of the journey to date: twenty miles and sixteen hundred yards in ten hours. The following day they made another long march. On the sixteenth they sighted land for the first time in three weeks. "My burst heels gave me great pain all day. Marshall dressed them to-night." They continued to make long marches down the glacier. Wearing finneskoes, they often fell on the blue ice.

January 21–25. On the twenty-first Shackleton wrote, "The heavy falls I had yesterday have so shaken me that I have been very ill to-day. I harnessed up for a while, but soon had to give up pulling and walk by the sledge; but, as the course has been downhill nearly all day and a fair wind has been assisting, the others have had no difficulty in getting along at a good pace, and we have covered 17 miles." The temperature was rising. On the twenty-third it was 8° F. The twenty-fourth was the longest day's work and one of the hardest of the journey so far. It began at 6:45 A.M. and ended at 9 P.M. For supper the party ate a single pot of hoosh and one biscuit per man. They had two days' food left and had to march forty miles over crevassed ice in order to reach the next depot. "I am all right again, though rather weak. We had a terribly hard time in the crevassed ice this morning, and now our sledge has not much more than half a runner on one side, and is in a very shaky state. However, I believe we are safe now." The following day they marched twenty-six miles. The weather was fine. The evening temperature was 12° F. "The food is all finished but one meal. No biscuit, only cocoa, tea, salt and pepper left, very little of these also. Must reach depôt to-morrow."

January 26–27. "Two days written up as one, and they have been the hardest and most trying we have ever spent in our lives, and will ever stand in our memories. To-night (the 27th) we have had our first solid food since the morning of the 26th. We came to the end of all our provisions except a little cocoa and tea, and from 7 A.M. on the 26th till 2 P.M. on the 27th we did 16 miles over the worst surfaces and most dangerous crevasses we have ever encountered, only stopping for tea or cocoa till they were finished, and marching twenty hours at a stretch, through snow 10 to 18 in. thick as a rule, with sometimes 2½ ft. of it. We fell into hidden crevasses time after time, and were saved by each other and by our harness. In fact, only an all-merciful Providence has guided our steps to to-night's safety at our depôt. I cannot describe adequately the mental and physical strain of the last forty-eight hours. When we started at 7 A.M. yesterday, we immediately got into soft snow, an uphill pull with hidden crevasses. The biscuit was all finished, and with only one pannikin of hoosh, mostly pony maize, and one of tea, we marched till noon. Then we had one pannikin of tea and one ounce of chocolate, and marched till 4.45 P.M. We had one pannikin of tea. There was no more food. We marched till 10 P.M., then one small pannikin of cocoa. Marched till 2 A.M., when we were played out. We had one pannikin of cocoa, and slept till 8 A.M. Then a pannikin of cocoa, and we marched till 1 P.M. and camped, about half a mile from the depôt. Marshall went on for food, and we got a meal at 2 P.M. We turned in and slept. Adams fell exhausted, but recovered and went on again. Wild did the same the night before."

January 28. "Thank God we are on the Barrier again at last. We got up at 1 A.M. this morning, had breakfast, consisting of tea and one biscuit, and got under way at 3 A.M. We reached the depôt in half an hour without any difficulty. The snow here was deep enough to carry us over the crevasses that had impeded our progress so much on the outward march. We had proper breakfast at 5 A.M. then dug out our depôt. The alternate falls of snow and thaws had frozen solidly in a great deal of our gear, and our spare sledge meter was deeply buried. We marched along till we were close to the Gap, then had lunch. At 1 P.M. we were through the Gap and on to the crevassed and ridged Barrier surface. We are now safe, with six days' food and only 50 miles to the depôt, but Wild has developed dysentery. We are at a loss to know what is the cause of it. It may possibly be due to the horse-meat. The weather has been fairly fine all day, though clouding up from the south towards noon, and we were assisted by a fresh southerly breeze up the slope to the head of the Gap. Indeed, we needed it, for the heavy surface and our dilapidated sledge made the hauling extremely hard. Just before we left the glacier I broke through the soft snow, plunging into a hidden crevasse. My harness jerked up under my heart, and gave me rather a shake up. It seemed as though the glacier were saying: 'There is the last touch for you; don't you come up here again.' It was with a feeling of intense relief that we left this great glacier, for the strain has been very hard, and now we know that except for blizzards and thick weather, which two factors alone can prevent us from finding our depôts in good time, we will be all right."

January 29–February 5. Inasmuch as it blizzarded next day, the men spent the time mostly in their sleeping bags, patching clothes. On the thirtieth Shackleton noted, "Wild is seedy to-day, but we hope that as soon as he reaches Grisi depôt he will be better. We have no variety of food, and only have four miserable thin biscuits a day to eke out the horse-meat. The plasmon is all finished and so are we ourselves by the end of the day's march. The sledge is also in a terribly bad state, but as soon as we reach the depôt all will be well." The following two days he wrote respectively, "Wild bad with dysentery" and "Wild very bad," and on the third day, "Wild and self dysentery; dead tired, bad surface, with undulations." On February 3 they reached the depot and picked up the second sledge. "All acute dysentery due to meat. Trust that sleep will put us right [after a march of only five miles over very soft snow]. Could go no further to-night. Wild very bad, self weaker, others assailed also. Bad light, short food, surface worse than ever."

The fourth: "Cannot write more. All down with acute dysentery;

terrible day. No march possible; outlook serious." But the weather was fine.

The fifth: "We are picking up the mounds well [those they had constructed]. Too weak on half ration to write much. Still hanging on to geological specimens. Please God we will get through all right. Great anxiety."

February 6–8. The following day he wrote, "All better and a better surface. Terribly hungry. Six biscuits per day and one pannikin horse-meat each meal. Picked up November 28 mound and made camp. I do trust this hunger will not weaken us too much. It has been great anxiety. Thank God the dysentery stopped and the surface better." The seventh: "Blowing hard blizzard. Kept going till 6 P.M. Adams and Marshall renewed dysentery. Dead tired. Short food; very weak." The eighth: "Started from camp in blizzard. Adams and Marshall still dysentery; Wild and I all right. Feel starving for food. Talk of it all day. Anyhow, getting north, thank God. Sixty-nine miles to Chinaman depôt."

February 9. "All thinking and talk of food."

February 10. "All thinking and talking of food."

February 11. "All our thoughts are of food. We ought to reach the depôt in two days. Now we are down to half a pannikin of meat and five biscuits a day. Adams not all right yet, and Wild shaky tonight. Good surface and following wind."

February 12–15. The party reached the depot on the thirteenth and ate Chinaman's liver. "It tasted splendid. We looked round for any spare bits of meat, and while I was digging in the snow I came across some hard red stuff, Chinaman's blood frozen into a solid core. We dug it up, and found it a welcome addition to our food. It was like beef-tea when boiled up." The fourteenth: "Burst lips our greatest trouble." Next day was Shackleton's thirty-fifth birthday. "I was given a present of a cigarette made out of pipe tobacco and some coarse paper we had with us. It was delicious."

February 16. "A fair surface to-day, but no wind. The sastrugi are disappearing. We are appallingly hungry. We are down to about half a pannikin of half-cooked horse-meat a meal and four biscuits a day. We covered 13 miles to-day, with the temperature from zero to minus 7° Fahr. There are appearances of wind from the south, long windy streamers of torn stratus. We are so weak now that even to lift our depleted provision bag is an effort. When we break camp in the morning we pull the tent off the poles and take it down before we move the things inside, for the effort of lifting the sleeping-bags, etc., through the doorway is too great. At night when we have come to camp we sometimes have to lift our legs one at a time with both hands in getting into the tent. It seems a severe strain to lift one's feet without aid after we have stiffened from the day's march. Our fingers are extremely painful. Some of us have big blisters that burst occasionally."

February 17–19. On the seventeeth the party marched in a blizzard. The wind was behind them. "We all have tragic dreams of getting food to eat, but rarely have the satisfaction of dreaming that we are actually eating. Last night I did taste bread and butter. We look at each other as we eat our scanty meals and feel a distinct grievance if one man manages to make his hoosh last longer than the rest of us. Sometimes we do our best to save a bit of biscuit for the next meal, but it is a much debated question whether it is best to eat all the food at once or to save. I eat all my lunch biscuit, but keep a bit from dinner to eat in the bag so as to induce sleep. The smaller the quantity of biscuits grows the more delicious they taste." The following afternoon they sighted Mount Discovery. "What a home-like appearance it has." The morning of the nineteenth they saw Mount Erebus. "The old landmarks are so pleasant."

February 20. "Started to get up at 4.40 A.M. It is almost a farce to talk of getting up to 'breakfast' now, and there is no call of 'Come on, boys; good hoosh.' No good hoosh is to be had. In less time than it has taken me to write this the food is finished, and then our hopes and thoughts lie wholly in the direction of the next feed, so called from force of habit. It was dull and overcast to-day, and we could see only a little way. Still we made progress, and at 4 P.M. we reached depôt A. The distance for the day was 14 miles, with 52° of frost. We sighted the depôt at 2.30 P.M., and now we have enough food to carry us to the Bluff Depôt. We had run out of food when we reached the depôt to-day, and we have had a good hoosh to-night. The unaccustomed pemmican fat made me feel quite queer, but I enjoyed the pudding we made out of biscuits and the tin of jam which we originally intended to have for Christmas Day, but which we left behind when on the way south in order to save weight. Our depôted tobacco and cigarettes were here, and it is difficult to describe the enjoyment and luxury of a good smoke. I am sure that the tobacco will make up for the shortage of food. I do not doubt but that the Bluff Depôt will have been laid all right by Joyce. Anyhow we must stake on it, for we have not enough food to carry us to the ship. Joyce knows his work well, and we talk now of nothing but the feeds that we will have when we reach the Bluff. That depôt has been the bright beacon ahead through these dark days of hunger. Each time we took in another hole in our belts we have said that it will be all right when we get to the Bluff Depôt, and now we are getting towards it."

February 21. "In ordinary polar work one would not think of travelling in such a severe blizzard, but our need is extreme, and we must keep going. It is neck or nothing with us now. Our food lies ahead, and death stalks us from behind."

February 22. The men made a good march this day. They came upon the remains of a noon camp of a party of four men with dogs. "We found three small bits of chocolate and a little bit of biscuit at the camp after carefully searching the ground for such unconsidered trifles, and we 'turned backs' for them. I was unlucky enough to get the bit of biscuit, and a curious unreasoning anger took possession of me for a moment at my bad luck. It shows how primitive we have become, and how much the question of even a morsel of food affects our judgment. We are near the end of our food, but as we have staked everything on the Bluff Depôt, we had a good feed to-night. If we do not pick up the depôt there will be absolutely no hope for us."

February 23. "Started at 6:45 A.M. in splendid weather, and at 11 A.M., while halting for a spell, Wild saw the Bluff Depôt miraged up. It seemed to be quite close, and the flags were waving and dancing as though to say, 'Come, here I am, come and feed.' It was the most cheerful sight our eyes have ever seen, for we had only a few biscuits left. These we at once devoured. The Grisi meat had given Wild renewed dysentery. After a short camp we pushed on. A flashing light appeared to be on the depôt, and when we reached it at 4 P.M., this turned out to be a biscuit tin, which had been placed in the snow so as to catch the light of the sun. It was like a great cheerful eye twinkling at us. The depôt had appeared much closer than it really was, because we were accustomed to judging from the height of an ordinary depôt, whereas this one was built on a snow mound over 10 ft. high, with two bamboos lashed together on top, and three flags. It was a splendid mark. Joyce and his party have done their work well. Now we are safe as regards food, and it only remains for us to reach the ship. I climbed up on top of the depôt, and shouted out to those below of the glorious feeds that awaited us. First, I rolled down three tins of biscuits, then cases containing luxuries of every description, many of them sent by friends. There were Carlsbad plums, eggs, cakes, plum puddings, gingerbread and crystallized fruit, even fresh boiled mutton from the ship. After months of want and hunger, we suddenly found ourselves able to have meals fit for the gods, and with appetites that the gods might have envied. Apart from the luxuries there was an ample supply of ordinary sledging rations. To-night we improvised a second cooking-stand out of a biscuit tin, and used our second Primus to cook some of the courses. Our dream of food has come true, and yet after we had eaten biscuits and had two pannikins of pemmican, followed by cocoa, our contracted bodies would not stand the strain of more food, and reluctantly we had to stop. I cannot tell what a relief it has been to us. There is nothing much in the way of news from the ship, only just a letter saying that she had arrived on January 5, and that all was well. . . . We now have to catch the ship [before her departure; the season was late and there was danger of her being frozen in], and I hope we will do that. Wild is better to-night. The temperature is plus 10° Fahr., fine and warm. I am writing in my bag with biscuits beside me, and chocolate and jam."

February 24–26. On the twenty-fourth the men marched fifteen miles in fine weather. On the twenty-fifth Shackleton noted, "We turned out at 4 A.M. for an early start, as we are in danger of being left if we do not push ahead rapidly and reach the ship." Marshall had dysentery again and "paralysis of the stomach." There being signs of a blizzard approaching, Shackleton considered him unfit to march. The men waited out the blizzard in their bags. "If Marshall is not better to-night, I must leave him with Adams and push on, for time is going on, and the ship may leave on March 1, according to orders, if the Sound is not clear of ice. I went over through the blizzard to Marshall's tent. He is in a bad way still, but thinks that he could travel to-morrow." The blizzard stopped next day and the men made twenty-four miles. "Marshall suffered greatly but stuck to the march. He never complains."

February 27–March 1. On the twenty-seventh Marshall's dysentery grew worse. Shackleton and Wild, leaving him in Adams's care, headed for Hut Point at 4.30 P.M. with one day's provisions, sleeping bags and the sledge. They marched until nine, had a hoosh, marched until 2 A.M. of the twenty-eighth, stopped for an hour and a half near White Island, without sleep, and marched again until 11 A.M., at which time they ate the last of their food. "We kept flashing the heliograph in the hope of attracting attention from Observation Hill, where I thought that a party would be on the lookout, but there was no return flash. The only thing to do was to push ahead, although we were by this time very tired." The weather turned thick. Shackleton abandoned the sledge.

"In the thick weather we could not risk making Pram Point, and I decided to follow another route seven miles round by the other side of Castle Rock. We clambered over crevasses and snow slopes, and after what seemed an almost interminable struggle reached Castle Rock, from whence I could see that there was open water all round the north. It was indeed a different home-coming from what we had expected. Out on the Barrier and up on the plateau our thoughts had often turned to the day when we would get back to the comfort and plenty of winter-quarters, but we had never imagined fighting our way to the back-door, so to speak, in such a cheerless fashion. We reached the top of Ski Slope at 7.45 P.M., and from there we could see the [*Discovery*] hut and the bay. There was no sign of the ship, and no smoke or other evidence of life at the hut. We hurried on to the hut, our minds busy with gloomy possibilities, and found not a man there. There was a letter stating that the Northern Party had reached the Magnetic Pole, and that all the parties had been picked up except ours. The letter added that the ship would be sheltering under Glacier Tongue until February 26. It was now February 28, and it was with very keen anxiety in our minds that we proceeded to search for food. If the ship was gone, our plight, and that of the two men left out on the Barrier, was a very serious one.

"We improvised a cooking vessel, found oil and a Primus lamp, and had a good feed of biscuit, onions and plum pudding, which were amongst the stores left at the hut. We were utterly weary, but we had no sleeping-gear, our bags having been left with the sledge, and the temperature was very low. We found a piece of roofing felt, which we wrapped round us, and then we sat up all night, the darkness being relieved only when we occasionally lighted the lamp in order to secure a little warmth. We tried to burn the magnetic hut* in the hope of attracting attention from the ship, but we were not able to get it alight. We tried, too, to tie the Union Jack to Vince's cross, on the hill, but we were so played out that our cold fingers could not manage the knots. It was a bad night for us, and we were glad indeed when the light came again. Then we managed to get a little warmer, and at 9 A.M. we got the magnetic hut alight, and put up the flag. All our fears vanished when in the distance we saw the ship, miraged up. We signalled with the heliograph, and at 11 A.M. on March 1 we were on board the *Nimrod* and once more safe amongst friends. I will not attempt to describe our feelings. Every one was glad to see us, and keen to know what we had done. They had given us up for lost, and a search-party had been going to start that day in the hope of finding some trace of us."

A relief party was immediately organized to rescue Marshall and Adams. Without rest, and with a meal of only bacon and fried bread, Shackleton led the party, which brought the stranded men to the ship. A photograph of Shackleton, Adams, Marshall and Wild, taken soon after they were reunited on the *Nimrod,* shows them looking unkempt, sun-darkened, haggard and as if they had suffered severe beatings on the face.

* A small hut erected by the Discovery Expedition for carrying out experiments in terrestrial magnetism—C.N.

12

CAPE ROYDS CONCLUDED

My ALARM CLOCK awoke me at six. The night had had an unexpected effect: the hut's foodstuffs no longer seemed strange, and the skis and sledges seemed to beckon as if I had once used them. I went outside. The sun was over Erebus.

Two guy wires had been looped over the hut to secure it against blizzards. On the right of the door an old sledge leaned against a wall. The door, originally hinged on the right or southern side, had been blown off in a storm long ago and was now hinged on the left side. It had been painted a brilliant orange, I presumed in modern times. There were two steps to the doorsill, the first quite high.

On the hut's northern side, where the stables had been, were bales of browned, weatherworn, still-wired fodder; venesta cases neatly stacked to form a wall; harness hanging from nails; rusty tin cans; a wooden puppy house; a large metal funnel; and a toilet seat made by cutting a round hole in the top of a crate. I wondered what the Shackleton expedition had done with feces, which do not decay readily at that latitude. We had found modern feces north of the wanigan, very dry, looking like plastic, and I had shoveled as many as I could find into latrine sacks to be taken back to McMurdo. Later today Murphy would roll three large empty fuel drums up to the helo pad for removal. This was Brandau's idea. Brandau had a passion about keeping Antarctica clean. There was old litter on the southern side of the hut too, including glass jars and many rusted cans.

I went inside the hut, where I picked up my copy of the second

volume of *The Heart of the Antarctic,* in which Shackleton had
set down some fascinating notes on the effects of severe hunger during the southern journey. I read:

"When we were living on meat our desire for cereals and far-
inaceous foods became stronger; indeed any particular sort of food
of which we were deprived seemed to us to be the food for which
nature craved. When we were short of sugar we would dream of
sweet-stuffs, and when biscuits were in short supply our thoughts
were concerned with crisp loaves and all the other good things dis-
played in the windows of the bakers' shops. During the last weeks
of the journey outwards, and the long march back, when our allowance of food had been reduced to twenty ounces per man a
day, we really thought of little but food. The glory of the great
mountains that towered high on either side, the majesty of the
enormous glacier up which we travelled so painfully, did not appeal to our emotions to any great extent. Man becomes very primitive when he is hungry and short of food, and we learned to know
what it is to be desperately hungry. I used to wonder sometimes
whether the people who suffer from hunger in the big cities of
civilisation felt as we were feeling, and I arrived at the conclusion
that they did not, for no barrier of law and order would have been
allowed to stand between us and any food that had been available.
The man who starves in a city is weakened, hopeless, spiritless,
and we were vigorous and keen. Until January 9 the desire for food
was made the more intense by our knowledge of the fact that we
were steadily marching away from the stores of plenty.

"We could not joke about food, in the way that is possible for
the man who is hungry in the ordinary sense. We thought about it
most of the time, and on the way back we used to talk about it, but
always in the most serious manner possible. We used to plan out the
enormous meals that we proposed to have when we got back to
the ship and, later, to civilisation. On the outward march we did
not experience really severe hunger until we got on the great
glacier, and then we were too much occupied with the heavy and
dangerous climbing over the rough ice and crevasses to be able to
talk much. We had to keep some distance apart in case one man
fell into a crevasse. Then on the plateau our faces were generally
coated with ice, and the blizzard wind blowing from the south
made unnecessary conversation out of the question. Those were
silent days, and our remarks to one another were brief and infre-

quent. It was on the march back that we talked freely of food, after we had got down the glacier and were marching over the barrier surface. The wind was behind us, so that the pulling was not very heavy, and as there were no crevasses to fear we were able to keep close together. We would get up at 5 A.M. in order to make a start at 7 A.M., and after we had eaten our scanty breakfast, that seemed only to accentuate hunger, and had begun the day's march, we could take turns in describing things we would eat in the good days to come. We were each going to give a dinner to the others in turn, and there was to be an anniversary dinner every year, at which we would be able to eat and eat and eat. No French chef ever devoted more thought to the invention of new dishes than we did.

"It is with strange feelings that I look back over our notes, and see the wonderful meals that we were going to have. We used to tell each other, with perfect seriousness, about the new dishes that we had thought of, and if the dish met with general approval there would be a chorus of, 'Ah! That's good.' Sometimes there would be an argument as to whether a suggested dish was really an original invention, or whether it did not too nearly resemble something that we had already tasted in happier days. The 'Wild roll' was admitted to be the high-water mark of gastronomic luxury. Wild proposed that the cook should take a supply of well-seasoned minced meat, wrap it in rashers of fat bacon, and place around the whole an outer covering of rich pastry, so that it would take the form of a big sausage-roll. Then this roll would be fried with plenty of fat. My best dish, which I must admit I put forward with a good deal of pride as we marched over the snow, was a sardine pastry, made by placing well-fried sardines inside pastry. At least ten tins of sardines were to be emptied on to a bed of pastry, and the whole then rolled up and cooked, preparatory to its division into four equal portions. I remember one day Marshall came forward with a proposal for a thick roll of suet pudding with plenty of jam all over it, and there arose quite a heated argument as to whether he could fairly claim this dish to be an invention, or whether it was not the jam roll already known to the housewives of civilisation. There was one point on which we were all agreed, and that was that we did not want any jellies or things of that sort at our future meals. The idea of eating such elusive stuff as jelly had no appeal to us at all.

"On a typical day during this backward march we would leave

camp at about 6.40 A.M., and half an hour later would have recovered our frost-bitten fingers, while the moisture on our clothes, melted in the sleeping-bags, would have begun to ablate, after having first frozen hard. We would be beginning to march with some degree of comfort, and one of us would remark, 'Well, boys, what are we going to have for breakfast to-day?' We had just finished our breakfast as a matter of fact, consisting of half a pannikin of semi-raw horse-meat, one biscuit and a half and a pannikin of tea, but the meal had not taken the keenness from our appetites. We used to try to persuade ourselves that our half-biscuit was not quite a half, and sometimes we managed to get a little bit more that way. The question would receive our most serious and careful consideration at once, and we would proceed to weave from our hungry imaginations a tale of a day spent in eating. 'Now we are on board ship,' one man would say. 'We wake up in a bunk, and the first thing we do is to stretch out our hands to the side of the bunk and get some chocolate, some Garibaldi biscuits and some apples. We eat those in the bunk, and then we get up for breakfast. Breakfast will be at eight o'clock, and we will have porridge, fish, bacon and eggs, cold ham, plum pudding, sweets, fresh roll and butter, marmalade and coffee. At eleven o'clock we will have hot cocoa, open jam tarts, fried cods' roe and slices of heavy plum cake. That will be all until lunch at one o'clock. For lunch we will have Wild roll, shepherd's pie, fresh soda-bread, hot milk, treacle pudding, nuts, raisins and cake. After that we will turn in for a sleep, and we will be called at 3.45, when we will reach out again from the bunks and have doughnuts and sweets. We will get up then and have big cups of hot tea and fresh cake and chocolate creams. Dinner will be at six, and we will have thick soup, roast beef and Yorkshire pudding, cauliflower, peas, asparagus, plum pudding, fruit, apple-pie with thick cream, scones and butter, port wine, nuts, and almonds and raisins. Then at midnight we will have a really big meal, just before we go to bed. There will be melon, grilled trout and butter-sauce, roast chicken with plenty of livers, a proper salad with eggs and very thick dressing, green peas and new potatoes, a saddle of mutton, fried suet pudding, peaches *à la Melba*, egg curry, plum pudding and sauce, Welsh rarebit, Queen's pudding, angels on horse-back, cream cheese and celery, fruit, nuts, port wine, milk and cocoa. Then we will go to bed and sleep till breakfast time. We will have chocolate and biscuits under our pillows, and if we want anything to eat in the night we will just have to get it.' Three of us would listen to this programme and perhaps suggest amendments and improvements, generally in the direction of additional dishes, and then another one of us would take up the running and sketch another glorious day of feeding and sleeping.

"I daresay that all this sounds very greedy and uncivilised to the reader who has never been on the verge of starvation, but as I have said before, hunger makes a man primitive. We did not smile at ourselves or at each other as we planned wonderful feats of over-eating. We were perfectly serious about the matter, and we noted down in the back pages of our diaries details of the meals that we had decided to have as soon as we got back to the places where food was plentiful. All the morning we would allow our imaginations to run riot in this fashion. Then would come one o'clock, and I would look at my watch and say, 'Camp!' We would drop the harness from our tired bodies and pitch the tent on the smoothest place available, and three of us would get inside to wait for the thin and scanty meal, while the other man filled the cooker with snow and fragments of frozen meat. An hour later we would be on the march again, once more thinking and talking of food, and this would go on until the camp in the evening. We would have another scanty meal, and turn into the sleeping-bags, to dream wildly of food that somehow we could never manage to eat."

Reading these pages, it seemed both strange and marvelous to be standing in Shackleton's hut.

Murphy was still asleep when I reached the wanigan. I heated water before waking him. He prepared a steak breakfast. Afterwards we hiked northward, intending to reach the southern limit of the pack ice. In a niche of the hills we came upon an old, rusty dump heap. Sometimes, when we climbed black hills with the consistency of sand dunes, our heels smoked with volcanic dust. Much of the terrain looked burned out. We crossed solid black rock. In the hill shelves and cups it could be almost oppressively warm but if you came within range of a wind you might get rapidly chilled. Standing on a hilltop, we saw the wanigan, the hut, the rookery, Flagstaff Point. The rookery seemed to be bathed by dappled poetic light even though the sky was cloudless. Its guano-tan was the sole warm color in the entire cape scene. The shore of Pony Lake nearest the rookery looked gentle. Although the sky was a pale blue, the color reflected in the lake was a gorgeous royal. Beyond the rookery we saw the dome of Mount Discovery, far to the south.

It was extremely pleasant to wander in this landscape. Erebus showed bare veined ribs. Its second crater looked quite clear of snow. There was a fascinating contrast between the black foreground—huge, strong, sweeping—and Erebus's delicacy, with its gentle slopes and sensuous, snowy sides. The black mass had been vomited out of Erebus's throat. We saw vistas of loaf-studded black terrain petering out toward the volcano's glacial slopes. We came to a pond in which skuas were bathing. The pond's shores were thick with coarse red algae; its waters were reddish. This was Shackleton's Green Lake. I could not understand why it had been so named. (Next day, coming upon it from a different angle, I saw a green cast to it.)

The skua is a powerfully built, gull-like, bipolar bird with a strong arched neck, a large, curved bill, and capable talons. The Antarctic skua has been described as resembling a small eagle. It has no hesitation in attacking man. Seeing us, the birds set up cries of alarm, cries somehow pathetic, like those of primitive women keening. Then they attacked, diving low in an effort to strike us with the leading edge of their powerful wings. One bird kept coming in at chest level, wing edges uplifted, tail fanned out, beak open. Some flew above us, hovered, and tried to defecate on us. When we passed beyond the lake they ceased attacking us en masse, but it was not possible to avoid being attacked from time to time as we moved northward, for they nested in the hills, and their nests were mere depressions in the lee of a rock, and their speckled white or tan or brown eggs were not easy to spot, nor their pearl-gray chicks.

It was exciting to encounter an erratic boulder occasionally— granite, gneiss, schist, porphyry, sandstone—brought by glaciers from the Western Mountains. They were a relief from the volcanic forms all around us. We gathered some rocks. Most were porous and dark gray or black but a few were the hue of old red brick. Some were heavy and contained feldspar crystals.

Encountering streams of noisy meltwater, we went as far north as Blacksand Beach, one of the few beaches in the McMurdo Sound area. There was pack ice abreast of it, hummocked and shredded by pressure. A long snow slope ran down like a road to it from the height on which we stood. It would have been fun to go down there but the snow was deep and looked soft. We might have disappeared in it.

We visited the rookery again and again; climbed to the end of Flagstaff Point; hiked to Green Lake a second time; studied the hut's interior at greater length; fiddled endlessly with the radio, which worked only off the generator and not well even then. And we hiked, hiked, eager to get a feel for the strange terrain that had become so familiar to Shackleton. On the third day, when our fingers showed deep cracks because of the extremely low humidity, a lone Adélie wandered up to the wanigan to peer inside and to study us at length, first with one eye, then the other. When he departed he cast several suspicious glances back at us.

The first night my legs had *taken* me to the Nimrod Hut. The second I had to direct them to it. The thrill was gone, and the smells in the structure were really not pleasant. Also, I had failed to encounter ghosts, nightmares or even just interesting dreams. I do not remember dreaming during either night.

13

~~~~~~~~~~~~~~~~~~~~~~~~~~~~

A VISIT TO VOSTOK STATION

IT IS RARE enough for an American in Antarctica to visit the Pole
Station. A visit to Vostok, the Russian base deep in the Antarctic
interior, is an even greater rarity, for there are only one or two flights
from McMurdo Station to Vostok each year, whereas flights from
McMurdo to the Pole are relatively frequent during the austral
summer. The two stations, roughly equidistant from McMurdo
(some 850 miles), are extraordinarily remote from the rest of the
world. There are no flights or traverses to either station during the
winter, when their sole communication with the outside is by
short-wave radio.

Vostok is the world's coldest known place. A temperature of
−126.9° F. was recorded there in August 1960. Situated at 78° S,
107° E, it is the station closest to the south geomagnetic pole and
is therefore excellently located for studies in upper-atmosphere
physics and in phenomena of extraterrestrial origin, such as cosmic
rays. The magnetic poles, because of local magnetic influences and
the poles' tendency to drift, do not indicate the axis of the earth's
magnetic field; a line drawn between them would not touch the
earth's center. The geomagnetic poles do mark that axis. Vostok's
absolute elevation, or altitude in terms of sea level, is about 11,500
feet. Its physiological altitude, in terms of millibars, is said to be
close to 12,500 feet. The difference is due to Vostok's being a low-
pressure area (there are numerous such areas in Antarctica). The
human organism responds as though it were at the higher elevation.

Built in 1955 for the International Geophysical Year, Vostok in

1971 had four buildings, with a complement of twenty-three men. Six of the crew had wintered over twice previously. The Russians at Vostok have a one-year tour of duty. By 1971 only one woman, a Russian, had visited the station, for a brief time during an austral summer. Vostok is resupplied annually by tractor train and by aircraft from the Russian coastal station Mirnyy, some eight hundred miles away. Vostok means East, Mirnyy means Peace. The stations were named after the two ships of the great Russian Antarctic explorer of the early part of the last century, Thaddeus Bellingshausen.

I wanted to visit Vostok for a number of reasons: to witness the operation of the Antarctic Treaty; to see my friend Dale Vance's new and exotic home; and to meet Russians on politically neutral territory, relatively speaking. A flight from McMurdo to Vostok dramatizes for Americans and Russians, perhaps better than any other single annual event, the benign international conditions that exist under the Antarctic Treaty, a treaty inspired by the highly successful international cooperation in Antarctica during the IGY. An editorial in the New York *Times* of December 9, 1969, suggested the extent and implications of the treaty.

"A decade ago this month the Antarctic Treaty was signed by the United States, the Soviet Union and ten other countries. With the passage of time, the example set by this treaty has grown enormously in significance.

"In effect, this pioneering compact declared the Antarctic to be a continent of peace, where men would cooperate for mutual advantage and for the advancement of science, where military activities would be prohibited and where territorial claims would be outlawed for at least thirty years. And so it has worked out—thus far. Even at the times of greatest tension in the terror-filled sixties—the Cuban missile crisis and the invasion of Czechoslovakia, for example—Russians, Americans, Britons and others have continued their work in the Antarctic undisturbed. They have helped each other as necessary, shared their knowledge and resources, accepted international inspection of their activities and generally behaved as friends and colleagues. In this coldest of the continents and the iciest of landscapes, the Cold War was abolished.

"There can be little doubt that this precedent helped to create the foundations of mutual confidence on which the great diplomatic landmarks of the past decade have been based, notably the test ban treaty of 1963, the space compact of 1967 and the nuclear non-proliferation pact of 1968. In effect, the Antarctic has become a political science laboratory, and the Antarctic Treaty a historic, successful experiment pointing the way for future progress toward international cooperation.

"Now the task is to apply the lessons learned from that experiment to all of the great contemporary problems where needless suspicion and rivalry waste huge resources and endanger earth itself."

Before I left McMurdo Station to camp at Cape Royds, Dale Vance and I had a long talk about his forthcoming role at Vostok, where he would live as the American exchange scientist from December 23, 1970, to January 10, 1972. On January 6, 1971, a new crew would replace most of the crew he would meet on December 23. He had great natural charm to go with his vigor, enthusiasm, optimism and good looks. Everybody at McMurdo was swept along by his warmth and was convinced he would make an excellent impression on the Russians. He was thirty-three, had dark-brown hair, wore horn-rimmed glasses, was six feet two inches tall and weighed about 175 pounds. He was born in Renfrew, Pennsylvania, had spent most of his childhood in Alva, Oklahoma, had a degree in electrical engineering from the University of Colorado, had wintered over at Byrd Station from November 1962 to December 1963, had spent the summer of 1968 at Pole Station, and was currently employed by NOAA (pronounced Noah and standing for National Oceanic and Atmospheric Administration), a federal agency. He lived in Boulder, Colorado.

He would operate upper-atmosphere-research equipment; two AC magnetometer setups; riometers (relative ionosphere opacity meters, which measure the attenuation of radio noise in the upper atmosphere); VLF (very low frequency) receiving equipment; and other equipment as well. The equipment was American and he would bring in many resupply items for it. If it broke down it was his job to do his best to fix it.

He would live and work in a Jamesway hut built by the United States Seabees in 1964. The hut would be heated by diesel fuel flown in with him: twenty-six drums weighing approximately five hundred pounds each, which would be railroaded out of the plane's rear ramp onto the snow as the pilot gunned his throttle. The Russians would furnish Vance with four things: companionship, electrical power, meals and the station's medical facilities. Vostok had two doctors, who doubled as dentists. He would have his share of station chores. He could live alone if he liked, or could ask a Russian to live with him. (His hut had an extra bunk.) He guessed that the hut was about a hundred yards from the station's center and that a handline ran from it to the station. If there wasn't a line there he would string one up.

"My name is chicken sukiyaki. I'm the world's oldest living ex-Kamikazi pilot. I'm going to *return*, like MacArthur to Corregidor," he said and laughed. His laugh was wholehearted and infectious.

He had taken a crash course in Russian with Berlitz. He estimated that three of the Russians at Vostok would speak good English. The rest would probably use some English words. He foresaw no problems for himself with the exception of those caused by possible political discussions. He hoped that his year would be mostly apolitical.

His amateur radio equipment, which he was taking along with him, would be absolutely essential to his happiness. "I would *not* go to Vostok without regular communication with my family. There's just no way it could happen." As a precaution against station power failure he was taking along a two-kilowatt generator for use with his "ham rig," as he called it. He planned to be on the air two to three hours a week, chiefly to talk with his family. His friend Steve Barnes of Boulder, mentioned earlier, would come up every Wednesday night at zero three hundred Zulu. (Zulu stands for Greenwich mean time.) There was no legal limit to how long Vance could use a phone patch but there were propagation-condition limits. There was only a certain time of day when he would be able to reach Colorado on twenty meters, his rig's wave length.

Although he had wintered over at Byrd Station, leaving his family this last time had been unusually difficult for him.

"The hardest thing I ever did was to walk away and leave my wife and two little kids back there. It was the first time I cried in the last . . . fifteen years. I'm afraid to talk to my kids now, because I know I'll cry. You know, I don't *do* that. I'm fairly hard-shelled, and I don't show emotion very often. I had a pretty tough time when I was down in '68. I'd been gone nearly two months and my little girl got on the phone and she said, 'Daddy, when are you coming home?' And it really got *to* me. I left my family in as good shape as I could. Going to Vostok is tough on my wife and it's tough on me.

But I think that it's very character-building. We'll both develop as individuals because of it. And it will help my professional career. The point is, *if* you hack it, *if* you make it, then you'll have something that no book and no amount of education can give you. My wife will have it much rougher back there, raising two children by herself for a year, than I'll ever have it at Vostok. *She's* the one who has the load and needs the courage."

He was not worried about the possible complexity of personal relations with the Russians in so small and isolated a station. There were going to be good people and some not so good, as there had been during his summer at the Pole and his winter at Byrd. What he wanted most was to be himself, to maintain his discipline and to achieve, as he put it, "respect in that peer group." The international aspects of the program had intrigued him from the beginning, as well as the adventure of wintering with the Russians. He had no desire to winter in an American station again. He thought he could represent "middle America" well and could do his bit for "Uncle Sugar."

Despite the fact that the Russians would provide him with meals, he was going to take along a certain amount of food, including twenty cases of beer, twenty-four bottles of whisky, T-bone and sirloin steaks, two turkeys, sweet potatoes, cranberry sauce, party cheeses, sardines, ice cream mix, bacon, lobster, shrimp, popcorn and oil, frozen milk, a hundred boxes of breakfast cereal, canned fruit and vegetable juices, five hundred tea bags, mixed nuts, instant freeze-dried coffee, peanut butter, beef stew ("Gosh, it might just taste so damned good to me some night after I've been eating kasha or something"), hot peppers, ketchup, and meat sauces. He planned to throw a steak dinner for the Russians on the Fourth of July, complete with charcoal and hickory-smoke salt. He would make his own charcoal at Vostok by burning some crate boards. "Maybe I'll wave an American flag, or post one on the wall." At Thanksgiving he would throw a turkey dinner.

He was also taking along canned cigars, sheets of Apollo 11 commemorative stamps, sixty Kennedy half-dollars, a sufficient number of specially engraved Zippo lighters to give one to each of the Russians, and two hundred hours of taped music. "What I found from my experience in the Antarctic is that it's not records, or just straight tapes you buy at the store, that are good, but music that you tape from the radio, with news, weather and sports. They're a comfort."

Finally, he was taking two items on the advice of Admiral Welch. During last year's visit to Vostok the admiral had been aced by the station's scientific leader, who was dressed in a white shirt, black tie and a fine-looking jacket.

"The admiral was taken aback. So the other day he said to me in a humorous way, 'You know what you could do? Outclass them!' So I'm taking an after-six dinner jacket and a bow tie. And I'll come walking into the dining room on midwinter's night dressed to the teeth."

On my return to McMurdo Station from Cape Royds on December 21 I received from Chris Shepherd the news that I would fly to Vostok Station on the twenty-third. Shepherd briefed me about the trip. Twenty men would go, in a C-130. There would be a crew of nine and eleven passengers, five of whom would be Usarps: Shepherd, Vance, Sergei Miagkov (the Russian exchange scientist at McMurdo), Russ Peterson (the scientific leader at McMurdo for the coming winter), and I. The Navy brass would be along, together with three Navy persons of lesser rank. On arrival we would help offload the C-130 before entering the station to meet the Russians.

Inasmuch as our hosts would serve us lots of vodka it was useful to remember that at Vostok's altitude one shot was equal to four at sea level, consequently it was easy to get wiped out. The Russians would treat us to a big spread. About an hour would be devoted to trading.

The morning of the twenty-third Vance, I and the three other Usarps were taken to Williams Field in a red power wagon that looked and felt like an armored truck. The cabin was isolated from the driver's cab. We sat on two opposing hard benches, with gear crowding us all round; climbed up the station and went through the Gap; passed Scott Base; then swung onto the ice shelf and were flung about as the vehicle ground and whined its way over the rough surface to the field.

We boarded the Herc, selected seats, stowed our gear and strapped ourselves in for the take-off. In my knapsack were three cartons of cigarettes and two cans of pipe tobacco I had purchased at the ship's store. The three-hour flight was uneventful. When one squinted through a porthole all one saw was the seemingly endless Antarctic plateau. I thought of Scott's western journey.

We exited from the front of the plane. Vance wore black wind-pants over his corduroys, a red parka, and new Japanese white mukluks with black trim and white laces. I was carrying his oscilloscope, a green box weighing about twenty pounds. The four turboprops never stopped turning.

We encountered a level white wasteland stretching to the horizon, thick, uneven snow, much glare, and a number of low-lying, extensive, rectangular, plywood-faced shacks and huts. The sky, sporting cirrus clouds, was a paler blue than at sea level. Snow crystals lay flat, large and gleaming, like mica flakes. The temperature was −29° F., but there was little wind. Vostok is usually spared the high, temperamental winds of the continent and the problem of snowdrift caused by them. In the sun's milky brilliance we would have felt comfortable if it hadn't been for the altitude. I recognized from photographs the two gleaming, 135-foot antenna towers which the United States Seabees had constructed in January 1964 for the International Year of the Quiet Sun program. They were secured by many guy wires.

Several Russians came up and greeted me with smiles. The greetings, in two languages, were very warm. I followed some of my companions into a tan building with a cursive sign in Russian over the door and found myself standing next to Admiral Welch.

"Take a look at *that*," he said.

Turning, I saw an adjoining square room containing a long table covered with white linen and crowded with such things as bottles of vodka and champagne; bits of bread smeared with black caviar and red caviar or containing thick, short slices of beluga; bars of Soviet chocolate; candy in cellophane wrappers; sliced pickles, salami, sardines, anchovies; cake; and cans of crab and lobster meat. At the head of the table were two small flags. On the wall behind these was a huge map of Antarctica.

A Russian asked me in English, "How do you feel?"

"Good," I replied.

"There is oxygen," he said, pointing to a tank hanging on a wall near a corner.

At my request he guided me to Vance's hut, which was closer to the station's center than I had expected, and urged me to be careful as I made my way down an ice mound to the door step. I deposited the oscilloscope and went to the rear of the plane to help with the offloading of Vance's cargo.

The wash of the turboprops was like a blizzard. We had been warned to be careful not to get frostbitten in it. But when you worked directly behind the lowered ramp you didn't feel it much. Our crew was sending crates and cartons down to the snow on rails. I was aware of black-clad figures working mightily, collecting the equipment and loading it onto the rear of a large, high, tracked vehicle. The Russians, almost all wearing black leather (their boots were heavy and coarse and in some instances were wrapped in black felt puttees), seemed eager to prove their hospitality by cornering the market on physical labor. No doubt, realizing that we had just come from sea-level McMurdo, they wished to spare us the effects of their altitude, which could be especially unpleasant if one exerted oneself physically. Their station was currently the highest on the continent and they themselves had had to adjust to it.

When the task was finished I went over to Vance's truncated, green-topped hut, which was near the Seabee antennas, and watched some Russians making a pile of his cartons near the entrance. It was odd to see that two of the cartons, now part of the remote Russian outpost, read "7 Up" and a third read "Budweiser." I wandered around the station until I realized that my cheeks were numb, my double-gloved hands were in intense pain, I was beginning to get a headache, my nape felt too cold and my heart was beating rapidly. I was the only person still outside.

I made my way into the reception hut, where, in the small vestibule in front of the dining room, there were packages of Russian cigarettes on a table. It was so warm in the place that my head soon ran with perspiration. I removed my cap and parka and threw them on a heap of clothes, but like my companions I continued to wear my windpants. It was strange to see so much heavy clothing being worn indoors: leather jackets and trousers, leather boots, bunny boots, mukluks, heavy shirts.

There were funny attempts at conversation between Russians who couldn't speak English and Americans who couldn't talk Russian. I knew a few Russian words and expressions. When a tall Russian asked me in Russian if I could speak Russian I replied in Russian that I couldn't. He insisted through an interpreter that I was Russian-born because my mustache, which I liked to think was cavalry-English, was in the Russian style. I resisted the temptation to admit I had been born in his country, having decided before the trip that such information might be misconstrued.

Many of the Russians had yellow gold teeth. One of them had white gold ones. One man's front uppers were all in yellow gold. To an American, such shining memories of prolonged visits to dentists' chairs were somewhat disconcerting. There was an emphasis on black in the Russians' clothes, suggesting sobriety or possibly a touch of puritanism. The heavy leather clothing reminded me vaguely of scenes from Tolstoy and Dostoyevsky.

Two tiny souvenirs of our visit were handed to each of us: a Leningrad pin and a Soviet fiftieth-anniversary pin. We were also given a cacheted photograph of Vostok, which we asked our hosts to autograph. There was a good deal of "busy" activity: arms reaching out to pin things, to sample Russian cigarettes, to write names. Meanwhile there was much excited chatter, squeezing of biceps, clapping of backs and shoulders.

Then trading began. Trading at Vostok serves the purpose of breaking the ice, of bringing strangers together informally. A Russian asked me if I wished to buy Russian boots or hats for dollars. I explained that I didn't have any dollars with me. Several Russians asked for *Playboy* magazine. Someone handed me a tiny, lacquered wooden figurine, in return for which I reached into my green nylon knapsack and gave him a can of pipe tobacco. This Russian brought over a friend and said haltingly that his friend (who had a serious face) was a "heavy smoker" and wanted to taste an American cigarette. I said I didn't have loose cigarettes, only cartons, which I was reserving for trading purposes. Although I repeated myself twice the Russians did not seem to understand me. I pulled out a carton and handed it to the serious Russian, saying several times, "No trade. Present." The serious Russian, who could not speak English, said something to his colleague, who said to me, "One moment, one moment, he will give you something." I protested that this was not a trade, but the serious-faced Russian dashed off somewhere and returned with a pair of brand-new, large, black canvas mittens, lined with brown fur of some sort, which he thrust upon me.

At a signal from the station leader we moved into the dining room and stood around the table. I found myself at the table's middle, facing a wall covered with posters. Behind me a large American flag was spread on the wall. On my immediate right a heavy-set man, his head shaven, his eyes slanted, gray, his face looking long and heavy with its black silken beard, spoke a bit of English, introducing himself to me as Roostom (spelled Rustom). When I told him my first name, which he pronounced with a rolled r, he embraced me powerfully and announced that we would be brothers, then handed me an enameled metal cup, inverted a bottle of vodka and let the liquid splash wildly into it. He himself used a paper cup of considerably smaller dimensions.

Somebody called for attention and the room grew silent. The station leader presented Admiral Welch with bottles of vodka. His remarks were translated by an interpreter. The admiral expressed his thanks. When these were interpreted there were American cries of "Hear! Hear!" To which the Russians responded with their equivalent of our "Hip hip hurrah!"

In 1966 the Russians at Vostok had presented the visiting Americans a document listing the Vostok personnel of that year. The admiral now returned this document (which all of us had signed on the plane), saying that he hoped it would be passed between the stations in the future. There were more hurrahs. Meanwhile there were toasts. Rustom Tashpalatov, who had catlike, shrewd eyes, complained that I wasn't drinking my share. I explained that it was my job to observe, therefore I had to stay sober. He said he agreed, but in a good-natured way he kept forgetting that he had agreed, and kept complaining. I found myself drinking a surprising amount of vodka. It tasted weaker than its American counterpart and seemed to have the delightful ability to lessen the effects of hypoxia.

Famished, I ate caviar and beluga voraciously, hoping I wasn't making a spectacle of myself. The beluga, the color of old ivory, was a marvelous fish. With a flourish of pride Rustom unwrapped a bar of chocolate and insisted I have a large piece. I discovered that the chocolate was just bitter enough to clear one's mouth of fish tastes and refresh one's desire for vodka. With the aid of gestures Rustom declared that he would drink bottoms up with me. Pointing to my temple, I said I had to keep a cool head. Up went his paper cup. He pretended to drain its contents at one swallow but I saw a good deal of liquid run over the sides, down his beard and onto the floor.

What did I do? he wanted to know. I said I was a writer. His eyes showed no comprehension. When I said I was an author he still didn't understand. Feeling ashamed to put myself even by remote inference in such company, I was forced to say, "Tolstoy,

Dostoyevsky, Turgenev." He broke into a great smile and from that moment looked and sounded very respectful.

A little later, while I was speaking with a slim, shortish man with a very pale forehead, again the words "writer" and "author" signified nothing and again I had to resort to the use of great Russian literary names. The man, who was a scientist named Valery Uliajov and had a badly sunburned nose, told me that Vostok had had a visit from a Russian writer, a humorist, and that the writer, after returning to Moscow, had cabled the station—Uliajov spoke the message in a mock-pompous tone—"In the interests of polar solidarity and out of respect for the nobility of polar man I am avoiding theaters, the company of women, and am ashamed to be consuming a full quota of oxygen instead of the two-thirds quota consumed at Vostok." Uliajov seemed to be delighted with this joke.

I gave him a can of pipe tobacco as a gift and he insisted on leading me to his hut so he could give me a present in return. It turned out that the hut was Vance's, which Uliajov was going to share briefly before going home. As you entered it you saw two bedcouches like bunks, divided by a low plywood partition, and automated machines, tools, boxes, benches, and two narrow corridors leading to a rear work space. The place was overheated. I began to perspire.

Uliajov showed me a wooden sword with which he had been knighted on his birthday at Vostok. He said the sword was a "heartly present" because it had been hand-made by its donor. Earlier, in the dining room, he had told me that the table's contents were an expression of the "hostility" of Vostok's residents toward their American guests. I had suggested that he meant "hospitality" and he had quickly corrected himself. He insisted now on giving me a brown woolen balaclava that he said had been used only at Vostok. I was impressed by its weight and thickness.

He said he was extremely respectful of writers. Gazing at me urgently with his blue eyes for what felt like a long time, he urged me to work for peace, adding that it was the sacred duty of writers and politicians to do so. In limited English he suggested that men today are dissonant but that in the future they will be remade from old parts of themselves and will have more brotherly feelings. His hair was light brown, his nose a fiery red, his small forehead almost sadly pale.

We returned to the dining room. The Americans went on a brief

tour of the station. Then the farewells began. On the surface they
were comical. You said good-by to somebody with a lunge of the
arm, a powerful squeezing of fingers, a pounding of the back, and
suddenly you were embraced, and your cheek was being rubbed
against a Russian cheek. You kept encountering faces you had already said good-by to, and gripping arms and squeezing shoulders
and clapping backs for the second and third times. Yet under the
surface there was something strangely moving. Was it due to the
altitude? To the vodka? Or was there more to these mad farewells?
We had gotten, however briefly and inadequately, to know each
other, to have regard for each other, and we would not meet again.
In this remote, hostile spot on the globe, we felt we were members
of a polar brotherhood and were trying to convey, however fool-
ishly, the fact that we meant well toward each other and that we
wished our two nations would do the same.

Shortly afterwards we went to our plane, whose four engines had
filled the station with a great background noise throughout our
visit. The plane seemed full of Russians eager to inspect it and to
indulge in a last bit of trading. I saw Rustom, hatless, vigorous, all
smiles. We embraced again. I told him I wanted to trade something
for his beard and I pulled it gently. A friend of his tweaked my
frozen mustache in reciprocal jest, hurting the roots more than he
realized.

I had seen little of Dale Vance during the visit. I had gathered
that he was busy looking after his gear. My last view of him came
when he ran up to the plane and climbed aboard, looking unlike
himself. His face was more pouchy than usual, his eyes were tired,
distressed. He was frowning. He told me that one of his briefcases
and a large box were missing. While several of us searched the
cabin, he disappeared.

It seemed quite awhile before the admiral came aboard and the
Russians departed. We took off at about 8:30, flew far out, turned,
made a pass at the station at a very low altitude, flew out again and
made a second pass. Figures were waving. The land was bare,
endless, white. The huts looked very vulnerable. I wondered what
Vance's feelings were now. He had to adjust to his new world, a
world without women and Americans, which would soon be socked
in by black winter.

We touched down at Williams Field at about 11:30. There was
a nasty ride back to McMurdo in the red power wagon. The ad-

miral's pink station wagon ahead of us slid off the rutted snow road and almost turned on its side. It was pulled clear with a rope by a white station wagon behind it. It was past 1 A.M. when I turned in.

Postscript

I spoke with Vance by phone patch several times during his year at Vostok. The phone would ring in the middle of the night in my home in Princeton, I'd find myself talking briefly with a ham operator in the States, then Vance would come on, sounding very clear. He ascribed his station's power to his antenna, which he described as a high-gain cubical quad on a thirty-foot mast. His call signal was KC4AAC. He was running a thousand watts single sideband and was confident of being able to reach anywhere in the world.

On one occasion it was a hundred below at Vostok when he called. He had had altitude trouble the first two weeks. The first week a doctor had monitored him with electrocardiograms and blood-pressure checks. After the third day Vance thought he would live but he still experienced shortness of breath. For a while his appetite had declined and he had had insomnia and headaches.

He was present when the tractor train arrived from Mirnyy January 6, 1971, with the new station crew. The train was met with the traditional bread and salt as well as with flares. He had made a good adjustment at the station and was happy to be regarded as just another member of the crew instead of as "the American." When an avid Communist tried talking politics with him, Vance declined on the ground that his, Vance's, love of his country overwhelmed his reasoning power when he discussed international politics. The things he had most trouble adjusting to in the beginning were the community drinking cup, the common hand towel, the slurping of liquids, the toilet that was a hole in the floor, and the crew's habit of downing a full glass of vodka at a gulp.

"There is nothing social about the way they drink. They are bent on self-destruction," he reported.

He visited me in Princeton in April 1972. As he spoke of some of his experiences at the Russian base, he played down the effects of extreme cold. He had thrown water into the air at −100° F. and, contrary to legend, it had invariably *not* popped like Chinese firecrackers and had *not* frozen before hitting the ground. And being out in minus a hundred did not feel significantly different from being out in minus fifty. On one winter occasion he and two or three companions had gone on a hike. Suddenly they realized that the station's lights had been turned off and that without them they had little chance of finding their way home. They had no signaling equipment with them. The temperature was around a hundred below and they had to keep moving hard to stay warm. Luckily someone at the station noticed they were out too long and that the lights were off. The lights were turned on and the hiking party made their way back to the base without injury.

What struck Vance most on his return to New Zealand was not women, not flowers, not animals, not trees, not grass—but the presence of children. It hit him very hard, he said, when he first saw the children in Christchurch.

14

~~~~~~~~~~~~~~~~~~~~~~~~~~~~~~~~~~~~~~

A FATAL CRASH IN THE DRY VALLEYS

On Christmas Eve there was a USARP-Navy party in the McMurdo wardroom, with free drinks. The little wardroom was crowded and noisy. Everyone seemed to be there. I saw Captain Swinburne, Captain Van Reethe and even Admiral Welch. Al Pretty, a mechanic who worked in the USARP garage, was costumed as Santa Claus. In the adjoining tiny movie theater were tuna sandwiches, cubes of American cheese, salami-and-cheese sandwiches. Several Kiwis, knowing that McMurdo's ice machines had broken down, had brought ice from Scott Base, cut by chain saw from the pressure hummocks on the ice shelf.

I had a chat with the tall, blond, no-longer-young pilot who had flown the C-130 to Vostok. He had empathetic eyes and a soft, retiring manner. He had not flown to Vostok before. As he had prepared to land, not knowing the wind direction, he had flown low over the station to note which way the station flags were blowing. He had requested Sergei Miagkov, who was in the cockpit, to ask Vostok for its wind velocity.

"Three meters per second," was the reply.

There was a scramble in the cockpit to translate this into miles per hour.

The pilot had been worried because the Russians had been lined up on both sides of the skiway.

"They were right on the runway itself. When I reversed the props, what if one didn't reverse? It rarely happens that they don't all reverse at the same time but it *can happen*. The plane would swivel around and go off the runway. That's all we'd need, to kill some Russians. I had to go right between them. I didn't reverse the props until I was well past them. It was a rough moment."

I heard a number of pilots say the continuing practice of exclusively using single-engine helos in Antarctica was sure to get people killed, for if you lost your engine for any reason you were likely to be in serious trouble, given the Antarctic terrain. They wondered when the Navy would get around to replacing the single-engine craft with twin-engine ones. A handsome, olive-skinned pilot predicted that when the Hercs got much older they'd have troubles similar to those of the Connies, with a tragic end; but he added that the Hercs could take a terrific beating. He spoke of very rough take-offs and of one he had made recently that had damaged his radar as well as some other instruments. Rattling off some numbers, he told me they were secret code between air and ground crews, used when aircraft were in flight. One number even meant, "Brass on board understands the code." Another meant, "A merry fucking Christmas." He said he hated loose women and complained that the new *Playboy* calendar "even shows hair" and was part of the national degeneration. He used more profanity than I had heard from one person in a long time.

I spoke with Brian Porter, leader of Scott Base, a short, straight-backed, gray-haired, balding man. Porter went to the Protestant service at eleven. A little later I peeked into the chapel. Chaplain Lesher, in black robes, was reading aloud from the Bible at a lectern on one side. Occasionally the worshipers sang to the accompaniment of the organ. A white pennant with a black cross flew from the chaplain's new flagpole beside the chapel, near the statue of Admiral Byrd.

After midnight I ran into Jim Brandau and two New Zealanders. Brandau, who was walking the Kiwis as far as the Gap, invited me to join him. The night was soft, furry. As Brandau and I turned back and headed downhill toward McMurdo he spoke of how Antarctica inspired him, how he loved the place, and related an anecdote about the ice cave in Erebus Glacier Tongue: about how beautiful it had been there and how awed he had felt and how he had asked the chaplain, who was also there, what kind of sermon he would preach in the cave if he had the opportunity.

The chaplain had replied, "About hell fire and brimstone," which had shocked Brandau a little.

Brandau spoke of his plan to remove latrine and other wastes from the Dry Valleys. He was a sensitive, intelligent and in some ways a remarkable man, as I had heard.

It was about 2 A.M. when I turned in. In the morning the station looked deserted. The mess hall was almost empty. There would be no flights today and little work.

From my journal:

"One experiences strange illusions which bring back the temperate world. You hear a distant sound outside and think, 'A crow,' then recall with some confusion that there are no crows here. You see from a truck an arrangement of crates on a field below and think, 'Skyscrapers,' then remember they're only crates, that skyscrapers belong in cities and that cities are mostly in temperate regions."

In the afternoon I attended a USARP party in Building 137, a Jamesway. Jim Elder, in charge of the Field Center, was stringing popcorn with a needle and thread and hanging long lines of it on a small plastic Christmas tree. People were snacking on filberts and on anchovy paste with crackers, and drinking whisky with ice-shelf ice that Gary Means had brought from Scott Base. We went to Christmas dinner in the chow hall. The large plastic Christmas tree in the chiefs' mess was festooned and illuminated. The recent warm spell made one feel less remote from home but, paradoxically, it also caused one's family to seem very far away.

In the evening, still thinking of home, I walked alone in dense fog almost as far as Scott Base. The road, glistening with meltwater rivulets, was asteam. I could not make out the New Zealand base at the point at which I turned back but I could faintly hear the howling of the huskies below me.

On my way to my quarters I passed the Field Center, where a new bronze plaque to the right of the door read: THOMAS E. BERG FIELD CENTER. DEDICATED TO THE MEMORY OF THOMAS E. BERG, USARP GEOLOGIST WHO WAS KILLED IN A HELICOPTER ACCIDENT NEAR MT. NEWALL ON 19 NOVEMBER 1969.

I had met Berg; also Jeremy Sykes, a New Zealand film director who had been killed with him. I had flown in the helicopter, Gentle 5, four days earlier. This was the helo that had been piloted by Brandau. I had often wondered about what had happened. I had heard rumors but the details were sparse and some were inconsistent. I resolved to ask Brandau to tell me what he knew about the crash.

Sitting in my room next morning, he related the following story.

He had headed towards Wright Valley and was just passing over a ridge off Mount Newall when there was an explosion in the engine compartment and the engine quit. For the previous hour he had been about 1,600 feet above the ground. Ten seconds later he would have been at least 2,300 feet above the ground. But at the time the engine went cold the ground was only 200 feet beneath him and it was a slope. If the ground had been level he thinks he would have been able to autorotate down.

"You have sufficient room to make an autorotation if you have a place to autorotate *to*. In fact, they recommend 500 feet for a 180-degree turn to an autorotation landing. In checking out the new people, and showing off a little bit, I've gone down to a hundred and eighty feet and closed the throttle and made a turn and then a landing. But at that altitude you have to do everything right. And you have to be right next to the runway, because you don't have a lot of room to maneuver in."

He believed he had three choices. He could make an abrupt 160-degree turn and go to the glacier behind him. But he would have to complete this turn and get into autorotation within the altitude of 200 feet. He could try to stretch his glide out beyond the slope. If he succeeded he would have another 1,200 feet in altitude to set himself up for a landing. However, he wasn't sure he could maintain his forward speed.

"In an airplane if you lose your air speed you stall and spin. In a helicopter you fall like a rock."

His third choice was the one he made. He tried to stick the tail into a snowbank and keep it there. But the tail didn't hold. The craft started sliding down the slope, which was partially snow-covered and partially dry, and its fuel tanks, which were beneath the cabin, ruptured and burst into flames. The helicopter picked up speed until it hit some rocks about 600 feet below.

There were eight persons on board: Brandau, the copilot, two crewmen and four passengers. One of the crewmen had been standing up to take pictures through the open cabin hatch. He came out running, then fell and gashed his thumb on a rock. Inasmuch as Brandau had partial control of the craft right down to the bottom he remained in the cockpit. At the bottom the helicopter made a 180-degree turn, the Plexiglas canopy tore off, and Brandau dove out and rolled. The landing gear had folded back, so he was some eight feet above the ground when he dove. The copilot threw himself out also.

There were people running around. Everyone was on fire. Brandau rolled on the ground until he got his flames out, then went to the cabin. He could see just one man, apparently in complete shock, standing back in a corner. Brandau went in and brought him out. It was Sam Grau, a New Zealander. Two other people rolled Grau on the ground. Brandau couldn't see anything more inside the helicopter.

"There just wasn't any way to force yourself back in."

There was the possibility of an explosion, so they all moved away from the craft. The helicopter, constructed of a magnesium-aluminum alloy, burned with great intensity. The only thing that could have put out the fire was Purple K powder. Brandau counted then and realized that only six men had escaped. Sykes and Berg were inside. Sykes had been seated on the middle of three seats on the starboard side. People on both sides of him had gotten out. Berg had been sitting opposite, just forward of the generator. Don Curry, sitting beside him, had also escaped.

"Sam Grau, whom I pulled out, was probably within seconds of being dead. His lungs were burned quite badly. His entire face was burned. And his eyes were burned closed. He thought his back was injured. We couldn't do much for him, but we gathered some of the hatches that had come off, and piled rocks and built a shelter for him. We had part of a sleeping bag that had been thrown out of the helicopter. We put this around him."

The temperature was about 15° F. Fortunately there was no wind. The men had saved some parkas. They removed the liners and were able to share the coats in this way. Two of the men would lie down on either side of Grau. He was shaking badly. While the men lay down they shook from being cold. So it was finally decided that if Grau did have a spinal injury the shaking would cause him more harm than his moving around. They got him up on his feet and walked him around between two of them.

A small first-aid kit was found; also a can of engine oil and one of white gas. All had bounced out of the helicopter. With the engine oil the men prepared three signal fires: on snow inside a Plexiglas hatch; in a depression scraped in the sand; and on a large rock with a depression in it. Only one of the men, a crewman, had fingers that had escaped burning. It was he who could still light matches. When the others put their hands into their pockets the pain became intolerable, so they kept them out and from time to time checked them for frostbite.

Brandau, knowing that another helicopter was in Wright Valley and would be coming out in about an hour, climbed to the top of the ridge and waited for it. He expected to be rescued by it. The crashed helicopter was still throwing flames twenty feet into the air, so the party did not light the signal fires. From the ridge Brandau could see Observation Hill some sixty miles away. It occurred to him that if he had a signaling mirror he could possibly attract McMurdo's attention. The helicopter from the valley flew by without spotting the burning helicopter.

Brandau descended to the group and sent his copilot, Mike Mabry, and one of his crewmen, Buddy English, to an emergency tent some seven or eight miles away. If for any reason they could not get the radio in the tent to work they were to proceed to Wright Valley near Meserve Glacier, some twelve miles away, where Brandau had put in a party the day before. The men would have to cross Wright Lower Glacier and Newall Glacier but these were not crevassed, and mostly they would be hiking on dry terrain, with adequate landmarks.

Soon a helicopter came looking for the party but missed them. Brandau had the second crewman lay rocks out in the snow down on a nearby glacier. The crewman made a large arrow. The party lit the signal fires. Two Hercs came by but saw nothing unusual. Brandau climbed to the top of the ridge again and was there when a helo flew over him. It was so close he could see the tread in its tires. Silhouetted against the sky on top of the ridge at 3,200 feet, he ran back and forth waving a scarf and was certain he had been spotted. But the helo kept on going.

"It was heartbreaking."

The crash had occurred at about 9 A.M. Meanwhile the helicopter burned itself out. There was little of it except five cylinders of the engine. But there were identifiable human beings among the remains: two human forms in the fetal position, the extremities burned off. Jeremy Sykes, the New Zealander, Brandau knew only superficially. But Tom Berg he had known quite well since 1963. He and

Berg had gone into the field together many times and dug down through four feet of permafrost with a gasoline-powered jackhammer to expose ledges that Berg was interested in studying. They would be out all day and would cook steaks with aluminum foil and charcoal. After a day's work they'd go exploring a bit. It was Berg, in 1964, who had shown Brandau where the petrified wood was near Allan Nunatak.

Mabry and English reached the first tent but were unable to transmit on its radio. English, exhausted, stayed there while Mabry hiked to Wright Valley, where he got on the radio and found himself talking to a Herc overhead. A helicopter came for him, then rescued the group at the burned helicopter, but not without difficulty in spotting them. Another helicopter picked up English. The rescues were accomplished some nine hours after the crash.

Grau, English, Curry and Brandau were the most seriously burned. All of them except Grau were sent up to Christchurch, where they recuperated away from the cold and dryness of Antarctica until their hands healed. Grau, whose face was a massive scab, was kept at McMurdo and given doses of antibiotics. He coughed up a great deal of black material. Both his lungs and his face healed, and his eyes were not permanently injured.

It was never learned why Berg and Sykes were trapped, nor what caused the explosion.

Fascinated by Brandau and enchanted with him, I was eager to learn some details of his life. He had been flying single-engine helicopters for seventeen years, as long as he had been in the Navy. During that time eight of them had cut out on him. In five instances there was no resultant damage. In the other three, "I didn't have a place to land," as he put it. He had been involved in a fatal crash in the waters off California, in which only he survived. When he tried to tell me about this crash his voice choked up and he couldn't go on.

He had been in Antarctica in 1963, 1964 and 1969. He expected to return in 1971. He had requested Antarctic duty. He thought that most of the Navy people who went there enjoyed their stay.

"I guess they aren't more career-minded. Coming here is obviously not the way to get command of a ship. I've never really been bitten by ambition. I've been bitten by the curiosity bug, I guess.

The relationship with people down here is not available anywhere else that I know of. Aboard ship you live in a society of men but there's a great deal less comradeship and respect for each other than you have here."

On the other hand, some people didn't like Antarctica.

"You have people who hate this place and are really bitter about being here, and they get back to Quonset and damn this place. I don't know where they want to go but they never seem to get there. Part of the wonder of this place is that you can get the whole history of it together, it's all within reach. When you walk out around Hut Point the footprints of Scott are not far gone. That rock that he described looks just about the same. You *can* get a kinship with history."

He spoke nostalgically of the McMurdo that had existed during his first year there.

"Everyone stood in the same chow line. The skipper of the squadron would come down and fall in behind the non-rated aviation mechanic. They used to have a smaller exchange, and a line would form outside, and one year, when Admiral Reedy was here, he had a chief of staff who was the very picture of a Prussian officer. One day Admiral Reedy stopped by the exchange and said, 'Oh hell, the line's too long.' I can still see his chief's being horrified at the idea of the admiral's waiting in line. A senator would get off the plane and pick up his own bag. Someone would tell him where to go. Now they haven't quite reached the shipboard idea of side buoys but there's definitely protocol. When a guy comes to the Antarctic he shouldn't get the feeling there's a gross surplus of people available to wait on him. My introduction to Antarctica was probably the proper one. I arrived here in all the gear that they dress you up in. They checked me into a hut. A fellow who had been in Deep Freeze Two was there. He said, 'I need some help.' And so about forty-five minutes after I got to Antarctica I was rolling a full barrel of piss down the streets."

He had flown seven kinds of helicopters and two kinds of jets.

"It's not really difficult flying down here. But it's different. If you're used to flying at altitudes, with navaids and essentially following the book, you're going to be severely limited down here, because a lot of times getting there and back is a matter of recognizing the way the snow has drifted and knowing that the character of the ice changes in a certain area. A lot of your flying down here is planning the next twenty seconds. If you're used to planning three or four hours ahead you might get worried."

He was born in 1933 on a farm in Iowa. His father and he were both born in the same house. His father died when Brandau was ten. Brandau moved in with a grandfather, and when the latter died Brandau moved to Mason City, a town of about 30,000 people. He said he had belonged to the lower middle class. "We didn't have a car but we lived quite comfortably." He had three sisters, two of them older than he. He went to junior college for one year and to the University of Iowa for two. He took a major in civil engineering "for no better reason than that I was good in mathematics and one brother-in-law was a civil engineer." He wasn't really interested in civil engineering. He joined the Navy during the Korean War and trained as a fighter pilot. "And just wanting to be checked out for something else, I volunteered for helicopter training, with the idea that I'd get back into jets, but I didn't really get back until twelve years later. That's a pretty fair helicopter check-out."

He was married and had two daughters, Paula and Peggie. His wife, Suzuko, was half Japanese and half Irish. He was considering retiring from the Navy in three years and becoming a farrier.

"I've worked around horses, and I own horses now, and I particularly want to do something using my physical strength. I'm quite strong and I get to really feeling down when I don't get exercise. There isn't anything available that a machine can't do better than a man, with a few obvious exceptions. A friend who's up in the mountains near Boulder says it's very reasonable to expect to shoe six to seven horses a day, every day you want to, at ten dollars a horse. They need shoes every two months. The income isn't a problem. I have sufficient money to get my two girls through college and I'm not interested in accumulating a lot more. I'll have sufficient money from the Navy so I won't have to do anything that's not interesting."

We discussed the maximum altitude capability of the H-34. I asked him what failed the craft on lift-off at high altitudes. Was the air too thin for it to grip?

"Well, we don't have a supercharger. Essentially the H-34 was built for sea-level work. Normally, to take off down here at the helo pad you can get airborne with about twenty-six hundred rpm and forty-five inches of manifold pressure. By the time you go through five thousand feet the maximum manifold pressure you can get at full throttle is around forty-three inches. As you go up, why, it just fades. Six thousand feet is probably a little high, but we set that as an arbitrary limit as far as putting in field parties goes."

I said that on the previous evening he had mentioned seeing the crater of Erebus. How had he been able to manage that?

"It takes a lot less power to fly than it does to land or to take off or to hover. What happens is, you have your rotor plane, and if you just hover about twenty feet above the ground you get a column of air moving down, and the rotor wash speed is about thirty-five knots, so you get a thirty-five-knot tube of air moving down. Well, you have to climb up through this. In effect you have to make a vertical climb of thirty-five knots. If you're moving off sideways it's fresh, still air and this will allow you to use about one third less power. I was going up Mount Erebus with one of the pilots one day and there was a low cloud bank we were coming over. He's got a lot of experience in other types but not in flying the Thirty-four much. I got up to six thousand feet. He says, 'The throttle's jammed. It won't go any further.' I said, 'That's all the far it goes, Mike.' 'Well, how do you get any more altitude?' 'Mr. Sikorski builds the first six thousand feet into the aircraft. The next seven thousand feet is pilot technique.' You need an updraft to get over Mount Erebus. You go back to your minimum required air speed, forty-five to fifty knots. Of course, you can put on your climb power but that runs out at about ten or eleven thousand feet. What you do is fly back and forth in this updraft until you get over the top."

He made it sound so very easy. I intended to ask him what would happen if you lost the updraft, or if it suddenly veered and deserted you, or if you made the mistake of encountering the downdraft on the opposite side of Erebus. But, remembering he had a flight to set up, he left in a hurry.

15

~~~~~~~~~~~~~~~~~~~~~~~~~~~~~~~~~~~~~~

CAMPING AT CAPE EVANS

EVANS IS A minor cape, a mere volcanic protuberance, of Ross Island, and if it had not served as the base of Scott's last expedition and as the base also of the Ross Island section of Shackleton's Endurance Expedition it would be interesting, probably, only because its skuary is the world's southernmost rookery. The remarkable characters and events of the two expeditions have lent to Cape Evans a depth of history, a tragedy and a nobility unmatched by any other single place on the continent. It was for obvious reasons that I wanted to camp there, again with Dave Murphy as my field assistant.

We were originally scheduled to lift off for the cape at 8 A.M. on Saturday, December 26, but the time was changed to 1 P.M. because the pilots, like everyone else, had been partying at McMurdo on Christmas Eve and Christmas Day. Our lift-off was delayed by fog until 1:30. We arrived at Evans a few minutes after two. Circling above the cape, which is some fifteen miles north of McMurdo, we saw the Scott hut below, on the beach of North Bay, and the small wanigan about 250 feet west of it. Evans is a shallow cape, blunt-nosed, pointing westward, and is full of cuplike depressions (at that time meltwater ponds) and great black boulders. It was much easier to set up camp there than it had been at Royds. The landing pad was on the beach, midway between the hut and the wanigan, and so we had to haul our gear only a short, level distance from the pad to our camp site. We staked down a handline between the wanigan and the hut and tested the experimental radio on batteries by calling McMurdo Station. The radio was not completely reliable even at this shorter distance from McMurdo but it worked much better than it had at Royds.

Murphy napped for several hours after we set up camp, using the single bunk on the seaward wall of the wanigan and putting his head in a crate to keep out the light. The wanigan, situated close to the beach and catching the light reflected from the sea ice and the Barne Glacier, was almost always brilliantly illuminated, even when the door was shut, for it had two windows, one on the north and the other on the east side. The northern window overlooked the Sound and the Glacier, the eastern one the Terra Nova Hut and its beach. Murphy had sprained a leg while skiing at Scott Base the day before and was now on a muscle-relaxing medication that made him sleepy. Also, he was using a chemical heating pad that turned very hot when you added a couple of tablespoons of water to it. While he slept I wandered around the environs, climbed a couple of ridges, then climbed Windvane Hill for its excellent views to the south and north. The hill was so named by the Scott expedition because an anemometer was established on it. Scott and his men often climbed the hill, and it was well known to the men of the *Aurora* section of Shackleton's Endurance Expedition.

On the hill, visible from many points on the cape, was a large, pale, rocked-down wooden cross, the base of which was a plaque with a printed inscription: SACRED TO THE MEMORY OF CAPT. A. L. A. MACKINTOSH, RNR, AND V. G. HAYWARD, WHO PERISHED ON THE SEA ICE IN A BLIZZARD ABOUT MAY 8, 1916, AND OF THE REVEREND A. P. SPENCER-SMITH, BA, WHO DIED ON THE ROSS BARRIER ON MARCH 6, 1916. A PAPER BEARING THIS INSCRIPTION, WRITTEN BY THEIR COMRADE A. K. JACK, WAS FOUND IN THE ICE-FILLED HUT BY THE NEW ZEALAND HUTS RESTORATION PARTY, 1960. JACK AND JOYCE, WHO MADE AND ERECTED THIS CROSS, HAD NOT ENOUGH TIME TO CARVE THE INSCRIPTION ON IT. THIS PLAQUE WAS ERECTED BY ANTARCTIC DIVISION, D.S.I.R., N.Z., 1962–1963. (The death of Mackintosh and Hayward was discussed in Chapter 2.)

From the hill I observed Skua Lake beyond the hut and the morainic ridge east of the hut that Scott had named the Ramp, then I walked along the beach toward the hut, which is very close to the Sound. The sea ice was still intact but the tidal crack was four or five feet wide and the ice nearby looked rotten in places, darker, wetter. There was still plenty of thick snow on the beach edge, in which meltwater had formed caves and tunnels whose icicles sparkled. From the beach one could see that a large chunk of the Barne Glacier had collapsed, forming a small embayment.

I was surprised by the amount of junk the warm summer had revealed around the outside of the hut and that the snow and ice had hidden from me during my visit of the previous year. Even the front of the hut was littered with broken bottles, rusty wire, wooden splinters, burlap and various odds and ends which were not only an eyesore but a foot hazard, and in the vicinity were foul, fishy smells of decaying ancient birds and seals. It seemed to me that this might be a case of carrying scholarly respect too far, to the point where it approached desecration. It would be an easy matter to deposit the litter in a shack built in the hills, where it could be saved for interested scholars, if any. Scott was a sensitive, orderly, aesthetically inclined man, and I imagined he would be distressed to know that so much offensive stuff lay all around his last home, stuff moreover which nobody could with certainty claim had been part of the camp during his time.

Aesthetically there's a marked contrast between this hut and the Shackleton one. The Shackleton one also has litter but not in the front, and it is mild—packing cases, fodder, some rusty tin cans—and there are no smells of putrefaction in its vicinity. The Shackleton hut leaves a very pleasant impression, which tends to inspire visitors with respect, whereas the ugly appearance of the immediate environs of the Scott hut may encourage visitors to take a casual attitude towards its contents. The poor impression was strengthened by a large pool of meltwater on the hut's southern side (the side away from the beach), in which junk was richly decaying.

I walked around the hut before entering it, and saw pony fodder, ropes, rags, boards, two outhouses, harness, rusty large cans, pieces of tubing, and a mummified tan dog curled in a fetal position, its skin intact, almost no skeleton showing, its excellent teeth exposed as if in a snarl. The dog was still wearing a broad, dark leather collar. The hut was not only much larger than the Royds one, it was also much darker and gloomier inside. I set up my cot, mattress and sleeping bag beside the old galley, which was close to the door. The cot ran parallel to the hut's length.

When Murphy awoke I said we ought to have a look at Skua Lake and at the strikingly conspicuous, light-brown conical mound halfway up the Ramp. The color of this mound was not in itself vivid but the contrast between it and the black hills was strong. He agreed. As we neared the lake our presence caused scores of skuas to leave its whitish, feather- and guano-strewn shores and soar above us like pearly leaves, wheeling against the cloudless sky in groups as though wind-scattered, and at times seeming to hang as still as kites. Occasionally a bird would dart at another and there would ensue a flurry of disagreement. The water, its crisping surface thick with feathers, appeared to be thoroughly polluted, but one was always thrilled to come upon a pond-sized body of fresh water in so high a latitude. We had not seen skuas in such profusion before. At Cape Royds we had at most encountered two dozen at a time. At Skua Lake there were several hundred. We wondered where they obtained food. At the Royds rookery seven miles to the north? At the McMurdo garbage dump fifteen miles to the south? The Sound was still frozen, and there was nothing at Evans to sustain them. Craning at them, we saw the sunlight pierce their outspread wing feathers.

Then, as though realizing belatedly that we were committing lese majesty, they stopped our further progress toward the conical mound by hurling themselves, screaming in alarm and anger, at us from all directions in a maneuver we called dive-bombing, for they occasionally ejected excreta at us. They kept us busy ducking.

It was exciting to stand your ground and let them come at you; to wait until the last moment, trying to frame a bird, to focus and to hold your camera steady, before dodging. Most of them gave the impression of bluffing, but a few flew so low and intensely they convinced us they had every intention of colliding. They swooped up at the last possible instant and at an altitude lower than where your neck had been, as photographs subsequently showed. Skuas are well known to be fierce, particularly when their nesting grounds are trespassed on. Although they gave the impression of being muscle-bound they were marvelous fliers. Their flight has been described as being more like that of a small eagle than a gull. We delighted in their beautiful maneuvers, their sudden climbs, dartings, peelings off, swoops, wheelings and bullet-like attack dives.

Rarely do skuas show their talons when diving, but one came at me chest high with talons extended. A cold pulse of fear swept over me as I imagined my eyes being raked. Being attacked by skuas had seemed at Royds a harmless sport provided your timing was adequate when ducking, although I remembered how Herbert Ponting, the gifted photographer of Scott's last expedition, had once received an unexpected strike across the eyes that had caused them to water for hours. It was his belief that the brim of his heavy felt hat, softening the blow, had saved his eyes from permanent injury. The skua that made the unusual pass at me seemed angrier than the others and more determined. Also, he flew lower, and there was something menacingly loose in the way his legs dangled. (When the other birds attacked, their legs were tucked under them.) His legs gave the impression not that he was crippled but rather that he was half demented. The coupled ideas—that he was demented and that I might be blinded—struck me simultaneously and I ducked very low, thinking we had better get out of there.

Murphy, wearing a red stocking cap, his face taut with excitement, had just finished dodging when a bird, having swooped on him from behind, struck him in the head. I heard as well as saw the blow, administered with the leading edge of the wing. Frightened, he threw himself prone. I ran over and stood cover for him as he rose. He rubbed his head thoughtfully, then we both laughed. Deciding we would return tomorrow armed with the two bamboo poles we had noticed leaning against the wanigan's southern exterior, we returned to the wanigan.

Murphy was justly proud of the tiny cave he had dug in the side of a nearby snowbank, from which he now extricated some food for dinner. We had tomato soup, steak, salt crackers with butter, frozen peaches, tea and a chocolate bar. Then we hiked over small black hills and ridges and across miniature black valleys in which colorless meltwater streams flowed noisily. We almost always had surpassingly beautiful views but despite them our eyes were often cast downward in a search for interesting rocks, ostensibly to bring back souvenirs for our friends but probably in an unconscious effort to find relief from the very grandeur around us. At Royds your eye was fascinated by the variety of sculptured forms. At Evans you felt more exposed to the great elements, and possibly for this reason also it was a comfort to lose yourself in the little world on the ground.

What a thrill it was to find a colored rock! The rocks were never large; the large ones invariably were the common black basalt. Nor were they to be seen in quantity. A thrifty hand had scattered them on those parts of the cape farthest from Erebus. Westward from the wanigan and on the tiny plateaus above it if you looked carefully and persevered you came upon a bit of precious color now and then in that black scape. There were brick reds, browns from coffee to rotten plum, umbers, and occasionally a bit of yellow scoria. The rocks contained tiny caves, and scalloped beaches, and tubes and tunnels, some of the last beautifully fluted.

At Royds I had felt the need for a geologist's hammer, so I had brought one to Evans. The hammer showed me how easy it was to slip into serious carelessness. I had not thought to bring protective glasses. Striking a large gray rock a sharp blow, luckily I shut my eyes at the same time. A piece of the shattered rock flew up and bounced off my left eye, stunning me with surprise and pain, leaving the eye sore for hours and causing me to wonder at my stupidity and the fact I had casually endangered my Ross Island project.

We came upon the black beach named West Beach by the Scott expedition. Here we found three tiny dried starfish, a sea urchin and a translucent brown coin shell, and almost stumbled on some dead Weddell seals, some fully skeletonized. Others were intact on the bottom and were skeletons only on top. One skeleton seemed to be lying on a sealskin rug. Its head showed signs of mummified skin: it seemed to be wearing a tight, ill-fitting skullcap. Some of the carcasses appeared to have been mummified long ago. A few were fresh enough to have renewed the process of decay in the unusually warm summer, consequently a nauseating fishy stench permeated the area.

We were attacked by four skuas. While two would come at you frontally the other two would disappear beyond the brow of a hill, gain altitude, then dive at you from behind or against your flank. They seemed to have an endless store of energy and determination. We looked around for signs of an egg or a fledgling. I was struck heavily across the left temple and ear by a skua I hadn't detected. It was a powerful blow, causing me to cry out instinctively. For a moment I wondered if I was going to pass out. It occurred to me then that it wouldn't do to be struck while standing on a cliff edge. Murphy, alerted by the sounds of the blow and my cry, ran frowning towards me. I assured him I was all right. A little later I was struck again, this time behind my right ear. Several skuas joined the first four. I decided to try to record on film just how low the birds dove. Murphy, standing out of range of their attacks and using one of my cameras and a 135mm lens, took a series of photographs of me ducking. In one I am shown almost squatting while a bird apparently attempts to rake my back. The birds were relentless, so, with my ears still ringing, we returned to the wanigan, took up the bamboo poles, then went back to West Beach, where the skuas promptly attacked us again, as though they had been waiting for us. Occasionally they hit the poles, which we held above our heads, but they were effectively prevented from striking our bodies.

Wandering closer to the sea ice, we discovered why the birds were so proprietary about the area. Nestled on the bare sand in the lee of a rib cage and thus more or less protected from the predominant southeasterlies, was a brown egg, beside which huddled a lovely, furry, pearl-gray chick with black eyes and a black beak, blending neatly with the skeleton and with the deep-gray or blackish beach sand. Having been alarmed by the cries of the adult birds, the chick stared uncertainly at us with alternate eyes. The tiny thing, surviving without real shelter in this, the world's southernmost bird breeding ground, stirred one's paternal feelings. We went quite close to it; and now the birds, having realized that we had outfoxed them, landed at a distance and grew very still, possibly out of fatalism, because they counted the chick and egg as already lost to us (as many an Adélie egg and chick had probably been lost to them), or because they cunningly hoped, in their fierce bird brains, that their sudden silence, calming us, would divert us from our murderous intent.

Afraid the chick might freeze when deprived for long of its parents' warmth, we hurried away, continuing westward to some other seal carcasses, from one of which Murphy managed to pry loose a canine tooth with a sheath knife despite the stench and despite the powerful grip of the mummified gums and the still strong, gleaming jawbone. We also climbed some capelike cliffs, from whose height we saw oil-green tidal cracks, blue patches of rapidly decaying sea ice, the light-bristling, chalk-textured snout of the Barne Glacier, and, serene above everything, the gently sloping sides of Erebus. Unlike Cape Royds, where the penguins make their various sounds and where the skuas cry plaintively as they scout above the rookery, Cape Evans has silences in which one listens, rapt, to the ringing of blood in one's ears and is aware of the mysterious purification of one's soul that seems to take place in them.

Some Weddells, basking on the sea ice just beyond the tidal crack near the wanigan, were making their weird noises when we returned from our hike. I felt I was too far from them to hear them clearly, so I went alone out onto a spit, but a meltwater stream gurgled so loudly it confused what I had come to listen to. However, it was fascinating to stand still beside the stream and observe the green algae waving in the current. Bits of plant life in this waste-land!

Murphy turned in early. I sat outside the wanigan. A solitary Weddell lay like a huge cigar on her side some twenty or thirty feet beyond the tidal crack. For hours she had been silent and had barely moved. Then, late in the long, white, beatific evening, graced by a few cirrus clouds containing touches of violet, lavender and rose, she had begun to "sing." She weighed, probably, close to a thousand pounds, yet from her girth issued what one might call "fairyland" sounds, marked by long pauses. Sometimes you heard a muted twang, with a minimum of resonance. Or the brief chirruping of a bird. Or noises reminding you of the gurgling of your stomach. Or the whistling and twittering of water disappearing down a drain. But mostly they brought to mind short-wave tuning whistles and static. She lay there hour after hour, possibly communicating with seals under the ice, or, like a bird, announcing a territorial impera-tive. Some miles out on the ice, near the cliffs of the Barne Glacier, were dashes which, through my binoculars, turned out to be other Weddells. Three or four Adélies could be seen determinedly march-ing far out on the sea ice, heading in the direction of Royds.

From my journal:

"We have not yet examined the interior of Scott's hut, which is a bit strange inasmuch as the hut is our chief reason for coming here. But we're surfeited with McMurdo and its artificiality—the hum of generators, the hot water, the abundance of food, the drink-ing in the wardroom every evening, and especially the round of holiday parties—and are exhilarating in the quiet, the birds, the seals, the sea, the mountain, the glacier, the ice, the volcanic land, the terrific sky. Tomorrow we'll turn to the hut, after we've had a brief respite from man.

"The razor sun on my cheek as I write near the wanigan door. No flies, insects. You expect them in this warm sun, with the brooks running. Find myself thinking of Cheechee nostalgically: of the trees, the summer sun, the green lawns, the pretty girls, Warner's bar, the buildings. This wanigan has two *Playboy* pinups. They're distracting, almost objectionable. Looking out the windows, you see the frozen Sound, the glacier, ice-covered Erebus, and you know that nakedness doesn't fit in here. The two girls are splendidly built and very pretty but they don't belong in this ice-land. You want to concentrate on what you have—the beauty, the historical perspective —not on what you lack: women."

When I left the wanigan after writing up my notes Murphy was already long and deeply asleep. As I walked beside the handline and approached the smelly litter heap that felt like a barrier between the hut (and Scott) and me I felt at moments a positive distaste, but once I was inside the structure I was brought back forcefully to the men who had lived in it and to their great stories, and although the place was very cold I had a brief look around before turning in.

I went to Scott's cubicle at the eastern end and observed the grimy remnants of what had once been there. His bunk. A reindeer-skin sleeping bag, dark, heavy, the leather dried out. A pair of worn-out shoes hanging from a nail. The sheath of a knife. A pair of very large hand-knitted gray socks. Leather mittens on a chair. The folding table on which Scott had written in his diary and on which he had carefully figured sledging rations, studied maps. On a shelf above the bunk was a copy of *The Green Flat and Other Stories of War and Sport,* by A. Conan Doyle.

I moved around the hut. An old leather bottle. Mukluks. Pins. Two large spools of thread, one white, one black. *The New Zealand Referee* of 1908. *The Weekly Press. The Illustrated London News.* A net. The mummified body of an Emperor penguin hanging from a hook. Folding chairs of wood and canvas. Iron cots with reindeer-skin sleeping bags. Rolls of cotton on a shelf. Vials, jars. A jar reading "Pure Carbolic Poison." Some reading "Thyroid Gland." Gauze bandages. Chloroform. Rectal suppositories. Rusted horse-blanket pins. Odds and ends of what resembled telegraph equipment. (They were perhaps related to the telephone line that had been strung between here and the Discovery Hut.) An electric lamp with the bulb still intact. Retorts, large flasks, glass tubing, chemicals, microscopic slides, an acetylene burner, a palette knife. Two spark plugs and a flywheel. Finneskoes. Hand-made leather boots. Brown sweaters hanging over the edges of rough-made wooden bunks. Seal-skin slippers. *The Canterbury Times,* Christchurch, New Zealand, Wednesday, July 1, 1908. *Tit-Bits,* February 3, 1907. *Starky and Company,* by Rudyard Kipling. Candles, candle holders, an old lamp, a work table with a spirit lamp. Carpenter's tools. Clips of rusted cartridges. Cans of "real Findon haddocks." Kegs of laundry soap. Cans of roasted veal. Savoy sauce. Jams: golden plum, damson, victoria plum. Meat sauces. Baking powder, baking soda. Pickles, onions, bloater paste. Patna rice, ham loaf, Moir's lunch tongue, baked beans, lentils, macaroni, pearl sago, ox tongue, potted beef.

I opened volume one of *Scott's Last Expedition*, a first edition of which I had with me, and read what Scott had written about the hut. On January 10, 1911, he wrote, "The hut is progressing apace, and all agree that it should be the most perfectly comfortable habitation. The sides have double boarding inside and outside the frames, with a layer of our excellent quilted seaweed insulation between each pair of boardings. The roof has a single matchboarding inside, but on the outside is a matchboarding, then a layer of 2-ply 'ruberoid,' then a layer of quilted seaweed, then a second matchboarding, and finally a cover of 3-ply 'ruberoid.' The first floor is laid, but over this there will be a quilting, a felt layer, a second boarding, and finally linoleum; as the plenteous volcanic sand can be piled well up on every side it is impossible to imagine that draughts can penetrate into the hut from beneath, and it is equally impossible to imagine great loss of heat by contact or radiation in that direction. To add to the wall insulation the south and east sides of the hut are piled high with compressed-forage bales, whilst the north side is being prepared as a winter stable for the ponies. The stable will stand between the wall of the hut and a wall built of forage bales, six bales high and two bales thick. This will be roofed with rafters and tarpaulin, as we cannot find enough boarding. We shall have to take care that too much snow does not collect on the roof, otherwise the place should do excellently well."

On the nineteenth he wrote, "The hut is becoming the most comfortable dwelling-place imaginable. We have made unto ourselves a truly seductive home, within the walls of which peace, quiet, and comfort reign supreme.

"Such a noble dwelling transcends the word 'hut,' and we pause to give it a more fitting title only from lack of the appropriate suggestion."

He stated in a letter written at this time, "Our residence is really a house of considerable size, in every respect the finest that has ever been erected in the Polar regions; 50 ft. long by 25 wide and 9 ft. to the eaves.

"If you can picture our house nestling below this small hill on a long stretch of black sand [the hut was some dozen feet above the sea], with many tons of provision cases ranged in neat blocks in front of it and the sea lapping the ice-foot below, you will have some idea of our immediate vicinity."

I undressed rapidly, slipped into my bag and immediately became aware of powerful and unpleasant odors. However, there was no other place in the hut that I could move my cot to, presuming that a change would be helpful. The hut was crowded and I felt crowded in it. My head was close to two cases of Fry's Pure Concentrated Cocoa and to a case of Heinz Baked Beans. Lying on my side, I stared at rows of enameled metalware hanging from hooks; at many chipped pitchers; at the galley stove and chimney, which had rusted badly. All the colors blended: mahogany, mauve, rust. I felt neither here nor there: not far enough from the door or close enough to the middle; up against a Nansen sledge on the door's left and close to the galley on the door's right. I assured myself that it made no difference where in the hut I slept.

I had never seen a ghost, so I had reason to believe I was not ghost-prone. Nor did I believe in ghosts except insofar as they might exist as projected images of one's imagination. As I settled into my bag I mildly hoped I would experience at least one powerful dream about Scott and his companions, a dream that would teach me something, and I would not have minded having a solid nightmare.

I heard sounds as of distant thunder. I knew the sky was still cloudless, so I wondered, as I fell off to sleep, if the imitation cannonading was caused by some shifting of the Barne Glacier, or by snowslides on the great Erebus slopes.

16

~~~~~~

ADVENTURES OF SCOTT'S TERRA NOVA

EXPEDITION

1. WINTER JOURNEY

THE MIDWINTER manhauling sledge journey made in 1911 between Cape Evans and Cape Crozier via Hut Point by Edward A. Wilson, Henry R. Bowers and Apsley Cherry-Garrard has been described by Cherry-Garrard as a chapter of his book, *The Worst Journey in the World,* the subject of which is not the journey but Scott's whole last expedition, of which the traverse was a spectacular part. Although Cherry-Garrard's account is well known, Wilson's official report on the journey, addressed to Scott and included in the second volume of *Scott's Last Expedition,* is still relatively unknown. Of the two accounts I favor, on the whole, Wilson's: it is by far the more authoritative and I prefer its cool tone to the sometimes overwrought one of Cherry-Garrard's. It may be noted that Cherry-Garrard's account often makes use of Wilson's.

The journey was made primarily for a scientific reason: in order to obtain freshly laid eggs at the Emperor penguin rookery at Crozier, at that time the only known such rookery in the world. The Emperors nest in midwinter in extremely adverse climatic conditions. Wilson wished to obtain eggs with their embryos intact. A subsidiary objective of the journey was to experiment with a variety of sledging diets under very difficult manhauling circumstances.

During the Discovery Expedition Wilson envisioned a midwinter journey to Crozier, and after the expedition he outlined the scientific reasons for and the advantages of such a journey. He did this in *National Antarctic Expedition, 1901–1904*, "Zoology," Part 2.

"The possibility that we have in the Emperor penguin the nearest approach to a primitive form not only of a penguin but of a bird makes the future working out of its embryology a matter of the greatest possible importance. It was a great disappointment to us that although we discovered their breeding-ground, and although we were able to bring home a number of deserted eggs and chicks, we were not able to procure a series of early embryos by which alone the points of particular interest can be worked out. To have done this in a proper manner from the spot at which the *Discovery* wintered in McMurdo Sound would have involved us in endless difficulties, for it would have entailed the risks of sledge travelling in mid-winter with an almost total absence of light. It would at any time require that a party of three at least, with full camp equipment, should traverse about a hundred miles of the Barrier surface in the dark and should, by moonlight, cross over with rope and axe the immense pressure ridges which form a chaos of crevasses at Cape Crozier. These ridges, moreover, which have taken a party as much as two hours of careful work to cross by daylight, must be crossed and re-crossed at every visit to the breeding site in the bay. There is no possibility even by daylight of conveying over them the sledge or camping kit, and in the darkness of mid-winter the impracticability is still more obvious. Cape Crozier is a focus for wind and storm, where every breath is converted, by the configuration of Mounts Erebus and Terror, into a regular drifting blizzard full of snow. It is here . . . that on one journey or another we have had to lie patiently in sodden sleeping-bags for as many as five and seven days on end, waiting for the weather to change and make it possible for us to leave our tents at all. If, however, these dangers were overcome there would still be the difficulty of making the needful preparations from the eggs. The party would have to be on the scene at any rate early in July. Supposing that no eggs were found upon arrival, it would be well to spend the time in labelling the most likely birds, those for example that have taken up their stations close underneath the ice-cliffs. And if this were done it would be easier then to examine them daily by moonlight, if it and the weather generally were suitable: conditions, I must confess, not always easily obtained at Cape Crozier. But if by good luck things happened to go well, it would by this time be useful to have a shelter built of snow blocks on the sea-ice in which to work with the cooking lamp to prevent the freezing of the egg before the embryo was cut out, in order that fluid solutions might be handy for the various stages of its preparation; for it must be borne in mind that the temperature all the while may be anything between zero and −50° F. The whole work no doubt would be full of difficulty, but it would not be quite impossible, and it is with a view to helping those to whom the opportunity may occur in the future that this outline has been added of the difficulties that would surely beset their path."

Wilson was thirty-nine and Bowers was twenty-eight when they died with Scott about a half-year after the Crozier journey. Cherry-Garrard was twenty-four when he joined the expedition.

The Outward March

The three men left the hut at Cape Evans the morning of June 27, 1911. They carried six weeks' provisions stored on two nine-foot sledges in tandem; a venesta case containing scientific gear for handling Emperor penguins and their eggs; and such items as a pickax, ice axes, a shovel, Alpine rope and a good deal of green Willesden canvas. The loads came to about 250 pounds per man. For food they had pemmican, biscuits and water. For drink they had tea, and they were always to have hot water before turning in for the night. Their plan was to experiment with different combinations of food. Each man started with his own proportion of the three items. The results of the experiment were designed to benefit the attempt on the Pole. They carried no sugar, and before long they were to experience an intense craving for sweets. They had a double tent, the inside of which they were to brush down scrupulously whenever they broke camp, a procedure that greatly diminished the collection of ice on the upper two thirds of the tent.

Wilson was the party's leader. He had selected his two companions. Of the three, only he had been to the Antarctic previously. He had made the journey between Hut Point and Cape Crozier twice during the Discovery Expedition but never in winter. Even he was to be appalled by the severity of the conditions they encountered.

That first day they were supported by a party of five men, two of whom turned back at Little Razorback Island and the rest a bit beyond the Glacier Tongue. They camped off Castle Rock at 8 P.M. The night was starlit. During the day the temperature had ranged from —14.5° to —15°. The minimum at night was —26°.

Next day the going was heavy over a surface of "rough, rubbly salt sea ice with no snow on it." They lunched in the Discovery Hut, then went around Cape Armitage and soon met the Barrier edge, mounting a snow slope onto the Barrier. The Barrier at this point was some twelve feet higher than the sea ice. Flowing down from it was a stream of very cold air, whose temperature was —47°. Cherry-Garrard, removing his mitts in order to haul the better on the sledge ropes as the men pulled the sledges up the slope, had all his fingers frostbitten. The result was blisters up to an inch long, the liquid of which froze and caused him great pain whenever he had work to do. The temperature during the night was —56.5°.

At 9 A.M. it was —49°. The day was clear and calm. Curtains of aurora covered much of the eastern sky both day and night. During the day's march the temperature remained at —50°. Cherry-Garrard's big toes were blistered by frostbite, as were Wilson's heel and the sole of one foot. Cherry-Garrard, who was near-sighted, had to work without spectacles because the lenses fogged up and froze. He was to write that the only good time out of a twenty-four-hour day was breakfast, and that the darkness was what made things so very bad, for you had difficulty seeing where you were going and where necessary articles were. You had to bend frozen clothes and canvas to your needs. It took four hours from the time of awaking to the time the men got into harness. Sweat froze, accumulated, shook down one's clothes as ice. At night it partly thawed in the sleeping bags. Both clothes and bags were often like sheets of armor plate, in Cherry-Garrard's description. Each man had a reindeer-skin bag but Cherry-Garrard's was too large for him, consequently he shook badly during the cold nights.

On June 30 the Barrier surface was so resistant the men had to relay the sledges one at a time—by faint daylight from 11 A.M. to 3 P.M. and by candle lamp from 4:30 to 7:45 P.M. They marched 3¼ miles but traveled ten miles to accomplish it. The hauling was like pulling through sand, for in the extreme cold the sledge-runners, unable to melt the snow crystals, merely turned them over and over. There was much silence among the men. Wilson counseled that they do everything slowly. A great deal depended on his knowledge and judgment as a doctor. Often, having asked his companions about the condition of their feet, he would decide whether to camp or to continue marching for another hour. Cherry-Garrard believed that a wrong decision could mean disaster, for if one man was disabled it probably meant death for all. Bowers, the small, compact man, affectionately known as Birdie because of his prominent aquiline nose, had the greatest amount of body heat of the party, in Cherry-Garrard's opinion.

The cold was so extreme that your clothes could freeze quickly in such a position that it was impossible for you to turn your head. On one occasion Cherry-Garrard had to manhaul for four hours with his head stuck up ludicrously. After that experience the party were careful to set themselves in a hauling posture before their clothes froze. The morning of the thirtieth the temperature was $-55°$; at lunch it was almost $-62°$; on making camp it was $-66°$. No one had imagined that conditions could be so bad at sea level in the close vicinity of Ross Island.

On July 1 and 2 the men relayed full days. Cherry-Garrard wrote, "Sometimes it was difficult not to howl. I *did* want to howl many times every hour of these days and nights, but invented a formula instead, which I repeated to myself continually. Especially, I remember, it came in useful when at the end of the march with my feet frost-bitten, my heart beating slowly, my vitality at its lowest ebb, my body solid with cold, I used to seize the shovel and go on digging snow on to the tent skirting while the cook inside was trying to light the primus. 'You've got it in the neck—stick it—stick it— you've got it in the neck,' was the refrain, and I wanted every little bit of encouragement it would give me: then I would find myself repeating 'Stick it—stick it—stick it—stick it,' and then 'You've got it in the neck.'"

On July 2 the men saw the first of the new moon. Wilson noted, "As it passed exactly behind the summit of Erebus it gave us an extraordinary picture of an eruption." Three toes of one of Cherry-Garrard's feet were frostbitten, as well as the heel and a toe of the other. The party were burning much oil to keep them going. During the night Cherry-Garrard pricked six or seven blisters on his fingers and got much relief.

In the mornings the men would stuff their personal gear into the mouths of the sleeping bags before the bags froze. Thus they had a plug that, when removed, permitted them to make a start at entering the bags at night. They often had cramps in legs and abdomen. Bowers's abdomen was especially vulnerable to cramps. Cherry-Garrard endured heartburn because of the large proportion of fat in his diet. Wilson insisted that they spend seven hours in their bags each night, whether they were able to sleep or not.

Of Wilson, Cherry-Garrard later wrote, "Always patient, self-possessed, unruffled, he was the only man on earth, as I believe, who could have led this journey."

Of his companions he wrote, "In civilization men are taken at their own valuation because there are so many ways of concealment, and there is so little time, perhaps even so little understanding. Not so down South. These two men went through the Winter Journey and lived: later they went through the Polar Journey and died. They were gold, pure, shining, unalloyed. Words cannot express how good their companionship was.

"Through all these days, and those which were to follow, the worst I suppose in their dark severity that men have ever come through alive, no single hasty or angry word passed their lips. When, later, we were sure, so far as we can be sure of anything, that we must die, they were cheerful, and so far as I can judge their songs and cheery words were quite unforced. Nor were they ever flurried, though always as quick as the conditions would allow in moments of emergency. It is hard that often such men must go first when others far less worthy remain."

On July 4 snow fell and nothing was visible by which to steer, so the men stayed in their bags. On the fifth the surface was worse than ever, and relaying was necessary. The minimum night temperature was −75.3°. Next morning it was −70.2°, at noon −76.8°, at 5 P.M. it was −77°.

On the seventh and eighth there was more relaying work to be done. Cherry-Garrard wrote, "Our hearts were doing very gallant work. Towards the end of the march they were getting beaten and were finding it difficult to pump the blood out to our extremities. There were few days that Wilson and I did not get some part of our feet frost-bitten. As we camped, I suspect our hearts were beating comparatively slowly and weakly. Nothing could be done until a hot drink was ready—tea for lunch, hot water for supper. Directly we started to drink then the effect was wonderful: it was, said Wilson, like putting a hot-water bottle against your heart. The beats became very rapid and strong and you felt the warmth travelling outwards and downwards. Then you got your foot-gear off—puttees (cut in half and wound around the bottom of the trousers), finnesko, saennegrass, hair socks, and two pairs of woolen socks. Then you nursed back your feet and tried to believe you were glad —a frost-bite does not hurt until it begins to thaw. Later came the blisters, and then the chunks of dead skin."

July 8: very hard relaying.

On the ninth, fog, mist and falling snow made relaying impossible, but the men could haul the two sledges simultaneously on the improving surface. Walking in finneskoes, they had a sense of touch, and they depended increasingly on the sound of their footsteps to tell them if they were on solid or crevassed ice. The crevasses were becoming more frequent. The pressured ice creaked, groaned, banged and boomed around them.

On the tenth a blizzard from the south-southwest blew all day, forcing the party to lie in their bags. The morning of the eleventh the temperature was a very warm 7.8°. The wind, now from the southwest, was still hard and squally. The men remained in the tent this day and the next. On the thirteenth, after digging out the tent and sledges, they made an excellent march: 7½ miles in 7½ hours. On the fourteenth they ran into one of the higher pressure ridges. Turning north from it, they encountered crevasses but succeeded in getting clear of them. Wilson believed they were now entering the true path of the southerly blizzard.

Next day they could see the moraine shelf that faced the Knoll. It was there they planned to build their "stone hut," as Wilson called it. (Cherry-Garrard called it an igloo; Wilson consistently referred to it as a hut.) Wilson wrote that they had a short, steep, uphill three miles' pull over very hard and deep-cut sastrugi before they reached the shelf. They pitched their final outward camp in a large snow hollow some hundred and fifty yards below the ridge where they intended to build the igloo. On the ridge were loose rock masses, including crumbly volcanic lava and various erratics; gravel; and hard snow that could be cut into paving-stone slabs: all the materials needed for the construction of the igloo. The spot they selected was some seven yards down on the ridge's lee side. They believed the igloo would be safe from the southerly wind but it was just here that, according to Wilson, the upward suction was to be at its greatest.

From this spot they had what Wilson called a magnificent outlook. In the east was the Barrier with its pressure ridges some eight hundred feet below them. In the north and northeast was the Knoll, beyond which was the frozen Ross Sea. In the south they could see the way they had taken in climbing to their present position. Mount Terror's summit was sharp against the western sky.

The Stone Igloo and the Penguins

On the sixteenth the party, using a pick and shovel, worked on the igloo by daylight and as long as the waning moonlight lasted, Wilson and Bowers collecting rocks and piling up snow slabs and gravel, and Cherry-Garrard building up the walls. The snow was so hard that the use of a pick was futile; large blocks had to be chipped out with the shovel. The men counted on soon having a comfortable home from which to make excursions to the Emperor rookery.

They built four rock walls, leaving a door gap in the lee end. They had brought along a board that they now used as a door lintel. The igloo was about eight feet wide and ten feet long. A nine-foot sledge served as a cross rafter to support the green Willesden canvas roof, which was secured by lanyards to heavy rocks. It took the party the light of three days to finish the igloo. On the eighteenth they tried to set the roof in place. The temperature was around $-27°$, with a strong south-southwest wind, a combination that made work virtually impossible.

The following day was calm. Inasmuch as the next to the last can of oil was running low, and the party had resolved to leave the last can untouched for the homeward journey, they decided to spend the day in reaching the Emperor rookery and obtaining some blubber for the blubber stove they had carried with them. They started down at 9:30 A.M. with an empty sledge, two ice axes, harnesses, skinning tools and Alpine rope. Roped together, they used the sledge as a protection against snow-bridged crevasses. They had great difficulty with ice slopes, ice cliffs and pressure ridges, and Cherry-Garrard went into crevasses half a dozen times. They heard the metallic cries of the penguins but, unable to reach the rookery, gave up the attempt for that day and in the failing light cautiously and with much difficulty retraced their steps.

On the twentieth they arose at 3 A.M., secured the igloo's roof, had breakfast and headed for the rookery before day broke at 9:30.

This time they tried a new way down and slid and crawled towards the sea-ice rookery, leaving their sledge behind at a space between the ice and the rock that was just large enough for them to crawl through one at a time. Occasionally they had to cut steps in snow and ice. Wilson noted that there were present in the rookery only about a hundred Emperor penguins instead of the couple of thousand he had seen in 1902 and 1903. The hundred formed "a compact group under the ice cliffs of the Barrier" not far from where the men stood.

Wilson and Bowers killed and skinned three birds, collected six eggs (according to Wilson; Cherry-Garrard says they collected five), then returned to the ice foot where Cherry-Garrard was ready to help them up with some rope. Three eggs survived the return journey to Cape Evans and eventually arrived safely in London.

On returning to the igloo the men flensed a penguin skin. The birds were well blubbered; the blubber was about three quarters of an inch thick. Supper was cooked on the blubber stove. The blubber oil burned much better than seal oil, in Wilson's opinion. He wrote, "I was incapacitated for the time being by a sputter of hot oil catching me in one eye."

About the incident of Wilson's eye Cherry-Garrard wrote, ". . . with great difficulty we got the blubber stove to start, and it spouted a blob of boiling oil into Bill's eye [Bill was Wilson's nickname]. For the rest of the night he lay, quite unable to stifle his groans, obviously in very great pain: he told us afterwards that he thought his eye was gone."

Next day a heavy wind tended to lift the igloo's canvas roof off its supporting sledge, so the men piled slabs of icy snow on the canvas to steady it. They spent the daylight hours in packing the walls with soft snow, then fetched their tent from the hollow below the moraine shelf and pitched it on the lee side of the igloo, close to the door. Afterwards they moved into the igloo for the night. The wind was negligible but the sky was overcast. At around 3 A.M. a blizzard blew suddenly from the south.

The Blizzard

By 6:30 A.M. of the twenty-second it was blowing very hard from the south-southwest, with heavy drift. Bowers, on awaking, dis-

MAPS

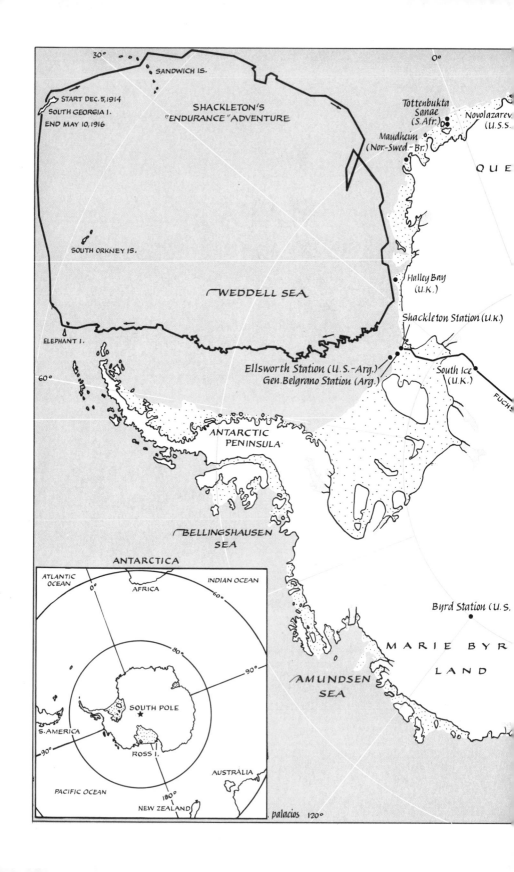

30°   0°

SANDWICH IS.

START DEC. 5,1914   SHACKLETON'S
SOUTH GEORGIA I.   "ENDURANCE" ADVENTURE
END MAY 10,1916

Tottenbukta
Sanae
(S. Afr.)   Novolazarev
(U.S.S.

Maudheim
(Nor.-Swed.-Br.)

QUE

SOUTH ORKNEY IS.

WEDDELL SEA

Halley Bay
(U.K.)

Shackleton Station (U.K.)

ELEPHANT I.

Ellsworth Station (U.S.-Arg.)   South Ice
Gen.Belgrano Station (Arg.)   (U.K.)

FUCHS

60°

ANTARCTIC
PENINSULA

BELLINGSHAUSEN
SEA

ANTARCTICA

ATLANTIC   INDIAN OCEAN
OCEAN   0°
            AFRICA   60°

80°

90°

S.AMERICA   Byrd Station (U.S.

SOUTH POLE   MARIE BYR
90°
                                   LAND
ROSS I.

AMUNDSEN
SEA

AUSTRALIA

PACIFIC OCEAN

180°

NEW ZEALAND   , palacios   120°

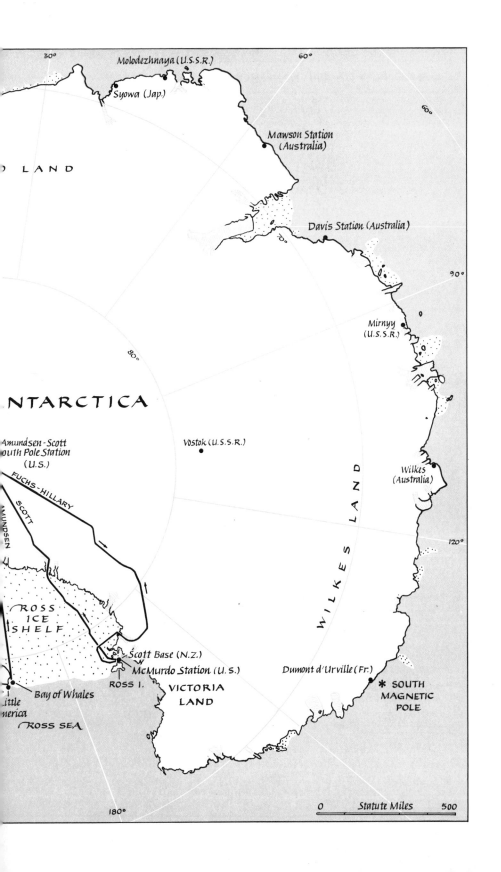

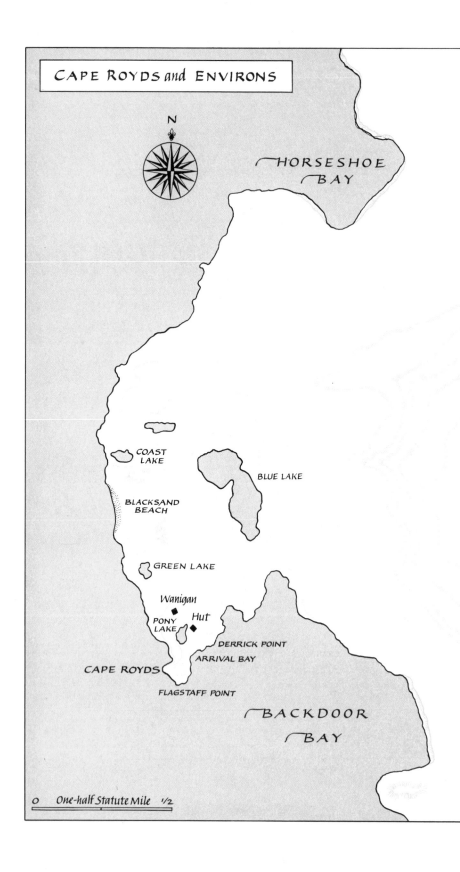

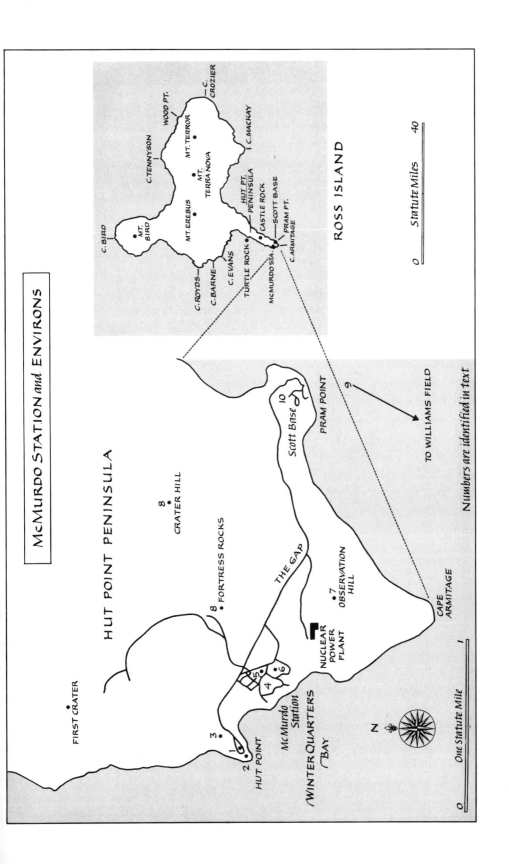

McMURDO STATION and ENVIRONS

HUT POINT PENINSULA

FIRST CRATER

HUT POINT

WINTER QUARTERS BAY

McMurdo Station

CRATER HILL 8

FORTRESS ROCKS 8

THE GAP

NUCLEAR POWER PLANT

OBSERVATION HILL 7

Scott Base

10

PRAM POINT

CAPE ARMITAGE

9

TO WILLIAMS FIELD

Numbers are identified in text

N

0   One Statute Mile   1

ROSS ISLAND

C. BIRD

MT. BIRD

C. ROYDS

C. BARNE

C. EVANS

MT. EREBUS

TURTLE ROCK

McMURDO STA.

CASTLE ROCK

SCOTT BASE

PRAM PT.

C. ARMITAGE

HUT PT. PENINSULA

MT. TERRA NOVA

MT. TERROR

C. MACKAY

C. TENNYSON

WOOD PT.

C. CROZIER

0   Statute Miles   40

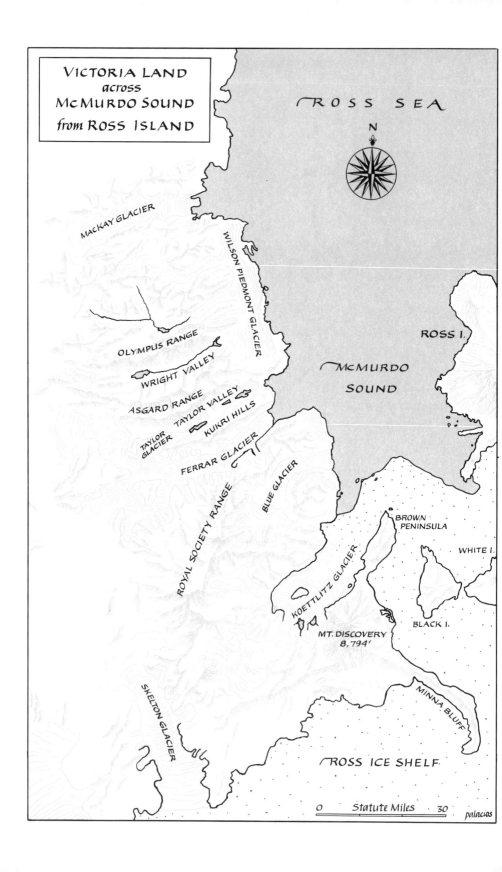

VICTORIA LAND
across
McMURDO SOUND
from ROSS ISLAND

ROSS SEA

N

MACKAY GLACIER

WILSON PIEDMONT GLACIER

ROSS I.

OLYMPUS RANGE

WRIGHT VALLEY

McMURDO
SOUND

ASGARD RANGE

TAYLOR VALLEY

TAYLOR
GLACIER

KUKRI HILLS

FERRAR GLACIER

BLUE GLACIER

ROYAL SOCIETY RANGE

BROWN
PENINSULA

WHITE I.

KOETTLITZ GLACIER

BLACK I.

MT. DISCOVERY
8,794'

SKELTON GLACIER

MINNA BLUFF

ROSS ICE SHELF

0   Statute Miles   30

palacios

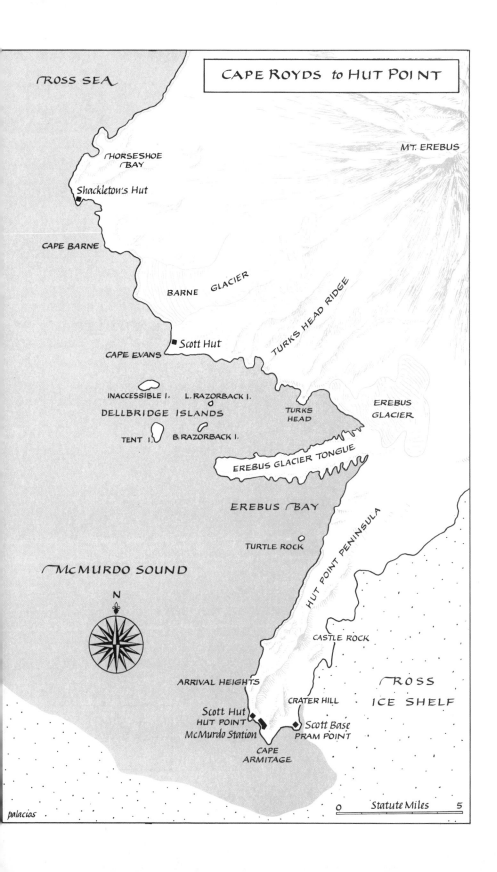

CAPE ROYDS to HUT POINT

ROSS SEA

HORSESHOE
BAY

Shackleton's Hut

CAPE BARNE

MT. EREBUS

BARNE GLACIER

TURKS HEAD RIDGE

Scott Hut

CAPE EVANS

INACCESSIBLE I.   L. RAZORBACK I.

DELLBRIDGE ISLANDS

TURKS
HEAD

EREBUS
GLACIER

TENT I.   B. RAZORBACK I.

EREBUS GLACIER TONGUE

EREBUS BAY

TURTLE ROCK

McMURDO SOUND

N

HUT POINT PENINSULA

CASTLE ROCK

ROSS

ARRIVAL HEIGHTS

CRATER HILL

ICE SHELF

Scott Hut
HUT POINT
McMurdo Station

Scott Base
PRAM POINT

CAPE
ARMITAGE

palacios

0   Statute Miles   5

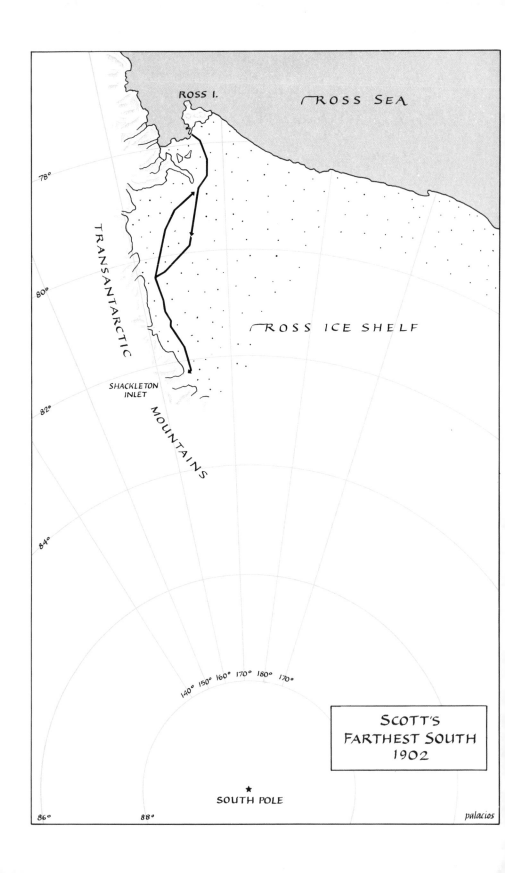

ROSS I.

ROSS SEA

TRANSANTARCTIC

ROSS ICE SHELF

SHACKLETON
INLET

MOUNTAINS

78°

80°

82°

84°

140° 150° 160° 170° 180° 170°

SCOTT'S
FARTHEST SOUTH
1902

★
SOUTH POLE

86°   88°

palacios

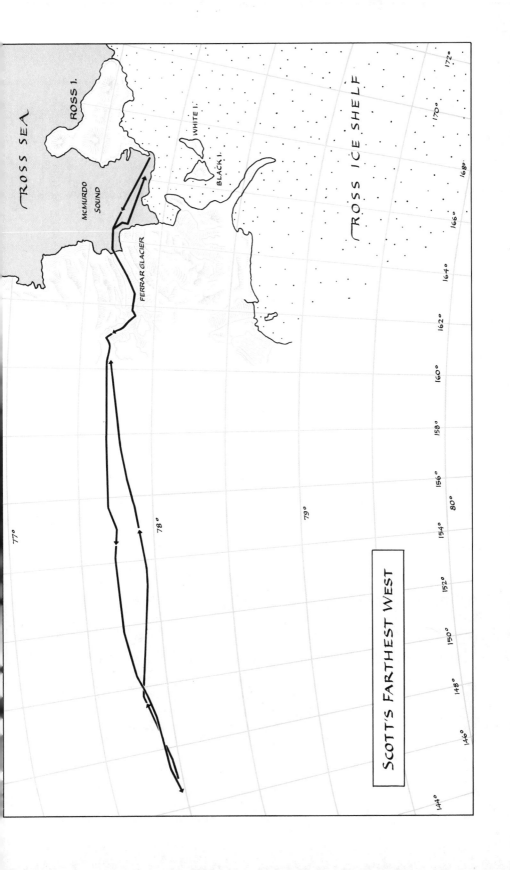

ROSS SEA

ROSS I.

McMURDO
SOUND

WHITE I.

BLACK I.

FERRAR GLACIER

ROSS ICE SHELF

SCOTT'S FARTHEST WEST

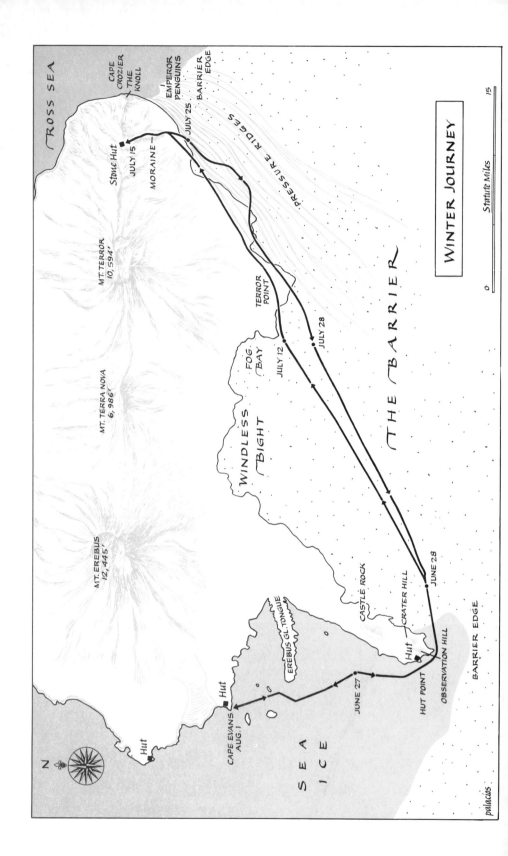

ROSS SEA

CAPE CROZIER
THE KNOLL
EMPEROR PENGUINS
BARRIER EDGE
Stone Hut
JULY 15
JULY 25
MORAINE

PRESSURE RIDGES

MT. TERROR
10,594'

MT. TERRA NOVA
6,986'

MT. EREBUS
12,445'

TERROR POINT

FOG BAY

JULY 12

JULY 28

WINDLESS BIGHT

THE BARRIER

JUNE 28

CASTLE ROCK

EREBUS GL. TONGUE

CRATER HILL

Hut

HUT POINT

OBSERVATION HILL

BARRIER EDGE

Hut

CAPE EVANS
AUG. 1

JUNE 27

Hut

S E A
I C E

N

WINTER JOURNEY

0   Statute Miles   15

palacios

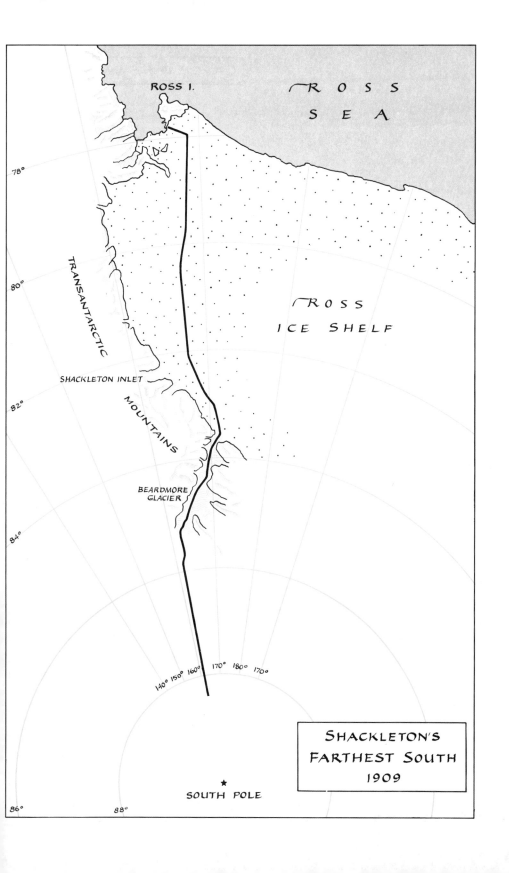

ROSS I.

ROSS
SEA

78°

TRANSANTARCTIC

80°

ROSS
ICE SHELF

SHACKLETON INLET

82°

MOUNTAINS

BEARDMORE
GLACIER

84°

140° 150° 160°   170°   180°   170°

SHACKLETON'S
FARTHEST SOUTH
1909

★
SOUTH POLE

86°   88°

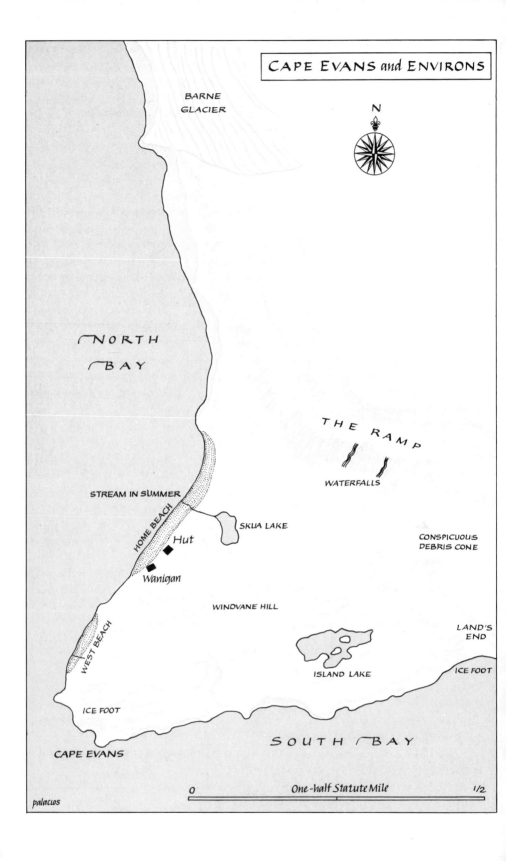

CAPE EVANS and ENVIRONS

BARNE
GLACIER

N

NORTH
BAY

THE RAMP

WATERFALLS

STREAM IN SUMMER

HOME BEACH

SKUA LAKE

Hut

CONSPICUOUS
DEBRIS CONE

Wanigan

WINDVANE HILL

LAND'S
END

WEST BEACH

ISLAND LAKE

ICE FOOT

ICE FOOT

SOUTH BAY

CAPE EVANS

0   One-half Statute Mile   1/2

palacios

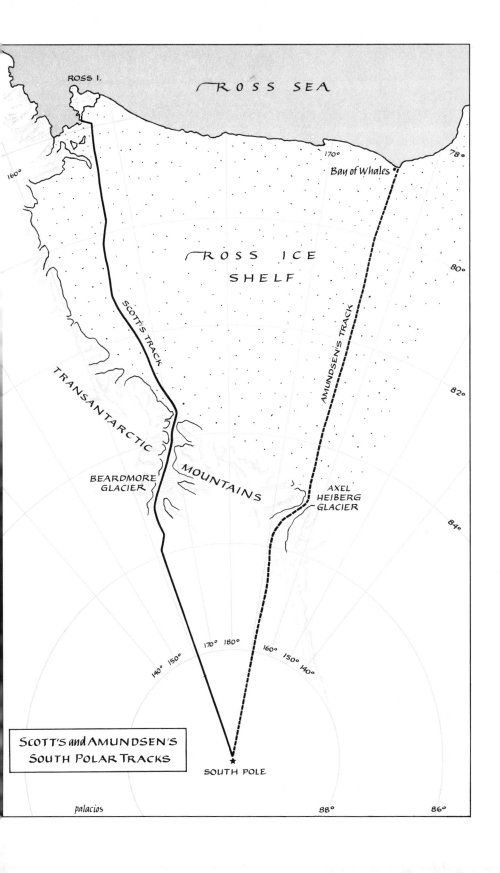

ROSS I.

ROSS SEA

170°

78°

160°

Bay of Whales

ROSS ICE

SHELF

80°

SCOTT'S TRACK

AMUNDSEN'S TRACK

82°

TRANSANTARCTIC

BEARDMORE
GLACIER

MOUNTAINS

AXEL
HEIBERG
GLACIER

84°

170° 180°

160°

150° 140°

140° 150°

SCOTT'S and AMUNDSEN'S
SOUTH POLAR TRACKS

SOUTH POLE

palacios

88°

86°

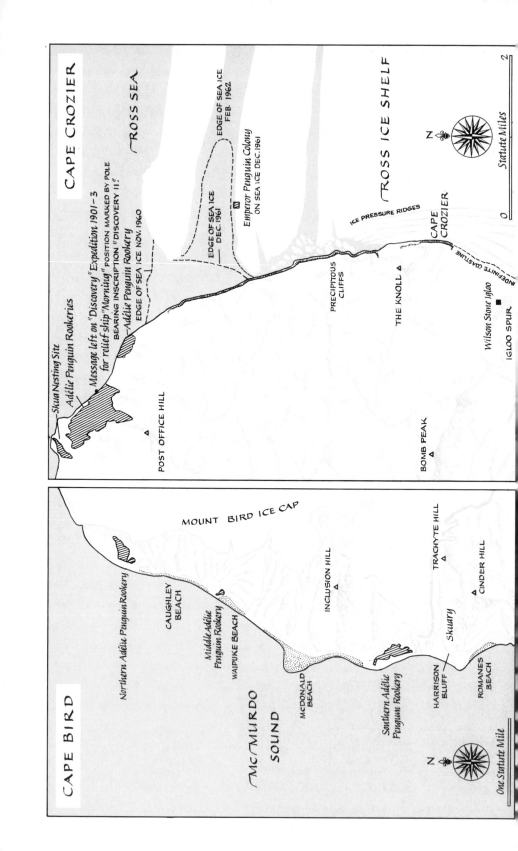

CAPE BIRD

MOUNT BIRD ICE CAP

Northern Adélie Penguin Rookery

CAUGHLEY BEACH

Middle Adélie Penguin Rookery

WAIPUKE BEACH

McDONALD BEACH

INCLUSION HILL

McMURDO SOUND

Southern Adélie Penguin Rookery

Skuary

HARRISON BLUFF

TRACHYTE HILL

CINDER HILL

ROMANES BEACH

N

One Statute Mile

CAPE CROZIER

ROSS SEA

Skua Nesting Site

Adélie Penguin Rookeries

Message left on "Discovery" Expedition 1901–3
for relief ship "Morning" position marked by pole
bearing inscription "DISCOVERY 11."

Adélie Penguin Rookery

EDGE OF SEA ICE NOV. 1960

EDGE OF SEA ICE
DEC. 1961

EDGE OF SEA ICE
FEB. 1962

Emperor Penguin Colony
ON SEA ICE DEC. 1961

POST OFFICE HILL

PRECIPITOUS CLIFFS

THE KNOLL

ICE PRESSURE RIDGES

CAPE CROZIER

ROSS ICE SHELF

INDEFINITE COASTLINE

BOMB PEAK

Wilson Stone Igloo

IGLOO SPUR

N

Statute Miles

0   1   2

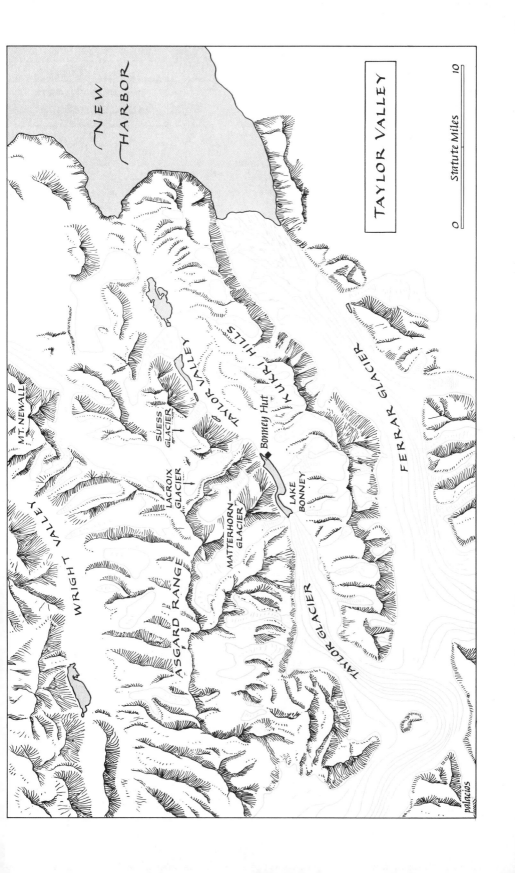

NEW HARBOR

MT. NEWALL

WRIGHT VALLEY

SUESS GLACIER

TAYLOR VALLEY

KUKRI HILLS

LACROIX GLACIER

ASGARD RANGE

Bonney Hut

MATTERHORN GLACIER

LAKE BONNEY

FERRAR GLACIER

TAYLOR GLACIER

palacios

TAYLOR VALLEY

0   Statute Miles   10

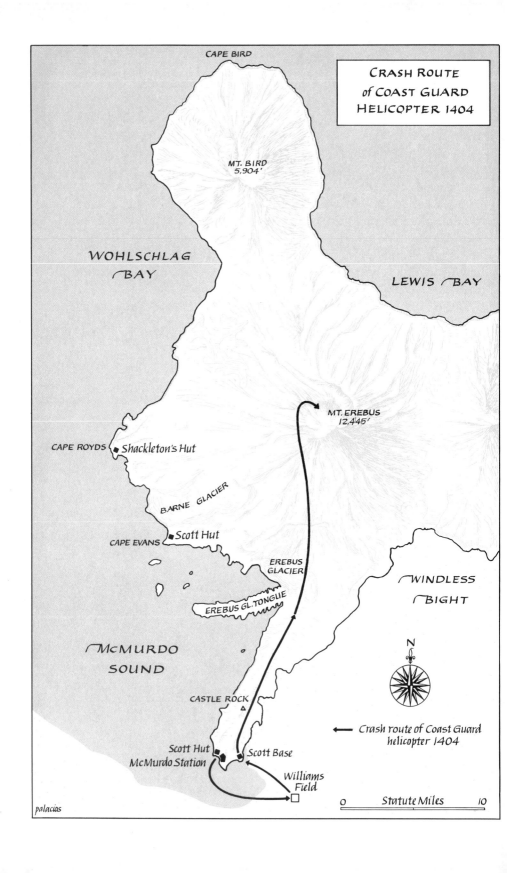

CAPE BIRD

CRASH ROUTE
of COAST GUARD
HELICOPTER 1404

MT. BIRD
5,904'

WOHLSCHLAG
BAY

LEWIS BAY

MT. EREBUS
12,445'

CAPE ROYDS ● Shackleton's Hut

BARNE GLACIER

● Scott Hut

CAPE EVANS

EREBUS
GLACIER

 WINDLESS
BIGHT

EREBUS GL. TONGUE

McMURDO
SOUND

N

CASTLE ROCK
△

← Crash route of Coast Guard
helicopter 1404

Scott Hut ■■ Scott Base
McMurdo Station

Williams
Field
□

palacios

0   Statute Miles   10

covered that the tent had disappeared; but the gear that had been left in the tent was intact. Bowers and Cherry-Garrard collected it and passed it to Wilson, who was in the igloo. Fortunately very little was lost. The finneskoes were there, as well as some smaller gear. Two flat parts of the cooker were missing; they were never found.

Cherry-Garrard wrote:

"I do not know what time it was when I awoke. It was calm, with that absolute silence which can be so soothing or so terrible as circumstances dictate. Then there came a sob of wind, and all was still again. Ten minutes and it was blowing as though the world was having a fit of hysterics. The earth was torn in pieces: the indescribable fury and roar of it all cannot be imagined.

"'Bill, Bill the tent has gone,' was the next I remember—from Bowers shouting at us again and again through the door."

He reported that Wilson and Bowers "sang quite a lot of songs and hymns, snatches of which reached me every now and then, and I chimed in, somewhat feebly I suspect. . . . The wind made just the same noise as an express train running fast through a tunnel if you have both the windows down.

"I can well believe that neither of my companions gave up hope for an instant. They must have been frightened, but they were never disturbed. As for me I never had any hope at all; and when the roof went I felt that this was the end. What else could I think? We had spent days in reaching this place through the darkness in cold such as had never been experienced by human beings. We had been out for four weeks under conditions in which no man had existed previously for more than a few days, if that. During this time we had seldom slept except from sheer physical exhaustion, as men sleep on the rack; and every minute of it we had been fighting for the bed-rock necessaries of bare existence, and always in the dark. We had kept ourselves going by enormous care of our feet and hands and bodies, by burning oil, and by having plenty of hot fatty food. Now we had no tent, one tin of oil left out of six, and only part of our cooker. When we were lucky and not too cold we could almost wring water from our clothes, and directly we got out of our sleeping-bags we were frozen into solid sheets of armoured ice. In cold temperatures with all the advantages of a tent over our heads we were already taking more than an hour of fierce struggling and cramp to get into our sleeping-bags—so frozen were they and so long did it take us to thaw our way in. No! Without the tent we were dead men."

Wilson wrote:

"Inside the hut we were now being buried by fine snow drift, which was coming through the cracks of the walls in fine spouts, especially through the weather wall and over the door in the lee wall. We tried to plug the inlets with socks, but as fast as we closed one the drift came in by another, and heaps of soft drift gradually piled up to 6 and 8 inches on everything. It seems that the strong wind blowing over the roof of the hut sucked it upwards and tried hard to lift it off, producing so much suction into the interior of the hut that the fine drift came in everywhere notwithstanding our day spent in packing every crack and cranny. When there was no more snow drift to come in, fine black moraine dust came in and blackened everything like coal dust. The canvas roof, upon which we had put heavy slabs of icy snow, was lifted clean off and was stretched upwards and outwards like a tight dome and as taut as a drum. There was no chafe or friction anywhere except along the lee end wall top, and there we plugged every space between the canvas and the wall stones with pyjama jackets, fur mits, socks, &. So long as the ice slabs remained on the top, moreover, there was no flapping and everything seemed fairly secure. Our only fear was that to allow of the admission of so much drift and dust through the weather wall there must have been openings in our packing—and we thought it possible that by degrees the upward tension might draw the canvas roof out. We could not be quite certain that the ice-slabs were not being eaten away. This, however, proved not to be our danger; the slabs remained sound to the end and the canvas buried in the walls did not draw anywhere at all, even for an inch.

"The storm continued unabated all day, and we decided to cook a meal on the blubber stove. We felt a great satisfaction in having three penguin skins to cook with for some days, so that we could last out any length of blizzard without coming to our last can of oil.

"We got the blubber stove going once or twice, but it insisted on suddenly going out for no apparent reason. And before we had boiled any water, in trying to restart it with the spirit lamp provided for the purpose, the feed-pipe suddenly dropped off, unsoldered, rendering the whole stove useless. We therefore poured the melted oil into tins and lamps for the journey home in case our candles ran out, and for drying or thawing out socks and mits."

The men, taking stock of their situation, resolved to do without a hot meal so long as the blizzard kept them physically inactive. They agreed that it was too hazardous to make inroads on their last can of oil in the uncertain hope of finding and killing a seal and improvising a new blubber stove.

On the twenty-third Wilson wrote, "Bowers estimated the wind at force 11 and noted it was blowing with almost continuous storm force, with very slight lulls followed by squalls of great violence.

"About noon the canvas roof of the hut was carried away, and the storm continued unabated all day, but latterly without much drift.

"It happened that this was my birthday—and we spent it lying in our bags without a roof or a meal, wishing the wind would drop, while the snow drifted over us.

"The roof went as follows. We saw, as soon as light showed through the canvas in the early morning, that the snow blocks on the top had all been blown off, and that the upward strain was now as bad as ever, with a greater tendency to flap at the lee end wall. And where the canvas was fixed in over the door it began to work on the heavy stones which held it down, jerking and shaking them so that it threatened to throw them down. Bowers was trying all he could to jam them tight with pyjama jackets and bamboos, and in this I was helping him when the canvas suddenly ripped, and in a moment I saw about six rents all along the lee wall top, and in another moment we were under the open sky with the greater part of the roof flapped to shreds. The noise was terrific, and rocks began to tumble in off the walls on to Bowers and Cherry, happily without hurting them, and in a smother of drift Bowers and I bolted into our bags, and in them the three of us lay listening to the flap of the ragged ends of canvas over our heads, which sounded like a volley of pistol shots going on for hour after hour. As we lay there I think we were all revolving plans for making a tent now to get back to Hut Point with, out of the floorcloth on which we lay—the only piece of canvas now left us, except for the pieces still firmly embedded in the hut walls. We were all warm enough, though wet, as we had carried a great deal of snow into the bags with us, and every time we looked out more drift which was accumulating over us would fall in. I hoped myself that this would not prove to be one of the five- or eight-day blizzards which we had experienced at Cape Crozier in days gone by."

By 6:30 A.M. the blizzard had subsided. The men lit the primus and had a hot meal, the first in twenty-four hours, the tent floor-cloth covering their heads. Then they went out to look for the tent.

"Everywhere," wrote Wilson, "we found shreds of green canvas roof the size of a pocket-handkerchief, but not a sign of the tent, until a loud shout from Bowers, who had gone more east to the top of a ridge than Cherry and I, told us he had seen it. He hurried down, and slid about a hundred yards down a hard snow slope, sitting in his haste, and there we joined him where he had found the whole tent hardly damaged at all, a quarter of a mile from where we had pitched it. One of the poles had been twisted right out of the cap, and the lower stops of the tent lining had all carried away more or less but the tent itself was intact and untorn.

"We brought it back, pitched it in the old spot in the snow hollow below our hut, and then brought down our bags and cooker and all essential gear, momentarily expecting the weather to break on us again. It looked as thick as could be and close at hand in the south."

They concluded that although it was very disappointing to have seen so little of the Emperors, given their present condition they had better start for Hut Point the next day. They made a depot in a corner of the igloo for possible future use.

By comparison with Wilson's account of the blizzard, Cherry-Garrard's, as of the whole winter journey, is flushed with excitement and sometimes verges on melodrama.

"I followed Bill down the slope. We could find nothing. But, as we searched, we heard a shout somewhere below and to the right. We got on a slope, slipped, and went sliding down quite unable to stop ourselves, and came upon Birdie with the tent, the outer lining still on the bamboos. Our lives had been taken away and given back to us.

"We were so thankful we said nothing. . . . If that tent went again we were going with it. We made our way back up the slope with it, carrying it solemnly and reverently, precious as though it were something not quite of the earth. And we dug it in as tent was never dug in before; not by the igloo, but in the old place farther down where we had first arrived. And while Bill was doing this Birdie and I went back to the igloo and dug and scratched away the drift inside until we had found nearly all our gear. . . . We loaded up the sledge and pushed it down the slope. I don't know how Birdie was feeling, but I felt so weak that it was the greatest labour. The blizzard looked right on top of us.

"We had another meal, and we wanted it: as the good hoosh ran down into our feet and hands, and up into our cheeks and ears and brains, we discussed what we would do next. Birdie was all for another go at the Emperor penguins. Dear Birdie, he never would admit that he was beaten—I don't know that he ever really was! . . . There could really be no common-sense doubt: we had to go back, and we were already very doubtful whether we should ever manage to get into our sleeping-bags in very low temperature, so ghastly had they become."

Return to Cape Evans

On July 25 the party made an early start for winter quarters but ran into a gale freshening from the southwest. According to Cherry-Garrard, "The strain and want of sleep was getting me in the neck, and Bill looked very bad." He thought that Bowers was by far the strongest of the group. The men were forced to camp after a march of only a mile. The gale continued during the night.

Cherry-Garrard wrote: "I was feeling as if I should crack, and accepted Birdie's eider-down. It was wonderfully self-sacrificing of him: more than I can write. I felt a brute to take it, but I was getting useless unless I got some sleep which my big bag would not allow. Bill and Birdie kept on telling me to do less: that I was doing more than my share of work: but I think that I was getting more and more weak. Birdie kept wonderfully strong: he slept most of the night: the difficulty for him was to get into his bag without going to sleep. He kept the meteorological log untiringly but some of these nights he had to give it up for the time because he could not keep awake. He used to fall asleep with his pannikin in his hand and let it fall: and sometimes he had the primus.

"Bill's bag was getting hopeless: it was really too small for an eider-down and was splitting all over the place: great long holes. He never consciously slept for nights: he did sleep a bit, for we heard him. Except for this night, and the next when Birdie's eider-down was still fairly dry, I never consciously slept; except that I used to wake for five or six nights running with the same nightmare—that we were drifted up, and that Bill and Birdie were passing the gear into my bag, cutting it open to do so, or some other variation,—I did not know that I had been asleep at all."

The gale did not end until all the daylight of the following day was gone, so the party made only half a day's march. Several times they found themselves stepping into snow-covered crevasses. Then the wind fell, the sky cleared and the temperature dropped from —21.5° at 11 A.M. to —45° at 9 P.M. The men pitched camp among the pressure ridges on snow that was soft and deep.

On the twenty-seventh the party started marching with the coming of daylight. During the day Wilson, having put a foot into a crevasse, shouted a warning but Bowers fell in and out of sight, hanging by his harness. Wilson wrote, "We were too close to one another in our harness and the sledge followed us and bridged the crevasse. I had hold of Bowers' harness, while Cherry lowered a bowline on the end of the Alpine rope into which Bowers got his foot, and then by alternately hauling on one and the other we got him up again. After this, for the next few days while we were on doubtful ground, I went ahead with 12 or 15 feet of rope on my trace, and so was able to give good warning and to change the course easily if I found we were getting on to bad ground."

Next day, making six and three quarter miles, the men came into view of the Western Mountains, Mount Discovery and Hut Point Peninsula. On the twenty-ninth they marched six and a half miles. The minimum temperature for the night was —66°. The following day they made seven and a half miles in perfect weather. There was much more daylight now.

Cherry-Garrard wrote:

"I do not think it took us less than an hour to get a hot meal to our lips: pemmican followed by hot water in which we soaked our biscuits. For lunch we had tea and biscuits: for breakfast, pemmican, biscuits and tea. We could not have managed more food bags— three were bad enough, and the lashings of everything were like wire. . . .

"The hoosh got down into our feet: we nursed back frost-bites: and we were all the warmer for having got our dry foot-gear on before supper. Then we started to get into our bags.

"Birdie's bag fitted him beautifully, though perhaps it would have been a little small with an eider-down inside. He must have had a greater heat supply than other men; for he never had serious trouble with his feet, while ours were constantly frost-bitten: he slept, I should be afraid to say how much, longer than we did, even in these last days: it was a pleasure, lying awake practically all night, to hear his snores. He turned his bag inside out from fur to skin, and skin to fur, many times during the journey, and thus got rid of a lot of moisture which came out as snow or actual knobs of ice. When we did turn our bags the only way was to do so directly we turned out, and even then you had to be quick before the bag froze. Getting out of the tent at night it was quite a race to get back to your bag before it hardened. Of course this was in the lowest temperatures. . . .

"I do not believe that any man, however sick he is, has a much worse time than we had in those bags, shaking with cold until our backs would almost break. . . .

"The horrors of that return journey are blurred to my memory and I know they were blurred to my body at the time. I think this applies to all of us, for we were much weakened and callous at the time. . . . I know that we slept on the march; for I woke up when I bumped against Birdie, and Birdie woke when he bumped against me. I think Bill steering out in front managed to keep awake. . . . The day's march was bliss compared to the night's rest, and both were awful. We were about as bad as men can be and do good travelling: but I never heard a word of complaint, nor, I believe, an oath, and I saw self-sacrifice standing every test. . . . 'You've got it in the neck, stick it, you've got it in the neck'—it was always running in my head.

"And we *did* stick it. How good the memories of those days are. With jokes about Birdie's picture hat: with songs we remembered off the gramophone: with ready words of sympathy for frost-bitten feet: with generous smiles for poor jests: with suggestions of happy beds to come. We did not forget the Please and Thank you, which mean much in such circumstances, and all the little links with decent civilization which we could still keep going. I'll swear there was still a grace about us when we staggered in. And we kept our tempers—even with God."

On the thirty-first they covered five and a half miles in as many hours by the time they reached the Barrier's edge off Pram Point. The temperature was −57°. They lunched on the sea ice, then made their way to Cape Armitage, and over rough sea ice from the cape to Hut Point. They camped in the Discovery Hut, where they had a relatively comfortable night, pitching a dry tent left there, lighting two primuses, drinking much cocoa and falling asleep between mouthfuls. They spent three hours in their bags before awaking at 3 A.M., hoping to reach Cape Evans before dinner. A strong easterly wind kept them in the hut. They started marching at 11 A.M. when the wind subsided, and camped for lunch at 4:30, having made eight miles from the hut.

They arrived at the hut on Cape Evans on the thirty-sixth day of their absence. The door of the hut opened and a voice said, according to Cherry-Garrard, "Good God! here is the Crozier Party." Cherry-Garrard reported that Scott remarked, "But, look here, you know, this is the hardest journey that has ever been made."

On August 2 Scott wrote in his diary, "The Crozier Party returned last night after enduring for five weeks the hardest conditions on record. They looked more weather-worn than anyone I have yet seen. Their faces were scarred and wrinkled, their eyes dull, their hands whitened and creased with the constant exposure to damp and cold, yet the scars of frostbite were very few and this evil had never seriously assailed them. The main part of their afflictions arose, and very obviously, from sheer lack of sleep, and to-day after a night's rest our travellers are very different in appearance and mental capacity. . . .

"Wilson is very thin, but this morning very much his keen, wiry self—Bowers is quite himself to-day. Cherry-Garrard is slightly puffy in the face and still looks worn. It is evident that he has suffered most severely—but Wilson tells me that his spirit never wavered for a moment. Bowers has come through best, all things considered, and I believe he is the hardest traveller that ever undertook a Polar journey, as well as one of the most undaunted; more by hint than by direct statement I gather his value to the party, his untiring energy and the astonishing physique which enables him to continue to work under conditions which are absolutely paralysing to others. Never was such a sturdy, active, undefeatable little man. . . .

"Wilson is disappointed at seeing so little of the penguins, but to me and to everyone who has remained here the result of this effort is the appeal it makes to our imagination as one of the most gallant stories in Polar History. That men should wander forth in the depth of a Polar night to face the most dismal cold and the fiercest gales in darkness is something new; that they should have persisted in this effort in spite of every adversity for five full weeks is heroic.

It makes a tale for our generation which I hope may not be lost in the telling."

2. THE SCOTT TRAGEDY

It is ironic that Scott, who invalided Shackleton home during the Discovery Expedition and who not only begrudged him the use of the Discovery Hut but all of the McMurdo Sound area as well, should have imitated certain major examples of Shackleton's Nimrod Expedition. Like Shackleton he brought ponies on his Terra Nova Expedition; like Shackleton he experimented with motorized transportation (two motor sledges in his case, not a motorcar as in Shackleton's); like Shackleton he headed due south on the Barrier instead of hugging the western coast as he had done previously; and like Shackleton he used the Beardmore Glacier as a means of crossing the Transantarctic Mountains and ascending to the polar plateau. This evidenced his respect for Shackleton; but he would have done well to avoid Shackleton's example in the use of motorized transportation and ponies and to heed Nansen's authoritative opinion (greatly valued by Amundsen) regarding the value of dogs in sledging. Cherry-Garrard wrote in *The Worst Journey in the World*, "Scott had set his heart upon the success of the motors. He had run them in Norway and Switzerland; and everything was done that care and forethought could suggest. At the back of his mind, I feel sure, was the wish to abolish the cruelty which the use of ponies and dogs necessarily entails."

As for Scott's luck with the ponies, Cherry-Garrard wrote in the same work, "We left New Zealand with nineteen ponies, seventeen of which were destined for the Main Party and two for the help of Campbell in the exploration of King Edward VII's Land. Two of these died in the big gale at sea, and we landed fifteen ponies at Cape Evans in January [1911]. Of these we lost six on the Depôt Journey, while Hackenschmidt, who was a vicious beast, sickened and wasted away in our absence, for no particular reason that we could discover, until there was nothing to do but shoot him. Thus eight only out of the original seventeen Main Party ponies which started from New Zealand were left by the beginning of the winter."

Amundsen's expedition of 1910–12, using Nansen's old ship, the *Fram*, originally intended as a North Polar voyage, dramatically

changed character when Amundsen reversed course at sea and
sailed to Madeira, from which he cabled Scott in Melbourne the
terse news: "Madeira. Am going south. Amundsen." This could
mean only one thing to Scott: that Amundsen intended to be first at
the Pole. Thus the race between the Norwegian and the English
parties began, a race that for a time Scott refused to acknowledge
to himself but which he increasingly admitted in his polar journey
diary.

Amundsen (1872–1928) sailed from Madeira to the Ross Sea
without calling at any port and established a base at the Bay of
Whales on the Ross Ice Shelf, in almost the very place that Shackleton a few years earlier had rejected as being too hazardous because
it was in danger of calving off from the shelf and floating out to
sea as a tabular berg. Amundsen was convinced that the shelf at
this point was grounded and therefore safe. The base placed him
some sixty miles closer to the Pole than Scott was at Cape Evans.
In later years Cherry-Garrard wrote that the Scott party had badly
underestimated Amundsen's abilities.

By 1910 Amundsen had had considerable polar experience. He
was not a newcomer to the Antarctic. He had been first mate on the
Belgica Expedition of 1897, which was the first to winter over on
the continent. He knew skiing, sledging and sledge dogs well and
was able to make brilliant decisions based on limited information.
Instead of depending, as Scott did, on the Beardmore Glacier route
to the polar plateau, he used the hitherto unknown Axel Heiberg
Glacier (which he named), and the glacier served him well. He
relied heavily on dogs. He did not mistrust them in polar work as
Scott did and he did not believe in the value of manhauling
sledges, in which Scott seemed at times to have an almost mystical
faith. Also, he had no qualms in following a carefully devised plan
to shoot dogs along the polar route and to feed them to the survivors, or in nourishing himself and his companions with dog cutlets.

He wrote in *My Life as an Explorer*, "All my experience in Polar
work had convinced me that dogs were the only practicable
draught animals for use in snow and ice. They are quick, strong,
sure-footed, intelligent, and able to negotiate any terrain that man
himself can traverse. Scott, on the other hand, had come South
equipped with motor sledges, which had immediately demonstrated
their impracticability over the surface of ice and snow. He had

brought also—and to these he pinned his fate finally—a number of Shetland [sic] ponies. I was confident that this was a fatal mistake, and much to my sorrow it was in part the cause of Scott's tragic end."

Amundsen landed on the ice shelf with one hundred sixteen dogs and erected a hut some two miles inland. He started for the Pole October 20, 1911 (Scott started November 1), with four companions, four sledges and fifty-two dogs and reached it December 14, beating the Scott party by a little more than a month. He remained at the Pole two days to fix his position. His polar journey was rapid and easy in contrast with Scott's.

When the Scott party learned of Amundsen's presence at the Bay of Whales (this was in February 1911), in the excitement and tension of the moment they resented him as an intruder, a deceiver, an adventurer and as someone who had no interest in scientific research but only wished to capture the Pole. On February 22 Scott noted in his diary (all quotations from him in this chapter are from the first volume of *Scott's Last Expedition*), "One thing only fixes itself definitely in my mind. The proper, as well as the wiser, course for us is to proceed exactly as though this had not happened. To go forward and do our best for the honour of the country without fear or panic.

"There is no doubt that Amundsen's plan is a very serious menace to ours. He has a shorter distance to the Pole by 60 miles—I never thought he could have got so many dogs safely to the ice. His plan for running them seems excellent. But above and beyond all he can start his journey early in the season—an impossible condition with ponies."

To his wife Scott wrote, "I don't know what to think of Amundsen's chances. If he gets to the Pole, it must be before we do, as he is bound to travel fast with dogs and pretty certain to start early. On this account I decided at a very early date to act exactly as I should have done had he not existed. Any attempt to race must have wrecked my plan, besides which it doesn't appear the sort of thing one is out for.

"Possibly you will have heard something before this reaches you. Oh! and there are all sorts of possibilities. In any case you can rely on my not doing or saying anything foolish—only I'm afraid you must be prepared for the chance of finding our venture much belittled.

"After all, it is the work that counts, not the applause that follows."

The Scott party were wrong in their judgment of Amundsen's character. Amundsen made no pretensions to being concerned with scientific discovery. His book about his expedition, *The South Pole*, exemplifies the vividness, modesty and admirable simplicity of his style in general. He was intelligent, brave and dedicated. With the Italian explorer, Umberto Nobile, he crossed the North Pole by dirigible in 1926. In 1928, when Nobile's airship, *Italia,* was wrecked on its return from the North Pole, Amundsen went to search for him, despite the fact that by then he had contempt for the man. He was lost over the Arctic seas and no trace of him was found.

Scott's polar journey was begun by the polar party of four—Scott, Wilson, Lawrence E. G. ("Titus") Oates and Petty Officer Edgar Evans—and two supporting teams of four men each, one of which included Bowers. Although the expedition's surviving ten ponies were helpful in many respects, they could not endure the severe conditions of the journey. Their fate was recorded by Scott in his diary.

December 5. "Noon. We awoke this morning to a raging, howling blizzard. The blows we have had hitherto have lacked the very fine powdery snow—that especial feature of the blizzard. Today we have it fully developed. After a minute or two in the open one is covered from head to foot. The temperature is high, so that what falls or drives against one sticks. The ponies—head, tails, legs, and all parts not protected by their rugs—are covered with ice; the animals are standing deep in snow, the sledges are almost covered, and huge drifts above the tents [sic]. We have had breakfast, rebuilt the walls [snow walls to afford some protection for the ponies], and are now again in our bags. One cannot see the next tent, let alone the land. What on earth does such weather mean at this time of year? It is more than our share of ill-fortune, I think, but the luck may turn yet. I doubt if any party could travel in such weather even with the wind, certainly no one could travel against it.

"Is there some widespread atmospheric disturbance which will be felt everywhere in this region as a bad season, or are we merely the victims of exceptional local conditions? If the latter, there is food for thought in picturing our small party struggling against adversity in one place whilst others go smilingly forward in the sunshine.

How great may be the element of luck! No foresight—no procedure —could have prepared us for this state of affairs. Had we been ten times as experienced or certain of our aim we should not have expected such rebuffs.

"11 P.M.—It has blown hard all day with quite the greatest snowfall I remember. The drifts about the tents are simply huge. The temperature was +27° this forenoon, and rose to +31° in the afternoon, at which time the snow melted as it fell on anything but the snow, and, as a consequence, there are pools of water on everything, the tents are wet through, also the wind clothes, night boots, &; water drips from the tent poles and door, lies on the floorcloth, soaks the sleeping-bags, and makes everything pretty wretched. If a cold snap follows before we have had time to dry our things, we shall be mighty uncomfortable. Yet after all it would be humorous enough if it were not for the seriousness of delay—we can't afford that, and it's real hard luck that it should come at such a time. The wind shows signs of easing down, but the temperature does not fall and the snow is as wet as ever—not promising signs of abatement."

December 6. "Noon. Miserable, utterly miserable. We have camped in the 'Slough of Despond.' The tempest rages with unabated violence. The temperature has gone to +33°; everything in the tent is soaking. People returning from the outside look exactly as though they had been in a heavy shower of rain. They drip pools on the floorcloth. The snow is steadily climbing higher about walls, ponies, tents, and sledges. The ponies look utterly desolate. Oh! but this is too crushing, and we are only 12 miles from the Glacier. A hopeless feeling descends on one and is hard to fight off. What immense patience is needed for such occasions!

"11 P.M.—At 5 there came signs of a break at last, and now one can see the land, but the sky is still overcast and there is a lot of snow about. The wind also remains fairly strong and the temperature high. It is not pleasant, but if no worse in the morning we can get on at last. We are very, very wet."

December 7. "The storm continues and the situation is now serious. One small feed remains for the ponies after to-day, so that we must either march to-morrow or sacrifice the animals. That is not the worst; with the help of the dogs we could get on, without doubt. [Two teams of twenty-three dogs driven by two men were being used to carry pony fodder and to lay depots for the returning parties.] The serious part is that we have this morning started our

Summit rations—that is to say, the food calculated from the Glacier depôt has been begun. The first supporting party can only go on a fortnight from this date and so forth. The storm shows no sign of abatement and its character is as unpleasant as ever. The promise of last night died away at 3 A.M., when the temperature and wind rose again, and things reverted to the old conditions. I can find no sign of an end, and all of us agree that it is utterly impossible to move. Resignation to misfortune is the only attitude, but not an easy one to adopt. It seems undeserved where plans were well laid and so nearly crowned with a first success. I cannot see that any plan would be altered if it were to do again, the margin for bad weather was ample according to all experience, and this stormy December—our finest month—is a thing that the most cautious organiser might not have been prepared to encounter. It is very evil to lie here in a wet sleeping-bag and think of the pity of it, whilst with no break in the overcast sky things go steadily from bad to worse (T. +32°). . . . Surely few situations could be more exasperating than this of forced inactivity when every day and indeed one hour counts."

December 8. "Hoped against hope for better conditions, to wake to the mournfullest snow and wind as usual. We had breakfast at 10, and at noon the wind dropped. We set about digging the sledges, no light task. We then shifted our tent sites. All tents had been reduced to the smallest volume by the gradual pressure of snow. The old sites are deep pits with hollowed-in wet centres. The re-setting of the tent has at least given us comfort, especially since the wind has dropped. About 4 the sky showed signs of breaking, the sun and a few patches of land could be dimly discerned. The wind shifted in light airs and a little hope revived. Alas! as I write the sun has disappeared and snow is again falling. Our case is growing desperate. Evans and his man-haulers tried to pull a load this afternoon. They managed to move a sledge with four people on it, pulling in ski. Pulling on foot they sank to the knees. The snow all about us is terribly deep. We tried Nobby [a pony] and he plunged to his belly in it. Wilson thinks the ponies finished, but Oates thinks they will get another march in spite of the surface, *if it comes to-morrow*. If it should not, we must kill the ponies to-morrow and get on as best we can with the men on ski and the dogs. But one wonders what the dogs can do on such a surface. I much fear they also will prove inadequate. Oh! for fine weather, if only to the

Glacier. The temperature remains +33°, and everything is disgustingly wet.

"11 P.M.—The wind has gone to the north, the sky is really breaking at last, the sun showing less sparingly, and the land appearing out of the haze. The temperature has fallen to +26°, and the water nuisance is already abating. With so fair a promise of improvement it would be too cruel to have to face bad weather to-morrow. There is good cheer in the camp to-night in the prospect of action. The poor ponies look wistfully for the food of which so very little remains, yet they are not hungry, as recent savings have resulted from food left in their nose-bags. They look wonderfully fit, all things considered. Everything looks more hopeful to-night, but nothing can recall four lost days."

December 9. "I turned out two or three times in the night to find the weather slowly improving; at 5.30 we all got up, and at 8 got away with the ponies—a most painful day. The tremendous snowfall of the late storm had made the surface intolerably soft, and after the first hour there was no glide. We pressed on the poor half-rationed animals, but could get none to lead for more than a few minutes; following, the animals would do fairly well. It looked as we could never make headway; the man-haulers were pressed into the service to aid matters. Bowers and Cherry-Garrard went ahead with one 10-foot sledge—thus most painfully we made about a mile. . . . By 8 P.M. we had reached within a mile or so of the slope ascending to the gap which Shackleton called the Gateway. I had hoped to be through the Gateway with the ponies still in hand at a very much earlier date and, but for the devastating storm, we should have been. It has been a most serious blow to us, but things are not yet desperate, if only the storm has not hopelessly spoilt the surface. . . .

"At 8 P.M. the ponies were quite done, one and all. They came on painfully slowly a few hundred yards at a time. By this time I was hauling ahead, a ridiculously light load, and yet finding the pulling heavy enough. We camped, and the ponies have been shot. Poor beasts! they have done wonderfully well considering the terrible circumstances under which they worked, but yet it is hard to kill them so early. The dogs are going well in spite of the surface, but here again one cannot get the help one would wish. (T. +19°) I cannot load the animals heavily on such snow. . . . In spite of some doubt in our outlook, everyone is very cheerful to-night and jokes are flying freely around."

The two supporting parties accompanied the polar party until December 21, when one of them turned back. Scott was determined that the polar party would manhaul. At the end of the year, according to a note on a flyleaf of one of his journals, he was forty-three, Wilson thirty-nine, Evans thirty-seven, Oates thirty-two and Bowers twenty-eight.

January 3, 1912. Scott informed the second supporting party that they would turn back next day, and decided to add Bowers to the polar party. "Bowers is to come into our tent, and we proceed as a five-man unit to-morrow. We have 5½ units of food—practically over a month's allowance for five people—it ought to see us through." This apparently last-minute decision to take a fifth man to the Pole has been the subject of much speculation and criticism, and it has even been wondered if the polar party might have survived had Bowers not been taken along. Cherry-Garrard, one of the members of the supporting parties, wrote in *The Worst Journey in the World,* "The final advance to the Pole was, according to plan, to have been made by four men. We were organized in four-man units: our rations were made up for four men for a week: our tents held four men: our cookers held four mugs, four pannikins and four spoons. . . . [Scott] changed his mind and went forward a party of five. . . ." Bowers had left his skis behind on December 31 and so, unlike his companions, he was obliged to walk, not ski, to the Pole.

January 4. "It is wonderful to see how neatly everything stows on a little sledge, thanks to P. O. Evans. I was anxious to see how we could pull it, and glad to find we went easy enough. Bowers on foot pulls between, but behind, Wilson and myself; he has to keep his own pace and luckily does not throw us out at all." Scott said good-by to the second supporting party. The polar party were on the summit, at an altitude of 10,280', when they camped for the night. The temperature was −16° F.

January 5. "A dreadfully trying day. Light wind from the N.N.W. bringing detached clouds and constant fall of ice crystals. The surface, in consequence, as bad as could be after the first hour." Scott discovered that he had miscalculated in one respect by taking Bowers along. "Cooking for five takes a seriously longer time than cooking for four; perhaps half an hour on the whole day." This meant a half hour lost from marching or from sleep. In the perilously close margins on which the party were proceeding, and in the length of time in which they would have to endure, the loss of a daily half hour could prove serious.

January 6–7. There was much hard manhauling during these two days. On the seventh Scott wrote, "I am awfully glad we have hung on to the ski; hard as the marching is, it is far less tiring on ski. Bowers has a heavy time on foot, but nothing seems to tire him. Evans has a nasty cut on his hand (sledge-making). I hope it won't give trouble." This is the first indication that Evans is not as well as the rest of the party. From now on he will go downhill steadily until his death at the foot of the Beardmore Glacier on February 17.

January 8. The men encountered their first summit or plateau blizzard and spent the day in their double tent. "Evans' hand was dressed this morning, and the rest ought to be good for it." Scott wrote of the virtues of his companions. "It is quite impossible to speak too highly of [them]. Each fulfills his office to the party; Wilson, first as doctor, ever on the outlook to alleviate the small pains and troubles incidental to the work; now as cook, quick, careful and dexterous, ever thinking of some fresh expedient to help the camp life; tough as steel on the traces, never wavering from start to finish.

"Evans, a giant worker with a really remarkable head-piece. It is only now I realise how much has been due to him. Our ski shoes and crampons have been absolutely indispensable, and if the original ideas were not his, the details of manufacture and design and the good workmanship are his alone. He is responsible for every sledge, every sledge fitting, tents, sleeping-bags, harness, and when one cannot recall a single expression of dissatisfaction with any of these items, it shows what an invaluable assistant he has been. Now, besides superintending the putting up of the tent, he thinks out and arranges the packing of the sledge; it is extraordinary how neatly and handily everything is stowed, and how much study has been given to preserving the suppleness and good running qualities of the machine. On the Barrier, before the ponies were killed, he was ever roaming round, correcting faults of stowage.

"Little Bowers [Bowers was 5′4″, if I remember correctly] remains a marvel—he is thoroughly enjoying himself. I leave all the provision arrangement in his hands, and at all times he knows exactly how we stand, or how each returning party should fare. It has been a complicated business to redistribute stores at various stages of re-organisation, but not one single mistake has been made. In addition to the stores, he keeps the most thorough and conscientious meteorological record, and to this he now adds the duty of observer and photographer. Nothing comes amiss to him, and no work is too hard. It is a difficulty to get him into the tent; he seems quite oblivious of the cold, and he lies coiled in his bag writing and working out sights long after the others are asleep. . . . Oates had his invaluable period with the ponies [of which he was in charge]; now he is a foot slogger and goes hard the whole time, does his share of camp work, and stands the hardship as well as any of us. I would not like to be without him either. So our five people are perhaps as happily selected as it is possible to imagine."

With regard to Bowers's ability to withstand cold, one may note that on the way from New Zealand to McMurdo Sound he almost daily drenched himself with cold water, at times having someone lower a bucket into the sea and pouring its contents over him two or three times as he stood naked on deck. His letters to his mother, quoted by Cherry-Garrard in *The Worst Journey in the World,* are remarkable for their keenness of observation, their precise detail, their liveliness and candor and their length. If he had not died on the polar journey he might well have become a great polar explorer and leader himself.

January 9–11. On the ninth the party surpassed Shackleton's farthest south. On the eleventh Scott noted, "I never had such pulling; all the time the sledge rasps and creaks. We had covered 6 miles, but at fearful cost to ourselves. . . . About 74 miles from the Pole—can we keep this up for seven days? It takes it out of us like anything. None of us ever had such hard work before."

January 12–15. On the twelfth Scott wrote, "Little Bowers is wonderful; in spite of my protest he *would* take sights after we had camped to-night, after marching in the soft snow all day where we have been comparatively restful on ski." Next day the party passed the 89th parallel. The altitude at night camp was 10,270 feet. The minimum temperature was −23.5°. On the fourteenth Scott wrote, "Oates seems to be feeling the cold and fatigue more than the rest of us, but we are all very fit. It is a critical time, but we ought to pull through." Oates was a taciturn man. At winter quarters one of his nicknames was the Old Pessimist. One wonders if such a temperament, so different from Shackleton's, is more likely than an optimistic, cheerful one to succumb to cold. Oates was the second of the party to die. The following day the men made their last depot. "It is wonderful to think that two long marches would land us at the Pole. We left our depôt to-day with nine days' provisions, so that it ought to be a certain thing now, and the only appalling possibility the sight of the Norwegian flag forestalling ours. . . . Only 27 miles from the Pole. We *ought* to do it now."

January 16. "The worst has happened, or nearly the worst. We marched well in the morning and covered 7½ miles. Noon sight showed us in Lat. 89° 42′ S., and we started off in high spirits in the afternoon, feeling that to-morrow would see us at our destination. About the second hour of the march Bowers' sharp eyes detected what he thought was a cairn; he was uneasy about it, but argued that it must be a sastrugus. Half an hour later he detected a black speck ahead. Soon we knew that this could not be a natural snow feature. We marched on, found that it was a black flag tied to a sledge bearer; near by the remains of a camp; sledge tracks and ski tracks going and coming and the clear trace of dogs' paws—many dogs. This told us the whole story. The Norwegians have forestalled us and are first at the Pole. It is a terrible disappointment, and I am very sorry for my loyal companions. Many thoughts come and much discussion have we had. To-morrow we must march on to the Pole and then hasten home with all the speed we can compass. All the day dreams must go; it will be a wearisome return. We are descending in altitude—certainly also the Norwegians found an easy way up."

January 17. "The Pole. Yes, but under very different circumstances from those expected. We have had a horrible day—add to our disappointment a head wind 4 to 5, with a temperature —22°, and companions labouring on with cold feet and hands.

"We started at 7.30, none of us having slept much after the shock of our discovery. We followed the Norwegian sledge tracks for some way; as far as we make out there are only two men. In about three miles we passed two small cairns. Then the weather overcast, and the tracks being increasingly drifted up and obviously going too far to the west, we decided to make straight for the Pole according to our calculations. . . . We have been descending again, I think, but there looks to be a rise ahead; otherwise there is very little that is different from the awful monotony of past days. Great God! this is an awful place and terrible enough for us to have laboured to it without the reward of priority. Well, it is something to have got here, and the wind may be our friend to-morrow. We have had a fat Polar hoosh in spite of our chagrin, and feel comfortable inside —added a small stick of chocolate and the queer taste of a cigarette brought by Wilson. Now for the run home and a desperate struggle. I wonder if we can do it."

January 18. "Decided after summing up all observations that we were 3.5 miles away from the Pole—one mile beyond it and 3 to the right. More or less in this direction Bowers saw a cairn or tent.

"We have just arrived at this tent, 2 miles from our camp, therefore about 1½ miles from the Pole. . . . The tent is fine—a small compact affair supported by a single bamboo. A note from Amundsen, which I keep, asks me to forward a letter to King Haakon! . . . Since lunch we have marched 6.2 miles S.S.E. by compass (i.e. northwards). Sights at lunch gave us ½ to ¾ of a mile from the Pole, so we call it the Pole Camp. (Temp. Lunch —21°.) We built a cairn, put up our poor slighted Union Jack, and photographed ourselves—mighty cold work all of it—less than ½ a mile south we saw stuck up an old underrunner of a sledge. This we commandeered as a yard for a floorcloth sail. I imagine it was intended to mark the exact spot of the Pole as near as the Norwegians could fix it. (Height 9500.) A note attached talked of the tent as being 2 miles from the Pole. Wilson keeps the note. There is no doubt that our predecessors have made thoroughly sure of their mark and fully carried out their programme. I think the Pole is about 9500 feet in height; this is remarkable, considering that in Lat. 88° we were about 10,500.

"We carried the Union Jack about ¾ of a mile north with us and left it on a piece of stick as near as we could fix it. . . . Well, we have turned our back now on the goal of our ambition and must face our 800 miles of solid dragging—and good-bye to most of the day-dreams!"

January 19. They found a Norwegian cairn and their own outward tracks and followed the latter to the "ominous black flag" that had revealed to them Amundsen's success. "We have picked this flag up, using the staff for our sail, and are now camped about 1½ miles further back on our tracks. So that is the last of the Norwegians for the present." They had heavy pulling in the afternoon. They were spotting their cairns without difficulty but knew they would feel anxious until Three Degree Depot, some 150 miles to the north, was reached.

January 20. "I think Oates is feeling the cold and fatigue more than most of us. . . . It is everything now to keep up a good marching pace; I trust we shall be able to do so and catch the ship. Total march, 18½ miles."

January 21–22. They were held up part of the twenty-first by a blizzard. The elevation was 10,000 feet. They had hard going over a bad surface. Next day Scott wrote, "I think about the most tiring march we have had; solid pulling the whole way, in spite of the light sledge and some little helping wind at first. . . . Ski boots are beginning to show signs of wear; I trust we shall have no giving out of ski or boots, since there are yet so many miles to go." The minimum night temperature was −30°.

January 23. The party encountered heavy winds. "The old tracks show so remarkably well that we can follow them without much difficulty—a great piece of luck. In the afternoon we had to re-organise. Could carry a whole sail. Bowers hung on to the sledge, Evans and Oates had to lengthen out. We came along at a great rate and should have got within an easy march of our depôt had not Wilson suddenly discovered that Evans' nose was frostbitten—it was white and hard. We thought it best to camp at 6.45. Got the tent up with some difficulty, and now pretty cosy after good hoosh.

"There is no doubt Evans is a good deal run down—his fingers are badly blistered and his nose is rather seriously congested with frequent frost bites. He is very much annoyed with himself, which is not a good sign. I think Wilson, Bowers and I are as fit as possible under the circumstances. Oates gets cold feet. One way and another, I shall be glad to get off the summit! We are only about 13 miles from our 'Degree and half' Depôt and should get there to-morrow. The weather seems to be breaking up. Pray God we have something of a track to follow to the Three Degree Depôt—once we pick that up we ought to be right."

January 24. "Things beginning to look a little serious. A strong wind at the start has developed into a full blizzard at lunch, and we have had to get into our sleeping-bags. It was a bad march, but we covered 7 miles. . . . At 12.30 the sun côming ahead made it impossible to see the tracks further, and we had to stop. By this time the gale was at its height and we had the dickens of a time getting up the tent, cold fingers all round. . . . This is the second full gale since we left the Pole. I don't like the look of it. Is the weather breaking up? If so, God help us, with the tremendous summit journey and scant food. Wilson and Bowers are my standby. I don't like the easy way in which Oates and Evans get frostbitten." They lay in their bags during the afternoon and the whole night.

January 25–28. On the twenty-fifth they postponed breakfast and skipped lunch. During breakfast the sun came out, affording enough light for them to see their old tracks. At about 2.30 they spotted the old depot flag. "We had lunch and left with 9½ days' provisions, still following the track—marched till 8 and covered over 5 miles, over 12 in the day. Only 89 miles (geogr.) to the next depôt, but it's time we cleared off this plateau. We are not without ailments: Oates suffers from a very cold foot; Evans' fingers and nose are in a bad state, and to-night Wilson is suffering tortures from his eyes." On the twenty-seventh Scott wrote, "A long way to go, and, by Jove, this is tremendous labour." The following day he noted, "We are getting more hungry, there is no doubt. The lunch meal is beginning to seem inadequate. We are pretty thin, especially Evans, but none of us are feeling worked out."

January 29–30. On the thirtieth, as on the previous day, they had a good march, but Wilson strained a tendon in his leg. He was in pain all day and the leg was swollen at night. "Of course, he is full of pluck over it, but I don't like the idea of such an accident here. To add to the trouble Evans has dislodged two finger-nails to-night; his hands are really bad, and to my surprise he shows signs of losing heart over it. He hasn't been cheerful since the accident. . . . We can get along with bad fingers, but it [will be] a mighty serious thing if Wilson's leg doesn't improve."

January 31. They reached Three Degree Depot and lunched an hour afterwards. Wilson favored his injured leg by walking beside the sledge. At night the leg was much less inflamed. "I hope he will be all right again soon, but it is trying to have an injured limb in the party." In the afternoon they picked up Bowers's skis.

February 1–5. The first: "Wilson's leg much better. Evans' fingers now very bad, two nails coming off, blisters burst." On the second Scott injured his shoulder in a fall on a very slippery surface. On the fourth he wrote, "Just before lunch unexpectedly fell into crevasses, Evans and I together—a second fall for Evans, and I camped. . . . The temperature is 20° lower than when we were here before; the party is not improving in condition, especially Evans, who is becoming rather dull and incapable. Thank the Lord we have good food at each meal, but we get hungrier in spite of it.

Bowers is splendid, full of energy and bustle all the time." Next day they encountered many crevasses. "Our faces are much cut up by all the winds we have had, mine least of all; the others tell me they feel their noses more going with than against wind. Evans' nose is almost as bad as his fingers. He is a good deal crocked up."

February 6. "We've had a horrid day and not covered good mileage. On turning out found sky overcast; a beastly position amidst crevasses. Luckily it cleared just before we started. We went straight for Mt. Darwin, but in half an hour found ourselves amongst huge open chasms, unbridged, but not very deep, I think. We turned to the north between two, but to our chagrin they converged into chaotic disturbance. We had to retrace our steps for a mile or so, then struck to the west and got on to a confused sea of sastrugi, pulling very hard; we put up the sail, Evans' nose suffered, Wilson very cold, everything horrid. . . . Food is low and weather uncertain, so that many hours of the day were anxious; but this evening, though we are not as far advanced as I expected, the outlook is much more promising. Evans is the chief anxiety now; his cuts and wounds suppurate, his nose looks very bad, and altogether he shows considerable signs of being played out. Things may mend for him on the glacier, and his wounds get some respite under warmer conditions. I am indeed glad to think we shall so soon have done with plateau conditions. It took us 27 days to reach the Pole and 21 days back—in all 48 days—nearly 7 weeks in low temperature with almost incessant wind."

February 7–10. The seventh: "Well, we have come through our 7 weeks' ice camp journey and most of us are fit, but I think another week might have had a very bad effect on P. O. Evans, who is going steadily downhill." On the eighth, despite a "beastly" morning with cold, strong winds, the party camped near a moraine under Mount Buckley and spent a part of the day "geologising." "We found ourselves under perpendicular cliffs of Beacon sandstone, weathering rapidly and carrying veritable coal seams. From the last Wilson, with his sharp eyes, has picked several plant impressions, the last a piece of coal with beautifully traced leaves in layers, also some excellently preserved impressions of thick stems, showing cellular structure. In one place we saw the cast of small waves on the sand. . . . Altogether we have had a most interesting afternoon, and the relief of being out of the wind and in a warmer temperature is inexpressible. . . . A lot could be written on the delight of setting foot on rock after 14 weeks of snow and ice and nearly 7 out of sight of aught else. It is like going ashore after a sea voyage." The following day "Wilson got great find of vegetable impression in piece of limestone."

February 11. "The worst day we have had during the trip and greatly owing to our own fault. We started on a wretched surface with light S.W. wind, sail set, and pulling on ski—horrible light, which made everything look fantastic. As we went on light got worse, and suddenly we found ourselves in pressure. Then came the fatal decision to steer east. We went on for 6 hours, hoping to do a good distance, which in fact I suppose we did, but for the last hour or two we pressed on into a regular trap. Getting on to a good surface we did not reduce our lunch meal, and thought all going well, but half an hour after lunch we got into the worst ice mess I have ever been in. For three hours we plunged on on ski, first thinking we were too much to the right, then too much to the left; meanwhile the disturbance got worse and my spirits received a very rude shock. There were times when it seemed almost impossible to find a way out of the awful turmoil in which we found ourselves. At length, arguing that there must be a way on our left, we plunged in that direction. It got worse, harder, more icy and crevassed. We could not manage our ski and pulled on foot, falling into crevasses every minute—most luckily no bad accident. At length we saw a smoother slope towards the land, pushed for it, but knew it was woefully long way from us. The turmoil changed in character, irregular crevassed surface giving way to huge chasms, closely packed and most difficult to cross. It was very heavy work, but we had grown desperate. We won through at 10 P.M. and I write after 12 hours on the march. I *think* we are on or about the right track now, but we are still a good number of miles from the depôt, so we reduced rations to-night. We had three pemmican meals left and decided to make them into four. To-morrow's lunch must serve for two if we do not make big progress. It was a test of our endurance on the march and our fitness with small supper. We have come through well. A good wind has come down the glacier which is clearing the sky and surface. Pray God the wind holds to-morrow. Short sleep to-night and off first thing, I hope."

February 12. This day they were in an extremely critical situation, getting caught in "a horrid maze of crevasses and fissures." "Divided councils caused our course to be erratic after this, and finally, at

9 P.M. we landed in the worst place of all. After discussion we decided to camp, and here we are, after a very short supper and one meal only remaining in the food bag; the depôt doubtful in locality. We *must* get there to-morrow. Meanwhile we are cheerful with an effort. It's a tight place, but luckily we've been well fed up to the present. Pray God we have fine weather to-morrow."

February 13–14. During the early morning of the thirteenth it was snowing so heavily the party could see nothing, so they stayed in their bags. They got up at nine, had some tea and one biscuit but no pemmican. They started marching and after a while Wilson spotted the depot flag. "It was an immense relief, and we were soon in possession of our 3½ days' food. The relief to all is inexpressible; needless to say, we camped and had a meal." Despite their grave difficulties Wilson looked for geological specimens. "Bowers has had a very bad attack of snow blindness, and Wilson another almost as bad. Evans has no power to assist with camping work." Next day: "There is no getting away from the fact that we are not going strong. Probably none of us: Wilson's leg still troubles him and he doesn't like to trust himself on ski; but the worst case is Evans, who is giving us serious anxiety. This morning he suddenly disclosed a huge blister on his foot. It delayed us on the march, when he had to have his crampon readjusted. Sometimes I fear he is going from bad to worse, but I trust he will pick up again when we come to steady work on ski like this afternoon. He is hungry and so is Wilson. We can't risk opening out our food again, and as cook at present I am serving something under full allowance. We are inclined to get slack and slow with our camping arrangements, and small delays increase. . . . The next depôt some 30 miles away and nearly 3 days' food in hand."

February 15–16. "We are pulling for food and not very strong evidently," Scott wrote on the fifteenth. "In the afternoon it was overcast; land blotted out for a considerable interval. We have reduced food, also sleep; feeling rather done." Next day he wrote, "Evans has nearly broken down in brain, we think. He is absolutely changed from his normal self-reliant self. This morning and this afternoon he stopped the march on some trivial excuse. . . . Perhaps all will be well if we can get to our depôt to-morrow fairly early, but it is anxious work with the sick man. But it's no use meeting troubles half way, and our sleep is all too short to write more."

February 17. "A very terrible day. Evans looked a little better after a good sleep, and declared, as he always did, that he was quite well. He started in his place on the traces, but half an hour later worked his ski shoes adrift, and had to leave the sledge. The surface was awful, the soft recently fallen snow clogging the ski runners at every step, the sledge groaning, the sky overcast, and the land hazy. We stopped after about one hour, and Evans came up again, but very slowly. Half an hour later he dropped out again on the same plea. He asked Bowers to lend him a piece of string. I cautioned him to come on as quickly as he could, and he answered cheerfully as I thought. We had to push on, and the remainder of us were forced to pull very hard, sweating heavily. Abreast the Monument Rock we stopped, and seeing Evans a long way astern, I camped for lunch. There was no alarm at first, and we prepared tea and our own meal, consuming the latter. After lunch, and Evans still not appearing, we looked out, to see him still afar off. By this time we were alarmed, and all four started back on ski. I was first to reach the poor man and shocked at his appearance; he was on his knees with clothing disarranged, hands uncovered and frostbitten, and a wild look in his eyes. Asked what was the matter, he replied with a slow speech that he didn't know, but thought he must have fainted. We got him on his feet, but after two or three steps he sank down again. He showed every sign of complete collapse. Wilson, Bowers, and I went back for the sledge, whilst Oates remained with him. When we returned he was practically unconscious, and when we got him into the tent quite comatose. He died quietly at 12.30 A.M. On discussing the symptoms we think he began to get weaker just before we reached the Pole, and that his downward path was accelerated first by the shock of his frostbitten fingers, and later by falls during rough travelling on the glacier, further by his loss of all confidence in himself. Wilson thinks it certain he must have injured his brain by a fall. It is a terrible thing to lose a companion in this way, but calm reflection shows that there could not have been a better ending to the terrible anxieties of the past week. Discussion of the situation at lunch yesterday shows us what a desperate pass we were in with a sick man on our hands at such a distance from home.

"At 1 A.M. we packed up and came down over the pressure ridges, finding our depôt easily."

The manner in which Evans died as well as the fact that he was the first of the party to go are sufficiently suggestive to lead one to speculate on the cause or causes of his death. Although Wilson spoke as a doctor he had no proof that Evans had suffered brain injury in a fall. Was it easier to believe in a fall than to suspect that Evans may have succumbed to malnutrition because, the largest and strongest worker of the group, he had experienced the most intense undernourishment, which itself may have been the cause of bad falls? Was Evans a victim of the notion of strictly equal rations that was adhered to in that time? Cherry-Garrard wrote in *The Worst Journey in the World,* "Seaman Evans was the first to crack. He was the heaviest, largest, most muscular man we had, and that was probably one of the main reasons: for his allowance of food was the same as the others."

There is another interesting possibility. Evans had camped previously with officers on sledge journeys but the polar journey, as far as I know, was the only extensive one he made in which he was the sole non-officer in a party of officers. (Wilson was a civilian but had officer status.) Can this unique position—at a time when distinctions between ranks, especially in England as contrasted, say, with the United States (and one may recall Scott's insistence on running his Antarctic expeditions along Royal Navy lines)—have had a marked and deleterious psychological effect on him? It was not simply a difference in rank that was involved: there were also differences in family background, education, speech patterns, income and so on. Scott speaks of Evans's "loss of all confidence in himself" as one of the factors in the man's death. However, I am not suggesting that Scott ought to be faulted for having overlooked (if indeed he did) such a factor in selecting Evans to be a member of the polar party. Quite possibly Scott chose Evans so that a representative of the "lower deck"—with proven great strength and eager usefulness—might share in the honor of reaching the Pole.

February 18–22. The party had five hours' sleep at the Lower Glacier Depot "after a horrible night," and proceeded to Shambles Camp, where the ponies had been shot. "Here with plenty of horse-meat we have had a fine supper, to be followed by others such, and so continue a more plentiful era if we can keep good marches up. New life seems to come with greater food almost immediately, but I am anxious about the Barrier surfaces." On the nineteenth the party struggled over bad surfaces. Next day Scott noted, "Same terrible surface; four hours' hard plodding brought us to our Desolation Camp, where we had the four-day blizzard. We looked for pony meat, but found none. . . . Terribly slow progress, but we hope for better things as we clear the land." On the twenty-second he wrote, "There is little doubt we are in for a rotten critical time going home, and the lateness of the season may make it really serious."

February 23–24. On the twenty-fourth he wrote, "Beautiful day— too beautiful—an hour after starting loose ice crystals spoiling surface. Saw depôt and reached it middle forenoon. Found store in order except shortage oil—shall have to be *very* saving with fuel— otherwise have ten full days' provisions from to-night and shall have less than 70 miles to go. . . . We had a really terrible surface this afternoon and only covered 4 miles. . . . It really will be a bad business if we are to have this pulling all through. I don't know what to think, but the rapid closing of the season is ominous. It is great luck having the horsemeat to add to our ration. To-night we have had a real fine 'hoosh.' It is a race between the season and hard conditions and our fitness and good food."

Concerning the oil shortage, Leonard Huxley, the editor of *Scott's Last Expedition* and the author of many of the book's footnotes, wrote, ". . . The tins of oil at the depôts had been exposed to extreme conditions of heat and cold. The oil was specially volatile, and in the warmth of the sun (for the tins were regularly set in an accessible place on the top of the cairns) tended to become vapour and escape through the stoppers even without damage to the tins. This process was much accelerated by reason that the leather washers about the stoppers had perished in the great cold. Dr. [Edward L.] Atkinson gives two striking examples of this.

"1. Eight one-gallon tins in a wooden case, intended for a depôt at Cape Crozier, had been put out in September 1911. They were snowed up; and when examined in December 1912 showed three tins full, three empty, one a third full, and one two-thirds full.

"2. When the search party reached One Ton Camp in November 1912 they found that some of the food, stacked in a canvas 'tank' at the foot of the cairn, was quite oily from the spontaneous leakage of the tins seven feet above it on the top of the cairn.

"The tins at the depôts awaiting the Southern Party had of course been opened and the due amount to be taken measured out by the supporting parties on their way back. However carefully restoppered, they were still liable to the unexpected evaporation and leakage already described. Hence, without any manner of doubt, the shortage which struck the Southern Party so hard."

February 25–26. On the twenty-sixth Scott noted, "The fuel shortage still an anxiety. . . . Only 43 miles from the next depôt. . . . We want more food yet and especially more fat. Fuel is woefully short. We can scarcely hope to get a better surface at this season, but I wish we could have some help from the wind, though it might shake us badly if the temp. didn't rise."

February 27. "We talk of little but food, except after meals. . . . It is a critical position. We may find ourselves in safety at next depôt, but there is a horrid element of doubt."

February 28. "Thermometer went below −40° last night; it was desperately cold for us, but we had a fair night. . . . Many cold feet this morning; long time over foot gear, but we are earlier. . . . Things must be critical till we reach the depôt, and the more I think of matters, the more I anticipate their remaining so after that event. Only 24½ miles from the depôt. The sun shines brightly, but there is little warmth in it. There is no doubt the middle of the Barrier is a pretty awful locality."

February 29–March 1. On the twenty-ninth Scott wrote, "Frightfully cold starting; luckily Bowers and Oates in their last new finnesko; keeping my old ones for present. Expected awful march and for first hour got it. Then things improved and we camped after 5½ hours marching close to lunch camp—22½ [miles]. Next camp is our depôt and it is exactly 13 miles. It ought not to take more than 1½ days; we pray for another fine one. The oil will just about spin out in that event, and we arrive 3 clear days' food in hand. The increase of ration has had an enormously beneficial result. Mountains now looking small. Wind still very light from west— cannot understand this wind."

March 2. "Misfortunes rarely come singly. We marched to the (Middle Barrier) depôt fairly easily yesterday afternoon, and since that have suffered three distinct blows which have placed us in a bad position. First we found a shortage of oil; with most rigid economy it can scarce carry us to the next depôt on this surface (71 miles away). Second, Titus Oates disclosed his feet, the toes showing very bad indeed, evidently bitten by the late temperatures. The third blow came in the night, when the wind, which we had hailed with some joy, brought dark overcast weather. It fell below −40° in the night, and this morning it took 1½ hours to get our foot gear on, but we got away before eight. We lost cairn and tracks together and made as steady as we could N. by W., but have seen nothing. Worse was to come—the surface is simply awful. In spite of strong wind and full sail we have only done 5½ miles. We are in a *very* queer street since there is no doubt we cannot do the extra marches and feel the cold horribly."

March 3. "We picked up the track again yesterday, finding ourselves to the eastward. Did close on 10 miles and things looked a trifle better; but this morning the outlook is blacker than ever. Started well and with good breeze; for an hour made good headway; then the surface grew awful beyond words. The wind drew forward; every circumstance was against us. After 4¼ hours things so bad that we camped, having covered 4½ miles. . . . One cannot consider this a fault of our own—certainly we were pulling hard this morning—it was more than three parts surface which held us back—the wind at strongest, powerless to move the sledge. When the light is good it is easy to see the reason. The surface, lately a very good one, is coated with a thin layer of woolly crystals, formed by radiation no doubt. These are too firmly fixed to be removed by the wind and cause impossible friction on the runners. God help us, we can't keep up this pulling, that is certain. Amongst ourselves we are unendingly cheerful, but what each man feels in his heart I can only guess. Putting on foot gear in the morning is getting slower and slower, therefore every day more dangerous."

March 4. "Things look *very* black indeed. As usual we forgot our trouble last night, got into our bags, slept splendidly on good hoosh, woke and had another, and started marching. Sun shining brightly, tracks clear, but surface covered with sandy frost-rime. All the morning we had to pull with all our strength, and in 4½ hours we covered 3½ miles. Last night it was overcast and thick, surface bad; this morning sun shining and surface as bad as ever. One has little to hope for except perhaps strong dry wind—an unlikely contingency at this time of year. Under the immediate surface crystals is a hard sastrugi surface, which must have been excellent for pulling a week or two ago. We are about 42 miles from the next depôt and have a week's food, but only about 3 to 4 days' fuel—we are as economical of the latter as one can possibly be, and we cannot afford to save food and pull as we are pulling. We are in a very tight place indeed, but none of us despondent *yet,* or at least we preserve every semblance of good cheer, but one's heart sinks as the sledge stops dead at some sastrugi behind which the surface sand lies thickly heaped. For the moment the temperature is on the —20°—an improvement which makes us much more comfortable, but a colder snap is bound to come again soon. I fear that Oates at least will weather such an event very poorly. Providence to our aid! We can expect little from man now except the possibility of extra food at the next depôt. It will be real bad if we get there and find the same shortage of oil. Shall we get there? Such a short distance it would have appeared to us on the summit! I don't know what I should do if Wilson and Bowers weren't so determinedly cheerful over things."

March 5. "Regret to say going from bad to worse. We got a slant of wind yesterday afternoon, and going on 5 hours we converted our wretched morning run of 3½ miles into something over 9. We went to bed on a cup of cocoa and pemmican solid with the chill off. . . . The result is telling on all, but mainly on Oates, whose feet are in a wretched condition. One swelled up tremendously last night and he is very lame this morning. We started march on tea and pemmican as last night—we pretend to prefer the pemmican this way. Marched for 5 hours this morning over a slightly better surface covered with high moundy sastrugi. Sledge capsized twice; we pulled on foot, covering about 5½ miles. We are two pony marches and 4 miles about from our depôt. Our fuel dreadfully low and the poor Soldier [a nickname for Oates] nearly done. It is pathetic enough because we can do nothing for him; more hot food might do a little, but only a little, I fear. We none of us expected these terribly low temperatures, and of the rest of us Wilson is feeling them most; mainly, I fear, from his self-sacrificing devotion in doctoring Oates' feet. We cannot help each other, each has enough to do to take care of himself. We get cold on the march when the trudging is heavy, and the wind pierces our warm garments. The others, all of them, are unendingly cheerful when in the tent. We mean to see the game through with a proper spirit, but it's tough work to be pulling harder than we ever pulled in our lives for long hours, and to feel that the progress is so slow. One can only say 'God help us!' and plod on our weary way, cold and very miserable, though outwardly cheerful. We talk of all sorts of subjects in the tent, not much of food now, since we decided to take the risk of running a full ration. We simply couldn't go hungry at this time."

March 6. "We did a little better with help of wind yesterday afternoon, finishing 9½ miles for the day, and 27 miles from depôt.

. . . But this morning things have been awful. It was warm in the night and for the first time during the journey I overslept myself by more than an hour; then we were slow with foot gear; then, pulling with all our might (for our lives) we could scarcely advance at rate of a mile an hour; then it grew thick and three times we had to get out of harness to search for tracks. The result is something less than 3½ miles for the forenoon. The sun is shining now and the wind gone. Poor Oates is unable to pull, sits on the sledge when we are track-searching—he is wonderfully plucky, as his feet must be giving him great pain. He makes no complaint, but his spirits only come up in spurts now, and he grows more silent in the tent. We are making a spirit lamp to try and replace the primus when our oil is exhausted. It will be a very poor substitute and we've not got much spirit. If we could have kept up our 9-mile days we might have got within reasonable distance of the depôt before running out, but nothing but a strong wind and good surface can help us now, and though we had quite a good breeze this morning, the sledge came as heavy as lead. If we were all fit I should have hopes of getting through, but the poor Soldier has become a terrible hindrance, though he does his utmost and suffers much I fear."

March 7. "A little worse I fear. One of Oates' feet *very* bad this morning; he is wonderfully brave. We still talk of what we will do together at home.

"We only made 6½ miles yesterday. . . . This morning in 4½ hours we did just over 4 miles. We are 16 from our depôt. If we only find the correct proportion of food there and this surface continues, we may get to the next depôt [Mount Hooper, seventy-two miles away] but not to One Ton Camp. We hope against hope that the dogs have been to Mt. Hooper; then we might pull through. If there is a shortage of oil again we can have little hope. One feels that for poor Oates the crisis is near, but none of us are improving, though we are wonderfully fit considering the really excessive work we are doing. We are only kept going by good food. No wind this morning till a chill northerly air came ahead. Sun bright and cairns showing up well. I should like to keep the track to the end."

March 8. "Worse and worse in morning; poor Oates' left foot can never last out, and time over foot gear something awful. Have to wait in night foot gear for nearly an hour before I start changing, and then am generally first to be ready. Wilson's feet giving trouble now, but this mainly because he gives so much help to others. We

did 4½ miles this morning and are now 8½ miles from the depôt
—a ridiculously small distance to feel in difficulties, yet on this surface we know we cannot equal half our old marches, and that for
that effort we expend nearly double the energy. The great question
is, What shall we find at the depôt? If the dogs have visited it we
may get along a good distance, but if there is another short allowance of fuel, God help us indeed. We are in a very bad way, I
fear, in any case."

March 9. No entry.

March 10. "Things steadily downhill. Oates' foot worse. He has
rare pluck and must know that he can never get through. He asked
Wilson if he had a chance this morning, and of course Bill had to say
he didn't know. In point of fact he has none. Apart from him, if he
went under now, I doubt whether we could get through. With great
care we might have a dog's chance, but no more. The weather conditions are awful, and our gear gets steadily more icy and difficult
to manage. At the same time of course poor Titus is the greatest
handicap. He keeps us waiting in the morning until we have partly
lost the warming effect of our good breakfast, when the only wise
policy is to be up and away at once; again at lunch. Poor chap! it
is too pathetic to watch him; one cannot but try to cheer him up.

"Yesterday we marched up the depôt, Mt. Hooper. Cold comfort.
Shortage on our allowance all round. I don't know that anyone is
to blame. The dogs which would have been our salvation have evidently failed. . . .

"This morning it was calm when we breakfasted, but the wind
came from the W.N.W. as we broke camp. It rapidly grew in
strength. After travelling for half an hour I saw that none of us
could go on facing such conditions. We were forced to camp and
are spending the rest of the day in a comfortless blizzard camp,
wind quite foul."

March 11. "Titus Oates is very near the end, one feels. What we
or he will do, God only knows. We discussed the matter after breakfast; he is a brave fine fellow and understands the situation, but he
practically asked for advice. Nothing could be said but to urge him
to march as long as he could. One satisfactory result to the discussion; I practically ordered Wilson to hand over the means of ending
our troubles to us, so that any one of us may know how to do so.
Wilson had no choice between doing so and our ransacking the
medicine case. We have 30 opium tabloids apiece and he is left

with a tube of morphine. So far the tragical side of our story. . . . Know that 6 miles [per day] is about the limit of our endurance now, if we get no help from wind or surfaces. We have 7 days' food and should be about 55 miles from One Ton Camp to-night, 6×7=42, leaving us 13 miles short of our distance, even if things get no worse. Meanwhile the season rapidly advances."

March 12. "We did 6.9 miles yesterday, under our necessary average. Things are left much the same, Oates not pulling much, and now with hand as well as feet pretty well useless. We did 4 miles this morning in 4 hours 20 min.—we may hope for 3 this afternoon, 7×6=42. We shall be 47 miles from the depôt. I doubt if we can possibly do it. The surface remains awful, the cold intense, and our physical condition running down. God help us! Not a breath of favourable wind for more than a week, and apparently liable to head winds at any moment."

March 13. No entry.

March 14. "No doubt about the going downhill, but everything going wrong for us. Yesterday we woke to a strong northerly wind with temp. —37°. Couldn't face it, so remained in camp . . . till 2, then did 5¼ miles. Wanted to march later, but party feeling the cold badly as the breeze (N.) never took off entirely, and as the sun sank the temp. fell. Long time getting supper in dark. . . .

"This morning started with southerly breeze, set sail and passed another cairn at good speed; half-way, however, the wind shifted to W. by S. or W.S.W., blew through our wind clothes and into our mits. Poor Wilson horribly cold, could not get off ski for some time. Bowers and I practically made camp, and when we got into the tent at last we were all deadly cold. Then temp. now midday down —43° and the wind strong. We *must* go on, but now the making of every camp must be more difficult and dangerous. It must be near the end, but a pretty merciful end. Poor Oates got it again in the foot. I shudder to think what it will be like to-morrow. It is only with greatest pains rest of us keep off frostbites. No idea there could be temperatures like this at this time of year with such winds. Truly awful outside the tent. Must fight it out to the last biscuit, but can't reduce rations."

"Friday, March 16 or Saturday 17. Lost track of dates, but think the last correct. Tragedy all along the line. At lunch, the day before yesterday, poor Titus Oates said he couldn't go on; he proposed we should leave him in his sleeping-bag. That we could not do, and induced him to come on, on the afternoon march. In spite of its awful nature for him he struggled on and we made a few miles. At night he was worse and we knew the end had come.

"Should this be found I want these facts recorded. Oates' last thoughts were of his Mother, but immediately before he took pride in thinking that his regiment would be pleased with the bold way in which he met his death. We can testify to his bravery. He has borne intense suffering for weeks without complaint, and to the very last was able and willing to discuss outside subjects. He did not—would not—give up hope to the very end. He was a brave soul. This was the end. He slept through the night before last, hoping not to wake; but he woke in the morning—yesterday. It was blowing a blizzard. He said, 'I am just going outside and may be some time.' He went out into the blizzard and we have not seen him since.

"I take this opportunity of saying that we have stuck to our sick companions to the last. In case of Edgar Evans, when absolutely out of food and he lay insensible, the safety of the remainder seemed to demand his abandonment, but Providence mercifully removed him at this critical moment. He died a natural death, and we did not leave him till two hours after his death. We knew that poor Oates was walking to his death, but though we tried to dissuade him, we knew it was the act of a brave man and an English gentleman. We all hope to meet the end with a similar spirit, and assuredly the end is not far.

"I can only write at lunch and then only occasionally. The cold is intense, —40° at midday. My companions are unendingly cheerful, but we are all on the verge of serious frostbites, and though we constantly talk of fetching through I don't think any of us believes it in his heart.

"We are cold on the march now, and at all times except meals. Yesterday we had to lay up for a blizzard and to-day we move dreadfully slowly. We are at No. 14 pony camp, only two pony marches from One Ton Depôt. We leave here our theodolite, a camera, and Oates' sleeping-bag. Diaries, &, and geological specimens carried at Wilson's request, will be found with us or on our sledge.

March 18. "To-day, lunch, we are 21 miles from the depôt. Ill fortune presses, but better may come. We have had more wind and drift from ahead yesterday; had to stop marching; wind N.W., force

4, temp. —35°. No human being could face it, and we are worn out
nearly.

"My right foot has gone, nearly all the toes—two days ago I was
proud possessor of best feet. These are the steps of my downfall.
Like an ass I mixed a small spoonful of curry powder with my
melted pemmican—it gave me violent indigestion. I lay awake and
in pain all night; woke and felt done on the march; foot went and
I didn't know it. A very small measure of neglect and have a foot
which is not pleasant to contemplate. Bowers takes first place in
condition, but there is not much to choose after all. The others are
still confident of getting through—or pretend to be—I don't know!
We have the last *half* fill of oil in our primus and a very small
quantity of spirit—this alone between us and thirst. The wind is
fair for the moment, and that is perhaps a fact to help. The mileage
would have seemed ridiculously small on our outward journey."

March 19. "Lunch. We camped with difficulty last night and
were dreadfully cold till after our supper of cold pemmican and
biscuit and a half a pannikin of cocoa cooked over the spirit. Then,
contrary to expectation, we got warm and all slept well. To-day
we started in the usual dragging manner. Sledge dreadfully heavy.
We are 15½ miles from the depôt and ought to get there in three
days. What progress! We have two days' food but barely a day's
fuel. All our feet are getting bad—Wilson's best, my right foot worst,
left all right. There is no chance to nurse one's feet till we can get
hot food into us. Amputation is the least I can hope for now, but
will the trouble spread? That is the serious question. The weather
doesn't give us a chance—the wind from N. to N.W. and —40° temp.
to-day."

March 20. No entry.

March 21. "Got within 11 miles of depôt Monday night; had to
lay up all yesterday in severe blizzard. To-day forlorn hope, Wilson
and Bowers going to depôt for fuel."

"Thursday, March 22 and 23. Blizzard bad as ever—Wilson and
Bowers unable to start—to-morrow last chance—no fuel and only
one or two of food left—must be near the end. Have decided it
shall be natural—we shall march for the depôt with or without our
effects and die in our tracks."

While dying, Scott, the sensitive, moody, brilliant person of
whom Cherry-Garrard wrote that he was one of the quickest men to

tears he had ever known; the once rather frail young man with an inclination to laziness; the self-made man with an early financial burden with respect to his parents; the man who took duty, responsibility and tradition with exceptional seriousness; the man of high literary and intellectual tastes: this man wrote a number of farewell letters. The one to Wilson's wife reads:

"If this letter reaches you Bill and I will have gone out together. We are very near it now and I should like you to know how splendid he was at the end—everlastingly cheerful and ready to sacrifice himself for others, never a word of blame to me for leading him into this mess. He is not suffering, luckily, at least only minor discomforts.

"His eyes have a comfortable blue look of hope and his mind is peaceful with the satisfaction of his faith in regarding himself as part of the great scheme of the Almighty. I can do no more to comfort you than to tell you that he died as he lived, a brave, true man —the best of comrades and staunchest of friends.

"My whole heart goes out to you in pity,

"Yours,
"R. Scott"

He wrote a letter to Bowers's mother:

"I am afraid this will reach you after one of the heaviest blows of your life.

"I write when we are very near the end of our journey, and I am finishing it in company with two gallant, noble gentlemen. One of these is your son. He had come to be one of my closest and soundest friends, and I appreciate his wonderful upright nature, his ability and energy. As the troubles have thickened his dauntless spirit ever shone brighter and he has remained cheerful, hopeful, and indomitable to the end.

"The ways of Providence are inscrutable, but there must be some reason why such a young, vigorous and promising life is taken.

"My whole heart goes out in pity for you.

"Yours,
"R. Scott

"To the end he has talked of you and his sisters. One sees what a happy home he must have had and perhaps it is well to look back on nothing but happiness.

"He remains unselfish, self-reliant and splendidly hopeful to the end, believing in God's mercy to you."

To Vice-Admiral Sir Francis Charles Bridgeman, Scott wrote:
"I fear we have shipped up; a close shave; I am writing a few letters which I hope will be delivered some day. I want to thank you for the friendship you gave me of late years, and to tell you how extraordinarily pleasant I found it to serve under you. I want to tell you that I was *not* too old for this job. It was the younger men that went under first. . . . After all we are setting a good example to our countrymen, if not by getting into a tight place, by facing it like men when we were there. We could have come through had we neglected the sick."

Scott's letter to James Barrie, the playwright, reads:
"We are pegging out in a very comfortless spot. Hoping this letter may be found and sent to you, I write a word of farewell. . . . More practically I want you to help my widow and my boy—your godson. We are showing that Englishmen can still die with a bold spirit, fighting it out to the end. It will be known that we have accomplished our object in reaching the Pole, and that we have done everything possible, even to sacrificing ourselves in order to save sick companions. I think this makes an example for Englishmen of the future, and that the country ought to help those who are left behind to mourn us. I leave my poor girl and your godson, Wilson leaves a widow, and Edgar Evans also a widow in humble circumstances. Do what you can to get their claims recognised. Goodbye. I am not at all afraid of the end, but sad to miss many a humble pleasure which I had planned for the future on our long marches. I may not have proved to be a great explorer, but we have done the greatest march ever made and come very near to great success. Goodbye, my dear friend,

"Yours ever,
"R. Scott

"We are in a desperate state, feet frozen, &. No fuel and a long way from food, but it would do your heart good to be in our tent, to hear our songs and the cheery conversation as to what we will do when we get to Hut Point.

"*Later*. We are very near the end, but have not and will not lose our good cheer. We have four days of storm in our tent and nowhere's food or fuel. We did intend to finish ourselves when things proved like this, but we have decided to die naturally in the track.

"As a dying man, my dear friend, be good to my wife and child. Give the boy a chance in life if the State won't do it. He ought to have good stuff in him. . . . I never met a man in my life whom I admired and loved more than you, but I never could show you how much your friendship meant to me, for you had much to give and I nothing."

To his wife Scott wrote:

". . . . I shall not have suffered any pain, but leave the world fresh from harness and full of good health and vigour. . . . We have decided not to kill ourselves, but to fight to the last for that depôt, but in the fighting there is a painless end.

"Make the boy interested in natural history if you can; it is better than games; they encourage it at some schools. I know you will keep him in the open air.

"Above all, he must guard and you must guard him against indolence. Make him a strenuous man. I had to force myself into being strenuous as you know—had always an inclination to be idle. . . .

"What lots and lots I could tell you of this journey. How much better has it been than lounging in too great comfort at home. What tales you would have for the boy. But what a price to pay."

Scott wrote other letters—to his publisher, Reginald Smith, to J. J. Kinsey, his great supporter in New Zealand, to his brother-in-law, to Sir Edgar Speyer, to Vice-Admiral Sir George le Clerc Egerton and to Admiral Sir Lewis Beaumont. There is no mention in *Scott's Last Expedition* or in Reginald Pound's biography of Scott's having written letters to Evans's wife and to Oates's next of kin.

Scott also composed a document that he titled "Message to the Public."

"The causes of the disaster," he wrote, "are not due to faulty organisation, but to misfortune in all risks which had to be undertaken.

"1. The loss of pony transport in March 1911 obliged me to start later than I had intended, and obliged the limits of stuff transported to be narrowed.

"2. The weather throughout the outward journey, and especially the long gale in 83° S., stopped us.

"3. The soft snow in lower reaches of glacier again reduced pace.

"We fought these untoward events with a will and conquered, but it cut into our provision reserve.

"Every detail of our food supplies, clothing and depôts made on the interior ice-sheet and over that long stretch of 700 miles to the Pole and back, worked out to perfection. The advance party would have returned to the glacier in fine form and with surplus of food, but for the astonishing failure of the man whom we had least expected to fail. Edgar Evans was thought the strongest man of the party.

"The Beardmore Glacier is not difficult in fine weather, but on our return we did not get a single completely fine day; this with a sick companion enormously inceased our anxieties.

"As I have said elsewhere we got into frightfully rough ice and Edgar Evans received a concussion of the brain—he died a natural death, but left us a shaken party with the season unduly advanced.

"But all the facts above enumerated were as nothing to the surprise which awaited us on the Barrier. I maintain that our arrangements for returning were quite adequate, and that no one in the world would have expected the temperatures and surfaces which we encountered at this time of the year. On the summit in lat. 85°, 86° we had −20°, −30° in the day, −47° at night pretty regularly, with continuous head wind during our day marches. It is clear that these circumstances come on very suddenly, and our wreck is certainly due to this sudden advent of severe weather, which does not seem to have any satisfactory cause. I do not think human beings ever came through such a month as we have come through, and we should have got through in spite of the weather but for the sickening of a second companion, Captain Oates, and a shortage of fuel in our depôts for which I cannot account, and finally, but for the storm which has fallen on us within 11 miles of the depôt at which we hoped to secure our final supplies. Surely misfortune could scarcely have exceeded this last blow. We arrived within 11 miles of our old One Ton Camp with fuel for one last meal and food for two days. For four days we have been unable to leave the tent—the gale howling about us. We are weak, writing is difficult, but for my own sake I do not regret this journey, which has shown that Englishmen can endure hardships, help one another, and meet death with as great a fortitude as ever in the past. We took risks, we knew we took them; things have come out against us, and therefore we have no cause for complaint, but bow to the will of Providence, determined still to do our best to the last. But if we have been willing to give our lives to this enterprise, which is for the honour of our country, I appeal to our countrymen to see that those who depend on us are properly cared for.

"Had we lived, I should have had a tale to tell of the hardihood, endurance, and courage of my companions which would have stirred the heart of every Englishman. These rough notes and our dead bodies must tell the tale, but surely, surely, a great rich country like ours will see that those who are dependent on us are properly provided for.

"R. Scott"

March 29. "Since the 21st we have had a continuous gale from W.S.W. and S.W. We had fuel to make two cups of tea apiece and bare food for two days on the 20th. Every day we have been ready to start for our depôt 11 *miles* away, but outside the door of the tent it remains a scene of whirling drift. I do not think we can hope for any better things now. We shall stick it out to the end, but we are getting weaker, of course, and the end cannot be far.

"It seems a pity, but I do not think I can write more.

"R. Scott

"Last Entry
"For God's sake look after our people"

Scott's penciled writing in his sledging diaries remained clear and firm to the end.

Some eight months later, on November 12, a search party led by Atkinson and including Cherry-Garrard and Charles S. Wright, found the tent. Covered with snow, it resembled a cairn. When it was dug out the party saw that Wilson and Bowers lay in their closed bags. Scott had thrown back the flaps of his bag and had opened his coat. He lay in the middle, with Wilson on his left and Bowers on his right. His arm was stretched across Wilson. Under the head of his bag was the green wallet which he had used for carrying his diary while sledging. The diary books were inside. On the floorcloth beside him were the letters he had written presumably on the days near the end when he had not made diary entries. Cherry-Garrard felt certain that Scott had died last.

Removing the tent poles, the search party let the tent cover the undisturbed bodies. Over the tent they erected a large cairn, on top of which they placed a cross. A futile search was made for Oates's body.

The world received the news of the tragedy in February 1913. This was at a time when England was feeling the menace of Germany and the probability of a rapidly approaching great conflict; as well as wondering whether her youth had grown too decadent to defend her adequately. There was talk of the threat of "the boys of the dachshund breed." A patriotic fervor was spreading, which was reflected in Scott's letters and his "Message to the Public."

In his failure Scott shook the Western world to a much greater extent than Amundsen had in his triumph. He did so for two reasons. One was his style as a man. Like Socrates he had shown the world how well a man could die. But unlike Socrates he had not died in the presence of living friends. He had gone out alone, apparently, writing until the end and hoping that his papers would be found on the ever-changing Barrier wasteland. The second reason was his style as a writer. It was the journals and letters that stunned a world and perpetuated his memory. One seeks with difficulty for another example of prose so calmly, so well and so nobly written under such dreadful circumstances. He had, by his eloquence, reaffirmed the value of the written word.

The deaths occurred on the Ross Ice Shelf, as the Barrier is now called, about 150 miles south of Hut Point. The cairn with its cross is no longer visible, having been blizzarded over decades ago. The tent and its bodies are no doubt buried many feet beneath the shelf's surface. They are slowly moving seaward. Some day they will drift northward to warm waters as part of a tabular berg and eventually will be given to the sea.

17

~~~~~~~~~~~~~~~~~~~~~~~~~~~~~~~

CAPE EVANS CONCLUDED

ON THE two or three occasions when I awoke during the night in Scott's hut I thought of Scott and of his companions on the tragic journey and of what they had had to endure before death released them; and my realization of what they and Shackleton and the latter's farthest-southing companions had managed to accomplish in an almost incredibly hostile country was buttressed by vivid recollections of my own trip to the Pole in November 1969 and by a remarkably low flight over the Beardmore Glacier on the return to McMurdo. Of my visit I had written:

"Early one morning my press companions and I headed for the Pole, where only the Americans have a station. To paraphrase a current politician, once you've seen one undersnow station you've seen them all, with this proviso: that you see the Pole Station first. Because of its historical significance, its remoteness, its hostility to life of every kind and degree, or if for no better reason than that, like Mount Everest, it's there, the Pole is the Mecca of all imaginative Antarctic residents and visitors, only a handful of whom get to visit it.

"It is still a difficult and hazardous traverse to the Pole from any Antarctic station. By the ski-equipped Hercules departing from McMurdo the trip takes three hours. The eight hundred and forty miles are covered pleasantly if noisily but perhaps with a certain apprehension if one is making the trip for the first time. How cold will it be? Will the altitude affect you after the sudden change from sea level? Will you be blinded by the light?

"Although my flight as a flight was routine, it was unique in one respect. It was carrying the first women ever to visit the Pole: five Americans and a New Zealander. Five were scientists and one was a science writer. The Navy was nervously determined that no one of them should have the unfair if accidental distinction of being the *first* woman to step down at the Pole. After some discussion among high-ranking officers the solution to the problem was found: lower the cargo ramp in the rear of the plane, disembark all passengers with the exception of Admiral Welch and the ladies, and have the latter descend the ramp arm in arm, the admiral in the middle. Navy photographers would record the historic event.

"As we neared the Pole we donned our waddle pants, lowered and secured our ear and neck flaps, closed the air valves in our bunny boots and checked our bear paws and fur-trimmed hoods. I glanced through one of the aft portholes and saw the vast, arid, blinding polar plateau. Warnings came over the intercom. The parka hood would eliminate our side vision, and the cap ear flaps and hood would dull our hearing, so it was best to exercise caution in one's movements. Several visitors in recent years, becoming confused, had wandered forward and had nearly been chewed up by the still-turning props. We were warned to be on guard against frostbite. The temperature at the Pole now was −49° F., the wind ten knots, making the effective temperature somewhat lower than −80° F. Unless we didn't mind losing skin we had better not touch metal with our bare hands, and if we had a range-finder camera it was wise not to touch the finder's metal rim with our cheek. Because of the Pole's considerable altitude we were advised to move slowly and to breathe often.

"But all went smoothly despite this last-minute counsel, much of which was a reiteration of earlier briefings. When we left the plane we waited for the cold to hit us but it didn't. What hit us was the light, for we had exited facing the sun. We were on a great flat desert plain and wherever we turned, there was the same glaring white featureless northern horizon. The sun hung low in the sky like a terrible spotlight. The snow was thick and extremely dry, the sky fantastically blue. Only man lent visual interest to the barrenness: vehicle and boot tracks, communications antennas, a khaki instrument dome, black fuel drums on a huge sled, a red cleated vehicle, a khaki rubber storage bladder for fuel. Some hundred feet away was the famous "barber" pole with its red and black stripes surmounted by a gleaming chromium-plated globe. We walked toward it and felt the effects of the altitude. Our breath issued in white streamers, frosting our glasses. Diaphanous steam rose and billowed from people and machines. My companions made me think of walking tea kettles. The red beard of one of the men had turned a brilliant white.

"I removed my bear paws, unzipped my parka and fumbled for the light meter and camera hanging from my neck. And now, as I shot the scenes, I at last felt the cold. My hands, even though covered by two pairs of gloves, ached and rapidly grew numb. I felt a strange satisfaction. After all, I told myself, I hadn't come more than thirteen thousand miles to experience warmth.

"We were photographed individually at the barber pole by official Navy photographers. Statistics on a sign were photographed with us. The ice cap in the Pole's vicinity is over nine thousand feet thick. The average temperature is $-57°$ F. The population is twenty-one. I remembered other statistics—the highest temperature recorded at the Pole is $5.5°$ F., the lowest $-113.3°$ F. The annual precipitation (in terms of water equivalent) is less than $2''$, as compared with Phoenix, Arizona's $7.2''$. I thought of the tragic contrast between Amundsen's and Scott's arrival at the Pole and remembered Scott's words from his journal: 'Great God! this is an awful place and terrible enough for us to have laboured to it without the reward of priority.'

"A Navy journalist, peering at my face, said the end of my nose was very white and advised that I go inside the station temporarily. I went to a wooden door and down a precipitous flight of wooden stairs, at the foot of which stood the station's medical officer, with whom I chatted while I warmed my nose with my hand. The tunnel extending from the stairs was encrusted with ice crystals. Its temperature was thirty or forty below. Other frostbite cases descended the stairs to be advised by the officer. This same pleasant young man doubled as the station's postmaster and later cacheted the group's envelopes and led some of its members on a tour of the station, showing them the tiny infirmary (one bed, rarely occupied), the communications room, the ham radio room, the food storage area, the snow melter, and his own tight quarters, all under the ice. The station had originally been constructed on the surface of the snow (during the International Geophysical Year, 1957) but drift snow had covered it, compacted into ice and was slowly crushing it.

The station would soon have to be abandoned. This was just as well in one sense, for the station had drifted with the ice cap away from the Pole. A new station, of superior design, would be built at the Pole itself in the early Seventies.

"We lunched in a small mess room, one wall of which was crowded with huge-breasted pinups. It was interesting to see the confrontation of these ladies of men's dreams with the real ladies casually consuming spaghetti with meat sauce, buttered bread chunks, mincemeat pie and coffee. The bread and pie were fresh out of the station's oven. We left on schedule after a visit of two hours, hearing that the ladies had been persuaded to leave souvenirs of their visit: a bobby pin, a comb, a pair of ear rings and a lipstick.

"If the flight to the Pole was dull because it occurred at too high an altitude for interesting sights, the return flight to McMurdo decidedly was not. It offered those few of us lucky enough to have access to a porthole a series of spectacular views of the Beardmore Glacier, which the pilot flew over at low altitudes, descending during one sequence to three hundred feet. The Beardmore is a landmark familiar to students of Antarctic exploration because it provided first Shackleton and then Scott with access to the polar plateau through the Transantarctic Mountains. Both the Shackleton and the Scott parties were in great danger on the glacier due to exhaustion, hunger and cold as they made their way back to Ross Island. The Shackleton party survived by a hair. The Scott group was trapped and destroyed by a blizzard on the Ross Ice Shelf not long after leaving the Beardmore.

"At first, after the wastes of the seemingly endless plateau, with its dead flatness except for occasional nunataks (mountain peaks visible above the ice cap), we saw delicate scenes such as the pale grays and gray-blues of a mountain range peeping out of snow. But soon we came on naked, barren, slate-gray mountains, vast, sprawled, showing the ribs of cliff edges. From a height the glacier looked like a bluish plain, behind which were serene mountains of a deeper blue, at whose foothills were the congregated gleaming points of something resembling a town. But actually these points were an array of sastrugi, crevasses and crumbling buttes reflecting the low-hanging sun and suggesting the vast forces involved in the ice cap's movement to the Ross Ice Shelf and eventually to the Southern Ocean. As we flew over long, parallel ice ridges the ice river's width seemed immense, the distant part looking smooth, level, fit for traverses, the foreground giving the impression of having been chewed up by a thousand half-tracks. Far away was a lesser glacier, tonguing down between mountains to add to the Beardmore's mass. A mountain range, pale slate with a hint of violet, crests capped by snow, rose out of a creamy sea. Now the plane descended rapidly and one saw pale-green, veined splotches of bare ice or splotches resembling ragged circles of boiling white metal. There were huge upward-curling flakes among wildly mixed-up tremendous crevasses, and gleaming wild waves, a frozen surf, great buttes, and immense sections resembling crumbling blue cheese."

Lying in my sleeping bag in Scott's hut, the one to which he had been fated never to return, it seemed to me almost beyond belief that he and his companions had accomplished so much in such a life-threatening country, not only in terms of geographical exploration and scientific discovery but in the refusal to lower their dignity under the most desperate of physical circumstances. It was inevitable, spending the night alone in his hut, with many of its original contents ranged around me, that I should feel a special closeness to him. It occurred to me then that although I had failed in my quest of encountering his ghost in the form of a dream, perhaps his spirit, which had long affected me, would do so even more strongly from now on.

From my Cape Evans journal entries:

"3:20 P.M. Have just awakened from a nap on the wanigan cot. Dave still asleep in his bunk. We walked to the conical mound and far beyond, were gone more than three hours, returned, had lunch of steak, frozen peaches and tea, were exhausted, so went to sleep. Am now sitting near the door. Cold wind out, fierce desert sun in a blue sky. Had a terrific time walking across a moonscape, but interspersed with brooks, rills, creeks, ponds, some with beautiful green or blue ice, one with pea-green ice. At Skua Lake were attacked by many birds and would have had a rough time if we hadn't had the bamboo poles. The poles are like pilgrim staffs, useful for walking and climbing over the madly uneven terrain. When the skuas and brooks aren't noisy (that is, when you're in a secluded place) you hear the soughing of skua wings or the tearing sounds as a diving bird suddenly puts out legs like brakes, and outspread tail and wings, and pulls up and away. Cries of alarmed birds—'Ah-ah-ah-

ah!' Very fast, staccato, and sounding mournful. Sometimes just an elongated 'Ah!' Cries of alarm as soon as they spot you, long before diving. When the alarm is sounded many skuas respond, rising for altitude, flapping for speed, gliding during the bombing run, coming straight at you but rarely hitting the poles, sometimes coming very close, especially when chicks are being defended. Very hard in the uneven terrain to see eggs or chicks, which are always sheltered in little depressions behind rocks. Louder cries, fiercer, more persistent attacks when chicks are involved. Beyond Skua Lake and beyond the cone (we came across many small cones, which seem to be glacial deposits) we were attacked by outlying skuas on ridges. Saw furry gray chicks, one very young, and another emerging from its shell. A wild scape, utterly enchanting, and it helps to know you're the only humans within miles. We hiked to Erebus's ice skirts and along them southward on a land ridge toward the great ice cape projecting into the Sound with its visible crevasses. The incredible light there near Land's End, had to wear sunglasses, and my beach glasses felt insufficient. Dave has a pair of mirrored glasses with a horizontal slit across the middle of the lens, and I think the lenses are double-gradient density. The exhilaration of climbing, of looking. During the hike we kept an eye peeled on the fog bank building up near the Western Mountains. It would not have been pleasant to have to make our way back to the wanigan in fog."

We climbed a good deal (but sometimes came to soft, furry hills down which we glissaded in our boots) over the extreme uneven-ness of the volcanic terrain, which was a dump heap of moraines, rocks, boulders, scoria and dust. Sometimes we made our way from boulder-crest to boulder-crest, or climbed over boulders that barred our way. The bamboo poles were very useful in this work. Wearing a red ski cap, a red parka, blue dungarees and mukluks, handsome in his thin blond mustache and struggling goatee, Murphy was as fine a camping companion as I could imagine: youthful, humorous, athletic, discreet, taciturn if need be, intelligent, and appreciative of Antarctica's wonders.

Looking down from the height of the Ramp, we saw a great deal of water running off Erebus's slopes: rivulets, creeks, fingers, ribbons, sheets, all racing toward the opalescent tidal cracks. We also saw numerous cuplike hollows that had become pools. Here and there we viewed ponds partially frozen over: pale blues, pale greens and a few lavenders, all marbled, a wondrous surprise after the monotony of the cape's cinder mass. In places the snowbanks showed plum colors or gentle lilacs. The contrast between the darkness of lava rock and the paleness of the snow, or between the boulders and the sky's purity, was not only extremely pleasing, it was also awe-inspiring. Life was largely absent here but this did not make the place depressing for us. We had much open sky and the regal blues and purples of the ponds to cheer us. A number of the ponds, with boulders rising from them, showed cool, gemlike colors, turquoise in the center. Upward on the Ramp we encountered many more large boulders than in the hut area, where the cape levels out. At times the cape looked like little more than a conglomeration of black boulders. We also saw the stark razorback of Inaccessible Island, and Big and Little Razorback Islands, and beyond them, in the south, Hut Point Peninsula and Cape Armitage.

The glare of Erebus's skirts, slopes, falls and glaciers became almost unbearable as we drew near them, leaving behind us the light-moderating influence of the black cape's badlands. They suggested thousands of brilliantly illuminated lily pads. We averted our gaze from them when we could.

The fact that Ross Island is of volcanic origin greatly adds to its interest and beauty. A more ordinary island would not be so extreme, so lunar in its scapes and so varied in its tiny forms. Far from feeling life-poor because of the lack of what recognizably looked like temperate earth, we were increasingly aware of the aesthetic realities, source and chief of which was Mount Erebus, stark, beautiful, a pennant of steam and smoke flying northward from its crater. Erebus is a shield volcano; that is, it is broadly rounded, with gently sloping sides, not conical like Mount Fuji. In size it is one of the world's major volcanoes, with an elevation greater than that of Fuji or Etna or Vesuvius.

A harsh, cold wind blew up from the southeast during our nap after the hike to Land's End. When I awoke I thought we might get socked in by weather, so while Murphy continued to sleep I climbed Windvane Hill to look around. There were clouds in the southeast and fog rising beyond the Barne Glacier. When Murphy awoke we went to West Beach, where we were immediately attacked by skuas, whose temper seemed to have been soured by the weather. I caught a sharp blow behind my right ear that I felt most of the day. Keeping an eye on the weather, we climbed ridges and hills on the western side of the cape. The wind continued to be piercing.

We visited the Terra Nova Hut before and after dinner. I had had enough of the hut's penetrating, unpleasant odors, which had caused me to wake up with a throbbing nose and head, so I decided to sleep in the wanigan that night. The southeast wind roared all night, shaking the little structure badly. At about 12:30 A.M. I went outside in longjohns to look at the weather. We had a lot of cloud cover now and the sun was not visible. Erebus too was obscured. I returned to my bag shivering, my hands numb. I awoke at five, went out briefly to look around (the cover had spread), lay in my bag till six, then got dressed and once more climbed Windvane Hill, where I could feel the wind's full force. The wind was about twenty knots, with gusts up to thirty.

At breakfast it was 18° outside and the temperature was falling. When I checked in with McMurdo he said it was 7° there and requested hourly weather reports. He wanted to know the wind's direction, its estimated velocity, including gusts, the surface conditions, the horizon visibility, the state of the cloud cover and whether any particles were blowing about.

From my journal:

"When one becomes cold one grows awkward, careless, one starts injuring oneself, mainly in small ways, bruising one's fingers, tearing nails from flesh, bumping into things, stumbling."

But when the wind swept down over the crest of the dark, boulder-studded hill behind us; when a hot drink was welcome; when we stamped our feet to sense life in them; when the two pairs of gloves each of us wore were inadequate outdoors; when our eyes flooded with tears in the wind—when this was the state of affairs we were pleased, for it countered some of our embarrassment of yesterday when we had sweated in the hills while climbing.

The cloud cover cleared a couple of hours after breakfast. Shortly afterwards a red helo brought four Navy cameramen to photograph the interior of Scott's hut with movie gear. We helped them to unload, served them coffee and later made lunch for them.

In the late afternoon we were taken out by helo and returned to McMurdo.

18

CONVERSATIONS WITH

SIR CHARLES WRIGHT

While at work on the final stages of the present book I published a condensed version of Chapter 23, "A Walk in Taylor Valley," in the *Antarctic Journal of the United States*. As a consequence of this I received, to my great surprise and pleasure, a letter from Sir Charles Wright, the only survivor of Griffith Taylor's geological party of the Terra Nova Expedition, the sole survivor of the Pole parties of 1911 and 1912, and one of the two survivors of the search party that had found Scott's tent. (Tryggve Gran, a Norwegian, is the other.) As a matter of fact, according to Cherry-Garrard, Wright had been the first to spot the tent. Wright was leading the party and was its navigator, so Cherry-Garrard is probably correct, according to Sir Charles.

This is not the place to detail the correspondence which ensued, nor my visit to Sir Charles's home on Saltspring Island, British Columbia, in May 1973 to interview him at length and in depth on tape. In a future volume I hope to publish taped interviews of persons who have had significant experiences in Antarctica. At that time I shall present in all their richness the long talks I had with Sir Charles. For the present purposes I can only include some excerpts from those conversations with the remarkable man who is a living link between the so-called heroic era of Antarctic exploration and the modern one. As a working scientist, Sir Charles made three trips to Antarctica in modern times. On his last one he was flown to his namesake valley (one of the Dry Valleys) by Brandau.

At the time of my visit to him he had just turned eighty-six but was still spry, energetic, witty and full of enthusiasm regarding the Antarctic. Living with him and his mementoes of those early days —over the head of my bed was an original and very beautiful water-color by Wilson of Mount Erebus and Castle Rock—it was eerie to think he had known Scott and those other now legendary figures of the Terra Nova Expedition. He was of medium height, had all his hair and wore thick-lensed spectacles. He had had a long and distinguished career as a scientist and a scientific administrator and had been knighted for his work as an administrator in the Admiralty during the Second World War. Far from being formidable, he was a delight to be with, was an adequate drinker and plied us both with various liquids in order to keep our voices well oiled, as he explained.

n: In what circumstances did you join the Terra Nova Expedition? You were at the Cavendish Laboratory.

w: That's right, I was doing research at the Cavendish—on what we called then penetrating radiation [cosmic rays]—and Dr. Griffith Taylor, who was a friend of mine at Cambridge, applied for and got appointed as physiographer on Scott's expedition. And then he brought up Mawson [later Sir Douglas Mawson], who had been with Shackleton's expedition, and Mawson gave us a talk and I decided that I ought to apply too. So I applied for a position as a physicist and was appointed in due course. Well, I was turned down straightaway at the start, and then, as I didn't like this, it didn't seem to be right and proper, he [Taylor] and I walked down to Cambridge, about fifty-five miles or so, next day in order to explain to Scott what a frightful mistake he would make if he didn't take me. So, I came away with the job and that was that.

n: Well now, when you say you were turned down. Did you have an interview with Scott?

w: No, no. My communications were by letter.

n: Some lesser person turned you down?

w: Yes. No, no, not that, it's just that either the post was already filled or—I believe it was somebody with pretty high qualifications had probably been appointed and had then been turned down by the doctors.

n: And when you say you walked down to Cambridge. Was this a lark or was it to save money or what?

w: It was a lark. It appealed to both Taylor and myself as a useful introduction.

n: Then was it Scott himself whom you saw?

w: Yes, and I was taken on as a chemist, of all things. It wasn't my line of country but they were looking for a chemist, so I was taken on as a chemist. [Laughs.] They didn't have one.

n: But he knew you were a physicist?

w: Yes.

n: Had you had Antarctica in your imagination or thoughts before this time?

w: Only from the point of view of getting to sea in order to make some experiments on board ship. That was my primary interest at the time. What we called penetrating radiation: what it was, where it came from and so on.

n: So the Antarctic side was merely an opportunity for you as a young physicist to get out into the field.

w: Well, it was a little more than that, a little more than that. One wanted to see what it was like too. [Said wistfully.]

n: Of course, Scott at that time was already a hero.

w: Yes, he was the big noise. He had Wilson with him as his scientific chief of staff. We were quite a large group—nine of us, I think, nine scientific blokes out of twenty-three.

n: You were undisturbed by being labeled a chemist on this expedition?

w: I knew I was going to be allowed to do what I wanted. I didn't mind being called a chemist. [Laughs.]

n: Now Cherry-Garrard, who speaks very highly—by the way, I'm very impressed by the fact that Atkinson, Cherry-Garrard and especially Scott all speak very highly of you. I have quotations from Scott's journals and I'm going to read them sometime on these chats. It would almost be embarrassing to have such fine things said about a young man of twenty-four. Cherry-Garrard speaks of you as the physicist and chemist of the expedition and later mentions you as being a meteorologist. And Atkinson speaks of you as being a very fine navigator.

w: That, in a way, I feel is the most important extrascientific part of the work I did there, and it came about simply because in my even younger days in Canada, in Ontario, I had the good luck to do some work in surveying. This helped enormously, it really did help enormously, and whenever I was on a party and the real navigator, that is, Lieutenant Evans [pronounced Leftenant], wasn't present I sort of automatically became navigator. It's not an easy job at all. It's not the kind of thing that could be, because on an expedition like that it's a job of keeping a straight line, shall I say, on the march, as much as anything. The magnetic pole is to the north of you quite a long way and the magnetic compass isn't very much good. The nearer you get to the geographical South Pole the more precise are the bearings from your compass needle to the south magnetic pole. In essence the job of navigating is being able to fix your position by sun, stars or some such thing, whatever it may be, to keep a good record of time with your pocket chronometer—everybody carried a chronometer—and to watch such things as the—well, you have the aurora and other things—and out of the corner of your eye being able to see something and keep track of the bearing of that line. But the real trouble comes when you cannot see the horizon. Gentle snowfall, no horizon, you're on ski, and you automatically focus on the tip of the ski. You must have your eye fixed on that one thing where the drift goes across the ski, the angle at which it slides across. And everything else—bits of cloud and all sorts of things you may see—help keep you straight. Once you're started on your compass then you've got to try to hold that bearing. The thing I did try once, and it worked very successfully, one of these days you can't see the horizon, you don't know where your focus is [chuckles], you don't know whether you're looking up there or looking down here, when you *do* see something ahead it literally hits you in the eye. On the way south, every lunchtime you make two cairns, and sometimes put a little bit of black stuff on top. I remember one occasion when I led our return party on the pole journey between two of these, about thirty feet apart, and one of the party said, "Do you think it's about time we were getting to one of these double cairns?" [Chuckles.]

N: Is the sledgemeter important to navigation?

W: Oh yes, it's very useful. But it's more useful for telling you when you've done your day's work. [Laughs.] Thirteen geographical miles a day on the main polar journey.

N: How did you regard yourself—primarily as a glaciologist on this expedition?

W: When I became one, yes. I had had no experience at all.

N: You became a glaciologist, if I may relate what you told me, because, one, you were eager to get away from headquarters, you wanted to be out in the field.

w: Yes, I wanted to see what was going on, I wanted to take part in field activities. I wouldn't have been able to if I had been tied to headquarters.

n: And you didn't want to be merely an assistant meteorologist to Simpson.

w: Yes. But I had to be it later on, in the second winter. I was helped greatly by the eager Tryggve Gran and others.

n: I think also you were interested in glaciology at this time because of the possibility of studying penetrating radiation on the ice. Was that not so?

w: Well, not specifically. It's not really related.

n: Then why did you want to be away from winter quarters?

w: [Chuckles.] Because I wanted to see something of the country, and I had hopes of being considered, at least, for the polar journey.

n: So you had in mind the idea of being a member of the polar journey.

w: Yes, oh yes.

n: Did you mention this to anybody?

w: No, I kept it to myself. You see, I wouldn't have had the opportunity if I'd been all mixed up with a whole lot of scientific work at headquarters.

n: I hope you don't object to my saying so, but this, I think, is a romantic side of you.

w: Romantic? *Don't* say I've got anything *romantic* about me! [Both laugh.] No, I admit that I'm an odd person. I've never concealed this even from myself.

n: Why do you say you're an odd person?

w: I'm an experimenter. The part of physics that interests me is experimentation, you see. Well, glaciology at that time was in a very sticky state, I thought. Practically all the work that had been published had been on glaciers in Switzerland, and that had been done over and over and over again. And nobody had taken any real interest in ice in real quantities, such as in Greenland or the Antarctic, where you measure glacier widths in miles, and lengths in hundreds of miles sometimes.

n: As a scientist, suddenly you saw a field that was virginal.

w: Yes, more or less. And to my mind it wasn't a bit of a handicap that I knew practically nothing of what had been written before.

Because my interest then became, partly at least, in—what shall we say—the internals of the glaciers: size and growth of the crystals and all that sort of thing.

N: Well, your enthusiasm must have been extraordinarily infectious, because very early in Scott's journals as published in *Scott's Last Expedition* he speaks of your great interest and of your energy and your conscientiousness and hard work and his hope of directing all this energy and interest towards the problem of the ice, of what we now perhaps call the Antarctic budget.

W: Yes. Well, you see, the field was open and the people who had taken an interest in glaciology before had more or less confined their attention to what happened in Switzerland—the Germans and the French, the Italians and the Swiss. They had been working and had little conception of the totality, nobody realized that practically all the ice in the world was in Greenland and the Antarctic.

N: Sir Charles, do you believe that there's such a thing as an Antarctic addiction?

W: It's really a queer thing but you know, you see those sunsets, perfectly lovely things. Makes you feel as if you've swallowed a rainbow. You feel you're part of nature is probably the best way I can explain it. I can't say it made me feel any more religious.

N: But you were not religious to begin with, were you?

W: No. Dr. Bill [Wilson] was. He was a marvel. He was a wonderful man, you know.

N: How was it possible for someone who was so scientifically oriented as he was to conduct services every Sunday and—

W: All to himself, sometimes.

N: And this apparently sustained him during the bad times.

W: Yes, yes.

N: He was more religious than Scott, do you think?

W: Oh yes. There's no question in my mind that Dr. Bill was the making of the expedition. Scott relied on him enormously. And that's why when we wanted to get something across to Scott we put it up to Wilson. Scott was the naval officer, the Royal Navy captain. He had his own quarters aboard ship and nobody else came in unless he invited him, that sort of thing. Very, very much alone.

N: This reminds me. When I was in Boulder a couple of nights ago and I talked with Dr. Victor Hessler, Dr. Hessler told me a very amusing anecdote that you had told him. You had told him some time ago that although it was a great privilege to go sledging with

Scott and share Scott's tent, there was a certain disadvantage, that Scott was *always* the naval gentleman, and that if you had to leave the tent in the middle of the night for private matters, you had to leave the tent regardless of how cold it was outdoors.

w: Yes. I thought that was stupid, of course, in really cold weather.

n: That's what Hessler told me.

w: Absolutely stupid. And it *is* absolutely stupid. When you consider the temperature and so on, why you shouldn't pump ship in the corner. [Laughs.] But everybody did it. I'm not sure that our own party on the return [from the top of the Beardmore Glacier] didn't show a bit of sense once or twice.

n: You think this was more typical of Scott than of Shackleton, who was a non-career naval man?

w: You know, I never asked Raymond [Priestley] what—maybe he never sledged with Shackleton, probably doesn't know. But I can't believe Shackleton was so stupid. I just can't believe it. It's silly. Silly beyond words.

n: When you were a member of the first supporting party on the polar journey, that was, according to Cherry-Garrard, a trek of 1,164 statute miles round trip, from Cape Evans to the top of the Beardmore. That was one of the longest treks on record.

w: Was it?

n: Yes. Now, I've never been on the Beardmore but I've flown very low over it, and from the plane it seems like a monstrous glacier.

w: It is. It's about sixty miles wide in one place.

n: Was it pretty bad sledging on it?

w: It was very, very hard. We killed the ponies at the bottom. They were finished anyway. The few that remained were shot. And then we started off on ski. But our party had been traveling quite a while on ski because, naturally enough, the people who were too busy with other things and didn't have sufficient time to give the ponies their exercise, they were formed from the beginning into a small party. Ours was called the Baltic Fleet. Now you wouldn't remember the Baltic Fleet, would you?

n: No.

w: Some Russian—Admiral Rojetzvenski?—took the Russian Baltic Fleet on instructions around to—well, the other side, right around off China, and they were wiped out by the Japanese, you see. They were traveling very slowly. So we were known as the Baltic Fleet. At any rate these were the oldest animals, the oldest and the least fit.

We'd been sledging a long time before we got to the Beardmore, and then when we got to one of the big depots, the first one after One Ton Depot, we came upon the party taking the motors out, or taking the motors part way and then manhauling the rest of the way. (And they joined up on the manhauling party then.) And Teddy Evans in particular had quite a long journey manhauling before we got to the bottom of the Beardmore, and I think wasn't really in awfully good shape on the way up. I think he had the beginnings of the scurvy that nearly finished him on the way back. At any rate our party, when the ponies were shot, consisted of Evans, who was in charge—Lieutenant Evans—and Atkinson, myself and Keohane. Keohane and Cherry-Garrard and Atch and I were all of the return party. Well, I don't know if it fits in now at all or not but it was dreadful work right at the bottom. It had been snowing for three days, very soft snow and very wet, the temperatures actually rose above the freezing point. Well, we made very poor time, and our party had the worst of it. I don't quite know what happened. But I think we were badly loaded, and also we didn't pay enough attention to cleaning off the bottom of the sledge, because with that high-temperature snowfall, down below bunches of snow would be frozen to the runners. Added to that, you were just sinking in anyway, so you were just plowing through the stuff. Just plowing through it. At any rate our party were making rather heavy weather of it, very heavy weather sometimes, and that, I think, is why Atkinson brought us back. So up to the Cloudmaker it was not very good going. I don't know how long it took.

* * *

N: Did you ever meet Shackleton, by the way?

W: Yes.

N: Under what circumstances?

W: I don't have much to talk about when one mentions Shackleton. I went with Priestley once just to shake hands with him at his headquarters. And then the other time was when he gave a talk at the Royal Geographical Society. A sort of private talk. I disagreed with him most heartily. His claim was that people only went to the Antarctic because they wanted to see new country and to be there first. Well, that's all right for lots of people, but all of our scientific people were at the meeting and we all took exception to this. But in essence if you give a different interpretation to "country" he's quite right. One goes there for a specific reason—either, as he says, to see new country, or to do something new and different and preferably important in a scientific way. But it's the same basic urge: something different. Curiosity, if you like.

N: Now, we were talking earlier about the trouble between Scott and Shackleton, and you felt—and this was a positive thing you had to say—that perhaps it was a good thing that Shackleton did get scurvy on the Discovery Expedition farthest southing—as a kind of motivation for Scott.

w: I think it could possibly have ended where it began, in 1902, if Shackleton hadn't made the next step forward. And for the same reason: chasing the Pole. After all, Scott's first objective was chasing the Pole. Although he had a lot of scientific blokes along, his first objective was to get to the Pole first, his second one was to give the scientific blokes a chance to do their work.

N: I know you went into many a crevasse on the Beardmore.

w: I led our party, I'm ashamed to say, into a real mess of crevasses, and I learned then for the very first time how much more difficult it is to see where you are going when you're going down-hill on a glacier than going uphill. For some reason or other the rough stuff sticks out, you can see it ahead going uphill. And I got just too close in to the west bank, to two glaciers coming down, actually at right angles—I called them the Cherry and Garrard Glaciers, I don't know what they are called now, only Cherry, or Garrard. I was too close in, and there was a frightful mixup there, it was such a mixup, it was really only a bunch of *séracs* sticking up, with snow in between, you know. And in fact when we got really stuck here, there was Atkinson down full length on his trace, there was me on top, the sledge lurching drunkenly over another crevasse, and Keohane, I think, just sort of halfway down one. It was a mess. I don't know how I got into it, because there was nothing to tell me, except that I was too close to the side. And I felt very ashamed of myself about this because Scott—he knew I was disappointed having to go back—he said, "Well, you've got a very important job going back, you'll have to see them back safely." [Laughs.] He put the responsibility on me, you see. Atch said, when we got him out of the hole, "Well, where do we go now?" I didn't know. All I knew was I had to get out of that mess quickly as possible, so I said, "Oh, straight ahead," but I sheared off very quickly, very quickly, to the right. [Chuckles.]

N: Sir Charles, Scott in his journal said that you seemed to take it very hard that you were told to go back.

W: Well, I did, and I think Scott was aware of this and he went out of his way to give me charge of the navigation of the outfit. No, I'll tell you why it was. I felt that I was the better man to go along than certainly one and maybe two of those who did. That's the way you look at these things, you know. Thinking in terms of Scott's objective that he would have been wiser if he'd taken me and left A or B perhaps.

N: I have some quotes from his journal about you, and he always talked about you as being in tremendously fit form. As a matter of fact, he compared you to Bowers in fitness although you hadn't gone through the winter journey, and he said that you took to sledging like a duck to water and that you were extraordinarily hardy, and so no doubt there was a great deal of truth in your intuition that you should have gone. You know, Cherry-Garrard wrote that he lived the rest of his life with physical changes that were caused during the winter journey. For example, some of his teeth cracked. And he speaks of his store of vitality, his capital of vitality, as having been seriously depleted by that journey.

W: Well, he came back asleep on his feet. He was absolutely cooked. You know, one foot in front of the other. He had an awful time, of course. All three of them did. And I think he's probably right, they asked of him too much. And this is what makes it the worst journey in the world. They could have turned back at any time.

N: Do you believe that you had permanent physical changes as a consequence of your life in Antarctica?

W: I don't think so. Cherry might have. [Pause.] Cherry had the worst of everything. It just happened, you know, that he had that winter journey. He had an easy time coming back with Atch and me [from the Beardmore], but he had the worst of the depot-laying party, when they lost these ponies. I've always been very sorry for Cherry, particularly because he was sent out with the dogs and with Dmitri, the Russian dog-boy, to pick up Scott at a certain time and a certain place—both, both. And this is completely, I think completely foolish, when you don't know—how can you, how can you pinpoint a place and a time both? And it does cramp one's style if you're told to be there at a certain time, and if the other party and you don't arrive at the same time, what's the poor lad to do? If he goes forward he may miss the other party, you see. And I think Cherry felt that in some way he hadn't quite done the best for Scott and his party. But that's Scott's fault. It's wrong, it's stupidly wrong, I think, to specify both time and place when you don't know anything about it.

N: According to Cherry-Garrard, you were the very first to spot the signs of the tent during the search.

W: Let me make this quite clear. Atkinson was in charge of the whole [search] party. It was decided during the winter that the right thing to do was not to try any more to relieve the northern party. At any rate we decided that we'd spend all our efforts at first to find out what had happened to Scott. We all had in mind what had happened on the first Scott expedition, when the Navy sent down half a fleet [chuckles] to help to free her [the *Discovery*] from the ice, and all unnecessarily. We were afraid that this sort of thing would happen unless we cleared it up. Well, Atkinson was in charge, there were thirteen of us left, and two were left back [at winter quarters] because they were injured by accident. We had some mules sent down and we had a few dogs left. Cherry and Atch and Dmitri were with the dogs, and I had the navigating business and was in charge of eight mules, I think. The dogs weren't awfully good, you know, they came from Siberia and used to be used on the postal services. Their route was always on a road and they hadn't been trained, like the Greenlanders, just to go blindly ahead if you told them in what direction to go. They had lost an awful lot of heart, they were not in very good shape after the previous summer, and they followed up after us. Well, I don't pretend to say that I was the first who saw it. How can one? But nobody—if anyone else did see it first, well, I don't know, it didn't occur to me to inquire, I saw the damn thing. It was a black spot on the ice on the starboard bow and, not knowing what it was except that it shouldn't be there, I had it all nicely laid out where the cairns were, you see, there was something black out there, so I went out on skis to see what it was, and told the party to carry on to the south. We were fitted out to go as far as the top of the Beardmore and have one day for research there. We didn't have much left, you see. At any rate, I went on, and I don't quite understand myself, really, but when I saw it was the tent I signaled the party to come in and I couldn't make them understand and I didn't feel it was right to shout, and this is the first funny thing, you see, I didn't think it was at all right to shout, like being in a cathedral. Finally I made enough signals to make them see what I wanted. The second funny thing was it didn't seem to me to be right to make our camp too close to the tent, so I made it about a hundred and fifty yards away. And then there was some discussion, I think, as to what we should do before Atkinson came up. Well, I wasn't having any of that, Atkinson was in charge and Atkinson had to be there when the tent was opened. So we did just that, and Atkinson came with the dogs about an hour later, I guess, I don't remember that, I don't remember it at all. So at any rate we waited for Atch and he opened up the tent and he and Cherry and I went in and had a look at the party of three—Scott, Wilson and Bowers—and closed it up again. Atkinson had taken out Scott's diary, and he read certain parts of it to everybody, the parts that made it clear that Evans had died on the Beardmore Glacier, and that Titus Oates had walked out into the blizzard, and so on—explaining why there were only three there. And then we got the bits of rock they had brought back, and collapsed the tent on them after taking away the chronometers they each carried. I got the idea that we'd get into trouble if we didn't bring these back to Greenwich, so I suggested to Atch, "Well, I think we'd better take these back, hadn't we," you see, so Atch dealt with Scott's chronometer, Cherry dealt with Dr. Bill's and I dealt with Birdie Bowers'. And then we collapsed the tent on them and built an enormous cairn on top.

N: Was there an examination of the bodies?

W: No.

N: Was it easy to identify each person?

W: Oh, heavens yes. They were very thin and so on, but they looked as though they were asleep. They were in their sleeping bags, except that Scott was half out of his sleeping bag and sort of leaning toward Dr. Wilson's bag. They had simply frozen to death.

N: Do you feel that you still remember these moments or are they memories based on your journals?

W: Oh, I remember this very well indeed. I was so surprised at myself. Why should I be diffident about shouting out and telling the party what to do? That sort of thing. Oh, it's very clear in my mind—if only because I couldn't understand myself.

N: In referring to your diary of that event do the details seem unreal to you? Does it feel as if another person experienced these events when you read the diary?

w: No.

n: You identify readily with your younger self in reading it?

w: Oh yes.

n: How is it that you never published your account of being a member of the search party?

w: Why should I? There's only one reason: if I get so hard up, or if Pat [one of his daughters] gets so hard up that she wants some money. I don't intend to publish it, but I'm going through it now and making it more readable. I'm going to leave a record, if I suddenly conk out, based on the diaries.

n: Do you feel it's too personal a matter? Is that why you didn't publish?

w: No. Nobody's asked me to publish. Why should I, anyway?

n: Sir Charles, you undoubtedly thought many, many times about the possible motive that Scott had for at the last minute taking Bowers along on the polar party which was set up for a group of four.

w: I don't understand it. The whole thing seems so queer. Quite obviously, as Birdie had left his ski behind—a little beforehand, they didn't go back to get them, you see—it looked as if he [Scott] had chosen his four and told them so. And then, somehow or other, something must have happened and he had second thoughts and took along a fifth man. Now what effect that may have had I don't know but it made things more difficult for the [Lieutenant] Evans party of three. How could they estimate—they had to re-make the ration bags week by week for three and five instead of four and four. It must have made things very different. I just don't know. [Long pause.] It doesn't make sense to me at all. What's Cherry got to say about it?

n: He thinks it was a very serious error.

w: Well, I do too. And I think it was a serious error in not making provision for using the pony meat. It was left as a casual extra. Any bit of pony not being covered up by snow would have spoiled, I guess. At any rate there was a little bit that was unspoiled, and everybody dipped into this as they went past, thank heavens.

n: Quite a number of people have felt that the selection of Bowers at the last minute was somewhat incomprehensible.

w: He should have selected him before.

n: Yes, and certainly with skis. If Bowers had been less indomitable he would not have made it without skis.

w: I can't imagine what kind of arguments Birdie must have made with him [Scott] to take him along. I can't think. . . . In fact, if he'd been in the Royal Navy I can't see him [Bowers] even daring to do it. But I can't see what form of argument he introduced that would enable Scott to make such a strange decision. I can't understand it.

n: Sir Charles, when you were going up the Beardmore with the rest of the group you must have been very much aware of the possibility of Amundsen's having reached the Pole.

w: No. I don't think anybody—I don't know how it came about but I don't think anybody had the idea that Amundsen would take a different route from the Beardmore. Once we reached the top of the Beardmore and had seen no signs of him we thought some catastrophe had happened.

n: Do you believe that Scott had a reasonable right to assume that the bodies and the papers would be found in the tent? I mean given the conditions of the Barrier.

w: Yes.

n: But isn't there a fair amount of drift snow, over eight months, on the Barrier?

w: Oh no, not as much as that, you know. You see, on the way south, every lunchtime we built up two cairns, and one cairn when we stopped at night. This was in order to help on the way back in case we didn't see the sun and couldn't get a bearing. But the plan of the search party was to go along, following as nearly as possible the route that they should have taken back, until we found a cache which had been picked up by Scott. And then backtrack, and on to the next cache. I was certain we'd find them, all right. I had a little map—I guess I've got it there [motions with his hand]— showing where the cairns were on the way south, and in fact I tried to have marked on this map where every stop was made by all the parties, including the motor party. And to actually find this little bit of the top of the tent sticking out was no problem. They were on line coming back. If they hadn't been we'd have gone on to the cache, the depot, before, you see, and then come back. We couldn't have missed them.

n: How do you account for the fact that Scott behaved so coolly and selflessly during his impending death?

w: Well, the first thing is that I'm sure he had in mind at the last the need for being found. I would have said, if I were one of that party and only eleven miles away from One Ton Depot, with all the water and stuff they wanted, I would have said the right thing to do was to get up and walk ahead *through* the blizzard. Eleven miles is not much, but if you're in a frightfully bad case already—legs, fingers all frozen—it's a bit of a handicap, even eleven miles. So I think that they decided the right thing to do was to make certain the world knew they had reached the Pole—they had a letter from King Haakon, you know [chuckles]—and it's my guess that what overweighed anything when they knew what a bad state they all were in was to see that the world knew what had been going on.

N: In short, what you're suggesting is that if they'd been marching and had died in their tracks they would not have been easily found.

W: They wouldn't have been found at all.

* * *

N: Sir Charles, yesterday I mentioned to you the fact that in my book I devote a paragraph or two to the fact that Edgar Evans for the first time was undertaking a long sledging traverse as the only non-officer in a group. And I suspect that this may have had a deleterious effect on him psychologically.

W: Well, it may be so. I don't know if you remember what happened to the northern party. They got the cave in the drift and ice and after they got settled in, Raymond Priestley said Campbell [the party's leader] did a very wise and useful thing: he drew a line across the floor of the cave and said, "Now this is for the officers and this is for the men, and anybody can say anything they damn well like in their own part." Now that's curious, I wouldn't have thought that that was a matter of importance, myself, but Raymond said afterwards it was a very wise thing to have done. Your surmise might very well have operated unfavorably on Evans. Now already, you see, he had cut his hand rather badly and didn't disclose the fact to Wilson, and this annoyed Scott a lot, of course, and it got blood poisoning, which doesn't help either, but nobody knows what actually happened. I suspect he fell down a crevasse, you know, and clawed his way out and that was that. But he might—well, I just don't know.

N: Sir Charles, if someone were to ask you—let us say a grandchild —"What are among your most vivid memories of the entire Terra

Nova Expedition, whether they were trivial or important?" what would you say?

w: What part of it is most memorable. Is that what you mean?

n: Yes.

w: Well, I find it difficult to say. There are two things that really shook me. One was finding Scott and the party there. I was completely stirred up at that time. I told you, I felt like being found in a cathedral with my hat on, that's the only way I can explain it. It all seemed wrong, first of all to talk in anything but low tones, and it seemed essential to me that we mustn't make camp too close to the tent—well, that shook me up, I'll never forget that, of course. But the thing that runs it rather close and is a quite different sort of thing [chuckles] is the time I got the wind up [scared] properly. This was during the return to Cape Evans on the sea ice. I had to bring back a small party. I don't know *who* was there. Except I remember Tryggve Gran, and I was very worried. We started off too soon and the ice—saltwater ice, it's very rubbery, even [when] that thick—and went along very happily on our way to Ice Tongue, and then we started a little bow wave moving ahead in front of the sledge. My trouble was: what's the right thing to do? Do I turn back or is it safe to go on? [Chuckles.] I didn't like it a bit. I thought, I ought to turn back, still I was obstinate enough to refuse to do it, regardless of the consequences. But I was scared, I was really scared that time.

n: And you were heading where?

w: From Hut Point up to Cape Evans.

n: At what time of year?

w: The spring of 1913.

n: You know that three years after that Mackintosh and Hayward were lost doing that, leaving Hut Point too early for Cape Evans.

w: Mm. Well, I was properly scared, it was the first time I was really scared. I put it down to being responsible. I believe that makes the difference. It was then that I almost for the first time realized what a difference there is for one's attitude, whole attitude, when you have the responsibility for other people as well as for yourself.

n: What would you say are your most vivid memories in modern times in returning to Antarctica?

w: [Chuckles.] Climbing up the ladder at Byrd Station. There were a few missing rungs, and anyway it was at a sort of angle, like that. That was hard work, last time I was there, in sixty-five. I was getting on in years.

N: Sir Vivian Fuchs wrote me recently and said he thought that you had been active in Antarctica as late as the age of seventy-nine.

w: Yes.

N: You were saying yesterday that Sir Raymond Priestley, who had been on both the Scott and the Shackleton expeditions, thought that he preferred Shackleton as a leader.

w: When things were sticky. When things were sticky give him Shackleton, he said. Very sticky. One of the kind of people who rise readily to an emergency. There are people, you know, like that.

N: He felt more comfortable in a dangerous situation?

w: In fact he thought—if you asked him I think he'd say—that Shackleton was a more human being. What I mean is that—now I don't quite know how to put it—I suppose he mixed better with his people. If you're in command, and particularly if you're in command for a long time, there are two ways of getting the best out of people. Let's put it this way. This is my private opinion. One is to order. The other is to turn it if you can into a game. If you can get two teams working against one another for some sort of a prize you're well away. And I think it's the better way of doing things than to issue orders with no argument or nonsense about it. I don't know what this is going to sound like or what impression you get from this. I did say before, Captain Scott was a Royal Navy captain, and on board ship the captain was God Almighty when there was no radio to tell him what to do. And Shackleton came up through another hawse-pipe, as it were. I'm only quoting him [Priestley], he said it to me more than once when I asked him about Shackleton. He said he thought the world about Shackleton, he thought the world about Scott, but they were two different kinds of people. Scott was the leader and Shackleton was one of the gang but pre-eminent, shall we say. I can't explain it properly but you know what I mean, of course.

N: Cherry-Garrard says in his book that Amundsen's abilities were underestimated by the *Terra Nova* people. That he was much more of an intellectual, much more a man of serious grasp of what he was doing, than the *Terra Nova* people thought.

w: Yes, I think that's fair enough. He had only one objective: get there and get there first. That's all that matters to a man like Amundsen. [Pause.] Well, he's a tough guy and he used his dogs in a way that we would never have done. If we'd had his dogs we wouldn't have treated them in the same way, we couldn't have borne to have fed the weakest to the strongest and so on, you see. I know perfectly well that this is why Shackleton and Scott chose to take ponies.

N: Are you speaking now as a Canadian? I mean this feeling about the use of dogs. Do you share that with the English?

W: Well, it's difficult to know. It all depends on the circumstances. You don't know until you bump up against them how you feel about things. But one always felt that Amundsen treated his dogs scurvily in order to get the best out of them, and Scott, you see, had had this experience on his first journey, he had had to kill the dogs, and this he couldn't stick at any price.

❈ ❈ ❈

N: Sir Charles, how much time do you suppose elapsed before you returned to Antarctica?

W: I left in 1913 and went back again toward the end of 1959.

N: Had you a desire to return before then?

W: I didn't have the opportunity. Well, I must have had this in mind for some time, because it takes a little bit of time to arrange things. I was at the Pacific Naval Laboratory, doing magnetic research, and had for some reason or other to go down to La Jolla, so I stopped off at Stanford University and had a word with Professor Helliwell and arranged for this conjugate-point experiment, you see. Well, it was just very, very convenient, with Byrd Station very close to the conjugate point of our Great Whale River station on Hudson Bay.

N: Did you return with the United States or the British Antarctic program?

W: With the United States program.

N: And you went to Byrd Station the first time?

W: Yes. I was at Byrd three times, I think.

N: What's so fascinating is that you left Cape Evans in 1913 and after a passage of so many years, suddenly you arrived by plane at Williams Field, and then at Hut Point, with all the enormous changes. I'm curious to know what the impressions were on you.

W: Well, I knew what to expect, you know. I'd been kept informed by NSF and other organizations. But I nevertheless was quite surprised to see these big C-130s landing on the ice and taking off.

And the techniques they used! One time they took me to the Pole, just for the purpose of going to the Pole, you see, and they had to deliver a great bagful of gasoline, and they had it on rails, kept the engines of the aircraft going, then opened the doors and just accelerated the aircraft, leaving the bag behind! [Laughs.] Yes, I thought the first man who thought of that deserved another medal.

N: When you first went back and saw the Discovery Hut there, with the storage tanks and so on, were old memories awakened?

W: Well, naturally. The fact was that the hut, and Observation Hill, and the cross that had been put up umpteen years ago—they didn't seem *very* different except there seemed to be more bare ground, less snow about.

N: Was it depressing to be there and to see these changes?

W: No, no, not at all. But I'll tell you one thing that gave me a frightful shock. I gave a talk once at Byrd, it was, and at the end of it one of the chaps got up and said, "Could you have got the bodies of Scott and his companions back?" I said, "Of course." And then I realized what it was all about. There's a fundamental difference between the American attitude and the British attitude. American casualties have been brought back from all over the world and been planted back at San Diego. It's quite amazing, it really is a strange thing to my mind. I'm sure there was not a single one of our party would have thought of it. This was the place where they had done their best work. Leave them there! Gosh! I got such a shock! [Chuckles.]

N: Sir Charles, was it Scott who named Wright Glacier in your honor?

W: Well, it appeared on the map, but Scott couldn't have approved it. The map as it stands at present wasn't drawn then. The truth of the matter is that the part of the glacier that we saw was named really by Griffith Taylor, I think. We were naming these things as we went along, any old thing, and then these were accepted.

N: You visited your namesake valley with Jim Brandau. He remembers the visit very vividly and fondly—I think this was in 1965—and in a letter to me you indicated that he put the wind up you.

W: Yes, he *did.*

N: Would you care to expand on that?

W: Well, he took me along—special trip, all by myself.

N: This was the first time you saw your namesake valley in modern times?

w: No, I had visited there before, by helicopter.

n: But this was the first time you went alone?

w: Yes, and the last time. I have a real admiration for that man, I think he's one of the nicest people I've ever met and one of the most competent. I'll never forget the time he took me over to Wright Valley to see the sights from the air, and I thought at one time when he was going over one of these steep, comb ridges, I thought that he was going to try and land, and I didn't see where he could possibly land on a slope of about sixty degrees on either side, there just was no land left on which to come down, but he had complete control of the thing in spite of the wind and the rest of it. I had thought he was going to land, and if he did I didn't know how I was going to get out. [Both laugh.]

n: What were your impressions of the valley on your first visit?

w: Well, it was a surprise to me. In the light of what I thought I knew I was surprised that there was so much of it. It's so much bigger than the Taylor Dry Valley. And to see from the air that gorge. It looks as if an incredible great mass of water and ice had come down and torn the steep sides.

n: Did you revisit Taylor Valley ever?

w: Oh, we spent quite a time there. On the lake.

n: Bonney Lake?

w: No, there's another one.

n: Lake Chad.

w: You know why? We had some, what we called bumf, paper rolls [toilet paper], made by a Lake Chad firm, whatever they were. And we drank this water, made tea out of it and so on, and there was a lot of magnesium sulfate or something in it, and thus we had to use a *lot* of paper. So—Griffith Taylor said, "Oh, we must call this Lake Chad." It was an awfully interesting time back then. I think the first surprise was to find that it was possible to find a fine place to put down your tent and go to sleep, and then wake up and have a stream of water in your sleeping bag. [Laughs.] As the sun came along. We didn't pay much attention to day or night. And then there was the time I'd gone off, doing something, and Taylor, who had a very curious mind, I mean filled with curiosity, at any rate he'd read that seals have a natural ability to catch things and play ball, the kind of things you see them doing down in California. So he untoggled from the sledge and slung the end of his harness, with the toggle on the end of it, to a seal that he'd met on the sea ice, and to his surprise on the second cast, I think it was—I heard about it afterwards—the seal caught it and waddled off to its hole, Griff unwillingly following. And the thing that struck me was Edgar Evans's remark, "You know, sir, his bloody face was as white as a bloody sheet." I've heard that since, but this was the first time I heard it put that way. Bloody face as white as a bloody sheet. [Laughs.] Well, I'd liked to have seen that. Fortunately the seal, just as he went into the water, let go, and Griff didn't go down with him. And then we moved across to the Koettlitz, and there it's an astonishing country. There was the glacier itself, quite wide, afloat at the end, and blown sand had drifted in with the wind and collected in all the crevices, then started eating its way in and down, and it left a most extraordinary landscape that Evans called, and again I heard this for the first time, "A few feathers."

N: It was almost untraversable, wasn't it?

W: Very difficult.

N: It has pinnacles.

W: Yes, pinnacles, and quite big chunks of ice. You could very often wind yourself round them but normally you just had to go up, and on the side facing south was a sort of plowshare effect. Flat slabs of ice, and the sun getting at the sand. We didn't go very far along the glacier, except we had to cross it on the way back. And there was where we met what seemed to me the most extraordinary thing: a headless fish. A great big fish, you know, but they had no heads. I still don't know why they had no heads. This was stuff that had been brought out in some way from the bottom of the sea. In fact we were walking on the floating stuff which originally had been right on the sea bottom, and the worst of that was that all the sponges there are silica sponges, and they had great big long strips of silica lying on the surface, they broke up into bits, you see, and our problem was how to get some ice or something which wasn't full of these silica strips. You had to strain them out with your teeth. It's one of the things that I didn't understand, why we didn't have severe trouble with our tummies.

N: Are you concerned about matters of conservation in Antarctica?

W: Yes, having seen, in 1959, the McMurdo base and the trouble they had in disposing of all the waste, and the numbers of people there, and everything thrown into the sea, you know, it worries one, it may be good for the euphausia and crabs and things like that but you've got to pay for it some time. And actually one feels now that we were far, far too careless, we were only a small party and it didn't matter, really, to dump the stuff on the sea ice and it went out and sank, but I feel we were very careless the way we killed the seals and penguins for fresh food. We didn't make the best use of them, anyway. The seal meat itself was not frightfully palatable, but seal's liver was awfully good, seal's liver was what we all went for in preference.

n: I understand that you also revisited Cape Evans.

w: Yes. There was quite a party—New Zealanders. . . . I can remember, but not his name, one New Zealander who was a lawyer, who had been brought down by air from Christchurch on a joy ride, you see, and one of the ways for the captain or admiral to get rid of him was to turn him out to go and visit the huts. They'd rigged it up very largely for my sake and for the sake of Quartermain— Quartermain was in charge of the restoration of the place—and they'd come to Ponting's photographic room and I was supposed to open it. [Chuckles.] I don't know whether I did or not, I don't remember it very much but there were lots of photographs taken on that occasion, including "Now, would you just point to your bunk?" you see, and you would point to your bunk, the thing was all in bits, it was really out of the place where the bunk *had* been. But I didn't get to Shackleton's hut that time. They had some senators and people like that from the States at the time, it was a special sort of little stunt.

n: Was this in '65?

w: No, I think it was 1960, tag end of the summer.

n: Let me ask you a rather sentimental question. What do you miss most in Antarctica? That is, is there anything about the place that haunts you, in a good sense?

w: [Chuckles.] Starvation. [Both laugh.] You know, one would dream things like . . . *apples*, apples. Heavens, what one wouldn't have given for one. Apples. Or . . . yes, porridge. But if you'd been offered an extra ounce of something, your choice of anything, really, an ounce a day of extra, I'm sure we would always have said, "More pemmican." More fat. Well, that's the thing that I've remembered very vividly.

23. *Interior view of Scott's hut on Cape Evans*

24. *An attacking skua, Cape Evans*

25. *Scott Base*

26. *A run on the ice shelf*

27.   *Sandstone, dolerite and the edge of a glacier in Victoria Land*

28. *Taylor Valley*

29. *Glacial meltwater in Taylor Valley*

30. *The Suess Glacier, Taylor Valley*

31.   *The crash scene on Mount Erebus*

32.   *A later view of the scene*

33. *Mount Erebus*

19

BRIEF STAY AT SCOTT BASE

THE MORNING after my return to McMurdo from Cape Evans I did some of those inevitable chores that help deplete one's precious Antarctic time: duplicated pages of my journal at the Chalet, air-mailed the photocopied pages to Joan, bought odds and ends at the ship's store in the personnel building, spoke at length about my program with Chris Shepherd at lunch, made arrangements to move to Scott Base at four, and selected the gear I wanted to take with me. I was no stranger to the Kiwi base but now my plan was to obtain a more intimate feel of it by spending two nights there. I remembered well the first time I had hiked there alone, some thirteen months previously, after which I had written:

"One morning I received permission to walk the two miles from McMurdo to Scott Base on condition that I was to phone the MAC (McMurdo) duty officer when I left McMurdo, when I reached Scott Base, when I departed from Scott and when I returned to McMurdo. Although the walk was safe enough, the weather in Antarctica is very uncertain and I could be caught in a blizzard or a whiteout, the latter a polar phenomenon in which the sky and the snow or ice reflect each other so completely that one loses orientation and feels as if he were in a bottle of milk. If caught in a whiteout one should sit it out until it passes. It may last an hour or two or a couple of days, depending on your luck. I suspected that the real reason for the calls was that I was a member of the tenderfoot press group and therefore a prime candidate for getting into trouble through ignorance and an excited imagination. Haunted by the ghosts of Scott and Shackleton, whose names and exploits were never distant from us on the ice, I might give way to the actor in all of us and play the role of OAE (Old Antarctic Explorer), taking a short cut across the crevassed ice or wandering off into the hills.

"I left McMurdo after an early breakfast, taking outlying lanes and seeing a fuel tank farm, crates stacked outside of warehouses, and fork trucks and bulldozers. As I climbed the Gap between Crater Heights and Observation Hill I came upon men constructing a tank which would hold more than two million gallons of fuel. The temperature was 4°, the wind velocity at McMurdo ten knots. But in the Gap were head winds of twenty knots and more, which brought the effective temperature down to −35° F. or lower. The winds made the going slow. Also, my Navy gear was heavy, the thermal boots caused my feet to drag and the way was still surprisingly steep. I had the neck and ear flaps of my cap down but side gusts burned my eyes, causing them to run copiously. When I put up my parka hood I discovered I couldn't secure it because one of the drawstrings was missing. The wind kept blowing it back over my shoulders. Finally I let it stay there, occasionally shielding my left eye, which felt frozen, with a hand. I had brought my bear paws along. Whenever I removed them, for example to adjust the hood, my hands in their double gloves ached, then went numb.

"On my right the island sloped away, black rock and white snow, to the bluish ice shelf which stretched out flat and immense to the horizon. On my left was a mottled, flinty, dark, volcanic hill of pumice-like stuff swept clean of snow and marked by regular vertical ridges that appeared to have been made by bulldozers. A hill further along on my left was furry with snow and on my right and somewhat ahead of me, far below on the white shore, was Scott Base, looking tiny with its antennas and green huts. I descended the steep road, slippery with brittle shards of volcanic rock, and became aware of the pressure ice at the coast's edge, its angular, uplifted, helter-skelter and vaguely frightening forms tinted with delicate blues and greens. Skuas were wheeling above the shoreline. Far out on the ice, almost indiscernible, was a cluster of specks that was Williams Field.

"A Kiwi led me past pressure ridges and over minor crevasses onto the ice to see some Weddells and their pups. The seals were massive, and the ice and snow in their vicinity were stained yellow, red and brown by the afterbirth. In this world of blacks, whites, greens and blues the warm afterbirth colors were very conspicuous. A seal observed us across her wiry whiskers, bawling cries of alarm if we drew closer than some six feet. Her pup's eyes were large, dark and soulful looking. When my companion, squatting, reached out a glove the pup suddenly snapped at it, just missing it. We threaded our way back among the pressure ridges with their jewel blues and cobalt shadows."

Named in honor of Scott, the base is located on Pram Point, a low, rocky projection on the eastern side of Hut Point Peninsula. In 1971 it consisted chiefly of nine prefabricated huts linked by corrugated iron tunnels or ways. The ways permit movement around the station regardless of the weather and without the loss of time that would be involved in changing clothes. Auxiliary buildings included two magnetic huts, two seismology huts and a large former hangar, now a garage and work space. The main reason for the present existence of the station was its scientific work. In 1971 Scott Base conducted experiments in seismology, geomagnetism, ionospheric physics, auroral and air glow, VLF (very low frequency) radio propagation, satellite tracking and meteorology. Its post office was the world's most southerly one to provide all postal and communications facilities, and it had its own set of stamps, known as the Ross Dependency series.

I was driven to the base in a Nodwell and taken in tow by Jim Barker, the deputy leader, a hearty, booming-voiced, sunburned, smiling, bright-toothed man whom I had met in the McMurdo wardroom. He led me to my quarters, the tiny hospital room in D Hut. (The station handled minor medical problems; more serious ones were treated at McMurdo.) The room had a speckled green linoleum floor and two small square windows that you opened and closed by a screw arrangement. It felt like a freighter cabin and was cold during the time I worked in it, even though I wore thermal underwear and a heavy wool shirt. Overhead was a bright electric bulb called a "glim" by Barker. The walls were painted enamel white. The several shelves were the same color; their facing and that of the windows was blue. On the shelves were medicines, dressings, first-aid kits and splints. In a corner, to the left of the door as you entered, was an old-style, high, wheeled, white metal bed, above the head of which was a ventilator. To the wall opposite the bed was attached a little plywood table that could be folded out of the way. It would serve as my desk.

To save on laundry (water was made by melting ice cut and transported from the ice shelf's pressure ridges) Barker asked me to use a sleeping bag instead of sheets. To my amusement the thin, zipperless khaki bag on the bed was narrower than a mummy bag. It was tricky to slip into it. You mounted the bed, braced your behind against the wall, set your feet into the bag and slowly snaked your way inside. Once you were inside it was difficult to move about. The bag had a pale blue liner and was provided with a pillow in a fresh case.

Barker, showing me around the station, introduced me to a number of friendly, attractive men. On the whole they were a youngish lot. They looked as if they had spent much of their lives outdoors in clean air; had keen eyes on the alert for humor; and smelled good in their heavy beards and rough, tweedy clothes. They knew they were being observed by someone collecting material for a book, yet they were unselfconscious in their gestures and speech.

I saw, among other things, the communications room, the post office, the scientific laboratory, the generator room, the communal room that served as mess hall, lounge, library and movie theater, the adjacent kitchen, the lavatory and the wash room. The lavatory had a hole and a honey bucket. A sign read PLEASE DO NOT EMPTY THE MOP BUCKET DOWN THE PISSER! The ways connecting the huts were very cold. In places you bent low to avoid obstructions. The heavy doors giving access to the huts were small. You stepped high over the lower part of metal door frames, bending in order to keep your head from coming into contact with the upper part. The doors had massive wooden or metal handles.

I had some New Zealand beer with Barker in the mess hall before dinner. Barker liked to use Maori words, such as potai (poetie) for head covering and smoko (smoe-koe) for tea break. The hall contained two long tables, each made up of three smaller, squarish ones. There were two table maps under glass, one of Antarctica, the other of New Zealand. The dinner, prepared by Frank Bonn, who was originally from England and was now a resident of Auckland, consisted of rare roast beef, broad beans, roast potato, Yorkshire pudding and a piece of fresh fruit. You picked up a plate, went to the kitchen and served yourself. You sat where you liked. You knifed up communal butter or jam without bothering to clean your knife of previous food; or at best you cleaned it on your slice of bread. When you finished eating you scraped your leavings into a container, placed the plate on a kitchen counter and dropped your utensils into a tin box half-full of soapy water. It was the duty of the house-mouse detail to wash the dishes and clean the hall. Food wasn't offered you in explosive quantities as it was at McMurdo.

There were twenty-two men at the base at present, excluding me. Two more residents were due to arrive that evening from the Pole. A few others were in the field. Eleven, including Brian Porter, Jim Barker and Frank Bonn, would winter over. The rest would return to New Zealand in February. All the current base personnel were on the ice for the first time. The personnel were selected by the station leader with the approval of the Antarctic Division of the Department of Scientific and Industrial Research.

After dinner I chatted with Brian Porter about needed repairs in the Cape Evans wanigan. I knew him from meetings with him at McMurdo and I liked and admired him. When you phoned him he always responded with furry yet unaffected softness. "Porter," he would say in an English accent, musically. He had a gentle, sometimes distant, at times ironical smile; was quite bald, with a fringe of attractive close-cropped gray hair; and was short, slender and handsome. He often wore a heavy, handmade, gray turtleneck sweater.

At eight there was a movie in the mess hall: *Midnight Lace*, with Doris Day and Rex Harrison, borrowed from the Navy at McMurdo. The mess hall was cool; you wanted to keep your hands wrapped in something. As soon as the film was over, men huddled close to the diesel-fired stove. The casual conversation was sprinkled with four-letter words, as it often was at McMurdo, and there were the usual sexual allusions.

One man asked Frank Bonn, "How are you?"

Bonn replied, "Still hanging. How's yours?"

Some of the men read Christchurch papers, snacked on bread, jam, tea, fruit, coffee. I spoke with Graham, the radio man, who told me that the base made regular phone calls to the States, Europe and elsewhere by short wave to New Zealand, then by cable. Unlike the phone patches from McMurdo these were two-way commercial calls. A call to the States cost $3NZ per minute. Graham said that quite a few people came from McMurdo on a regular basis to make calls.

I slept deeply and awoke very hungry. Out of overpoliteness I hadn't eaten enough at dinner. For breakfast I had two poached eggs, bacon, homemade bread, butter, black-currant jam, gooseberry jam and tea. Also available were smoked cod warmed in water, fried eggs, marmalade and coffee. An American rock singer was being played on the Philips stereo machine. The mess hall was warm and cozy now. I chatted with Brian Jackson, the tall young base information officer, who was from Dunedin and who admired the work of and had once interviewed Janet Frame, the New Zealand novelist, for N.Z.B.C. (pronounced N Zed B C). Jackson was interested to learn that Janet Frame and I were friends. I spoke enthusiastically about her work to him.

During the morning I wandered around the base's vicinity, fascinated by the razorbacked slabs of pressure ice, yellowish in places, that had been pushed up by the ice shelf. The Ross Ice Shelf has its northwestern terminus at Ross Island. Its northern side, facing the Ross Sea and stretching eastward from Cape Crozier, is some four hundred nautical miles or roughly four hundred and seventy statute miles long. The shelf is approximately the size of France; this gives one some idea of the continent's vastness. The shelf is believed to be afloat although attached to the continent, and its thickness has been judged to be between eight hundred and a thousand feet. It is the largest in the world, is in slow motion, moving generally in a northerly direction, and presses against the eastern shore of Ross Island, a shore much of whose outline is conjectured only. It is this pressure that causes the chaotic upheavals known as pressure ice. Antarctica's uniquely tabular bergs are tabular because they are formed by ice calving off the ice shelves. On occasion immense tabular bergs have been encountered by ships. An iceberg approximately the size of Connecticut was reported some years ago.

Now I saw blocks of ice, huge shapes jutting out of the shelf's flatness (the shelf had a pale, bluish-lilac tint), that looked as if they had been tossed about at random. The pressure ice was no place for a novice to explore: it contained crevasses, some of them hidden because they were snowbridged. Beyond it were several basking Weddells.

Near the base's entrance was a sign listing air distances to some major cities. Wellington: 2536. London: 10588. Moscow: 10501. Buenos Aires: 4449. Paris: 10382. Washington: 9214. Capetown: 4603. Brussels: 10520. Oslo: 11085.

After attending the morning tea break at ten, I went to my room, where my hands turned very cold as I wrote in my journal. Glancing at them, I realized it was not a smart idea to cut your nails short if you went camping in the high southern latitudes. When your nails were short, flesh tended to separate from them, and the dirt under them was difficult and painful to remove. At lunch I was invited to go sledging with the huskies and to join an ice party afterwards.

Few nations nowadays keep dogs. The trend for some time has been all to motor toboggans, which don't run off without you, don't fight each other and aren't carnivorous. Scott Base legitimately feeds its dogs seals under the Antarctic Treaty, but occasionally I heard grumbling at McMurdo about the misuse of Weddells in order to hold to a tradition now anachronistic. Whether the Kiwis continue to use dogs in addition to motor toboggans more out of a sense of tradition and romance than for other reasons, I do not know. No doubt they get good work out of the dogs in the field. Sometimes the dogs and sledges are airlifted to distant work sites by the United States Navy. But it seems to me in keeping with New Zealand's slower and more nostalgic pace in the world for Scott Base to continue to use dogs.

Shortly after 1 P.M. I walked with two dog handlers northward along the coast to where the huskies were staked out. The handlers were young, strong and bearded. One I knew only as Ken; the other's name was Mac Riding. Riding had a magnificent, brown, patriarchal beard, a fine nose and clean, engaging, sharp eyes, but he cut a strange figure in his mechanic's coveralls streaked and spotted with grease, in his filthy, broken-vizored cap (the vizor hung limply on his forehead, making the cap remind one of the little fatigue article worn by the Japanese Army in World War II), and greasy white thermal boots. I wondered where these affable Kiwis, newcomers to the ice, had learned to handle huskies.

The dogs had been born in Antarctica and would die there. As they sensed our coming they began to howl, bark and whine, at first gently and in fits and starts, as if unsure we were heading their way; then, as we came in sight, loudly and continuously; and from their compound rose an uproar of wild sounds that to the handlers were by now probably ordinary but that to me were electrifying, for they not only vividly stirred thoughts of Scott, Shackleton and

Amundsen but told of harnessed energy, runs on the ice shelf and potential savagery.

Siberians and Greenlanders with eyes suggesting an oriental look, the dogs were spaced on chains attached to a long wire to prevent their getting at each other. Like their counterparts of the old days, these charming, friendly-looking animals, who bounded against you and licked your face, sometimes had murder in their hearts for their fellows. They were work dogs, used to and needing to work, and they lived a dog's life. Their compound was urine-stained, and spotted with dark feces that had sunk deep in the snow, and they themselves were stained with urine and seemed to smell of it. They were half-wild creatures who endured extreme cold for much of the year, subsisted on fishy seal meat and occasional human caresses, and probably daydreamed of coupling, running and fighting. They were wet and dirty; their tan, creamy or brown fur was heavily matted; they looked pent-up, irascible.

The area was dirty, tracked upon; contained both hard and soft snow; the deep ruts made by a bulldozer; snow mounds; ice mounds; and, beside a small crevasse (called a "slot" by the Kiwis), the re-mains of many seals, especially flippers. To the east were slabs and hummocks of bluish pressure ice, to the west the black and white slopes of Ross Island. Also visible were the ribs of White Island on the ice shelf, and Mount Erebus in the north, steaming heavily.

Only nine dogs would be taken out for the day's run. The pack howled, barked and pranced to get the handlers' attention in the hope of being chosen. There were twenty-one dogs at the base. Riding said that tomorrow there would be twenty. One, a nine-year-old bitch who still hadn't shed all her winter coat, who no longer pulled well in the traces and was no longer worth what it took to feed her, would be killed. Riding would shoot her.

After each dog was harnessed he was lifted by the collar so his forelegs were in the air and was brought to the sledge in this manner to keep him from taking off and disappearing in his frenzy of activ-ity. Snorting, grunting, heaving, pulling, whining, barking and lunging, he was led to the traces. Ken, Riding's assistant, wore a white woolen ski cap over long brown hair, blue coveralls over heavy clothing, and orange mukluks. Like Riding he was sunglassed and barehanded.

By the time Osman, the leader and the last of the dogs to be harnessed (an Osman was a leader on Scott's last expedition), was brought to the head of the double line of dogs, I was seated on my parka at the end of the Nansen sledge, my back wedged against the sturdy sledge back, my heels propped against a long weighted cardboard box covered by a green canvas and well roped down. I had been told to dress warmly. Hatless and gloveless, I was sweating, for the sun was sharp and the compound was protected from the winds by hills and pressure ice. Riding warned me to hold on: the dogs would take off like a shot and go flying over the shelf ice until the steam was out of them.

However, they were slow getting started, the sledge was on wet deep ruts, and suddenly they tangled and were a great furry mass of contorted, snarling, slashing bodies. Possibly certain personal grudges were being settled. The impression I received was that the dogs were biting at random, with those on the bottom getting the worst of the fray. The guttural snarling was intense and moving. The handlers, carrying heavy rope knouts, rushed silently to the heap and flailed at it. Despite their fury the huskies made no passes at the men. But it was some time before they responded to the blows.

We made another start (Ken was sitting in front of the cardboard box) and almost overturned on a sharp slope. The snow shone with diamonds and rainbows as we tore across fresh surfaces, over old ruts and came close to spilling as we crossed narrow crevasses. I saw bloody ears and legs. One dog limped and whined and was pulled and dragged during the entire run. Riding remarked in a disturbed voice that there was no help for it, the dog would have to learn the hard way. On the flying snow I saw drops of bright blood. When the pack showed signs of slackening, Riding, clinging to the end of the bouncing sledge (the shelf's surface was rougher than it looked, as I knew from my trips on it in Nodwells) and breathing heavily just behind me, and occasionally and accidentally rapping my bare head with the handle of his ice ax, shouted, "Ready, dogs! Ready, dogs! Ready, ready, ready, dogs!" Or "Osman, you dirty bastard!" Or "You bloody cunt!" Or "Come on, you fucking bastards!" "Ready, dogs! Ready ready *ready*, dogs!" Soon he was hoarse.

We were sledging at what felt like great speed over patches of sastrugi, over deep, rough-textured, virginal snow and over stretches of pale blue glacial ice. On our left was Erebus; on our right were Black and White Islands; receding behind us were Pram Point and

Cape Armitage. The dogs, silent, were running as though for their lives.

Suddenly we were following vehicle tracks and Riding cried, "Look at the bloody fuckers! They're too used to roads! Koo-woo-woo! Koo-woo-woo-*woo!*"

Koo-woo-woo was the signal to Osman to turn to the right. Osman blandly ignored it.

Then Riding ran as fast as he could to the right of Osman and ahead of him, a flying bearded broken-vizored figure, hoping Osman would follow him, shouting, "Osman! Osman! Osman you bloody stupid bastard! Koo-woo-woo! Osman! Koo-woo-woo-Osman! Osman you fucker! Koo-woo-woo-woo!"

But for a long time Osman didn't respond. When he did, Riding cried, "Good Osman! Good dog! Ready, dogs! Ready, dogs! Ready ready ready ready, dogs!" and away they flew, and Riding had to run with all his might across soft snow in his huge bunny boots to catch up.

Once Riding cried out, possibly for my benefit, "Every dog handler has to swear at his dogs!" Another time, when Osman was lagging and Riding had to run to the head of the line to urge Osman to follow him, Riding cried, "A dog handler has to set an example!"

I thought of Amundsen's highly trained dogs, who, if they had disobeyed, would have immediately felt the whip. Not that Amundsen had been insensitive to dogs; he had loved them. It was that his mission and his life had depended on them.

Occasionally, when the dogs were allowed to rest briefly, Ken left the sledge and anchored it by plunging the point of his ice ax through a round metal device attached to the traces. During the rest periods the dogs were busy with latrine matters (the feces were black, probably because of a diet of Weddell meat), and one became aware of the deep, dark odor of the dogs' farting.

When we came to a snow cairn with a little red flag on a pole they ran over the cairn and broke the pole. They tried now to turn right to head for the base, which was no longer visible to the naked eye. Riding shouted several times, "Osman! Uh-rrrr-uh!" (He rolled the "r" on the tip of his tongue.) This was the signal for Osman to turn left. Osman took his time before complying. The dogs broke into another fight and again the handlers had to knout them to stop it.

The Nansen sledge was comfortable; it felt as if it had built-in shock absorbers.

Returning to the base, we crossed several crevasses, into one of which a dog disappeared. But he quickly emerged, being yanked out by the others, and Riding shouted, "Tighten the traces, you bloody fuckers!"

I was on the sledge for more than two hours. It was a marvelously interesting, exhilarating and profane ride.

I was let off near the ice party, which was in a tiny valley, a trough between hummocks in the pressure. There was a great deal of glare. The five bearded men wore sunglasses. The group was cutting ice from the top of a pressure ridge north of the base and loading it in great milky cubes onto two huge yellow sledges in tandem, with high, fencelike sides. Two men were using power saws that sent steamlike smoke against the blue sky and were so noisy one of the loaders, a blond young scientist, covered his ears with his hands. It was hot, heavy work and the three loaders strained under the loads. Full of dynamic, extreme motion, they reminded me of figures, say of smiths at a forge, in certain of Goya's paintings. The loaders had removed parkas, hats and shirts and were laboring in white or navy wide-mesh net undershirts of the kind I had seen in Christchurch shop windows.

Two of the men wore baggy windpants. One of these was a man named Jim, who was in his early forties but looked much older with his serious face and the many gray streaks in his thick brown hair. Wearing crampons over his boots, Jim was working at the very top of the hummock, cutting the ice in steps. When he jackknifed away from me I saw what looked like a pair of empty cerise standing windpants. His assistant, wearing blue dungarees, a black turtleneck and a black ski cap, gracefully crowbarred the ice blocks, causing them to tumble down to the loaders.

I waited until the sledges were filled, then rode back toward the base on the tail of one. They were pulled by an orange Caterpillar bulldozer with NZARP painted on it. When the bulldozer got stuck on a steep slope a Nodwell had to be fetched to pull it free with winch and cable. The bulldozer then tried to winch up the sledges, which were on the edge of a deep crevasse about two feet wide. The cable harness broke and the sledges were temporarily abandoned. I continued to the base on foot in the company of the ice party.

During dinner I asked some of the men how they had learned

about positions being available at the base. Without exception they had answered advertisements in the New Zealand papers. Later I hitched a ride to McMurdo by Navy truck, picked up my mail and hitched one back to Scott Base in time for the evening smoko. In the communications room I drank a couple of cans of Piel's Real Draft Beer with two Kiwis while some Americans waited in the tiny post office next door to make calls to New Zealand and the States. The sun was deliciously warm this evening and pellucid as it poured through windows, luring you into believing there was still plenty of time before nightfall: take it easy, mate, have another beer, another chat. I got chilled working in my room before turning in in the very light but thermally adequate bag atop the white hospital bed.

I arose at 6:30. After breakfast I wandered around the area north of the base for close views of pressure ice and a chance to stare at serene, smoking Erebus. My left thigh was troubling me. Its underside had been sore for almost a week, making it painful for me to sit in certain positions and impossible to touch my toes. When I returned to my room and tried touching them for ten minutes the consequence was twofold: I failed, and the thigh was in considerable pain for a couple of hours afterwards. It was depressing to have to consider one's body in Antarctica while one still had much urgent work to do that required one to be fit and on the move.

The Candy Wagon (USARP power wagon) picked me up at 1:30 and took me back to McMurdo Station, where I reported to the Dispensary across the fast-running, silvery meltwater stream from the chow hall. Examining the thigh, a medical corpsman declared that a muscle was in spasm as a result of dehydration, adding that dehydration was a fairly common human ailment on the ice. I checked my memory but could not recall that it had been a problem mentioned by either Scott or Shackleton. He urged me to drink lots of water and gave the thigh a heat treatment on a hospital bed, during which I fell into a deep sleep lasting more than an hour. The other beds were vacant. When I awoke, the plastic Christmas tree in the room looked friendly with its illuminated, colored little lights. I listened awhile to the pleasant murmuring of the voices of two corpsmen in a nearby office. Before releasing me, the corpsman handed me a box of light green pills called parafon forte, saying they would relax the muscle and warning they might make me sleepy. I had a hunch it was the same kind of pill that had caused Dave Murphy to sleep so much in the Cape Evans wanigan.

I went to my room in the Lodge. Chris Shepherd phoned me about the icebreaker. I reminded him that I needed to board her while she was still north of Ross Island. He told me not to worry and said one of her two helos would pick me up on Saturday or Sunday (this was Thursday). Meanwhile I would be on standby, ready for immediate departure; a Coast Guard helo from an icebreaker might appear unexpectedly.

While plodding through chores (cleaning gear, unpacking, packing, finding places for new acquisitions, duplicating pages of my journal, writing and mailing letters, doing some laundry), I realized suddenly, with a sense of something like horror, that I had only ten days left on the ice and that I still had many impressions to receive and much data to mine and record. I wished I could stay on longer but I knew my chances of receiving an extension were slim. Even scientists had difficulty in obtaining an extension. From the scientific point of view, the view that my sponsor, the National Science Foundation, naturally took, my program was marginal. When I considered this fact together with the condition of my thigh it was hardly surprising that I grew a bit depressed.

20

<hr>

ABOARD THE ICEBREAKER

STATEN ISLAND

ON THE LAST DAY of the year a mimeographed bulletin appeared in the chow hall, announcing in blue ink:

NEW YEAR'S EVE
PARTY
IN DOWNTOWN MCMURDO
AT THE O'CLUB
Music by "Sweet ART and his SWINGERS"
Horses Ovaries and free booze
1930 UNTIL 0200
31 DECEMBER 1970
BRING YOUR OWN GIRL—UNACCOMPANIED
LADIES NOT ADMITTED

From my journal:

"1 January 1971. I stayed in the wardroom and movie theater, where a party was going on, until about 10:15 last night, then went to my room, intending to do some chores and return for the midnight scene, but felt very sleepy, lay down on my back, fell asleep thinking about women, awoke at about 11:40, thought I'd get up but decided I was too short on sleep, undressed and turned in.

"The wardroom itself wasn't lively but the theater was. There was plenty of food in the theater: a heaping mound of reconstituted dehydrated shrimp with a hot red sauce; salami; frankfurter bits; hot meat balls; cold cuts and so on. And there was music: Art with an electric guitar, somebody with an electric harmonica and a third man with an electric banjo. These were later augmented by more electric banjos. The bass sounds were tremendous, drowning out almost all others and booming back and forth in the small, floor-slanting room.

"When I entered the wardroom I immediately encountered four Kiwis in their usual dress: heavy beards, flowing hair in the hippie style, heavy dusty boots, plaid woolen shirts, brown tweed trousers. They greeted me warmly by name, asked if I had deserted Scott Base. I spent some time with them before moving to the bar and asking for a beer. The two bartenders, servicemen, were very alert, serving rapidly and intelligently. Other Kiwis were playing the dart game at the theater end of the wardroom and being pleasantly noisy about it. Among them were Graham the communications man, partially recovered from his cold (he was sick my last night at Scott Base), Mac Riding the dog handler and Neil the carpenter. I asked Riding if the bitch had been shot. He said no, they hadn't been able to find 'ammo.' I had seen him fooling with a black automatic yesterday morning. I said, 'Good. She has another day. Seal meat is cheap. Why not let her live?' 'She's a work dog,' he said. 'Work dogs must work. Every day she sees the others go out to work and she's left behind. That's crool. It's crool to the dog. When a work dog can't work—pop.' He put a finger to his temple.

"There was a terrible din in the wardroom because of the bass sounds, which drowned out even the loud singing of Art and his companions. Some Kiwis, including Mac, Neil and Graham, went into the theater, got hold of a mike on a stand and sang a long funny bawdy song, accompanied by Art on the electric guitar. John Noyes, holding a tall glass with a teacolored drink, kept giggling in an uncharacteristic way. Bawdiness is typical of the McMurdo area. There's a terrific emphasis on intercourse, genital parts, sex jokes, pinup girls. In the science lab at Scott Base are some startlingly suggestive pinups in color, and somewhere at Scott is a black-and-white version of the seductive naked girl that hangs in the wardroom. Having had two beers and feeling sleepy, it was at this time that I left the theater, meaning to return.

"I was sleeping very deeply when I was awakened by an insistent knocking at my door. Standing at the door were Willis Nelson, recently returned from the Lassiter Coast and waiting for a flight to

Christchurch, and a Navy commander, Venzke, the Coast Guard liaison officer. Venzke had come to assure me, after wishing me a Happy New Year, that he would instruct the commanding officer of the second icebreaker, the *Staten Island*, to take me aboard as far out as possible. He explained that you can see Erebus at a great distance, that to take me aboard at a point where Erebus isn't visible would probably be impractical but that I would go aboard at the farthest practicable point. The first icebreaker, the *Burton Island*, was already too close to do me any good—it was probably off Royds. He said he would call the c.o. of the *Staten Island* tonight and tell him to prepare to send for me; that Chris Shepherd had talked with him about me and my need to go aboard.

"Apparently Willis had mentioned my urgent desire to get aboard as far out as possible and they had spontaneously decided to rouse me, reassure me and wish me a Happy New Year. Willis wore a party hat on his bald brown dome. He's an older man with thick spectacles, a gray mustache, brilliant teeth. His body is very white and rather thin. His neck, face and head are extremely brown from living in the field. He's a geologist with the Geological Survey.

"I went promptly to sleep again and awoke at seven. Feel I want to call Joan from Scott, where I could put through a call *today*.

"11:50 A.M. I walked over to Building 33 (Antarctic Support Activities) and told Venzke I'd like to take the *Burton Island* for a while to see the unbroken ice and to experience its being broken, then proceed to the *Staten Island* for long-range views. He explained that the two ships will cut ice side by side, that the *Burton Island*, now off Royds, will take a week to ten days to make it to McMurdo, so I'll have both experiences on the *Staten Island*. He'll 'firm up' plans for me at noon today and I'll probably be picked up this evening. I'll pack and be on standby. I explained that I have to give a talk Sunday at 7:30, and would I be able to come to McMurdo for it, then if necessary return to the ship? He said, 'No problem,' all would be arranged. It would be fine if I could spend more time on the ship than between this evening [Friday] and Sunday afternoon but I'm scheduled to fly to Crozier Monday morning.

"Called Scott Base. They don't think they can get calls through to the States today. The traffic from Wellington, through which they must move, will be considerable. But they could make a call tomorrow. However, I'll be on the ship tomorrow. Called the ham shack and signed my name on the phone patch list in the chow hall. *Would* like to speak to Joan and Susy.

"I still get illusions. A bit of fuzz floats down on a piece of paper and I think it's a fly or a mosquito, then catch myself and realize there are no flies, mosquitoes at this latitude. Dave Murphy was with the enlisted men last night. 'They're *animals*. One guy got his teeth kicked in. Another had his face slashed.' George Lacey told me before he left for the field that last New Year's Eve there were several fights in the streets, that he heard a voice in the night calling for help, picked up a shovel and ran outside, saw two guys, extremely drunk, wrestling harmlessly and *both* calling for help. So he went back to sleep.

"2:15 P.M. Am waiting for a phone patch and packing for the ship. There's never an end to things to be done. Did some laundry and other chores. Wonder where I'll get time to prepare for the Sunday talk. At least I'm not sitting around waiting, as some people unfortunately are obliged to do. Willis, back from the field, trying to fill the time before flying to Cheechee. People waiting to go into the field or waiting for cargo that's been delayed.

"2:45 P.M. It feels like night because I just talked with the girls and it's night where they are. At home it's 9:45 P.M. December 31. Spoke through Arkansas. At first the patch was poor, voices sounded fantastically treble, like canaries singing, or crazy bass, then it settled down.

"6:50 P.M. Finished dinner. Am getting ready for the *Staten Island* helo, which is coming for me at 9:15. Will return to McMurdo about 4:00 Sunday for my talk, so I'll have a couple of hours to prepare for it. Chris said it's all right for me to prolong my stay here some five or six days but I'll lose time on the New Zealand end. He leaves for Christchurch on the eighth for a planning conference there."

The two icebreakers, part of Task Force 43, would cut a channel through the softening, thinning sea ice to McMurdo for the tankers and cargo ships that would follow them and resupply the station. Today, with few exceptions, only those who work the ships that annually and briefly visit McMurdo Sound have the privilege of encountering Ross Island from the sea as Ross, Scott and Shackleton did. The visitor to the Ross Dependency sector almost invariably boards a plane in Christchurch and hours later finds himself, a bit bewildered, on the ice at Williams Field, staring at Cape Armitage or Mount Erebus and suspecting he has lost something in not arriving slowly.

I wanted to see the island's classic landmarks at a distance, to observe the pack and sea ice at close range, to witness the movement through pack and the breaking of sea ice, and to sense what it's like to be in Antarctic waters. These were the reasons I had had myself scheduled to spend some time on an icebreaker and to be flown to the ship before it reached the island.

In the first edition of Ross's book there is a lithograph captioned BEAUFORT ISLAND AND MOUNT EREBUS, DISCOVERED 28TH JANUARY, 1841. Beaufort is seen in the left of the illustration, Erebus in the middle and right. The height and shape of Erebus are greatly exaggerated. Erebus does not appear to be the gently sloping, shield volcano that it is but one with a high cone. And neither Mount Bird nor Mount Terror is visible. Ross's people, using triangulation methods while at sea, obtained a surprisingly accurate elevation for Mount Erebus: 12,400 feet. Today the mountain is thought to be fifty feet higher. The Scott and the Shackleton expeditions reached excessive elevations for the mountain through the use of barometric devices.

Ross named Beaufort Island, "a small high round island," after Captain Francis Beaufort of the Royal Navy, Hydrographer to the Admiralty, "who was not only mainly instrumental in promoting the sending forth our expedition, but afforded me much assistance, during its equipment, by his opinion and advice."

Of Erebus he wrote, "The discovery of an active volcano in so high a southern latitude cannot but be esteemed a circumstance of high geological importance and interest, and contribute to throw some further light on the physical construction of our globe." Erebus was erupting at the time. "At 4 P.M. [January 28] Mount Erebus was observed to emit smoke and flame in unusual quantities, producing a most grand spectacle. A volume of dense smoke was projected at each successive jet with great force, in a vertical column, to the height of between fifteen hundred and two thousand feet above the mouth of the crater, when condensing first at its upper part, it descended in mist or snow, and gradually dispersed, to be succeeded by another splendid exhibition of the same kind in about half an hour afterwards, although the intervals between the eruptions were by no means regular. The diameter of the columns of smoke was between two and three hundred feet, as near as we could measure it; whenever the smoke cleared away, the bright red flame that filled the mouth of the crater was clearly perceptible; and some of the officers believed they could see streams of lava pouring down its sides until lost beneath the snow which descended from a few hundred feet below the crater, and projected its perpendicular icy cliff several miles into the ocean."

Ross spent some time sailing eastward to observe the face of the ice shelf. He described the discovery of the shelf. "As we approached the land under all studding-sails, we perceived a low white line extending from its eastern extreme point as far as the eye could discern to the eastward. It presented an extraordinary appearance, gradually increasing in height, as we got nearer to it, and proving at length to be a perpendicular cliff of ice, between one hundred and fifty and two hundred feet above the level of the sea, perfectly flat and level at the top, and without any fissures or promontories on its even seaward face. What was beyond it we could not imagine; for being much higher than our mast-head, we could not see any thing except the summit of a lofty range of mountains extending to the southward as far as the seventy-ninth degree of latitude." These mountains, named by Ross in honor of William Edward Parry, under whose command he had served in four Arctic voyages, were proved by Scott's first expedition to be non-existent.

On February 16 Ross again saw Erebus erupting. "During the afternoon we were nearly becalmed, and witnessed some magnificent eruptions of Mount Erebus, the flame and smoke being projected to a great height; but we could not, as on a former occasion, discover any lava issuing from the crater; although the exhibitions of to-day were upon a much grander scale."

Ross named Mount Terror after his ship, *Terror*, and Cape Crozier after the captain of the *Terror*, Francis Rawdon Moira Crozier. He named Cape Bird after the senior lieutenant of the *Erebus*, Edward Joseph Bird.

Some sixty years later Scott described his impressions on first entering McMurdo Sound. "The night of the 21st [of January 1902] was gloriously fine. By 8 A.M. we were in the middle of McMurdo Sound, creeping slowly, very slowly, through the pack-ice, which appeared from the crow's-nest to extend indefinitely ahead. But a few miles separated us from the spot where we were ultimately to take up our winter quarters, and as we got to know this scene so well it is interesting to recall some extracts from what I wrote when first we gazed on it: 'To the right is a lofty range of mountains with one very high peak far inland, and to the south a peculiar conical mountain, seemingly ending the coastline in this direction; on the left is Mount Erebus, its foothills, and a glimpse of Mount Terror. The Parry Mountains cannot be seen ahead of us. In the far distance there is a small patch like a distant island. Ross could not have seen these patches, and a remnant of hope remains that we are heading for a strait, not a bay.'"

Ross had erroneously believed that Erebus was connected to the mainland and, as we know, that the body of water between Ross Island and Victoria Land was a bay.

At 8:45 P.M. I carried my gear to the upper helo pads, just below the Chalet, and left it there, waiting for the Coast Guard helicopters to appear. Two helicopters from the *Burton Island* arrived first, stayed awhile, then flew to Williams Field to refuel. The Coast Guard helos were HH-52As and had a hull and pontoons in addition to wheeled landing gear. They were turbine-powered, single-engine, and looked sleeker and roomier than the Navy's H-34s. The cockpit did not sit high as in the latter, and you entered it from the passenger cabin.

I went down to the hangar, where I ran into Shepherd and Venzke. Shepherd kidded me about being eager to take off for the icebreaker and persuaded me to join him and Venzke in his Jamesway hut, Building 137, for some beer.

The two helicopters from the *Staten Island* landed at 9:15. When I saw them coming in I went down to the pads and met the ship's skipper, Captain Stanley G. Putzke, and put my gear aboard one of the craft. The skipper disappeared with Venzke while I joined the two pilots, who asked to be shown the wardroom. This was their first visit to the ice. The wardroom looked strangely dark and empty after all the recent partying. The pilots were wearing black rubber survival suits under their flight suits. Complaining of being too hot, they stripped the survival suits off. I led them to BOQ2, a Jamesway, and found Jim Brandau and a friend of the younger of the two pilots. Brandau, wearing loose-fitting longjohns, made a pot of coffee.

After some talk in the BOQ2 bar in the proximity of large photographs of naked women, the pilots and I went to the hangar, where we remained until Captain Putzke showed up at about eleven. The captain entered one helo, I the other, and we all lifted off for the ice-breaker. During take-off I was belted in as usual. As we soared above the Sound I unstrapped myself and belted myself to a long heavy canvas strap hanging from the ceiling. The strap allowed me to stand at the very edge of the open cabin hatch while I shot photos. The wind sweeping into the cabin was very cold. Occasionally I had to stop shooting, close the hatch and rub my hands together to make them continue to function.

We flew northward quite far out from the island, passing several miles west of Castle Rock. A great cloud streamer ran southward from the crest of Erebus. It was close to midnight now, the sun was nearing its lowest point of the day, and there was a soft, nostalgic light everywhere. In the south the sky was a pale bluish green; its zenith was a mild, clear, watery blue. The Glacier Tongue's southern cliffs were agleam. Much of the sea ice was under cloud cover and was therefore bluish and subdued, but some of it was alive with a dappling light. The textured sea ice showed pimples, sastrugi, and gray and ivory blotches. Off Cape Royds we flew over the *Burton Island,* a pretty toy sitting on ice marked by ripples, cones and something resembling pebbles. The lane the ship had cut showed beautifully grained brash. We saw at a glance the ship, water beyond it, and beyond the water the farflung western ranges. The ship's smoke cast violet shadows onto the sea ice.

What was most enchanting, perhaps, was the delicacy of the light and colors, especially in the sky, which was tinted with lazy, horizontal lemons and limes, as well as with rose and a pale magenta. A cloud bank above Beaufort Island in the north (Beaufort rose from the sea some miles to the northwest of Cape Bird) hung softly, with hints of dusty gray. Near Beaufort were stretches of ice gleaming dully in the low-lying sun. On the milky saddle between Mounts Erebus and Bird were glowing ivories reflecting the spotty cloud cover there.

We began to see strange patterns in the lilac-washed sea ice, the beginnings of long cracks, and what looked like roads far below. We spied the Sound's head, water with pack in the north, and the dark cliffs of Mount Bird under their mantle of snow-ice. The whole vicinity of the northwest end of Ross Island had the softness of scenes long but now only faintly remembered, rising up from the fairy-tale world of one's earliest childhood. Portions of the sea ice and sea were a burnished brass. The patches of thawed sea in the foreground, royal blue, in places verging on black, added greatly to the scene's haunting magic.

I had never heard anyone speak of the great beauty of pack ice as seen from the air. Leaning out of the hatch so I could look straight down, I became aware of the abstract pack-ice patterns, composed of octagons, squares, triangles, rectangles, ellipses and ovals. I was stunned by the infinitely varied patterns of black and white; by the marvelous, almost musical variety of forms; by the subtle greens in oily sea streaks; and by the slow, soft sweep of Mount Bird. Erebus was seemingly everywhere, smoking, overpowering. The sea in the direction of Cape Bird was now a glossy, sweet, rich blue. Beaufort Island sat alone, an abstract stony figure, small, humpbacked, at the horizon's edge, with a vast sky all round it. Part of the sky above it was a faint, transparent cirrus. Just above the horizon were bands of ivory merging into pale greens. In the foreground, floating upon the deepest possible blues, were masses of pack.

I spotted the *Staten Island* north of Ross Island, heading south towards the Sound. The perfectly mirrored ship, trailing a series of ripples, was sailing on burnished clouds. The serenity and breadth of the scene, and the reflections of the cloud-figured sky in the placid, limpid, frigid water, were breathtaking. I could not believe the amount of beauty I had been explosively exposed to. As we began to descend towards the ship I saw beyond it a large floe, then Beaufort again, naked, gray, like the back of a wild hog; also the ship's wake, suggestive of streaming long hair. I found myself looking straight down at the white-outlined, stern-deck helo pad, marked by a bright red circle. The ship's prow seemed to be fast in ice between two cuts it had just made. The ice had the color of old ivory; its markings resembled those of a thoroughly weathered plank.

Although the ship looked tiny, like the *Burton Island* she had a length of 269 feet, a beam of 63 feet, a displacement of 6,000 tons, and an authorized allowance of 14 officers and 167 enlisted men. She was built by the Western Pipe Company of San Pedro, California. Under the terms of a lend-lease agreement she was turned over to the U.S.S.R. in February 1944 and given the Russian name *Severny Veter*, meaning *North Wind*. She remained a Russian icebreaker until the end of January 1952, when she was returned to the United States Navy at Bremerhaven, Germany. Between 1952 and

1956 she was used by the Navy in the Arctic. Her first Antarctic voyage was made in 1956 as part of Operation Deep Freeze II.

I was welcomed aboard the *Staten Island* by the ship's executive officer, Commander James N. Schenck, who introduced me to several officers on the bridge, took me to the wardroom and then led me to my bunk in the visiting officers' quarters two decks below. The crowded bunks, some already occupied by sleeping forms, reminded me of photographs of oldtime steerage. There were no portholes here. The quarters were only dimly illuminated by one or two weak electric bulbs to permit sleep. I had the middle bunk on one side of a very narrow corridor. The bunk was high off the deck, and, as I later discovered, it took some doing to slide into it without slamming your head against the metal side of the bunk above. It was a bit like sandwiching yourself between two slices of bread. When you lay on your back it was not possible to flex your knees, and the upper bunk felt surprisingly close to your nostrils. Getting out of the bunk was even more funny than getting into it. You could not sit up and let your legs dangle before dropping down onto the deck. You had to execute a roll-and-drop maneuver. It was not a good bunk for veterans of lower-back trouble.

I had expected to be assigned a stateroom so I'd have a place to work in, therefore I was a little surprised to find myself in the midst of loud engine sounds and the roaring sounds made by the ship's attacks on the ice. But I was not disappointed, for I could sense the possibility of literary material in my situation. I stowed my seabag and other gear where I could, spoke briefly with several young and eager Kiwis who were on their way to Scott Base and who had heard that I had lived there, then followed the executive officer to the captain's cabin, at the door of which the x.o. left me.

Captain Putzke, a gentle, reserved, soft-spoken man with a thoughtful air, offered me a nightcap, which I declined with the explanation that I had work to do before turning in. The skipper then called for apple juice. It was brought by a dark-skinned steward. We drank a couple of glasses before the skipper turned in. I made my way alone to the bridge, which was commanded now by a young, affable, blond junior lieutenant. We were still north of Ross Island, between the island and Beaufort Island, and I was relieved and delighted to be able to see the classic view: Mount Terror on the left, partially behind Mount Bird, Mount Bird massive in the middle, and Mount Erebus on the right: the three rounded volcanoes, two of them extinct, that formed a clustered trinity and were the quintessential landmarks to the early explorers arriving from the lower latitudes. Mount Terror showed a bit of a crater. Mount Bird seemed to have none. You could see Mount Erebus's second crater clearly, as well as its third and youngest crater at the crest. I could not make out Cape Crozier or the ice shelf to the east.

Working mostly outside, occasionally I got very cold, especially in the feet (I was wearing my hiking boots), which I couldn't manage to warm up despite visits to the wheelhouse. We were heading directly toward the low-lying sun, and the frozen sea glared terrifically. When the prow swung for a little while to the west or east it was a relief not to have the sun in one's eyes. The sun and ice flared powerfully through one's sunglasses.

The ship never stopped working. Picking up momentum, it rammed the seemingly solid sea ice, which was some nine or ten feet thick here. The icebreakers do not cut the ice; they ride up onto it, and their weight cracks it. Then they back off down the lane they have cut, reverse direction, gather speed, and ram again. The ships have rounded sides and are capable, by means of a ballast system, of rolling to help the ice crack. When the prow rams and climbs the ice there's a great growling, snarling and hissing, and the hull roars as the larger ice chunks scrape against it. Momentarily you're unsure of your footing. Then the ship slides back, or settles through the newly formed cracks. There are a few moments of quiet and stability before it backs off.

At times I saw the ship's superstructure blue-shadowed on the frozen Sound, or its brown smoke fouling the crystal air. I saw the cone of Mount Discovery south of us; floes of pack; and between the floes, chunks of jewel-green, freshly upturned sea ice. The water was vivid blue when you looked down upon it, the ice a faint amethyst. Through binoculars the western ranges, with their snowfields and glaciers, showed extremely sharp. The pack, containing many fine jades, looked very rough when you glanced across it towards Ross Island. The meeting of forces, ship against ice, was very alluring, almost hypnotizing.

It was after 3 A.M. when I made my way down the steeply pitched steel stairways to my quarters. For a while I wasn't sure I had found my quarters. They were in darkness except for the dim glow of a low-slung red light near the door, far from my bunk. I groped my way to the head, recognized it and was certain then where I was.

But I couldn't see well enough to make out bunks or sleeping forms. I didn't like the idea of fumbling down the narrow, cluttered corridor toward my bunk and possibly touching sleeping men. What to do? Return to the deck and spend the rest of the night working? Or tell the young lieutenant on the bridge about my predicament? Then I remembered that while packing for the ship, almost as an afterthought I had tossed a tiny flashlight into my green rucksack. I crawled to my gear, felt around, located the sack, and found the little flashlight that had served me well in Christchurch but which I had had no occasion to use on the ice. I was all smiles when my fingers embraced it.

After sleeping an hour or so—the bunk was hard, and I was distant from the breeze offered by a ventilator—I had to urinate (I had been drinking a lot of water), so I went to the head again, on entering which I hit my right toe against a metal upright. The toe's pain made a harmony of pain with that of my sore, dehydrated thigh. My situation for some reason struck me as being very funny.

Next morning the captain invited me to use either his cabin or an adjoining stateroom for my office. I accepted gratefully.

From my journal:

"2 January 1971. Saturday, 8:05 A.M. Off Mount Erebus, somewhat north of Royds. The skipper, and I gather most if not all the crew, are new to the Antarctic but veterans of the Arctic. Home port is Seattle. The young Kiwis told me about the rough voyage, the ship sometimes listing forty degrees. Last night the skipper said he expected the ship to be off Royds by morning but it wasn't. It was about abreast of the northern slope of Erebus and going in circles to cut big pieces out of the ice so that any wind that came up might send the ice northward. The *Burton Island* was visible now, working to the south of us.

"9:30 A.M. The skipper is extremely friendly. He has offered me a tour of the ship and has placed his helos at my service whenever they're not in official use. I'm being treated handsomely, and the bunk down below, where the engines throb and vibrate and roar and where you really feel the collisions between the ship and the ice, is an added windfall of humor and color. A general rattling of things in this stateroom. At times the ship itself seems to rattle. But it doesn't roll much. The Sound is smooth, and there's little wind.

There's no inclination to be sick. The ship lurches, though, when she hits a large mass of thick ice. The stateroom is opposite the captain's and shares his head, which has a stainless steel basin and john, also a shower, all spotless. I suppose it's because I'm growing tired that I begin to think how pleasant it will be to return to Cheechee and see those lovely minis, the green-bordered streets, enjoy the bar at Warner's, sleep long, maybe go for a swim. The Coast Guard helo pilots saying yesterday they can't understand why anyone would want to come here. The skipper saying he loves the Arctic but can't 'see' the Antarctic. 'I'm a practical man. I know it's beautiful down here, with mountains. But what good are they? Maybe it's good enough that the place is a scientific laboratory. I don't know.' They look skeptical when I say I love the place, and surprised when they learn I've returned to it. This morning, by the light of other bunks, I found a light above mine, but last night I didn't know it was there. The placed looked black even after I stood awhile and let my eyes get used to it. But I had been on the bridge, looking into the sun, so my night vision was temporarily impaired.

"Another low-latitude illusion: yesterday at McMurdo my eye was caught by a long stocking being blown in a brown streamer on the ground. I thought, 'Women!' Then I saw it was a kind of crepe paper, probably used for wrapping things, and remembered that there are mighty few women down here on the ice, and even fewer who might be wearing sheer hose.

"2:35 P.M. We're off the Barne Glacier, tackling some heavy ice. The going is slow. The ship shivers and heaves, sometimes as though in heavy weather. The day is typically brilliant. We work side by side with the *Burton Island*. We ram the ice about one and a half ship's length. When we come to a halt with grinding, rending, cracking sounds we back off a good distance, pick up speed and grind forward again.

"4:45 P.M. Lunched with the skipper, Venzke and Chris Shepherd in the skipper's cabin. Hot vichyssoise, asparagus tips rolled in ham, delicious french fries in strips, tomato and lettuce, a carrot and radish salad, and vanilla ice cream with chocolate topping—all with linen and a thin reddish drink. I returned to the deck as Chris and Venzke departed by helo. It's nippy on the bridge. Men working very seriously there, steering a course. Many skuas following the ship for garbage. Occasionally Adélies, on seeing us, rush madly for the water, tobogganing, then plunge out of the water in upward dives, then submerge. Some Weddells."

Once I saw Erebus with cloud streamers that seemed to have exploded from its crater. Its northern slope, showing rock masses, looked grainy. At times the Western Mountains looked empty, rough, razorbacked, dangerous.

The two ships, working together, made huge cracks in the ice between them. Each ship cut its own channel but the strategy was to chop up the cracked ice between the channels, forming a broader lane that hopefully the winds would clear of brash. If the winds failed, the brash would freeze and the ships would have their work to do again. The upper portion of the freshly broken ice (the portion that had originally faced the sky) was white; the lower was pale blue. It was fascinating to watch the ice crack and break up around the ship, showing vivid blues, or tannish undersides.

The icescape was very desolate. A helo pilot, gazing at it, said to me, "How'd you like to enlist? It's not fit for a man." There was a faint sickle moon in the northern sky, east of a brilliant sun.

The skuas had gathered on the floes near us. Some of the men threw food out to them. I had heard stories about the cruelty of enlisted men toward skuas, whom they despised because the birds preyed on the Adélies. Once, standing on the bridge deck, I noticed a man two decks below handling a rod whose hook he had baited with a chunk of raw meat. Grinning, he prepared to cast. Fortunately an officer happened along, noticed what I was observing and called down to a chief below, "Chief, I don't think that's a good idea." The enlisted man took his rod indoors.

It would be useful to have a booklet prepared explaining the ecological balance in Antarctica and the terms of the Antarctic Treaty that protect fauna, and to distribute it to all American hands entering Antarctic territory. It would be no cure-all but it might in some instances prevent sadistic behavior through a better understanding of the predation roles played by certain fauna in the high southern latitudes.

At dinner the skipper said he hadn't had much sleep of late; he was often interrupted by phone calls. (There were many dial phones on board.) A sign at the door of his cabin requested you to press a buzzer before entering. Once, as I came in from the bridge, I awoke him as he was dozing on the couch.

I said, "I'm sorry. Sorry about that."

"This is quite a place," he said.

We dined alone on rock lobster, rolled chicken and ham, boiled potatoes, salad, mixed vegetables and canned fruit cocktail.

He said, "The Arctic is fascinating because of the Eskimos. It looks as if God didn't make the Antarctic for man. He made it just to be here."

His practical mind was troubled by the unexploited Antarctic.

"There's a mint of money to be made in the Arctic. What's there to be made here?"

He spoke of how lonely he felt when driving across an American desert.

"Some people like the desert. Not me. I push down on the accelerator. I want to get *through* it, to be with people."

"Am bothered by my left leg, which seems to be worsening. Feels like a cold in it, if you can have such a thing. And I think it's worse when I'm outdoors. Haven't been taking the green pills on shipboard; didn't want to feel sleepy. But tonight I'll take two, and tomorrow also. One writes, writes, but the essential beauty eludes one. Maybe that's why one wants to come back. Am haunted by a desire to capture some of that beauty out there: disemboweled foaming ice, showing blues and greens; the naked sky with the medusa sun, the rays like streaming hair.

"3 January 1971. 10:35 A.M. Abreast of the Dellbridge Islands. Am surprised we didn't make more progress during the night. I thought we'd be off Erebus Glacier Tongue by now. We're about 9½ miles from McMurdo. Have been able to see Ob Hill since yesterday: very clear, with what looks like smoke rising from it. Can it be volcanic dust? At about 11:45 two chaplains, one Protestant, one Catholic, will fly aboard from McMurdo, hold services (this is Sunday), lunch with the captain. I'll return to McMurdo with them. I got up late this morning, a bit past eight, having taken two green pills last night. Slept deeply but at times was aware of my left leg aching in certain positions. Had breakfast in the wardroom and chatted with a young helo pilot, then went to the bridge, greeted the skipper, took in our position and shot some photos. Relief to find a wide cloud cover and mild windless air. The cover protects one from sunburn, varies the views, puts the scenes in a lower key. But there's still plenty of glare. In places, say on Erebus's upper slopes and on

Hut Point Peninsula beyond the Dellbridges, the cloud cover allowed light to seep through and dapple the scenes below. The Dellbridges look black, harsh. Scott described them as inky. 11:20. Fell into a deep sleep in my chair. The green pills are working. Feel stiff and sore throughout my body.

"Last evening a red-bearded pilot asked me if I cared to go on a flight. I said, "Sure," and went with a helo to retrieve a tall red metal target barrel (for the ships to sight by in cutting the channels) and place it farther down the line on the ice. Before the flight the pilot asked me if there was anything special I cared to see. I said yes, pointed Cape Evans out to him, said I wanted to check the door of the wanigan there. So after we finished with the barrel work we headed for Evans, I indicating to the pilot where to go. The door looked secured. I was relieved, for it was a helo crewman, not I, who had shut it when Dave and I departed. I was worried about it, it's hard to shut.

"The captain this morning expressed surprise the ice continues three feet thick and rather soft. He had thought it would be thicker as we approached Hut Point. But we need a good wind to blow the brash out. The ships will be at McMurdo sooner than he had expected. His is the command ship of the two, and the other captain at lunch yesterday, Frank E. McLean, is the skipper of the *Burton Island*. The ships will remain at McMurdo about a month, then cruise around Antarctica, visiting Mirnyy, among other stations. Today the ships will stand side by side, touching (this is feasible in ice), and services will be held.

"1:25 p.m. I watched the ships join. Captain Putzke maneuvered the *Staten Island* from the outside wheel, standing on a platform and wearing a khaki cap, khaki trousers and a dark windbreaker. He moved the bow up to the stern of the *Burton Island*. A plank was set between the ships, roped down, a net rigged beneath it. There was little if any tidal or wave motion to be felt. The *Staten Island* now very steady, its engines silent. Occasionally I feel a rolling in my body.

"Men breaking out beards all over the ship. Everyone extremely appreciative of New Zealand women. New Zealand described as 'a bird-watcher's paradise,' with the shortest minis, beautiful legs. Used binoculars on the bridge this morning, could make out the Polar Party Cross on Ob Hill. Exciting to study Erebus's slopes and crevasses. Such beauty, and so inhospitable to man. Something fine in that. Good to see places that frustrate man, belittle him."

I flew out late that afternoon, sorry to have to depart so soon from such an interesting and hospitable home. But I was glad to have some solitary time in my McMurdo room to prepare at least briefly for my talk in the Chalet that evening, the topic of which was, as I recall, "Looking for the ghosts of Scott and Shackleton."

21

~~~~~~

WILSON'S IGLOO AND CAPE CROZIER

DURING MY TALK in the Chalet on Sunday evening Brandau was present in the balcony, and afterwards, downstairs, I overheard him saying something to Chris Shepherd that alerted me. Shepherd was replying that I was too tired and would not go on another flight. I asked Brandau what he had in mind. He said he wanted to fly me tomorrow morning up to Cape Evans, then down around Hut Point, Pram Point, Cape Mackay and up to Cape Crozier. He would thus roughly retrace by air the route that Wilson, Bowers and Cherry-Garrard had taken in their midwinter trek. I quickly said I'd go, adding that although I had checked the Evans wanigan door from a flying Coast Guard helo I wanted to double-check it on the ground to make sure the wanigan was secure for the winter.

When we lifted off, Hut Point was a mess of rotten ice, brownish tidal cracks, famous hut, point of volcanic land, silver fuel tanks. Erebus came into view, and the two icebreakers working abreast of each other and resembling toys, and the Dellbridge Islands, and Erebus Glacier Tongue and Castle Rock. We landed between the Terra Nova Hut and the wanigan and waited while the crewman ran to check out the door. When he reported it to be tightly shut, we took off and headed south over the sea ice and had a close look at Danger Slope and Arrival Heights. McMurdo was entirely free of snow and ice now, and the ice of the anchorage was rapidly breaking up. I saw the Lodge, the Chalet, Crater Hill, the nuclear power plant, and then there were Cape Armitage, black, deserted, and the Gap, green Scott Base, and Erebus flaming in whites and blues.

The boundary of the eastern shore of Ross Island is indefinite, being covered by pressure ice, and by ice and snow in the form of glaciers, cascades and slopes flowing from the island's interior. We were quite far out on the ice shelf when we passed Erebus, whose sensuous eastern slopes, lovely with dappled light, looked more creamy than the textured shelf beneath us. We saw Windless Bight and the gentle protuberance of Mount Terra Nova, and fascinating compositions, some in whites, off-whites and chalk whites, and many crevasses, some on the lower Erebus slopes, others on the Aurora and Terror Glaciers. (The Aurora runs between Mount Erebus and Mount Terra Nova down to the bight; the Terror runs down to it between Mount Terra Nova and Mount Terror.) The larger crevasses were spectacular: great bluish gashes. As we left the bight behind and passed Cape Mackay we saw small black hills descending from Mount Terror to the shelf and making fine contrasts with the bluish-white island snow masses. Mount Terror did not look imposingly high, probably because of the saddle between it and Mount Terra Nova on the left. Mount Terror was a dull lilac-white except for slashes of glowing white caused by light falling through breaks in the clouds. In the foreground, below the mountain's chief mass, was a maze of pale blue crevasses.

We circled over Wilson's stone igloo and landed near it on a black knoll or spur about eight hundred feet above the ice shelf. The igloo seemed to be closer to the shelf than I had expected it to be. Some of the lower portions of the rock walls were still in place. One saw pieces of bamboo pole; parts of the skins of the Emperor penguins the three men had killed in the Crozier rookery and dragged here in order to flense them and use the blubber in the blubber stove and thus conserve oil; some blubber; pieces of pale Willesden canvas; a wooden box; either a khaki sock or a khaki balaclava (I couldn't make out which); a shirt; a ball of twine; some rusty bits of metal; pieces of rope and wire; and a bit of broken board.

Brandau said the floor of the igloo, together with these remnants of that remarkable trek from Cape Evans to Cape Crozier, were usually encased in ice. Today there was some ice skim on the water that covered the floor. I thought of all that had occurred here back in 1911 and wondered if a wanigan shouldn't be built over these souvenirs to protect them.

A cold wind was blowing off the shelf. Brandau searched the ground in the vicinity of the igloo, picked up something and handed me a tiny piece of black volcanic rock with black hairy lichen on it. He meant for me to have it as a remembrance of the visit. I gratefully accepted it.

We lifted off. Approaching the shelf's edge, we flew over stretches of fragmented, grated, lacerated ice. We saw cracks, cracks everywhere, of all widths and lengths, open, gray, running in many directions. The waste-ice reminded me of that of the Beardmore Glacier. It was very exciting to swoop low over it. The Ross Sea, lying beyond the shelf, at first glimpse resembled an indigo ribbon. The shelf edge as seen from above was jagged and sugar-white, with an embayment some miles to the east. Suddenly we saw the full sea itself, free of pack, not blue but lead-colored, for the cloud cover gave the water a somber look. Yet there was beauty in the contrast between sea and shelf, both of which, because of their uninterrupted size, were liberating to look at after the writhing volcanic masses of the island. I hadn't realized to what an extent I had felt land- and ice-locked. Near the ice cliffs four Killer whales were crisping the sea's surface.

We turned now to view the Crozier cliffs, black, basalt, some eight hundred feet high. Beyond and above them white snow masses rested in the cradles of black hills. In this direction the mostly blue sky contained some pale gray cirrus. It was thrilling for me to see the meeting of cliffs, ice shelf and sea which I had read about in Ross, Scott, Shackleton and Cherry-Garrard. It was not far from here that Ross had discovered the great Ice Barrier, of which he wrote in his book:

"It is impossible to conceive a more solid-looking mass of ice; not the smallest appearance of any rent or fissure could we discover throughout its whole extent, and the intensely bright sky beyond it but too plainly indicated the great distance to which it reached to the southward. Many small fragments lay at the foot of the cliffs, broken away by the force of the waves, which dashed their spray high up the face of them."

The first edition of his book contains a small engraving captioned CAPE CROZIER AND MOUNT TERROR. He wrote, "Mount Terror was much more free from snow [than Mount Erebus], especially on its eastern side, where were numerous little conical crater-like hillocks, each of which had probably been, at some period, an active volcano;

two very conspicuous hills of this kind were observed close to Cape Crozier."

In *The Voyage of the "Discovery"* Scott discussed Cape Crozier, its Adélie rookeries and the Barrier at length. "From Cape Crozier," he wrote, "the land turns sharply to the south in a magnificent black volcanic cliff in parts 700 or 800 feet sheer above the sea. The barrier edge extends at right angles from the southern end of the cliff, and at first has a very rugged appearance where the ice-mass presses past the land, but within a few miles it settles down into its uniform wall-like aspect."

In January 1902 he, Royds and Wilson climbed the highest of several volcanic cones in the vicinity of Crozier, recording an elevation of 1,350 feet for it. Scott wrote:

"Perhaps of all the problems which lay before us in the south, we were most keenly interested in solving the mysteries of this great ice-mass. Sixty years before, Ross's triumphant voyage to the south had been abruptly terminated by a frowning cliff of ice, which he traced nearly 400 miles to the east; such a phenomenon was unique, and for sixty years it had been discussed and rediscussed, and many a theory had been built on the slender foundation of fact which alone the meagre information concerning it could afford. Now for the first time this extraordinary ice-formation was seen from above. The sea to the north lay clear and blue, save where it was dotted by snowy-white bergs; the barrier edge, in shadow, looked like a long narrowing black ribbon as it ran with slight windings to the eastern horizon. South of this line, to the S.E. of our position, a vast plain extended indefinitely, whilst faint shadows on its blue-grey surface seemed to indicate some slight inequality in level; further yet to the south the sun faced us, and the plain was lost in the glitter of its reflection. It was an impressive sight, and the very vastness of what lay at our feet seemed to add to our sense of its mystery."

While viewing the Crozier cliffs I also saw the triangular-shaped trench in the sea ice, pebbled-looking and dirty, in which the Emperors had their rookery (the world's best-known Emperor one) and in which some fifty or sixty Weddells were now basking. The birds had already gone north. We saw spots of pea-green water and pale, jewel blues in the pressure ice.

We landed near the Jamesway at Cape Crozier and were greeted by Dietland and Christine Müller-Schwarze, a German-born couple whom I had met at Skyland, Virginia. They were biologists employed by Utah State University. This was their second austral season at Crozier, where they were studying antipredator behavior of Adélie penguins. On the brief walk between helo pad and Jamesway we passed nesting young skuas whom Dietland Müller-Schwarze fed daily and whom he had partially tamed. Beyond the hut was a falling slope on which, a good distance away, was a large Adélie rookery. From what I saw of it the place felt barren, stony and not very interesting visually. It was notoriously windy but not even a small breeze blew now.

It was my intention to camp here with the Müller-Schwarzes a few days, and in a sense my present visit was a scouting one. But when, over tea in the Jamesway, I learned that no leopard seals or Killer whales had been sighted from Crozier during the past couple of weeks; when I added to this the fact it was too late in the season to observe the Emperor penguins; when, in addition, I heard I would be living with these two attractive, intelligent but rather formal people in this overheated hut that contained a white tablecloth, white napkins, an armchair or two, a small plastic Christmas tree and a very delightful woman who belonged to someone else, and when I contrasted this style of camping in Antarctica with the one I had encountered at Royds and Evans, I decided to camp at Cape Bird instead, for I had heard that at Bird there were leopard seals, Killer whales and a simple wanigan. I did not have the option of camping at both places. I was due to leave the ice January 11, a week from today, and was greatly pressed for time. However, I did not have the heart to dampen Dietland Müller-Schwarze's ardor about Crozier, so I didn't tell him now about my change of plans. He spoke of skuas and Adélies in a very excited way and at length, imitating them with facility and passion.

On leaving Crozier we headed south and inland, rising quite high, to about 8,500 feet, according to my barometric altimeter, and received extraordinary views, chiefly in black and white, of a startlingly beautiful world done as if with a sensuous and sensitive brush. We saw snow-filled small black volcanic craters and the dusty blue of ice in craters blown free of snow. At this altitude the ice shelf seemed smooth and without crevasses, but we could still make out the long pressure waves alongside the black island. The eastern sky was milky and about the same hue as the shelf, so we could just barely distinguish the horizon line. In the northeast, far away, two or three tawny bands of light glowed between cloud cover and shelf. We looked out over Lewis Bay in the north, and saw Cape Bird and Beaufort Island in the northwest, and pack ice there, and in the far distance Victoria Land with its mountains. As we approached some of the clouds at cloud-height they resembled steam or fog. I experienced intensely and again and again the excitement and joy of flight. I knew that at 8,500 feet we had exceeded the normal maximum altitude capability for our craft, the H-34, and I wondered how Brandau had managed to do it and whether he was riding an updraft, but I had little time to think about this; so many scenes of great interest seemed to be demanding my attention.

And then I had a view of Mount Erebus and its surroundings from the northeast, and I saw the dark Fang to the north or right of Erebus, and the smoke plume flying northward from the crater, and the whole of the volcano's long eastern slope, treacherous with cascades and cliffs that fell to the pressure ice and the shelf, and some of the black Dellbridge Islands, and Observation Hill, and Cape Armitage, and the Royal Society Range and the glistening piedmont glaciers just north of it. The blues of the crevasses directly under us were so pure as to be stunning. I was shooting the volcano through the windshield. Noticing this, Brandau silently swung the craft around so I had unobstructed shots through my open hatch.

We flew southward, then turned west and crossed Hut Point Peninsula and flew over Erebus Glacier Tongue. A glacier flowing westward from Erebus, the Tongue's mass cracks and crumbles, forming dirty trenches full of jagged ice forms, wrenched, torn, flung about, as it drops from the island onto the Sound on which it floats. In the trenches we also saw soft, creamy snow blobs suggesting fresh plaster and containing commas of beautiful pale blues. The most marvelous color was the cobalt of the deeper crevasses. The Tongue's serrated scimitar shape curves slightly northward. Its cliffs, which at a distance look clean and firm, were in such a crumbled state they reminded me of the sides of a rotten tabular berg. Erebus rose beyond this chaos, its crest obscured by clouds fiery in a sunburst. We were moving low. At one point we skimmed the sea ice and looked *up* at the luminous greens of the broken cliffs. We saw Weddells craning to see us, and some humping snakelike to seal holes, and we saw a hole gory with blood. We flew round and round, and the little knobs of my cameras seemed to whirl as they reflected our rotors.

Then we flew low past the icebreakers working together off Castle Rock and landed at McMurdo. As soon as we got out of the helo Brandau, smiling, pumped my hand and said, "Chuck, I have to congratulate you. You're the only man I've ever taken on this flight who didn't run out of film. I've taken all kinds of people, many of them professional photographers, and I've warned them to take plenty of film along, but they always ran out."

He asked if I had any film left over. I said yes, two rolls. He couldn't seem to get over the fact. He told various people at the station about it and mentioned it publicly a year and a half later in New Hampshire. I was frankly more than a little puzzled by his being impressed, and still am. I just happened to have jammed a lot of cans of film into my pockets.

~~~~~~

22

CAPE BIRD AND WILLIAMS FIELD

THAT EVENING I dropped by the wardroom. I was wearing khaki corduroys and a khaki work shirt. Billy Blackwelder, a helo pilot who was a good friend of mine, asked me where I got my clothes.

"Army and Navy store."

He said he'd be damned if I wore khaki, I'd wear Navy greens from now on, and he took his shirt off and handed it to me.

I said, "Billy, you don't want to do that."

"Fuck you if you don't want my shirt," he said.

I said, "Hell, Billy, you know I feel honored."

"You hummer, I'll get you a *dozen* of them," he said. "You're a Navy man now. Don't you go wearing those Coast Guard khakis any more."

So Blackwelder and I exchanged shirts. His shirt had LCDR BLACKWELDER printed over the right breast pocket and VXESIX over the left one. It fitted me perfectly.

Some Coast Guard officers, loosening up, started laughing a lot, a number of Kiwis at one end of the bar were shooting crap, and soon there was a fair amount of profanity abroad. So then Blackwelder, right foot thrust forward solidly with a stamping sound, torso leaning strongly forward, eyes not lingering on anything or anybody, sang leather-voiced such songs as "There She Goes," "Half of a Photograph," "I Can't Help it if I'm Still in Love with You," "I Really Don't Want to Know," "Half as Much," "I Can't Stop Loving You" and "There Stands the Glass." Singing with him, you could not listen to him and watch him without becoming mesmerized, for he was handsome, young, athletic, had a powerful neck, his eyes were as serious and devoted as if he was singing hymns, he never paused between songs, only stamped his right foot hard and thrust it forward solidly and leaned forward to signal the beginning of a new one, and lowered his chin a moment until it almost touched his chest, and held his glass high, and his eyes, half-glazed, burned with that sacred light (bourbon; almost extinguished now), and his voice never faltered or cracked, and his repertory was delightfully extensive.

So then he started throwing coins onto the floor, shouting, "Sweepers! Sweepers! Get the hell out of here!"

And John Dana slammed coins onto the floor.

And I slammed coins onto the floor.

And Blackwelder threw a dollar bill down.

And a Navy officer who had just come in threw down a dollar bill.

And John Dana, related (so he said) to Richard Henry Dana of *Two Years Before the Mast,* kept wildly side-kicking coins and bills under the bar, often missing them, and grinning apple-cheeked, with a pointed gray chin, his eyes sometimes lost in folds of skin, and saying something sober now and again and managing to look sober.

So then Blackwelder said somebody impartial was needed to collect the sweepers as a gift to the new bartender. I was selected. So I gathered the sweepers on my hands and knees, added a dollar bill, and the money was placed in a glass and the glass set on the bar. The new bartender, an enlisted man, smiled and said nothing.

Then Dana, crying he'd be back in a minute, ran outside and returned with Blackwelder's portable tape recorder and some cassettes and played old songs, and somebody said, "John, what in hell happened to your head?" and Dana's dark head was gray on the temple now and there was dirt on his right shoulder and right thigh, and his right hand was bleeding, and he grabbed a brown paper towel and clenched it in a fist and wouldn't let anybody examine his hand. Finally he admitted he had slipped, and everybody laughed, so he said what a slide to second it had been, he had slid completely across the street.

"But nobody saw me!" he said very rapidly. "There were no witnesses! I looked around and checked that out!"

There was a lot of shouting and laughter and it was very good to be there in that small, overheated hut.

When Jim Brandau came in for a Coke he told me he might fly to Cape Bird tomorrow, and if he did he would take me along. I left soon afterwards and turned in, hoarse from shouting and singing.

Next afternoon as I approached his helo Brandau said quietly, "Chuck, you'll sit in the cockpit."

I harnessed and belted myself in, donned my helmet, checked my cameras and film. Off we went, rising quickly, surely, as Brandau always rose, but instead of heading out above the sea ice we went high and inland over the ham shack at Pogo, getting excellent views of McMurdo Station and Arrival Heights. Then we were at Castle Rock and observing the Dellbridge Islands and the gleaming Glacier Tongue with its bluish cliffs, and Erebus's icefalls. I was surprised to see a Coast Guard helo, 1360 of the *Burton Island*, on our port side and somewhat behind us. Brandau explained that it was accompanying us so its pilots could have a look at the McMurdo-Bird route. Examples of how lovely the route can be showed up below us: beautiful crevasses on the Erebus slopes, in some places fine curved parallel chalk marks indicating snow bridges, in others bluish or greenish upthrusting cracks. Then we were over the saddle between Mounts Erebus and Bird and soon we were above black hills and rushing through masses of vapor (clouds) and, breaking out, we saw blue water, ice floes, Beaufort Island, pack ice, pancake ice, brash, some small rotten bergs, the Western Mountains, and we descended rapidly and landed on long, broad, dark Caughley Beach. The *Burton Island* helo landed behind us.

Brandau went off alone onto the shore ice. Chris Shepherd, who had been seated in the cabin, and the Coast Guard people climbed the steep, soft, scoria trail to the Kiwi camp on a hillside plateau. I remained on the beach, waiting for Gary Means of the McMurdo Biolab, who was approaching the shore in a trimaran. Means said Cape Bird was the most beautiful place he had seen in the McMurdo area. He was particularly impressed by the sea here, covered by the constantly moving ice floes. He said the great access to the sea, to penguins, to seals and skuas was far superior to that at Crozier. And he was pleased by the fact the living quarters were quite close to the water's edge. He said the Kiwis, who were his hosts, were very friendly and hospitable.

For about two weeks prior to coming to Bird, while he was still at McMurdo, he had been unable to catch any fish. He had thought that if he could get to open water he might get some. Cape Bird had both open water and the trimaran. He had hoped to catch *borchgrevinki*, the kind he and Feeney had caught off McMurdo, but he was able to get only *bernachii*, a closely related species. He suspected the *borchgrevinki* had moved back under the permanent ice shelf. He had caught the *bernachii* with a baited trap made of wire screen, with an opening at each end which permitted entry but not exit. The trap was lowered from the trimaran and left off shore in two hundred yards of water, tied to a float. The trap had been lost when an ice floe tore the float away.

Means had then gone out with two Kiwis to help them take samples of the sea bottom. While doing so several whales sounded about half a mile away. Means and the Kiwis approached the whales for a better look. The whales were black on top, with a distinctive dorsal fin, and were an off-white underneath. Nine of these Killer whales were breaking the surface in unison. As the trimaran drew closer the whales moved away from it.

"Finally they approached a large solid ice floe which they appeared reluctant to go under. They began swimming back and forth along its edge. We approached to within about thirty yards and cut the engine. They kept swimming back and forth as we watched."

He said it was his belief that Killers wouldn't attack a man; he didn't know of one substantiated incident in which they had done it. When I mentioned Ponting's experience on Scott's last expedition he expressed skepticism. I said that Scott, Shackleton and other explorers who had spent years in Antarctica had been convinced that Killers were ferocious and would go for ponies, dogs, anything they could get, and would even, in packs, attack the giant blue whale. What did he imagine, from their point of view, was so special about man? He only smiled. Sunburned, he looked happy in his golden beard. Cape Bird had done him good.

Some time later Brian Jackson of Scott Base was to inform me that the Cape Bird trimaran was the first to be used in Antarctic seas and that it was named the *R. V. Clione* after an abundant swimming mollusk in McMurdo Sound.

Means and I climbed up to the wanigan on a height above the beach. It had two sections, the larger containing the bunks and a small kitchen area, the smaller a well-stocked biology laboratory. It was extremely crowded now. It reminded me of how the wanigan at Cape Evans had felt when the Navy cameramen had descended on Dave Murphy and me.

Six young scientists were currently working at Bird, five Kiwis and an American. The latter was a student at the University of Canterbury in Christchurch. Two of the Kiwis were husband and wife; they lived in a tent apart from the wanigan. One of the scientists was studying the behavior and breeding ecology of Adélies; a second the ecology of freshwater lakes in the Cape Bird area; a third the structure of sea-bottom animal communities at the cape; a fourth the summer season cycle of plankton communities off Bird; a fifth the behavior of young skuas which hadn't yet taken breeding partners; and the sixth was making a general survey of the sea bottom.

Barbara Spurr, young, small and pretty, prepared tea and coffee and served slices of a large cake that had been sent down from Christchurch as a Christmas present. Her husband, Eric, the group leader, seemed to be a very affable host. I could hardly have guessed that the Cape Bird Kiwis were very irritated by our sudden arrival and that their irritation would have consequences for me personally.

I went down to the beach to look around. The ice was idyllic in the still water. A group of Adélies trooped along in single file on the ice edge, tobogganed in places and dove into the water to fish. Four of them walked stolidly up the beach, occasionally glancing back at me to see what I was up to. Then the other visitors came down the hill and we flew out and saw the texture of the sea ice, rotten, darkly pocked and splotched; and rivulets from the hills bringing a coffee stain into the Sound; and a group of gleaming streams resembling a delta; and the sun bristling in dots and blotches on the water; and the dirty Fang Glacier snaking down between dark hills; and suddenly we were over the Terra Nova Hut at Cape Evans; and we went to Cape Barne close by, glimpsing two vivid green ponds, each in a small volcanic canyon, and touched down. The Coast Guard helo was no longer with us.

Brandau shut down the engine, saying, "I want to get some rocks for Lois Jones."

Lois Jones had headed the team of four women scientists who had worked both in Taylor and Wright Valleys in the austral summer season of 1969–70.

Following him a brief distance inland over small hills, I saw him leaning over a white mound.

"How can it be white in all this volcanic blackness?" I wondered.

He handed me a large piece of crystalline white rock (mirabilite), saying it would turn to powder if exposed to humid air. We gathered several pieces and returned to McMurdo, where after supper we sealed them in plastic bags at the Biolab.

That night, in a private conversation with me in the corridor outside my room, a highly educated and intelligent man (whom I shall call Wilkes) was very negative on the subject of Williams Field. He had visited the field that day and now he spoke of how "filthy" and "disorganized" it was and of how you had to be very careful to avoid meltwater pools. I wondered why he bothered to indulge himself in this way about the place to me, knowing as he did that I was in love with Antarctica and was planning to visit the field in the morning for a close look around.

Wilkes was usually critical in his reactions to Antarctica. He sometimes sounded as if he had come to the continent as its self-appointed critic. For example, he often spoke of the Antarctic heat wave, saying half-jokingly how embarrassing it was for him to receive letters from a friend in Vermont, where it was now twenty below, and how apparently one came to Antarctica to escape the current cold wave in the States.

Conditions at Williams Field were indeed serious due to the unusually warm weather but only miles away, in the island's interior, the temperature might be dangerously low. And the weather at McMurdo could change within hours. Last year, approximately at this time, the station had experienced a blizzard that had deposited twenty-four inches of snow. The temperamental Antarctic weather could repeat this virtuoso performance if it chose.

Wilkes had recently visited Wright Valley for about four hours.

"I wouldn't like to live there," he had told me afterwards. "The fresh water is almost entirely lifeless."

In the hurried, special circumstances of Antarctica one is obliged to make rapid judgments of men, and these are more lasting than not. There was a man, whom I shall call Biscoe, who came to my attention by his use of water in the Lodge head. Only he of all the people I ever saw in Antarctica allowed faucets to stream at full force while he washed his face and hands. Only he didn't make use of the drain stop, seemed oblivious of the rule that water must be used sparingly. And the manner in which he washed called attention to itself. He made several kinds of loud blowing noises as he uncertainly threw water onto his face.

In Christchurch he had begun to grow a beard. For weeks it was a gray stubble. In a young man such a lack of dignity would have been overlooked. But there were lines under Biscoe's eyes and in his jowls that suggested he ought to be more aware of the figure he cut. I came to associate him with a scrubby look and with the silly look of a middle-aged man playing the Antarctic swashbuckler. When I lived at Scott Base he came to the ice caves there one day to take photographs. Later, at dinner, I overheard some Kiwis speak derisively about him. They said he had brought along two Navy cameramen to photograph *him* while he photographed the caves.

Biscoe always seemed to be too aware of himself and to be preening. It wasn't only I who had this impression of him. The word about him got around without my help. Soon he was making requests to go here and there which kept being turned down by the civilian authorities. He was always asking people for the time. This trait alone would have queered him. It was astonishing that he should allow himself to be without a timepiece in Antarctica. (Inexpensive watches were for sale in the ship's store.) On one occasion he woke me very late at night to borrow an alarm clock, explaining he had to get up early to go somewhere with somebody. And then he woke me very early next morning to return the clock before departing.

When I went to Williams Field I found the meltwater pools, the soft, mushed-up ice and snow and the conditions very hazardous to aircraft. The control tower looked squat on its low red building. White Island, which seemed only several miles away, was placid with masses of snow and slate-colored bits of land. There was a good deal of cloud cover. In the south, under the cover, was a thin blue sky. From where I stood in the control tower section I sensed the thickness and moistness of the ice-shelf snow. The shelf stretched away to the east and south as if to infinity. There were a couple of Jamesways around, with their dark arched roofs, and several red boxlike shacks on huge skis. Each of the shacks had a primitive wooden stairway of five steps. In places the snow had been piled into masses ten or fifteen feet high. In the distance, near the runway (which was ten thousand feet long), was parked a great red tracked vehicle, the crash truck. The western ranges were visible under the cover.

While having a morning beer in the little wardroom in the control tower section I learned that there were men who lived so contentedly in the central compound they rarely went to McMurdo, that metropolis.

"There's little reason to go there," an officer said. "Those guys have their own food, movies, activities and friends."

I also heard that there were still rarer types, living in the control tower area (a suburb of Willy proper), who didn't visit the chief compound for days.

"We're self-sufficient here. We even have our own pinups."

Yes, the men said, conditions at the field were difficult. One helo crewman had stepped onto some ice and had gone up to his armpits in water. He had cut his hands while trying to crawl out. He was pulled out by a hovering helo after a thorough chilling. The bulldozers, Nodwells and other large tracked vehicles churned the snow into a soft, deep, powdery stuff. Taking off and landing were increasingly hazardous. Wings had a way of dipping dangerously while a plane was taxiing.

It took some effort to slosh around. The footing was uncertain and you didn't quite know how far you were going to sink at any point. Occasionally I skirted meltwater pools, some of which looked to be several feet deep. The less-used areas of the compound hadn't been scraped clear and were difficult to cross on foot. Some skuas were feeding on bits of food.

The field seemed only remotely related to a regular airfield. It felt like a hodgepodge, a series of improvisations. Its surface was chopped up, thick, rutted, and showed the treads of vehicles and the ski marks of Hercs. One saw fuel tanks, antenna towers, generators, crates. Some of the Jamesways sported signs.

One sign read: THE RESORT CROWD. HOME OF THE BAD GUYS.

Another read: THE GHETTO.

The dispensary was a red structure with a red cross over the door. To the left of the door, in red, blue and green, was a fancy vertical sign, containing a painted thermometer and the legend:

FAMOUS DISPENSER OF CURES AND GRADUATE PHYSICIAN, SPECIALIZING IN DYSPEPSIA, SCURVY, CARBUNCLES AND BOILS, LUNG FEVER AND GOUT. WALK IN.

23

〜〜〜〜〜〜〜〜〜〜〜〜〜〜〜〜

A WALK IN TAYLOR VALLEY

THE CONTINUATION of the Transantarctic Mountains that fringes the coast of Victoria Land on the western side of McMurdo Sound and that Scott unofficially called the Western Mountains contains mountain ranges, foothills, and scores of glaciers and valleys. Some of the names in this region are colorful: Killer Ridge, Purgatory Peak, The Pimple, Mount Dromedary, Obelisk Mountain. Many of the valleys, large and small, are free of ice as a result of deglaciation and are therefore known as the Dry Valleys, although in the austral summer they may be rich in meltwater flowing from the receding glaciers. They are strange, rare and rather sterile oases in a continent of ice and have fascinated explorers and scientists since their discovery by Scott's first expedition.

They reveal extensive outcrops of bedrock; consequently they offer scientists an opportunity to glimpse the geology of the continental margins. In a number of instances their surface-frozen lakes act as solar heat traps; the waters of the lake bottoms may be as warm as the middle seventies Fahrenheit. Such lakes provide material for wonder as well as study. The valleys are characterized by low mean temperatures, very low humidity and frequent and high winds. They are earth deserts within the vast ice desert of the continent, and contain ventifacts, sand dunes and mushroom rocks. Evidence that post-glacial processes have begun is not lacking; soils have started to form, and algae, mosses and lichens are to be found. It is not surprising that since the International Geophysical Year the Dry Valleys of the so-called McMurdo Oasis—there are several other, lesser oases in Antarctica—have received the special attention of geologists, geomorphologists, glaciologists and botanists. The deglaciation of the McMurdo Oasis is not fully understood. It does not necessarily suggest an ebbing of the Antarctic ice cap in general. The question of whether the cap is increasing or decreasing, known as the Antarctic budget, is still unresolved.

The most famous and one of the largest of the Dry Valleys is Taylor Valley, first explored by Scott during the Discovery Expedition. In *The Voyage of the "Discovery"* Scott used the plural form, referring to the valleys. But Shackleton, in *The Heart of the Antarctic*, referred only to "the Dry Valley," meaning the still unnamed valley that Scott had found. And Griffith Taylor, the geologist on Scott's last, Terra Nova Expedition, who was the first to understand that the Ferrar Glacier is really two glaciers in apposition (that is, that the two are Siamese twins, in a sense), adhered to Shackleton's usage. Scott later named both the Taylor Glacier, formerly the northern arm of the Ferrar, and Taylor Valley in honor of the geologist. Historically, Taylor Valley was the original Dry Valley. Extending from the Antarctic ice plateau on the west to McMurdo Sound on the east, and lying just north of the Kukri Hills, it was once entirely occupied by the Taylor Glacier. The glacier has receded toward the plateau from much of the valley and has diminished both in depth and width, but what is left of it still constitutes a mighty ice river, more than sufficient to plug up the valley's western end.

At Scott's request Taylor explored the valley in January 1911. He wrote enthusiastically about it in a chapter of *Scott's Last Expedition:*

"A strong keen wind was blowing up the valley, but the most remarkable feature of this region prevented it from becoming obnoxious. There was no drift-snow! Imagine a valley 4 miles wide, 3000 feet deep, and 25 miles long without a patch of snow—and this in the Antarctic in latitude $77\frac{1}{2}°$ S. . . . Between the serrated crests of the giant cliffs towering five or six thousand feet above us were cascading rivers of ice. These hanging glaciers spread out in great white lobes over the lower slopes of dark rock, and in some cases the cliffs were so steep that the lower portion of the tributary glacier was fed purely by avalanches falling from the ice fields above. And, most amazing of all, not a snow-drift in sight. It was warm weather most of the time we spent in Dry Valley—rising sometimes above freezing-point—and everywhere streams were tinkling among the black boulders, so much so that this valley, in spite of its name, was certainly the wettest area I saw in Antarctica!"

I had been scheduled to camp in Taylor Valley with Roy E. Cameron and three of his colleagues so I could observe the work of scientists in the field while I was experiencing a Dry Valley. Cameron, of the Bioscience Section, Jet Propulsion Laboratory, California Institute of Technology, was interested, among other matters, in developing a life detection system that might be used on the forthcoming Mars probes and that might illuminate the problem of planetary quarantine of materials brought back from extraterrestrial environments. In his words, "Although Antarctica does not possess a Martian environment, it can serve as a useful model of ecology for design, testing, and extrapolation. The naturally harsh environmental conditions of the Antarctic provide a valuable testing ground for space exploration and manned bases."

But the Cameron party changed its plans and camped in the Mount Howe region near the Pole during the time I was available for a stay in Taylor Valley. As a consequence I visited the valley on my own on January 7, 1971, spending a long and wonderful day in the excursion. I took with me as my field assistant ("buddy") David Dreffin, the personable, tall, heavily bearded, blue-eyed and sensitive man in his early twenties who monitored the equipment in the red cosmic ray shack on the road between McMurdo Station and Scott Base.

Dreffin and I breakfasted together the morning of the seventh and reported to the helo hangar at 8:45. I was happy to learn that Jim Brandau would be our pilot, and was delighted when he invited me to fly in the cockpit. As I swung myself through the cockpit port hatch the crewman, standing below me, remarked, "Most people try to go in body first." It was nice to realize I had learned how to swing my right thigh over the seat while the rest of me still clung outside. I eased myself down and reached for my harness. Brandau, entering from the starboard side, said, "You've become more agile."

The helicopter lifted off, hovered, then sideslipped over the edge of a hill, seemingly ready to plunge onto the rotten sea ice. During that first moment of helo flight my abdominal muscles still tight-

ened. The craft banked sharply to starboard. Sensing myself slipping toward Brandau's powerful shoulder, I leaned in the opposite
direction. My belly responded by settling down.

My head is very large. I could never find a communications
helmet to fit it. Usually I had to force a helmet down over my head,
helping my ears by flattening them one at a time. On this occasion
I began by wearing Brandau's helmet, roomier than most. I basked
in it. But at New Mountain he asked if I wouldn't switch with him,
for the one he had was giving him trouble. After New Mountain I
felt my head was in a mind-cracking vise. However, what I experienced that day was so stunning that even considerable physical
discomfort lost its force.

Brandau could have flown directly across the Sound to the mouth
of Taylor Valley and up the valley to Lake Bonney, our destination.
This would have entailed a trip of approximately seventy-five miles.
Instead, he went by a roundabout way in order, as he later casually
mentioned, to expose me to some unusual sights. The length of our
outward flight was roughly one hundred and seventy-five miles.

As we drew near to Brown Peninsula—the tip of the peninsula is
about twenty miles southwest of Hut Point—we flew low over vast
fields of chaotic ice, much of which, mixed with morainic deposits,
resembled mudflats. Dark silt lay between the morainic ridges. We
encountered a few patches of dirty snow. Water was visible in the
form of pools and rivulets but none was blue. We had a cloud cover
now and the water, failing to catch a blue sky, showed black. It was
a black-and-white scene, for both ice and snow were entirely and
unusually white, although a dirty, messy white. I was totally un-
prepared for such a wild wasteland, which was unlike anything I
had ever seen. At times we crossed great furrows and ridges, like
plowed black land that had been snowed upon long ago. At others
we viewed mazes of ruts and crisscrosses that suggested an alluvial
delta. It was impossible, from the helicopter, to judge the depths of
the streams, or whether the ice surface would support a human
body, but the area looked thoroughly untraversable. Everything
was a stark black and white except for a bit of thin blue sky far,
far to the west.

We swung north and crossed the mouth of the Koettlitz Glacier,
which is some twelve miles wide. The Koettlitz, about forty miles
long, flows between Brown Peninsula and the mainland to the Ross
Ice Shelf at the head of McMurdo Sound. With the exception of

the piedmont glaciers it is the largest glacier west of the Sound. Its eastern side is full of ridges, icefalls, gullies and undulations; its western half is marked by deep thaw streams, bastions of pinnacled ice, silt, and ridges of moraine materials. Discovered by Scott's first expedition, it was named by Scott for Dr. Reginald Koettlitz, physician and botanist of the expedition.

In the glacier's mouth we saw fantastic blue ice forms, some of which must have been a hundred feet high. Blue? Not the subtle glacial pastel. I mean a blue bluer than the desert sky; a riotous candy blue. What we saw was as unbelievable and pleasurable as fairy tales: snow and ice forms looming out of fields of ice: teahouse kiosks, turrets, battlements, cliffed islands, Swiss lake dwellings. And blue ice streams snaking along in a stupendous nightmare of slow motion. The blue showed despite the cloud cover, so I assumed it was in the ice itself. What a scene it was: the glacier so spacious, we flying quite low, and all these varied shapes against the powder blues of the basic glacial ice. The exotic formations were caused by erosion, by sublimation of ice, and by variations in the tempo of melting, the latter being due to the debris the glacier was carrying, the darker portions, absorbing more heat, melting more rapidly than the lighter ones. The ice river was moving and depositing a vast amount of material and was exerting pressure against the land and against the sea ice. It caused the sea ice adjacent to its mouth to look utterly chaotic. Meltwater ponds were as fascinating as the ice shapes. Observing them, I imagined I was seeing non-objective paintings, or cross-sections of agate, moonstone, coral, pearl.

All the while, as if for the first time, I kept experiencing that special kinaesthetic thrill that comes from flying in a helicopter cockpit. And I imagined I was a bird: fluttering, hovering, suddenly darting. The experience was rhapsodic, and was marked by a stroboscopic-like flicker that the whirring rotors made across the instrument panel and my eyes. I was working with my two 35mm cameras close to the limit of my intensity and I felt marvelously well. Brandau, as usual, was an inspiration to me. He handled the craft with art. And it was astonishing how conscious he was: he seemed to observe everything: the helicopter, the scenes, my actions, even my moods.

We caught glimpses of the inland, white plateau. There, in the west, the sky was clear, a deep blue near the zenith. Heading for

Marshall Valley, we approached the strange, denuded brown land with its mountains, glaciers and valleys that I had wanted for so long to visit. The tops of hills and mountains were often obscured by clouds. At times we flew through clouds that felt like fog. We crossed Marshall Valley and went up Miers Valley, seeing the Miers Glacier and Miers Lake, then came to the Blue Glacier with its many icefalls. The Blue Glacier is rather short and is not fed directly by the plateau ice cap. Smaller glaciers, spilling down hills, pour from the plateau into it. In places we saw splotches of textured ice in many vivid hues of green and blue. Brandau flew to the glacier's head, where we had close views of the frozen, broken falls. We were at quite a height now, around 5,000 feet. I leaned out of my hatch into the windstream and glanced back. Along the horizon, right to left, tiny yet still recognizable, were Cape Armitage, Observation Hill, the Gap, Crater Hill, Castle Rock, Hut Point Peninsula and the Turks Head Ridge. The Ridge was the Erebus icefalls back of Cape Evans. Erebus was hidden by clouds.

We flew above Overflow Glacier to the Ferrar Glacier, then headed west along the Ferrar's southern side. The Ferrar Glacier, some thirty-five miles long and from three to six miles wide, lies between the Royal Society Range and the Kukri Hills. It was named after Hartley T. Ferrar, geologist of the Discovery Expedition. The Kukris, named by the same expedition, are so called because of their supposed resemblance to a Ghurka knife. Serrated, dark brown, in places tan, their crests now laced, cottoned and curtained by pearly clouds, with glaciers hanging down the crests and meeting the great highway of the Ferrar, they were very beautiful. The Ferrar is rather a rotten glacier, chopped up, highly textured, with many meltwater courses and numerous dirty areas due to silt material. It has long dark lines running down its length.

"I have a feeling I'm satiating you," Brandau said.

But if my eyes and brain were satiated—*could* I be satiated who was due to leave this continent so soon, possibly never to return? —my will and fingers were not, they were as eager as ever to bring back a report of a world beyond belief.

Hugging the golden, barren mass of Briggs Hill, with its gray cottony clouds that seemed to be falling down its slopes—the hill met the Ferrar sharply—we approached Cathedral Rocks, those massive, brown, spired mountains so well known to Scott and

Shackleton that are the northern terminus of the Royal Society Range. The tops were now brilliantly sunlit and etched with snow.

"I get a shiver up my spine every time I see them," Brandau said.

We saw areas of pure white snow, some on glaciers subsidiary to the Ferrar, others on mountain sides; naked brown or tan hills that gave the impression of being made of brass; jagged mountain tops; crumbling icefalls. On our left we passed first Table Mountain, whose top was swathed in clouds, then the Knobhead, the latter, showing slabs of dark brown dolerite interspersed with strata of tan sandstone, resembling a terra cotta pyramid. Glancing westward up Windy Gully with its icefalls and crevasses, we had glimpses of the great, high, bleak plateau and of nunataks on it, and, in the foreground, saw New Mountain on the right or northern side of the Gully and Terra Cotta Mountain on the left of it. We flew low over some Windy Gully icefalls that suggested a mass of whipped cream that had suddenly been frozen while being frothed.

"Let me have some smoke," Brandau said.

Windy Gully is famous for its katabatic (gravity-caused) winds that sweep from the plateau down to McMurdo Sound.

The crewman tossed a bomb out through the cabin hatch. The craft banked, swiveled, turned to the direction from which it had come.

"The wind usually blows forty knots here," Brandau said.

Seeing the purple smoke column wanly rising, he cried, "My God, it's absolutely calm!"

We touched down on New Mountain close to the Windy Gully ice river. New Mountain, not far from the plateau, is the easternmost spur of a group of mountains and valleys that includes Pyramid, Finger, Maya and Aztec Mountains and Turnabout, Beacon, Furnell and Arena Valleys. There were patches of snow on New Mountain but most of the mountain was bare. Looking eastward at the bad weather we had left behind, we saw a world boiling and steaming in a huge cauldron. The Ferrar Glacier seemed to be emitting volumes of steam.

We left the helicopter briefly to hunt for "ashtray" rocks. They are of sandstone and resemble beautifully formed ashtrays of various sizes and depths. Most of them have a single concavity but some have two or even three. They are formed by chemical weathering and by the winds. The rims are sometimes so highly polished you think they're coated with a film of oil until you touch them. An ashtray rock is not easy to come by unless you happen to have helicopter time at your disposal and a pilot like Brandau who knows where New Mountain is and is willing to fly roundabout to take you to it. He once said to me, apropos of Antarctica, "There are people here who don't like this place. They travel in a straight line between two points." He knew several such rare and out-of-the-way places as New Mountain. As I had myself learned, he gathered things not for their possession but for the pleasure of giving them away, and of stimulating interest in the continent. But he was careful not to broadcast his special knowledge, for he disliked the thought of a general hunt for souvenirs, and of the latter's depletion.

We took off again and flew west briefly over Windy Gully, then northwest over the land mass of which New Mountain is a part, crossing a rich, brown, denuded, sterile land of peaks, crags, valleys, and of large amphitheaters composed of bands of sandstone alternating with ribbons of dolerite. Bad weather, moving in from the east and north, was filling the amphitheaters with smoke-colored clouds. The Lashly Glacier was part of the distant background, as were the Lashly Mountains. Tabular Mountain, in the middle ground, looked remarkably fine: pale, gray, a suggestive thin wash setting off the spectacular brilliance of the terra cotta areas. Coming around east of Pyramid Mountain—both Pyramid and Finger Mountains had a terra cotta appearance and the area between them formed an amphitheater full of creamy snow—we had views of the head of the Taylor Glacier, which resembled a steaming cauldron: the weather was thick there. The icefalls there gave the impression of being in great motion. Beyond the Taylor, the Asgard Range rose out of agitated clouds. Finger Mountain, well known to the early explorers, swung in a tight arc, the fingertip pointing southeast. The Taylor moves down from the north side of New Mountain. At Cavendish Rocks it is apposite to the Ferrar Glacier. It is some thirty-five miles long, from two to ten miles wide and flows from the Victoria Land plateau into the west end of Taylor Valley, north of the Kukri Hills.

We crossed its upper reaches, then swung eastward over Pearse Valley, in which we saw a small, lovely blue and green lake. As we left the valley we picked up the Taylor Glacier again, whose cliffs appeared to be several hundred feet high. The glacier's surface was a pale, dusty blue, with patches of white; occasionally it was daubed with circular tan spots indicating rock and boulder debris.

Flying eastward alongside the Taylor's northern edge, we caught sight of the Kukris with their glaciers that hung like loose tongues. The Catspaw Glacier sprawled over two or three hills opposite the Kukris. The valley's hills were a fine, dark gray. When illumined directly by the sun they looked almost tan. The Taylor receded from us like a triangle down the valley. Its surface as we moved eastward began to show crevasses and rotten low spots. At times we flew beside its eroded cliffs with their embedded boulders and soil. One large place in the cliffside was splotched by what looked like egg yolk. Reaching the glacier's easternmost snout, we came to Lake Bonney, which stems from it. We landed at Bonney Hut on the shore of the lake.

The green, A-frame hut was more substantial and better-equipped than I had expected. At one time it had been used by scientists for prolonged stays. There was a smaller, storage shack nearby. The hut contained provisions, a large stove, a large generator, ceiling lights, a sink, cots, chairs, cooking utensils and, in case one had forgotten what naked women looked like, many pin-ups in color. It lacked blankets and sleeping bags. Brandau, showing us how to operate the stove, said we would be picked up at about eight. We accompanied him to the helo pad, near which were several empty fuel drums and a rock cairn, and watched him take off. It was now almost noon. Dreffin and I agreed to skip lunch in order to have more time for walking. He had consumed five or six eggs at breakfast; he said they would hold him. I had had a small breakfast but I was too excited to eat now.

In the vicinity of the hut there was no way to cross over to the north shore of the lake. We wanted to approach the snout of the Matterhorn Glacier, so we hiked eastward until we reached an isthmus separating Lake Bonney from a smaller lake. Here we moved to the valley's northern side. It was a boulder-strewn valley with a gray pebbly floor and with numerous glaciers tonguing down from above. The very dry hills were brilliantly sunlit. We came to the shores of a pond. Our boots sank in the porous soil. Proceeding along the pond's northern shore, occasionally we leaped across meltwater streams, Dreffin flying through the air with stilt-like legs. He was wearing a black cap, a plaid woolen shirt, a USARP parka, baggy black windpants, standard-issue hiking boots and large sunglasses.

We reached higher, firmer ground. The hills rose on both sides of us to a naked, dazzling sky. I recalled the grays and blacks of Royds and Evans, the volcanic darknesses of McMurdo. When I turned around to look back, I saw the Taylor Glacier filling the valley floor thickly. There was something hauntingly strange here. Then I realized what it was: the absence of birds over dry land.

No life stirred that the naked eye could discern. The world seemed purely inorganic. No leaves or weeds to rustle in a breeze; no treetops to sough or sigh. There was no wind. If and when we left the sound of meltwaters we would encounter the great Antarctic silence.

We came upon what I thought of as "mysterious" tracks, of about four persons, heading eastward and going persistently and intelligently, selecting the middle ground to avoid unnecessary climbing over debris hills, finding the best way among boulders, moraines and across streams, and often following little trails that I suspected were old meltwater courses. Occasionally, when the ground was very hard, almost bony, we lost the tracks. Then we hunted for them, for our "friends," as we called them, or for our predecessors and trailmasters, as I thought them. Given the facts of life in Antarctica, I was fairly certain that the makers of these tracks were no longer in the valley. I would have been informed of the fact at McMurdo if they were. So who were they and how long ago had they been here? And had they been just legging it along like ourselves, going as far as the spirit moved them?

When we came abreast of the Matterhorn we stared up at its rotten, vertically striated snout suspended on the northern hillside above us, and at the ice boulders strewn in a helter-skelter mass directly below the snout. We listened to the sounds of a brook rushing westward past us, and to the noises of waters flowing from the dying glaciers and trickling over the dry earth and being sponged by the earth. I stared in wonder at the brook. There were freshets aplenty in the McMurdo environs this summer, but those were volcanic-milky, whereas this one at my feet was limpid, crystal, inviting us to drink. We drank and moved on.

The valley at times doubled and tripled because of long morainic hills. The glacial debris made this place a rock hunter's paradise. Then we found that the valley had subtly turned; we were no longer able to look back and see Lake Bonney. Sometimes the footing was soft, laborious; we slid, lost ground. Near the Lacroix Glacier we heard meltwater rushing among boulders and under giant slabs of fallen glacial ice. At times the valley floor bristled with light glancing off rocks, many of them erratics. We found numerous interesting stones: granites, marbles, chalks, conglomerites; others suggesting coke or cinders; some pink with gray veins, or plum flecked with bits of ivory, or rose and resembling glazed clay; others burnt coffee, angelic white. Many had been sculptured by the winds in such a way as to be lovely to gaze at and to handle. A grapefruit-size piece of marble, cracked, irregular in shape, whitish in places, yellowish and glazed in others, contained deep, grainy, burnt-rust little holes. One long stone, heavy, gray, had been streamlined and polished to an especially pleasing result. We came to moraines like earthworks. Occasionally the valley floor looked dunelike in its freedom from morainic clutter.

We reached a mummified crabeater seal, one of some half dozen, including pups, we had encountered on our way. We studied this phenomenon, reported as long ago as Scott's first expedition, and wondered, as Scott's people and no doubt the makers of the tracks had, how the seals, whose habitat is salt water, had gotten so far up the valley. If I remember correctly, carbon-dating experiments indicate that the youngest of the specimens is some two hundred and fifty years old, the oldest five thousand. But, for special and technical reasons, there is some doubt as to the accuracy of the carbon-dating method as applied to the seal specimens in the Dry Valleys. The seal's hide felt as hard as wood. Some of the bleached, curved bones, off which the light glanced brilliantly, were exposed.

When we were close to the Nussbaum Riegel (rock bar), which protrudes northward from the Kukri Hills and almost cuts the valley in two, we turned back. But before doing so we climbed to the top of a hill of shards and rocks and viewed the Suess Glacier to the east of us, with its sensuous, gentle fall down the north slope on our left. A small, ice-covered lake, with patches of snow, beautiful with pale greens, blues and touches of lavender, lay between us and the glacier. Clouds were by now moving into the valley's western end, causing us to wonder if the helicopter would be able to pick us up on schedule. If it wouldn't, we could make do for the night by firing up the stove in Bonney Hut. On our way back we ascended the slope to the Matterhorn's high, massive, clifflike snout, under which we rested. Looking across the valley from this shadowed vantage point, I had the feeling I was viewing two large Egyptian pyramids atop the sunlit Kukri Hills, whose dryness and color reminded me of the Sahara near El Gîza.

Moving now into the last lap back, and doing it by a more southerly route, on the opposite side of the valley from which we had come, we reached what looked like an alluvial delta. On the shore of a little lake as green as jade were the remains of another crabeater seal. The lake rippled in a wind, its surface aflame with whitecaps. Waves of gratitude to all those who had made my being here possible swept over me. In this mood I reached Bonney Hut.

The stove, the generator, the cots, chairs, a sink that emptied into a tub; shelves with canned rations; our gear flung about; and Dreffin gulping a long time from his canteen, then leaning back on a cot in a corner, wild-eyed with fatigue, without his large sunglasses, his long brown hair askew, his long legs lying as if broken at the knees, observing me, wondering perhaps what my next move would be. I left that look and that huge beard and went outside to gaze at the lake's frozen cap and at the glacier beyond, then reentered the hut and prepared a supper of K rations. Afterwards I cleaned up and looked through a window at the brilliance, the radiance. Dreffin still sat asprawl.

I went outside again, walked along the shore, then stood very still, listening to Antarctica's silence (the wind had died down), now exquisitely broken as bits of floating, iridescent ice flakes, colliding with icicles, tinkled like tiny musical glasses. Some three billion human beings were teeming on the surface of the earth. I was one of a handful who had been lucky enough to walk at the world's very edge.

24

CRASHING ON MOUNT EREBUS

I was scheduled to fly in a Navy helicopter, an H-34, from McMurdo Station to Cape Bird at 1 or 1:30 P.M. January 9. My mission was to become acquainted with the layout of the cape while camping there; to observe if possible some predation activities of leopard seals against Adélie penguins; to observe Killer whales if to my good fortune any showed themselves; and to witness the work and life of scientists in the field.

As we have noted, the Kiwis at Cape Bird were irritated by the unexpected descent on January 5 of what in their view was an unconscionably large number of American visitors. It should be emphasized that this was not the first unscheduled appearance of Americans during the season—at least that was what Brian Porter later told me—and that the Cape Bird Kiwis believed such visits were serious interruptions of their scientific work. They made their feelings known to Porter at Scott Base during a scheduled radio contact. Porter communicated their displeasure to Chris Shepherd, who informed me the morning of January 8, the day after my walk in Taylor Valley, that both Porter and the cape Kiwis were now doubtful whether I, as an American, a non-scientist and one of the January 5 visitors, was welcome to camp at the cape, considered both by New Zealand and American authorities to be New Zealand territory.

I immediately looked up Porter at Scott Base and underscored my

The names and residence states of my companions in the crash are fictitious for reasons that will be obvious to the reader.

innocence in the episode. When I asked if he had lodged a complaint with the Operation Deep Freeze people he replied he did not wish to create an "incident." I said I could understand his desire to underplay the affair but that I took no pleasure in being a scapegoat. I asserted that I did not consider my mission to the cape a light matter in my program of gathering material for my book, that I was sorry the Kiwis at Bird, whom I liked, felt affronted, and that I would do everything I could to mollify them, not only for my mission's sake but because I was sure there had been a misunderstanding concerning the attitude of McMurdo regarding the unfortunate visit. I certainly could not believe that a man like Brandau, the pilot of one of the helos, was capable of behaving tactlessly in such an instance. I promised to bring the cape Kiwis whole cartons of foods, such as fresh fruits and vegetables, that they were in very short supply of.

Porter, now sympathetic to my cause and probably influenced by the fact I had recently been a happy member of the Scott Base community, convinced the cape Kiwis to let me camp there. But he was told by them, or so he informed me, that I must come alone and bring a tent: I would not be welcome to share the wanigan; I would have to live alone and apart from them. They indicated they would cooperate minimally with me, that I would have to look after my own safety and that I would have no need of a field assistant, who would only serve to clutter the scene.

I was obviously in for an interesting time at Bird. I wished I wasn't quite as tired and as short on sleep as I was, but I was not seriously troubled. The Bird people were young and pleasant; their irritation would wear off; and I had no doubt they would eventually accept me as their friend. However, their insistence on my bringing a tent gave me something to think about. Living in a small unheated tent in Antarctica is one thing; trying to write in one is quite another. The wanigan at Bird had four bunks, all currently occupied. But it also had a fair amount of floor space, as I had seen, and Gary Means had slept on the floor and I had hoped to do the same and to use the structure's facilities at least for the physical part of writing in my journal.

As it turned out, the matter of the tent was crucial. If I hadn't brought the tent along on the flight toward Cape Bird on January 9 my three companions and I probably would not have survived the crash experience, at least not without permanent injury. Also, because I expected both to live and to work in the tent, I brought along two cot mattresses rather than one. I intended to use one under my sleeping bag, the other I planned to employ as a work surface on the tent's floor. The extra mattress too proved important to our safety. During my conference with Porter the latter asked me to do Scott Base two favors: to deliver an ice ax and a packet of mail to the cape Kiwis. The ice ax played a role in the crash story.

As for the tent itself, I selected an Air Force survival tent because, never having used this type, I wanted to familiarize myself with it. It is not a tent one person can easily load gear into. It has two entrances, which are tubelike, wormlike and double-layered. You crawl in order to reach the interior. Such entrances help keep wind out and body heat in but because they create a potential trap it's a good idea to have a sheath knife on you or very handy, for in case of fire you would need to cut your way out rapidly. I wanted to set up the tent quickly and efficiently. Also, I had no intention of hauling my considerable gear alone from the beach up to the cliffside plateau on which I was to camp. So I requested the services of a field assistant on a turnaround flight.

The assistant, with whom I was acquainted superficially, was Van Enderby, twenty years old and from Arizona. A tallish, lean man in excellent physical condition, he was reserved, reticent and always quietly eager to be of help. From the look of his legs in jeans and his feet in boots and from the way he carried himself I took him to be a strong hiker. I had rarely encountered him except when I had had occasion to visit the field party processing center. Like Dave Murphy, he was a Holmes & Narver employee there. I selected him under urging from his boss (this was not Jim Elder), who, when I indicated that I wished to take Dave Murphy because I knew, liked and trusted Murphy, protested that I had already "done more than enough" for Murphy and that, in all fairness, I ought to consider the needs of other deserving young men. His boss informed me that Enderby hoped to become a geologist; that he would be very grateful for any opportunity to get away from McMurdo and see some other part of the island, even if only on a turnaround flight to Bird; and that he was entirely capable of preparing me to camp at the cape.

As I have already suggested, few persons working in Antarctica today have the chance to see the place extensively; most have the feeling, I suspect, of being marooned. Young non-scientist civilians like Enderby would put in long work weeks in the warehouse-like

Field Center, and on their days off had only McMurdo, Scott Base and a few hikes in their vicinity to vary a quite monotonous life. It was understandable that Murphy was envied by his fellow employees for having camped at Capes Evans and Royds.

Murphy told me *he* wanted very much to accompany me to Bird, for he had never seen the island's terrain north of Royds. I had the unhappy task of explaining that although I much preferred to have him with me on the turnaround flight, the pressure was on me again to stop "favoring" him on my field trips; and that because I felt harassed by lack of time I had decided not to buck the pressure and had accepted Enderby.

Now, as to who was to fly me to Bird: Brandau was out of the picture, for he was scheduled to depart from McMurdo for Christchurch at 12:30 or 1 A.M. of the ninth in connection with a planning conference, along with some DVs and Shepherd and Putzke, the skipper of the *Staten Island*. In the wardroom the evening of the eighth Billy Blackwelder told me he would fly me. At breakfast on the ninth, however, Dan Biggerstaff, known as Biggee, informed me that *he* would fly me, adding that Brandau had asked him and Blackwelder to look out for me during his absence and that they meant to do it.

I headed for the helo hangar at a bit before 1 P.M. of the ninth, leaving Enderby at one of the lower helo pads to handle my gear, which he was offloading from a truck and which he had prepared and gathered at my instructions but not under my personal supervision, for, as I had told Murphy, I was greatly pressed for time. I had turned over to him the key to my Field Center cage, in which my camping gear was stored, with both verbal and written instructions regarding my needs, including the special foods I wished to present to the cape Kiwis and which he would have to obtain from the Navy commissary, and had helped him load my stuff onto the truck. I was not carrying a radio; the Kiwi radio contacts with Scott Base would suffice to keep McMurdo Station informed of my whereabouts and safety.

Biggerstaff emerged from the hangar to inform me there was too much cloud cover today over the McMurdo-Bird route—or, at any rate, too much for the H-34. The McMurdo-Bird route fringed the island's western coast; I had flown over it when I had gone up to Bird. By contrast, flying in a helo over the island's deep interior was considered to be extremely dangerous for several reasons, a major one being the fact that Mount Erebus, with its ice-sloped, crevassed and ice-falled sides, occupied so much of the island's mass, and a forced landing might be most hazardous. I make this point now because of its considerable relevance to the crash tale. Not that the coastal route was viewed as safe by VXE-6 helo pilots; on the contrary, they referred to it half jokingly as "the suicide route."

Biggerstaff said some of the flight to Bird would have to be made under the cover—the cover, massive, was both low and high—and at times probably over water instead of ice: it was well known the sea ice was rapidly breaking up north of Royds. If an H-34, with only tricycle landing gear, had to ditch in water it would sink with the certain and quick death of all on board because of the water's temperature. He said actually it was illegal for an H-34 to fly over water in Antarctica. But a Coast Guard helo, the H-52, with its hull fuselage and pontoons, could fly over water with a fair degree of safety, for unless it hit the deck too hard it would remain afloat, certainly long enough for a rescue attempt. If I still wanted to fly to Bird today a Coast Guard helo, the one on the upper pad below the Chalet, was prepared to take me.

Biggerstaff said maybe I ought to consider postponing the flight.

I said no, I was fast running out of time and preferred to fly now.

And so the decision was made. Later, during the massive search for us, he convinced himself he should have scratched the flight— he had the authority to do so—and felt very bad when, for a time, my companions and I were given up for dead. He and I were very fond of each other. In addition, he had Brandau's request that he and Blackwelder look out for me to add to his burden of guilt and sadness.

I regretted having to switch from the H-34 to the H-52, for I had hoped Biggerstaff would ask me to fly in the cockpit. I had no reason to think the Coast Guard pilot, whose identity I did not yet know, would invite me to share his cockpit. No other Coast Guard pilot had invited me to do so. I would not ask him to share it. I had never asked a pilot for a favor and I had resolved I never would. The pilots had enough to do without my imposing on them.

Biggerstaff said the Coast Guard pilot was Stu Palmer (of the *Staten Island*), now in the hangar. I went inside the hangar, greeted Palmer and told him I would fly with him to Cape Bird. Palmer delayed the flight some ten or fifteen minutes while he had a leisurely cup of coffee. I could not recall whether I had flown with him before but I knew him from both the *Staten Island* and the McMurdo wardrooms. As a matter of fact, I had bought him a drink or two in the McMurdo wardroom the previous evening.

He was a quiet, reserved man whom I took to be about thirty-two or thirty-three, with straight brown hair, a long and wispy brown mustache, a soft-skinned face that gave you the impression he had the lightest of beards, a soft-voiced drawl (he was from Georgia) and with dark eyes lidded in a manner that suggested an owl's. I didn't know if he was a family man and don't know now. I never felt a desire to lessen the distance between us, possibly because I sensed a dark side in him that I didn't feel in the other Coast Guard pilots I knew. He was remote not only with me and other civilians but with military men as well. He often sat alone in one of the mentioned wardrooms, aloof from the singing or hilarity around him. At least this is how I remember him. Perhaps I'm confusing his behavior after the crash episode with his behavior before it. He was rather handsome and of good height. I imagined he was popular with women. But he didn't give the impression of being vain; this I liked in him. I sensed he might be soft physically by my standards, that he disliked being in Antarctica, that he hadn't chosen to come here, and that he felt much more comfortable in semi-tropical places. I sometimes even wondered if he hated the continent I loved so much.

We climbed to the upper pad, where I found that my gear was already aboard. The crewman walked to the front of the craft while Enderby and I climbed aboard and began strapping ourselves in. Palmer, boarding the craft, said he had to fuel up at Williams Field. In the H-52 the pilot enters the cockpit via the cabin; cabin and cockpit are on the same level.

Then Palmer surprised me by asking, "Chuck, would you like to sit in the cockpit?"

"Yes *sir!*" I replied in delight.

I went to the copilot's seat, harnessed myself in, squeezed the spherical helmet onto my head and plugged it into the intercom system. The helmet was so tight I wondered if I'd be able to endure it all the way to Bird. The direct flight from McMurdo to Bird takes about forty-five minutes but we would be stopping en route at Scott Base as well as Williams Field. We lifted off and headed down and around the tip of Cape Armitage, then north. From a distance and a height the exotic airfield, a dark, speckled mass on the huge white sheet of the ice shelf, with three rows of Jamesways, the latter re-

sembling dashes, seemed like a tiny, otherworldly settlement. It was
fascinating to watch the place, including its runway to the right
of the control tower, and the dark line of the old bus route leading
off to the left, looming to meet us. Vehicle tracks ran southward;
almost none went north. Mount Terror was dappled with light.
Mount Erebus rose on the left, its crest clear, but cloud cover was
already halfway up its western slopes. More cover was moving in
from the west.

We touched down, shut off the engine, took on fuel and flew
briefly over the shelf to the New Zealand base to pick up the packet
of mail I had promised Porter I'd deliver to Bird. I already had the
ice ax, which he had given me at the conclusion of our recent conference. Palmer did not shut down the engine at the Kiwi base.
We were on deck just long enough for my friend Paul, with the
blond beard, who managed the Kiwi post office and who was standing by for our arrival, to run out, ducking under the spinning rotors,
and hand me the packet through my open hatch.

We lifted off and proceeded toward Bird but with, for me, this
significant difference: whereas I had automatically expected us to
retrace our way around Cape Armitage and go briefly westward
past McMurdo, then north along the western coast, we crossed
gleaming, low-lying Hut Point Peninsula itself and headed for black
Castle Rock, which we soon passed. Still frozen McMurdo Sound, an
expanse of whites, lilacs and pale blues, was speckled with cloud
shadows, in the midst of which one of the icebreakers, too tiny for
identification without binoculars, looked very vulnerable. Some blue
sky was still visible directly above us but the western ranges were
rapidly dimming behind curtains of weather. In the northwest, that
is, in the direction of Cape Bird, there was a great deal of thick,
ominous looking cover.

We took to hugging the glaring, crevassed slopes of Erebus. Wondering why Palmer was going so far and so dangerously inland, why
in other words he wasn't following the traditional route as our flight
plan required, I told myself vaguely that that was his business, not
mine, and continued with my own, which was the use of my two
cameras, but shot without my usual enthusiasm, for one reason because the scenes were no longer fresh for me and for another because my hatch views were badly obstructed by the H-52's port
pontoon, as a consequence of which I was forced to aim through
the dusty, streaked windshield. I hadn't counted on the pontoon's

posing such a considerable photographic problem; I realized then I had been spoiled by the H-34. I felt myself resisting a growing irritability, which was not aided by the pressure the helmet was exerting on my temples and by Palmer's silence, broken once when he asked me if I knew the way to Cape Bird. I replied that I did, at which he looked relieved.

In retrospect I realize I should have wondered at that look, which possibly suggested he would do well to return to McMurdo and not encounter, in a state of doubt as to where he was, that northwestern terrain and that cover which in conjunction threatened to be a hazard to our safety. It occurred to me he might have heard of Brandau's feat in taking an H-34 over Erebus and that he meant to emulate him with the H-52. If that was his intention I hoped he was a damn good pilot, for despite the H-52's greater maximum altitude capability than the H-34's (by some 4,000 feet), I had about three hundred pounds of stuff on board and a field assistant whom I judged to weigh, clothed, in the neighborhood of a hundred and seventy-five pounds. I also trusted he had asked VXE-6 helo pilots lots of intelligent questions about what was involved in climbing the atmosphere close to Erebus and had elicited informed replies.

We now began to climb, not fitfully but steadily. Both pilot and copilot had two altimeters: a barometric one indicating elevation above sea level, and a radar one showing elevation above the ground. I observed my barometric altimeter with fascination.

At 8,000 feet we were inland from Cape Royds. Looking down at the cape, I made out portions of its seaward side. Its upper slopes were covered by massive clouds resembling vast steam explosions. As we continued to climb I saw many crevasses—curved machete slashes—some of them snowbridged, and many clifflike rock slopes. The sky was still blue but beyond the large second crater, that is, north of it, hung a great white cloud bank. We were hugging the precipitous slope of the second crater and encountering more and more naked rock. Looking down and immediately westward, I saw little more than a sea of clouds. But far, far to the west, above the cover, was serene blue sky.

At around 11,500 feet we saw Erebus's crest clearly. Light smoke, probably mixed with steam, was issuing from the crater. We were on the volcano's northwest side and close to the top of the clifflike second crater. Erebus has three craters, the third being the topmost. We saw many rock outcrops, for here the mountain was exposed to the warming effects of the summer sun, which, as we know, slowly dips as it rounds the sky counterclockwise, reaching its nadir at midnight, when it is above the Pole.

Palmer said calmly, "I'd like to clear it but we've got too much weight."

At about 12,000 feet he said, "It's as high as she'll go," yet he seemed to be pushing the craft to go still higher.

Erebus's crest felt very close to us. At moments we seemed to be heading directly for it. During my current visit to Antarctica I had several times imagined Erebus to be Ross Island's godhead, and its crest to be the mountain's face, remote from mortals, a legendary place where great prophecies were pronounced. This despite my knowledge of the meaning of the name. In Greek mythology Erebus is a son of Chaos and also the dark nether place through which souls pass on their way to Hades. At times I had thought of the mountain as a symbol of Antarctica, a continent both extraordinarily beautiful and dangerous. I had seen the mountain from many sides, always at normal distances. What I was now experiencing were abnormally intimate views of the northwestern side of that face.

I made out Beaufort Island on our left and some open sea to our right. It occurred to me I should ask Palmer to abandon this madness and take me immediately to Cape Bird as scheduled. But I was not about to cry chicken.

"If he wants to keep climbing that's his business," I thought.

What an idea: as if my life were not my business.

The craft was straining; it seemed to be trembling. My altimeter registered more than 12,500 feet. The reader will recall that the elevation of Mount Erebus as indicated on current official maps is 12,450 feet and he will no doubt wonder if, since we were higher than this, we could see into the crater itself. I should like to remind him that the figure of 12,450 feet represents elevation based on triangulation at sea level, and that my readings were in barometric terms, that Mount Erebus is in a low-pressure area, and that in such terms its elevation is approximately 13,300 feet. I saw some open sea, a lot of pack ice, and the watery horizon in the north, where there was still a good deal of lovely blue sky. Cape Bird was under thick cover.

We were approaching the crest from the northwest now. It rose to a mildly sloping peak, at the top of which was some dark stuff with the hue and texture of an ash heap. I was shooting through the windshield and through a strange apparition: a distorted reflection of a helmet surrounding a mongoloid face. At the crest, in addition to the ash heaps—the central one was the largest and darkest—were some snow and some precipitous rocky areas; the gullies of the latter were snow-filled. There was a moment when we seemed to be almost on a level with the top of the mountain. I was shooting out of my hatch now. We were spiraling very slowly clockwise. Beyond the heaps was the smoking crater itself.

I was both willing and ready to take advantage of the situation if we cleared Erebus, yet I kept silent, whether because I had something to gain by Palmer's overflying the crater or because I was determined not to cry chicken I shall probably never know. Technically the pilot is solely responsible for his craft, and nothing I said or failed to say could mitigate this fact. But I *might* have succeeded in persuading him to descend if I had tried. Possibly he had gone too far out on a limb and needed me to save his face. Perhaps if I had felt less distance between us in our wardroom meetings I would have been kinder and have given him, presuming he needed and wanted it, the overt excuse to lose altitude voluntarily.

I am not unaware of the fact he may have taken a great risk in a desire to do me a service, as he had already done me one by inviting me to sit in the cockpit with him, and that I was responding meanly. Or, knowing that I was gathering material for a book about Ross Island, he may have tried to impress me in the hope of playing a role in it. On the other hand, inasmuch as I would have been much safer in the cabin than in the cockpit during a crash, and inasmuch as he was inviting a crash by his rashness, he may have done me a disservice by inviting me to share the cockpit. These are subtle and painful matters and have puzzled and troubled me ever since.

Suddenly we seemed to hang still. Then we descended quickly, not flying but falling. Yet it was not a vertical fall but a forward one, as if we were trying to land too rapidly.

Palmer cried in a brittle, bitter tone, "We've got a downdraft! We're going down!"

For an instant I thought he meant we had merely failed to clear Erebus. Then I realized that our single, turbine-powered engine had air-starved in the too-thin air. This was bad enough. In addition we were being shoved down by a powerful downdraft.

And so Palmer had made the mistake of flying around to the opposite side of the updraft. The updraft, on the southeast side of

Erebus, was due to the prevailing southeasterly, that bitter, life-endangering wind that swept down from the polar plateau and across the Ross Ice Shelf. The downdraft was on the northwest side. Until this moment, and during the other helo flights I had been fortunate enough to experience in a cockpit, I had enjoyed the feeling of having nothing between me and the outside world but a thin Plexiglas shell. Now I felt I was in a free fall, with not even the shell to protect me, and that on impact the back of the craft would slam against me.

The wild, desolate, rocky landscape rose up to greet us. Strangely, I thought for a moment that Palmer was possibly trying to land somewhere—anywhere—in order to have a look around or to think things through. I hoped he retained enough control of the craft to be autorotating but I could not really believe he had sufficient altitude for an autorotation or that an autorotation was possible in such a downdraft.

A white mass of snow came at us, magnifying with great speed and intensity. There were gray and black boulders and rock aprons and shoulders everywhere. There was insufficient time to experience fear, yet there was time for fascination, for observation and above all for acute experience.

Palmer, shouting "Mayday! Mayday! Mayday! Any station! Any station!" desperately flipped toggle switches.

The snow and ice masses rose up and slammed us. We bumped, buckled, spun around, skidded. I wondered if I was about to be killed. Suddenly we were motionless. There was a terrific silence. I unfastened my harness, removed my helmet, realized I was in one piece and that my cameras, which hung from my neck, hadn't been damaged. The engine had quit. The rotors were still. We weren't on fire.

Palmer, having unharnessed himself, jumped up, his face contorted, and shouted, "Fuck! Fuck!" in disgust and exasperation, flipping some overhead switches.

"Take it easy, Stu," I said.

I went outside for a look around. The crest looked unbelievably close, and bad weather was moving in from the west and north. It was obvious the latter would soon engulf us. We had dropped down onto a colorless world: nothing but blacks, grays and whites. The blue of the sky was so rapidly being transfigured into a milky gray it hardly counted as a color; in any event it would not be a color for long. The only colors were those we had brought with us: for example, the brilliant red of my USARP parka. The helo's tail pointed in the direction of the crest. The cockpit faced rock aprons, huge black and gray boulders and two large ice fumaroles just beyond the boulders. In the crest's direction was a series of parallel-like and horizontal rock ridges, rising one above the other, interspersed with boulders and patches of snow and ice. The smoke issuing from the crater beyond the ash heaps was blowing away from us. On the craft's starboard side were more rock aprons and boulders. On its port side was a long stretch of naked and fairly level rock; but there too were many boulders the helo had miraculously missed. We had come down on the upper portion of the plateau of the second crater, whose great cliff was not too distant in the direction of the ice fumaroles. I wondered how it would have felt if we had gone spilling down that cliffside.

It struck me as being about the worst place for a ditching imaginable: difficult for single-engine helos, the only kind available in Operation Deep Freeze then, to ascend to for a rescue; almost impossible for them to start an engine at if it conked out; death to walk down from past the rock and ice cliffs and ice slopes and ice falls and crevasses I knew about from extensive reading, from studies of high-altitude photographs and from having observed some of them at first hand from helicopters. Doubting that my companions suspected what a man-killer Erebus could be, I resolved to keep such knowledge to myself as long as possible.

An examination of the craft revealed that the landing gear had been badly damaged. We had hit the deck on the port side. The port tire had blown. The port wheel had been slammed out of position on its axle. The struts connecting the port pontoon with the fuselage had been telescoped and their covering shredded. The pontoon was almost vertical instead of horizontal. The small tail wheel had been partially rammed into the fuselage. The starboard wheel had been bent out of shape. Its tire was almost flat. But the pontoon looked all right. The helo was resting on its hull and tipping strongly to port. One of the rotor blades was almost only head-high.

We were now all outside and greatly relieved to be uninjured. It seemed a miracle that we had found a bit of level, snow-covered ground among all the rocks and boulders. Also miraculous was the fact we hadn't come down in straightforward, tricycle fashion. If we had, we would have had sufficient momentum to pile up on the boulders and burst into flames. Coming down on one side had caused us to swivel around and skid sideways; this had given us sufficient traction to brake us short of disaster. And fortunately the snow had been soft and deep enough to act as a shock absorber. If we had hit down on ice or flat rock we would have pancaked.

Studying the damage, once again Palmer cried "Fuck!" in despair, his face showing anguish. It was inevitable that such behavior, coming from the leader of our group, would be infectious. The crewman's face trembled, he worked to control his emotions, he said "Fuck" in a low voice, bit his nether lip and swung his head from side to side. But Enderby looked stolid although pale. I learned from him later, at McMurdo, that he had thought Palmer had landed deliberately.

Palmer said as if to himself but very clearly, "I'm going to be shipped out."

He remarked several times how lucky we were one of the rotor blades hadn't hit the snow; if it had, we would have been flipped over. He entered the cockpit and tried to start the engine. The crewman stood by outside with a fire extinguisher. We had plenty of battery power but the engine could not grab hold. I had heard a story about a Coast Guard helo going too high somewhere on Erebus, landing, shutting down its engine and being unable to start it without the help of other helos, special batteries and special equipment. And that hadn't been near as high as we now were. Palmer called out to the crewman that he had a red warning light indicating fire.

"Look for a fire!" he shouted.

The crewman replied he didn't see any sign of a fire but that smoke was pouring out of the exhaust. The smell of fire in the cabin was too strong to be ignored. I asked Enderby to remove my survival tent and gear from the craft and to set the tent up as best and as quickly as he could at a sufficient distance from the helo to protect it if the helo burned. Whether the craft burned or not, we would need the tent if the temperature kept dropping. I told him not to bother staking the tent down thoroughly.

"Just secure it against a possible gust of wind. Then give me a hand with the food."

I started lugging cartons out of the craft. The effects of the altitude, which became apparent the moment one moved about or worked, were unpleasant now: breathlessness, a pounding of the heart, dizziness, quick fatigue, the possibility of blacking out. But they were mild for me as compared for my companions. I was surprised when, quite early, the crewman complained of a vicious headache. Then Enderby and Palmer said they had very bad headaches too. I explained my lack of a headache to myself as being the result of all the swimming I had done and the oxygen hunger I had deliberately endured.

After a while the smoke stopped and the smell of fire disappeared. We were still warm from the craft's heating system. Things could be worse. They could also be somewhat better: for example if the HF (high frequency) radio was functioning. But the HF radio required a lot of juice, and we had lost the radio with the engine's failure. You lose your single engine and go down, and to help along your morale you also lose your HF radio.

Palmer fetched a line-of-sight hand radio and walked around the craft, saying, "Mayday! Mayday! McMurdo! McMurdo! Any station! Any station! This is copter one four zero four down on the northern slope of Mount Erebus!"

He handed me the radio—it was small, with a flexible, tubelike antenna—and asked me to keep calling. So I walked around outside and pressed the transmission button and said over and over, "McMurdo Station, McMurdo Station! Mayday, Mayday, Mayday! McMurdo Station, this is helo one four zero four down on the northern slope of Mount Erebus!"

But I felt very dubious about the effort, for the gadget was a line-of-sight thing, and Erebus was between us and McMurdo.

Again Palmer tried to start the engine and again he received a fire signal. Coming outside, he told me he believed the engine was all right but that the air was too thin to permit the engine to take hold.

He said, "We'll have to walk to a ridge overlooking McMurdo and use the hand radio from there. Chuck, you know Ross Island best. Can we walk to the top?"

I said it would be foolhardy to try it. Visibility was poor and getting worse. We were going to be socked in very shortly. The temperature was rapidly dropping. We might have to contend with bad ice slopes, even crevasses. And we had no crampons, no rope and only one ice ax. Furthermore, we had the altitude effects to contend with.

Palmer walked around examining the craft, uttered a few more "Fucks," then turned to me and said, "Chuck, I'm sorry to have gotten you into this place."

"Forget it, Stu, it's okay."

Labels on image:
VICTORIA LAND
← ROSS ISLAND
ROSS SEA
ROSS
ICE
SHELF
TRANSANTARCTIC
MOUNTAINS
← SOUTH POLE

1

*Victoria Land, Ross Island, the Ross Sea, the Ross Ice Shelf, the Trans-
antarctic Mountains and the South Pole photographed by polar satellite
Nimbus 4 from six hundred miles above the earth.*

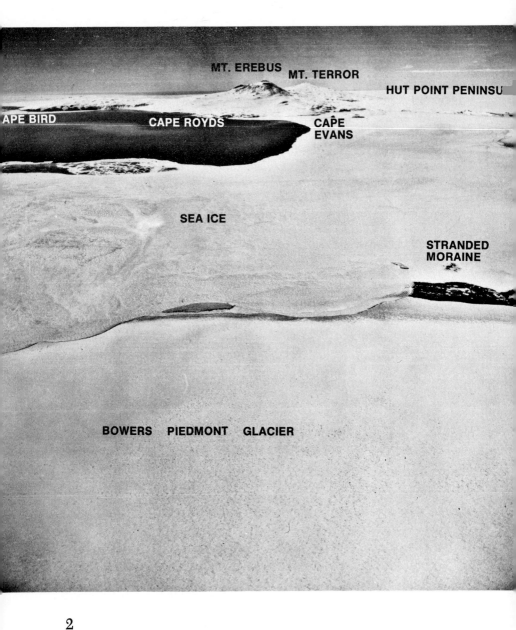

2
Ross Island seen from the west at an elevation of 15,700 feet. The photograph was taken December 6, 1956.

The northern part of Ross Island seen from the east at an elevation of 19,000 feet. The photograph was taken November 5, 1958.

MT. EREBUS

MT. TERROR

CAPE BIRD

PACK ICE

CAPE CROZIER

ROSS ICE SHELF

3

4

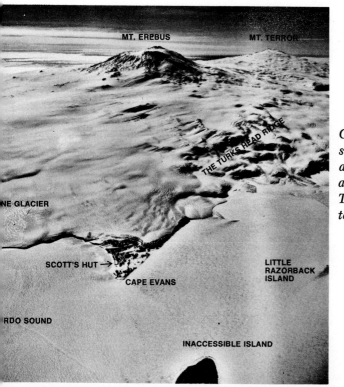

MT. EREBUS

MT. TERROR

THE TURKS HEAD RIDGE

NE GLACIER

SCOTT'S HUT →

CAPE EVANS

LITTLE RAZORBACK ISLAND

RDO SOUND

INACCESSIBLE ISLAND

Cape Evans and vicinity seen from the west at an elevation of about 14,000 feet. The photograph was taken December 2, 1956.

5

Scott in his "den" in winter quarters at Cape Evans.

Ernest Shackleton

6

Shackleton's southern party on board the Nimrod shortly after their farthest southing. Left to right: Wild, Shackleton, Marshall, Adams.

7

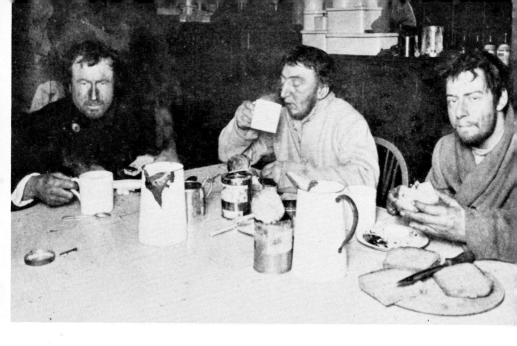

·8 and 9

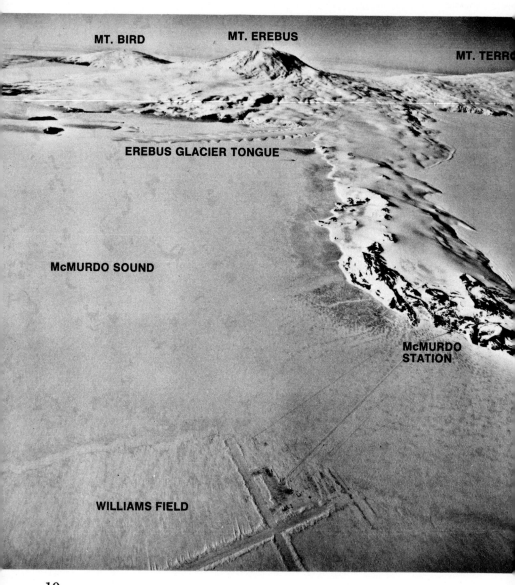

MT. BIRD   MT. EREBUS   MT. TERRO

EREBUS GLACIER TONGUE

McMURDO SOUND

McMURDO
STATION

WILLIAMS FIELD

10

Ross Island seen from the south at an elevation of 16,000 feet. The photograph was taken November 14, 1959.

11

Mount Erebus seen from an altitude of about 20,000 feet. The view is to the south. In the foreground is the Fang and just beyond it the Fang Glacier. South of the volcano is Hut Point Peninsula, at the southern tip of which can be seen Observation Hill. The long object with the serrated edges lying between Mount Erebus and Observation Hill and stemming from the right of the peninsula is Erebus Glacier Tongue. Beyond the peninsula, left to right, are the Ross Ice Shelf, White Island, Black Island and the prominent cone of Mount Discovery. The arrow indicates the approximate position of the Coast Guard helicopter crash site.

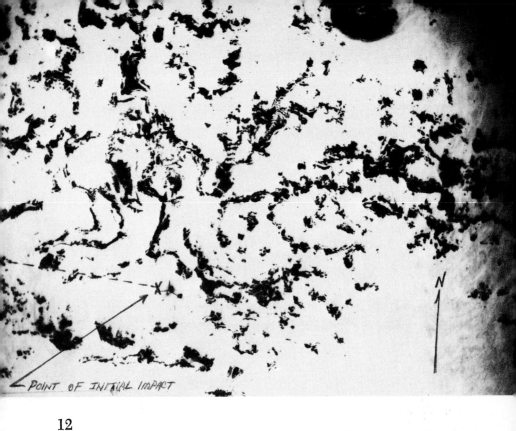

POINT OF INITIAL IMPACT

N

12

The helicopter crash site as seen from the C-130 circling over us. The photograph vividly exemplifies the difficulty of locating us from the air solely by visual means. Aside from the bits of color offered by the helicopter and the tent, color that went unnoticed by the crew of the helicopter that saw our Very flare, only the geometric pattern of the rotors indicates our presence in the mazelike landscape.

"We'll *have* to get to a ridge," he said. "If not up there, then a lower one, maybe lower than here. Van and I will look for a ridge."

I advised him to stay on outcrop whenever possible and to probe with the ice ax when he was on snow.

He said, "Hell, let's walk down the mountain and get away from this altitude."

I said, "You wouldn't get three hundred yards before you'd be dead. There are snowbridged crevasses. You could fall through and go down thirty or forty feet. Even if you survived the fall and we had rope and gear and know-how to rescue you with, there'd be little time. Down there, below the surface, you'd be at mean temperature, probably fifty or sixty below. And there are icefalls and ice slopes. We have no belaying equipment, only one ice ax, and no knowledge of the safest way down. The best way down I know about is at Royds, but we're too far north of that. And how would we see in that mass of clouds? We wouldn't stand a chance."

He looked startled.

"We're trapped," I said. "We'd better stay close to the craft. It's our best chance of being found."

I wanted to say more. I wanted to ask, "Why don't you drain the helo's fuel and lubricant while they're still warm, so we can use them for heat and for smudge pots?"

For it was standard polar survival procedure to drain fuel and lubricant immediately after a crash.

But I could sense that he still hadn't accepted the fact the craft was here to stay, that he was hoping the engine would somehow fire, catch hold and extricate us from our most unusual predicament; and clearly I was eager to share his hopes even though I wondered vaguely if the engine system had been damaged in the crash, for otherwise I would have said what was on my mind; or wouldn't I?

Much was uncertain. Had McMurdo heard our HF mayday signal? But even if it had, it knew neither our identity nor our location. Was the hand radio working?

And so Palmer and Enderby headed southwestward, Enderby probing the way and Palmer looking unearthly in his huge helmet. If they remained as much as possible on the plateau on which we found ourselves, which contained a substantial amount of outcrop, and if they used the ice ax responsibly they would be reasonably safe. Soon they disappeared below a nearby ridge, leaving me alone with the crewman.

25

~~~~~~~~~~~~~~~~~~~~~~~~~~~~

THE HELICOPTER

I WALKED to an outcrop to study the crash scene from a distance and to view the helo, this poor kitelike box that through mismanagement had fallen out of the sky; this outpost of civilization in a bleak and savage wilderness; this comfortable "home"; but a home which, because it was a metal fuselage, was a heat sink, beautifully capable of dissipating our body heat into space; therefore a home that could destroy us if we depended overmuch on it; this representative of high technology, costing half a million dollars, but a technology, as for example in the case of the HF radio, that had failed us; or that we had significantly failed.

The cloud cover that had been steadily moving in on us had by now engulfed us like a thick fog. Who would have dreamed it had the audacity to climb so high? At times one had to resist the notion it was malevolent. For weeks Erebus had been clear. Now, in the increasing warmth of the austral summer, more and more seawater was free of its frozen state and creating massive fogs and clouds. The cover made the largest, blackest boulders appear to be faint gray shadows in a vast milky stuff. Visibility was seventy-five to a hundred feet. Beyond that range, in every direction, including overhead, was a potentially murderous white wall. What a thing to happen at a time when we had strayed grossly from our flight plan! We might as well be underground for all the good it would do to set off flares and smoke bombs.

The crewman, wearing a white spherical helmet, a khaki flight suit, light khaki flight gloves and beat-up desert boots, was standing uncertainly in front of the open hatch. He was a gracefully tall man with a pleasant, easy-smiling, longish face. Little brown hairs sprouted from his bony chin in what, hopefully, was the beginning of a beard. I had paid little attention to him. One saw helo crewmen but looked through them. What did we have in common? Usually very little. But this present crewman and I had a good deal, despite the fact that we had been born greatly apart, he in Illinois in 1950, I in Russia in 1915. We might well die together; or, if not together, in tandem. And I believe we also felt the uncommon bond of representing life in a mostly inorganic world. I thought "mostly" in the faith there must be little outposts, faint strains, of life here, even though none were presently visible.

Realizing that I didn't know his name, I walked over and asked what it was. It felt odd to be making such a request inasmuch as we had crashed and worked together and he had been addressing me as Doc. But I had been uncertain as to whether we would lift off and remain strangers to each other. Now I knew we were not going to take off—not in one four zero four, which had found its last resting place. We were going to get to know each other before we were out of this.

"Jack Eights," he replied.

I gave him my name but he called me Doc throughout the episode although Palmer and Enderby called me Chuck. He looked unhappy. I suspected he felt very lonely. I knew I did, yet I had relished the feeling of loneliness, or rather of being alone, in Taylor Valley and at Capes Evans and Royds. Four had been diminished to two; temporarily it was only he and I against raw nature here in the form of Erebus: Erebus the white, the beautiful; an angel capable of vomiting up molten lava, of destroying life with either heat or cold.

I asked him to help me secure the tent. We were lucky the wind was mild, but would it continue to be? Our lives might depend on the tent. He worked at the ropes and poles while I hammered at the rock pegs with a fire extinguisher. We had thin cylindrical metal pegs, meant for Cape Bird, instead of square wooden ones. In snow and ice and in a steady, grinding wind the metal pegs, providing less friction, would work loose more readily. The sound of metal on metal ricocheted around us. The temperature was dropping steadily.

Occasionally Eights looked on the verge of panic. Once he said harshly to himself, "Fuck! What am I doing here?"

He was, as we know, only twenty. When I saw him like this something paternal stirred inside me.

"We'll be all right," I said.

Glancing up, he asked hopefully, "Think so, Doc?"

"Yes. I wouldn't miss this for anything."

He smiled. He seemed more relaxed after that. Possibly I represented for him the responsibility and reliability of middle age. And perhaps he had already begun to doubt Palmer's ability to bring him intact out of the situation and had begun to look to me to do it. Maybe he was impressed by my relative calmness, which resulted, I believe, from my being acquainted with the facts of life in Antarctica. Also, I was fascinated by everything and was trying to observe and remember acutely. What must have seemed a naked disaster to him seemed to me at times, in addition, a remarkable opportunity.

There was more work to be done, but his head was splitting, and I was breathing very heavily and rapidly. We rested awhile, watching the weather. He drew out his sheath knife, saying, "Doc, I've always wanted to stick this into a helo and now I can."

I laughed. But, not wanting to witness the sticking, I turned away and walked to a distant outcrop to take a few shots of the boulders showing in the cover. It occurred to me that if he was temporarily mad enough to tilt with a dead helo he might also be sufficiently unhinged to stick a knife into a man. I went back to him. He said his feet were numb. His boots could be called boots only by extravagant courtesy. I suggested he stand on rock because rock, being dark, had absorbed the sun's heat better than snow and ice, which had reflected it back. We made our way across hard, squeaky snow to an outcrop near the ice fumaroles, going on the path we had probed earlier with the ice ax. His feet felt better on the rock.

If our luck had been bad before, it became rotten now: the cover got so thick it approached the dreaded whiteout condition. In response, the outcrop grew bitterly cold. Soon it made little difference to our feet whether we stood on rock or snow. We glanced skyward longingly, hoping the cover would break up and permit the sun to give us back our body heat. I judged our present temperature to be about five below.

Eights entered the cockpit and said through the open starboard hatch he thought the engine would start if we had some sunlight to warm it and a head wind to blow air into the turbine intake. There was still plenty of battery power. The engine made lots of noise, spewed smoke out of the exhaust and emitted a strong smell of fire. A red warning light flashed on the instrument panel.

Emerging from the craft, Eights murmured, "Christ, Christ, we're fucked," his lean face showing despair.

He asked me to spray a long fire extinguisher's contents into the turbine intake as he again tried to start the engine. The carbon dioxide in the extinguisher was depleted; only air was coming out; hopefully the latter would help the engine to grab hold. I climbed onto the fuselage and did what he requested. The effort was useless. Without a thicker air mixture the engine was dead.

I wandered off in the direction Palmer and Enderby had taken, going farther from the helo than before, intending to shoot the scene so I would be able to convince myself, in the event we were rescued, that the weather had been as bad as it now looked. I saw narrow, long, green crevasses. Although it seemed unlikely, judging by the terrain, that I would encounter wider ones, I could not be sure, so I made my way with some caution. The mostly white craft would not easily be visible from the air. The bottom of the hull was white, as were the cabin and the engine housing. A red stripe ran down the back of the cabin. The front exterior of the cockpit as well as the tail were red. The rotors were black, with orange tips. Up on the turbine housing were the numerals 1404.

I had stopped at a large deep cleft in some rock. Glancing into the cleft, I saw a patch of pink lichen: the non-human life I had hoped was here with us.

"Doc?" Eights called anxiously.

I headed toward him to see what he wanted. He left the helo to meet me.

"We'd better not get separated," he said, handing me a khaki plastic whistle with a braided black cord.

I didn't blame him for not wanting to be left alone in a place where everything was so unfamiliar and threatening. He had recently arrived on the ice for the first time. He had been living on the warm, crowded *Staten Island*. He had visited warm, crowded McMurdo. And now he was near the top of Mount Erebus, with his life's supply of heat steadily diminishing.

He was such a nice-looking boy, and possibly he had been thinking of his parents, or of a girl friend, or of places in Illinois he especially liked, or of some chore he had meant to do on the icebreaker, or was wondering by what sour luck he had been chosen for this flight, *my* flight, designed solely to deliver me to Cape Bird, and probably he realized I might have decided, had I felt less pressed for time, to scratch it, considering the state of the cover. Was the cover as thick along the coastal route as it was up here? It struck me, from the little I knew of such things, as being capable of lasting many days. If it stayed a long time would we handle ourselves badly or well? I was still ignorant of facts I would soon acquire. I believed then that we possessed the means to fight the cover and the mountain with a sporting chance of coming through, even if we had to hold out for weeks. I wonder now how much of my reaction to Eights was guilt for my having had a share, such as it was, in causing his predicament.

It seemed to me that Palmer and Enderby had been gone too long. We had crashed at approximately 2:30. It was now past a quarter to four. Where were they? Would they find their way back in this white stuff? What if one or both had fallen into a crevasse? What if they were lost?—they were without shelter or food. And they were lightly clad. Palmer, as we know, had on only his helmet, his flight suit, his flight gloves, flight boots. And Enderby had on a USARP parka, whose hood he had pulled over his head—I didn't know what kind of shirt he was wearing under it, but I assumed it was the standard heavy woolen one—blue jeans, hiking boots and black gloves. I knew how cold they must feel: I myself was lightly clad for this temperature. I wore thermals, a black cap, a wool shirt, threadbare tan cotton corduroy trousers, a USARP parka, black double gloves and my own hiking boots, and I had begun to experience fits of shivering, as had Eights. The cold that was penetrating our bodies was sending alarm signals to our brains, crying as if in panic, "Beware! Beware! Parts of you are in danger of freezing!" Adrenalin flowed accordingly, whether you wished it to or not. If Palmer and Enderby died it would be a poor beginning to a tragedy that might have the added horror of being long drawn out, with Eights and me following them but more slowly because we had the tent, food and the helo. We ought to have decided how long they would be away. How stupid it had been of us not to have formed a plan. We had had no right to improvise so casually.

Warning Eights I intended to use the whistle, I walked a fair distance in the direction in which I had last seen them and blew a long blast, hoping I would hear a cry in return. I heard nothing human. It was not easy to blow hard at this altitude. You got dizzy; you wondered for a moment if you were going to black out. Between blasts you listened to the eerie Antarctic silence, interrupted now only by the hum of the wind as it caressed jagged volcanic boulders and your ears. I blew half a dozen times at intervals of about five minutes, becoming increasingly alarmed, for I knew that our best chance for survival was to stick together, to remain near the helicopter and to keep up our morale.

I returned to the craft, where Eights had broken out smoke bombs, flares and a Very pistol with shells. I asked him to fire the pistol at the cover overhead. The flare rocketed up, burst, divided into two brilliant red mushrooms and fell, dying. It came nowhere near reaching the cover. Taking inventory of our signaling devices, we resolved not to use them unless the cover lifted and we heard a plane.

Not long afterwards Enderby and Palmer appeared slowly out of the mists southwest of us, looking very tired, Enderby still carrying the ice ax. I was relieved to see them. We were all together again; we hadn't done anything irreversibly stupid. Palmer was shivering; he was obviously unwell for some reason. He said the hand radio was useless; its battery was too cold. Enderby's face was red and drawn. He reported that his feet had gotten wet and were very numb. By questioning Enderby, who gave me the impression of being more stolid than stoical, I learned that they hadn't heard the whistle—what had muffled it? ridges? the cover? the thin air?—and that they had had no trouble following their tracks on their way back. They had not found the ridge they had been seeking, one overlooking McMurdo. They had reached several ridges but each had given way to another. Feeling the cold badly, with the altitude fatiguing them, and having trouble with altitude headaches, they had decided to go no further. What Enderby and Palmer did not reveal then for some reason (I learned it from Enderby back in McMurdo after our rescue) was that Palmer had taken two spills, slamming down on his back so suddenly and hard as to cause Enderby to be seriously alarmed.

Palmer was silent now and his glances tended to be averted. Was it because he suspected he had already said too much by declaring, "I'm going to be shipped out?" Why had he taken Enderby instead of Eights on his search for a ridge? Because he wanted to avoid the sense he had abandoned the passengers? Probably he was still stunned by the falls. I wish now I had known about them. Such knowledge might have lessened my resentment of him. I caught myself thinking, "Going over Erebus is a game in which there can be no sympathy for failure."

Yet there were crucial questions, such as whether he had autorotated—I doubted he had—that I failed to put to him in order to spare him possible embarrassment. His mental state was important to our safety; he was still our leader, who would pull us through. I failed utterly at this time to grasp our true condition, for example to take stock of our survival gear. Much later, on reviewing the episode, I was astonished it had taken me so long to grasp the real situation.

A strong north wind came up and whipped the tent flaps, strings and openings. Enderby pounded at the tent stakes and checked the poles and ropes. I thought, "Prepare yourself for a long stay and prepare the others." We gathered in the tilted helo cabin, which still felt warmer than the outside, and shut the hatch. I told Palmer what I had already explained to Eights about the metal fuselage being a heat sink. He was skeptical. He said the cabin was a good place to remain in; it was more roomy and more comfortable than the tent. I said that the tent, being much smaller than the cabin, was easier to warm with our bodies. He remained dubious even when our feet began to freeze from contact with the floor.

It slowly became clear to me that there was a failure of leadership on his part. He seemed unwilling or unable to take command, and was understandably reluctant to hand it over to me. However, it became increasingly unnecessary for him to relinquish it formally. As he turned more and more inward the two young men looked to me for suggestions and orders and I found myself having with painful embarrassment to take over his role out of necessity.

He asked me—I was closest to the cockpit—to see what the windshield thermometer read. I reported it was at $-25°$ C., or about $-15°$ F. The two scales begin to merge at low temperatures. At forty below there is no difference between them. They diverge again below that figure. The wind had a permanent feel to it.

And now, quite suddenly, certain unpleasant facts came to light. Enderby stood up, looked at me with a pale face full of embarrassment, and said in a small voice, "Chuck, I forgot to bring my survival gear."

It struck me as especially ironic that he, who worked in the Field Center, which was supposed to know something of the hazards of Antarctica, should be guilty of this lapse. Perhaps he had thought, "It's only a turnaround flight. We're in the middle of a heat wave. Why bother to drag my survival bag along?" But probably he hadn't. The history of Antarctica was dotted by people who had taken the continent for granted, sometimes to their sorrow. Now his sorrow was mine also, for I would have to share my survival gear with him. Of course, he had not known the weather was foul on the McMurdo-Bird route. Still, that route was as long a flight as you could make on Ross Island, and he ought to have taken survival gear along on even a short flight: it was the rule, designed to save limbs and possibly lives.

Then Eights told me that the helicopter's four survival packs, each weighing about fifty pounds, were not on board. They had been removed for the shuttle flights between McMurdo and Willy Field and, through some confusion, had not been replaced. Furthermore, he said, he had brought no personal survival gear and nor had Palmer. Palmer, staring at the floor, remained remote and silent.

The harsh facts of our situation were now beginning to take full hold of me. My companions had trifled with Antarctica. They had been lulled by the heat wave at McMurdo; by the comforts provided by the nuclear plant; by the security suggested by all the aircraft and heavy equipment and men. I was by far the oldest of the group, with the least chance of coming through, despite my good physical condition. When I considered that my ability to survive would be greatly lessened by my having to spread my gear thin to help my companions a bitterness rose temporarily to my palate. My careful habits had proved insufficient to my safety. The lesson was simple: it was not enough to provide for yourself unless you were traveling alone.

An intuition caused me to ask Enderby suddenly, "Did you pack matches in my gear?"

Enderby paled, looked stunned.

"No. I forgot."

I turned to Eights.

"Are there matches on board?"

"No, sir."

"Anybody got any matches?" I asked.

There was no reply.

We were losing moisture with some rapidity. When one of us spoke, clouds of steam escaped him. The continent was notoriously dry; its air was like a sponge. But now we had the added complication of the special dryness of high altitude. It seemed obvious to me—a thought that I expressed to my companions—that our lives would first be threatened by severe dehydration, which would cause certain organs to collapse, and that somehow we would have to make a fire and heat snow to make water. The snow outside was already too cold to put in one's mouth safely, and the temperature was steadily falling.

By now the engine's lubricant had no doubt congealed and could not be drained; it should have been drained within a half to three quarters of an hour after the crash. With the lubricant and using wicks we could have made flares as well as smudge pots. But the helo's fuel was still fluid at this temperature. We could drain it, using a section of the canopy or some other article as the container. We could improvise a stove out of a large can or whatever else was handy and, using bits of gravel or small rocks as a base, pour fuel on them and burn the fuel for heat, for making water, for thawing food and for cooking. The helo's fuel, if carefully conserved, could last us quite awhile. But it was useless without matches. If the sun were out and we had a magnifying glass—perhaps one of my camera lenses could be used as one—we might make a fire, for the sun was strong in this dry air, especially at our altitude, despite the fact that it hung low over the horizon. However, given our cloud cover, I did not think we had a right to be optimistic about its reappearing soon. I wondered if the helo's battery could be used to make sparks and then a fire, and wondered also how long the battery would hold up at this low temperature. Possibly it was already dead.

Eights's feet were the first to go. I pulled my mukluks out of my orange seabag—they were rated to forty below, I had been told in Christchurch—and gave them to him. He had no headgear aside from his helmet, and only his flight suit and flight gloves. I gave him my khaki woolen balaclava and a pair of heavy gray mittens. To Enderby I handed fresh woolen socks to replace his wet ones. Palmer had no headgear other than his helmet. I had no headgear to give him. I handed him a double pair of gloves to be used in addition to his thin flight gloves. Luckily he was wearing sturdy leather boots, as was Enderby. My own boots were inadequate: the soles had been ripped by my climbing around the volcanic terrain of Royds and Evans. My feet felt frozen, especially the left one, which had been run over by a car and which, ever since, had been the weak one. My legs were turning numb. After considering the matter a moment I asked if it was all right if I put on my windpants, explaining that I was losing sensation in my legs.

"Hell yes!" Palmer said loudly out of his silence.

I said, "This gear belongs to all of us."

Then—I hated myself for doing it, for I had only one pair of windpants—I pulled them out of the survival bag, removed my boots, laboriously donned the black pants, then put the boots on again, my head spinning with the effort of bending over, my hands thick, clumsy, my thoughts murky. I felt guilty, nasty for wearing the windpants when no one else had windpants. On the other hand, only Eights had mukluks and he was delighted to have them and to know he was not going to risk the loss of his feet. Then I thought that, after all, the pants were mine and that I was the oldest of the group and presumably the least able to take the thing that might be coming: a tremendous test of our ability to cling to life. A second thought came forcefully: at what price was it worth hanging on? At the cost of one's honor? Then I thought that if we had all brought our survival gear and the helo's four survival packs we wouldn't be in a very bad way unless a long-lasting blizzard blew up. We could set up a couple of tents and be comfortable in our sleeping bags. We could rest and sleep the time away until we were found, even if it took a couple of weeks.

Well, we were in for it and it would take a few miracles to get us out. I was convinced we must soon move into the tent. I could say simply, "I'm moving into the tent" and let whoever wanted to follow me follow. But that would humiliate Palmer and lower his morale still further. If it continued to decline, his will to survive would fall with it; with a weak will his chances of survival would greatly lessen and he might do something to decrease them further: for example, he might take a serious fall. If one of us suffered badly the others would have to minister to him. In the process we would lose our own narrow margin of safety and we might all go down into irreversible damage or death. So I refrained from saying, "I'm moving into the tent" not out of altruism but out of self-interest. For the clear fact was that our lives depended on each other.

26

~~~~~~~~~~~~~~~~~~~~~~~~~~~~~~~

THE TENT

IT WAS NOW about four forty-five, two and a quarter hours after
the crash. Our mayday signals had obviously not gotten through,
for if they had we would have heard C-130 engines overhead long
since. We should have reached Cape Bird at about two-thirty or
two-forty and notified McMurdo Station of our arrival. By an hour
later McMurdo had no doubt become thoroughly alarmed. I expected that the coastal route between McMurdo and Bird was
being completely although hazardously searched. Cape Bird had
probably already been visited. We wondered if a SAR (search
and rescue) Condition was in full operation.

We took stock of our means of survival. We had one Air Force
survival tent, designed for single or double occupancy, one Bauer
sleeping bag, two cot mattresses, one ice ax, one canteen of water
(already frozen), a good deal of food, much of which would need
thawing out, and no apparent means of making a fire. We also had
the helo's insulation and a lightweight brown blanket that I assumed belonged to the helo but whose ownership I have not been
able to establish with certainty. Enderby later told me it may have
been part of my camping gear; he wasn't sure. In addition we had
the clothes we were now wearing and a pair of bear paws in my
seabag that no one, I think out of delicacy, used because it was the
only pair among us.

Our situation was not good but it could have been much worse.
No one had been injured in the crash. We had a tent and therefore
were not obliged to stay in the helo. Without a tent we would have

been forced to remain in the craft, for we lacked the tools for digging body trenches in the hard snow. We had the sleeping bag, which, when unzipped, could serve as a blanket. We had the brown blanket. We had the survival gear I had brought along.

The cold began to feel savage. The temperature was steadily falling and the wind was still rising. The metal fuselage was rapidly draining us of body heat even though we tried to avoid metal contact. When I repeated forcefully that we would freeze in the cabin, Palmer said, "Maybe we'd better move to the tent."

I asked Eights to strip the cabin of its insulation and told Enderby to crawl inside the tent and prepare a flooring with the stuff we would hand him. Palmer and Eights stripped the helo of everything that looked useful, including the seats, and handed it to me. I carried the stuff to the tent about twenty or twenty-five feet away and gave it piecemeal to Enderby through the complicated, wormlike entrance. All I saw of Enderby during this operation was his hands. I also passed to him the two cot mattresses, the canteen and the sleeping bag.

When I crawled in to examine his handiwork I made my way through a billowing red tube of light material, then through some white, gauzelike stuff that served as a curtain-door, and fouled myself at times as though in a shroud—I felt like a crawling blind man —and even the extra little exertion of getting down on all fours made itself felt by a wild beating of my heart. I was surprised to see how neatly he had arranged things. He had spread the helo insulation on the tent floor, the mattresses side by side on the top of the insulation, and had made a blanket of the sleeping bag. It all looked unexpectedly cozy.

"What a fine boy he is!" I thought.

We gathered together our necessaries and set them down near the tent entrance, that is, the one facing the summit. The opposite one Enderby had tied into a great knot as a protection against the wind. We had a Very pistol and shells, flares, smoke bombs, dye markers, and cartons and crates of food: fruit, vegetables, bread, frozen steaks, frozen rock lobsters, even milk chocolate.

Palmer and I agreed on a plan: to huddle in the tent and to try to ward off permanent damage while we got used to the altitude. Each man's thermal margin was so small, even in the tent, as we were soon to discover, that if one of us had reached an irreversible stage, with the psychological consequences this would have entailed, and required ministering to, the others would probably have gone down in domino fashion. Eights asked me how long it would take to get used to the altitude. I replied that the effects would probably increase before they diminished. My friend Dale Vance, now at Vostok Station, had felt fairly good there the first day but for the next ten had had headaches, insomnia and some nausea. We were approximately as high as Vostok.

You sensed that the altitude was like an animal, lurking to assail you, and although you were cautious, being by now aware of its potency, it worked on you suddenly: when you were walking or working or even just standing still and talking. It made you breathless, caused your speech to be fuzzy, disarranged your thoughts. Your words came out too slowly or mixed up. It was easy to do something stupid or dangerous. In addition, the altitude prevented you from warming up by jogging in place. To try jogging was to invite blacking out or vomiting. However, the altitude effects were inconstant and fortunately they were infrequent. But my companions were plagued by intense headaches which I took to be as bad as migraines. In addition to the altitude, always you sensed the power and personality of Erebus. This domineering, remote volcano now had an intimate place in our minds, our lives and perhaps in our death.

Glancing at my companions—we were still outside—I found myself wondering who would outlast whom. I thought of my age. In nine days I would be fifty-six. How long would my heart endure the demands being put on it? It beat very rapidly and pounded even when I did not exert myself. I told myself I must not think about my age: I must put all negative thoughts aside if I meant to survive. I must keep up my morale and the morale of the others. Above all I must behave well. For this, in the end, was what it was about, my having come to Antarctica. It was the subject that had intrigued me so long and intensely: getting at the heart of a magnificent, wild continent. Whenever I remembered my wife and daughter and thought of what my death would mean to them I put them quickly out of mind. I could not afford to let myself be softened by sentiment. Anyhow—and this struck me as very odd—I felt that my truest loyalty was to my present companions, strangers to me. It was with and for them I must behave well; but primarily it was for myself.

And then there was the cold: that thief of one's life's warmth.

We kept glancing hopefully at the sky, and when the scud showed patches that seemed thinner than usual our hearts sang, and we grinned, cracked jokes. If the sun were to come out we'd be *warm*. My left foot was worrying me; it had begun to lose all feeling.

Palmer entered the tent. Enderby was outside somewhere, Eights was in the helo cabin. We needed rocks with which to secure the tent flaps in order to minimize the seepage of wind in the tent. I took the ice ax to some boulders and tried to break chunks off. The volcanic stuff was unbelievably hard. All I managed to achieve was to stimulate my hands with the shock of the blows. One would need a pickax to dent such material. Eights, having emerged from the cabin, suggested inflating the helo's one-man life rafts and placing them against the sides of the tent; this would to some extent hold down the flaps. We inflated the rafts but not to much effect. Later, when we were huddling in the tent, we would feel minutely the variations in the wind's strength. When the wind subsided, the tent grew noticeably warmer. When it rose, we immediately felt threatened, and involuntary alarm signals went off throughout our bodies, various appendages crying out that they were in imminent danger of dying.

I walked to a distant outcrop to take some photographs. Returning to the helo, I found Eights standing in front of the cabin hatch, munching on a chunk of cabbage. In one gloved hand he held a whole head, from which he had cut a hunk with his sheath knife. He had thrown the outer leaves onto the snow. Picking them up and tossing them into the cabin, I said, "Our lives may depend on these. There's no telling how long we may have to hang on. Don't throw *anything* away."

He stopped eating.

I thought, "Stu has made no move to inventory the food and to prepare to ration it. What's he thinking of? Is he positive we'll be rescued? Doesn't he realize this cover can hang on for days, during which fatigue will worsen, causing irritation, illness, accidents? But first will come the dehydration."

As if reading my mind, Eights asked, "Why can't we eat snow, Doc?"

I said the temperature of the snow was now probably twenty or twenty-five below; that the temperature of a freezer compartment in a house refrigerator was about five above; that the snow would injure lips, tongue and palate.

He said, "We've got lots of fruit."

"Which will be like billiard balls soon."

I went to the cockpit to read the thermometer. It registered $-35°$ C., the equivalent of $-31°$ F. The wind was blowing steadily. What was the effective temperature? Fifty, sixty, seventy below?

Eights and Enderby crawled into the tent. I followed them. We lay on our backs under the sleeping-bag blanket at right angles to the entrance and would continue to lie like that, without the luxury of lying on our sides. Any motion on the part of one of us disturbed the others and robbed them of body heat. I was nearest the entrance. Farthest from me was Palmer, lying parallel to me; next to him was Eights, lying opposite him; and next to Eights was Enderby, lying opposite me.

The unzipped sleeping bag wasn't large enough to cover us adequately. We shifted the brown blanket from time to time on an emergency basis. My right side and thigh, only partially covered, grew very cold. I asked Enderby how his feet were. He said he had lost feeling in them. I invited him to place them under my parka, which he did. I felt like crying about him. He had come on a simple turnaround flight and now he might die here. He and Eights aroused painful fatherly feelings in me. Of the four of us they had the most to lose by dying now; it was right that they were in the middle, where it was warmest. I had the least to lose. I had lived a long and complex life, containing its share of tragedy, and I did not discover a strong desire to cling to it.

My own feet were a problem, especially the left one. For a while I hoped they would recover under the blanket—we had removed our boots—but I realized slowly it was not responding. I tried wiggling the toes. I rubbed it against my right foot. I curled the right foot over it. Finally I handed Enderby my two left gloves and asked him to put them on my left foot. Slowly the foot came around but then my right foot began to go. At the same time I felt sleepy; I wanted to sleep in order to conserve strength. But if I slept I would fail to stay on guard for my foot's sake. How would it be to return to the world footless? So I determined not to sleep unless my whole body was secured. Meanwhile it became plain that it wasn't just my right foot that was in trouble but my right side from the hip down.

Palmer said, "I'm not going to make it if my left leg doesn't get more cover," and Eights rearranged himself, in the process unavoidably rearranging Enderby and me, and the brown blanket was passed to Palmer temporarily.

We huddled close together, shivering fitfully. It was remarkable how small our margins of body heat were. We would all have to be on a constant alert if we were to succeed in warding off permanent damage.

We were struck by what the red tent did to colors. The green sleeping bag had become a deep navy blue, my red parka a pale yellow-orange. Eights kept commenting on this transmutation of colors. He seemed more relaxed now, although once I overheard him saying to Enderby, "Every once in a while I feel panicky." He cracked jokes and exhibited a comic, mugging side. He could not seem to let go of the subject of colors.

Then we heard C-130 engines in the north for a while; in the south; in the west. So there was no doubt the search was on. One wanted to shout, "Here we are!" and to send up flares. We took turns crawling out of the tent to see if there was a break in the cover. Each exhausting effort dissipated some of our body heat. Each shivering returning man brought in more cold.

Invariably the report was, "It's the same."

I thought, "If only there was a tiny Plexiglas window in the top of the tent, through which we could observe the weather. What a lot of body heat it would save!"

For a while all we wanted was for the cover to break up. That would signify *the next step,* without which there could be no help for us. The long hours passed.

Then, to my great astonishment, Palmer asked casually, "Would anybody mind if I smoked?" and broke out a little lighter.

And Eights, asking the same question, withdrew from a pocket an identical lighter.

"Great Christ!" I thought. "I'm dealing with children!"

One charitable explanation I could put on their having failed earlier to reveal the existence of the lighters was that they were positive we were not in a genuine survival situation; we could carry on our lives in normal fashion; we were sure to be rescued. But if that was the case why had they shown signs of panic? Were their minds, then, dissonant with their bodies? Did their minds say, "There's nothing to worry about. I'll be taken care of."? Or did they say, "There's too much to worry about, and I'll just smoke to comfort myself."? Another charitable explanation was that they had misunderstood, or had failed to grasp, or had disagreed with, or had discounted, my warnings of the dangers of dehydration. A less charitable one was that it graveled them to be helped by a middle-aged civilian, a writer at that, somebody who typically spent much time on his behind.

At any rate, we could make a fire after all! I, a non-smoker, did not enjoy the prospect of the small tent's being filled with smoke. Apparently an abstainer could not escape cigarette smoke even near the crater of Mount Erebus. But if smoking was good for Palmer's and Eights's morale, I was for it—for the moment. So I did not raise an objection. Enderby didn't either. Nor did I ask why the lighters hadn't been mentioned previously. Anyhow, I hoped they would not enjoy smoking at this altitude and would quickly give it up. I was wrong. They seemed to find comfort in it.

We were all sitting up now. The tent felt very crowded but not as much as when we were prone on our backs, our heads against the tent walls or helo seats, our chins thrust down, cricks developing in our napes and in our throat muscles. The narrow tent was not meant for use by persons lying at a right angle to the entrances. How long would it take before such crowding made us exceedingly irritable, debasing the quality of our social behavior, lowering our will to survive and causing a proneness to accidents?

The problem arose of where to put the cigarette ashes. Palmer offered his helmet. I suggested to Eights he use some tinfoil from one of the milk chocolate bars we had with us. He did. He was greatly intrigued by the vivid, electric green of the cigarette flame. He had begun to expand. He was very charming now, I thought. Often, happening to glance his way, I discovered him staring intently at me. He and Palmer finished their cigarettes and we lay down again.

The time slipped by. At one point I focused sharply on Joan, my wife. I felt I was communicating with her. I imagined saying intensely to her, "Lift the cloud cover. It's an urgent matter. If you wish for it hard enough it may go away." Then it struck me that if there *was* anything to ESP I might alert her to my situation, which would be terrible, for it would make her aware of her inability to help me. So I quit this game.

I thought I was a bit old for my heart to be beating as hard, as fast and as strangely as it was. It hammered against my chest cavity like a live, wild thing: jumping, twisting, bouncing in a way I had never experienced. When I had swum hard my lungs had worked hard in rhythm with my heart. Now they worked heavily but quietly while my heart, like some wild caged bird, beat so powerfully I experienced it as a unique, alien entity, some small but mad bit of life that had gotten trapped inside me and was frantically trying to escape. I think it was the altitude that caused it to behave like that. If it was fear, it was for me an entirely new kind, without overtones in my mind and in other parts of my body, as far as I knew. I do not recall feeling fear during the episode, not fear in the very personal sense; certainly at times I was alarmed for us as a group. Quietism seemed to have possessed me. I felt ready to die peacefully; I knew that freezing was a peaceful death. It did not seem at all like a big deal to take off. It felt, as a matter of fact, like a pretty good moment for me to go, and I was comforted by the fact I was well and specially insured. It occurred to me more than once that, financially speaking, I was probably worth more dead than alive. I wondered how long this little bird in my chest could keep beating its wings in such a mad way and I thought what a messy situation it would be for all of us if I had a heart attack.

My bare left hand was in a parka pocket with a furlike lining. My double-gloved right hand lay on my chest. Now and then I was aware that the middle finger of my right hand was slowly assuming a hook shape and that the knuckle was extremely sore. Once, when I removed the gloves and glanced at the hand, I saw that the tendon was taut and whitish under the palm flesh. It was very difficult for me to straighten the finger. I wondered what had happened to it.

There were hours of silence, during which I asked myself what my resources for hanging on were. It seemed to me that Erebus could be personified as cunning and that if I was to survive I must be more cunning than it. I must be more cunning than I had ever been in my life. Above all I must not fight the mountain head on. I noticed that if I kept my face beneath the blanket my face became warm from my breath, and that the energy conserved in not having to warm my face as much as when it was exposed, went into warming my right thigh and foot, making their temperature bearable. This was not something I imagined; I tested it. With my face exposed, my right thigh and foot felt achy, numb. With my face covered they began to relax with more heat. It was an example of being cunning, I thought. I reported this minor discovery to my companions, although without using the idea of cunning; they soon confirmed it. I also noticed that whenever I sat up I had strong abdominal cramps and felt on the verge of vomiting. To vomit would mean to leave the tent and lose much body heat. So I took to sitting up very slowly, calming the cramps with an effort of mind and not mentioning them in order to keep the group's morale as high as possible.

Palmer announced that he needed "to take a dump" but would try to hold it in. Defecation meant leaving the tent and exposing yourself to cold and wind. A trifle, perhaps; but by their sum a series of trifles could determine if you survived or not.

I resolved I would try to survive. But for whom? My wife? My daughter? Myself? It seemed redundant, self-serving, meaningless to survive for oneself. Although it was clear to me that I ought to try to survive for my daughter's sake because of her youth (she was thirteen), I felt the need to survive for my wife, who, I told myself, needed me more than she knew. And so when I felt very tired—I hadn't had a good night's sleep in days and last night I had slept for four hours—and on the verge of not caring any longer what happened to me, of drifting off somewhere—to sleep or gangrene or death—I thought of her needing me, and then my eyes opened wide beneath the sleeping-bag blanket, and that popping open roused me with a lunge to full consciousness, or to superconsciousness, as it seemed to me then. Over and over, thinking of her needing me, I came wide awake and determined I would *live*. If I didn't have the will to live for myself there was no doubt I had it for her. Perhaps this exercise in determining to live for someone else was also a part of being cunning.

Occasionally I realized how silent it was when the wind died down. This was the great Antarctic silence: a ringing of blood in one's ears. But mostly I didn't hear it because my breathing was heavy: my chest rose and fell with force to provide me with sufficient oxygen, and if I started to drift off toward sleep I would awake with the feeling I was out of breath.

Cunning: I warned my companions not to eat bread because bread was gas-forming and because the expansion of gases at twelve thousand feet was considerable as compared with that at sea level. Dale Vance had overeaten at one of his first meals at Vostok and had lain on his back for hours, gasping. Sea level? By air miles we were so close to it, and to McMurdo, and to warmth and security.

I wondered at times why Palmer didn't try to use the HF radio on battery power. I knew I was ignorant on the subject and so I didn't mention it to him. I assumed the HF radio required more juice than the battery could provide. About a year later I happened to be talking with Jim Brandau about this matter. Brandau asked me if we had heard planes while we were on Erebus. I said yes, often. He looked surprised. He said it took a lot of power to send HF signals that would bounce off the ionosphere and go beyond the horizon, more power, probably, than could be obtained from a battery, but that Palmer should have tried the HF radio on battery in an effort to contact the planes within sound of us, and that he might have succeeded.

Palmer was perhaps at least partially in a state of shock. He had taken two bad falls, as we know. They had occurred because he had failed to notice that certain patches of snow were a lighter shade than others and had not avoided them. Such patches often indicate a thinner layer of snow over ice and can be treacherous to walk on. Enderby had stayed clear of them. He had either failed to warn Palmer or Palmer had ignored the warning. As Enderby described the falls to me when we were back at McMurdo, Palmer's legs had flown from under him; he had landed heavily on his back; and he had reacted with great surprise and a good deal of bewilderment. Probably the two falls influenced his subsequent abandonment of any serious effort to provide leadership for our group. Such falls were what could come of ignorance. They were also the result to some extent, I suspect, of hubris. A more modest man would have walked in Enderby's tracks, especially inasmuch as Enderby carried the ice ax and occasionally probed the snow with it.

Some months after the crash episode it occurred to me that the state of one's conscience during a crisis can determine whether one behaves badly or well. Thus the fact that I was the only one of the group with survival gear placed me in the position of the giver rather than the receiver and left me with a fairly clear state of mind. Palmer was in the worst position of us all: he had brought us onto Erebus and was now technically responsible for our welfare. Affecting his behavior must have been the realization that his career if not his life had abruptly reached a turning point.

The extraordinary thing is that not once during the long hours when we waited for a rescue did any of us ask him, at least so far as I know, any direct, pertinent questions which might have revealed his motives, his intentions or what precisely had happened; nor did he offer such information. I suppose we had better things to think and talk about than what was now in the past. We were concerned with our future, or rather with the question of whether we had one. I suppose too that a sense of delicacy prevented us from raising questions that might have injured his morale. He turned inward almost from the start and psychologically moved increasingly away from the rest of us. From time to time he coughed, and once he said he believed he had pneumonia.

There were various practical aspects of the question of being cunning. For example, when I lay with my face exposed and opened my eyes now and then, I didn't mind the pink, dappled light of the red tent—how misleading that light was! how it always tricked us into thinking the cloud cover was lifting!—but when my face was under the blanket and I then had to uncover my eyes and look around the tent, the light was atrocious, it assaulted my eyeballs violently, causing nerves to throb madly all the way from my eyes deep into my head, and I knew I could not sustain many such seizures without becoming snow-blind. So I developed a little strategy to minimize the assault. I covered my eyes with my fingers, slowly opened my eyes, then tentatively, carefully, spread my fingers until the light was bearable. It was strange that the light was so intense while the cloud cover was so thick.

Cloud cover: that was mostly what I thought about, wondering when it would lift and asking myself how to be patient, even if I had to wait for days. Patience too was a way of being cunning. Unless you were patient Erebus would surely defeat you. You must be as simple-minded, in some ways, as a penguin. At Cape Evans in the nasty, bone-destroying southeast wind that had come off the polar plateau and the ice shelf, I had observed Adélies lying on their breasts out on the sea ice, seemingly asleep, waiting for the bad weather to pass. This was what I too must do. And it was what we were doing: lying low, waiting for that momentous time when we would be able to use our flares and smoke bombs. The cover was endlessly on my mind and endlessly the subject of tent conversation when there *was* conversation. Mostly there was none; there were vast silences when it was easy to assume my companions were asleep. The silences conserved energy. They allowed us to animalize in this primitive moment, to sink somewhere inside ourselves to a secret place where we could concentrate entirely on clinging to what strength each of us had. But what if the cover hung on day after day? Would there come a time when we would crack?

There were also less pleasant aspects of being cunning. Palmer was snoring, which meant he was asleep and regaining strength; he would be in better shape than I in the morning. In a crisis—as if this in the tent was not enough to justify the name of crisis—he would outlast me. So I began to think what I could do to be more cunning than he.

Hours passed, passed. He and Eights lit up again.

I said half jokingly, "Easy on those lighters. Our lives may depend on them."

Neither Eights nor Palmer responded to the remark. I was profoundly irritated by Palmer's failure to requisition the lighters for the common good. When they lit up a third time, I resolved that at the fourth I would ask them to stop smoking and make the lighters common property. I hoped the confrontation would not be ugly. Fortunately it never came.

Palmer finally couldn't hold it in any longer; he crawled outside to "take a dump," returning with a rueful expression and reporting, "It froze while I was wiping it."

I suggested it wasn't necessary to move our bowels in the open. We could defecate in the cabin's large metal cabinet that contained cans of lubricant. It would be a simple matter to line the cabinet's bottom with a helo seat cover. This would permit us to dispose of the feces from time to time. One could shut the hatch and keep out the wind, and one would have the cabinet's side to sit on. My companions agreed, so I removed my gloves, withdrew a Swiss army knife from a parka pocket and cut away a seat cover. To my surprise, although the cover was very cold the foam rubber inside it was much warmer, and the styrofoam was even warmer. These materials were not as efficient heat conductors as the plastic cover. So this too was an aspect of being cunning: saving body heat by using as pillows foam rubber and styrofoam instead of whole seats.

At times my abdominal cramps rose to a pitch and I too felt I might need to defecate. I held on, hoping I wouldn't vomit. I thought how disastrous violent indigestion could be in our circumstances.

At one point, to make sure I hadn't been mistaken, I made a special trip to the cleft in the outcrop where I had seen the lichen.

There the bit of life was, a striking pink suggesting the warmth of human blood. What a lonely, dreary place the lichen lived in, yet its existence deeply comforted me by suggesting that even here there were fascinating things to occupy one's mind, however little of one's life might be left.

Occasionally we heard planes. They always sounded far away. How long would they keep looking for us? Palmer said they'd never quit; this was no civilian matter; the search would continue until the mystery was solved. It was comforting to hear it but was it a reasonable view? I doubted it. We might have fallen into the open sea without a trace, or into a giant crevasse. The search could not go on indefinitely. If it stopped, *then* what would we do?

Unlikely though it may seem, at times I was glad to be in this spot, for if I survived, what a tale I would have to tell! Over and over a gear slipped in my thinking as I projected myself into the future and found myself a rare bird, one who had crashed on Erebus and lived. It was pleasant and perhaps necessary for me to dream like this; it lessened the burden of waiting; but the dreams always ended abruptly when, with a thud, I recalled I was in the present and that my future might never come.

Several times I donned my boots and left the tent to observe and to take photographs. It was very pleasant to be alone. What a beautifully subtle if menacing scene it was! In my mind I threw my life away on each of these solitary excursions. If one died now one would have the satisfaction of knowing one had died fairly well. The glow that one could not be robbed of and that sustained one again and again was the knowledge that one was behaving decently, as far as one knew. This knowledge was the best gift one had, and the best one could hope to bring down off Erebus.

Saying his headache was killing him, Eights went to the helo and fetched a first-aid kit, which contained morphine but no aspirin.

"Shall I take some morphine, Doc?" he asked.

I said if he did he would fall into a deep sleep and wouldn't know if he got badly frostbitten. I told him where in the cabin he could find my toilet kit and get aspirin from it. He swallowed two or three tablets of aspirin without water, but his headache did not respond. Enderby said *his* headache was going away.

A little later Eights sat up, broke out a bar of milk chocolate and ate some of it. Palmer said nothing, so I said, "Stu, I don't think we have a right to eat at will. We should ration everything we've got. There's no telling how long it will be before we're found. We may have to hold out for weeks."

Palmer said, "I thought it was the other way around, that we eat as much as we want while we're still in good shape."

"Stu," I said, "you're still fresh from McMurdo, from the ship. You're well fed. The time may come when we'll desperately need food and water to survive."

He thought a moment, then suggested we all eat a bit of chocolate and an apple to stave off hunger. My companions each placed a small apple in an armpit, meanwhile munching chocolate.

Later, lying with my eyes closed, I found myself thinking, "You son of a bitch. You threw my life away."

But I knew I must stop resenting him, for if I didn't I would soon hate him, and his knowledge of the hatred might lower his morale even lower than it was. Without high morale we could not show the volcano what human beings were capable of. No, in this place Palmer and I were one, bound together like Siamese twins. To hate him, or just to resent him, was to threaten my own morale and survival as well as that of the two young men.

The hours passed: in silence. Always, except for the wind and the sound of engines, there was silence. Then the engines faded out. Did this mean the search had stopped temporarily? If so, when would it be resumed? If we were not found in time when *would* we be found? *We* knew we were all right but those searching for us were no doubt wondering in what condition they would find us, if find us they did. Occasionally I saw myself with their eyes, for I had come so close to not being all right that it was as if I had tasted the experience of being smashed, frozen. *If* we were found, how would it happen? And if we were *not* found?

The ceasing of the engines brought apathy. There was no longer an urgent need to check on the cloud cover, for even if the cover lifted now, what good would it do us if there were no planes in our vicinity? The hours were passing without signposts. On eternity's edge time itself grew apathetic.

27

FOUND

AFTER a time we heard engines again. They sounded quite low and seemed to be helos. I scrambled out of the tent. An engine approached, dimmed. Another seemed to draw close but faded. The cover was too thick for me to see planes. I returned to the tent.

Lying half-conscious, I thought I heard a helo coming close and *above* us. The sound was very faint but I was sure it belonged to a helo. I alerted Eights, who, after listening a moment, agreed with me. I shouted to Enderby to take a look. He was more agile than I. He rushed out in stockinged feet. The engine sounded louder.

Then we heard his electrifying cry: "I *see* it!"

We had left the loaded Very gun in an open carton beside the entrance shroud.

I shouted, "Fire the Very pistol directly at him!"

I heard the gun go off. Eights was tearing outside.

"They *see* us!" Enderby cried.

In that twinkling everything changed for us.

"Wave him off! Don't let him land!" Palmer shouted.

This was sound advice, for we had not selected and marked a landing pad, nor indicated by smoke bomb the wind direction.

A moment later Eights cried that the helo was dropping two survival packs. Palmer and I were fumbling with our boots. My hands were not cooperating. I crawled through the shroud, belly cramping, head swimming. Palmer was behind me, coughing heavily.

A Coast Guard helicopter was departing beyond a high ridge just to the right of the crater. On that side of the crest the sky had cleared a bit and the sun was showing milkily. My watch read precisely midnight, which meant it was due south where the sun was. We didn't realize then that the helo would not return until about 2:30.

Eights and Enderby retrieved the survival kits, which contained no headgear and footgear but which did have matches and fat white candles and lots of mosquito netting. We laughed. We felt wonderfully refreshed.

I went to the helo cabin, where my two caseless cameras were white with frost, removed the lens covers and began shooting the damage to the helo, knowing the Navy would want close-up shots for the investigation that was sure to come. It was not easy to keep one's mind clear at that altitude while portions of one's body kept sending signals warning of the danger of irreversible frostbite. One had to caution oneself to do everything in slow motion. It was now as well as earlier that one's practice with cameras in the temperate zone became crucial. While I was photographing the telescoped strut that ran from the fuselage to the port pontoon, Eights stripped metal from it, commenting on how easily it came away. Later he amused himself by lobbing red flares into the mouths of the two ice fumaroles. The red glow was very conspicuous in the fuzzy gray world.

When the cameras ran out of film I carried them into the tent and rewound the cassettes as slowly as I was able. I was still wearing the double gloves. I could feel from the tension of the rewind knob that the film remained intact. Back at McMurdo, trying to reload cameras while wearing the gloves, I had failed in the experiment, as I had failed when wearing only the large, bulky shell. I had no alternative now but to reload the cameras with naked hands. I had not brought along anti-contact gloves but in any case they would have prevented only adhesion of skin to metal, not frostbite. I remembered what had happened to the fingers of my right hand when, earlier in the crash episode, frustrated by a Very pistol shell that was stuck in its casing, I had removed the gloves from that hand and freed the shell. It had been strange to the point of fascination to observe the fingers rapidly turn a dead white almost to the knuckles. Since metal and skin had been extremely dry there had been no adhesion.

The frost on the cameras had by now seemingly ablated. I touched the cameras tentatively and found that my fingers did not stick to them. As I reloaded, my fingers burned, and turned very white, and then I lost feeling in them but they kept responding to my commands. Going outside to continue shooting, I discovered that the lenses were frosted over by condensation of moisture from the tent's interior. I set the cameras on the floor of the open helo cabin, where they cleared by ablation, then shot skid marks, pontoons, wheels, struts.

Before we were found—and it was still by no means certain we would be rescued: the cloud cover was playing tricks over the summit—it had seemed to me that there was really a simple equation inherent in our situation. I had been fairly sure our lives had been forfeited. The only relevant question was, it had struck me, would one die well or badly. If by some miracle we were rescued, I had thought, the sole thing of lasting value one could hope to bring off this mountain was the knowledge one had behaved well. Frankly, I had not relished the prospect of having to deal, for the rest of my life, with the memory that I had behaved otherwise.

Failure to do one's duty, duty being for example work one had committed oneself to, in my case to bring back data gathered during my visit to the continent, was an element in behaving badly. If I failed to take pictures during such an episode what could I tell myself later? That I had been too cold, tired, sleepy, numbed, frightened? But such excuses, if they didn't wash now, and they didn't, would hardly wash later. I would have to deal with the fact I had let myself down, and I wasn't ready to pay so considerable a price. As a result, I had few qualms about risking parts of my body by leaving the tent periodically to take photographs. Besides, it was fruitful to confront oneself alone from time to time; and keeping busy helped one to be mentally resilient. In addition, I had thought, if we died on the mountain, the photographs, when found, would be a partial record of what had happened to us as well as a suggestion that I had died while at work rather than in a state of funk. And if we should be rescued they would be a record of what had occurred.

At about 12:30 a Herc appeared and flew under the high cover in huge circles over us. He never let go of us, and once he made a low pass and I gathered he was shooting us. It was a tremendous morale boost to have him up there.

Still shooting, in a while I realized I had better warm my left foot. And my hands had gone strangely very bad despite the double gloves. So I crawled into the tent to work on the foot.

Palmer, sitting under the brown blanket, was warming a stockinged foot with a lighted candle. The candle's green flame was close to his foot and the blanket.

I thought, "He's showing the same poor judgment he showed when he tried to overfly Erebus. If this tent goes up in flames, and presuming we escape, all our gear will go with it and we may well go under even though we've been found, for there's no telling how long it will be before they come for us, or *can* come for us."

I said, "Take it easy with the candle, Stu," but he didn't respond.

I asked Eights where the hand radio was. He said he had tried to communicate with the rescue helo both by beep and by voice but had failed even to pick up the craft, and had got so disgusted he had thrown the radio into the crashed helo's cabin.

"They should have dropped us a radio so they could tell us their plans," he said. "Or at least they could have dropped us a note."

When Palmer tired of the candle Eights asked for it and warmed his naked right hand over it, staring at the flame, and the flame singed the elbow of Enderby's parka and came close to the tent wall. Then, after I warned him, Eights set the candle down on a small piece of styrofoam and studied it, fascinated by the flame's unbelievably pure and intense green.

He and Enderby wondered aloud when the rescue attempt would be made and how. Would Coast Guard helos hazard an attempt? Or would a Herc try to skylift us out one at a time?

Palmer said, "They're not going to skylift *me*. You get a hell of a jerk when they do that. And you'd freeze to death before they pulled you inside."

The speculation between Enderby and Eights continued awhile.

Palmer said, "They can't take us out all together. We'll probably go out two at a time. We ought to decide who's going out first."

For myself, I didn't care whether I went out first or last. We had been found, and if I were the last to be scheduled to go, and got socked in by weather for days, my position was known, I'd have the sleeping bag to myself, and matches and candles, and I could lie low, and drink enough water to keep from getting seriously dehydrated, and I'd be fine.

I said, "I volunteer to go last."

After an awkward silence he said, "I'll go out with you."

"Take it easy," I told myself. "He did behave well in looking for the ridge. He did wave the helo off. He did invite you to fly in the cockpit with him. And possibly he did autorotate, select the landing spot, save our limbs if not our lives."

But later, when I returned to the tent after shooting some more while my companions were under the sleeping bag, Eights said, "You and I will go out last, Doc."

I said, "I thought Stu and I were going last."

"Stu's not feeling too good," Eights said.

Palmer said nothing.

As I slid beneath the blanket I expected to resent or even to hate him. I was wrong. My resentment seemed to have burned itself out at the time when I had told myself I couldn't afford it. Actually, I felt paternal toward him now, as I did toward the two young men, and discovered, on looking back on the long hours of hoping, that at times I had already felt that way toward him. I discovered also that I *had* been afraid at times, in little bursts, but that the essential thing was not whether one was afraid but whether one's fear could be controlled.

Then suddenly we heard a helo approaching—with that beautiful familiar chopping sound—and we were lacing our boots and crawling outside, and we spotted not one but two Coast Guard helicopters circling over Erebus, and the scene was unreal, for here we were on this ice and snow and rock shelf, and there was the red tent, well staked down, its rope taut, the cloth brilliant, and the stricken helo leaning to port, heavy on its hull, and Eights setting off violet smoke bombs, and up there was the volcano's summit, obscured by scud and smoke, and beyond the summit was a milky, wan sun, the summer sun that for months never set, the sun that had burned me badly at Royds, and up there in that fairyland the two helos were circling, feeling their way carefully, and I thought, "My God, that's hairy," and I wondered if they too would air-starve, and meanwhile the Herc watched over all of us, and I tried with all my might to observe and remember everything.

We had selected a landing pad—an apron of sloping, almost naked rock not too far from the tent—and Eights and Enderby now marked it with my green rucksack and some food cartons, and Eights signaled the first rescue helo (1377, from the *Staten Island*) to a landing. I naïvely stood nearby and watched the helo touch down. The blizzard caused by the rotors hit me full in the face, and my eyes were blasted by ice and snow particles. Blinded, I whirled to give the blizzard my back. After a moment, glancing at my frosted cameras sitting on the cabin floor, I saw that the lenses, or rather the UV filters, were white with snow. I wiped them clean with a gloved finger.

The pilot of 1377, Neil Nicholson, whom I knew, dressed lightly but looking confident and warm, left the craft and walked rapidly to 1404, his helmet making him look like a megacephalic Martian out of a science fiction tale. He came up beside me. I was studying my gear on the cabin floor, deciding what I had to take out with me. He touched my arm and asked with a glance of concern, "Are you all right?"

It struck me suddenly as extremely remarkable that the eerie, immense and in some ways marvelous silence of Mount Erebus was being shattered by 1377's barbaric sounds; yet I was grateful for those sounds; they were made by a *live* engine; and I found myself responding with a new and special intimacy to the noises a helo made as against those made by a C-130 like the one circling, circling above us.

I shook my head affirmatively.

Again he asked, "Are you all right?"

Again I shook my head.

"We've got to get out of here fast," he said. "The weather is very bad and may close in again. Leave everything behind except maybe a camera."

"I'm not leaving without my professional gear," I said.

He glanced at my face, shrugged, and walked away.

Enderby fetched the Kiwi mail from the cockpit and handed it to Palmer, who ran to 1377 and boarded it. Meanwhile the second rescue helo had disappeared. I hoped it hadn't crashed. It would be terrible if someone got killed while trying to save us. Taking my cameras, I went to an outcrop near 1377 and observed what Nicholson, his crewman (who was wearing a brilliant red flight suit) and Eights were doing to mark the pad for the second helo. A vivid red line was drawn on the outcrop to indicate the position of the front of the cockpit. Smoke bombs marked the position of the rear wheel. Nicholson had hung my blue towel from a tent pole as a wind sock and was now marking the pad with flares, dye markers and smoke bombs. The preparations were very colorful in the gauzelike, black-and-white terrain: red, orange and purple smoke poured along the base of the pad, was caught by the rotor blasts and sent north-ward, southward and then directly at me, choking me. Feeling tremendously lucky to be there with cameras that seemed to be functioning well, I believed this was my best moment on the ice. I kept warning myself to remember to check light meters, to advance frames slowly, to double-check focus, to compose carefully, and above all to work in slow motion, being mindful of the effects of high altitude on one's judgment.

Then I realized that my double-gloved hands had been scream-ing for some time, as if they were being crushed by giant pincers, and I wondered vaguely why they were making such a fuss—my face felt fine—and I wondered if reloading the cameras barehanded had something to do with it. The fact was that the double gloves were not sufficient protection for hand work at that temperature. One needed to wear bear paws to be comfortable. As we know, I had brought a pair in my survival bag but one of my companions was now using them. Anyhow, it was not possible to take photo-graphs while wearing them.

And then Neil Nicholson stripped to the waist and replaced the towel with his undershirt because the towel was too heavy to flutter in the current breeze, and I thought, "It's thirty below and he has a small, very white paunch. He has a great deal of body heat from the warm helo to be able to do that."

I intended to photograph him like that but my hands failed to respond to my orders. All feeling had left them. I was not to regain full sensation in the finger ends for from six to eight months, and at this writing a certain amount of circulatory and neural damage seems to be permanent. I let my cameras hang from my neck while I clapped my gloved hands together. It was like clapping boards, for all the feeling there was in it. Enderby ran over to me and handed me the bear paws he had been wearing, and he ran to the helo and boarded it, and I kept slamming my hands together in the bear paws.

Suddenly Nicholson, now in the cockpit with his copilot who had never left the helo and who had not shut down the engine, raced the rotors for liftoff, and I stood there idiotically, having already forgotten what had happened when 1377 had hit the deck. My face felt as if it were hit by a metal curtain, and pellets of ice stung my eyeballs. I wheeled, and hung on to the outcrop, digging with my toes and bracing to be kept from being blown off. The helo's liftoff caused such a whiteout that for whole minutes nothing could be seen. The whiteout cleared, and, by God, there was the second helo, descending, and Eights ran to the pad and signaled it in.

"Let's *go!*" he shouted to me, and boarded the craft.

With gear hanging from my shoulders and cameras from my neck, I ran to the hatch and fumbled to climb aboard, but my knees were weak, my hands couldn't clutch, and my gear was pulling me backwards toward the pad. It was a high step to the cabin floor. The bearded crewman, warm, fresh, reached out above me, grabbed my armpits and with a tremendous jerk hauled me aboard.

I removed my gloves and fumbled with my seat belt. The crewman, noticing I was having trouble, belted me in. My hands were dead white, especially from the knuckles to the nails. To the left of my seat I felt a current of warm air. I hung my left hand down in it. The crewman bent over to increase the air flow. I warmed my hands in it alternately until they hurt very badly and I knew they would be all right. Eights slouched back in his seat, his long legs outstretched, his arms limp. His eyes were closed. The crewman offered us coffee. I had given up drinking coffee about a year ago, so I declined it.

"Gee, Doc, take it," Eights said. "At least it's warm to hold."

I accepted a cup.

The bearded crewman with his large blue eyes and foreign-sounding name—he was older than the usual crewman and looked mellower, wiser, perhaps also sadder—stared at us with a gentle, pensive, fatherly smile, now and then glancing almost lovingly at us. Eights, grinning, showed me a raised thumb.

"We're on our way down, Doc," he said. "I'll get the gear back to you."

I patted his knee and said, "You're a good boy, Jack. You behaved well."

His eyes filled with tears.

A little later he leaned toward me and in the roar of the engine and rotors said, "He said an admiral is going to greet us," by *he* meaning the bearded crewman.

I thought, "The admiral's in Cheechee, and no admiral is going to greet us in the middle of the night," but I let him have his pipe dream.

I sat staring at the floor and feeling the warmth slowly returning to my body.

Stepping down at the helo pad at McMurdo, where it was startlingly warm and bright, I glanced at my watch. The wheel had come full circle. We had crashed at about 2:30 P.M. It was now several minutes past three in the morning.

I remember the extraordinary emotion I felt at that moment, when I expected McMurdo to be the ghost town it usually was at that hour. What seemed like a wave of human bodies slowly, methodically moved towards us, surrounding us, not speaking much, just smiling. Many people had been unable to sleep, apparently. They wanted to be at the pad when we got back.

While on the mountain I was convinced the crash episode didn't really get to me. A phone patch I had with my wife the day after I was rescued will give the reader some idea of what the experience did to me and how painful it was to recall it.

I was a bit reluctant to talk with her but I had been told that news releases had already gone out, and if she must learn about what had happened it was best she learn it from me and in advance. Would I behave well with her? Would I keep up my guard? For I must reassure her of my safety and well-being and must not let anything in my voice betray the emotions which I seemed to believe I had never had on Erebus. The distance between us was great, phone patches hard to come by, I must make my point casually and well. If I wasn't up to it it was better not to phone her at all.

The phone near my room in the corridor of the Lodge rang. It was the ham operator, asking if I was Charles Neider and how long I was going to talk. I explained that this was a high-priority patch approved by the x.o., that I was one of the guys who had crashed on Erebus and that as far as I knew there was no time limit on the patch.

"Yes, sir," he said.

I hung up, went to my room, drank some more scotch, lay down on my bed and stared at the ceiling, my heart pumping fast and hard.

The phone rang again. It was the same voice, this time saying, "Stand by, please. Don't hang up."

While my hands that had experienced a frost change went cold with nerves and suspense, I waited, feeling naked in the corridor and hoping no one would come along during the call.

Then she was on: that voice I knew so well, with a lilt and a gaiety, and I said, "There's something I want to tell you. If you read or hear about a helicopter accident down here and my name is mentioned don't be concerned. I'm fine, as you can hear from my telling you. I was involved in a crash. We crashed near the summit of Mount Erebus but were rescued after twelve hours and are all in good condition. So you're not to be concerned."

She asked for details. I provided them.

She said, "I'm flabbergasted."

Now and then, for example when I told her about my hands and glanced at them, my heart grew cold, I felt I was melting away, my voice dropped in pitch, it sounded unlike itself, my throat trembled, I did not dare to speak, I struggled to regain control, my jaws clamped shut, my eyes threatened to grow moist, something threatened to babble out of my voice box, and I grew icy with fear, for I must above all, above all carry it off well and not let her suspect there were unresolved forces fighting inside me, trying to overwhelm me, unman me. I kept thinking with horror that the sole purpose of this call was to spare her anxiety and that I was in great danger of doing precisely what I wanted to avoid. There were moments of hard silence when I lost my voice and when something terrible seemed to be threatening me. The silences terrified me. They must not be allowed to give me away. She must not realize that I was wrestling with something tremendously powerful, that one moment I was calm, objective, serene, then suddenly I was beset, especially when I spoke about myself in some detailed way. She must not be permitted to realize the horror of the wrestling match I was so unexpectedly going through. I fought, fought, rescued some semblance of a voice, managed a bit of humor and perspective.

"Is there anything the matter? Are you all right?" she asked.

"I've been drinking scotch. I guess I've drunk a fair amount," I said, relieved to have an excuse.

Then she said, perhaps glad to change the subject because of what she probably suspected, "Aren't we going over our time?"

I explained that this was a high-priority patch.

My feelings about continuing the patch were mixed. I was glad to be speaking with her but I obviously couldn't trust myself, and just as my heart on Erebus had seemed to be throbbing wildly in a rhythm all its own, so now my voice and jaws seemed to have deserted me for very urgent tasks and messages, they seemed to need to cry out something with enormous strength, something of highest priority, but also something which I was convinced would shame me. I knew my task if they didn't: it was to handle this call gracefully and with only one objective: my wife's peace of mind. If I flubbed it she would be badly upset, would decide I was covering up a serious injury, and I would not get another patch for some time, and a letter to her trying to set things right could take a long while reaching her.

Some merciful force appeared from nowhere to help me through. I steadied myself, and at last I managed to sign off decently. Once I hung up, that terrifying wrestling match ceased. I walked like a half-dead person to my room, lay down, closed my eyes and listened to echoes of the conversation, hearing significant parts of it and feeling I had made it by the skin of my teeth.

Exhausted, gathering my forces as best as I knew how, I was no longer prepared to believe I had been emotionless on Mount Erebus.

28

~~~~~~

SAR CONDITON I*

How WARM and bright it felt at McMurdo when we stepped off the helos!

The crowd that approached and surrounded us seemed to be observing us closely, as if we were ghosts. I wondered if all survivors of a taste of death felt for a time like ghosts.

In 1415, on the way down from Erebus, sensing the possibility of a loss of face by a too strong show of emotion, I had cast about for a way to defend myself. Humor, I had decided: the mask of comedy.

"You all right?" Dave Murphy asked, frowning despite his smile, and studying me searchingly.

"I *told* you I'm rugged," I replied.

We laughed.

The medic who escorted us to the ambulance drove us up the hill not to the front of the Dispensary but the rear, and ushered us in, and didn't request us to remove our boots to spare the linoleum the ravages of volcanic grit.

"Any injuries?" he inquired.

Palmer said, "Chuck, tell about your hands."

I spoke briefly about them.

"We can use some aspirin," Palmer said.

The medic countered, "Not without the doctor's orders."

But the medical officer wasn't on duty at this hour.

* This is the name applied to an all-out search and rescue mission. SAR rhymes with far.

Drawling in his Georgia accent, Palmer said, "We've had head-aches all night and we need some *aspirin*."

There was a pause.

"You probably have altitude headaches," the medic said.

"Yes, indeed we have altitude headaches and we don't need to be told what's perfectly obvious. What we need is some *aspirin*."

There was a bite in Palmer's voice.

The medic gave each of us two tablets of aspirin.

On Erebus, after 1377 had found us, Palmer had said, "Hell, they'll open the wardroom for us. *They'll* get us a bottle."

"Any chance of getting a shot of scotch?" I asked the medic. "We could use it."

The medic went to a storeroom and returned with eight minia-ture bottles of blended whisky. He gave each of us two.

Dave Murphy, who was waiting outside the Dispensary, walked with me toward my room.

"Van looked *bad* when he got off the helo," he said.

"Bad?"

"He looked real *bad*. We all thought so."

I had caught glimpses of Enderby and he had looked fine to me: tall, straight, like a young lumberjack.

"What do you mean? Was he pale?"

"He looked very *bad*. He kept smiling too much."

I thought, "Great God, don't they realize where Van has been?"

"I don't agree," I said. "He looked good to me."

I heard my voice quivering. Its pitch was lower than normal. And my hands felt strange. There was no sensation in the finger ends. The skin there felt as if it was half an inch from the flesh.

"Did he look any different from the rest of us?"

"You all looked bad. You were joking and smiling too much."

I thought, "Don't you understand that at least part of it is due to our being, suddenly, strangers to ourselves? We flew into a new dimension."

For a moment the bridge of communication was down. I felt alone and very tired. He came into my room and sat on my bed while I sipped the whisky.

He said, "I was *so pissed off* because I couldn't go with you on the flight. Then I realized it could have been me instead of Van who was dead."

When he left I shut the door, pulled the drapes and removed my clothes, wondering if it was really true my family and friends would hear from me again. I fell asleep.

Awaking, I sensed I had slept enough. But a glance at my clock showed me I had slept about three hours. I went across the corridor to the head. Since I was here last—that was on Saturday, which was yesterday, but it felt like several days ago—broad ribbons of masking tape had been stretched across the two toilet cubicles and the two urinals. On them had been hand-printed: SECURED. WATER HOURS. The water-making system had apparently broken down. The four wash basins were free, however.

As I washed I realized how strange my finger ends were to me. They felt fat, calloused; were swollen; they tingled in an unpleasant way and felt dangerously slow and stupid in hot water. The middle finger of my right hand was curved like a hook in the direction of the palm. The knuckle was swollen and very sore.

After dressing I went outside. The station was deserted. The sun shone, shone. It was always gleaming and glaring somewhere.

I thought, "Anybody fearful of the ghosts of night might do well to consider the advantages of a place where the nights are brilliantly sunlit. God, how beautiful. How I love this place, those mountains, that ice, that sky, this air that's so dry it cracks your fingers to the quick out in the field."

When I ran into Enderby later in the day he told me that he too had been unable to sleep much. I met Biggerstaff near the chow hall.

Grinning, he said, "Son, we kissed your ass good-by."

I went to the Dispensary, where I was told there had probably been nerve damage to my fingers. Sometimes it could take as long as a year for the sensation to return; sometimes the sensation came back in a matter of months. The injured knuckle was straightened and splinted. The medic who treated it said it had suffered a contusion and must not be moved. With the splint on it was impossible to put the hand in a glove. He said I could not go camping with my hands the way they were. It was frustrating to write in my journal with a splinted hand.

Next day, Monday, I flew to the *Staten Island*, with whose executive officer I had some business to discuss. On the flight deck I encountered Jack Eights, who greeted me warmly and told me, with a good deal of surprise, that he had suddenly been hit very hard this morning by the realization of what had happened.

"I was shook up, Doc," he said wonderingly, his eyes moistening.

I said I understood very well what he meant.

After a discussion with the x.o. in the skipper's cabin I was invited to dinner in the wardroom. I sat on the x.o.'s right, at the head of the table. Palmer sat at the end of the table, looking remote. On my way out of the room I asked him how he was.

"I hurt in every bone in my body," he replied.

On Tuesday afternoon I had a talk with Dave Murphy in my room, during which, at my request, he gave his impressions of the SAR.

"They called us at the Field Center at about three o'clock and said that they had set up a SAR for you. About five o'clock Fritz, myself, Steve Kellaway, Jim [Elder], Lokey . . . all went down to the Chalet and were waiting for calls. We stayed down there and just listened to tapes [of music] and waited. It got to be about six o'clock and they said, 'Still no change.' Seven, eight, 'Still no change.' We kept debating about where you'd gone and whether you had a chance or not. *I* thought you went in the water. And if you got *in* the water I figured you were dead—from exposure if not from drowning. *I'd* given up. I *hoped* that you'd come back but I actually didn't think you'd come back, because of the route that you were supposed to take. We sat around. Finally, at about eleven o'clock, I guess, we decided to have something to eat and we went on up to the Field Center and had some lobster. It was pretty quiet. We didn't say much. We were mostly talking about your chances and if the copters could find you. I took a shower, and some of the others took showers, and we kept waiting around. At twelve-thirty, I guess, they finally called and said they'd found you. Whew! It was a great relief!

"It was kind of funny, because we'd go down to the helo pads and see all those helos coming *in* and *out,* and *in* and *out,* and yet— I don't know—the Seabees and the ASA were having a basketball game, and you'd hear this cheering. It didn't seem right, for some reason. I guess a lot of people didn't even know about it, maybe that was the thing. It just seemed—certain people knew about it and certain people didn't—but it seemed somehow not right. A helo would land and we'd all rush to the windows of the Chalet with binoculars and would watch, and see them shaking their heads. I guess about ten o'clock we heard there was a patch of cloud cover on Erebus and that that was just about the only place left. And that's where they found you. *No one thought that you'd be up there.*

No one at all. I went over to the bar, Steve and I, about seven, and one of the Kiwis, Paul Christianson, said that you had landed there [Scott Base] and had flown toward Erebus. It never dawned on me to say anything about it. I thought he had gone over Castle Rock, over the Tongue and then out. About six-thirty they heard somebody giving a count up to nine and back down. But they couldn't raise it. I guess that wasn't you but they thought it might have been. We were really concerned. Once they called up and asked if Van had his survival gear. And we called back and said no, he didn't even have mukluks on, he had regular boots. And this caused a lot of concern. And then they asked if you had brought your radio along. We whipped up to the Field Center and there it sat in your cage, so—'Nope, no radio.' It turned out you didn't have this, you didn't have that."

"How could you tell that Van didn't have his gear?"

"See, when I went down to take Sergei out I saw you and Van walking to the helo pad, and all he had on was boots and his blue jeans. And he and I had loaded the truck and I knew he didn't throw a survival pack in. And he didn't come back to the Field Center, where we keep the survival packs. It really surprised all of us, because that's the first time Van has gone out without survival gear. He's pretty conscientious about that."

"Was it MAC Center that was asking these questions?"

"I believe so, because Fritz was up at Air Ops, and he'd keep sending back these messages—go check on them. They wanted to know if you had a tent, how many sleeping bags, what kind of gear you had, and food, and they asked if you had a stove, and I said no, I didn't believe so, because you were going to eat off the Kiwis—I thought the Kiwis would do the cooking. I knew you had frozen food but I didn't think that would do much good. And then I knew you didn't have any water except what you had in the canteen, and that you had no way of getting water either, unless you just ate snow, which is kind of a slow process. But I imagine you could if you wanted to. I was thinking it could have been me, very easily. I guess the reason Van got to go instead of me was because I was supposed to go on a trip over to the Dry Valleys, and they just wanted to give him a chance to get out in the field, because he *was* going to winter over, at that time. I was relieved that I wasn't along. Then I felt kind of sorry that *I* hadn't gone instead of Van, because I thought I could do a better job. All I could think of was—you were in the water. You knew it was serious when, about ten to five, you saw these Hercs go up and all these helos go up. One Herc had just come in from Cheechee. They refueled him, let him get his mail off, then he was gone looking for you. They had this tremendous group of people going out and searching . . . for four people. One other thing they wanted to know was how many people were on board. They didn't know, for a while, whether the chaplain had gone out or not. Because he was supposed to go [as far as Cape Evans]. Those Coast Guard helos don't have the capacity, I guess, of those large grasshoppers [H-34s]. And so in the shuttles to and from Willy Field they took the survival gear out that they usually have in there—for maximum load going back and forth. They just didn't put it back in, I guess."

"Did you happen to know why he went up, knowing he didn't have any survival gear?"

"I had no idea whatsoever. It was a nice day out. Been nice since the Coast Guard got here. They haven't seen a whiteout, I don't think, yet. They haven't been here when the wind goes racing through here and you're cold in your parka and you put on your windpants and heavy boots. If they'd come here in October, when *we* did—it's *cold*. This has been the warmest season down here in a long time. Most people didn't even go to the mess hall. It would be almost deserted. A lot of people just stayed by their radios. Sat-track [the satellite tracking station] set up their radio for the helo frequency. Trace, over at Sattrack, heard the pilot tell them, 'We found them!' People that knew, and were closely involved, were just waiting. Like all the Holmes and Narver and USARP people. Most people thought either they would have found you in the first two or three hours or they weren't going to find you at all. We all went down to the Chalet and sat around in Chris's office, listening to tapes. Emmett Herbst wasn't around. He was at Operations. I saw him at dinner. He was just . . . kind of quiet. He didn't say much at all. He was worried, really worried. Kind of felt sorry for him. The first day after Chris Shepherd leaves, and Emmett's the boss, and now this happens. Everybody was really worried. No one was sleeping. We got the news that they'd found you and were attempting a rescue—I guess between twelve and one. We went down and watched the helos. One guy was practicing hovering. One helo was getting fitted out with baskets, and they wanted to get another basket for *this* helo. He must have been practicing hovering, because he'd get up maybe four or five feet off the ground and just keep it, just steady, right there—very little motion. They expected to winch you up. They thought they'd have to take you up in a basket. Al Pretty was three or four years in the Coast Guard. He was wondering why they didn't use belts. They got a belt, I guess, that goes around your legs and through your arms and it would be much better than to winch you up in a basket. It's small and compact. They were fooling around with this long basket. There was quite a lot of activity. At around five o'clock they had two helos in the hangar, being fixed. They shoved them *out* of there. Those mechanics were *cracking*. One Coastie helo was in there, and one of those large grasshoppers. They got that Coastie up in the air. Each time a helo would come in the Coastie pilots and the other pilots would get together. They were sitting out in front of the helo hangar, talking and looking up at the sky. We sat up in the Chalet, listening to tapes and drinking a few beers."

I heard from several people that the SAR Condition was handled extremely well. Someone said it was conducted like a detective story. Many persons visited McMurdo Center to observe a large map of Ross Island, on which grid lines were checked off as soon as a plane had searched a particular area. After the first two or three hours it was thought we had gone down into the waters off the coast or into a great crevasse. People were sent out to gather whatever information they could. It was heard at the helo hangar that Palmer had ruminated aloud that day, both on his ship and in the hangar, about possibly going up and having a look at the crater. A young Kiwi working on a road near Scott Base declared he had seen a *white* helo land at Scott, pick up a package without shutting down its engine and take off across the peninsula in the direction of Erebus. His story was doubted but he insisted it was true. When the two bits of information were put together it began to be surmised where Palmer had gone, and the search turned to the volcano's crest.

For a while the two rescue helos considered winching us up while hovering. But hovering requires much power, and because of the altitude this idea was abandoned.

The executive officer of McMurdo Station, Commander Balchunis, told me that at one point they were debating whether to bring us out one at a time. He rejected the idea because it seemed too possible that one or two of us might have to be left behind because of foul weather, with bad morale resulting. So it was decided to bring us out two at a time, with two helos working together.

Seven aircraft and two icebreakers were involved in the SAR. The aircraft were two C-130s, two Navy H-34s and three Coast Guard H-52As; the ships were the *Staten Island* and the *Burton Island.* The *Staten Island* was in the vicinity of McMurdo Station during the SAR Condition. At the beginning of the SAR the *Burton Island* was located twenty-five miles north of Cape Bird, enroute to Hallett Station. It was requested to reverse course and to proceed to the Cape Bird area and conduct SAR operations there. Coast Guard involvement in the SAR was extensive. The ships were used as communications platforms, heliports and helo refueling stations.

At 1:43 P.M. 1404 left McMurdo for a scheduled, two-hour daylight VFR (Visual Flight Rules) flight. In a VFR flight the aircraft is flown free of clouds and is controlled by visual reference to the ground. This is in contrast with IFR (Instrument Flight Rules) flight, in which the craft may be flown in the clouds and controlled by flight instruments and electronic ground aids to navigation. In IFR flight a craft is provided with traffic separation by a ground station. In VFR flight the pilot provides his own separation from other traffic.

After taking off from Scott Base, Palmer called McMurdo Center and said, according to the accident board's Findings of Fact, "Be advised 404 is going to take a direct route to Cape Bird, we're going along just the [western] edge of Mount Erebus."

I do not recall hearing him say this. Possibly I was switched off the intercom during this transmission or was busy with my cameras and failed to notice it. In deciding to go to Cape Bird via the direct route he was deviating from the standard helo route chart, a copy of which was aboard 1404. The standard route had been established by VXE-6 for search and rescue purposes. Thus when he got into trouble after deviating from the standard route it made search and rescue operations much more difficult. The above call to McMurdo Center was the last transmission from 1404 recorded by the Center, and so the HF radio never got through. But some of the distress messages sent on the line-of-sight gadget, the PRC-63 emergency radio, were received, somewhat uncertainly, by C-130 320 and H-34 Gentle 4, who reported hearing 1404 calling Any Station at about 2:50 P.M., or some twenty minutes after the crash.

[The Findings of Fact also stated that Palmer, prior to the flight, was aware that 1404's four survival packs were not aboard and that he decided not to load them when he saw that a considerable part of my gear consisted of survival equipment. Obviously, I did not have survival gear sufficient for four persons. Also, much of my survival gear was in a closed seabag. It would have required superhuman vision for him to have seen what it consisted of. The findings are incorrect in some other respects. They state that the elapsed time between the accident and the rescue was "slightly over ten hours." It was twelve hours. They conclude that 1404 came to rest on the "south west (true) side of Mount Erebus." The site was on the northwest side. They say I suffered "slight" frostbite in all the fingers of my right hand. Both hands were equally affected. Whether the frostbite was slight I cannot as a layman say. Probably it was, although it was uncomfortable and somewhat uncanny to be deprived of sensation.]

After a single aircraft search proved negative and after repeated attempts to establish communications with 1404 were unsuccessful, SAR Condition II was set at 3:30 P.M. At 4:35 P.M. SAR Condition I was set and an all-out search was ordered.

H-34 Gentle 4 went to Cape Bird and reported that we had never arrived there. It searched the top of Mount Bird; some of the lower slopes of Mount Erebus; Cape Evans; and the terrain between Mount Erebus and Mount Terra Nova. H-34 Gentle 3 had a look at Cape Royds, Cape Evans, Erebus Glacier Tongue and the upper slopes of Mount Erebus. At 9:12 P.M. it recommended a search of the northwest side of Mount Erebus in the neighborhood of the Fang Glacier, where the cloud cover appeared to be lifting. This was an important recommendation inasmuch as it stimulated 1377, whose crewman spotted us, to have a look there.

CG 1360 checked the coastal route and had a look at the western and southern slopes of Mount Erebus. CG 1415 checked Cape Crozier, the top of Mount Erebus and Cape Bird. CG 1377 checked the Fang Glacier; made a contour search of Mount Erebus at 12,000 feet; checked Mount Terra Nova; Mount Terror; Cape Evans; and then, at 11:59 P.M., spotted us on the northwest slope of Erebus.

The Coast Guard has generously granted me permission to publish the deposition made by Neil Nicholson, pilot of 1377, for the accident board. I reprint the deposition as I received it. The material in brackets is mine.

STATEMENT MADE BY LCDR N. A. NICHOLSON 7878, USCG INTO THE
EVENTS LEADING TO CG HELO NR. 1377's SEARCH, SIGHTING AND RESCUE
OF THE CREW AND PASSENGERS OF DOWNED CG HELO NR. 1404:

During the initial phases of search CG-1377 was in a downed
maintenance status (phase check). I had talked with Chief BURNS
and he said that the phase check was in the final stages and work
would continue to ready CG-1377 to join the search. I was concerned that the crew may feel an urgency or rush to complete the
check. I stressed to Chief BURNS several times that we were in no
rush and to use ample time conducting the final phases of the
check. During most of this phase, the search area had two CG
HELOS, two Navy HELOS and one or two C-130s.

I had been keeping close tabs on the progress of the search in
MAC Center where a coordinated effort was being made to locate
subject helo and crew.

At approximately *2000L* [8:00 P.M. local time] the air search
had been going on for approximately three hours with most of the
probable areas covered. One of the areas of concern was the upper
levels of Mt. EREBUS which had been covered by a cloud layer
during this search effort. CG-1377 was reported ready for test. At
2046L [8:46 P.M.] CG-1377 was A/B [airborne] enroute Williams
Field to conduct required flight test. Pilot LCDR N. A. NICHOLSON
with crew AE2 [Aviation Electricians Mate Second Class] T. Lee.
Upon satisfactorily completing the test flight CG-1377 was refueled
and returned to McMurdo to pick up co-pilot LT J. G. CARROLL
7855, USCG. *2125L* [9:25 P.M.], CG-1377 departed McMurdo
Center, initial instruction, search grid S.E. [northwest]* Fang
Glacier and upper limits of Mt. Erebus. Conduct [should have read
"Contact"] on-scene-commander 320 [that is, the on-scene-commander was in C-130 320]. Departing McMurdo Station we proceeded direct to the grid S/E [northwest] side of Mt. Erebus and
weaved a search [flew back and forth over the track line to achieve
a wider area of detection] while gaining altitude up the face of
Mt. Erebus and Fang Glacier area. We were able to climb to an
altitude of approximately 10,000 feet but were unable to proceed to
the top due cloud cover. We then held a clockwise contour search of

---

* The reasons for using grid directions in polar navigation are technical and complicated and are partially due to the fact that the convergence of lines of longitude at
the poles increases the difficulty of polar navigation. In essence, a grid system ignores
the convergence. I shall not try to explain the reasons in this book meant for the
general reader. The directions given in brackets are true directions.

the 10,000 foot level of Mt. Erebus. The area of search was considered very hazardous and offered very little in the way of an emergency landing area. The area of search was 99% snow white [the ground was 99% covered by snow]. During the search I wondered how easy it would be to fly over a white helo lying on its side with minimal high visibility areas exposed. Our search altitude varied from approximately 600 to 1000 feet which I felt was high, but safer due to the hazardous areas.

On completion of the limited search around Mt. Erebus, we proceeded to conduct a track line search [a search along a line between two geographic points] to Mt. Bird. We searched the upper immediate levels of Mt. Bird and ended up on the grid s/w [northeast] side. At this time we were directed to search the grid south [north] side upper limits of Mt. Terra Nova and Mt. Terror. Clouds were forming along the grid sides of the mountains and we decided to depart and conduct a tracklines search along the Hut Peninsula. After a short period of search along the Hut Peninsula we decided to take a look around the Cape Evers [Evans] area then back up to Mt. Erebus for a final try prior to refueling. At this time the clouds were still visible but visibility appeared to be improving. After climbing to the upper limits of Mt. Erebus (Plateau Area) we decided that the visibility had improved enough to take a look in the area of the crater. The aircraft had a sloppy control feeling like (down wind landing, mushy) and we were flying 40–50 knots with 100% NF NR, Temp −25° C. [That is, total available engine power was being delivered to the rotor. Rotor revolutions per minute (RPM) were 100%, or 212 RPM (normal).] The airspeed, ground relationship seemed unusual probably because of TAS [true air speed, or the speed of a helicopter through an air mass without regard to the wind]. At approximately 12,500-feet we got a look into the crater, which was filled with clouds. About this time we were proceeding to reverse course and the crewman yelled he had subject sighted. *1159L* [11:59 P.M.] The pilot & co-pilot followed with sighting of the flare and then Helo. The weather at this time was a partial obscuration 1–1½ miles [the sky was partially obscured by clouds; visibility was 1–1½ miles] with clear patches and every now and then a scattered cloud drifting through the area. On initial sighting we were approximately ½ to ¾ miles away. I recall first of sighting the flares, then the red parts of the Helo, followed by a red tent that had been constructed. We made several passes over the site and tried to make radio contact with the ground personnel, to make sure everybody was O.K. We finally sighted four personnel who appeared to have no injuries. We also dropped two survival bags, ASK-2 kits [air-droppable survival kits] in the site area.

At this point I was concerned about several factors:

a. Was the visible moisture of any danger? [Were clouds in the area likely to form ice on the helicopter?]

b. I would prefer a cover Helo prior to attempting a pick-up.

c. I knew we could not pick-up everybody at this time, and how much of a load could I pick-up?

d. I had not established a landing area at this time and felt a basket [standard Coast Guard basket used to lift personnel] would be required for any hover hoist attempt.

e. My torque was fluctuating approximately 15%?? [The torque gauge measures power delivered to the gear box and ultimately to the rotor head. In normal operations the torque should not fluctuate. In this instance there might have been a gauge malfunction.]

f. Height altitude on crew vrs time.

With the satisfaction that the ground crew was O.K. I decided not to rush into a hasty attempt. I decided to take my time, refuel, get a back up Helo, consult the handbook, lighten the Helo and check the weather. McMurdo was informed of our intentions and after refueling at Williams Field to 750⚡ (lbs), we arrived at McMurdo Station at *0042L* [12:42 A.M.]. A helo CG-1415 from the CGC BURTON ISLAND was enroute McMurdo Station at this time. We had removed radios and unnecessary gear from the Helo to get it down to the lightest weight. I had satisfied myself that the Helo could handle the job and the weather man said icing was not likely to occur in the visible moisture at the existing temp: −25° C. I talked with CPO [Chief Petty Officer] BURNS on the flux torque [fluctuating torque] and he did not think this was an area for concern.

In the meantime, LCDR SCHILLING [pilot of 1415] had arrived at McMurdo. After comparing figures we departed McMurdo Station at *0155L* [1:55 A.M.]. CG-1377 was the lead Helo and our intention was to try and establish a landing site and pickup one or two personnel each. CG-1415 to follow, making the second pickup. After several passes over the site area we had established several things.

a. Definite wind line [direction of wind] (via smoke signal from ground personnel).

b. Helo landing area (large flat slanting rock—pointed out by ground personnel, slanted in direction of wind).

c. A low, slow pass over the area, torque required approximately 60% at 100% NF NR. [The power setting was 60% of total available engine power.]

d. No indication of turbulence in landing area.

There were no unusual problems during the approach and a hover type landing was accomplished (blew up snow on hover but ground contact was maintained). The rock made a very good platform for landing but would present problems with a change of wind direction. (Due to being narrow & the slant.) While making sure everybody was still O.K. we marked the helo pad with the dye end of a flare. [If the smoke end of a flare is held close to the snow it will mark or dye the snow.] We also marked spots to put the main gear. A wind indicator was made from one of the tent poles and a T-shirt. I had burned my fuel down under 500 lbs and decided to take two of the four passengers.

Take-off was normal using approximately 85–90% torque, 100% NF NR. CG-1415 made a landing and picked up the two remaining passengers. Both helos arrived at McMurdo Station at *0308L* [3:08 A.M.], and despatched subjects to waiting ambulance.

I would like to extend a "Well Done" to LCDR L. M. SCHILLING 6892, USCG and crew of CG-1415 for their excellent performance during the demanding final stages of this rescue. A "Well Done" should go to LT JOHN G. CARROLL 7855, USCG, co-pilot of CG-1377, whose excellent performance helped to make this mission a success. Last but not least, a special note to CG-1377's crewman, AE2 W. A. LEE 375 872, USCG whose aggressive spirit and initial sighting helped to make a happy ending to this story.

[*Signed*]

N. A. NICHOLSON

DATED: 22 January 1971
On Board, USCGC STATEN ISLAND (WAGB-278)
Moored, McMurdo Station, Antarctica.

[Signed]

WITNESSED: YNC H. W. USHER, JR
260 468, USCG.

29

~~~~~~

EPILOGUE

THE READER has probably wondered why 1404's engine air-starved at around 12,000 feet whereas the engines of its two sister craft, the craft that rescued us, did not. An explanation of this question requires a few words on the subject of the maximum altitude capability of the HH-52A, as it is officially known.

According to information provided me by the Coast Guard, the above capability varies greatly and is dependent on several factors, such as air mass conditions (temperature and stability), aircraft weight, and type of flight: normal or hover. For example, the maximum altitude of an HH-52A operating at a gross weight of 8,300 pounds is limited to approximately 10,200 feet at a minimum airspeed of twenty knots and a maximum airspeed of fifty knots. An HH-52A operating at a gross weight of 7,000 pounds is capable of climbing to and maintaining level flight at an altitude of approximately 16,000 feet. In general, normal operations of the HH-52A at a medium gross weight of 7,000 pounds can be conducted up to an altitude of approximately 12,000 feet.

Leaving aside such an important question as air stability (in our case a downdraft), the crucial question related to the crash of 1404 is that of weight. The official Findings of Fact of the accident investigating board state that Palmer "was aware, prior to the flight, that the survival packs were not aboard. He decided not to load them when he observed that a considerable part of the cargo consisted of survival equipment and to load the survival bags would place the aircraft over 8,100 pounds, (maximum normal weight for operations), on take off." The findings also state that the bags "weigh 50 pounds each, or a total of 200 pounds."

By Palmer's own estimate, therefore, 1404 at the time of take-off from Williams Field with a full fuel load weighed no less than 7,900 pounds (subtracting 200 pounds from 8,100 pounds). And this is assuming that the findings are correct in stating, "In addition to passengers and crew the aircraft carried cargo manifested at 147 pounds, consisting of food, survival equipment and some personal effects of Mr. Neider."

The figure 147 is a strange one in that it presumes to be so precise. I do not know who manifested my cargo at 147 pounds. I do know that my cargo was not weighed before the flight and that my own estimate of its weight was 300 pounds. My cargo consisted of a tent, tent poles, metal pegs, tent ropes, an ice ax, a sack of mail, a sleeping bag, a cot, two cot mattresses, a canteen of water, a seabag full of heavy survival clothes, photographic equipment, a suitcase full of professional gear (notebooks, books, maps, tape recorder, cassettes, batteries, etc.), a good deal of regular clothes and personal equipment, and boxes and cartons of food, including frozen steaks, frozen rock lobsters, vegetables, fruit, bread, chocolate bars and so on. I believe that my estimate of my cargo's weight is more accurate than the estimate listed in the Findings of Fact. If my estimate is correct, then the craft weighed 7,900 pounds plus another 150 pounds, or a total of 8,050 pounds. However, I won't press the point. At 7,900 pounds the craft obviously did not possess, at normal operations, a maximum altitude capability of 12,000 feet, by the Coast Guard's own understanding of the craft's capability.

On the other hand, 1404's two sister craft had been stripped down, so that they had more lift than usual. And when it came to the rescue itself, the rescue pilots knew exactly where they were going; they knew the winds on the route that day and could avoid or make use of them; they were ready for the unexpected; they carried a minimum of fuel; and their helos had been stripped especially for the rescue operation.

In talks with Jim Brandau long after the crash I reached the conclusion that above a certain altitude and at certain conditions flying a helo is an art, not a science; that is, that it depends on "feel" and on other similar factors as well as on knowledge, skill and experience. Let me offer an example of the kind of thing he told me. Sometimes, when you're falling in a helo and are perilously close to the ground, you ought *not* to try to pull away from the ground, for such a maneuver will reduce airstream and cause rotor stall. Instead, you ought to head *for* the ground to pick up lift, then skim ahead or even bounce if necessary. As in a car skid, you should do the opposite of what you would want to do instinctively. He said that Palmer may have faced this situation in the downdraft and reacted poorly to it—presuming he still had an active engine, which I doubt. Also, much can depend on your knowledge of and ability to utilize local winds.

I was originally scheduled to leave the ice January 11. Shortly before the crash I had received from Chris Shepherd an extension until the eighteenth. My plan had been to spend several days at Cape Bird, a day at McMurdo and then to camp at Vanda Station, a Kiwi base in Wright Valley, before leaving Antarctica. The accident, with its effect on my hands, made it unwise for me to undertake Antarctic camping in the immediate future.

A more important consideration was that I needed to set down in my journal as soon as possible my impressions of the crash episode, and I could do this with maximum efficiency only at McMurdo. Also, the Coast Guard, which was conducting the investigation of the accident, felt it was urgent that my three rolls of crash films (the existence of which I had made known to VXE-6 pilots immediately on my return to McMurdo) be made available prior to the accident board's arrival in Antarctica. The films, Kodachrome II, could be processed in only one place in New Zealand: Wellington. I decided to take them there myself. And so it was agreed I would leave the ice for Christchurch by C-130 at 1 A.M. of the fourteenth.

On the thirteenth I was up at six for an early breakfast, during which I listened with fascination to my breakfast companion, the South African vertebrate paleontologist James Kitching, whom David Elliot had spoken to me about. Kitching had returned from the field a few days ago with a precious cargo of reptilian fossils which was locked in a Field Center cage. He would take the same plane out as the fossils did. He was a tall, wiry, bone-dry man with brilliant black eyes and a dry manner of speaking. His face and hands were very sunburned. During the meal he belittled his legendary ability to spot bits of fossil bone in places already combed by colleagues. He spoke of life in the bush and seemed to know a great deal about bush lore.

At 9:30 P.M. Enderby drove up to the Lodge in a truck and took me and my personal gear to the small plywood bus booth near MAC Center. I waited alone in the unheated structure until Father Crawford, a priest from Christchurch, wearing Navy clothes, joined me. A bit later a stout, tall lieutenant commander from personnel came in, followed by Louis Halle, an American professor of international relations who lived in Geneva and who had got stuck at Byrd Station during the SAR.

A large Navy truck drove up. The back of it had a canvas top and sides. The four of us sat in pairs on opposite benches. As we climbed to the Gap, I glimpsed McMurdo. The road beyond the Gap had been torn up badly by meltwater. The driver was going fast. All of us except Halle, who was hatless, held on to arched wooden beams above our heads to keep our skulls from smashing into them. Once, we flew into the air and came down very hard on the wooden benches. Suddenly we went over what felt like a boulder, and Halle's head cracked against a beam. He looked intensely startled, wide-eyed, alert and in pain. Grabbing hold of the beam with one hand, with the other he explored the top of his head. We heard the moaning, barking and yipping of the Scott Base huskies.

The truck stopped beside two trackmasters. Our gear was put in one. We entered the other and lumbered across the ice shelf. At Williams Field we made our way to the galley hut and dined at a small table. Father Crawford was solicitous about my canvas bag, which I wore over my shoulder by a broad strap and which contained my data: films, journals and tapes. At my request Enderby had sealed the bag in heavy plastic against the possibility of ditching in an aircraft. Some time between one-thirty and two in the morning we boarded a Herc.

Christchurch was not summery at 55° F., although the previous week its temperature had been in the nineties. But it was bright, expansive and rich with summer greens and miniskirts. In the USARP warehouse at Harewood Airport I changed from Antarctic clothes to my summer ones, the latter fetched from a stored suitcase. The large warehouse door was open; the place was drafty; I shivered a little. Riding in a cab to the Holiday Lodge on Colombo Street downtown, I stared at the trees, the little houses with their gardens in bloom, the shops, the green fields of Hagley Park, the narrow, winding, willow-shaded Avon. After depositing my canvas bag in a bank vault I soaked a long time in a hot bath.

I awoke during the night, went to a window and looked out at the churchyard beyond the driveway, at the street light and at the black sky. I smelled flowers, heard the rustle of trees. I remembered McMurdo, the Western Mountains, and thought of the fact that it was daylight down there. At Williams Field as I had slogged across the slushy ice shelf to the Herc I had looked forward to seeing Christchurch with its summer and girls. Both girls and summer felt strangely remote from me now. Nor did I react to night as I had expected. After my first visit to Antarctica I had been startled by the beauty of a dark sky and by the relief of having one overhead after a bright day. Perhaps spiritually I was still on the ice now.

I encountered Jim Brandau only briefly in Christchurch.

He said dryly, "I thought I told you all about what it's like. Why did you have to find out for yourself?"

An important consequence of the 1404 crash was that the accident convinced Operation Deep Freeze to replace VXE-6's helos in Antarctica (all were single-engine craft, and if you lost your engine you were likely to be in serious trouble) with twin-engine turbine-powered Hueys (the UH-1N), whose rated maximum altitude capability was about 25,000 feet.

Almost exactly a year after the crash, Brandau, who was back on the ice and flying one of the new helos, put two Kiwi geologists down on the Fang Glacier so they could gather some rocks for study. Then, after circling Erebus's crater, he set out to find the crash site, the approximate location of which Dan Biggerstaff, also in Antarctica, had marked on a map for him. Shepherd, in the cockpit with Brandau, spotted the site. Brandau set the Huey down on the rock apron we had used as a pad for the rescue helos. It was a fairly warm day, about 4° F., with excellent visibility and with no downdraft.

To Brandau's surprise the survival tent was still perfectly upright, its stakes, ropes and the life rafts all in place. The inside of the tent was filled with compacted snow that had turned to ice which Brandau later described to me as being as hard as glacial ice. He guessed the snow had blown under the poorly rocked-down tent flaps. He tore the entrance away to get at the interior, meaning to chop down to the floor with an ice ax to retrieve some things I had left behind. The ice ax proved inadequate for the job. Also, he got winded. Near the entrance were the Very pistol, a sheath knife and a carton of rock lobsters. They were put aboard the Huey.

He found 1404 had been blown onto its side. The open cabin was ice-filled but the cockpit was clear. With gusto Brandau cut foot supports in the helo's fuselage, using his ice ax, entered the cockpit and retrieved Palmer's sunglasses, which he meant to deliver to Palmer at McMurdo (Palmer was at McMurdo with his ship). Brandau, laughing while relating the incident to me, said he had always had to be so careful about helos, and now, suddenly, it was very liberating to be able to chop away at one. I was reminded of Eights's pleasure in his freedom to stick a sheath knife into 1404.

The group, which included the crewman and a man from the Field Center, climbed to the summit, where Brandau picked up for a souvenir a piece of pumice-like rock with a yellowish stain made by sulfur fumes.

On June 24, 1972, in his house in North Kingstown, Rhode Island, Brandau showed me some 8mm films he had taken of the crash site. I was startled by details that neither he nor Shepherd had mentioned to me. The bright red of the tent had faded to a sickly flesh color. Through the torn-away entrance peeped a spot or two of the original red. I had expected to see the tent bulging with ice. I was wrong. The sides were a good deal slacker than they had been on our departure from Erebus, probably because the pegs had worked loose. One could not tell, from the films alone, that the tent contained ice. A bank of snow half as high as the tent pressed against the tent's western side, the side closest to the abandoned helo. I gathered that this snow had been caught by a life raft, although I couldn't see the raft myself. The tent, with its faded color and slack sides, looked much smaller than I remembered it to be. It was a bit strange to think it had sheltered four men in a crisis and had possibly saved their limbs if not their lives.

Also extraordinary for me was the appearance of the helo. I realized now that it was one thing to be told it had been blown onto its side. To *see* it in that position was to have a powerful and completely surprising visual impression. The craft's white underbelly, which faced the tent, showed in large, black, stark letters the legend: USCG. The fuselage resembled a huge cigar, but what complicated this image were the strange protuberances on the northern end, which turned out to be the pontoons. One pontoon seemed to be suspended above the fuselage, the other to be crushed beneath it. As far as I could make out, the helo's red color hadn't faded. An east wind had blown the helo over in the direction away from the tent. Probably the open hatch, allowing the cabin to gather the wind like a sail, had caused the motion toward the west. Although I viewed the films three times, each time the helo struck me as almost unrecognizable at first: it suggested a grotesque modern sculpture.

Long after the accident Shepherd, looking puzzled, asked me in Washington why there was a pole sticking up between rocks near the tent. For a moment I did not know the answer. Then I remembered. The pole had been used with Nicholson's T-shirt to make a wind sock. Who knows where that T-shirt is now?

APPENDIX 1

SAR Log [9 January 1971]

From: Deep Freeze Southern Regional SAR Coordinator
To: Deep Freeze SAR Command
Subj: Narrative Report of SAR Mission 9 January 1971
Ref: (a) CNSFAINST 3130.1D

1. In accordance with reference (a) the following narrative is submitted concerning SAR Mission involving Coast Guard Helicopter D1404 on 9 January 1971.

2. Coast Guard Helicopter D404 departed Scott Base at 1406M [2:06 P.M.][1] and called MAC Center enroute to Cape Bird by a direct route. C130 V320 and H34 gentle (4) reported hearing D404 calling any station at approximately 1450M [2:50 P.M.]. SAR II condition was set at 1530M [3:30 P.M.] after repeated attempts to establish communications with D404. At 1635M [4:35 P.M.] SAR Condition I was set and an active search ordered.

One C130 from VX6, 2 H34 helos from VX6 McMurdo, and 2 H52 Helos from USCGC BURTON ISLAND were utilized as SAR aircraft.[2]

Two H34s (Gentle 3 and Gentle 4) were launched from McMurdo at 1649M [4:49 P.M.], one to search the coastal route to Cape Bird and the other to search the direct route. USCGC BURTON ISLAND, located 25 miles from Cape Bird and enroute to Hallett [Station], was requested to reverse course, proceed to Cape Bird area and support helo operations there. The BURTON ISLAND's 2 H52 helos were launched, CG360 at 1730M [5:30 P.M.] and CG415 at 1745M [5:45 P.M.], to search the Cape Bird/Lewis Bay area and the slopes of Mount Erebus.

The C130 (V320) was designated on scene commander and all search aircraft were assigned 234.0 MGS and 8997 ECS as SAR frequencies. SAR aircraft were refueled as necessary during the search and returned on station. Search routes and areas were revised with cloud cover preventing a thorough search of the upper slopes of Mount Erebus. As cloud

---

[1] The material in brackets is mine.
[2] This is an incomplete statement, as can be seen from the SAR Log, which lists two C-130s and three H52s (as well as the two H34s) as involved in the search. There are several discrepancies between this summary and the Log, which I have not tried to account for.

cover lifted on Erebus the search was extended towards the peak and CG helo 377 joined search from McMurdo.

At 2359M [11:59 p.m.] (10 Jan)[3] CG Helo 377 reported sighting the lost helo on Mt. Erebus. He reported it to be in an upright position and that at least two persons were outside firing flares. Closer surveillance revealed that all four occupants were near the downed helo and apparently uninjured.

C130 (V320) remained overhead while CG 377 returned to McMurdo for fuel. Two helos CG 377 and CG 415 (both H52As) departed McMurdo to attempt rescue at 0156M [1:56 A.M.]. CG 377 landed first (0247M) [2:47 A.M.] and picked up two persons and CG 415 landed (0251M) [2:51 A.M.] and picked up the other two. C130 (V320) remained overhead until both helos were enroute to McMurdo, then returned to Williams Field, landing at 0305M [3:05 A.M.].

The rescue helos landed at McMurdo at 0311M [3:11 A.M.]. The four occupants of CG 404 were taken to McMurdo Dispensary, checked by the medical officer[4] and released. The SAR condition was secured at 0311M [3:11 A.M.] 10 Jan 71.

Enclosure (16)   T. L. Johnston—LT USN

INCIDENT RECORD OF SAR ON USCG HELICOPTER 404

320—LC-130 BUNO 48320, VXE-6
G3—Gentle Three LH-34, VXE-6
G4—Gentle Four LH-34, VXE-6
319—LC-130 BUNO 48319, VXE-6
415—HH52A, USCG
377—HH52A, USCG
360—HH52A, USCG

SAR COND. II set at 0330Z
SAR COND. I set at 0435Z

Notes: Last radio contact 0206Z. LC-130 BUNO 48320 heard 404, but was unable to contact him. 404 initiated a radio call to "any station."

ALL TIMES ZULU[5]

0449—G4 off NZCM.
0451—G3 off NZCM.

---

[3] This is inaccurate. The time is a minute before midnight, the day still 9 January.
[4] This too is inaccurate, as the reader knows.
[5] Zulu stands for Greenwich Mean Time. Midnight Zulu equals Noon McMurdo Station.

0500—LC-130 319 On-Scene-Commander/G3 visually sighted hut at Cape Bird.

0512—G4 on top of Mt. Bird.

0518—USCGC BURTON ISLAND advised to launch helos.

0522—319 going down to look at Mt. Bird.

0525—USCGC BURTON ISLAND advised to turn back to Ross Island and not launch helos.

0529—LC-130 320 off NZCM.

0530—G4 reports 404 never arrived Cape Bird.

0538—320 assumed On-Scene-Commander. G3 circled Mt. Erebus enroute to NZCM.

0549—USCGC BURTON ISLAND 7 mi. E of Beaufort Is. returning Cape Bird.

0550—G3 Erebus Glacier Tongue.

0551—G3 low route Royds/G4 Mt. Erebus/USCG helos 415 and 360 launched from USCGC BURTON ISLAND 415 was off at 0545Z enroute to Lewis Bay, 360 off at 0530 enroute Cape Royds.

0602—360 Cape Royds.

0606—G4 enroute Cape Evans for landing.

0607—320 Grid North of Erebus.

0609—G4 on Cape Evans.

0614—G3 on Cape Evans.

0624—G3 slope of Erebus Grid West (enroute)/G4 Scott Base searching between Mt. Erebus and Mt. Terra Nova.

0630—360 on Cape Route. 415 landing Crozier.

0635—G4/G3 advised to search between Erebus and NZCM. 360/415 advised to search between Erebus and Mt. Bird.

0647—320 rounding Crozier. G4 south of Erebus returning NZCM.

0651—G3 grid east of Erebus Glacial Tongue.

0654—USCGC BURTON ISLAND 5 mi. west of Cape Royds proceeding north along coast.

0656—360 proceeding grid east up Erebus.

0700—G4 lost HF over tongue (climbed 10.5 over lip).

0703—320 proceeding overhead Erebus.

0708—360 and 415 proceeding to top of Erebus.

0721—G3 Erebus slope.

0726—G4 5 mi. W of Royds.

0740—360 descending below 10,000.

0742—320 retains On-Scene-Commander.

0745—G3 returning NZCM.

0747—415 vicinity of Mt. Bird. 360 vicinity of Erebus.

0800—360 grid north Erebus 9.5. 415 on deck Cape Bird.

0804—G4 returned NZCM.

0808—320 requests 415 and 360 return for fuel and crew change/360 returns to BURTON ISLAND, 415 returns to NZCM.

0840—360 off Cape Bird enroute BURTON ISLAND.

0904—G3 departed NZCM at 0844 enroute Erebus, direct Scott Base, Hut cliffs, north Erebus 7000 climbing. 320 at Cape Bird 500 ft.

0907—G3 grid east Erebus 9.5.

0912—G3 grid north Erebus 11.5 recommends search grid SE on Fang Glacier, cloud cover appears lifting.

0920—G3 circling to east of Erebus 10.0.

0924—320 climbing for another look at Erebus.

0928—377 enroute grid SE Erebus to Fang Glacier.

0933—G3 grid E. Erebus 7.0 descending.

0947—G3 Mt. Bird circling.

0950—377 Fang Glacier proceeding E 500 ft.

1000—G3 enroute NZCM retracing flt. path long arm of peninsula from Erebus. 377 grid 090 from Erebus 12.0 proceeding in clockwise contour search.

1015—Concentrating search to Terra Nova and Terror Mts. as recommended by CO. G3 proceeding Crozier, search grid N Terra Nova enroute.

1019—377 proceeding grid S of Terra Nova.

1020—320 proceeding to NZCM.

1040—G3 proceeding grid W down slope of Terra Nova direct Terror Mt.

1053—377 grid 180 from top of Terra Nova—1045 at 6.5 proceeding grid W enroute Terror Mt. begin search of grid 8 slope.

1102—G3 proceeding to Lima-Lima.

1108—377 proceeding at 8.0 from Terror to Hut Point Peninsula.

1111—G3 search grid N. Terror and return NZCM. Presently over Crozier 2.5.

1117—377 Grid N. Erebus criss-cross to Hut Point Peninsula.

1121—G3 3.0 grid N. Terra Nova.

1123—320 proceeding grid N. of Erebus to circle.

1126—G3 returning NZCM.

1132—320 Cape Bird proceeding to Beaufort Is.

1140—320 Mt. Bird circling. 377 Scott's Hut.

1147—320 enroute Beaufort Is.

1150—377 Fang Glacier 8.0.

1152—377 Mt. Erebus 10.0/320 direct Mt. Erebus/377 reports crater out of clouds.

1155—377 reports top of crater is clear.

1157—377 12.5 grid SE Mt. Erebus.

1158—320 Bird direct Erebus.

1159—*Helo 404 sighted.* NE side Erebus, green flare sighted, two persons moving in area. True north side, uphill from Fang Glacier about 12.2 Helo cocked port side down. Reported by 377.

1205—377 returning NZCM. Fuel state .5.

1210—320 making another pass at party.

1215—320 possibly four persons in sight.

1220—377 Williams Field for fuel. 320 all four persons standing and appear in good shape.

1242—377 on deck NZCM.

1245—415 off ship direct NZCM.

1310—415 Erebus Glacier Tongue.

1312—415 on deck NZCM.

1330—320 reports party 22NM on 180 radial Williams Field Tacon.

1351—320 Ops Normal.

1356—377/415 off NZCM enroute to 404 site.

1411—377/415 grid SE climbing to 8.0.

1428—377/415 over 404 site.

1431—377 on deck 404 site.

1434—377 reports all persons in good shape.

1447—377 off site. Two pax aboard.

1449—415 on site.

1451—415 off site, two remaining pax aboard.

1453—377 reports considerable damage to port landing gear of 404. Rest will follow on deck report.

1507—377 arrived NZCM/discharged pax to ambulance.

1511—415 arrived NZCM/discharged pax to ambulance.

SAR SECURED AT 1511Z

APPENDIX 2

SAR Log [9 January 1971] "Translated" and Unscrambled

P.M.

4:49—Gentle 4 takes off from McMurdo.

4:51—Gentle 3 takes off from McMurdo.

5:00—C-130 319 is appointed on-scene-commander. Gentle 3 sights the wanigan at Cape Bird.

5:12—Gentle 4 is on top of Mt. Bird.

5:18—The *Burton Island* is advised to launch its helos.

5:22—319 goes down to have a look at Mt. Bird.

5:25—The *Burton Island* is advised to return to Ross Island and not launch its helos.

5:29—C-130 320 is off McMurdo Station.

5:30—Gentle 4 reports that 1404 never arrived at Cape Bird. 1360 takes off from the *Burton Island* enroute to Cape Royds.

5:38—320 is appointed on-scene-commander. Gentle 3 circles Mt. Erebus enroute to McMurdo.

5:45—1415 takes off from the *Burton Island* enroute to Lewis Bay.

5:49—The *Burton Island* is seven miles east of Beaufort Island and is returning to the vicinity of Cape Bird.

5:50—Gentle 3 is over Erebus Glacier Tongue.

5:51—Gentle 3 takes the low route to Cape Royds. Gentle 4 is in the vicinity of Mt. Erebus.

6:02—1360 is at Cape Royds.

6:06—Gentle 4 is enroute to Cape Evans with the intention of landing there.

6:07—320 is south of Erebus.

6:09—Gentle 4 is on Cape Evans.

6:14—Gentle 3 is on Cape Evans.

6:24—Gentle 3 is enroute to the eastern slope of Erebus. Gentle 4 is searching the terrain between Erebus and Mt. Terra Nova.

6:30—1360 is on the cape route. 1415 lands at Cape Crozier.

6:35—Gentle 3 and Gentle 4 are advised to search the terrain between Erebus and McMurdo. 1360 and 1415 are advised to search the terrain between Mt. Erebus and Mt. Bird.

6:47—320 rounds Cape Crozier. Gentle 4 is south of Erebus enroute to McMurdo.

6:51—Gentle 3 is west of Erebus Glacier Tongue.

6:54—The *Burton Island* is five miles west of Cape Royds and proceeding north along the coast.

6:56—1360 is climbing the western side of Erebus.

7:00—Gentle 4 loses HF contact over Erebus Glacier Tongue, having climbed to 10,500 feet and over a lip of Erebus.

7:03—320 proceeds over Erebus.

7:08—1360 and 1415 are heading for the top of Erebus.

7:21—Gentle 3 is over a slope of Erebus.

7:26—Gentle 4 is five miles west of Cape Royds.

7:40—1360 is descending to below 10,000 feet.

7:42—320 retains its rank of on-scene-commander.

7:45—Gentle 3 is returning to McMurdo.

7:47—1415 is in the vicinity of Mt. Bird, 1360 in the vicinity of Mt. Erebus.

8:00—1360 is at 9,500 feet over the southern slope of Erebus. 1415 is on deck at Cape Bird.

8:04—Gentle 4 is returning to McMurdo.

8:08—320 requests 1360 and 1415 to return for fuel and crew change. 1360 proceeds to the *Burton Island,* 1415 to McMurdo Station.

8:40—1360 is off Cape Bird, enroute to the *Burton Island.*

8:44—Gentle 3 departs from McMurdo enroute to Erebus via Scott Base.

9:04—Gentle 3 is north of Erebus at 7,000 feet and climbing. 320 is 500 feet above Cape Bird.

9:07—Gentle 3 is over the western side of Erebus at 9,500 feet.

9:12—Gentle 3 is over the southern slope of Erebus at 11,500 feet and recommends a search of the northwest side of Mt. Erebus in the neighborhood of the Fang Glacier, where the cloud cover appears to be lifting.

9:20—Gentle 3 circles to the eastern side of Erebus at 10,000 feet.

9:24—320 climbs for another look at Erebus.

9:28—1377 is enroute to the northwest side of Erebus in the area of the Fang Glacier.

9:33—Gentle 3 is west of Erebus at 7,000 feet and descending.

9:47—Gentle 3 is circling Mt. Bird.

9:50—1377 is over the Fang Glacier and proceeding east at 500 feet above the ground.

10:00—Gentle 3 is enroute to McMurdo along the arm of Hut Point Peninsula. 1377 is conducting a clockwise contour search of Erebus at 12,000 feet.

10:15—The search is being concentrated on Mt. Terra Nova and Mt.

Terror, as recommended by the commanding officer. Gentle 3 is proceeding to Cape Crozier with the intention of searching the southern slope of Mt. Terra Nova enroute.

10:19—1377 is heading for the north side of Mt. Terra Nova.

10:20—320 proceeds to McMurdo.

10:40—Gentle 3 heads for the eastern slope of Mt. Terra Nova on a direct route to Mt. Terror.

10:45—1377 is at 6,500 feet and proceeding east enroute to Mt. Terror.

10:53—1377 is east of the top of Mt. Terra Nova.

11:02—Gentle 3 is heading for Lima-Lima, a checkpoint.

11:08—1377 is proceeding at 8,000 feet from Mt. Terror to Hut Point Peninsula.

11:11—Gentle 3, having searched the southern slope of Mt. Terror, is enroute to McMurdo. It is over Cape Crozier at 2,500 feet.

11:17—1377 is south of Erebus and crisscrossing to Hut Point Peninsula.

11:21—Gentle 3 is south of Mt. Terra Nova at 3,000 feet.

11:23—320 is proceeding south of Erebus with the intention of circling the mountain.

11:26—Gentle 3 is enroute to McMurdo Station.

11:32—320 is over Cape Bird and heading for Beaufort Island.

11:40—320 is circling Mt. Bird. 1377 is over Scott's Hut at Cape Evans.

11:47—320 is enroute to Beaufort Island.

11:50—1377 is at the Fang Glacier at 8,000 feet.

11:52—1377 is at 10,000 feet over Erebus. It reports that the crater is clear of clouds. 320 is heading directly toward Erebus.

11:55—1377 reports that the top of the crater is clear.

11:57—1377 is at 12,500 feet over the northwest slope of Erebus.

11:59—1377 sights a green flare, then 1404 on the northwest side of Erebus. Two persons are seen to be moving in the area. 1404, cocked port side down, is uphill from the Fang Glacier at about 12,200 feet.

A.M.

12:05—1377 is returning to McMurdo. Its fuel state is .5.

12:10—320 makes another pass at the stranded party.

12:15—320 reports possibly four persons to be in sight.

12:20—1377 is at Williams Field to refuel. 320 reports that all four persons are standing and appear to be in good shape.

12:42—1377 is on deck at McMurdo Station.

12:45—1415 takes off from the *Burton Island* enroute to McMurdo.

1:10—1415 is over Erebus Glacier Tongue.

1:12—1415 is on deck at McMurdo.

1:30—320 reports the stranded party to be twenty-two nautical miles on a 180 radial from the Williams Field Tacon. [A Tacon is an electronic ground navigation aid.]

1:51—320 reports Operations Normal.

1:56—1377 and 1415 take off from McMurdo enroute to the 1404 site.

2:11—1377 and 1415 are over the northwest slope of Erebus, climbing to 8,000 feet.

2:28—1377 and 1415 are over the 1404 site.

2:31—1377 is on deck at the 1404 site.

2:34—1377 reports all four persons to be in good shape.

2:47—1377 takes off with two of the stranded passengers.

2:49—1415 is on deck at the 1404 site.

2:51—1415 takes off with the two remaining stranded passengers.

2:53—1377 reports considerable damage to 1404's port landing gear.

3:07—1377 lands at McMurdo and discharges its two passengers to a waiting ambulance.

3:11—1415 does the same.

THE SAR IS SECURED AT 3:11 A.M.

APPENDIX 3

Conquest of Mount Erebus

Inasmuch as Mount Erebus plays so prominent a role in the geology of Ross Island and in my experiences on the island, I have thought it worth presenting an account of the mountain's conquest, which hopefully will afford the reader an intimate sense and some understanding of the volcano. Unless otherwise ascribed, the quotations are by Shackleton from *The Heart of the Antarctic.*

The work by the Nimrod Expedition of settling into winter quarters was accomplished by March 3, 1908. Shackleton was eager to make a depot-laying journey to the south in preparation for his announced attempt on the Pole the following austral summer. However, open water still intervened between Cape Royds and Hut Point, making it impossible not only to move southward but in the direction of Victoria Land as well. This situation left one important present undertaking within the expedition's reach: the conquest of Erebus. An ascent to the crater was considered desirable because "the observations of temperatures and wind currents at the summit of this great mountain would have an important bearing on the movements of the upper air, a meteorological problem as yet imperfectly understood." Also, it was expected that the climb would reveal some interesting geological facts.

For the summit party Shackleton selected Thomas W. Edgeworth David, Douglas Mawson and Alister Forbes Mackay. David, at fifty the expedition's oldest member, was a geologist, Mawson was the expedition's physicist and Mackay was a surgeon. The summit party were to carry provisions lasting ten days. The supporting party were to be provisioned for six. The latter consisted of Jameson Boyd Adams, Eric Stewart Marshall and Sir Philip Brocklehurst. The attempt on Erebus was to be under Adams's command until it was time for the supporting party to head back toward winter quarters. The summit party were then to be commanded by David. Shackleton gave Adams the option of continuing to the crater if he thought it feasible for his party to make the ascent with its limited means.

March 5. The ascent was begun at 8:30 A.M., with one eleven-foot sledge. The sledge, together with its load, weighed 560 pounds. All hands at Cape Royds helped lift the sledge over the rocky ridge behind the hut and to pull it over the slopes of Back Door Bay, across Blue Lake and part way up the snowy slopes of the mountain. At this point the Mount Erebus double party proceeded alone, going up a snow slope and avoiding crevassed glaciers. They had to portage the sledge over a glacial moraine. Making their way up a small glacier, they had at times to work on their hands and knees on "smooth blue ice thinly coated with snow." The parties camped at about 6 P.M. some 2,700 feet above sea level and about seven miles from the hut.

March 6. During the morning's climb the gradient grew much steeper and the sledge capsized frequently because of sastrugi running obliquely to its course. Camp was made at an altitude of 5,630 feet after a day's march of three miles. That night the temperature was —28°. At this second camp a depot was made of the sledge, part of the provisions and some of the cooking utensils. "In the ascent of a mountain such as Erebus it was obvious that a limit would soon be reached beyond which it would be impossible to use a sledge. To meet these circumstances the advance-party had made an arrangement of straps by which their single sleeping-bags could be slung in the form of a knapsack upon their backs, and inside the bags the remainder of their equipment could be packed."

March 7–8. The morning of the eighth Adams decided that both parties would attempt to reach the summit even though his own party was handicapped in certain respects. Unlike the summit party, his carried a three-man sleeping bag, which meant that one man had to lug the bulky article. And instead of having broad straps for carrying their knapsacks they had only rope. Also, they had no crampons for either their ski boots or their finneskoes. The joint party began the day's climb with tent poles as part of their equipment but after marching half a mile decided it would be impossible to ascend the mountain with the poles, so they returned to the depot and left the poles there. The Erebus party now had two tents, sleeping bags, cooking apparatus, and provisions for three days. Each man carried about forty pounds. "The snow slopes became steeper, and at one time Mackay, who was cutting steps on the hard snow with his ice-axe, slipped and glissaded with his load for about a hundred feet, but his further downward career was checked by a projecting ledge of snow, and he was soon up again." The party camped at an elevation of about 8,750 feet. The temperature was —20°.

"Between 9 and 10 P.M. that night a strong wind sprang up, and when the men awoke the following morning they found a fierce blizzard blowing from the south-east. It increased in fury as the day wore on, and swept with terrific force down the rocky ravine where they were camped. The whirling snow was so dense and the roaring wind so loud that, although the two sections were only about ten yards apart, they could neither see nor hear each other. Being without tent-poles, the tents were just doubled over the top ends of the sleeping-bags so as to protect the openings from the drifting snow, but, in spite of this precaution, a great deal of snow found its way into the bags. In the afternoon Brocklehurst emerged from the three-man sleeping-bag, and instantly a fierce gust whirled away one of his wolfskin mits; he dashed after it, and the force of the wind swept him some way down the ravine. Adams, who had left the bag at the same time as Brocklehurst, saw the latter vanish suddenly, and in endeavouring to return to the bag to fetch Marshall to assist in finding Brocklehurst he also was blown down by the wind. Meanwhile, Marshall, the only remaining occupant of the bag, had much ado to keep himself from being blown, sleeping-bag and all, down the ravine. Adams had just succeeded in reaching the sleeping-bag on his hands and knees when Brocklehurst appeared, also on his hands and knees, having, by desperate efforts, pulled himself back over the rocks. It was a close call, for he was all but completely gone, so biting was the cold, before he reached the haven of the sleeping-bag. He and Adams crawled in, and then, as the bag had been much twisted up and drifted with snow while Marshall had been holding it down, Adams and Marshall got out to try and straighten it out. The attempt was not very successful, as they were numb with cold and the bag, with only one person inside, blew about, so they got into it again. Shortly afterwards Adams made another attempt, and whilst he was working at it the wind got inside the bag, blowing it open right way up. Adams promptly got in again, and the adventure thus ended satisfactorily. The men could do nothing now but lie low whilst the blizzard lasted. At times they munched a plasmon biscuit or some chocolate. They had nothing to drink all that day, March 8, and during the following night, as it would have been impossible to have kept a lamp alight to thaw out the snow. They got some sleep during the night in spite of the storm. On awaking at 4 A.M. the following day, the travellers found that the blizzard was over, so, after breakfast, they started away again at about 5.30 A.M."

March 9. The angle of ascent was now steeper than before: 34°, or a rise of 1 in 1½. The men made use of bare rocks as much as possible, for the snow slopes, being steep and hard, would have necessitated the cutting of steps with ice axes, and the loss of energy and time. Occasionally there was no choice; steps had to be cut across slopes to other rocks which could be climbed. Brocklehurst, wearing ski boots instead of his finneskoes, felt his feet growing very cold yet decided against changing footgear. The extreme cold and the high altitude were beginning to affect the party strongly. At one point Mackay, after cutting steps while carrying his heavy load, fainted.

"Having found a camping-place, they dropped their loads, and the members of the party were at leisure to observe the nature of their surroundings. They had imagined an even plain of névé or glacier ice filling the extinct crater to the brim and sloping up gradually to the active cone at its southern end, but instead of this they found themselves on the very brink of a precipice of black rock, forming the inner edge of the old crater. This wall of dark lava was mostly vertical, while, in some places, it overhung, and was from eighty to a hundred feet in height. The base of the cliff was separated from the snow plain beyond by a deep ditch like a huge dry moat, which was evidently due to the action of blizzards. These winds, striking fiercely from the south-east against the great inner wall of the old crater, had given rise to a powerful back eddy at the edge of the cliff, and it was this eddy which had scooped out the deep trench in the hard snow. The trench was from thirty to forty feet deep, and was bounded by more or less vertical sides. Around our winter quarters any isolated rock or cliff face that faced the south-east blizzard-wind exhibited a similar phenomenon, though, of course on a much smaller scale. Beyond the wall and trench was an extensive snow-field with the active cone and crater at its southern end, the latter emitting great volumes of steam, but what surprised the travellers most were the extraordinary structures which rose here and there above the surface of the snow-field. They were in the form of mounds and pinnacles of the most varied and fantastic appearance. Some resembled beehives, others were like huge ventilating cowls, others like isolated turrets, and others again in shape resembled various animals. The men were unable at first sight to understand the origin of these remarkable structures, and as it was time for food, they left the closer investigation for later in the day. . . . The camp chosen for the meal was in a little rocky gully on the north-west slope of the main cone, and about fifty feet below the rim of the old crater."

When Brocklehurst mentioned that he had lost all feeling in his feet some time ago Marshall examined them and found that both big toes were black and that four others, although less severely affected, were also frostbitten. Marshall and Mackay, the surgeons in the party, treated Brocklehurst's feet by warming and chafing them. (Chafing is no longer considered wise as a treatment for frostbite; it can harm already injured tissues; warming as soon as possible is the treatment now advised.) Then Brocklehurst's feet were covered with dry socks and with finneskoes stuffed with sennegrass, and after lunch at 3:30 P.M. he was left in the three-man sleeping bag while the rest of the party went off to explore the second crater.

"Ascending to the crater rim, they climbed along it until they came to a spot where there was a practicable breach in the crater wall and where a narrow tongue of snow bridged the névé trench at its base. They all roped up directly they arrived on the hard snow in the crater and advanced cautiously over the snow-plain, keeping a sharp look-out for crevasses. They steered for some of the remarkable mounds already mentioned, and when the nearest was reached and examined, they noticed some curious hollows, like partly roofed-in drains, running towards the mound. Pushing on slowly, they reached eventually a small parasitic cone, about 1000 ft. above the level of their camp and over a mile distant from it. Sticking out from under the snow were lumps of lava, large felspar crystals, from one to three inches in length, and fragments of pumice; both felspar and pumice were in many cases coated with sulphur. Having made as complete an examination as time permitted, they started to return to camp, no longer roped together, as they had not met any definite crevasses on their way out. They directed their steps towards one of the ice mounds, which bore a whimsical resemblance to a lion couchant and from which smoke appeared to be issuing. To the Professor [David] the origin of these peculiar structures was now no longer a mystery, for he recognised that they were the outward and visible signs of fumaroles. In ordinary climates, a fumarole, or volcanic vapour-well, may be detected by the thin cloud of steam above it, and usually one can at once feel the warmth by passing one's hand into the vapour column, but in the rigour of the Antarctic climate the fumaroles of Erebus have their vapour turned into ice as soon as it reaches the surface of the snow-plain. . . . Whilst exploring one of the fumaroles, Mackay fell suddenly up to his thighs into one of its concealed conduits, and only saved himself from falling in deeper still by means of his ice-axe. Marshall had a similar experience at about the same time."

March 10. "After breakfast, while Marshall was attending to Brocklehurst's feet, the hypsometer, which had become frozen on the way up, was thawed out and a determination of the boiling-point made. This, when reduced and combined with the mean of the aneroid levels, made the altitude of the old crater rim, just above the camp, 11,400 ft." At 6 A.M. the party, with the exception of Brocklehurst, started for the summit of the active crater. Their progress was slow. The altitude and the cold made breathing very difficult. The summit was reached at 10 A.M.

In *The Heart of the Antarctic* Shackleton quoted from the report of the ascent supplied him by David and Adams.

"We stood on the verge of a vast abyss, and at first could see neither to the bottom nor across it on account of the huge mass of steam filling the crater and soaring aloft in a column 500 to 1000 ft. high. After a continuous loud hissing sound, lasting for some minutes, there would come from below a big dull boom, and immediately great globular masses of steam would rush upwards to swell the volume of the snow-white cloud which ever sways over the crater. This phenomenon recurred at intervals during the whole of our stay at the crater. Meanwhile the air around us was extremely redolent of burning sulphur. Presently a pleasant northerly breeze fanned away the steam cloud, and at once the whole crater stood revealed to us in all its vast extent and depth. Mawson's angular measurement made the depth 900 ft. and the greatest width about half a mile. There were at least three well-defined openings at the bottom of the cauldron, and it was from these that the steam explosions proceeded. Near the south-west portion of the crater there was an immense rib in the rim, perhaps 300 to 400 ft. deep. The crater wall opposite the one at the top of which we were standing presented features of special interest. Beds of dark pumiceous lava or pumice alternated with white zones of snow. There was no direct evidence that the snow was bedded with the lava, though it was possible that such may have been the case. From the top of one of the thickest of the lava or pumice beds, just where it touched the belt of snow, there rose scores of small steam jets all in a row. They were too numerous and too close together to have been each an independent fumarole; the appearance was rather suggestive of the snow being converted into steam by the heat of the layer of rock immediately below it."

The party calculated the mountain's elevation, made a traverse around the crater, collected specimens of feldspar crystals, pumice and sulphur, then returned to their camp, which they left almost immediately, having decided to descend 8,000 feet this day in order to reach the base of the main crater. At one point they deliberately glissaded down a long, steep névé slope after sending their loads down the slope ahead of them. They descended 5,000 feet between 3 and 7 P.M. and camped at the sledge depot.

March 11. The sledge was packed by 5:30 A.M. and the final march begun. "They now found that the sastrugi caused by the late blizzard were very troublesome, as the ridges were from four to five feet above the hollows and lay at an oblique angle to the course. Rope brakes were put on the sledge-runners, and two men went in front to pull when necessary, while two steadied the sledge, and two were stationed behind to pull back when required. It was more than trying to carry on at this juncture, for the sledge either refused to move or suddenly it took charge and over-ran those who were dragging it, and capsizes occurred every few minutes. Owing to the slippery nature of the ground, some members of the party who had not crampons or barred ski-boots [ski boots with leather bars across the soles] were badly shaken up, for they sustained innumerable sudden falls. One has to experience a surface like this to realise how severe a jar a fall entails. . . . Marshall devised the best means of assisting the progress of the sledge. When it took charge he jumped on behind and steered it with his legs as it bumped and jolted over the sastrugi, but he found sometimes that his thirteen-stone weight [182 pounds] did not prevent him from being bucked right over the sledge and flung on the névé on the other side."

The party reached their first camp at about 7:30 A.M. Threatened by the approach of a southeasterly blizzard, they took stock of their condition. They were very tired. Their oil supply was almost finished. One of the tents, having been accidentally burned, had a large hole in it. And a primus stove had been made temporarily useless as a consequence of the glissade. They decided to leave the sledge and the equipment and to make a dash for Cape Royds.

At about 11 A.M. Shackleton happened to be outside the hut for a moment. "[I] was astonished to see within thirty yards of me, coming over the brow of the ridge by the hut, six slowly moving figures. I ran towards them shouting: 'Did you get to the top?' There was no answer, and I asked again. Adams pointed with his hand upwards, but this did not satisfy me, so I repeated my question. Then Adams said: 'Yes,' and I ran back to the hut and shouted to the others, who all came streaming out to cheer the successful venturers. We shook hands all round and opened some champagne, which tasted like nectar to the way-worn people. Marshall prescribed a dose to us stay-at-home ones, so that we might be able to listen quietly to the tale the party had to tell."

Unlike his other toes, one of Brocklehurst's big toes failed to recover from the effects of frostbite. On April 6 Marshall amputated it with the aid of chloroform.

David, at Shackleton's request, wrote a summary of the scientific observations of the climb, which Shackleton quoted in his book.

". . . . Among features of geological interest may be mentioned the fact that the old moraines left by a former gigantic ancestor of the great ice barrier, ascend the western slopes of Erebus to a height of fully 1000 ft. above sea-level. As the adjacent McMurdo Sound is at least three hundred fathoms deep, this ice sheet when at its maximum development must have been at least 2800 ft. in thickness. We noticed that in addition to these old ice barrier moraines, there were moraines newer than the period of greatest glaciation. They had evidently been formed by glaciers radiating from Erebus. . . . The frequent glows on the steam cloud above the crater, and at the actual edge, as seen from our winter quarters during the winter months, prove that molten lava still wells up into the crater. The fresh volcanic bombs picked up by us at spots four miles distant from the crater and lying on the surface of comparatively new snow are evidence that Erebus has recently been projecting lava to great heights. . . . The ice fumaroles are specially remarkable. . . . No structures like them are known in any other part of the world. . . .

"From the above brief notes it will be obvious that Erebus is very interesting geologically on account of its unique fumaroles, its remarkable felspar crystals and rare lavas, as well as on account of its having served as a gigantic tide gauge to record the flood level of the greatest recent glaciation of Antarctica, when the whole of Ross Island was but a nunatak in a gigantic field of ice. From a meteorological point of view, its situation between the belt of polar calms and the South Pole; its isolation from the disturbing influence of large land masses; its great height, which enables it to penetrate the whole system of atmospheric circulation; and, above all, the constant steam cloud at its summit, swinging to and fro like a huge wind vane, combine to make Erebus one of the most interesting places on earth to the meteorologist."

APPENDIX 4

Taking Photographs in Antarctica

In addition to the obvious photographic problem that Antarctica poses, that of extremely low temperatures, there are two others: static electricity due to very low humidity, and condensation. Inasmuch as Antarctica is a vast continent one can expect to encounter considerable variations in temperature due to differences in latitude, elevation and to local weather conditions as well as to season.

On my second trip there was no problem about getting my photographic equipment down to Antarctica. The United States Navy flew it there before my arrival. But there were problems inherent in getting the exposed film safely out. It seemed quite simple until one got immersed in the details. Why not airmail the cassettes home in batches? Well, if a Navy plane got into trouble while flying between McMurdo and Christchurch it might ditch some of its cargo, of which my film might be a part. In addition there was the normal hazard of loss during mail transit. Or the film might be irradiated by X rays at some point on their way home; airport guards were on the outlook for weapons and explosives. Or it might be held up somewhere in the tropics and damaged by heat and humidity. I could send the cassettes home by Navy ship, but if I did they would leave the continent perhaps as long as two months after my departure, and the film might deteriorate during its passage through equatorial waters.

Before leaving for the Antarctic in December 1970 I decided that there was only one solution acceptable to me. I would take out films, together with tapes and journals, on my person. Which is what I did. I loaded them in a canvas rucksack that I purchased in New York for the purpose, had the sack sealed in heavy plastic at McMurdo and kept it attached to my person all the way from McMurdo to my home with one exception, when I deposited it in a bank vault in Christchurch for about a week.

Photographic film grows brittle as its temperature decreases. At the very low temperatures one may encounter in the Antarctic it can easily break. Frame advancing when cameras are very cold should be done not at the speeds common to temperate zones but in increments of millimeters. Before embarking on my second trip to the continent I practiced such advancing whenever I could. I also practiced rewinding film very slowly, for rewinding at normal speeds in Antarctica may well result in an entire roll of film being scarred by static electricity. I also practiced frame advancing and rewinding and focusing and setting shutter speeds and depressing the shutter-release button while wearing gloves of varying weights. And I practiced looking through the rangefinder while holding the camera slightly in front of my cheek, for at very low temperatures, touching the metal rangefinder piece with your cheek may result in the skin adhering to the metal or being burned by it. This was boring but necessary work, the purpose of which was to make special handling of cameras automatic in Antarctic conditions. Once I arrived in Antarctica it would be too late to train myself; I would not have the time.

People who expect to go to the very high latitudes and to the high elevations in Antarctica would do well to bring rangefinder cameras rather than reflex ones, for the latter have a greater tendency to freeze because they have more moving parts. It is also useful to bring winterized cameras if one expects to spend much time in extremely cold places. In such a camera the normal lubricant has been replaced by graphite powder. During both of my visits to Antarctica I brought along 35mm rangefinder cameras with normal lubricants. However, when I was in very cold places I kept the cameras under my parka except for the times when I was using them, and I avoided keeping them out for prolonged periods. I was lucky in never having a camera freeze on me and in never having film break.

I needed to bring much other gear with me, such as tape recorders, tape cassettes, binoculars, journals, etc., so I had to limit myself in the matter of photographic equipment. In addition to two Leica cameras, an M4 and an M2R, I brought along a table tripod, cleaning materials and a hundred rolls of thirty-six exposure color film on my second trip. I brought three extra lenses (28mm, 90mm and 135mm), but because of the special conditions of my program did not often use lenses other than a 35mm f/2 Summicron on the M4 and a 50mm dual range f/2 Summicron on the M2R. All the lenses were equipped with UV filters, which are necessary for color film if one is to avoid the harsh cold blue that one otherwise tends to get in Antarctica. The filters are also valuable in protecting the lenses. One can use skylight filters rather than UV ones but I prefer the latter, although they are slightly "colder." A yellow filter is recommended for black-and-white film. Each of my cameras had its own Leicameter, coupled to the shutter speed. The meters worked on cadmium sulfide batteries. Batteries tend to drain at low temperatures. The preservation of the meter batteries was an added reason for keeping the cameras warm. Some Antarctic photographers have suggested the advisability of taking meter readings of the back of one's hand rather than of the highly reflective and deceptive ice and snow surfaces. I did not find it necessary to follow this advice.

Because of the intense light of the austral summer I used Kodachrome II film exclusively. I did not use black-and-white film at all although I brought some with me. The light enabled me to take advantage of Kodachrome II's slow speed, fine grain and faithful color range and values. With so much light coming from all directions, from the azure sky, from glaciers, sea ice, ice shelves, ice caps and sometimes from bright clouds, it is easy to obtain overexposed pictures. As a precaution against this possibility and because Kodachrome II lends itself well to slight underexposure, whenever possible I stopped down the speed by one stop. I say the speed because in many instances I preset the apertures in order to minimize the amount of work I had to do in the settings. I selected apertures that I thought would be optimal for each particular lens. This meant that in such instances I had only to check the light meter, set it, focus, compose and shoot. I tried to make my work as simple as possible so I could concentrate on composition and on handling the cameras according to the necessities of low temperature and humidity. On occasion I checked the light meters against each other. Whenever their readings varied much—probably the variations were due to those in battery strength—I selected an intermediate figure.

The intensity of light in Antarctica makes light leaks during reloading or during changing of lenses out of doors a very real threat. When you are in the field away from your shelter there is usually nothing that casts a shadow. Of course, you will turn your back to the sun but sometimes it is worth removing your parka and reloading or changing lenses under its protection despite the cold. However, when one is cold one becomes increasingly awkward and accident-prone. It is then one is most likely to make a serious error, such as inserting a bayonet lens improperly or keeping a camera open too long, either at the lens mount or at the loading area, thereby allowing a bit of grit to enter the shutter or the film compartment.

One must remember not to blow on a lens to remove a mote of dust. If you forget, this mistake will cause condensation of your breath and will require patience while you wait for the frost covering the lens to ablate. If you intend to bring a very cold camera into a relatively warm and humid shelter it is wise to seal it in a plastic bag first and, if possible, to let it warm up gradually, otherwise condensation will form on the instrument, and some of the moisture may work itself inside the camera and remain there to freeze it next time you carry it outdoors.

Camping out at low temperatures can be a problem. If the temperatures are low enough one may wish to share one's sleeping bag with a couple of cameras to prevent their freezing and to keep the light-meter batteries from draining. Camping on volcanic Ross Island, where winds are frequent, also presents the hazard of volcanic grit, so great care had to be taken during reloading and during handling of cameras in general, and the cameras were kept covered when not in use. Despite all the care I took—I cleaned the cameras often—I found them feeling gritty at times and I wondered if a particle was damaging the film.

Those photographers fortunate enough to visit the historic Scott and Shackleton huts on Ross Island are advised that the light-absorbing power of the age- and smoke-stained wood walls in the huts is considerable. One is likely to obtain underexposed pictures if one doesn't compensate by adding a stop or two to what the light meter suggests. Bracketing is advisable whether one is using available light or not. Unfortunately the usual visitor is given only a brief time to spend in them. I had the best luck with available light, but then I had the advantage of camping out on Capes Royds and Evans, where two of the huts are located, and of living in the huts, so I had ample time to experiment. But I did not learn the results of the experiments until I had the films developed after I returned to my home.

I had two special rules for myself: never to snapshoot, and to compose absolutely in the camera. Despite the fact that many scenes were breathtaking in their interest and beauty, I told myself to shoot only when I could not resist doing so. One reason was that I had no way of readily replenishing my film supply. A more deep-seated reason was that I knew that snapshooting would inevitably lead to sloppy techniques in general.

When working from the cockpit of helicopters, as I often did, sometimes on long flights, the operation was even simpler in one respect: I would set the focus at infinity and generally leave it there, for the scenes I was shooting were appropriate, for the most part, to the setting. But an essential feature of such work is that one must constantly check the light meters, for with rapid changes of scene and posture inherent in helicopter flight one encounters changing landscapes and cloud conditions, and of course a great deal depends on whether one is shooting away from, in the general direction of, or even directly into, the sun.

Photography in the cockpit of the Navy H-34 helicopter, which was the craft most frequently at my disposal, poses certain special problems. You are sitting in the copilot's seat on the port side, wearing a huge spherical communications and safety helmet. From the pilot's point of view as well as your own it is obligatory that you wear the helmet, for without it communication between you is not possible: the roar of the engine, the rotors and the windstream is too great. The helmet projects so far in front of your forehead that it is impossible for you to bring the camera very close to your cheek. You must consider this discrepancy when sighting through the viewfinder. Between your legs is a moving control stick with its button that operates the intercom portion of your helmet. Immediately on your left is a large lever that is also in motion. In front of your feet are two pedals in motion. Only the balls of your feet rest on the floor. Your heels hang in space; below them is the front of the passenger cabin. There is almost no place on the heavily vibrating and sharply slanting top of the instrument panel where you can rest anything safely. Your lap is no resting place because your legs are divided by the control stick, and on the occasions when you forget yourself and press your legs together you grab the stick with your knees and interfere with the pilot's control of the craft—your stick, lever and pedals are connected with his.

The windshield is almost always dusty and streaked, so you will not want to shoot through it unless you have no alternative. You shoot through your hatch, which you can slide open or shut at will. The caseless cameras are slung around your neck. You have left your parka and gloves in the cabin below. When you open the hatch the cockpit cools off very rapidly and soon you are very cold. You are wearing a heavy wool shirt with two breast pockets that you meticulously keep buttoned except when you need to use them. In the right one are cassettes of unexposed film. In the left you deposit the exposed cassettes. It is of some importance that you do not grow confused about these pockets if you are to avoid wasting time reaching for a cassette that you intend to load into a camera, only to find it has no visible film tag end, proof it has been rewound. Meanwhile the act of handling is not without hazards, for usually the hatch is open, the windstream is strong, creating suction in the cockpit, and it takes no special imagination to see an exposed cassette or the cover of the camera's film compartment being whipped out of your numb fingers and go flying out of the craft.

The enormity of the light in that dry, almost inky sky is something to consider. Whereas the pilot has lowered the sun shield in his helmet, thus protecting his eyes, you have not, for the shield is a further barrier between you and the viewfinder; in addition you are eager to see the scenes in their true colors so you can compose color values accordingly as well as be in a position later, when the film has been developed, to judge if the transparencies have recorded what you believe your naked eyes saw. But at times you are forced to lower the shield to avoid sun-blindness, which can put you out of business very painfully for days. You try not to shoot when the shield is down.

By pressing a small lever you can permit your shoulder harness to give you a surprising degree of leeway if you wish to project your torso far out of the cockpit in order to shoot scenes below you, behind you or ahead of you. Sometimes you feel almost divorced from the craft. If you are flying low, even over a hard, glacial surface, the air turbulence caused by the rotors distorts the scene below you as if heat waves are rising from it, so you do not shoot straight down at such times. When you shoot ahead of you the windstream stops your breathing and makes your eyes run. You constantly monitor the meters; you try to check them for every shot. Using reading glasses in such circumstances is out of the question, so you squint, being aided by the light's brilliance and by the fact you have marked on the meters with a china marker pencil the aperture numbers you have preset on the cameras. From time to time you monitor the cameras themselves to be sure the aperture and the rangefinder settings have not been moved accidentally.

You try to keep abreast of the changing scenes. Is this scene best caught by the wide-angle lens? If so, use the M4; don't confuse it with the M2R. Ought you to do this one vertically? The pilot is watching you. You tell yourself to behave smoothly, easily, never angularly. You pretend you're alone. You keep watch on the frame numbers, which will warn you when the cassettes are running low on film and when, if upcoming scenes are of special interest, you ought to stop shooting. You try to avoid letting both cassettes run out of film simultaneously, waiting for a lull in the visual excitement before rewinding one cassette and proceeding to reload.

You remove the camera film cover and carefully place it in your left breast pocket, then button the flap down. You hope you'll be able to remove the cassette without trouble, but how often your numb, extremely dry fingers slip helplessly off it, and you do wish the manufacturer had built a better grip on the cassette than the tiny knurled knob, meant for more temperate conditions. Probably it is the dryness of skin that makes it so difficult at times to remove the cassettes. Or do they stick because the cameras are cold? You consider licking your fingers but decide they may acquire a film of ice or even stick to the metal.

It was always painful to have to rewind so slowly while being aware of the fantastic scenes slipping by. But I had taught myself patience at home and I knew that it was one of my best photographic assets in Antarctica. What a relief it was to have both cameras full or almost full of film, ready for shooting even though shooting, at heart, was not what the matter was truly about. The matter was seeing and remembering well enough so I could later make entries of value in my journal. I was primarily a writer and as such had to defend myself against the alluring encroachments of photography. I could not afford to let the cameras do too much seeing for me. I regarded my films primarily as a form of data subservient to the book I planned to write. I was aware of the danger of letting my own medium, language, be overwhelmed by the camera's infinitely greater ability to record visual events. This was an added reason why I shot only when I could not resist doing so. I at least *tried* to see first with my own eyes, fully enough for a scene to make some impression on my brain before I gave way and pressed the button. But many times I was very glad to have the cameras with me, for in the awesome places of Antarctica I realized nakedly the limitations of language in describing what I saw.

I was very lucky with my photographic work in the Antarctic. Of the exposed film I brought back with me from my second trip I destroyed about 8.9 per cent, which left me with something over 2,600 transparencies.

Regarding the behavior of my cameras during the crash episode. Although I did not see the results until later, it seemed extraordinary how well my unwinterized Leicas were performing. Their behavior in such extreme conditions reinforced my longstanding faith in my Leitz equipment and this confidence was ultimately confirmed by the transparencies. I first saw the crash photographs in Wellington, where I had the crash films specially developed so the Coast Guard could make copies to be used by members of the accident board en route to Antarctica from the States. Sitting in my hotel room and viewing the slides, I wondered if I had really been involved in such a bizarre episode.

GLOSSARY

ablation: surface waste of ice or snow by melting or evaporation.

Air Ops: Air Operations.

aneroid barometer; aneroid: an instrument used for measuring atmospheric pressure, in which the pressure moves a pointer by distorting a metallic surface.

annual or *sea ice:* ice that breaks up during the austral summer, as distinguished from the so-called permanent ice of glaciers, ice shelves and the ice cap of the inland Antarctic plateau.

ASA: Antarctic Support Activities.

autorotation: in the present volume, emergency unpowered descending helicopter flight in which the spin of the rotors, due partially to momentum and partially to the passage of air across the blades, decreases the speed of the descent. The rotors act as a sort of parachute. Under certain conditions of autorotation the pilot has a limited control over his craft.

balaclava: heavy woolen masklike headgear that covers the neck and most of the face.

Barrier: see Great Ice Barrier.

bear paws: large gauntleted fur-back leather mittens.

BOQ: Bachelor Officers' Quarters.

brash: small fragments and nodules of ice, resulting from a floe breaking up.

bunny boots: large, heavy thermal boots capable of providing protection against extremely low temperatures.

Buno: bureau number. Each aircraft has a number as it comes off the assembly line.

calving: natural breaking off of part of an ice shelf, glacier, glacier tongue or iceberg, resulting in the formation of a berg.

canvas tank: a canvas "hold-all" containing food bags and strapped to a sledge.

Centigrade: the conversion of a Centigrade temperature into a Fahrenheit one is accomplished by multiplying the Centigrade figure by 9/5 and adding 32.

CG: Coast Guard.

Cheechee: Christchurch, New Zealand.

chopper: helicopter.

Clements building: a modular building with 4×8-foot panels for both top and sides, developed especially for Antarctic use by the United States Navy and prefabricated by the Clements Company.

Connie: the C-121 Super Constellation four-engine propeller aircraft.

crevasse: a crack in a glacier or ice shelf. It can vary greatly in width and depth and can be either exposed or deceptively snowbridged.

DV: distinguished visitor.

emergency Oxo: Shackleton was probably referring to the original "Oxo," which was and still is a meat-extract fluid that, when mixed with hot water, provides a stimulating, beefy drink. I am informed by the manufacturers of the product, Brooke Bond Oxo Ltd., that although they have no record of Shackleton's having used the product, they do know that Scott used it in Antarctica.

erratics: rocks, usually ice-worn, that have been carried by a glacier from their original position.

F.: Fahrenheit.

fast ice: sea ice that is attached to land.

finneskoes: boots, including the soles, made of fur. The early explorers used "finnesko" for the plural form, as they also did "ski" for skis. Finneskoes provided warmth but little traction.

fumarole: a subsidiary vent in the side of a volcano, from which issue various gases and water vapor. Ice fumaroles are the result of condensation and freezing of the water vapor around and above fumaroles located in very cold places.

Gentle: the code name for aircraft of VXE-6. Each squadron has its own code name.

geographical mile: see knot.

Great Ice Barrier: early name for the Ross Ice Shelf.

head: U. S. Navy term for toilet facility.

helo: helicopter.

Herc or *Hercules:* the C-130 four-engine turboprop jet aircraft.

hoosh: pemmican soup; that is, pemmican cooked with snow.

hummock: a rough ridge or small hill of ice, usually formed by pressure.

hypsometer: an instrument used to estimate elevation in mountainous regions by measuring the boiling points of liquids.

the ice: a term used by Antarctic hands to designate the white continent.

Ice Barrier: see Great Ice Barrier.

ice foot: fringes of ice skirting parts of Antarctic shores and often formed by sea spray.

IGY: International Geophysical Year (1957–58).

Kiwi: New Zealander.

knot (as a unit of speed): one knot equals one nautical or geographical mile per hour. A nautical mile (the international unit, used by the United States since 1959, is 6,076.115 feet or 1852 meters) is approximately the equivalent of 1.1 statute miles. A statute mile (5,280 feet) is approximately equal to .91 of a nautical mile. Differing from the international unit, the British nautical or geographical mile, known also as the Admiralty mile, is equal to 6,080 feet or 1853.2 meters.

MAC Center: McMurdo Center.

manhauling: hauling sledges by the sole use of manpower.

mukluks: high, canvas, felt-lined boots with thick rubber soles, designed to afford protection at very low temperatures.

navaids: electronic aids to navigation.

nautical mile: see knot.

névé: the packed, hard-frozen snow of a snow field, containing minute ice crystals.

NSF: National Science Foundation.

nunatak: an island of bare land, in some cases the top of a high mountain, projecting through a snow field or ice sheet.

Ob Hill: Observation Hill.

pack ice or *pack:* broken sea ice or broken ice of floes, caused by wind, temperature and current.

pancake ice: small circular pieces with raised edges.

pannikin: a small cup or pan.

pemmican: dried and powdered beef to which a relatively large percentage of fat has been added.

permanent ice: a term used relatively, as distinguished from annual or sea ice; the ice of glaciers, ice shelves and the ice cap of the inland plateau.

plasmon: a milk-protein health food, carried in powdered form during sledging traverses by the Scott and Shackleton expeditions; also used as a food supplement, for example in the manufacture of sledging biscuits.

P.O.: Petty Officer.

pram: a Norwegian-type skiff. Pram Point on Ross Island was so named by the Discovery Expedition when it was necessary to use a pram while traveling in open water between the point and Winter Quarters Bay.

pressure ice or *pressure:* ridges, hummocks and upthrust sharp masses of ice caused by the collision of slowly moving permanent ice with a land mass.

primus or *Primus:* an oil-burning stove, often used for cooking during sledging traverses in polar regions.

red ration: pea meal and bacon powder.

rep: representative.

rotten berg: an iceberg that has been wasted by winds, ablation, sublimation and the action of waves. Usually it no longer has the typical tabular form of the Antarctic berg.

rpm: revolutions per minute.

SAR Condition: Search and Rescue Condition.

sastrugi (singular: *sastrugus*): irregularities, often wavelike, formed by the wind on a snow plain or ice field.

scurvy: the dreaded vitamin-C deficiency disease, whose cause was not known at the time of Scott's two Antarctic expeditions and Shackleton's Nimrod Expedition.

Seabees: members of construction battalion units of the United States Navy.

sennegrass: a type of Norwegian hay used as a moisture-absorbing packing in finneskoes.

sérac: a pointed ice ridge in a crevassed area.

skua: a large, gull-like, fearless bipolar bird with flight characteristics that have been described as being similar to those of a small eagle. The Antarctic skua preys on Adélie penguins, eating their eggs and chicks.

snout (of a glacier): a glacier's lower extremity.

statute mile: see knot.

st.: stone (as a unit of weight).

stone: a British unit of weight—fourteen pounds.

sublimation: direct passage from the solid to the gaseous state, used here to denote the change from ice to water vapor.

tank: see canvas tank.

USARP: United States Antarctic Research Program, a division of the Office of Polar Programs of the National Science Foundation.

Usarp: a member of USARP.

USCGC: United States Coast Guard Cutter.

UV: ultraviolet.

venesta case: a strong and relatively light packing case made of cemented and pressed layers of wood and used by the Scott and Shackleton expeditions.

VIP: very important person.

VXE-6: the air arm of Task Force 43, the latter also known as Operation Deep Freeze.

wanigan: a boxlike modern refuge shelter, usually made of plywood and containing survival foodstuffs and gear.

whiteout: a dangerous polar weather and optical phenomenon in which the sky and the snow or ice reflect each other so thoroughly that one seems to see only a two-dimensional white mass and consequently is disoriented.

Willy or *Willy Field:* Williams Field.

wind forces: they are logged according to the Beaufort Scale, which in the early days of Antarctic exploration ranged in number from 0 to 12, in description from Calm to Hurricane, and in miles per hour from 0 to 92. The scale now ranges from 0 to 17, with a maximum wind velocity of 136 miles per hour.

x.o.: executive officer.

Zulu: phonetic for z, standing for zero meridian of longitude (the meridian of Greenwich, England).

INDEX

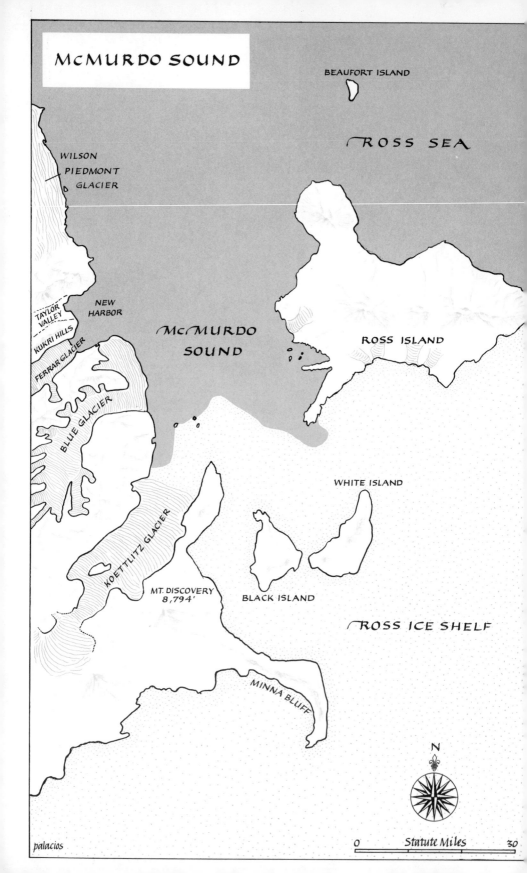